# 'Aryanisation' in Hamburg

## Monographs in German History

# 'ARYANISATION' IN HAMBURG

## The Economic Exclusion of Jews and the Confiscation of their Property in Nazi Germany

Frank Bajohr

**Berghahn Books**
New York • Oxford

Published in 2002 by Berghahn Books
www.berghahnbooks.com

© 2002 English-language edition, Berghahn Books
© 1997 Hans Christians Druckerei und Verlag (GmbH & Co.), Hamburg
Originally published as *Arisierung' in Hamburg. Die Verdrängung der jüdischen Unternehmer 1933-45.*

**Library of Congress Cataloging-in-Publication Data**

'Arisierung' in Hamburg. English
    'Aryanisation' in Hamburg : the economic exclusion of Jews and the confiscation of
their property in Nazi Germany / Frank Bajohr.
        p. cm. -- (Monographs in German history ; v. 7)
    Includes bibliographical references (p.  ) and index.
    ISBN 1-57181-484-1 (cl. : alk. paper) -- ISBN 1-57181-485-X (pb. : alk. paper)
        1. Jews--Persecutions--Germany--Hamburg. 2. Holocaust, Jewish
(1939-1945)--Germany--Hamburg--Economic aspects. 3.
Antisemitism--Germany--Hamburg--History--20th century. 4. Jews--Legal status, laws,
etc.--Germany--Hamburg. 5. Jewish property--Germany--Hamburg. 6. World War,
1939-1945--Confiscations and contributions--Germany--Hamburg. 7. Hamburg
(Germany)--Ethnic relations. I. Title. II. Series.

    DS135.G4 H3274 2001
    943'.515004924--dc21                                                    2001043586

**British Library Cataloguing in Publication Data**

A catalogue record for this book is available from the British Library.

Printed in the United States on acid-free paper.

# Contents

# INTRODUCTION

## *The destruction or 'Aryanisation' of Jewish businesses in Nazi Germany*

One of the biggest transfers of property in contemporary German history took place with the 'Aryanisation'[1] and liquidation of so-called Jewish enterprises[2] under the National Socialists, its magnitude only exceeded by the property confiscations of the Soviet Occupation Zone and the German Democratic Republic after 1945. Yet, the destruction of the economic livelihood of the Jews has met with only limited interest from historians. Overshadowed by the mass murder of millions of European Jews, 'Aryanisation' has not been treated as a historiographical subject in its own right until today.

Years ago, the 'Nestor' of Holocaust research, Raul Hilberg, underlined the functional connection between economic expropriation and the subsequent annihilation of the Jews, understanding the 'definition', 'expropriation', 'concentration' and 'annihilation' of Jews as logical consequences of a complex 'destruction process'.[3] Similarly, there is a broad consensus among academic historians writing on the subject that the destruction of the economic livelihood of the Jews should be treated as a part of National Socialist anti-Jewish policy. Historians have interpreted the 'exclusion' and 'Aryanisation' of Jewish enterprises as ideologically motivated elements of anti-Jewish policy, which, although built on economic hostility to the Jews and carrying economic consequences, were not primarily determined by economic interests. After all, the National Socialists had never concealed their view that the 'Jewish question' represented 'a national and racist, not an economic, question'.[4]

A counterinterpretation was first advanced by Marxist–Leninist historians who emphasised 'the responsibility of German finance capital for the persecution and murder of the Jews'.[5] However, their one-sided stress on economic interests proved to be an argumentative dead-end and their work presented no empirical evidence to support this hypothesis.

Notes for this chapter begin on page 11.

Another interpretation advanced by Götz Aly and Susanne Heim viewed the 'Aryanisation' and liquidation of Jewish businesses in the light of economic, utilitarian calculation rather than ideological factors. In their study *Vordenker der Vernichtung*, they characterised the economic expropriation of the Jews on the pattern of the Viennese model as an act of economic modernisation aimed at the structural purification of 'overcrowded' economic spheres, a policy which then became a blueprint for occupation and extermination policy in Eastern Europe.[6] This interpretation was likewise rejected by many historians, who accused the authors of rationalising National Socialist policy and of neglecting the policy's ideological dimensions.[7]

Academic research on the economic exclusion of the Jews under National Socialist rule was launched in the 1960s with the pioneer study of Helmut Genschel on 'The displacement of the Jews from the economy in the Third Reich'.[8] Genschel's work made clear that this process did not develop in a linear and consistent fashion, but was marked by contradictions, periods of delay and phases of tactical restraint. Genschel therefore differentiated two phases in the 'creeping persecution of the Jews' – 1933–35 and 1936–37 – both characterised by antisemitic campaigns and simultaneous state restraint. Only after Schacht's dismissal as Economics Minister in the autumn of 1937 was a state-enforced policy of economic exclusion instituted, leading to the 'legal exclusion' of the Jews from economic life in November 1938.

This version of the development of the economic exclusion of the Jews, which also influenced later analyses of National Socialist anti-Jewish policy,[9] focused on the activities of the government and central authorities and was tied to a view of the policy process as seen 'from above'. Because Genschel did not have recourse to research on either regional anti-Jewish policy or the situation of those affected by the policy, important aspects of the expropriation process remained unclarified. Genschel's analysis completely overlooked the regional anti-Jewish activities of the National Socialists' party organisation, for instance.

By contrast, Avraham Barkai, who we must thank for the second groundbreaking monograph on the economic exclusion of the German Jews, placed the perspective of the victims at the centre of his study.[10] In pointed contrast to the structuralist analysis of anti-Jewish policy in general, and to Genschel's interpretation in particular, Barkai emphasised the intentionality and continuity of the policy of economic exclusion of the Jews. He characterised the early years of National Socialist rule as a mere 'illusion of a grace period' and rejected assumptions about protected or sheltered areas for the economic activity of Jews. Whereas Genschel judged the success of the National Socialists' efforts to exclude the Jews up to the autumn of 1937 to have been 'rather poor'[11], Barkai spoke of a 'far-reaching 'Aryanisation''[12] which had developed to the point that after the autumn of 1937 only a small residue of Jewish economic activity remained to be liqui-dated. Barkai expressly cast doubt on the protection which Genschel believed to have been given to Jewish enterprises by Schacht as Reich Economics Minister. A continuous expropriation process would leave no room for talk of a 'protective' policy, and correspondingly the dismissal of Schacht in the autumn of 1937 could not have marked a 'turning-point' for the economic exclusion of the Jews.[13]

The two analyses of the economic exclusion process advanced by Genschel and Barkai stand in clear contrast to each other. The first provides a structural/his-torical model based on phases, focused on the behaviour of the Reich institutions and the disunity and contradictoriness of the process. The second is based pri-marily on the perspective of the victims, which, although not denying the variety of different facets of anti-Jewish policy, does emphasise its systematic nature and continuity. Both of these positions appear frequently in the controversy between 'intentionalists' and 'structuralists',[14] though neither of the authors treated above could be clearly assigned to either of these two historiographical 'camps'.

Only recently have researchers begun to examine the practices of the author-ities responsible for 'Aryanisation', as well as the wider circle of participants and beneficiaries of the process. Gerhard Kratzsch turned to the previously over-looked *Gau* Economics Advisers of the NSDAP (the *Gauwirtschaftsberater*, GWB), laying out, on the basis of a complete review of the archival evidence, a study of the operation of the NSDAP's regional economics machinery in the 'de-Judaisation' of the medium-sized economy of *Gau Westfalen-Süd*.[15] In contrast to Avraham Barkai, who suggested that NSDAP *Gau* Economics Advisers proved 'ideal executive organs in the continuing process of displacing Jews from eco-nomic life'[16], Kratzsch made a considerably more cautious assessment of the activities of the *Gau* Economics Adviser in *Gau Westfalen-Süd*. This official was only 'involved' in 'de-Judaisation', and 'participated' in it on a legal basis. More-over, the development of 'de-Judaisation' could not be described as having run 'to plan'.[17] How generally it might be possible to apply this characterisation, which Kratzsch undermines with his own portrayal of events,[18] will be a subject of the present study.

While the attitude of the German population to the persecution of the Jews has attracted a higher level of interest from researchers in recent years,[19] still lit-tle is known about the position of German business and the behaviour of the purchasers of Jewish property. Avraham Barkai has described them in a tentative overview as 'sleeping partners' of the National Socialist regime who profited from rearmament and from National Socialist anti-Jewish policy without play-ing a leading political role.[20] Many middle-class 'Aryanisers' of Jewish property were enriched by the crimes of the National Socialists, and other captains of industry became 'accomplices'. This behaviour cannot be understood without the 'contribution of antisemitic prejudice'.[21] Peter Hayes has examined the attitude of big industry in Germany to the economic exclusion of the Jews in a contribution that displays an exceptional breadth of research; he describes their behaviour as a combination of distance and even rejection on the one hand, and involvement on the other.[22] The attitudes of big business should be differentiated from that of the middle class antisemitic followers of the National Socialists, not least from a chronological perspective. For instance, the relatively small number of 'Aryanisations' of large Jewish enterprises before 1937 corresponded to the lack of active support that large-scale industry showed for the persecution of the Jews. Its reservations were eroded over time, though on the whole leading German industrialists were less involved in 'Aryanisation' than the average German entrepreneurs were.[23]

All of the research fields and controversies raised for discussion here – the development of 'Aryanisation' and economic exclusion policies, the role of the authorities, the attitude of business and the behaviour of those who acquired property that had belonged to Jews – will be taken up at various points in the course of the present book. This work focuses not only on the sale and liquidation of businesses in a narrow sense, it sees 'Aryanisation' as an all-encompassing displacement process whose political and social underpinnings and historical context have to be analysed as well.

The study is also consciously conceived as a regional study. In view of the present state of research, the level of concrete description and analysis needed can only be provided by a regional case study, not by an overview at the wider level. Beyond this, there is also an important thematic motive for the examination of the economic exclusion of the Jews and 'Aryanisation' in the context of a regional historical approach. Hardly any other aspect of the National Socialist persecution of the Jews holds – as will be shown here – such relevance to regional history, since for a long time the institutions at the Reich level were relatively passive actors in the economic exclusion process, and the development of Reich-wide instructions was often far behind developments on the local and regional levels.[24] To give one example of many, on 1 March 1938, the Reich Economics Ministry prohibited the assignment of public contracts to Jewish firms; the situation in which such a decree would have been relevant had long disappeared as by that time there were no more towns or regions in Germany in which Jewish businesses could still receive such contracts. After the oft-announced special economic laws against the Jews had failed to develop beyond the discussion stage, the Reich only played a regulating role in the process of 'Aryanisation' in 1938, but even then delegated practical responsibility for the policy to regional institutions and concentrated on the confiscation of Jewish assets through taxes and compulsory charges.

In addition, in spite of radical anti-Jewish Reich laws like the 'Nuremberg laws' of 1935, the centralisation of anti-Jewish policy making was only instituted in any comprehensive sense in 1938. Up to this point in time, the position of the Jews across Germany, as well as the behaviour and competences of the regional authorities responsible for persecuting them, had varied enormously. In National Socialist Germany there were no islands of humanity. Nevertheless it made a great deal of difference to a Jewish entrepreneur whether his or her business was conducted in Hamburg, in Nuremberg, or in a small town. More than was the case for any other aspect of anti-Jewish policy, economic questions, like the validity of welfare vouchers for redemption at Jewish businesses, were regulated differently in almost every German town or region, and even differed from neighbourhood to neighbourhood. While recipients of welfare assistance in Hamburg could still redeem their welfare vouchers in Jewish businesses in 1937, in neighbouring Harburg-Wilhelmsburg this had been forbidden since 1933.[25] Similarly, there were substantial regional differences with respect to the position of the NSDAP *Gau* Economics Advisers, who occupied a central role in the economic exclusion of the Jews.

In sum, 'Aryanisation' was far from a process carried out 'from above' by means of the simple execution of Reich-wide orders. If the process of the economic exclusion of the Jews is to be described fully, both a regional historical analysis and a systematic regional comparison are necessary. In this way not only will the fundamental features of regional anti-Jewish policy have to be examined, but decision-makers, antisemitic activists, profiteers and the representatives of a variety of interests must be covered as well. In addition, counter-forces and hindrances to the execution of anti-Jewish measures, the reasons for tactical restraint and the reactions of the Jews concerned deserve more detailed attention, as the attempt to replace the classic picture of anti-Jewish policy 'from above' by the stereotype of autonomous social development inevitably ends in a deterministic dead end.[26]

The objectives outlined here can hardly be met given the present state of research. There is no lack of regional histories of the persecution of the Jews under the National Socialists,[27] but the economic exclusion of the Jews and 'Aryanisation' for the most part occupy only marginal parts in these. Most local and regional studies limit themselves to a summary overview; they contain useful bits of information, but they cannot replace a comprehensive investigation.[28] On the subject of 'Aryanisation' there are at present only two monographs that have been written at a local level, namely the research by Barbara Händler-Lachmann and Thomas Werther on Marburg[29] and that by Alex Bruns-Wüstefeld on Göttingen.[30] Both studies meticulously describe the displacement of the Jews from economic life, although, ultimately, they deal with small to middle-sized towns which were of rather marginal importance in terms of the economic activity of the German Jews – thus, despite the impressive wealth of detail they provide, it is impossible to draw general conclusions from them. We still know almost nothing about the destruction of businesses in centres of Jewish life such as Berlin, Frankfurt am Main, Breslau and Hamburg – to name only the four largest Jewish communities in Germany. The following study sees itself both as laying the foundations for this work at a regional level and also as a stimulus for further comparative research.

The first chapter focuses on the social carriers of antisemitism working 'from below', who, as early as the spring of 1933, and independent of the policy of the National Socialist state, were pressing for the economic 'exclusion' of the Jews. This introductory chapter examines the scope and impact of the antisemitic terror created by the SA and of the initiatives taken against Jews by middle-class professional associations and businessmen. However, the limitations to these initiatives will become clear from a few individual examples of the constraints imposed in the initial phase of National Socialist rule by the state itself because the uncompromising pursuit of antisemitic principles would have presented an obstacle to the goals of the consolidation of its rule and the stabilisation of the economy.

These quite complex influences on National Socialist anti-Jewish policy – notably the economic structure and situation of Hamburg – will be described in more detail in the introduction to the second chapter. They gave a regional specificity to anti-Jewish policy in Hamburg in the first years of the National Socialist regime which stands out clearly in comparison with the anti-Jewish policies of other cities and regions. At the focal point of this second chapter stand the decision-makers, who defined Hamburg's anti-Jewish policy and the reactions of the Chamber of Commerce and the townspeople in Hamburg to the economic discrimination against the Jews, and the various anti-Jewish measures instituted up to 1937. These are compared (wherever this is empirically possible) with measures taken in other regions and with those taken at the Reich level in order to assess the specific profile of National Socialist anti-Jewish policy in Hamburg.

The third chapter focuses on the victims, and sketches the economic and demographic situation of the Jewish minority in Hamburg under the National Socialists. It outlines the repression that Jewish firms faced in their everyday work, and describes the possibilities for, and obstacles to, stabilising the economic position of those in the 'Jewish economic sector'. Among the 'counter-strategies' developed by Jewish businessmen there were both legal and 'illegal' attempts at salvaging property, as well as numerous initiatives on the part of the Hamburg banker, Max Warburg, to come to a political settlement with the National Socialists by which the situation of the persecuted Jews could be improved.

The fourth chapter attempts to determine at what point in time the transition to the systematic 'de-Judaisation' of the economy of Hamburg was launched and the 'illusion of a grace period' finally ended. This transition has encouraged historical research in general, and Helmut Genschel in particular, to focus on the 'change of course' in the Economics Ministry of the Reich in the autumn of 1937. By contrast, I have attempted to show that even earlier than this the economic 'exclusion' of the Jews had already heightened dramatically – both through the activities of the NSDAP *Gau* economic machinery and, significantly, the tightening of exchange policy (little noted in historical research to this point), following which, the Hamburg Foreign Exchange Office became a much-feared institution through its work in liquidating Jewish enterprises.

Chapters V and VI centre on the 'Aryanisation' and liquidation of Jewish businesses in 1938–39, when the Reich successfully eliminated the Jews from the business world through ordinances which gave the process an appearance of legality. In this period the 'Aryanisation' of Jewish firms climaxed, finally becoming something of a 'race for personal enrichment'. The examination in these chapters of the behaviour of decision-makers and participants will particularly focus on commercial industry and on the behaviour of the people who acquired Jewish property and other beneficiaries of the expropriation of the Jews. The modalities and effects of the economic 'exclusion' of the Jews are worth particular attention: their economic implications, the balance of Reich and regional interests and the material benefits which accrued to figures from within the National Socialist Party. The perspective which this affords makes clear how much arbitrary, corrupt and nepotistic activity took place behind the 'legal' façade of government policy.

After the 'de-Judaisation' process in Hamburg was more or less completed in 1939–40, the economic 'exclusion' and expropriation of the Jews was pursued in those territories which had been annexed and in those conquered in the Second World War. This new phase cannot be easily separated from the previous one, since many enterprises from Hamburg were involved in the 'Aryanisations' in the occupied territories and the population of Hamburg profited from the expropriation of the whole of West European Jewry, their possessions being transported to Hamburg and auctioned to the population there. The seventh chapter, conceived as an overview, sketches the extent of this material profit, which involved a considerable portion of the population in the policy of annihilating the Jews.

Not all aspects and consequences of the economic exclusion and 'Aryanisation' policies will be treated comprehensively in the following examination. This study does not look at the restitution of Jewish property after 1945, which must be the subject of a separate research project.[31] On similar grounds the history of the Jewish community in Hamburg between 1933 and 1945[32] and many sub-themes of the processes of expropriating and 'Aryanising' Jewish foundations[33] will not be dealt with, or will be dealt with only in passing.

The archival sources used for this regional study appear to give solid support to the conclusions outlined above, though a few gaps remain in the archival materials that survive. The late occupation of the town by British troops on 3 May 1945 left the National Socialists with sufficient time to destroy important documents covering their 12 years in power. This meant the loss of almost all of the holdings of the institutions involved in the authorisation and implementation of the policy to exclude Jews from the economy. This applies in particular to the records of the Central Office of the Reich Governor, the NSDAP *Gau* leadership, the NSDAP *Gau* economic machinery and the Trade, Shipping and Industry Department, whose records relating to 'Aryanisation' policy were almost totally destroyed. In addition the so-called 'de-Judaisation files' of the Reich Economics Ministry were burned at the war's end. From February 1945 the Ministry instructed all regional institutions responsible for the 'Aryanisation' policy to destroy the relevant files, and to prevent them from falling into the hands of the Allies 'under all circumstances'.[34] Other collections of papers – notably those of the Chamber of Commerce in Hamburg – have proven elusive despite a meticulous search.[35] In attempting to reconstruct the destruction of the Jewish business world the absence of these documents made precise quantification of specific measures more difficult, and in some respects impossible. Without the records of the NSDAP *Gau* Economics Adviser, which contained political and economic assessments, a detailed biographical analysis of those people who acquired Jewish property has proven impossible.

Conversely, an in-depth examination of the surviving records in the Hamburg State Archive provided extensive and diverse sources from the Senate and administrative department collections. Combining these with the collections in the federal archives in Koblenz and Potsdam, the Berlin Document Centre, the Special Archives in Moscow, the Netherlands State Institute for War Documentation in Amsterdam (NIOD), the archives of the *Forschungsstelle für Zeitgeschichte* in Hamburg, the Judicial Authority in Hamburg, the archive of the Chamber of Handicrafts, the company archives of the banking house M.M. Warburg & Co. and of Beiersdorf AG, and a range of documents from private collections, an overall picture can be built up that covers a wide range of perspectives.

In the course of this examination it became clear that two collections of records were of particular importance. First there are the almost totally preserved collections of the Foreign Exchange Control Office (*Devisenstelle*) of the Lower Elbe Regional Finance Office (the *Landesfinanzamt Unterelbe*, subsequently renamed the *Oberfinanzdirektion Hamburg*), recently made available to researchers in the Hamburg State Archive. In addition to the general files, the subject files for criminal proceedings relating to currency exchange controls and the files covering emigration are particularly valuable sources of material. In three areas they provide especially important information: the participation of the Exchange Control Office and the financial bureaucracy in the economic 'exclusion' of the Jews, the 'illegal' attempts of Jews to save their property and the almost total financial plundering of individual Jews after the 'Aryanisation' of their property.

Secondly, the restitution files of the Reparations Chamber (*Wiedergutmachungskammer*) of the Hamburg State Court proved in some areas to contain a rich collection of material. At present they are still on an attic floor above the Hamburg civil law courts and comprise exactly 27,534 files,[36] covering approximately 47,000 separate proceedings – a figure that suggests the enormous scope of the 'Aryanisations' and property confiscations carried out under the National Socialist regime. On the basis of 'fiduciary petitions' (*Treuhand-Anmeldungen*) a total of 8,625 files were laid before the Jewish Trust Corporation for Germany (JTC), which represented the interests of Jews who had been murdered. The majority of files on individual property petitions derive from the restitution law for the British Occupation Zone of 12 May 1949 and the Federal Restitution Law of 19 July 1957.[37]

Two-thirds of the proceedings dealt with by the Reparations Chamber related to the confiscation of furniture, movable goods, insurance, jewellery and valuable objects of all kinds, and to taxes and compulsory payments or deliveries. A good quarter of the proceedings related to the 'Aryanisation' or seizure of property, while approximately six per cent were concerned with the investigation of especially interesting company 'Aryanisations'.[38]

The records provide information on the development of the restitution proceedings after 1945, and also contain much information on 'Aryanisation' before that time, including, among other items, biographical reports and information about individual Jews, letters, reports, licences and sales contracts, and legal documents submitted by both parties with respect to restitution of property owned by Jews and the duties of those who acquired their property to make restitution. These documents permit an exact reconstruction of the process of 'Aryanisation' despite the loss in many cases of all of the files of the institutions responsible. They also clarify the behaviour of the parties that acquired the 'Aryanised' property as much as they do the behaviour of the institutions involved in the sale and confiscation of property. However, these documents can only be used after agreeing to the strict conditions imposed for the protection of individuals and of personal information, which, among other things, has meant that most of those who acquired Jewish property have been treated anonymously. Avraham Barkai has rightly written, in discussing this, of a 'harmful' data protection act[39] that still guarantees complete protection for perpetrators sixty years after the event.

Whereas the restitution documents have proven valuable for a qualitative analysis of 'Aryanisations' and confiscations of property, the enormous scale of the

47,000 individual proceedings – listed only in the form of an alphabetical card index – rule out any attempt at a detailed quantitative evaluation. Nevertheless, on the basis of the 'Aryanisation' lists of the Regional Finance Office and by means of a search in the lists of the Reparations Chambers and the card index of the Reparations Office, it has been possible to put together a sample of around three hundred company 'Aryanisations'. These constituted only part of all sales of businesses but nevertheless they make possible not only a qualitative analysis of the process of the economic exclusion of the Jews but also the beginnings of a quantitative analysis of that process.

This book originally appeared in German in 1997 under the title *'Arisierung'* *in Hamburg. Die Verdrängung der jüdischen Unternehmer 1933–1945*. My thanks go to many people for helping in the completion of this project. Especial thanks are due to

- the Director of the *Forschungsstelle für Zeitgeschichte*, Prof. Dr Arnold Sywottek, Prof. Dr Axel Schildt, Prof. Dr Arno Herzig, Dr Uwe Lohalm and Dr Beate Meyer for their critical review of the manuscript and many recommendations for improvements,
- colleagues and collaborators from the archives I have used, especially Dr Peter Gabrielsson and Jürgen Sielemann from the Hamburg State Archive, who spared no effort to quench my 'thirst' for documents, as well as the Director of the State Archive, Prof. Dr Hans-Dieter Loose, who granted permission speedily enough for me to be able to cover many of the document collections,
- the Hamburg Board for Science and Research, and particularly Dr Walter Schindler, for its financial support, and Dagmar Wienrich for help with much time-consuming research,
- the former Director of the *Forschungsstelle*, Prof. Dr Ulrich Herbert, who gave much stimulation to this work and gave me the opportunity to present my initial research findings at his Freiburg research colloquium,
- a multitude of colleagues within and beyond the *Forschungsstelle* for their support, for the suggestions they made and for their stimulating conversation. To name but a representative few, these included Thomas Jersch, Friederike Littmann, Jörg Morré, Prof. Dr Monika Richarz, Jan Philipp Spannuth and Dr Michael Wildt,
- and last but not least I wish to thank my translator George Wilkes, as well as Inter Nationes e.V., which sponsored this translation.

# Notes

1. A racist neologism, the term 'Aryanisation' grew out of the official discourse of the 1930s and referred in a narrow sense to the transfer of so-called 'Jewish' property to 'Aryan' ownership. It was also used, however, as a synonym for the whole process of the economic exclusion of the Jews, although at the same time the National Socialists employed the term 'de-Judaisation' – another term used in a racist sense – for this as well. In the analysis which follows, 'Aryanisation' and 'de-Judaisation' are employed as terms for the whole process of economic exclusion. No official definition for either concept was given in any of the enactments, orders and legal commentaries of the time. One semi-official commentary uses them without reflection – Alf Krüger, *Die Lösung der Judenfrage in der deutschen Wirtschaft. Kommentar zur Judengesetzgebung*, Berlin, 1940.

2. This book uses 'Jewish enterprises' to refer to companies that were in the possession of persons who fell into the National Socialist definition of 'Jews' and were therefore subjected to economic discrimination and exclusionary measures. What was decisive in the classification of individuals or businesses was not the self-understanding of those affected – of whom not a few had converted to Christianity and did not consider themselves to be Jews – but the ascription of Jewishness by others on the basis of National Socialist race theory. For this reason, the terms 'Jew' or 'Jewish enterprise' should either be paraphrased or, as established National Socialist categories, be placed in inverted commas. This will have to be dispensed with here, however, or the text could easily become overburdened with quotation marks or complicated paraphrases (e.g., Jew = so-called Jew according to the criteria of National Socialist race theory).

3. Raul Hilberg, *The Destruction of the European Jews*, 3 vols, New York, 1985 (revised and enlarged from the editions of 1961 and 1982), p. 53ff.

4. Cited from 'Die Ausschaltung der Juden', in *Die Deutsche Volkswirtschaft. Nationalsozialistischer Wirtschaftsdienst*, No. 33/1938, p. 1197.

5. Kurt Pätzold, *Faschismus, Rassenwahn, Judenverfolgung. Eine Studie zur politischen Strategie und Taktik des faschistischen deutschen Imperialismus (1933–1935)*, East Berlin, 1975, p. 25; ibid., 'Von der Vertreibung zum Genozid. Zu den Ursachen, Triebkräften und Bedingungen der antijüdischen Politik des faschistischen deutschen Imperialismus', in Dietrich Eichholtz and Kurt Gossweiler, eds, *Faschismusforschung. Positionen, Probleme, Polemik*, Köln, 1980, pp. 181–208. Cf. also Klaus Drobisch, Rudi Goguel and Werner Müller, *Juden unterm Hakenkreuz*, Berlin, 1973, which maintains, on the one hand, that 'Aryanisation' and the persecution of the Jews had become a fundamental goal of the 'monopoly bourgeoisie', in order 'to repel or to completely shut out troublesome competition from power in the state' (p. 13) and, on the other hand – particularly in the first years of National Socialist rule – that the persecution of the Jews had been subordinated to 'the external and domestic political objectives of the "monopoly bourgeoisie" as a [tool for] diversionary rhetoric and for ideological brutalisation' (p. 135). Such argumentative inconsistencies indicate the difficulties of looking at the persecution of the Jews and at 'Aryanisation' solely in the light of economic interests. On the very real primacy of the '*Weltanschauung*' in National Socialism, see Ulrich Herbert, 'Arbeit und Vernichtung. Ökonomisches Interesse und Primat der "Weltanschauung" im Nationalsozialismus', in Dan Diner, ed., *Ist der Nationalsozialismus Geschichte? Zu Historisierung und Historikerstreit*, Frankfurt am Main, 1987, pp. 198–236.

6. Götz Aly and Susanne Heim, *Vordenker der Vernichtung. Auschwitz und die deutschen Pläne für eine neue europäische Ordnung*, Hamburg, 1991, pp. 33–43.

7. For criticism of this view of 'Aryanisation' see below Ch. V; on the continuing interpretation of National Socialist extermination policy see, *inter alia*, Hermann Graml, 'Irregeleitet und in die Irre führend. Widerspruch gegen eine "rationale" Erklärung von Auschwitz', *Jahrbuch für*

*Antisemitismusforschung*, 1(1992), pp. 286–295; Ulrich Herbert, 'Rassismus und rationales Kalkül. Zum Stellenwert utilitaristisch verbrämter Legitimationsstrategien in der national-sozialistischen "Weltanschauung"', in Wolfgang Schneider, ed., *'Vernichtungspolitik'. Eine Debatte über den Zusammenhang von Sozialpolitik und Genozid im nationalsozialistischen Deutschland*, Hamburg 1991, pp. 25–35; Norbert Frei, 'Wie modern war der Nationalsozialismus?', *GG* 19 (1993), pp. 367–387; Dan Diner, 'Rationalisierung und Methode. Zu einem neuen Erklärungsversuch der "Endlösung"', *VfZ* 40 (1992), pp. 359–382; Bernd Jürgen Wendt, 'Der "Holocaust" im Widerstreit der Deutungen', in Arno Herzig and Ina Lorenz, eds, *Verdrängung und Vernichtung der Juden unter dem Nationalsozialismus*, Hamburg 1992, pp. 29–74. In his most recent investigations, Götz Aly has modified his one-sided interpretation of the extermination of the Jews based on population economics and has concentrated on analyzing the political practice of the institutions responsible for the deportations and resettlements. Cp. Götz Aly, *'Endlösung'. Völkerverschiebung und der Mord an den europäischen Juden*, Frankfurt am Main, 1995.

8.  Helmut Genschel, *Die Verdrängung der Juden aus der Wirtschaft im Dritten Reich*, Göttingen, 1966.

9.  Uwe Dietrich Adam, *Judenpolitik im Dritten Reich*, Düsseldorf, 1972.

10. Avraham Barkai, *From Boycott to Annihilation: The Economic Struggle of German Jews, 1933–1943*, Hanover and London, 1989. A third monograph on the economic exclusion of the Jews by Johannes Ludwig, *Boykott – Enteignung – Mord. Die 'Entjudung' der deutschen Wirtschaft*, Hamburg, 1989, does present interesting material, but does not advance beyond a journalistic treatment of individual cases to a systematic examination of the underlying issues.

11. Genschel, *Verdrängung*, p. 140.

12. Avraham Barkai, '"Schicksalsjahr 1938". Kontinuität und Verschärfung der wirtschaftlichen Ausplünderung der deutschen Juden', in Walter H. Pehle, ed., *Der Judenpogrom 1938. Von der 'Reichskristallnacht' zum Völkermord*, Frankfurt am Main, 1988, pp. 94–117, citation from p. 95.

13. Barkai's view was also recently supported by Albert Fischer, *Hjalmar Schacht und Deutschlands 'Judenfrage'. Der 'Wirtschaftsdiktator' und die Vertreibung der Juden aus der deutschen Wirtschaft*, Cologne, 1995. Fischer's characterisation of Schacht's antisemitism stresses the halfheartedness and ineffectiveness of his interventions. A comprehensive, regional and trade-specific analysis of the historical impact of Schacht remains to be undertaken, however, and it could only be achieved through detailed research into regional and trade-specific variation. Thus Christopher Kopper has recently advanced the thesis that, confronted with Jewish private banks up to 1938, Schacht had in practice exercised a protective function: Christopher Kopper, *Zwischen Marktwirtschaft und Dirigismus. Bankenpolitik im 'Dritten Reich' 1933 bis 1939*, Bonn, 1995. Albert Fischer however has a considerably more sceptical view, see Albert Fischer, 'Jüdische Privatbanken im "Dritten Reich"', *Scripta Mercaturae*, 28. Jg., Heft 1/2, 1994, pp. 1–54.

14. The literature on this long-standing historiographical dispute since then has hardly become more clear. Cf. Ian Kershaw, *The Nazi Dictatorship: Problems and Perspectives of Interpretation*, London, 1985.

15. Gerhard Kratzsch, *Der Gauwirtschaftsapparat der NSDAP. Menschenführung – 'Arisierung' – Wehrwirtschaft im Gau Westfalen-Süd*, Münster, 1989.

16. Barkai, *Boycott*, p. 64.

17. Kratzsch, *Gauwirtschaftsapparat*, p.115f.

18. Kratzsch stressed at a number of points that the activities of the GWB had been limited to cooperation with 'legally instituted measures, implemented by organs of the state', but nevertheless proceeded from there to other places that the GWB had encompassed in the 'Aryanisation' process through more or less self-authorisation on a party-political – and not even a 'legal' – basis. On these inconsistencies see ibid., pp. 116, 146.

19. David Bankier, *The Germans and the Final Solution*, Oxford, 1992; Ursula Büttner, ed., *Die Deutschen und die Judenverfolgung im Dritten Reich*, Hamburg, 1992; Hans Mommsen and Dieter Obst, 'Die Reaktion der deutschen Bevölkerung auf die Verfolgung der Juden 1933–1945', in Hans Mommsen and Susanne Willems, eds, *Herrschaftsalltag im Dritten Reich*, Düsseldorf, 1988, pp. 374–421; Ian Kershaw, 'The Persecution of the Jews and German Popular Opinion in the Third Reich', *LBI YB* 26 (1981), pp. 261–289; Otto Dov Kulka, '"Public Opinion" in Nazi Germany and the "Jewish Question"', in Michael R. Marrus, ed., *The Nazi Holocaust*, Vol. 5, Westport/London, 1989, pp. 115–150.

20. Avraham Barkai, 'Deutsche Unternehmer und Judenpolitik im "Dritten Reich"', *GG* 15 (1989), pp. 227–247.

21. Cp. also Avraham Barkai, 'Volksgemeinschaft, "Arisierung" und der Holocaust', in Herzig and Lorenz, eds, *Verdrängung*, pp. 133–152.

22. Peter Hayes, 'Big Business and "Aryanisation" in Germany, 1933–1939', *Jahrbuch für Antisemitismusforschung*, 3(1994), pp. 254–281.

23. Ibid., p. 272.

24. As Wolf Gruner has recently pointed out in this respect, the institutions which – like the German Municipal Congress, the *Deutsche Gemeindetag* – existed in between the Reich and regional levels played a pivotal coordinating function in the pursuit of anti-Jewish policy. Cf. Wolf Gruner, 'Die öffentliche Fürsorge und die deutschen Juden 1933-1942. Zur antijüdischen Politik der Städte, des Deutschen Gemeindetages und des Reichsinnenministeriums', in *ZfG*, 45. Jg., Heft 7/1997, pp. 597–616; ibid., *Der geschlossene Arbeitseinsatz deutscher Juden. Zur Zwangsarbeit als Element der Verfolgung 1938–1943*, Berlin, 1997, p. 332.

25. Cf. Uwe Lohalm, 'Hamburgs öffentliche Fürsorge und die Juden 1933 bis 1939', in Arno Herzig, ed., *Die Juden in Hamburg 1590 bis 1990*, Hamburg, 1991, pp. 499–514.

26. The most recent example is the attempt of Daniel Jonah Goldhagen to underline the consistency of an alleged 'eliminationist antisemitism' as a 'national project' of the Germans. As his examinations of National Socialist anti-Jewish policy after 1933 show, the consistency of his argument can only be sustained at the price of selective and one-sided interpretations. It is thus no surprise that the author describes regional differences as 'tertiary deviations' from 'ground-level perspectives'. Cf. Daniel Jonah Goldhagen, *Hitler's Willing Executioners: Ordinary Germans and the Holocaust*, New York, 1996, p. 133.

27. For the most important regional studies, see *inter alia*: Regina Bruss, *Die Bremer Juden unter dem Nationalsozialismus*, Bremen, 1983; *Dokumente zur Geschichte der Frankfurter Juden 1933–1945*, ed. by the *Kommission zur Erforschung der Geschichte der Frankfurter Juden*, Frankfurt 1963; Hans-Joachim Fliedner, *Die Judenverfolgung in Mannheim 1933–1945*, 2 vols, Stuttgart 1971; Dieter Goertz, *Juden in Oldenburg 1930–1938*, Oldenburg, 1988; Peter Hanke, *Zur Geschichte der Juden in München zwischen 1933 und 1945*, Munich, 1967; Arno Herzig, ed., *Die Juden in Hamburg 1590 bis 1990*, Hamburg, 1991; Ulrich Knipping, *Die Geschichte der Juden in Dortmund während der Zeit des Dritten Reiches*, Dortmund, 1977; Arnd Müller, *Geschichte der Juden in Nürnberg 1146–1945*, Nuremberg, 1968; Günter von Roden, *Geschichte der Duisburger Juden*, Duisburg, 1986; Paul Sauer, ed., *Dokumente über die Verfolgung der jüdischen Bürger in Baden-Württemberg durch das nationalsozialistische Regime*, 2 vols, Stuttgart, 1966; Herbert Schultheis, *Juden in Mainfranken 1933–1945, unter besonderer Berücksichtigung der Deportationen Würzburger Juden*, Bad Neustadt a.d. Saale, 1980; Arno Weckbecker, *Die Judenverfolgung in Heidelberg 1933–1945*, Heidelberg 1985; Josef Werner, *Hakenkreuz und Judenstern. Das Schicksal der Karlsruher Juden im Dritten Reich*, Karlsruhe, 1988; Klaus Werner, *Unter der Herrschaft des Nationalsozialismus 1933–1945 (Zur Geschichte der Juden in Offenbach am Main, Vol. 1)*, Offenbach, 1988; Wolfgang Wippermann, *Die nationalsozialistische Judenverfolgung (Das Leben in Frankfurt zur NS-Zeit, Vol. 1)*, Frankfurt am

Main, 1986. A comprehensive catalogue of materials can be found in Michael Ruck, *Bibliographie zum Nationalsozialismus*, Cologne, 1995, pp. 370–394.

28. Britta Bopf, 'Zur "Arisierung" und den Versuchen der "Wiedergutmachung" in Köln,' in Horst Matzerath, Harald Buhlan and Barbara Becker-Jákli, *Versteckte Vergangenheit. Über den Umgang mit der NS-Zeit in Köln*, Cologne, 1994, pp. 163–193; Irene Diekmann, 'Boykott - Entrechtung - Pogrom - Deportation. Die "Arisierung" jüdischen Eigentums während der NS-Diktatur. Untersucht und dargestellt an Beispielen aus der Provinz Mark Brandenburg', in Dietrich Eichholtz, ed., *Verfolgung - Alltag - Widerstand. Brandenburg in der NS-Zeit*, Berlin, 1993, pp. 207–229; Gerhard Kratzsch, 'Die "Entjudung" der mittelständischen Wirtschaft im Regierungsbezirk Arnsberg', in Arno Herzig, Karl Teppe and Andreas Determann, eds, *Verdrängung und Vernichtung der Juden in Westfalen*, Münster, 1994, pp. 91–114; Dirk van Laak, 'Die Mitwirkenden bei der "Arisierung". Dargestellt am Beispiel der rheinisch-westfälischen Industrieregion 1933–1940', in Ursula Büttner, ed., *Die Deutschen und die Judenverfolgung im Dritten Reich*, Hamburg, 1992, pp. 231–257; Stefan Rheingans, 'Ab heute in arischem Besitz. Die Ausschaltung der Juden aus der Wirtschaft', in Anton M. Keim/ *Verein für Sozialgeschichte Mainz*, eds, *Als die letzten Hoffnungen verbrannten. 9./10. November 1938. Mainzer Juden zwischen Integration und Vernichtung*, Mainz, 1988, pp. 53–66; Monika Schmidt, 'Arisierungspolitik des Bezirksamtes', in Karl-Heinz Metzger *et al.*, eds, *Kommunalverwaltung unterm Hakenkreuz. Berlin-Wilmersdorf 1933–1945*, Berlin, 1992, pp. 169–228; Wolfram Selig, 'Vom Boykott zur Arisierung. Die "Entjudung" der Wirtschaft in München', in Björn Mensing and Friedrich Prinz, eds, *Irrlicht im leuchtenden München? Der Nationalsozialismus in der 'Hauptstadt der Bewegung'*, Regensburg, 1991, pp. 178–202; Arno Weckbecker, 'Phasen und Fälle der wirtschaftlichen "Arisierung" in Heidelberg 1933–1942', in Norbert Giovannini *et al.*, eds, *Jüdisches Leben in Heidelberg. Studien zu einer unterbrochenen Geschichte*, Heidelberg, 1992, pp. 143–152; Falk Wiesemann, 'Juden auf dem Lande. Die wirtschaftliche Ausgrenzung der jüdischen Viehhändler in Bayern', in Detlev Peukert and Jürgen Reulecke, eds, *Die Reihen fast geschlossen. Beiträge zur Geschichte des Alltags unterm Nationalsozialismus*, Wuppertal, 1981, pp. 381–396; Hans Witek, '"Arisierungen" in Wien. Aspekte nationalsozialistischer Enteignungspolitik 1938–1940', in Emmerich Talos *et al.*, eds, *NS-Herrschaft in Österreich 1938–1945*, Vienna, 1988, pp. 199–216; Jörg Wollenberg, 'Enteignung des "raffenden" Kapitals durch das "schaffende" Kapital. Zur Arisierung am Beispiel von Nürnberg', in ibid., ed., *'Niemand war dabei und keiner hat's gewußt.' Die deutsche Öffentlichkeit und die Judenverfolgung*, Munich/Zürich, 1989, pp. 158–187, 263–267. Jacob Toury has undertaken a trade-specific and regional-historical study profiling Jewish textile company owners in Württemberg and Baden. Jacob Toury, *Jüdische Textilunternehmer in Baden-Württemberg 1683–1938*, Tübingen, 1984.

29. Barbara Händler-Lachmann and Thomas Werther, *'Vergessene Geschäfte - verlorene Geschichte'. Jüdisches Wirtschaftsleben in Marburg und seine Vernichtung im Nationalsozialismus*, Marburg, 1992.

30. Alex Bruns-Wüstefeld, *Lohnende Geschäfte. Die 'Entjudung' der Wirtschaft am Beispiel Göttingens*, Hanover, 1997.

31. Jan Philipp Spannuth will focus on this theme in the course of a dissertation he is undertaking. By way of a preliminary study, in 1994 he published a master's thesis on the subject. Cf. Jan Philipp Spannuth, *Die Rückerstattung jüdischen Eigentums nach dem Zweiten Weltkrieg. Das Beispiel Hamburg*, Hamburg (master's thesis) 1994.

32. On this subject, Ina S. Lorenz will publish a comprehensive documentary compendium. See also her documentation on the history of Hamburg's Jews in the Weimar Republic: Ina Lorenz, *Die Juden in Hamburg zur Zeit der Weimarer Republik. Eine Dokumentation*, 2 vols, Hamburg 1987.

33. On the history and 'Aryanisation' of Jewish foundations, see the dissertation which Angela Schwarz is now preparing. See also her essay on Jewish housing foundations in Herzig, ed., *Juden*, pp. 447–458.

34. *Bundesarchiv Potsdam* (BAP), Reichwirtschaftsministerium, 8042, circular on the treatment of documents relating to 'de-Judaisation', letter from Dr van Hees to the President of the Government of Wiesbaden of 16 February 1945. Cf. also Hayes, *Big Business*, p. 272.

35. The archives of the trade associations at the Hamburg State Archive (*Bestand Gewerbekammer*) include sources from Hamburg handicraft particularly from the period before 1933, while the collection of the Hamburg Chamber of Handicraft (*Bestand Handwerkskammer*) only contains insignificant, fragmentary collections for the years 1936–1948 and the *Handwerkskammerarchiv* almost exclusively consists of primary material from the period after 1950. The reason for the striking lack of documents for the National Socialist period could not be determined.

36. This arises in particular from the documentary numbering system. Thus, *Akten* Z 1 - Z 15.934 (15,934 files) constitute the proceedings conducted on the basis of the restitution law for the British Zone. The files for cases conducted on the basis of the Federal Restitution Law are contained in file numbers Z 20.000 - Z 31.599 (11,600 files). Where the 'shortfall' between 15,934 and 20,000 comes from could not be determined here.

37. On compensation and restitution, see Constantin Goschler, *Wiedergutmachung. Westdeutschland und die Verfolgten des Nationalsozialismus (1945–1954)*, Munich, 1992; Ludolf Herbst and Constantin Goschler, eds, *Wiedergutmachung in der Bundesrepublik Deutschland*, Munich, 1989. On the situation of the Jews in the British Zone of Occupation, see also Ursula Büttner, *Not nach der Befreiung. Die Situation der deutschen Juden in der britischen Besatzungszone 1945–1948* (ed. by the *Landeszentrale für politische Bildung Hamburg*), Hamburg, 1986.

38. Cf. the statistical evaluation in Spannuth, *Rückerstattung*, p. 63f.

39. Barkai, *Unternehmer*, p. 237.

# Chapter 1

# ANTISEMITISM 'FROM BELOW' DURING THE FIRST PHASE OF NATIONAL SOCIALIST RULE

## Antisemitic Riots, 1933–34

'Jew farewell – here comes Germany', Emerentia Krogmann noted in her diary a few days after Hitler took power on 30 January 1933, an event which she experienced in Berlin in the company of Schacht, Himmler, Ribbentrop and other senior figures in the National Socialist party.[1] These words – penned by the wife of the future 'Mayor-in-Office' or 'Governing Mayor' (*Regierender Bürgermeister*) of Hamburg, Carl Vincent Krogmann, born into a middle-class Huguenot family in Hamburg – expressed an expectation which was widespread among the adherents of National Socialism: 30 January 1933 was, for them, the point in time at which they were to put into practice the antisemitic principles that had for many years been the subject of National Socialist propaganda and to destroy the alleged 'Jewish influence' over political, economic, and cultural affairs in Germany.

During the final years of the Weimar Republic, the National Socialists' anti-Jewish agitation had been toned down for tactical reasons,[2] nevertheless, antisemitism took on great significance from a programmatic perspective in so far as it enabled the diverse range of ideological components of National Socialism to be brought together in an apparently cohesive *Weltanschauung*. Anti-Marxism, anticapitalism and antidemocratic thought in National Socialism, when looked at through the prism of an antisemitic struggle against 'Jewish Bolshevism', 'Jewish bigwigs and black marketeers' and the 'Jewish Republic', could be traced back to a single underlying cause: 'the Jews' as the supposed root of all evil, who therefore had to be 'exterminated root and branch'[3]. Antisemitism – as the National Socialist economic theorist Gottfried Feder put it – was also of the utmost importance as an 'instinctive substructure for the movement',[4] integrating the heterogeneous group of adherents of National Socialism.

It therefore required no starting signal from above to spark off the 'savage' antisemitic campaign of terror which marked the seizure of power by the National Socialists in 1933–34. Many acts of repression against Jewish citizens – and this was especially true of these months – were not the product of a deliberate anti-Jewish policy on the part of the National Socialists, enforced through legislative and administrative measures, but were prompted by an antisemitism from below that proved resistant to the calls for moderation which leading National Socialists made out of tactical considerations, with one eye on the international reaction and another on Hitler's conservative coalition partners. Politics and terror under the National Socialist regime were mixed together in a seamless web, though terror from below was also a means to an end,[5] enhancing the interaction between 'spontaneous popular wrath' and the antisemitic initiatives taken by the government. Nonetheless the radicalism and momentum of the National Socialist movement meant it was only partly giving in to pressure from the new regime. The reality was more complex than might be suggested by a simple picture of a meticulously coordinated, carefully prepared and efficiently executed 'dual strategy'.

One incident, pregnant with symbolism, typified the general situation at the time: the torchlight procession in Hamburg on 6 February 1933, uniting both SA and Stahlhelm formations on the occasion of the National Socialists' assumption of power in the Reich. During the parade SA units cried 'Perish Judah'[6] and sang 'When Jewish blood spurts from the knife', which – as one SA report remarked – 'caused a most cold sobering-up among the hitherto enthusiastic populace'.[7] Because of this, Böckenhauer, the most senior SA leader in Hamburg, ordered in a circular of 8 February 1933 that all SA units refrain from singing such 'bloodthirsty songs' in future.[8]

Such appeals had no impact on the determination of party activists 'to have a final reckoning with "the Jews" and not to allow themselves in any way to be hindered from tackling this by "cowardly considerations"'.[9] At the end of March 1933, an SA group stormed the Jewish slaughterhouse area and forcibly obstructed the slaughter of animals according to Jewish ritual.[10] At the beginning of April 1933, six National Socialists gained entry to the apartment of a Jewish trader, a Mr Moritzsohn, in the Hammer Landstraße, 'in order to make a search of the house'. While two of them held the maid of the absent Moritzsohn in check with a pistol, the others rooted through all of the cabinets in the apartment and stole 40 Reich Marks (RM) from a money box.[11] At the beginning of May 1933, an SA contingent arrested Dr Max Plaut in his capacity as board member of the German

Israelite Community (*Deutsch-Israelitische Gemeinde*) and ordered him to open
the community treasury and to hand over the money in it. When Plaut refused,
he was carried off to the nearby SA premises and abused.[12] A few days later, on 11
May 1933, the shop windows of several Jewish businesses in Hamburg were
smashed.[13] In the Grindel quarter near the university, one of the main centres of
Jewish population in Hamburg, SA members held brazen 'Jew hunts' in the
spring of 1933, and again in 1934,[14] in which Jewish citizens were harassed and
beaten up.

Outbreaks of 'mob antisemitism' were not a new development in the spring
of 1933, but had already appeared on the agenda in previous years. In the Grindel
quarter, a series of cemetery desecrations and antisemitic attacks had already taken
place in 1931–32 which made it 'at times dangerous' for Jews 'to go over the
Grindelallee in the evening'.[15] Nevertheless, the situation which developed in the
spring of 1933 was very different. In this earlier period, perpetrators were pursued
by the police and courts, and the representatives of democratic Hamburg publicly
assured the harried Jewish community of their solidarity and support. In March
1931 the Mayor of Hamburg, Petersen (German State Party, *Deutsche Staatspartei*),
the Chair of the SPD parliamentary group, Podeyn, and representatives of the
German People's Party (*Deutsche Volkspartei*, DVP), the Centre Party and the
*Reichsbanner Schwarz-Rot-Gold* took a public stand against antisemitism.[16] In the
spring of 1933, by contrast, the Social Democrats themselves were among those
being persecuted, and convicted cemetery desecrators now represented the new
state authorities – for instance, National Socialist Ludwig Krautsdorfer was now
a member of 'Kommando z.b.V.' (a commando unit on special orders) under
Police First Lieutenant Kosa.[17]

The extent of the antisemitic attacks of 1933–34 is hard to evaluate. An
indication of how extensive they were is offered by the many complaints from foreign consulates – especially those from Southern Europe – about the abuse of
their citizens by SA units, who frequently mistook Southern Europeans for
Jews.[18] Indeed, even a consulate employee could be attacked and beaten up by a
troop of SA men, as one secretary at the Greek Consulate in Hamburg was at the
end of March 1933, on the grounds that they had an 'appearance like a Jew'.[19]

Police investigations against the perpetrators were, as a rule, only pursued in
those cases which had diplomatic consequences and where it was feared that there
might be damage to Germany's image abroad, while in general Jews could no
longer count on the protection of the police from violent attacks. When two SA
men mistreated a Jewish welfare recipient at the welfare benefit office at the
Klosterwall in August 1933, there was no serious intervention by the police.[20]

The reluctance of the police to take action against National Socialists responsible for violent attacks was primarily a result of the privileged situation of the SA

in the initial phase of the National Socialist seizure of power. On 14 March 1933, by authorisation of SA Chief Ernst Röhm, Hamburg's *SA-Oberführer* Böckenhauer became the 'Special Commissar of the *Obersten SA-Führer* to the Hamburg State Government'.[21] Over 300 Hamburg SA members were officially installed as auxiliary policemen on 20 March 1933[22] and thereby took over a state function – strengthening still further a self-confidence that was already high because of the seizure of power at the Reich level on 30 January 1933 and in Hamburg in March 1933. Occasionally, even their 'Aryan compatriots' had to endure the insults hurled at them by members of the SA.[23]

This situation pitted an SA running wild in an orgy of violence against an intimidated Hamburg police force, which – at least in the spring of 1933 – still included many Social Democrats who were openly mocked by the SA[24] and whose authority was not taken seriously.[25] In order to curb SA attacks on the police, the Hamburg SA leadership first introduced a fining service and later even a special command to bring unruly SA members into line, so as 'to avoid the usual conflicts between members of national organisations and uniformed police officers'.[26]

The reason that the appeals of the Hamburg SA leadership to its members to behave in a 'dignified, calm and chivalrous' manner and with 'iron self-control and discipline'[27] were so ineffective for so long was that they were accompanied by simultaneous appeals 'to strike without mercy' – each SA member was duty bound 'to use a fist if confronted with an opponent of the SA or of the Movement'.[28] SA members could thus be sure that their leadership would unofficially give their tacit assent to attacks on, and molestation of, Jewish citizens.

This only changed with the elimination of the SA as a powerful political actor in the wake of the 'Röhm Affair' in 1934. The arrest and murder of Röhm and of many other SA leaders coincided with a shocking antisemitic incident in Hamburg that occurred during a pack march of the Hamburg 'old guard'.[29] On their march at the end of June 1934 the 'old guard' abused an old man in his car because he looked 'Jewish'.[30] When it turned out, however, that the victim, far from being a German Jew, was the Portuguese Consul-General, Foreign Minister von Neurath was forced to make an official apology and advocates of 'hooligan antisemitism' in the Hamburg NSDAP were even forced onto the defensive within the party. The membership cards of the 'old guard', whose activities Gauleiter Kaufmann regarded with some scepticism,[31] were publicly not extended. After the elimination of Röhm, the Supreme Party Court of the NSDAP initiated internal proceedings against senior SA leaders in Hamburg. The trials did not deal with their responsibility for antisemitic attacks, but focused exclusively on their private lives.[32]

In mid-1934, violent antisemitic attacks died down in Hamburg, although they were rekindled again in 1935 and 1938. For Hamburg's Jews, the experience of unrestrained 'hooligan antisemitism' was significant in so far as it showed the potential that National Socialism held to deprive them of protection from the forces of law and order, leaving them open to the threat of violence.

## Middle-class Antisemitism

The National Socialist seizure of power in 1933 was not only characterised by violent attacks by the NSDAP's agitated antisemitic following, but also by an economic antisemitism that was particularly common in the middle class and which led, in 1933, to a large number of activities aimed directly at the destruction of the businesses of the German Jews.

These actions were supported primarily by trade associations which felt particularly affected by the global economic crisis. After the National Socialists took power, many saw a good opportunity to exclude Jewish members from the trade associations and thereby to improve the commercial opportunities of those who remained. These efforts were particularly notable in the professional associations where even before 1933 there were already complaints about the 'overcrowding' of their occupations, and where there had already been pressure to limit the number of licences granted, as for instance was the case in the legal profession.

In 1929 the Hamburg lawyers' association had seen a sharp conflict over the allocation of 'poverty cases paid from the state's coffers', a development that underlined the poor income situation of many attorneys.[33] In the Free Hanseatic City of Hamburg, where, at one lawyer per 2,195 inhabitants, the density of lawyers in the population was almost double that of the average in the Reich as a whole (3,930),[34] demands for a *numerus clausus* for lawyers at the bar thus fell on fruitful ground, while the Federation of National Socialist German Jurists (*Bund Nationalsozialistischer Deutscher Juristen*, BNSDJ), composed primarily of younger jurists, turned vehemently against such initiatives.[35]

In the spring of 1933, however, the conservative and National Socialist tendencies within the Hamburg bar united behind repressive measures against quite another group, Jewish lawyers. On 11 March 1933, members of the Hanseatic Lawyers' Chamber belonging to the NSDAP, DNVP, DVP and Stahlhelm took an 'Oath of Loyalty to the Government of National Rebirth'[36] and joined together to form a 'Working Committee of Nationalist Lawyers of the Hanseatic Cities' (*Arbeitsausschuß nationaler Anwälte der Hansestädte*). The main task of the Working Committee was to execute 'the necessary preparations for curbing the number of Jewish lawyers'.[37]

Another professional association which proceeded with ruthless exclusionary methods against Jewish members was the Reich Federation of German Real Estate Brokers (*Reichsverband Deutscher Makler*, RDM). In 1933, the Hamburg

Regional Group of the RDM, led by its Chairman, Hartmann, decided to exclude all Jewish members from the Reich Federation. This step was all the more remarkable because it was made in spite of the express opposition of the RDM national leadership, the Hamburg *Staatsamt* (the regional seat of government) and the Reich Interior Ministry.[38]

Such exclusions became even more crucial for those Jews for whom practising a profession was tied to membership of a professional association. Jewish street and market traders, for example, who could no longer belong to the Reich Federation of Itinerant Traders (*Reichsverband ambulanter Gewerbetreibender*) were not given a licence to set up stall in markets or fairs on the grounds that this privilege was restricted to members of the Reich Federation.[39]

Where middle-class professional associations refused to exclude Jewish members from their ranks, National Socialist and antisemitic professional associations were in some cases set up to put pressure on the established association. If the established association gave way and introduced an 'Aryan Paragraph', in most cases nothing stood in the way of a merger of the professional associations.[40]

In addition, antisemitic campaigns were carried out by middle-class entrepreneurs who had organised in the context of the National Socialist Combat League for the Commercial Middle Class (*Kampfbund für den gewerblichen Mittelstand*). Even before 1933, boycotts against Jewish firms of every size had been initiated and were brought together under the umbrella of the NSDAP, with antisemitic middle-class interest groups like the Combat Group against Department Stores, Consumer Unions and Large Chain Firms (*Kampfgemeinschaft gegen Warenhaus, Konsumvereine und Großfilialbetriebe*), the Association of German Businessmen (*Arbeitsgemeinschaft deutscher Geschäftsleute*) and the Combat League for the Preservation of the German Middle Class (*Kampfbund zur Erhaltung des deutschen Mittelstandes*).[41] Because of the small membership of these unions, the economic effects of the anti-Jewish boycotts they initiated remained slight before 1933. This changed after the National Socialists took power, with the Combat League for the Commercial Middle Class gaining many new members[42] who were obligated to break off all business relations with Jewish firms or face exclusion from the League. Trade with Jews in Hamburg was already noticeably affected by the customer boycott organised by the Combat League in 1933. Thus, for instance, a boycott organised by the Combat League for the Commercial Middle Class against the Hamburg florist A.M. Jacobsen & Sons, a Jewish wholesaler, sent the firm into bankruptcy in 1933–34.[43]

Under the leadership of the newly mandated Hamburg State Commissioner for the Middle Class, Christian Bartholatus, the Combat League also organised 'Brown Fairs' in Hamburg, which presented the products of middle-class enterprises and warned against buying from Jewish stores.[44]

In fliers distributed in many parts of Hamburg, the General Association of German Craftsmen, Businessmen and Tradesmen (*Gesamtverband deutscher Handwerker, Kaufleute und Gewerbetreibender*) advised the 'German housewife' to buy only in German stores so that money would not pass 'through department stores or one-price stores to Jewish or foreign capital'.[45] For the antisemitic propaganda campaigns of the National Socialist organisations, the *Graphische Kunstanstalt Schultz GmbH*, headquartered in Wandsbek, produced metre-long propaganda banners with the inscription: 'Anyone who buys from Jews is a traitor to the German people'.[46]

By no means was nation-wide or regional pressure from above required for campaigns against Jewish firms to be set in motion in the spring of 1933. After the National Socialists took power, many middle-class party members involved in business saw that a good climate had developed in which to denounce their Jewish competitors and to turn the supposedly favourable political climate to their personal private business advantage, thereby repaying themselves materially for their hitherto idealistic support of the National Socialist movement. The support of the new regime seemed to them to be so self-evident that they made no attempt at all to seek state or party agreement. In this way, from the spring of 1933, numerous antisemitic initiatives were unleashed against Jewish enterprises from below, developing into full-blown campaigns. The following examples of the campaigns waged against the Hamburg firms Beiersdorf and *Deutscher Tuchversand* (Detuv) show this clearly.[47]

## The Campaign Against Beiersdorf AG

In 1933, with over one thousand employees in its main Hamburg plant alone, Beiersdorf AG was one of the most successful manufacturers of pharmaceutical products in Germany. Its success was chiefly due to two Jewish pharmacists, Dr Oscar Troplowitz and Dr Otto Hanns Mankiewicz, whose products – *Nivea*, *Leukoplast* and *Labello* – were market leaders in Germany and abroad.[48] After the death of these two innovative founders of the firm, important functions in the management of the company were taken by assimilated Jews like the Chairman of the Board of Executives, Dr Willy Jacobsohn, board members Dr Hans Gradenwitz and Dr Eugen Unna, and the Chairman of the Supervisory Board, Dr Carl Melchior from the Jewish *Hausbank* M.M. Warburg & Co., which held a block of shares that gave it a majority at shareholders' meetings.

After the Nationalist Socialist seizure of power, the Beiersdorf management was confronted by an antisemitic campaign in which almost all of the company's rivals were involved.

The campaign was launched by the Hamburg firm Queisser & Co., whose own product – *Lovana Cream* – was in direct competition with Beiersdorf's skin cream products. In March 1933 next to the firm's title it added the motto 'The pure Aryan factory in South Eimsbüttel', and announced in a circular to its customers 'that our whole firm is purely Aryan and patriotic'.[49] The head of the company, consul and party member Alfred Queisser, was descended from 'old farming stock in the Lausitz region, where his family history has evolved continuously from 1600'. Finally, the recipients of the letter – pharmacists and drugstore owners – were bluntly told to do business with Queisser: 'You will now take great steps to recommend this kind of national extraction rather than Jewish specimens.' Queisser made even more direct demands in advertisements he placed in April 1933 in the *Illustrierter Beobachter* and other publications: 'Use Jewish skin cream no longer! *Lovana Cream* is at least as good, cheaper and purely German!'[50] Representatives of the Queisser enterprise went so far as to suggest to pharmacists that they were 'assigned by a political organisation to manufacture a skin cream to replace Jewish *Nivea* cream'.[51]

With this broadside, the Queisser company launched a campaign which several more of Beiersdorf's competitors quickly joined; Wolo G.m.b.H. from Freudenstadt in the Black Forest, in which the manufacturer Otto Böhringer had a share of 50%, distributed tens of thousands of yellow stickers carrying the motto: 'Anyone who buys *Nivea* products is supporting a Jewish company!'[52]

Lohmann A.G. from Fahr am Rhein, a sticking-plaster manufacturer, sent a circular to doctors asking them to support their 'German colleagues' and styling itself as a victim of 'international capital', which was seeking 'to expand to the detriment of purely German firms'.[53] All of the firms mentioned here also joined the Society for the Interests of German Brands (*Interessengemeinschaft Deutsche Marke*) headquartered in Dresden-Lockwitz, which led the call for a battle against the 'international web of Jewish big capital' and in favour of the 'union of all German Christian – that is to say Aryan – manufacturers of German perfumes and quality soaps'.[54] The Society for the Interests of German Brands represented a radical middle-class antisemitism which was aimed not only against Jewish competitors – principally Beiersdorf – but also against the established representative association of the trade, the *Verband deutscher Feinseifen- und Parfümerie-Fabriken e.V.*, urging it to implement the principles of racist antisemitism in the *Verband* as a whole.

At the beginning of May 1933, the Society for the Interests of German Brands raised its campaign against Beiersdorf to a new level, mobilizing the *völkisch*-nationalist press against the company. In its edition of 4 May 1933, the *völkisch*-nationalist newspaper *Fridericus* accused Beiersdorf of having camouflaged its real nature since the firm's foundation by taking the name of an Altona pharmacist and of trying to get around the boycott of German goods abroad by presenting itself as a 'Jewish' enterprise. The article culminated in a threat: 'The German people will not allow itself to fall into the position in which Jewish companies from Germany compete with German businesses, dressing themselves up to look German while abroad they seek to displace German businessmen by running around with frizzy Jewish curls.'[55]

When the Society for the Interests of German Brands reproduced thousands of fliers with the *Fridericus* article, adding the motto 'Does this interest you, then, German businessmen?', Beiersdorf could no longer ignore the antisemitic witch-hunt – especially after disconcerted pharmacists began turning to the Beiersdorf headquarters for an explanation. Some had even cancelled their orders. Placed in this difficult situation, the Beiersdorf management saw no way out other than to head off the campaign with 'voluntary Aryanisation'. On 18 April, the Jewish executive board members, Dr Willy Jacobsohn and Dr Hans Gradenwitz, and another member who in National Socialist terminology was 'half-Jewish', Dr Eugen Unna, resigned, while the two Jewish members of the supervisory board, Leo Alport and Dr Carl Melchior, announced their resignation at the next shareholder's meeting.[56] When M.M. Warburg & Co. converted its majority shares in Beiersdorf into common stock,[57] executive board member Christian Behrens was able to announce publicly on 24 April that the majority of Beiersdorf shares were once more 'in Christian hands'.[58] The Jewish executive president, Jacobsohn, like all of the other Jewish employees of the firm, was not dismissed but was moved to Amsterdam and from there directed Beiersdorf's foreign business. His replacement, 'Company Führer' Carl Claussen, fulfilled the critieria for being of 'Aryan' extraction while also representing continuity in the firm in so far as he was married to a niece of the Jewish founder of the firm, Troplowitz.[59]

With this internal restructuring of the firm, Beiersdorf had prepared itself for an offensive against its competitors in the Society for the Interests of German Brands, although the newspaper *Der Stürmer* immediately attacked Beiersdorf's counter-offensive as a 'typically Jewish' diversion.[60] In the period that followed it became clear that Beiersdorf's campaign had succeeded in obtaining the support of influential figures in the state, the party and industry. Thus, on 15 May 1933, Beiersdorf was awarded a certificate as a 'German enterprise' from the Reich leadership of the Combat League of the Commercial Middle Class.[61] Likewise, the newly founded National Association of German Health Product Industries (*Nationalverband der Deutschen Heilmittelindustrie*) showed little inclination to make itself the defender of the personal profits of particular members. Executive board member Hans Schwarzkopf – though a member of the NSDAP – took a clear position on the side of Beiersdorf, and assured the firm in a letter that the 'dubious' campaign of their detractors had also encountered 'absolute opposition within the party'.[62] From the perspective of the National Association, the greedy campaigns of individual member firms jeopardised the credibility of the often-proclaimed National Socialist corporatist order and also raised the threat of incalculable distortions to the economy, particularly where, as in the case of Beiersdorf AG, they were dealing with a large enterprise with a leading position in the market.

For this reason, Beiersdorf was also supported by the Hamburg Economics Department under the leadership of NSDAP *Gau* Economics Adviser Dr Gustav Schlotterer, who explained to the NSDAP Reich Press Office that antisemitic campaigns ran against 'the economic policy goals pursued in Hamburg for the maintenance of employment opportunities'.[63]

The Reich Economics Ministry, to which Beiersdorf AG had turned for assistance,[64] gave similar arguments against isolated antisemitic initiatives. In a circular of 8 September 1933, Reich Economics Minister Dr Kurt Schmitt, a member of a discussion circle of leading industrial figures together with Hamburg bankers Max Warburg and Carl Melchior which sought to moderate the impact of anti-Jewish policy on business life,[65] prohibited any differentiation between 'Aryan' and 'non-Aryan' firms, and vehemently opposed efforts to boycott Jewish businesses: 'Such a distinction, aimed at a boycott of non-Aryan firms, will necessarily lead to substantial disturbances for economic reconstruction since unfavourable responses in the labour market would become unavoidable due to operational restrictions imposed on firms affected by the boycott.'[66]

With such support coming from all around it, the Beiersdorf management now went onto the offensive and submitted claims for sizeable damages against the firms which had taken part in the campaign against the company. The move did not lead as far as court proceedings, however, since the NSDAP Reich leadership wished to avoid a public legal condemnation of their antisemitic party membership at all costs, and the *Nationalverband der deutschen Heilmittelindustrie e.V.* finally negotiated a settlement prohibiting the companies which had joined the campaign against Beiersdorf from continuing it further.[67] In a circular to its customers, the management of Beiersdorf described this result as 'somewhat meagre' but at the same time emphasised 'that by our accommodating behaviour we have gained sympathy in decision-making circles which are more important to us'.[68]

Beiersdorf's strategy of building trust among the National Socialist leadership was subsequently repeated time and again when faced with antisemitic incidents and the 'covert campaign'[69] in the period which followed. On the whole it was successful, since it assured the company management of official protection from repression. However, this moderate outcome, and the ultimate collapse of the antisemitic campaign were only made possible by virtue of the coincidence of four specific conditions that were woven together in the Beiersdorf case.

First, the initiators of the campaign against Beiersdorf had chosen the 'wrong' time to act. In spring 1933, the highest priority of the new National Socialist regime was to consolidate its power, which meant giving due consideration to the National Socialists' right-wing conservative coalition partners, to international opinion and to the objective of eliminating mass unemployment. For these reasons the regime adopted a degree of tactical moderation in its anti-Jewish policy, above all with respect to economic questions.

Secondly, although the measures taken against Beiersdorf had been a serious threat, they were not able to destroy the company because the decision-making bodies of the state and NSDAP did not support them. The lesson given by the antisemitic campaign against Beiersdorf demonstrates that without the active support of the state, antisemitism from below had only sporadic effects, and fizzled out.

Thirdly, the size of Beiersdorf and its significance for Germany's economic policy as a whole played a decisive role in the decision of both state and party to support the company. During the global economic crisis, Beiersdorf had not dismissed a single worker. Had it been otherwise, Reich institutions like the Economics Ministry would hardly have shown any favour to Beiersdorf. The owners of small Jewish businesses facing similar attempts at repression at the time could count on no such support.

Fourth, this official support only applied to Beiersdorf after it had undergone a 'voluntary Aryanisation' and thereby sought to demonstrate its 'good behaviour' on a political level.

### The Detuv Affair

In the spring of 1933, almost in parallel with the antisemitic attacks against Beiersdorf AG, a further antisemitic campaign developed against another Hamburg firm, again from among the ranks of the commercial middle class.

Before 1933 the Jewish fabric company Adolph Frank & Co. K.G. – for which a Jewish businessman Albert Levy was personally responsible as a key shareholder – had had great success, in, among other things, selling fabric to private households on a payment-plan basis. Given the general decline in income during the global economic crisis, dispatching cheap fabrics for do-it-yourself dressmakers proved a great source of profit for the company.

So as not to jeopardise their position in the market by provoking National Socialist boycott measures, Albert Levy and his partner Leopold Garfunkel decided to 'Aryanise' the presentation of the business at the beginning of 1933. In March 1933 they created another company, German Fabric Dispatch Ltd (*Deutscher Tuchversand GmbH*, Detuv), into which they brought the bulk of their previous company Adolph Frank & Co. K.G.; the entire purchasing infrastructure, personnel, a part of the business premises and above all the firm's account – in total worth 700,000 RM.[70] Three 'Aryan' businessmen were added as partners in Detuv with a share worth 21,000 RM. The sole managing director was Alois Mainka, a former sales representative of the Adolph Frank factory who as an 'old fighter' in the NSDAP had supplied clothing to clients such as the office of the NSDAP *Ortsgruppenleiter* of Neumünster since 1929.[71] Although formally under 'Aryan' management, Detuv was in fact the distribution division of the Adolph Frank factory, to which, moreover, it was tied by fixed delivery contracts.

In the following months, an antisemitic campaign was launched against Detuv's new structure. The campaign was led by the State Association of North German Dressmakers (*Landesverband Norddeutscher Schneiderinnungen*), which, in the wake of the 'national uprising', saw that the time was ripe to rid itself of an irritating source of competition. In a number of articles in their newsletter the dressmakers waged a polemic against Detuv, branding it the 'worst parasite on the dressmaking craft'[72] and attacking it as a Jewish cover firm. A classic modernisation conflict, in which a company with modern distribution methods placed competitors working with antiquated handicraft under pressure, was redefined here as a model for the antisemitic argument of the 'avaricious Jew' pulling the rug out from underneath 'honest German handicraft'.

The 'Aryan' partners in Detuv reacted to the campaign with counterarguments and sworn assurances, ultimately seeking an injunction at the Hamburg State Court when the campaign continued into 1934. The court rejected Detuv's complaint, however, describing the company as 'camouflage' for the 'continuing business of the firm Adolph Frank & Co., currently working behind an Aryan façade'.[73]

When the State Association of North German Dressmakers once again renewed its campaign against Detuv on the strength of the State Court's opinion, it unexpectedly introduced another institution into the conflict. The NSDAP *Gau* Economics Adviser, who in the years that followed would enforce the 'de-Judaisation' of Hamburg industry, in this case took the side of the firm that was being threatened. On the grounds of the 'threat to the economic peace' it represented he forbade the dressmakers from publishing the court ruling in their newsletter and threatened that if need be he would take the publisher responsible for a breach of his prohibition into 'protective custody'. In addition, the Hamburg Economics Department also took the side of Detuv and gave it a certificate as an 'Aryan' enterprise.[74]

The dressmakers did not respect the prohibition issued and published extracts of the judgment in their newsletter of 1 August 1934. The *Gau* Economics Adviser then removed the *Obermeister* of the Hamburg Dressmakers from his post and blocked any further continuation of the campaign by bringing in the Gestapo. In a letter to the attorney of the North German Dressmakers he described the legal constitution of Detuv as completely 'normal'. His decisive intervention was 'in the interests of the German national economy ... so that many German employees not be made to go without bread'.[75]

For the Jewish company owners this constellation of interests did not provide long-term security, just a temporary period of grace. The initial attitude of the *Gau* Economics Adviser and the Hamburg Economics Department to the campaigns against Beiersdorf and Detuv had demonstrated that the new Hamburg state and party leaderships would not support the radical antisemitism of the middle class at any price, and were temporarily ready, and in a position, to make tactical compromises. In this respect, the Detuv affair had shown that in the first phase of their period in power the National Socialists themselves overturned a judgment of a state court, intervening in favour of a Jewish businessman when employment calculations made this appear opportune.

## The Boycott of 1 April 1933

With antisemitism fermenting from below and the Reich leadership focusing on consolidating its power and other pressing considerations, the organised boycott against Jewish businesses and legal and medical practices of 1 April 1933 functioned as an outlet for channelling the pent-up hatred of Jews among National Socialist activists, allowing them at the same time to prove their faithfulness to the party's antisemitic principles.[76] As was the case in Hamburg, where in mid-March the SA blockaded department stores, many cities and regions witnessed 'unauthorised' boycott initiatives against Jewish firms[77] that put the new National Socialist Reich government in a difficult position with respect to its followers.

The official reason for the 1 April boycott, launched on the strength of a personal decision by Hitler,[78] was the allegation that 'horror stories' were being spread abroad against National Socialist Germany. On 28 March, the Reich leadership of the NSDAP issued an announcement to this effect and a day later a detailed notice fixed the launch of the organised boycott of Jewish businesses, goods, doctors and lawyers 'promptly' for Saturday, 1 April 1933.[79]

In Hamburg the new National Socialist Senate stirred up anti-Jewish opinion with a carefully worded press release in which 'foreign elements' were blamed for price rises in stores – in particular in the woven goods trade – in order to disturb the economic life of the population. For this reason the Senate decided – this was the basic thrust of this transparent piece of propaganda – 'to use draconian means ruthlessly to suffocate these attempts'.[80]

On 29 March 1933, Hamburg Gauleiter Karl Kaufmann delivered a half-hour radio broadcast fulminating against both 'Jewish finance capital' and 'international social democracy', which he accused of 'betraying the Fatherland' through a 'propaganda campaign of lies and horror stories'.[81] Playing cleverly on widespread anxiety within Hamburg's export trade, he declared that this was inflicting 'untold damage on the image of our father city' and on its economic interests. With respect to the real core of these alleged horror stories, the abuse of Jews and foreigners by the Hamburg SA, about which the Gauleiter had known for a long time through a variety of written complaints,[82] Kaufmann deliberately remained silent. He described the accusations of rampant antisemitism that were put by the Jewish community in Hamburg, the *Deutsch-Israelitischen Gemeinde*, as 'lame' and 'whinging'. It was the responsibility of the 'Jewish guest people' to eliminate the causes of antisemitism themselves. These he described as the disproportionate numbers of Jews in particular industries and occupations, which he sought to buttress with the most fantastic numbers.[83] From there he proceeded to demand 'equality for the Germans in their own Fatherland'. By this time, the victims of the press campaign in Hamburg were already deprived of any right to argue against the propagandistic torrent of words from the Gauleiter, who in his broadcast had threatened to refuse to tolerate 'any tendentious report against the Senate and Reich government'.

Before the Hamburg SA were deployed outside Hamburg's businesses on 1 April, another political grouping attempted to make its name by positioning itself at the forefront of the boycott. Uniformed propaganda troops from the Combat Group of Young National Germans (*Kampfring junger Deutschnationaler*) marched through the shopping areas of Hamburg with placards bearing slogans such as 'Don't run after foreign goods – Germans should buy from Germans', attracting considerable attention.[84] For the National Socialists in Hamburg, the adoption of their combat methods by a young right-wing conservative tendency was clearly undesirable and the Combat Group of Young National Germans was banned in May 1933.[85]

While otherwise the situation in Hamburg before 1 April remained calm, in the neighbouring town of Altona the boycott of Jewish businesses had already begun on 29 March. It may be that this early launch of the boycott formed the background to the accusations addressed by the police chief of Altona, Hinkler, to Krogmann, the mayor of Hamburg, 'that the police in Hamburg are proceeding too cautiously with respect to the Jewish question'.[86] In Altona, Hinkler had imposed upon Jewish businesses the duty of putting up yellow signs showing they were 'Jewish businesses', threatening them with a fine or imprisonment if they did not comply.[87]

The type of discrimination marked by this threat did not, however, go far enough for Hamburg's Senator for the Interior, Alfred Richter, who imposed upon the 'Aryan' business people of Hamburg an obligation to identify themselves. They were to assure on a placard 'that the business concerned is not a Jewish enterprise, that it will not employ any Jewish workers and that it is free of Jewish capital'.[88] Falsification of information would lead to the immediate closure of the business.

Thus, without any legal basis to do so, Hamburg's Interior Senator had introduced an extraordinarily far-reaching definition of a 'Jewish business'. At the same time, he sought to isolate them by stigmatizing them and blocking any grounds for a show of solidarity which other 'Aryan businesses' might have staged for their Jewish counterparts.

The effects of the proclamation could be seen not only in the placards hung in shop windows, but also in the eagerness of 'Aryan' business circles to reinforce the proclamation, with large numbers of declarations and advertisements being placed in the Hamburg daily newspapers. Thus the Salamander shoe factory assured readers that it 'was under German management, only used German material and only gave wages and bread to German workers';[89] the owners of the Elsner shoestore were described as 'genuine German and Christian men';[90] the 'genuine German Peiniger fabric store' declared that it wished not to be mistaken 'with similar-sounding firms which have been set up in the area';[91] and the drugs wholesaler Iwan Budnikowsky published details of his place of birth (Perleberg), his denomination (Lutheran) and his Prussian citizenship 'in order to counter false rumours about my person'.[92] Advertisements promoted 'German fabric',[93] 'German sweets'[94] and 'German wool',[95] the 'German cash register',[96] 'German typewriters'[97] and the 'German quality bicycle',[98] 'German eggs'[99] and 'German butter'.[100] One oriental carpet store in Hamburg even advertised its products as 'German carpets'.[101] By contrast, a small measure of dissidence among Hamburg shopkeepers could be detected on the day of the boycott when some – against instructions – decided not to describe themselves as 'Aryan' or 'German', but as 'old Christian' businesses, even if such a statement did not always conceal a conscious act of nonconformity.[102]

At 10 o'clock on 1 April, SA men were placed outside all Jewish businesses in Hamburg and placards inscribed 'Don't buy from Jews' were fixed to the shop windows, or the warning 'Look out, Jews' was daubed in red paint on the window panes. Fliers were also handed out to passers-by and antisemitic literature was sold. Because it was sabbath, many Jewish store owners, particularly in the Grindel quarter, had their stores shut the whole day.

Press reports unanimously praised the 'admirable discipline'[103] of the SA and pronounced that the reason that there had been no incidents was because, in the run-up to the boycott, the Hamburg Gauleiter had already guaranteed that 'no Jews would even have one hair bent'.[104] However, Jews were in fact exposed to violent attacks by the SA. Two SA men beat up a Jewish passer-by so brutally that his eardrum burst. Only through the courageous intervention of another passer-by were worse injuries avoided.[105]

The reactions of the population of Hamburg to the boycott on the whole fell into two categories. Curiosity had clearly driven many of Hamburg's residents into the centre of town. The newspapers reported that 'hundreds of thousands had come into the town in order to observe the extent of the boycott'.[106] Their mood appeared to one observer, however, to be 'depressed, unhappy; most could not support [this] in their inner self'.[107] The rejection of the boycott, at least among parts of the population of Hamburg, could even be detected between the lines of the National Socialist-controlled press. Thus the *Hamburger Nachrichten* mocked those 'primitive and even perverse minds that had completely failed to understand what this was about'.[108] The Hamburg police authorities also admitted in a public announcement that 'in some Jewish businesses there was a demonstrative traffic of left-radical elements'.[109]

Hans J. Robinsohn of the fashion store *Gebrüder Robinsohn*, acknowledged this type of 'protest customer' in his memoirs, who demonstrated their rejection of the National Socialists – particularly in the initial period of the National Socialist regime – by buying in Jewish stores.[110] The turnover of the fashion store on 1 April had fallen to barely one-tenth of the normal level, though the number of cash-till receipts amounted to one-third of the normal figure – a sign that many customers had only entered the store out of opposition to the regime and just bought a small item.

Hamburg physician Dr Hans Bruno reported demonstrative visits to his practice by many of his patients on the day of the boycott. During a house visit on one of the days that followed, one patient for whom he had prescribed a diet told him: 'Doctor, I cannot keep the diet because first I have to eat all the eggs we bought at Jewish stores on the day of the boycott.'[111]

Likewise, Dr Henriette Necheles-Magnus, a physician from Wandsbek, reported many gestures of loyalty from among her patients: 'The patients kept coming with flowers, with small gifts: "We want to show you what we think of this type of politics." "I am not ill, Doctor, I have come to see how you are." A small piece of handicraft, the "boycott blanket", still lies in my room today. A patient crocheted it for me in those days as a sign of her affection.'[112]

The customers of a shoe store in Altona which the SA prevented locals from entering decided to place their orders by telephone.[113]

When Lutheran pastor Heinrich Schwieger intervened with NSDAP County Leader Heinz Morisse on behalf of the boycotted Jewish salesman J. Scharfstein – although he was a supporter of the National Socialists – a fierce argument broke out which he later reported to his bishop:

I asked him whether he thought the Jew should open his business again, to which he answered: never. At that I thought I had to say something about justice, that Scharfstein had lost his son at the front in the naval batallion in Flanders (war volunteer in 1914!), that he himself was a religious Israelite who had never made a secret of his ethnic and religious beliefs and in my community had quietly done much, much good. Whereupon Herr Morisse answered with a laugh: now more than ever. He still considered it necessary to ask me as an old soldier from the front where I had been then, what I as a pastor had suffered and how generally the whole church had failed. He thought that we would have now had a different outlook on the world. I added nothing to this friendly observation, which he still found it necessary to underline by asking whether I had any special interest in the defence of the Jew, except for noting that I had to bear the brunt of his anger. If he had no appreciation of the conscientious doubts expressed to him by German men, I would feel sorry for him.[114]

In assessing such demonstrative gestures of solidarity, account should of course be taken of the fact that during the two months after 30 January 1933, the National Socialist dictatorship had not consolidated its hold in any way. Above all, the all-encompassing network of repression and social control which effectively paralysed all opposition in later years was still not fully developed.

The National Socialists drew a sobering conclusion from the behaviour of the population. At a meeting of the National Socialist Lawyers' League in Hamburg at the end of April 1933, the boycott was openly described as a mistake and the reaction of the population was described as unsatisfactory.[115] Not even NSDAP party members followed suit in boycotting Jewish businesses. As late as the beginning of January 1934, the administrative head of the NSDAP's Hamburg *Gau*, Henry Meyer, complained in a public statement that 'members of the party or of its subsidiary organisations buy in Jewish department stores in uniform or with party badges on'.[116] Significantly, the fact that National Socialists were buying in Jewish stores was not the primary object of criticism, the problem was that they did so wearing their uniform.

The reaction of Hamburg's business community to the boycott of 1 April 1933 partly followed the same lines as the official propaganda that was disseminated by the new rulers. Some middle-class radical antisemites in the larger firms, associations and industrial federations sent telegrams to their business partners elsewhere in the world describing reports of the persecution of Jews and foreigners in Hamburg as 'untrue' or dismissing them as 'malicious and fabricated rumours'. Though the British popular press published a few sensationalist articles that were not based on the facts,[117] the generally accurate, if unsympathetic, international press response[118] did not justify writing indignant letters of protest that made excuses for what had taken place. The authors of these telegrams included the Union of Traders on the Hamburg Exchange (*Verein der Getreidehändler der Hamburger Börse*), the Union of Firms in Hamburg involved in the Coffee Trade

(*Verein der am Caffeehandel betheiligten Firmen in Hamburg*), the Union of Tea Traders of Hamburg and Bremen (*Verein der Hamburg-Bremer Teehändler*), *Frachtkontor GmbH* and the Hamburg Rotary Club.[119] The Hamburg firm Olff, Köpke & Co. distributed four thousand copies of an explanation to its foreign trading partners in which it certified the National Socialists' 'exemplary discipline and order' and described reports of attacks on Jews, Communists and Social Democrats as 'slanderous inventions'.[120]

These statements from individual companies and industrial federations, so unlike the distanced attitude of the population of Hamburg to the April boycott, were primarily motivated by economic self-interest. Boycott initiatives against German goods abroad had hit Hamburg's heavily export-oriented industry so hard that reports that glossed over National Socialist rule in Germany – prompted by personal conviction or tactical motives – were now deliberately being circulated.

This was, moreover, a product of Hamburg industry's unhealthy tradition of spreading propaganda abroad, conducted primarily through the 'Enlightenment Committee' (*Aufklärungsausschuß*) of the Hamburg Chamber of Commerce.[121] Since 1924 the Enlightenment Committee, of which the Bremen Chamber of Commerce was a member from 1931, had worked in secret to place tens of thousands of propaganda articles in the foreign press, through a large network of trusted collaborators, in order to improve Germany's image after the defeat in the last war. The articles stressed, on the one hand, the competitiveness of German industry and the quality of German products and, on the other, the restrictions imposed by the Treaty of Versailles and the refutation of the alleged 'war guilt lie'.

Thus, before 1933, the work of the Enlightenment Committee was already identified uncritically with national myths and legends that did less to serve the cause of 'enlightenment' than to cloud Germany's historical responsibility. In the light of this underlying attitude it is not surprising that after 1933, foreign reports of the persecution of the Jews and concentration camps met with a well-established defensive reflex: there was no readiness to check whether the horror stories were accurate. With the assumption of power by the National Socialists, the Committee entered fully into the spirit of National Socialist propaganda and developed into the most important international news service of the Third Reich,[122] linked to the Reich Propaganda Ministry on a contractually regulated basis.[123]

From its foundation the managing director of the Enlightenment Committee was Dr Kurt G. Johannsen, a former Hamburg gymnasium teacher,[124] who, after 1933, turned out to be a fanatical National Socialist. In his position, Johannsen could count on a large number of illustrious collaborators and above all on the foreign contacts of Hamburg industrialists. One of his collaborators, Count Zeppelin, urged Johannsen to show the 'folks' abroad 'that, in contrast with what you believe, German industry and intelligence did not disappear with the emigration of Jews from Germany, but that even without them we are able to preserve what before the war we Germans were well-known for and famed around the whole world for having made'.[125] Hamburg companies were so involved in the work of the Enlightenment Committee that, among other things, they prepared reports about Jewish calls for boycotts abroad which the Committee also sent to the Reich Propaganda Ministry and to the Foreign Office.[126] In return they received assistance with developing arguments against the boycott of German exports prepared by the Committee's managing director, Dr Johannsen, using excerpts from the standard texts of antisemitic literature.

One surviving example, circulated by the 'Association of Hamburg Shipowners' (*Verein Hamburger Rheder*), justified what it described as 'current events' – meaning the boycott of 1 April – as 'a reaction to developments that have taken place since 1918'.[127] Johannsen's first tack was to expand on the allegedly extensive influence of Jews in politics, industry, culture and science in Germany, which he put down to the 'high number of Jewish officials and party functionaries in the Social Democratic and Communist parties'.[128] Johannsen also tried to prove the 'inferiority' of the Jews in a pamphlet in which he meditated on 'Jews as criminals' and on the 'extensive racial degeneration of Jewry'.[129] That this important organ of the Hamburg Chamber of Commerce promoted a primitive antisemitism highlights that such attitudes were in no way confined to the grassroots of the NSDAP or to the middle class.

### First Dismissals of Jewish Employees

The antisemitic climate of the spring of 1933 was not only expressed in campaigns and attacks on Jewish businesses and factories, it also led to the first dismissals of Jewish employees, which many companies were ready to make 'voluntarily' (this was particularly true of public limited companies). Chain stores and high street stores assumed an inglorious pioneering role in this process. Having long been a target of the National Socialists' propaganda among the middle class they now hoped to gain political credit for dismissing their Jewish employees quickly.

In January, a first foretaste of the debates in the spring of 1933 was given by a conflict which broke out in the Hamburg City Parliament (*Bürgerschaft*) over the licencing of a Woolworth branch in the Barmbek neighbourhood. The NSDAP caucus opposed the granting of the licence, trying to present itself as the voice of middle-class interests in Hamburg.[130] On 11 March 1933, a few days after the National Socialists took power in Hamburg, SA members blocked the entrance to the Karstadt store in Mönckebergstraße and forced the store management to close the building. On the same day, SA members marched on the Tietz department store on Jungfernstieg and also forced other Hamburg department stores and high street stores to close down for the day. The new National Socialist police chief, Dr Hans Nieland, took no steps to halt the SA's arbitrary attacks, but merely noted with cold cynicism 'that no illegal force would be used against the public'.[131]

Confronted by the 'unruly' actions of the SA, and under internal pressure from the National Socialist Factory Cells Organisation (*Nationalsozialistische Betriebszellen-Organisation*, NSBO) – the organisation that coordinated the work of National Socialist representatives in commercial enterprises – the managers of Karstadt AG decided on the radical step of dismissing all its Jewish employees on 1 April 1933 without notice. Shortly before that, all of the Jewish members of Karstadt's supervisory board had announced their resignation so that they would not have to agree to the dismissals. Dr Fritz M. Warburg, a member of the board from Hamburg, explained to Karstadt's executive board that because of the political developments of recent weeks he could no longer take part in important decisions, 'especially in the area of personnel policy', without being in danger of difficult conflicts of conscience.[132]

Karstadt's official explanation for these dismissals, which affected many employees in Hamburg, generated much attention as it made reference to the legal position of German Jews in the business world even before many of the regulations in this area had been introduced. Two years before the passing of the 'Nuremberg Laws', the management of Karstadt AG assumed that Jews were no longer 'useful and equal citizens' and therefore that they were also no longer 'equal as co-workers'. The author of this declaration, Dr Ahlburg, a Karstadt lawyer, dug deep into the arsenal of vulgar antisemitic stereotypes and went so far as to claim 'that the members of the Jewish race are today no longer fully equal citizens, and that they be regarded as alien intruders in the Germany national body, whose position of power, built on the ruins of the world war and with the help of war mutineers in Germany, will have to be completely destroyed and eliminated if the German people and German culture are not to be ruined'.[133]

In the months that followed, this 'lowest level of demagogy' – as Dr Ernst Spiegelberg of the bank M.M. Warburg & Co. described it[134] – encouraged the activists of the NSBO to undertake yet more antisemitic initiatives to test how much further the company's managers could be pressurised. An NSBO representative at the Karstadt store in Mönckebergstraße attached a sign to the purchasing office at the beginning of October 1933 which declared that 'non-Aryan reps' were 'not wanted'. Once people had begun to tell Jewish salesmen not to come to the store, it took a major intervention from the company directors to get rid of the sign again.[135]

A similar tactic was practiced by the SA and NSBO at the Hamburg branches of *Einheitspreis-AG* (EPA). When, at the beginning of April 1933, three Jewish members of the supervisory board – Dr Ernst Spiegelberg, Julius Oppenheimer and Paul Braunschweig – and one executive board member, Hans Lindemann, resigned from their offices,[136] NSBO representatives felt encouraged to resort to even more radical measures, demanding the resignation of all Jewish executive board members, as had already happened at Karstadt AG. On instructions from the NSBO the staff of the Harburg and the three Hamburg EPA branches went on strike in order to lend weight to their demand, eventually forcing the resignation of the executive board members.[137] Such receptivity to the demands of the National Socialists did not, however, prevent the Hamburg Senate from imposing a supplementary penalty on EPA, Karstadt, Tietz and Woolworth in the form of a 'department store tax', analogous to the Prussian goods tax supplement of twenty per cent introduced retroactively from 1 April 1933.[138]

Just as department store chains like Karstadt and EPA displayed an eager servility in the face of demands from the National Socialists, so too did a number of banks which, before 1933, were exposed to the same type of attacks from antisemitic middle-class National Socialist propagandists.[139] The *Deutsch-Südamerikanische Bank* in Hamburg had already let all of its Jewish employees go in August 1933.[140] This mass lay-off of Jewish workers, unusually quick for a bank, was probably due to the influence of the chair of the executive board, Hermann Victor Hübbe, who, as an NSDAP member from 1931 and President of the Hamburg Chamber of Commerce from 1933, belonged to the younger, pro-National Socialist generation of Hamburg businessmen. In addition, the parent company of *Deutsch-Südamerikanischen Bank*, Dresdner Bank, which until its denationalisation in 1937 was strongly influenced by the state and subsequently became deeply involved in the 'Aryanisation' of Jewish enterprises, showed little consideration in its handling of Jewish employees. In the course of 1933 it dismissed a total of 219 employees on predominantly 'racial' grounds.[141] At the end of June 1933 the two deputy directors, Dr Mosler and Dr Freund, both Jewish, received a four-line letter of dismissal from the personnel department which contained not one word of gratitude despite the more than 25 years of service they had given to the company – a procedure that the Hamburg banker Max M. Warburg described as 'barbaric' and about which Dr Mosler observed sarcastically after his dismissal that, 'by comparison, Karstadt had gotten rid of its employees in an exemplary fashion'.[142]

The dismissal of large numbers of Jewish employees highlighted the indirect impact of antisemitism from below with exceptional clarity, since the management in many companies – whether from fear, overeager obedience or antisemitic conviction – readily gave in to pressure from below and parted from their Jewish workers. The first year of National Socialist rule was marked by a great variety and range of antisemitic activities. These were partly encouraged or accompanied by supporting measures from above – especially from the NSDAP Reich leadership, Reich ministries and other central authorities – as was the case, for instance, on the occasion of the Reich-wide April boycott of 1933. However, in some respects they were also not supported or often even opposed at these levels, as a number of individual attacks on Jewish businesses revealed.

The total number of those damaged by these anti-Jewish activities and their actual economic effects are, even in hindsight, still difficult to determine. Many Hamburg Jews nevertheless found the experience of this persecution and the atmosphere in Hamburg after the National Socialists took power so oppressive that even in the first six months of 1933 thousands emigrated rather than remain in such uncertain circumstances.[143]

## Notes

1. *Staatsarchiv Hamburg* (StAHH), *Krogmann Familie I, Bestand Carl Vincent Krogmann*, C 15, I/1, extract from the diary of Emerentia Krogmann, written for her children.
2. See Gerhard Paul, *Aufstand der Bilder. Die NS-Propaganda vor 1933*, Bonn, 1990, pp. 236–239.
3. Thus Hitler already in a statement of 6 April 1920, cit. from Hitler, *Sämtliche Aufzeichnungen 1905–1924*, ed. by Eberhard Jäckel and Axel Kuhn, Stuttgart, 1980, p. 120.
4. Citation from Helmut Berding, *Moderner Antisemitismus in Deutschland*, Frankfurt am Main, 1988, p. 204.
5. On this see in particular the references in Adam, *Judenpolitik*, p. 46.
6. *Archiv der Forschungsstelle für Zeitgeschichte* in Hamburg (referred to below as *Archiv FZH*), 11/S 11, diary of Luise Solmitz, 6 February 1933.
7. StAHH, NSDAP, B 197, circular from the Hamburg SA *Untergruppe*, 8 February 1933.
8. Circular in ibid.
9. Genschel, *Verdrängung*, p. 50.
10. StAHH, NSDAP, B 202, letter from Deputy Gauleiter Henningsen to the Hamburg SA *Untergruppe*, 28 March 1933.
11. StAHH, NSDAP, B 112, announcement by the state police of 12 April 1933.
12. StAHH, *Familie Plaut*, D 39/4, letter from Dr Max Plaut to the *Sonderkommission der Kripo Hamburg* (undat.).
13. Special Archives, Moscow, 721-1-2339, p. 47, communication from the Hamburg-Altona local group of the *Centralverein deutscher Staatsbürger jüdischen Glaubens*, 12 May 1933.
14. StAHH, NSDAP, B 112, Hamburg state police (*SS-Standartenführer* Streckenbach) to *SA-Brigade* 12, 7 August 1934, re. riots in the Timpe café, Grindelallee 10. The Timpe café was a traditional meeting place for left-leaning Jews in Hamburg interested in culture.

15. Arie Goral-Sternheim, *Im Schatten der Synagoge*, Hamburg, 1989, p. 29. Cf. also Ina Lorenz, *Die Juden in Hamburg zur Zeit der Weimarer Republik. Eine Dokumentation*, 2 vols, Hamburg, 1987, here Vol. 2, pp. 1000–1073.

16. *Hamburger Anzeiger*, 27 March 1931, '*Front gegen Intoleranz und politische Verwilderung*'.

17. On Krautsdorfer's career, see *Justizbehörde Hamburg*, preliminary legal investigations against Karl Kaufmann, *Landgericht Hamburg*, 14 Js. 28/49, p. 303.

18. On incidents of this kind, see StAHH, NSDAP, B 112.

19. Ibid., announcement from *Polizeihauptmann* Abraham, 29 March 1933.

20. StAHH, NSDAP, B 202, note by the *Unterstützungsstelle*, 9 August 1933.

21. *Bundesarchiv Koblenz* (BAK), NS 22/259, letter from Böckenhauer, 17 March 1933, to the *NSDAP-Gauleitung Hamburg*. Cf. also the question put by Kaufmann to *Reichorganisationsleiter* Ley on 25 March 1933 with respect to Böckenhauer's competences.

22. StAHH, NSDAP, B 262, circular from the *Chef der Ordnungspolizei*, 17 March 1933.

23. E.g., 'You are passing by the state; if you don't do it correctly, I will kick you in the ass!' Citation from StAHH, NSDAP, B 109, Harry Vogler to *Reichsstatthalter* Kaufmann, 7 July 1933.

24. StAHH, NSDAP, B 262, SA *Standarte* 15 to the Hamburg *Untergruppe* of the SA, 10 June 1933. Thus the police were described *inter alia* as '*Reichsbanner* shit'.

25. StAHH, NSDAP, B 114, *Chef der Ordnungspolizei* to the Hamburg SA *Untergruppe*, 11 May 1933.

26. StAHH, NSDAP, B 202, *Polizeibehörde* to *SA-Brigade* 12, 29 May 1934.

27. StAHH, NSDAP, B 112, instruction sheet for the *Scharführer* of *Sturm* 72.

28. Ibid., circular from *SA-Oberführer* Böckenhauer, 21 June 1933.

29. Officially the '*Alte Garde*' included all NSDAP members with a membership number under 100,000, who had already been a member of the party before 1928.

30. *Archiv FZH*, 912 (*Alte Garde, Gau Hamburg*).

31. Cf. Kaufmann in the *Hamburger Tageblatt*, 18 May 1935: 'The Führer has not fought this fight in order at the end of the day to set up a union of old veterans.'

32. In this, visits to the brothel in uniform, *inter alia*, played a central role. Cf. Berlin Document Centre, Fust, Herbert, SA-P, excerpts from the files for the proceedings of the *Obersten Parteigericht*, 21 January 1935.

33. *Hamburger Echo*, 5 May 1929.

34. Figures can be found in *Lübecker General-Anzeiger*, 23 August 1929.

35. *Hamburger Fremdenblatt*, 3 March 1933.

36. *Hamburgischer Correspondent*, 12 March 1933.

37. *Hamburgischer Correspondent*, 7 April 1933. On the exclusion of Jewish lawyers from the Hamburg courts, see Ch. II.

38. StAHH, *Staatsamt*, 106, communication from the Hamburg Legation in Berlin to the Hamburg *Staatsamt*, 30 November 1933. On the approach of the *Reichsinnenministerium* to this question, see Adam, *Judenpolitik*, p. 88.

39. Cf. the letter from Jakob Boldes, a Jewish market trader in Hamburg, to the *Reichsinnenministerium*, 19 January 1934, BAP, *Reichswirtschaftsministerium*, 13862, pp. 68–71.

40. Cf. the situation among independent commercial agents, who had organised themselves traditionally in the *Centralverband Deutscher Handelsvertreter-Vereine* (Central Federation of Associations of German Commercial Agents), created in 1886. As controversies developed in the Federation over aspects of the 'Jewish question' in 1933, a *Bund Nationalsozialistischer Handelsvertreter* (Federation of National Socialist Commercial Agents) was formed. On 23 January 1934, both federations united by order of Rudolf Hess into the *Reichsverband Deutscher Handelsvertreter und Geschäftsreisender* (Reich Federation of German Commercial Agents and Travelling Salesmen), to which Jews were no longer allowed to belong. See BAP, *Reich-*

*swirtschaftsministerium*, 9258, letter from the *Centralverband Deutscher Handelsvertreter-Vereine* to Rudolf Hess of 6 September 1933.

41. BAP, *Reichswirtschaftsministerium*, 13859, communication from the *Schutzgemeinschaft der Großbetriebe des Einzelhandels und verwandter Gruppen e.V.* (Defence Association of Large Retail Businesses and Associated Groups (Reg'd)) to the *Reichsinnenministerium*, 13 August 1932.

42. The rush of applications for membership of the local Hamburg group of the *Kampfbund* was so large that on 1 July 1933, a block on the acceptance of new members was imposed. Cf. *Hamburger Nachrichten*, 14 June 1933.

43. Letter from A.M. Jacobsen & Söhne, an import-export firm specializing in accessories for florists, to the Hamburg *Handelskammer* of 17 August 1933, re. customer boycott organised by the *Kampfbund*, *Gruppe Blumengeschäftsinhaber*, Archiv Handelskammer, 100.B.1.5.

44. See *Hamburger Tageblatt*, 9 September 1933, on 'Brown Fairs' at 'Cap Polonio'.

45. Flier from the Eppendorf *Kreisamt* of the *Gesamtverband deutscher Handwerker, Kaufleute und Gewerbetreibender*, 12 December 1933, Special Archives, Moscow, 721-1-2339, p. 46.

46. Cf. the advertising leaflets of the *Graphische Kunstanstalt Schultz GmbH, Wandsbek-Hamburg* in ibid., p. 43.

47. On the following see also Frank Bajohr and Joachim Szodrzynski, '"Keine jüdische Hautcreme mehr benutzen". Die antisemitische Kampagne gegen die Hamburger Firma Beiersdorf 1933/34', in Herzig, ed., *Juden*, pp. 515–526.

48. On the development of the Beiersdorf firm, see the festschrift *100 Jahre Beiersdorf 1882–1982*, Hamburg, 1982; Ekkehard Kaum, *Oscar Troplowitz. Forscher - Unternehmer - Bürger*, Hamburg, 1982.

49. Circular from Queisser & Co. 'To our dear customers', March 1933, *Werksarchiv Beiersdorf, Fach* 130.

50. Advertisement text in ibid.

51. Ibid., solemn declaration by Ernst Schirrmacher, 20 May 1933.

52. Ibid., letter from the delivery warehouse in Stuttgart to Beiersdorf headquarters, 2 June 1933; also there a copy of the sticker.

53. Ibid., communication from Lohmann AG, 25 April 1933.

54. Ibid., circular from the *Interessengemeinschaft Deutsche Marke*, May 1933.

55. *Fridericus*, No. 19/1933, 4 May 1933.

56. Letter from Beiersdorf AG to the Hamburg *Amtgericht*, 18 April 1933, *Werksarchiv Beiersdorf, Fach* 130.

57. Ibid., M.M. Warburg & Co. to P. Beiersdorf & Co. AG, 24 April 1933.

58. Ibid., declaration by the managers of the company, 24 April 1933.

59. Because he had refused to divorce his Jewish wife, Claussen was relieved of his post in 1944, on Himmler's orders. Cf. Claussen's de-Nazification papers in the *Werksarchiv Beiersdorf, Fach* 132, and the interview with Georg W. Claussen of 11 June 1990 (interviewer Beate Meyer), *Archiv Hamburger Lebensläufe - Werkstatt der Erinnerung* at the *Forschungsstelle für Zeitgeschichte in Hamburg.*

60. '*Die Nivea Creme Juden*', in *Der Stürmer*, No. 34/August 1933.

61. Reich leadership of the *Kampfbund für den gewerblichen Mittelstand* to P. Beiersdorf & Co., 15 May 1933, *Werksarchiv Beiersdorf, Fach* 130.

62. Ibid., letter from Hans Schwarzkopf to Beiersdorf AG, 30 May 1933.

63. Ibid., communication from the *Behörde für Wirtschaft* to the *Reichspressestelle* of the NSDAP, 6 October 1933.

64. Ibid., communication from Beiersdorf AG to the *Reichswirtschaftsministerium*, 2 September 1933.

65. See below Ch. III; on the initiative of these industrial leaders see Hayes, *Big Business*, p. 257 ff.

66. Circular from the *Reichswirtschaftsministerium*, 8 September 1933, *Werksarchiv Beiersdorf, Fach* 130.

67. See for example the settlement with Queisser & Co. of 21 June 1933, ibid.

68. Ibid., circular from Beiersdorf AG, 26 June 1933.

69. Cf. the letter from the Frankfurt distribution store to Beiersdorf head office (undated), ibid.

70. Cf. Judgment of the Hamburg *Landgericht*, Z VI 349/34 of 13 July 1934, StAHH, *Justizbehörde I*, II Ba Vol. 2, No. 6.

71. Ibid., letter from Dr Drögemüller to the editors of *Der Schneidermeister*, 23 August 1934.

72. Ibid., newsletter of the *Landesverband Norddeutscher Schneiderinnungen*, No. 8/1934, 1 August 1934, p. 2.

73. Citation as in Hamburg *Landgericht* judgment Z VI 349/34, 13 July 1934, p. 9, ibid.

74. Letter from Dr Drögemüller to the editors of *Der Schneidermeister*, 23 August 1934, ibid.

75. Letter from Deputy *NSDAP-Gauwirtschaftsberater* Otte to Dr Breiholdt, 31 August 1934, ibid.

76. Thus runs the convincing thesis of Karl A. Schleunes, *The Twisted Road to Auschwitz. Nazi Policy Toward German Jews 1933–1939*, new edition, Urbana and Chicago 1990, pp. 62–91.

77. Examples in Genschel, *Verdrängung*, p. 44ff. On boycott actions in Kiel, Schwerin, Göttingen, Gleiwitz and the Ruhrgebiet, see *Hamburger Tageblatt*, 28 and 29 March 1933.

78. Cf. diary entry of Joseph Goebbels, 26 March 1933: 'He has carefully considered the situation up there in the isolation of the mountains and has now come to a decision.' Cited in *Die Tagebücher von Joseph Goebbels. Sämtliche Fragmente*, ed. by Elke Fröhlich, Vol. 2, Munich, 1987, p. 398.

79. *Hamburger Tageblatt*, 29 March 1933.

80. '*Der Senat warnt Judá*', *Hamburger Tageblatt*, 29 March 1933.

81. Radio broadcast of Kaufmann, 29 March 1933, in the *Archiv des Norddeutschen Rundfunks*, WR 23771/1. Extensive excerpts are published in the *Hamburger Tageblatt* of 29 March 1933.

82. Cf. the letters in StAHH, NSDAP, B 109, 112.

83. Thus, for example, Kaufmann calculated the percentage of Jews among the lawyers of Hamburg at 43%. Even the antisemitic propaganda published by the Hamburg *Handelskammer* at the same time put the figure at only 25%. Cf. '*Material gegen den Boykott des deutschen Außenhandels*', StAHH, *Krogmann Familie I, Bestand Carl-Vincent Krogmann*, C 15 I/7. The proportion of 'non-Aryans' in Hamburg, including 'Jewish *Mischlinge*', amounted to 31% of all lawyers. See below, Ch. II, 'The "Law for the Restoration of the Professional Civil Service"'.

84. *Hamburger Nachrichten*, 30 March 1933 (morning edition) and 31 March 1933 (evening edition).

85. *Hamburger Nachrichten*, 30 May 1933. The boycott followed on 29 May 1933, based on the *Verordnung des Reichspräsidenten zum Schutze von Volk und Staat* (the 'Decree of the Reich President for the Protection of People and State') of 28 February 1933.

86. StAHH, *Krogmann Familie I*, diary of Carl Vincent Krogmann, C 15 I/7 (entry of 2 April 1933).

87. *Hamburger Nachrichten*, 31 March 1933.

88. Proclamation of the Hamburg *Polizeibehörde*, *Hamburger Nachrichten*, 1 April 1933.

89. Advertisement in *Hamburger Tageblatt*, 30 March 1933.

90. *Hamburger Tageblatt*, 30 March 1933.

91. Advertisement in the *Hamburger Nachrichten*, 1 April 1933.

92. *Hamburger Tageblatt*, 31 March 1933.

93. Advertisement of the *Verband deutscher Uniformtuchfabrikanten e.V.*, *Hamburger Tageblatt*, 9 April 1933.

94. Advertisement of the Alsterdamm fashion store, *Hamburger Tageblatt*, 9 April 1933.

95. Advertisement of the Christofstal towel factory, *Hamburger Tageblatt*, 9 April 1933.
96. Advertisement of the Anker-Werke, *Hamburger Nachrichten*, 1 April 1933.
97. Advertisement of H. Reeck G.m.b.H., *Hamburger Tageblatt*, 2 April 1933.
98. Advertisement of the Triumph bicycle factory, *Hamburger Tageblatt*, 2 April 1933.
99. Advertisement of Eierlager Zentrum, *Hamburger Tageblatt*, 2 April 1933.
100. Advertisement of Hammonia butter wholesalers, *Hamburger Tageblatt*, 6 April 1933.
101. Advertisement of Tefzet carpets, *Hamburger Tageblatt*, 9 April 1933.
102. Diary of Luise Solmitz, entry of 1 April 1933, *Archiv FZH*, 11/S 11.
103. Citation as in *Hamburger Nachrichten*, 2 April 1933.
104. Thus Gauleiter Kaufmann on 29 March 1933. *Hamburger Tageblatt*, 29 March 1933.
105. Galerie Morgenland, ed., *'Wo Wurzeln waren...' Juden in Hamburg-Eimsbüttel 1933-1945*, Hamburg, 1993, p. 93f.
106. *Hamburger Nachrichten*, evening edition, 1 April 1933.
107. Diary entry of Luise Solmitz on 1 April 1933, *Archiv FZH*, 11/S 11.
108. *Hamburger Nachrichten*, 2 April 1933.
109. Report of the *Polizeibehörde* in *Hamburger Nachrichten*, 2 April 1933.
110. Hans J. Robinsohn, 'Ein Versuch, sich zu behaupten', in *Tradition*, Vol. 3, Issue 4/ 1958, pp. 197–206, here pp. 197, 200. Arie Goral-Sternheim plainly regards this as a 'historical fairy tale', Arie Goral-Sternheim, *Schatten*, p. 33.
111. Citation (translated) from: recordings of Dr Hans Bruno, p. 27, *Archiv Werkstatt der Erinnerung, Forschungsstelle für Zeitgeschichte*, 211a.
112. Cited as in Henriette Necheles-Magnus, 'Anhängliche Patienten - opportunistische Kollegen', in Margarete Limberg and Hubert Rübsaat, eds, *Sie durften nicht mehr Deutsche sein. Jüdischer Alltag in Selbstzeugnissen 1933–1938*, Frankfurt am Main, 1990, p. 50.
113. Susanne Goldberg, Ulla Hinnenberg and Erika Hirsch, 'Die Verfolgung der Juden in Altona nach 1933 in den Berichten der Zeitzeugen', in Herzig, ed., *Juden*, pp. 577–587, here p. 578.
114. Letter from Schwieger in the *Nordelbisches Kirchenarchiv*, Kiel, B IV.
115. Curt Menzel, *Minderheitenrecht und Judenfrage. Zwei Vorträge, gehalten am 17. Februar und 28. April 1933 im Bund Nationalsozialistischer Deutscher Juristen in Hamburg*, Beuern o.J., p. 18.
116. Declaration of 2 January 1934 in *Hamburger Tageblatt*, 6 January 1934.
117. Cf. for instance the report of the *Daily Mirror* of 24 March 1933: 'Fourteen hundred Jews have been tortured and murdered in the city of Hamburg alone during the Hitler terrorism now sweeping Germany.'
118. Cf. the outspoken factual reports of the *New York Times* of 30 March 1933, StAHH, *Senatskanzlei-Präsialabteilung* (Senate Chancellery-Presidential Division), 1933 A 35/34.
119. *Hamburger Nachrichten*, morning editions of 31 March and 1 April 1933; *Hamburger Tageblatt*, 31 March 1933.
120. Cf. StAHH, *Senatskanzlei-Präsialabteilung*, 1933 A 35/34, letter from Olff, Köpke & Co. to the Hamburg Senate, 31 March 1933.
121. On the development of the '*Aufklärungsausschuß*' from the early 1920s onwards, see StAHH, *Staatliche Pressestelle* I-IV, 7938, Vol. 1ff.; letter from the President of the *Handelskammer*, Hermann Victor Hübbe, to *Reichsminister* Joseph Goebbels of 30 June 1933, StAHH, *Aufklärungsausschuß Hamburg-Bremen*, 1.
122. HAPAG *Aufsichtsratvorsitzende* Emil Helfferich described the *Aufklärungsausschuß* in his memoirs as the 'most effective overseas propaganda service that we possessed in the Third Reich in Germany.' Cf. Emil Helfferich, *1932-1946. Tatsachen*, Jever, 1969, p. 65.
123. See the agreement between the *Reichspropagandaministerium* and the *Aufklärungsausschuß* of 1 July 1933, StAHH, *Aufklärungsausschuß Hamburg-Bremen*, 1.

124. Cf. the personal records of Johannsen, who committed suicide as the Allies marched into Hamburg in 1945, in StAHH, *Aufklärungsausschuß Hamburg-Bremen*, 2.

125. Letter to Wilhelm Burchard-Motz from Count Zeppelin, who served the *Aufklärungsausschuß inter alia* as a translator, 10 August 1937, StAHH, *Familie Burchard*, B 9 b 4.

126. StAHH, *Aufklärungsausschuß Hamburg-Bremen*, 9, Vol. 9, see *inter alia* letter from H. Rost & Co., Alsterwall 62, to the *Aufklärungsausschuß*, 11 February 1935.

127. Material against the boycott of German international trade (1933), StAHH, *Familie Krogmann I*, Carl-Vincent Krogmann, C 15, I/7.

128. Ibid., p. 2.

129. Ibid., pp. 15,17.

130. Cf. *Hamburger Tageblatt*, 11 January 1933: 'National Socialist advance at the sitting of the City Parliament'.

131. *Frankfurter Zeitung*, 12 March 1933.

132. Letter from Dr Fritz M. Warburg to *Geheimrat* Fellinger of 29 March 1933, *Archiv M.M. Warburg & Co., Einzelkorrespondenz Februar 1933-Februar 1935 (Nicht durch das Sekretariat)*. The other members of the *Aufsichtsrat* who resigned were Dr Gustav Gumpel, Dr Norbert Labowsky, Julius Oppenheimer, Albert Schöndorff and Dr Arno Wittgensteiner. Cf. *Hamburger Tageblatt*, 3 April 1933.

133. Copy in *Archiv M.M. Warburg & Co., Einzelkorrespondenz Februar 1933-Februar 1935 (Nicht durch das Sekretariat)*. The text of the declaration was also published in *Das Schwarzbuch. Tatsachen und Dokumente. Die Lage der Juden in Deutschland 1933*, ed. by the Comité des Délégations Juives, Paris 1934, p. 380ff. On the 'voluntary Aryanisation' of Rudolf Karstadt AG, see also Rudolf Lenz, *Karstadt. Ein deutscher Warenhauskonzern 1920–1950*, Stuttgart, 1995, p. 175ff.

134. Dr Ernst Spiegelberg to *Geheimrat* Fellinger of 6 June 1933, *Archiv M.M. Warburg & Co., Einzelkorrespondenz Februar 1933-Februar 1935 (Nicht durch das Sekretariat)*.

135. Memorandum by Dr Fritz M. Warburg, 6 October 1933, *Archiv M.M. Warburg & Co., Einzelkorrespondenz Februar 1933-Februar 1935 (Nicht durch das Sekretariat)*.

136. *Hamburger Tageblatt*, 4 April 1933.

137. *Hamburger Tageblatt*, 12 May 1933, *Vossische Zeitung*, 12 May 1933.

138. *Hamburger Tageblatt*, 24 August 1933. On National Socialist policy towards department stores, see also Heinrich Uhlig, *Die Warenhäuser im Dritten Reich*, Cologne, 1956.

139. Cf. on this subject Kopper, *Marktwirtschaft*, pp. 18–50.

140. Letter from the board of the *Deutsch-Südamerikanische Bank AG* to Carl Goetz of 31 August 1933, citation as in *OMGUS - Finance Division - Financial Investigation Section, Ermittlungen gegen die Dresdner Bank 1946*, ed. by the *Hamburger Stiftung für Sozialgeschichte des 20. Jahrhunderts*, Nördlingen, 1986, p. 86.

141. OMGUS, *Dresdner Bank*, p. 86.

142. Letter from Mosler to Dr Ernst Spiegelberg, 7 July 1933 and reaction from Max M. Warburg, 11 July 1933, in *Archiv M.M. Warburg & Co., Einzelkorrespondenz Februar 1933-Februar 1935 (Nicht durch das Sekretariat)*.

143. In 1925 a total of 19,904 'believing Jews' lived in Hamburg. This figure had already decreased to 16,973 in the census of 16 June 1933. Cf. *Die Volks-, Berufs- und Betriebszählung in Hamburg am 16. Juni 1933. Nachtrag zum Statistischen Jahrbuch für die Freie und Hansestadt Hamburg, Jahrgang 1933/34*, Hamburg, 1935, p. 13.

# Chapter II

# DECISION-MAKERS AND TRENDS IN NATIONAL SOCIALIST ANTI-JEWISH POLICY IN HAMBURG, 1933–1937

## Underlying Factors and Problems for National Socialist Anti-Jewish Policy-making in Hamburg

As a result of the various anti-Jewish initiatives of the first year of their rule, the National Socialist leadership, on the Reich level as well as in Hamburg, faced a confusing overall situation which presented them with a tactical dilemma. On the one hand, a brutal antisemitism from below had mobilised its own party grassroots, as well as a wide section of the middle class, and had produced a climate which seemed favourable to the displacement of the Jews from economic life. On the other hand, tactical considerations with regard to the economic situation, to the National Socialists' conservative coalition partners and to the attitude of foreign observers, pushed the regime in the direction of moderation.[1] Thus, for instance, in Hamburg, the Senator responsible for economic policy had at times to withdraw the prohibition of ritual slaughter announced after Jewish dock workers in North Africa had refused to unload ships from Hamburg.[2] Reactions in Hamburg to the street terror of the SA also threatened to cause problems on an international level, as did the middle-class antisemitism that aimed at the elimination of the Jews from the economy and at structural changes favourable to the middle classes.

The attempt to channel mob antisemitism from below through the boycott of 1 April 1933 had altogether proven a failure. It had no lasting effect on Jewish store and company owners, nor did it gain any particular sympathy from the general population, which rejected the 'street politics' of the antisemitic activists.

---

Notes for this chapter begin on page 88.

One cause of the city government's caution in pressing the economic 'exclusion' of the Jews that was of particular importance was Hamburg's economic situation. The economic structure of the Hanseatic city displayed a number of special features which did not exist in other large German cities. Nowhere else was the proportion of the workforce employed in the trade and transport sector so high and the percentage involved in the industry and craft sector so low.[3] In 1925, 16.9 per cent of the inhabitants of the Reich worked in the trade and transport sector, whereas in Hamburg the figure was 42.5 per cent, while only 32.1 per cent of the population in Hamburg were engaged in industry and craft (Reich average – 41.3 per cent).[4] The orientation of Hamburg's economy towards trade and shipping stood in stark contrast to the policy of autarky of the National Socialists, from which industry and agriculture gained the most. The one-sided strengthening of the domestic economy over foreign trade meant that in the early years of the National Socialist regime Hamburg's unemployment figures declined only gradually. The job-creating measures of Hamburg's National Socialists made no more than a slight impact on this. In 1934, of all the large cities of over 200,000 inhabitants, Hamburg registered the lowest decrease in its unemployment figures.[5] From the beginning of 1933 to the end of 1934 unemployment fell from 167,207 to 111,872. This corresponded to a decrease of a mere 33 per cent, whereas the average for the Reich fell by 57 per cent in the same period. On the Reich level, this meant that Hamburg was officially recognised as an economically 'distressed area' up until 1938.

In the early years of National Socialist rule, the persistently poor economic situation led to some tension and discontent among the population. This emerged during the referendum of 19 August 1934, when over 20 per cent of the electorate of Hamburg voted against a merger of the offices of the Reich Chancellor and the Reich President in the person of Hitler. The proportion of 'no' votes in Hamburg was thus twice as high as the average figure in the rest of the Reich. In this regard, Gauleiter Kaufmann commented that the election results were 'the deepest disappointment of the many years I have been active in the party'.[6]

In this situation of continuous economic crisis and widespread discontent, the maintenance of current levels of employment enjoyed first priority where the question of Jewish enterprises arose. At this point in time the collapse of Jewish industries would have worsened the economic situation and atmosphere still further and thus would have increased the threat to the stability of the National Socialist regime.

The regime's international considerations also had a moderating effect on anti-Jewish policy in view of Germany's international isolation. In an international port and commercial city like Hamburg, hardly any of the measures of the new powers went unnoticed. The National Socialists in Hamburg had seen this clearly after the attacks of SA units against foreigners. No doubt they had suppressed all critical domestic opinion by bringing the press into line. This made the unrelenting reports of the international press seem all the more unpleasant. 'Hamburg is' – Gauleiter Kaufmann concluded in November 1934 in a conversation with Hitler – 'exposed to the eyes of the world', its port formed an 'open border' that acted strongly in favour of 'foreign propaganda'.[7]

The experience of the National Socialist regime in Hamburg was that even apparently minor measures unleashed a sizeable response from the international press, and this was particularly true of anti-Jewish policy. When, for instance, in August 1933, the Hamburg Senate decreed that the Heinrich Heine memorial be removed from the city park on the ground that he had 'crassly slandered the German people',[8] the Senate saw itself confronted not only with anonymous petitions from outraged citizens but also with comments from the US, 'Should Hamburg lose its good old reputation?' one incensed German-American asked the Hamburg Mayor.[9] Attached to his letter was an article from an American newspaper entitled 'Hamburg, Hitler and Heine' that condemned the decision of the Senate as an act of cultural barbarism.

Of course, the National Socialists in Hamburg did not regard the traditional reputation of Hamburg as a liberal commercial city as being of great importance, liberalism being in their view a sign of weakness. All the same, the deterioration of the position of Hamburg's foreign trade could not be a matter of indifference to them. The economic consequences of an antisemitic policy were made clear in a letter that an American trading company sent to the Hamburg Chamber of Commerce with regard to the renaming of the steamship *Albert Ballin* with the name *Hansa*.[10] As an antisemitic measure, the renaming had made a 'poor impression' in American importing circles, the firm informed the Chamber of Commerce. It continued: 'That further damage would be caused to German export trade today's blind German government will not see. In fact we welcome that the name Albert Ballin will not be attached to a steamship sailing under a flag which signifies only hate, envy, terrorism ... Yes, instead of "Hansa" the steamship should have been named "Hate", which would have been still more accurate.' The letter ended with the far-sighted prophecy: 'He who sows hatred will reap hatred.'

Similarly, Hamburg's trade situation received the attention of a range of boycott committees which had formed, above all in the US and Great Britain, in reaction to the National Socialist persecution of the Jews. In the US a 'Joint Boycott Council' was established with the support of the American trade unions, which, among other objectives, worked against the import and sale of German goods by monitoring ship's cargoes, calling for boycotts and introducing boycott posts.[11] In Great Britain, a 'Jewish Representation Council for the Boycott of German Goods and Services' existed, and besides this a 'Non-Sectarian Anti-

Nazi League to Champion Human Rights' launched activities in other European countries as well as in the US.[12]

With respect to the diplomatic and international economic isolation of National Socialist Germany from mid-1933, i.e., after the Reich government first passed a series of far-reaching antisemitic laws, it began to urge caution in the conduct of an anti-Jewish policy. Jews were to have full freedom of action in the economic arena. On 6 July 1933, Hitler explained at a meeting with Reich Governors that the National Socialist 'revolution' had 'come to an end'. 'To destroy the economy is not National Socialism', he told his subordinates, and admonished them that: 'To delve further into the Jewish question means to throw the whole world into turmoil again.'[13] The Prussian Minister President, Hermann Göring, described the international isolation of Germany in a speech of 25 April 1933 as 'unparalleled'. It was not, Göring continued, going to be possible to 'achieve what we wish to easily'.[14] Even a fanatical antisemite like Reich Propaganda Minister Goebbels stressed at the German Trade and Industry Congress that no special laws would be insisted upon for Jews in the industrial field.[15] As was mentioned above, the Reich Economics Ministry sent a similar memorandum to the German Trade and Industry Congress on 8 September 1933. On 17 January 1934, Reich Interior Minister Frick warned, in a circular letter, against the application of the so-called Aryan Paragraph in the 'free economy'.[16] In 1933 there was a department in the Reich Economics Ministry for the 'Prevention of Improper Interventions into the Economy', known more generally as the 'Jewish Protection Department', which sought to counter individual antisemitic attacks in the business world.[17] If one were to include in addition the circulars sent by Reich Economics Minister Schacht in the years that followed arguing against anti-Jewish measures in the economy, euphemistically characterised by many historians as a policy aimed at protecting Jews,[18] it might leave the impression that up until 1937 the economic activities of Jews had been conducted in a sanctuary protected by the state. The evaluation of Avraham Barkai is closer to the truth: the period before 1937 had been a mere 'illusion of a period of grace'[19] during which an official policy to displace the Jews from the German economy was initiated. Barkai has rightly pointed out that in the context of the everyday life of Jews in National Socialist Germany, the idea that Jews had any liberty to conduct economic affairs was a chimera.

This at first barely discernible displacement process can only be reconstructed in all its complex ramifications if the countless regional variations on anti-Jewish policy and their respective actors in each region are taken into account. The following investigation therefore broaches the question of whether and how the specificities of the economic situation in Hamburg also influenced regional anti-Jewish policy. Does a distinctive profile of anti-Jewish policy in Hamburg emerge from a study of the underlying conditions in the region, or did Hamburg, on the contrary, limit itself to implementing ministerial edicts and the laws of the Reich? Did the regional government in Hamburg follow the orders of the Reich verbatim or did it interpret them in the light of its own interests? Did it oppose the measures laid down by the Reich if they ran against its own interests? All these questions turn on the relationship between Hamburg and the Reich, and hence they only describe one level of regional anti-Jewish policy. In order to be able to assess it more accurately, it is important to go beyond this and to compare it with the anti-Jewish policy of other cities and regions. In a systematic comparison between the anti-Jewish policies of Hamburg and Munich at the end of the chapter, the variation between regional approaches to anti-Jewish policy will be shown more clearly. First, however, a closer examination of the decision-makers charged with anti-Jewish policy in Hamburg, of their attitudes to the 'Jewish question' and of the structures of National Socialist rule in the city is needed since they were so important to the shaping of National Socialist anti-Jewish policy in Hamburg.

## Anti-Jewish Policy: Regional Decision-Makers

After the Reichstag elections of 5 March 1933, a coalition was formed in Hamburg on March 8 comprising six National Socialists, four German Nationalists, a member of the German People's Party and one from the German State Party.[20] The new head of the Senate was First Mayor (*Erster Bürgermeister*) Carl Vincent Krogmann, who had risen to prominence in Hamburg as a member of the circle around Hitler's economic adviser Wilhelm Keppler and as a leading figure among a younger, pro-National Socialist generation of businessmen, though at the time of his election he had not yet become a member of the NSDAP. The National Socialists had intended Krogmann to present the party's acceptable face to the middle classes so as to reconcile Hamburg commercial circles, which up until 1933 had been somewhat sceptical, to the new regime.

In bringing the State of Hamburg into line and dissolving the Hamburg City Parliament, the formal position of Krogmann, soon given the loftier title of *Regierender Bürgermeister*, was strengthened to an extraordinary extent. The State Administration Act (*Landesverwaltungsgesetz*) of 14 September 1933 expressly gave him the power to issue decrees to the senators – as the other ministers were known – of the state government.[21] In practice, however, Krogmann's power was eroded more and more in the years that followed. On 16 May 1933, the appointment of Gauleiter Kaufmann to the position of Reich Governor (*Reichsstatthalter*) for Hamburg had already created a constitutional dualism which would inevitably weaken Krogmann's position in the long term. From 1935 Kaufmann, who in 1933 had placed one of his henchmen, Secretary of State Georg Ahrens, at Krogmann's side, intervened more and more forcefully in the business of government. In July 1936 he was formally named 'Führer' of the Hamburg state government by Hitler,[22] under circumstances which were humiliating for Krogmann.[23]

Although Krogmann protested against his progressive exclusion from the exercise of power, he nevertheless displayed an obsequious, if completely characteristic, servility and subservience even in these protests.[24] His once-proud title *Regierende* (officiating or governing) *Bürgermeister*, was sarcastically altered by many in Hamburg to *Regierter Bürgermeister*, or 'governed mayor'.[25] When the Hamburg authorities were divided in the 'Greater Hamburg Act' of 1937 into a State Authority directly under the Reich and a 'Municipal Authority' governed by German Municipal Code (*Deutsche Gemeindeordnung*), Kaufmann absorbed the oversight of both authorities into his office, demoted Krogmann to the rank of a First Councillor of the Municipal Authority[26] and fobbed him off with some additional honorary offices without influence.[27]

There was little Krogmann could do about the progressive erosion of his power. As a party member from 1933 he had no power base in the NSDAP; his upper-class origins made him an outsider in the petty bourgeois and plebeian NSDAP; his manners clearly diverged from the traditions of the party. 'I hated the buddy-buddy atmosphere and the drinking sessions to which many National Socialists were accustomed from the times of the struggle', Krogmann would reflect later.[28] This reluctance, he added, 'caused him great damage' in the party.

Krogmann tried to compensate for his position as an outsider through a particularly ideological fanaticism.[29] Among the fundamental components of his *Weltanschauung*, which, according to his own statements, he took eclectically from the writings of Houston Stewart Chamberlain, Richard Wagner and Paul de Lagarde,[30] he adhered to antisemitism with the rigidity of the late convert. In terms of the implementation of National Socialist anti-Jewish policy in Hamburg, Krogmann was hardly going to be the moderating influence that sections of the Hamburg population had publicly hoped he would be.[31] Instead, Krogmann clearly supported the antisemitic policy of the new regime. He thus took an active role in the dismissal of Jews from company boards and from the Hamburg Chamber of Commerce. When, in 1933, the Chamber of Commerce attempted to help Jewish members to keep their posts, he responded with an unambiguous refusal.[32] In April 1934, he distanced himself from the attempts of Hitler's economic adviser, Wilhelm Keppler, and the Reich Economics Ministry to create a legally consolidated economic position for the Jews: 'I cannot share this point of view. Everywhere, Jews are becoming too impudent again.'[33] In similar language in a discussion of the Jewish question with Himmler and Heydrich in February 1935 he lamented 'the increasing impudence with which these people [the Jews] are again behaving in Germany'.[34] In public speeches Krogmann held forth about Jews on a level to which not even the most primitive among Hamburg's National Socialists would have stooped: in a public speech on 3 July 1938, he inveighed against the 'mendacity of the Jewish world press' and the 'advocates of international Jewish capitalism'.[35]

In clear contrast to the unrestrained antisemitic fanaticism of the *Regierende Bürgermeister*, the public speeches of Gauleiter Kaufmann on the 'Jewish question' displayed a notable moderation. Kaufmann's antisemitic speeches were primarily delivered to party functionaries on occasions at which this antisemitism had great significance for the emotional integration of party comrades.[36] By contrast, in addresses given in public he conspicuously avoided antisemitic expressions. Before middle-class audiences, Kaufmann even posed as a critical observer of his own party, openly admitting 'mistakes', 'excesses' and 'gaffes'.[37] Unlike Krogmann, Kaufmann had the ability to adapt to changing situations flexibly and to make political decisions conditional on shifts in his political environment.

With respect to Hamburg's continuing economic problems, Kaufmann's highest priority was the internal political stability of the National Socialist regime. This called for a strategy of caution and a pragmatic arrangement with the traditions of 'red' Hamburg and the city's bourgeoisie, to which he made concessions that went beyond mere rhetoric.[38] Kaufmann was not unaware that the 'hooligan antisemitism' of the NSDAP and of radicalised middle-class politicians attracted little sympathy from the workers or the middle class, as had become apparent in Hamburg in the spring of 1933. In 1935, when the antisemitic terror revived once more in Hamburg, Kaufmann publicly warned against antisemitic 'troublemakers' and 'wild' poster campaigns 'which deal in rabble-rousing ways with the struggle against Jewry'.[39] Nevertheless, this in no way prevented him from spending a good two weeks with the worst antisemitic 'rabble-rouser' among the National Socialists, the Franconian Gauleiter Julius Streicher, in order to organise a joint mass rally in Hamburg.[40] Kaufmann approached the riots during 'Reich Crystal Night' in November 1938 in a similarly contradictory manner. Though given prior warning, and having been politically responsible for the attacks, he subsequently distanced himself from the destruction caused in a speech to the Hamburg Chamber of Commerce, thus placing himself at the forefront of the widespread criticism which had developed in Hamburg.[41]

Whether Kaufmann's public calls for moderation suggested difficulties in controlling the excited antisemitism of the party grassroots or part of a wicked double game by which the Gauleiter sought to pose before the wider public as a trustworthy representative of law and order cannot be determined with any certainty. There is no doubt, however, about his deep-seated antisemitic convictions.

Where he feared no negative consequences for public opinion or industry in
Hamburg, Kaufmann stuck to his antisemitic principles with extreme obstinacy.
When a Jew from Hamburg was to be licenced as an accountant, Kaufmann
informed Reich Economics Minister Schacht in 1936 'that the [more lenient]
position of the Economics Minister of the Reich and of Prussia is politically difficult to accept and should not be upheld'. It was more important, Kaufmann lec-
tured the minister, 'that difficulties be confronted when it comes to pushing
through the Nuremberg laws against all resistance'.[42]

In spite of Kaufmann's exceptionally powerful position as Gauleiter (from
1929), Reich Governor (from 1933), 'Führer' of the Hamburg State Government
(from 1936), Leader of the Hamburg State and Municipal Authorities (from
1937–38), Reich Defence Commissar in Defence District X (from 1939) and
Reich Commissar for German Maritime Shipping (from 1942), the authoritarian
reform and development of the political system in Hamburg responded to, and
was moulded by, the particularistic and even anarchic tendencies governing Hamburg's anti-Jewish and other policies. The implementation of the 'Führer principle' appeared to promote transparent and streamlined decision-making structures
only because this principle took no account of the division of labour of modern
industrial societies or of the complexity of these societies. In practice, chaotic and
contradictory leadership structures developed that led to precisely the kind of
bureaucratic freewheeling and conflicts over authority that the 'Führer principle'
was supposed to overcome.[43]

Kaufmann soon felt overloaded by the constant growth of his powers. Seeing
the organisation of administrative mechanisms according to the National Socialist principle of the 'leadership of men'[44] primarily in terms of the application of
personnel policy, alongside the state authorities he installed a growing network of
agents directly responsible to him.[45] These rivalled the traditional administrative
organisation and, like a parasite, contributed to the creeping subversion of the
bureaucratic state organisation. As early as 1946, the journalist Walter Petwaidic
described this system of rule, not without justification, as 'authoritarian anarchy',[46] and those historians who have put the 'functionalist'[47] case have added
further concepts to this characterisation such as 'institutional anarchy',[48] 'the
organisational jungle'[49] or 'organised chaos'.[50]

Such tendencies emerged in Hamburg at the outset of the 'Third Reich', as
they did all over the Reich, with a tide of (in many cases self-appointed) 'State
Commissars', who appeared in nearly all areas of political life in the context of
Gleichschaltung – the imposition of National Socialist control over German society. To the consternation of the leaders of the National Socialist regime, the Commissars obstructed this process in many ways, placing their own personal interests
before all other objectives.[51] The Hamburg 'State Commissar for the Adminis-

tration of Allotments' represented a particularly bizarre facet of this 'Commissar Chaos'.[52] Similarly, the Hamburg administrative machinery directed by the city's senators was rife – particularly in the early years of the National Socialist regime – with a grotesque proliferation of competences. It expanded in a particularly unrestrained fashion among these senators when, according to some witnesses, it became clear that the incoming *Regierende Bürgermeister*, formally responsible for the city's government, possessed no knowledge of either politics or administration.[53] That petty bureaucratic politics also affected anti-Jewish policy in Hamburg[54] was in part a consequence of these circumstances.

Particularistic tendencies were also promoted by the many special Reich authorities in Hamburg that were created when whole areas of policy were put under the authority of the Reich. By 1942 their number had risen to 28.[55] They included such important institutions as the Reich Trustee for Labour and the Reich Propaganda Office, and, more importantly still, large parts of the security apparatus represented by the police and judiciary. The power Kaufmann wielded as Reich Governor gave him a general right to information about these special Reich authorities, but he could not give them direct orders. He therefore relied upon a personal rapport with the heads of the authorities and in this way succeeded in many cases in gaining considerable influence, as he did for instance with the Hamburg Gestapo. Here he came to a personal arrangement with *Reichsführer SS* Heinrich Himmler, but also defended his regional spheres of interest with particular obstinacy.[56] With respect to other special Reich authorities such as the Chief Financial Administration, Kaufmann frittered away his time in bureaucratic battles over specific questions without ever gaining the right to give orders. That Kaufmann clashed with the Chief Financial Administrator Georg Rauschning over the auctioning of goods taken from Jewish refugees and furnishings from the houses of deported Jews[57] illustrates the significance of these conflicts in terms of anti-Jewish policy. In these, as in most other cases, there was no question of a difference over principles; rather the conflict was prompted by competing institutional interests.

Chaotic and persistent conflicts could be seen not only in the relationship among state institutions, but also in the relations between the state and the NSDAP in Hamburg. In contrast to many of the so-called '*Flächengaue*' in rural areas, the NSDAP in '*Stadtgau*' Hamburg had made limited inroads into areas within the city government's competence. Only some branches and regional offices of the Hamburg NSDAP assumed tasks previously performed by these authorities.[58] These institutions included the National Socialist People's Welfare (*Nationalsozialistische Volkswohlfahrt*, NSV), which offered substantial competition to the public institutions responsible for welfare, the Hitler Youth (*Hitlerjugend*, HJ) as well as League of German Girls (*Bund Deutscher Mädel*, BDM), which had a near-monopoly in youth work and care issues, as well as the Office of the NSDAP *Gau* Economics Adviser, which had substantial powers in questions relating to the retail trade and to handicrafts, in particular with respect to the 'Aryanisation' of Jewish enterprises.[59]

While in many rural regions – at least before 1937 – the NSDAP district leaders (*Kreisleiter*), in addition to their party title, also held the office of district councillor or mayor[60] and thereby, in their person, overcame the separation between party and state, in Hamburg district leaders were prevented from taking over state functions. On the one hand, this was a product of the special constitutional position of Hamburg which, until the reform after the 'Greater Hamburg Act' of 1937, knew of no division between the areas of responsibility of state and community, with the result that the German Municipal Code (*Deutsche Gemeindeordnung*) issued in 1935 could not be implemented in Hamburg for some time. On the other hand, the extreme centralisation of authority in Hamburg limited the opportunities for the NSDAP to exercise influence through regional 'party sovereigns'. Only when the Hamburg administration was itself decentralised in 1943, after the heavy aerial bombing of Operation 'Gomorrha', were the NSDAP's district leaders furnished with the authority to give orders to the newly created district branches and local offices of the administration.[61]

In practice, the comparative separation of state and party in Hamburg did not lead to the level of harmony that was desired, but rather to a host of long-standing conflicts. The political leaders of the NSDAP in Hamburg – released from all state responsibility – developed a particularly strong tendency to behave like ideological 'watchdogs'. Their self-perceived status as guardians of the ideological principles of National Socialism expressed itself – in particular with respect to the 'Jewish question' – both in keeping a watch on, and controlling, opinion, and in spurring antisemitic actions that would create a new political environment and put state and local administration under pressure from below.[62]

NSDAP functionaries brutally pilloried those who did not share their opinion of what was the correct position on the 'Jewish question'. With great satisfaction the National Socialist *Hamburger Tageblatt* published the names of officials and employees of the state authorities who had bought goods in Jewish stores or consulted Jewish doctors.[63] The Jewish population of Hamburg suffered particularly heavily from the repression and control imposed by NSDAP party officials. A typical example of the many denunciations is the memorandum of the NSDAP district office chief responsible for local government cited above, which complained to Mayor Krogmann about the behaviour of 'Jews on public transport'[64] – at bus stops Jews showed a 'really Jewish insolence' and pushed 'to the front with no consideration' in order to occupy seats that were still free. A 'Jewish brat of about 14 years old' had systematically 'smeared' the hand grips of a bus 'with jelly', and male Jews deliberately sought out overcrowded railroad cars so as 'to rub up against the knees of German women and girls' seated there. The pornographic fantasies of this particular Nazi make clear how far National Socialist anti-Jewish policy had created a political space for the unleashing of the basest instincts of party functionaries, allowing them to make a show of their hate-filled antisemitism.

## The Attitude of the Chamber of Commerce and Business Circles in Hamburg to National Socialist Anti-Jewish Policies

For National Socialist anti-Jewish policy to become accepted in business and industry, and in order to be able to drive out Jewish industry gradually, the institutions of the state and the agencies of the NSDAP were also dependent on the cooperation of self-governing economic bodies within the National Socialist system of government. The registration, liquidation or 'Aryanisation' of Jewish firms would inevitably encounter difficulties where the main figures in business did not participate in these measures, or opposed them outright.

It is not surprising therefore that the coordination of public and state views during the early period of *Gleichschaltung* also involved the Hamburg Chamber of Commerce.[65] At the same time, this policy was implemented in a remarkably moderate form in the hope of not disturbing the traditional business leadership of Hamburg by a more radical approach. Whereas the Hamburg Retail Association (*Hamburger Detaillistenkammer*) was taken over by National Socialist activists in a coup in the spring of 1933, the Chamber of Commerce underwent a 'voluntary' takeover with the 'support' of four state commissars. On 16 June 1933, Hermann Victor Hübbe presented himself to the plenum of the Chamber of Commerce as the new President, while his predecessor Carl Ludwig Nottebohm was demoted to Vice-President.[66] Seventeen members – including all Jewish and 'half-Jewish' members like Rudolf Petersen, Franz Rappolt and Max Warburg – were forced to withdraw from the general assembly of the Chamber of Commerce. Seventeen others remained in the Chamber of Commerce and eighteen new members were nominated, including confirmed members of the National Socialist Party like Joachim de la Camp, a businessman, or the coffee broker and National Socialist President of the City Parliament, C.C. Fritz Meyer.

With the appointment of 33 year-old Hermann Victor Hübbe, a generational shift was achieved from the largely 'National Liberal' older generation to younger, pro-National Socialist businessmen who had rallied around the new Hamburg Mayor, Carl Vincent Krogmann, and who, unlike the older generation, did not reject direct state intervention in economic life.[67]

Despite these reshuffles and increasing state encroachments on its economic decision making imposed by the *Gleichschaltung*, which reached a new high-point in August 1934 when the Reich Economics Minister placed industrial associations and chambers of commerce under his supervision, the Hamburg Chamber of Commerce insisted on its independence even under National Socialist leadership. This applied as much to anti-Jewish policy as it did to other questions. While the 'Enlightenment Committee' of the Chamber of Commerce developed into a National Socialist and antisemitic propaganda instrument, involving many trading companies in doing the National Socialists' dirty work in their attempts to rebut the 'horror stories' spread by Germany's critics, this attitude was not characteristic of the Chamber of Commerce as a whole, nor of the business community of Hamburg in general during the first years of National Socialist rule: Hamburg's business leadership tended to view the National Socialists' anti-Jewish policy with scepticism. For instance, the Chamber of Commerce continued to have their communications printed by the Jewish firm Ackermann & Wulff Nachflg. although the Gestapo and the Hamburg Economics Department opposed it. In response to official complaints, the Chamber of Commerce explained that it had 'to be free [to make] its economic decisions'.[68]

In other questions too, the Chamber of Commerce made clear that it did not wish at this time to be actively involved in the displacement of Jewish firms from the economy. For example, it refused to issue to the 'Rewe' firm a table of Jewish import companies on the ground that it did not want to become entangled in anti-Jewish boycott campaigns.[69] In May 1936 it released an internal memorandum to this effect.[70] The move limited the distribution of information about the 'Aryan quality of a company owner' to authorities and public bodies. Information was to be 'completely' denied to firms or private individuals. Moreover, mentioning 'membership of a race' was forbidden in any such information, the only differentiation permitted being that between 'citizens of the Reich' and 'those currently not citizens of the Reich'. The Chamber of Commerce only deviated from this basic position in 1937/38, when the release of information about Jewish enterprises was revised on the basis of new nationwide decrees. Even then, in January 1938, the SS security service (*Sicherheitsdienst*, SD) complained of supposed 'infringements' evidenced by the decision of the Hamburg Chamber of Commerce to withhold information about Jewish businesses.[71] The Chamber of Commerce based its restrictive attitude on an instruction from the Reich Economics Ministry that forbade 'special campaigns' against Jewish enterprises.

Underlying this approach there appears to have been a thorough scepticism of Nazi race policy. Refusal to go along with this policy affected not only many circles in the working population, but also many within the city's economic elite. Thus, particularly in the early years of the National Socialist regime, the *Ham-*

*burger Tageblatt*, the newspaper of the National Socialists in Hamburg, denounced the lack of 'race consciousness' among the Hamburg bourgeoisie and stirred the petty-bourgeois resentment of its readers against the 'riff-raff from Harvestehude and Uhlenhorst' (the residential areas preferred by Hamburg's bourgeoisie).[72] In July 1935 the paper attacked the wife of a lawyer who had objected indignantly to antisemitic campaign posters that had been stuck on the shop window of an 'Aryan' store, warning the owner 'that some ladies did not like this and would not buy in such stores'.[73] Under the headline 'Lawyer's Wife Defends Jews', the *Tageblatt* took up the incident, commenting that 'one must first of all take a deep breath of air to stay calm. That such things could still occur today shows us with unmistakable clarity that certain "kind" circles in particular do not, or do not want to, understand National Socialism. Probably the latter is correct and it is only because these "certain circles" are on friendly terms with the local Jews, since they also have the necessary money to cultivate a nice society in a big way. Indeed, in these "certain circles" men are only judged by their earnings. If that is sufficient, all other things play absolutely no role, least of all the race question.'[74]

In March 1935, *Regierende Bürgermeister* Krogmann publicly responded to voices from the business community that had been critical of the National Socialists' 'race policy'. The forum he chose was a particularly social occasion in Hamburg, namely the traditional *Liebesmahl* banquet of the East Asian Union (*Ostasiatischen Verein*). Before this audience, Krogmann criticised those who believed 'themselves able to deny absolutely the concept of race and especially that of the Aryan race'.[75] The German people could only 'become great and strong' if it struggled to develop a 'strong race consciousness'. The factor of 'decisive importance' in this respect was the 'Jewish question'. In order to appease anxious listeners, Krogmann emphasised that the National Socialists would proceed in this respect with moderation, 'and indeed in a very much more humane manner than has otherwise usually been the case in the course of world history'.

Although this observation was a mockery of the policy which had developed in reality, the General Consul of the Union of South Africa congratulated the Mayor on his speech on the 'race question', noting that he believed the policy was an 'extremely fortunate' one.[76] He wrote to assure Krogmann that it was correct to respond openly to the 'sceptics' among the business community in this area: 'Indeed these old chaps are slow in getting things into their heads.'[77]

The observation of the General Consul about the 'old chaps' suggests that it was primarily the older businessmen who were sceptical of National Socialist race policy. Grounded in the bourgeois outlook of the *Kaiserreich* with its esteem for private economic individualism, they regarded measures against Jewish enterprises as improper state interventions into economic affairs and also rejected the methods – such as the organised boycott – by which these interventions were affected. Hamburg banker Cornelius von Berenberg-Goßler, although a member of the NSDAP, condemned the boycott of 1 April as 'unheard of' and 'medieval', and entrusted to his diary the admission that the anti-Jewish attacks had made him feel ashamed before his foreign and Jewish business friends.[78]

Support for, and rejection of, anti-Jewish policy frequently cut straight through the bourgeois families of Hamburg, with divisions, as a rule, falling along generational lines. Even before 1933, the Counsel of the Chamber of Commerce Dr Eduard Rosenbaum, a Jew and a man with an intimate familiarity with the Hamburg business class, had detected clear differences between the attitudes to National Socialist ideology held by the older and younger generations. When, after the Reichstag elections of July 1932, he had been asked by older business-men what they could do against the growth of the NSDAP, he told them, 'Take a look at what your sons are reading.'[79] Rosenbaum observed that the thinking of the younger generation was heavily influenced by the intellectual Right of the Weimar Republic. It no longer thought along 'class' lines, but instead spoke of '*völkisch*' interests.

It was from this generation that the new President of the Chamber of Commerce, Hermann Victor Hübbe, came. Born in 1901, Hübbe belonged to the *Kriegsjugendgeneration*[80] whose chief experience of the bourgeois professional world had been at a time of crisis and decline. Because of this, the businessmen of this generation were open to ideas that looked heretical to their fathers – from the notion of a 'planned national economy',[81] championed, for instance, by the newspaper *Die Tat*, to *völkisch* antisemitism. Following this *völkisch* antisemitic argument, Hübbe railed at the 'machinations by Jews abroad against Germany', which he attributed to the 'rabble-rousing' of a 'Jewish Central Committee'. He told the Reich Economics Ministry, 'These circles can only be put to work if there is a comprehensive information campaign for national and self-conscious patri-otic groups abroad to confront energetically the subversive influence of Jewry as a whole and the force of Communism partly identified with it.'[82] In the summer of 1933, Hübbe considered it appropriate to send Eduard Rosenbaum into pre-mature retirement with the observation that it must be hard 'to belong to such a rootless race'.[83]

By contrast, his father Anton Hübbe never made a secret of his scepticism of the National Socialists and as late as 1931 financed the publication of a book enti-tled *Hold the Door Open!*,[84] edited by members of the SPD, the German State Party (*Deutsche Staatspartei*) and the German People's Party (DVP) and directed explicitly against the Hamburg National Socialists and their economic policies. After 1933 he kept in touch with Jewish acquaintances such as the banker Max Warburg, with whom he abruptly severed ties, however, when the National Socialists photographed them together and publicly denounced him.[85]

Similar intergenerational differences emerged in another Hamburg commercial family, the Witthoeffts. Franz Heinrich Witthoefft – an international trader and owner of the firm Arnold Otto Meyer and a member of the generation born around 1863 – had already played a significant political role in the Weimar Republic as a DVP delegate in the National Assembly and as a Hamburg senator.[86] Although towards the end of the Weimar Republic he switched over to the National Socialists – as a member of the 'Keppler circle' he was one of the most prominent proponents of Hitler taking office as Chancellor, becoming a member of the NSDAP in 1933 – he rejected their anti-Jewish policies. He gave his backing to the sponsorship for Jewish scientists given by the Hamburg Scientific Foundation (the *Hamburgische Wissenschaftliche Stiftung*) and indignantly resigned from the Rotary Club when it demanded an 'Aryan certificate' from its members.[87] Writing to his former DVP colleague Max Warburg, with whom he remained in contact after 1933, he admitted at the beginning of 1934 'that quite a few things [had] developed in ways other than those we had all hoped [for]'.[88] However, Witthoefft's son, Peter Ernst, was a convinced antisemite and justified the measures of the National Socialists against the Jews on the grounds that the Jews had 'gone somewhat too far in their outrages'.[89] In his view, the foreign reports about Germany under the National Socialists were just the 'bawlings of the international Jews'.[90]

It would be a mistake to exaggerate such differences of opinion and turn them into a 'generational conflict'. As the example of Franz Heinrich Witthoefft shows, support for the NSDAP and rejection of antisemitism were by no means mutually exclusive. In the older generation, too, there were convinced antisemites such as Ricardo Sloman, a businessman who hoped to popularise National Socialist racial hygiene theories by publishing obscure tracts on the subject.[91] Moreover, almost no-one in the older generation committed themselves to the cause of defending the persecuted Jews. Their scepticism of National Socialist racist antisemitism which contradicted the class-based values and standards of the traditional commercial bourgeoisie and the primacy of the 'capabilities' of the individual, did not lead them to any active solidarity with the Jews. Among the few exceptions – mentioned above – was Cornelius Freiherr von Berenberg-Goßler (born in 1876), who took up the defence of his many 'Jewish' friends without consideration of the consequences for himself. Thus, after direct negotiations with Himmler's adjutant, *SS Gruppenführer* Wolff, he was able to arrange the release of his friend Fritz Warburg from the custody of the Gestapo in April 1939.[92]

Nevertheless, such selfless commitment was exceptional. For a fair summary of the behaviour of most businessmen one might take the self-critical conclusion of Alwin Münchmeyer, a banker, 'We did nothing and thought little about it.'[93]

In the same way, the Chamber of Commerce kept out of decisions on Jewish policy as much as possible until 1937/38.[94] It did not participate in the 'elimination' of Jewish companies, but equally did not oppose it. Public doubts were only expressed if the 'elimination' of Jewish enterprises or their 'Aryanisation' threatened, or was felt to present a potential threat, to their own position.

In January 1939 Gauleiter Kaufmann dismissed such doubts in a speech before the Chamber of Commerce:

> Aryanisation has certainly unsettled a few Hamburg Aryans. I have been informed that there are rumours that elderly gentlemen have seriously contemplated whether and in which year of grace this very type of Aryanisation would happen to them. One could only think of, discuss or expect this if one was not familiar with the racial problem or was not sure about one's own race. Such statements are so childish – excuse this expression – that they should really be the cause of some serious concern. I would like to ask you, where you encounter such apprehensions, to exorcise these men of such figments of their imagination, with heartwarming clarity and, if it should increase the impact you have, by referring to me, for anyone who is industrious will remain at the same level he was previously at in economic terms.[95]

The doubts of 'elderly gentlemen' about 'Aryanisation' were primarily prompted by their ideal of law and order. By dispossessing a businessmen of their economic livelihood, the National Socialist State made a deep intrusion into the realm of private property which ran against the middle-class sense of security. Many therefore interpreted 'Aryanisation' as a foreboding of a 'brown Bolshevism' to come.

## The 'Law for the Restoration of a Professional Civil Service'

The 'Law for the Restoration of a Professional Civil Service' (also known as the Civil Service Act, *Berufsbeamtengesetz*, or BBG), announced by the Reich government on 7 April 1933,[96] represented the 'first comprehensive law involving economic discrimination against the Jews'.[97] It was intended both to eliminate opponents of National Socialism from public office, and, conversely, to facilitate the infiltration of the state apparatus by National Socialists. It was also designed to remove Jewish civil servants from public service.[98] Apart from civil servants, those affected by the law included employees and other workers in the state administration as well as officials in bodies established under public law and, indirectly, professional groups such as doctors and lawyers whose licence to practice was likewise made dependent on their 'Aryan identity'. In addition to the dismissal of public employees, the wave of dismissals of Jewish employees from private enterprises already dealt with above was also in many respects based on the definitions set out in the Civil Service Act.

Although the BBG was promulgated at the beginning of April 1933, the dismissal of Jewish officials was not proceeding quickly enough in the eyes of many newly appointed National Socialist regional potentates. Thus, on 28 March 1933, Frankfurt *Oberbürgermeister* Krebs ordered the suspension of all Jewish officials and the dismissal of all Jewish employees – without waiting for any legal grounds on which to base his order – as a 'defensive measure' against foreign propaganda and 'horror stories'.[99] Similarly, in other cities like Dortmund, National Socialists undertook anti-Jewish 'cleansings' without any legal basis.[100] In Hamburg, by contrast, a Senate enquiry gathering information from all departments[101] brought to light the fact that in March/April 1933, no such dismissals had been made,[102] with the notable exception of the dismissal of the Jewish Councillor of State Leo Lippmann in March 1933. By 31 May 1933, a total of only 22 people had been dismissed from public service.[103] The manifold regulations of the BBG when it came into force thus represented the first effective instrument used in the comprehensive purging of state personnel.

Paragraph 2 of the BBG was aimed at removing professionally unqualified 'partisan' appointees – *Parteibuchbeamten*. The truth was that such officials had not existed in Hamburg before that time, (typically) being first appointed on a large scale by the National Socialists.[104] Paragraph 2a dealt with Communist officials who were to be dismissed, like other so-called *Parteibuchbeamten*, without pension rights.

Finally, according to Paragraph 3, officials of 'non-Aryan extraction' were to be sent off into retirement. 'Non-Aryans' already included persons with just one Jewish grandparent[105] and 'non-Aryan' descent was 'to be assumed in particular if one parent or grandparent belonged to the Jewish religion'. The Reich Interior Minister radicalised this vague formulation further in a circular to all Reich governors on 1 September 1933. The circular underlined that 'birth, race, blood' was the determining factor in deciding 'Aryan' extraction, not religious confession.[106] Thus, one could be considered 'non-Aryan' even if one's grandparents had never belonged to the Jewish religious community but did have 'Jewish parents according to racial criteria'. Nevertheless, the Hamburg Senate decided not to adhere to the guidelines from the Reich Interior Ministry and in its place developed a more flexible procedure. Here the 'minimum condition' for recognition as an 'Aryan' was having four grandparents all of whom had been baptised as children. In special cases a decision could be taken 'without in-depth examination' which did not exclude the possibility of choosing to apply the harsher conditions of the Reich Interior Ministry.[107] Thus, the Hamburg Senate reserved for itself the right to define the concept of 'Jewishness' variously according to 'religious' or 'racial' criteria.

The grounds for this arbitrary regulation become clear after reviewing a few individual cases in which the Senate was content with its 'minimum condition'. These cases related to officials and lawyers from old Hamburg bourgeois families whose forefathers had married middle-class Jews who had assimilated and converted to Christianity in the nineteenth century.[108] In this regard the regulation represented a concession by the Hamburg National Socialists to their bourgeois coalition partners in the Senate.

On the intervention of Reich President von Hindenburg, exceptions were made to dismissals made under Paragraph 3 for Jews who had fought at the front, for fathers and sons of those who had fallen in the First World War and for 'non-Aryans' who had entered public service before 1 August 1914. Those Jewish officials who were removed from office received only seventy-five per cent of their pensions – and even then only if they could show a minimum of ten years of uninterrupted service.[109] These discriminatory regulations also applied to officials dismissed from public service under Paragraph 4 of the BBG because of their political affiliation. Paragraph 5 of the BBG regulated the transfer of officials to another department with a lower rank, while Paragraph 6 enabled employers to shunt officials off into retirement 'to simplify the administration'. In this case the position they left free was not to be filled again.

In Hamburg, dismissals effected in conformity with the BBG were made by the regional Reich Governor on the recommendation of the Senate.[110] In practice, measures were prepared and implemented by the personnel departments of the various authorities and the State Office (*Staatsamt*) working together with the Hamburg NSDAP's *Gau* Bureau for Officials (*Gauamt für Beamte*), which submitted recommendations to the Senate for the implementation under the BBG.[111]

The majority of dismissals in Hamburg affected teachers in all types of schools as well as professors and lecturers at the university. According to a list drawn up in 1938, the dismissals in Hamburg made under the terms of the BBG affected a total of 792 teachers, university teachers and officials charged with the supervision and administration of schools.[112] Those dismissed from service included internationally acclaimed Jewish academics such as the philosopher Ernst Cassirer, the art historian Erwin Panofsky, the jurist Albrecht Mendelssohn-Bartholdy and the psychologist William Stern.[113] Those dismissed as 'non-Aryans' under Paragraph 3 of the BBG totalled seventy-six, or 9.6 per cent of the total number of those dismissed, whereas even the proportion of those classified as politically unreliable under Paragraph 4 was only 4.5 per cent (36 individuals). The overwhelming majority of those affected – six hundred and sixty-four individuals (83.8 per cent) – were retired early under Paragraph 6 in pursuit of a reduction in the numbers of officials serving in the administration.

Similar numerical ratios characterised the dismissals in the general and internal departments of the State of Hamburg. Of the 2,666 officials employed here, three hundred and fifty-three were affected (13.2 per cent), of whom again more than four-fifths – 81 per cent (286 individuals) – were dismissed under Paragraph 6. The proportion of those dismissed as 'non-Aryans' pursuant to Paragraph 3 was lower here at 2.8 per cent (10 individuals) than was the case among teachers and university teachers, while by contrast the 'politicals' dismissed under Paragraph 4 – 15.3 per cent (54 individuals) – represented a higher proportion than was the case in the teaching profession.[114] While the proportion of senior officials dismissed amounted to 16.4 per cent, at the lower levels it was only 9.7 per cent.[115]

The actual number of Jewish officials and employees dismissed was however substantially larger than the numbers of those classified under Paragraph 3 suggests. Those 'non-Aryans' who, until 1933, had expressed only vague sympathies for republican parties were generally classified under Paragraph 4.[116] In addition, the highest-ranking Jewish official in the Hamburg administration, the State Councillor of the Finance Deputation, Dr Leo Lippmann, was dismissed as 'politically unreliable' under Paragraph 4 although Lippmann had never belonged to a political party and was the embodiment of the non-political 'professional civil servant'. When asked about this, Georg Ahrens – Director of the Hamburg State Office – told him that there was 'not the least thing' against him and the classification was purely made at the discretion of the Senate.[117] The Senate had probably selected this apparently arbitrary category only because Lippmann had been an official before 1 August 1914 and therefore fell under the rule covering exceptions to Paragraph 3.

The great majority of 'non-Aryan' officials and employees were nevertheless not dealt with under either Paragraphs 3 or 4, but were instead pensioned off under Paragraph 6 on grounds of the need for the 'simplification of the administration'. For instance only 5 Jewish judges and state attorneys were dismissed under Paragraph 3 against the 22 retired under Paragraph 6.[118] Paragraphs 4 and 6 of the BBG thus developed from a law that claimed to treat each individual case with its own particular solution into one in which all of the law's general categories were used arbitrarily against 'non-Aryans'. The state simply bypassed the legal provisions for exceptions to the law. Jewish soldiers who had fought at the front and older officials could thus be pensioned off arbitrarily under Paragraphs 4 and 6 and the lengthy certification procedures with questions relating to definition of 'Aryan' and 'non-Aryan' descent – like the artificial dilemma over a 'religious' or 'racial' interpretation of the concept of Jewishness – could also be sidestepped.

This impression of arbitrary, capricious behaviour becomes stronger when we take a closer look at some decisions of the Hamburg Senate relating to individuals. At the end of 1933, the Reich Interior Ministry asked the Hamburg

Reich Governor to dismiss the National Socialist Mayor of Bergedorf, Albrecht Dreves, who had taken office on 16 June 1933.[119] Through research into his ancestry it had been established that Dreves had two 'fully Jewish' great-grand-parents and one 'fully Jewish' grandparent on his mother's side and thus fell into the BBG's definition of a Jewish *Mischling*, or a Jew of mixed blood.[120] Because Dreves had, however, belonged to the NSDAP since 1927, and Reich Governor Kaufmann recognised that he had given great service in the 'national uprising', the Hamburg Senate opposed the instruction to dismiss him. On 29 November 1933, Reich Governor Kaufmann and the Senate concurred in a joint decision that the dismissal of Dreves 'ought only to be undertaken, and done in an hon-ourable manner, if an appropriate position for Dreves was found in the eco-nomic sector'.[121] When the Reich Interior Ministry persisted with its demand, Dreves was transferred, in August 1934, to be a director of the *Hamburger Frei-hafen-Lagerhaus-Gesellschaft*, although this company also fell under the provi-sions of the BBG. Shortly thereafter Dreves even moved up to the Office of the Chairman of the Board and with it drew a salary that was considerably larger than that which he had received as Mayor of Bergedorf. Despite his classification as a 'Jewish *Mischling*', Dreves was also allowed to wear the uniform of a District Office Director – *Kreisamtsleiter* – of the NSDAP.[122]

One 'Aryan' kindergarten teacher, Hildegard K., could not have even hoped for this kind of obliging treatment when a local NSDAP group and the *Gau* Per-sonnel Office of the Hamburg NSDAP complained about her to the State Office.[123] The charge made against her was that she had maintained, not inti-mate, but nevertheless friendly contacts with a 'half-Jew'. She had 'accompanied' him 'on walks' and helped him 'unpacking goods in the store'.[124] Although the Senator for the Interior supported the kindergarten teacher, Senator Ahrens as Head of the Hamburg State Office pressed for her immediate dismissal. Which legal grounds Ahrens took this position on remains obscure, since even intimate relations between 'Aryans' and 'non-Aryans' were not punishable before the 'Nuremberg laws' were decreed.

In view of his attitude in the Hildegard K. case, it might seem at first glance somewhat surprising that Senator Ahrens himself also supported a 'half-Jewish' employee of the 'People's Welfare Service', the *Volksfürsorge*. In 1935, the employee was dismissed without notice after 16 years of service because NSDAP *Kreisleiter* Arthur Lenz, Head of Personnel of the People's Welfare Service, wished to make his organisation 'free of Jews'.[125] If in this case Ahrens opposed the Party's request, it was only because the employee had lodged a complaint with the 'Office of the Führer', and the Reich Economics Ministry had drawn the attention of the Head of the State Office to the unequivocal legal position according to which 'Jewish *Mischlinge* were to be treated absolutely equally in the same areas of business as persons of German blood'.[126] After repeated interventions the People's Welfare Service declared itself ready to make a one-off compensation payment.

In each of the three cases the State of Hamburg did not decide the course it would take on the basis of existing legal principles but sought to deal with the specific situation presented by the case. In both of the first two cases the interests of the NSDAP turned on balancing suitable provision for an 'old fighter', on the one hand, and the exclusion of 'non-Aryans' from German society, on the other, while the third case was only dealt with according to the legal requirements because the 'Office of the Führer' and the Reich Economics Ministry pressed for their observance. All three cases are indicative of a collapse of security under the law and the normative principles of state government.

Any Jew who survived the first wave of dismissals on the grounds that he or she fell under the exceptions to the rules outlined in Paragraph 3, nevertheless had no security under the law from that time onwards and was subject to continuous pressures and threats of dismissal. This applied especially to officials and employees of the lower and middle ranks of the administration, which, after 1933, took in numerous 'old fighters' of the NSDAP who went out of their way to harass their Jewish colleagues. Many managers took these conflicts as a cause to dismiss their Jewish employees for 'disturbance of the peace in the workplace'. One striking example of this is the case of the Jewish civil servant Julius Plaut, dismissed in May 1934 from the Department of Welfare.[127] After the National Socialists took power, the severely disabled veteran who had fought at the front was confronted with a series of humiliations that began with his transfer from the Office of the Adviser on Professions (*Amt des Berufpflegers*) to the department archives where he was exposed to harassment and insult from his National Socialist colleagues. This finally culminated in a dispute, described by Plaut in a formal complaint to the Hamburg Reich Governor:

> I replied to Herr S. that he was a liar and his behaviour was more like that of a Communist than that of a National Socialist, that I had also fought and shed blood for him. To that S. replied: 'You, Jew, did not fight for Germany, you fought for your Jews!' When I countered that I was a Christian, he said: 'For me there is only race!' On one of the last days on which I was working in the archives, S. in my presence whistled the tune: 'Haven't you seen little Cohn?' He also harassed my colleague P., who is otherwise a peace-loving, calm and accommodating man … so much that he no longer gave me any information and no longer greeted me. I would also like to note that I have been equally troubled from the time of my transfer to the Archive by a Frau H., who is known in the administration and amongst colleagues as an exceptionally intolerant National Socialist, who was annoyed because of my Hitler salute, which I held and hold it to be my duty to give. Thus she once said to me, speaking straight into my face, that I had no right to give it, and that she would make sure that I would be dismissed for it.[128]

Despite Plaut's complaint the Welfare Department persisted with the notice which it had served – on the ground that he had 'repeated differences with colleagues'.[129] This argument made Jewish employees practically responsible for antisemitic disturbances. In view of the arbitrary approach taken by the authorities it is no wonder that only a few Jewish officials were able to remain in their posts up to 1935, the last being finally dismissed on 31 December 1935.[130] Whereas many of the Social Democrats and Communists dismissed under Paragraph 4 of the BBG were shortly thereafter discreetly taken back into the service of the Hamburg authorities – one incomplete list from the year 1937 mentioned a total of 43 cases[131] – for 'non-Aryans' no such concessions were made. In addition, the BBG prevented a whole generation of younger Jewish clerks, lawyers and academics from entering state service and thus from pursuing their careers in Germany.

No figures exist for the total numbers of 'non-Aryan' officials and public employees employed or dismissed in Hamburg because they were never compiled. This was primarily a result of the method of certifying ancestry, which was dealt with in very different ways from department to department. Certificates of Aryan extraction were first introduced for officials of the State of Hamburg in 1937/38.[132] Until then the certification procedure was limited to senior officials,[133] new employees and promotions. By contrast, some departments – like the Welfare Department – had already given all of their officials application forms for certificates in 1934.[134] Aryan certificates were dealt with even more inconsistently for the employees of the State of Hamburg. Whereas some authorities like the Office for Construction had required a certificate of 'Aryan' extraction from their employees in 1933, this was not the case in the Trade, Shipping and Industry Department, where only new employees and employees receiving promotion needed certificates, while a third group of departments did not require the certificates at all.[135] As this example makes clear, behind the regime's 'totalitarian' façade loomed a widespread tendency towards particularism across the different departments – and indeed this was true even when a central area of the National Socialist *Weltanschauung* was affected, as was the case with the certification of 'Aryan' descent.

Because the regulations of the BBG also extended into occupations which were not part of the public services – for example public corporations, public joint-stock companies and mixed public-private commercial concerns[136] – the Civil Service Act affected the economic life of the Jews particularly drastically. Following instructions from the Prussian Ministry of the Interior, even businessmen who owned private lotteries had to submit to the 'Aryan Paragraph'.[137]

On 22 April 1933, instructions from the Reich Ministry of Labour prevented 'non-Aryan' doctors from working in medical insurance companies.[138] The regulations provided for exceptions that were analogous to the regulations of the BBG for war veterans, the fathers and sons of those who had fallen in the war, and doctors who had been in medical insurance work before 1 August 1914. It would not be possible to calculate with any precision the number of Jewish doctors in Hamburg who were affected by the directive on the basis of the sources available. In 1934, Dr Willy Holzmann – the Chair of the Hamburg Chamber of Physicians (*Hamburger Ärztekammer*) and also Head of the Office for Racial Policy of the Hamburg NSDAP – calculated that the total number of 'non-Aryan' doctors in Hamburg was three hundred and forty, of whom two hundred and sixty-seven were also Jewish in terms of their religion.[139] One register compiled in November 1936 listed two hundred and seventy-five 'non-Aryan' doctors still working in Hamburg, of whom one hundred and sixty-six were licenced to work as health insurance doctors.[140] In other words, between forty and fifty per cent of all 'non-Aryan' doctors in Hamburg may have continued to practice.[141] This corresponded to the average numerical ratios which pertained at Reich level, where four thousand of nine thousand 'non-Aryan' doctors were able to continue practising as licenced health insurance doctors.[142] By July 1938, their total number in Hamburg had declined to one hundred and ninety-five,[143] and finally, on 30 September 1938, these too lost their licence.[144] With special permission thereafter fourteen Jewish doctors were able to continue to practice for a further period as 'medical care-givers' (*Krankenbehandler*).[145]

The Hamburg Chamber of Physicians, under the direction of Holzmann, was firmly committed to the fight against their Jewish colleagues. On the initiative of the Chamber, the register of doctors in the Hamburg telephone book of 1933 was expanded to include comments about the 'racial origin' of the doctors listed.[146] The instructions published by the Reich Ministry of Labour on 17 May 1934 dealing with the registration of licenced health insurance doctors also encouraged the Chamber to take further action against Jewish doctors. The directive excluded doctors from the profession if there was 'a significant factor weighing against their person' or if they did not offer a guarantee of 'unqualified commitment' to the National Socialist state.[147] On the basis of this directive the Hamburg Chamber of Physicians removed licences for all doctors against whom criminal proceedings had been initiated, without waiting for the opening of the main proceedings, nor for the verdict. In this way a Jewish gynaecologist, Dr L., lost his licence even though the district court of Hamburg later acquitted him of the charge of conducting 'commercial abortions'.[148] In order to prevent the acquittal of Jewish doctors in the future, the Clerk of the Chamber of Physicians, Dr Matthies, asked the Senator for Judicial Affairs to consult in such trials only with experts 'who, by virtue of their medical experience, by virtue of their *Weltanschauung* and by virtue of their work for the National Socialist state offered a guarantee that the correct decision would be made in defence against parasites on the body of the German *Volk*.[149]

Like doctors, Jewish lawyers were also devastatingly affected by measures taken by the National Socialists to exclude them on the basis of the BBG. Two hundred and one of the six hundred and forty-six lawyers in Hamburg were 'non-Aryan'.[150] At thirty-one per cent, the proportion of lawyers in Hamburg who were 'non-Aryan' was twice as high as it was for the Reich as a whole. Even before achieving equal civil rights in the course of the nineteenth century, Jewish university graduates had shown a preference for the liberal professions since they gave them the greatest freedom from professional restrictions. It was also easier to achieve a respected position in society. Their concentration in the largest cities was caused not least by the liberal, more anonymous atmosphere which contrasted with the intolerance of small towns and their often rigid social restrictions.[151] Ignoring this historical context, the National Socialists considered the concentration of Jews in the legal profession to be a sign of 'Jewish infiltration'. In the wake of the antisemitic terror of the spring of 1933 they began to restrict the ability of Jewish lawyers to practice in early April 1933. The 'Law on the Licencing of Lawyers' (*Gesetz über die Zulassung zur Rechtsanwaltschaft*) of 7 April 1933, passed on the same day as the BBG, enabled them to withdraw the licence of 'non-Aryan' lawyers up to 30 September 1933.[152] Exceptions, as in the BBG, were only made for war veterans, fathers or sons of those killed in the war, and lawyers who had been licenced before 1 August 1914.

In Hamburg, Justice Senator Curt Rothenberger withdrew Jewish judges from duty in criminal courts by changing the division of labour as early as the end of March 1933[153] and limited Jewish lawyers to working on legal aid cases and as defence attorneys.[154] These measures, however, fell far short of the anti-Jewish measures taken at the same time by the ministers of justice in Prussia and Bavaria.[155] After the National Socialists had organised antisemitic disturbances and riots at the Berlin courts, the acting Prussian Justice Minister Kerrl asked, on 31 March 1933, that all Jewish judges, state lawyers and legal officers submit requests for retirement forthwith. Jewish lawyers were to present themselves at court in future only in the same proportion of the total number of trials as the percentage of the Jewish population of Prussia. On the same day, the acting Justice Minister of Bavaria, Dr Hans Frank, retired all Jewish judges, state and official attorneys, banned Jewish lawyers from entering the courts and forbade Jewish notaries from practising their profession.

Whereas in other parts of the Reich, gangs of SA thugs stormed the courts and regional ministers of justice undertook radical measures to exclude Jews in order to pacify what was alleged to be 'popular anger' against them, the situation in Hamburg remained remarkably quiet. On 31 March 1933, Justice Senator

Rothenberger ordered that 'all molestation of Jewish judges and lawyers is to be strictly avoided and must be completely stopped'.[156] On 4 April 1933, he wrote to the Reich Interior Minister to support the regulations giving favourable treatment to Jewish war veterans in the context of the forthcoming BBG.[157] In a paper setting out its basic principles at the beginning of April 1933, the Hamburg Justice Department recalled the need for restraint in measures against Jewish lawyers and to take account of the 'special local conditions' in Hamburg.[158] Since both commercial enterprises and the consular corps employed many Jewish lawyers, anti-Jewish measures would 'not' create a 'favourable' impression on international opinion.

Did this represent a specifically 'moderate' course on the part of the Hamburg judicial authorities, distinct from the radicalism of anti-Jewish measures in other regions? This assumption is not confirmed by an examination of exclusions effected under the act with respect to the legal profession. On the basis of this act, by September 1933 seventy out of two hundred and one 'non-Aryan' Hamburg lawyers had lost their licences.[159] This ratio – 34.8 per cent – corresponded approximately to the levels in other states in the German Reich. In Prussia the act led to the dismissal of 32.2 per cent of all Jewish lawyers, and a total of 40.5 per cent lost their jobs by 'voluntary' dismissals.[160] Moreover, at the first meeting of state justice ministers held after the National Socialists took power on 22 April 1933, Justice Senator Rothenberger took the floor out from under any speculation that Hamburg might go its own way and demonstrated his close solidarity with his colleagues. The ministers aired their grievance that the regulations of the BBG were too mild, compelling them to make exceptions to their considerably more radical regional regulations. 'Guidelines kill action', complained the head of the Prussian Ministerial Department of Justice, Roland Freisler, who also wished to test the 'mental outlook' of Jewish war veterans and to distinguish between 'those who had fought at the front' and 'those who had only smelled the front'.[161] To be true to their task 'of creating revolutionary facts ... the duty of state ministers to use their judgment' had, in such cases, 'to be able to be exercised as freely as possible and without restriction'.

According to the records of the meeting, the Hamburg Justice Senator declared that he agreed with this thinly veiled call to break the law[162] and gave the impression to his fellow ministers that he himself was a representative of this radical antisemitism. Rothenberger had pressed the Reich Interior Minister for a milder version of the BBG, but carefully concealed this now. In this, Rothenberger revealed some of his most characteristic patterns of behaviour: opportunistic and pragmatic where it served his career and finely attuned to the 'spirit of the times', attributes which would carry him into the office of Undersecretary of State in the Reich Ministry of Justice.[163] Once figures like Rothenberger had accepted the antisemitic fundamentals of National Socialist policy, they found themselves increasingly radicalised, since every tactical gesture of restraint necessarily appeared 'cowardly' and 'half-hearted', and by contrast each radical initiative appeared to be quite consistent with the new regime's outlook. Striking a political profile within the fractious crowd of National Socialist decision-makers was only possible by pursuing a particularly radical position. This was the starting-point for the escalation of National Socialist anti-Jewish policy, contributing greatly to the development of the 'Final Solution'.

## Public Contracts and Jewish Enterprises

The general collapse of the purchasing power of the masses in the global economic crisis had driven countless companies into bankruptcy or to the brink of economic ruin. When Hitler's regime finally reversed the deflationary policies which the Brüning government had pressed and turned to a policy of deficit spending, it meant that public contracts and other supporting measures took on a central role in the revival of economic activity. For many economically weakened Jewish enterprises, survival depended to some degree on whether or not they would be able to compete for public contracts under the new regime.

The new government of the Reich initially gave an unambiguous answer. Whereas it did not allow newlyweds to use their loan for purchasing goods in Jewish businesses, causing heavy damage to Jewish retail traders,[164] in its assignment of public contracts it developed a far less rigid approach. On 14 July 1933, the government issued instructions for this purpose, according to which 'ethnic Germans' 'were to be preferred', wherever their tenders and those of 'non-Aryan' suppliers were of equal quality.[165] At the same time, however, it warned against 'lengthy searches for Aryan descent' or 'snooping', and raised the 'persisting economic conditions' which suggested restraint with respect to measures that would raise the high levels of unemployment still further.

The guidelines, thus, did not exclude Jewish businesses from public contracts, though they guaranteed them no long-term legal security because Nazi policy was linked to the economic context of the time. Eventually, two circulars from the Reich Ministries for Economics and Finance of March and May 1938 'corrected' the guidelines of 1933 and prevented Jewish companies from being able to compete for public orders.[166]

At the beginning of 1933, the relatively moderate Reich guidelines had been preceded in many cities and regions by the publication of decrees which were considerably harsher, restricting public contracts to 'Aryan', 'German' or 'Christian' firms, for instance on 2 March 1933, in Thuringia,[167] on 25 March in Baden,[168] on 27 March in Cologne,[169] on 22 March in Oldenburg,[170] on 29 March in Bremen,[171] on 31 March in Karlsruhe,[172] in Dortmund[173] and on 24 March in Munich, where suppliers were asked to fill in declarations of their Aryan descent.[174] Many of these regional regulations were maintained in open contradiction to the guidelines issued by the Reich thereafter and were rarely revised because of interventions from 'above'. Speaking of one such remonstration, Gauleiter Bürckel of Saarland-Pfalz declared publicly: 'We old Nazis don't care one bit what the posh Nazi higher-ups say.'[175]

In contrast to many local and regional authorities, the Hamburg Senate had proceeded without making special regulations, and on 22 July 1933, it adopted the recently released Reich guidelines.[176] Thus, even in the years following 1933 Jewish firms were able to bid for public contracts. The Hamburg Senate's moderate line was soon, however, countermanded by a number of partially contradictory orders from Gauleiter and Reich Governor Kaufmann. Probably because of complaints from within the Party, at the end of July 1934, Kaufmann instructed that before any contract was given to a Jewish company the Department of Industry was to give an opinion on the basis of which he would make a personal decision. Shortly afterwards he informed the Senate via his liaison officer 'that the greatest possible restraint was to be used in giving contracts to "non-Aryan firms"'.[177] A little later again, Kaufmann made the granting of contracts to Jewish firms dependent on the vote of the NSDAP *Gau* Economics Adviser.

In view of the Gauleiter's opposition to granting contracts to Jewish firms, in October 1934, the Hamburg Senate made renewed efforts to deal with this question. On 22 October 1934, the Senate issued confidential guidelines which made a clear break with the set of principles that had previously been in use. Now, the Senate showed itself to be a willing agent of the Gauleiter. Following the new guidelines would mean that in the future public contracts with Jewish enterprises would be blocked even when a Jewish business had made a considerably better offer than its 'Aryan' competitors. Underlying this decision was the assumption that 'in many cases non-Aryan firms competed unfairly in order to obtain business with the government – as well as on propagandistic grounds – whatever happened'.[178] Only in 'absolutely exceptional cases', and only with the prior certification of the *Gau* Economics Adviser, was there to be any deviation from this principle from now on. As the Senate's decision was in obvious contradiction to the guidelines laid down at Reich level, it was given orally to the senior officials in the administration and their subordinates.

The available sources do not make possible a clear enough reconstruction of decision-making processes in Hamburg at the time to enable us to judge if this form of news transmission left a lasting impression on departmental heads in Hamburg or if the content of the decree met with general rejection. What is clear, however, is that the Senate's decree was not carried out in practice. In view of their notorious financial difficulties some senior officials hoped not to have to forego the comparatively cheap tenders by Jewish suppliers, which often produced goods more efficiently and were therefore able to sell more cheaply than their 'Aryan' competitors.

The police administration continued to buy part of its office supplies from the Jewish supplier Alex Loewenberg after it had ascertained that 'Aryan' suppliers had likewise bought some of their products from Loewenberg and had sold them on to the authorities, taking a mark-up for themselves.[179] Though the Hamburg State Office insisted once more on a Senate decree on 22 October 1934, according to which no public contracts were to be granted to Jews,[180] the decree was not fully complied with until 1938.

Similarly, before 1938, the Welfare Department, which had one of the largest budgets of any department in Hamburg, persisted in not excluding Jewish businesses from welfare services.[181] Indeed, the President of the Welfare Department, Oskar Martini, sent an instruction to all welfare offices on 14 November 1933, to the effect that those in need of assistance were also to be provided with the equipment desired, even 'if the supplier is a non-Aryan'.[182] Moreover, in view of its difficult budget situation, the Department bought large supplies of used clothing from Jewish pawnbrokers and second-hand dealers. This did not imply a rejection in principle of National Socialist antisemitism, as the President of the Health and Welfare Department made clear in a letter to SA Oberführer Heuser. He described it as 'unfortunate' that they continued to be dependent on 'these people', 'It seems that no Aryan has yet been born to do this dirty trade, while at the same time it is not without consequence to the Department whether we buy a used but good suit for 15.- RM at a junk dealer's or for 30.- RM in an Aryan clothing store.'[183]

Over the years, however, this position put department heads under more and more pressure. They faced the petty bourgeois antisemitism characteristic of the trade guilds and industrial associations pressing for the removal of Jewish firms from the lists of suppliers to the authorities. Thus, the Chamber of Handicrafts pleaded for the exclusion of a Jewish shoe store owner from the list on the grounds that he had 'with the capabilities of the singularity of his race been able … to find access to the authorities and to displace other businesses'.[184]

The only exception among the guilds were the opticians, who sought to protect Jewish members and even complained when Jewish firms were struck off the authorities' lists. Meanwhile some opticians who had, until that time, not been certified as suppliers, denounced their Jewish competitors.[185] 'It is a carricature [sic] of our National Socialist state that Jews and comrades of Jews may continue to supply the same without check and I, as before, am not allowed to', one National Socialist optician protested to the economic section of the Health and Welfare

Department.[186] Such individual initiatives did not alter the basic approach of the Department to the provision of welfare services by Jewish businesses.

This did not, however, prevent some Welfare Department branch heads from proceeding on their own account with actions against Jewish businesses, thereby in practice reversing the position of the leadership of the Hamburg administration, as it were, from below. Some Welfare Department branch heads supplied the papers of welfare recipients who had bought goods from a Jewish business with a note threatening that if this were repeated they would not refund the amount of the purchase.[187] The owner of one Jewish department store, a Herr Bucky, complained to the Welfare Department that one of his customers had reported 'that he had been yelled at by someone in your office charging that she had bought goods in my store'.[188]

That some Welfare Department local offices responded with an increasingly restrictive approach was, to some degree, also due to the pressure which NSDAP local offices exerted on the administration. For example, Dr Becker, the 'liaison officer' of the NSDAP to the Hamburg administration, pressed for payments to Jewish businesses to be 'forestalled as much as is possible' after a complaint had been made by the local office of the National Socialist Craft, Trade and Commerce Organisation (*Nationalsozialistische Handwerks-, Handels- und Gewerbeorganisation*, or *NS-Hago*) about some of the offices of the Welfare Department.[189] In August 1935, NSV Hamburg leader Senator Wilhelm von Allwörden said that the position of the Welfare Department towards purchases made in Jewish stores was 'no longer tenable'.[190] A few days later, the President of the Health and Welfare Department, Dr Ofterdinger, made reference to the changed economic situation reported in the Reich guidelines of 14 July 1933.[191]

Although National Socialists both within and outside the administration pushed for the total exclusion of all Jewish businesses from making public deliveries, seeking to use the highly charged climate of antisemitism in the run-up to the Nuremberg Party Congress of 1935 for their own ends, the underlying position of the Welfare Department did not alter. In this respect the numerous instructions from the Reich Economics Minister and Reichsbank President – Schacht – were not insignificant: Until the 'revision of the position of the Jews in economic affairs', Schacht had forbidden all measures against Jewish businesses to be taken on an individual basis.[192]

Under pressure because of the antisemitic initiatives of the NSDAP and a few craft associations, confronted by demands for restraint from the Reich Economics Ministry, confused by contradictory instructions from the Reich Governor, the Senate and the senior officials in the various departments, as well as by their arbitrary practical implementation, the heads of the Hamburg administration awaited clear guidance on the situation from decisions taken at Reich level. Thus, on 5

October 1935, the Head of the Hamburg State Office recommended that the
hapless heads of department await eventual implementation regulations for the
Reich Citizenship Act, from which they could expect a greater degree of legal clarity over the position of Jews in economic affairs.[193] At the same time, the Hamburg Economics Department undertook the only identifiable attempt to clarify in
detail the position of the state with respect to Jewish businesses, so as to end the
multiplicity of conflicting instructions and the contradictory interpretations
placed on regulations in their implementation within the administration in Hamburg. They prepared a draft letter for the *Regierende Bürgermeister* Krogmann to
be sent to the 'Führer's Economics Representative', Wilhelm Keppler, with the
request that detailed clarification be given. In the letter, the Hamburg authorities
listed a whole range of unresolved questions about the state's relations with Jewish enterprises for which 'a variety of understandings' existed in the Hamburg
authorities.[194] Among these open questions was the assignment of public contracts to Jewish businesses and the demand, often addressed to the authorities, to
give preference to 'Aryan' companies over Jewish ones.

Since the letter never got beyond drafting stage and the position of the Jews
in economic affairs was not fixed by law – because Hitler deliberately avoided giving the Jews any legal position, even a limited one[195] – the question of whether
or not public contracts should be given to Jewish companies continued to be
open. A final clarification of this was arrived at only in 1937/38 in the course of
the incorporations following the 'Greater Hamburg Act', which made homogen-
ising the regulations necessary. This meant that the areas incorporated into Hamburg which had previously been part of Prussia and had often been considerably
more radical in their treatment of the 'Jewish question'[196] no longer gave public
contracts to Jewish firms from 1933.

For example, from the end of March 1933 the welfare office of the city of
Harburg-Wilhelmsburg had attached to its vouchers an additional note 'Not
valid for Jewish businesses, wholesale or retail stores.'[197] The Hamburg practice
of allowing Jewish businesses to deliver supplies and to redeem their welfare
vouchers thus met with no support from the Harburg-Wilhelmsburg city council. The head of the Harburg welfare office, Prellwitz, rejected the Hamburg regulations as an 'impossible state of affairs' which gave the instructions from the
Reich Economics Ministry 'a rather pro-Jewish interpretation'.[198] For this reason
he unabashedly demanded that the President of the Hamburg Welfare Department 'adapt the practice of the Economics Division there to the predominant
trend of opinion'.

In December 1937, when it emerged that the authorities in Hamburg and
Harburg could not agree on common regulations, the debate was submitted to
the Reich Governor for Hamburg, Kaufmann, for a final decision. After the dis-

missal of Schacht as Economics Minister in November 1937 and the intensification of the antisemitic measures of the ministry under Schacht's provisional successor, Göring, Kaufmann rejected the previous directive from Schacht and decided to introduce the more radical Harburg regulation in Hamburg as well.[199] By 1 April 1938, Jewish companies were to have been struck off the lists of suppliers and the credit vouchers of welfare offices were to be marked with the note 'Not valid for Jewish businesses'.[200] Thus Hamburg finally submitted to a regulation which many cities and regions had been applying since the spring of 1933.[201]

## Displacement and Early 'Aryanisations' through State Intervention

Although the legal position of Jews in economic affairs was not at first restricted by a comprehensive act at Reich level, and until the end of 1937 the Reich Economics Ministry held firmly to its fundamental position that Jews were to remain unhindered in the open market, a process of creeping 'Aryanisation' was set in motion in 1933, by which Jewish firms were more or less 'voluntarily' sold or were 'quietly' liquidated without a sale. Beyond that, an increasing number of Jewish company owners were forced into 'Aryanising' their holdings by statutory or administrative measures of the various Reich ministries. Since a number of misconceptions persist in the scholarly literature on the scope, timing and context of this state-enforced 'Aryanisation policy', the following section treats this complex series of 'Aryanisations' through examining a few selected industries and occupational groups in greater depth. The focus is not only on measures, procedures and disputes at Reich level, but also on how they were reflected in the policies of the Hamburg state leadership.

Among those Reich ministers who proceeded to rule particularly inflexibly on questions relating to Jewish enterprises in their areas of responsibility, the Minister for Public Information and Propaganda, Dr Joseph Goebbels, did so with exceptional effect. Beyond his press and propaganda tasks, Goebbels' position as President of the Reich Chamber of Culture (*Reichskulturkammer*, RKK),[202] created in the autumn of 1933, gave him an instrument for taking over and controlling the whole cultural life of Germany, since in practice all cultural activity was from now on tied to membership of one of the seven subsections of the RKK.[203]

Contrary to a widespread misconception in such research as has been published on the subject[204] Jews were in no way excluded from membership in the Reich Chamber of Culture. Neither the Reich Chamber of Culture Act, nor the first executive regulation of 1 November 1933, contained an 'Aryan Paragraph'.[205] However Paragraph 10 of the regulation made membership in one of the subassociations of the RKK dependent on possession of the 'necessary reliability and suitability'. Deploying this vague formulation, Goebbels set out, from the beginning of 1935, to eliminate the many Jewish businesses active in cultural life. His initiatives were not linked chronologically or causally with the 'Nuremberg laws' issued in September 1935, nor were they primarily focused on art and antique dealers.[206] On the contrary, they dealt with all Jews active in 'cultural business'. The measures introduced from the beginning of 1935 affected the owners of bookstores, publishing companies and second-hand bookstores and also the owners of music and radio stores and cinemas.

In March 1935, most Jewish art galleries and bookstores in Hamburg received a letter from the division of the Reich Chamber of Culture responsible for them which argued that 'non-Aryans' did not have the necessary reliability or aptitude to take part 'in the promotion of German culture in a manner corresponding to *Volk* and *Reich*'.[207] They were therefore told to sell their business to an 'Aryan' or to wind it up within a short period. Almost none of those who had received the letter appear to have accepted their elimination from economic life without putting up some resistance. The owner of the 'Burstah art gallery', Walter Dosse, and Jewish publisher and bookstore owner Dr Kurt Enoch, a veteran and a highly decorated officer, went to the Hamburg Economics Department and requested their support. The Economics Department declared its unreserved support for the Jewish business owners and argued that the professional disqualifications that had been issued contradicted all of the declarations of fundamental principle of the highest levels of the Reich. The Department referred explicitly to the decree issued by the Reich Interior Minister of 17 January 1934, which forbade the application of the 'Aryan Paragraphs' in private industry.[208] The Department requested that the Hamburg Legation in Berlin intervene at the Reich Chamber of Culture on behalf of the Jewish company owners.

In preceding years, Hamburg's Legation in Berlin had already acted several times on behalf of the economic interests of Jewish businesses. To give one example, in January 1934, speaking on behalf of the Hamburg authorities, the economic adviser of the Legation, Kurt Langguth, had criticised the exclusion of Jews from economic associations. Through the introduction of the Aryan Paragraphs a 'fake idealism' was covering up the pursuit of self-interest by members of the Chamber, 'to raise their own commercial income at the expense of others and thereby eliminate their Jewish competitors' without themselves having to go to any effort.[209] Among Hamburg's administrative bodies, the Hamburg Legation argued most emphatically for the importance of prioritising economic stabilisation over an unregulated policy of displacing Jewish businesses. The Legation stuck to this maxim, not only writing to intervene with the President of the Reich

Press Association and the Reich Chamber of Fine Arts, but also writing to request support from the Reich Economics Ministry.[210]

The Reich Chamber of Culture took some time before it sent a reply. Only after repeated interventions from the Hamburg Legation did the 'Legal Adviser' of the Reich Chamber of Culture, Dr Karl-Friedrich Schrieber, decide to give the Legation a 'confidential' message – orally, not in writing, as was typical of the procedures of the Reich Propaganda Minister and of the Reich Chamber of Culture. On 4 May 1935, the Legation informed the Hamburg State Office of the substance of the conversation: 'From the conversation [held] in person with Dr Schrieber this *confidentially* [emphasis in the original] means that according to the view taken in the Ministry, which is based on a personal decision of the Minister, a basic lack of reliability and suitability are to be assumed of non-Aryans in cultural matters even though the non-Aryans concerned were war veterans. This personal and confidentially shared information is intended only for the internal instruction of the State Office and Economics Department and may not be communicated externally.'[211]

By means of this clandestine procedure, not regulating the ban on 'non-Aryans' in the occupations concerned by decree but informing those affected individually on the basis of a vague authorising paragraph, Goebbels was attempting to circumvent the fundamental opposition of the Reich Economics Ministry. The Propaganda Ministry appeared at first to have been successful in using this tactic. As the Hamburg Legation reported to the State Office, the Reich Economics Ministry had initially registered its opposition very half-heartedly.[212] It had thus placed no fundamental question mark behind the measures taken by the Propaganda Ministry, but instead merely pleaded for longer transitional periods for the firms affected.

It was in this sense that on 4 November 1935, Reich Economics Minister Schacht entered the conflict with a letter to Goebbels, which he copied to Hitler. Although Hitler did not intervene in favour of his Economics Minister, the dispute between Schacht and Goebbels did not end in a clear victory for the Propaganda Minister either.[213] Instead, in January 1936, Goebbels began a temporary retreat and let it be known by way of 'Reich Culture President' (*Reichskulturwalter*) Hinkel that 'all measures aimed at the de-Judaisation of trade associations and federations of occupations dealing with the economic aspects of culture...[were to be] abandoned'.[214] By that time, two hundred and seventy-three 'non-Aryan' bookstores and publishers, to name just one group affected by the campaign, had already been excluded from the Reich Cultural Association. At the end of 1936, however, the Propaganda Ministry intensified its anti-Jewish activities to include book and art dealers who were 'related by marriage' to Jews. The resultant special measures, which were accompanied by constant interventions from the Reich Economics Ministry, were still in force in 1938.[215]

Hamburg's Legation in Berlin also continued to take up a position in favour of Jewish company owners in special cases. These initiatives were mostly unsuccessful. On 31 March 1937, Hamburg's envoy in Berlin, Peter Ernst Eiffe, reported to the State Office that Goebbels and Hitler had personally 'ordered that no exceptions could be made'.[216] In response to the intensification of the antisemitic campaign at Reich level, Eiffe felt a growing unease about his interventions, despite the fact that they referred to the difficult economic situation in Hamburg and were not based on any philosemitic sentiments. Eiffe reported to the State Office that it was 'naturally always a difficult task to appear to represent the interests of a Jew or a person related by marriage to Jews. Experience teaches how easily the reproach can be made that we are impeding the implementation of the Aryan legislation in Hamburg.'[217] The basic position of Hamburg, to give absolute priority to the stabilisation of the economy even if it did not signify any defence of Jewish interests per se, nonetheless appeared to Eiffe to be too difficult to press in Berlin. Speaking with a Jewish textile manufacturer, Eiffe demonstrated a willingness to press this point, but he seems to have had no more than limited room for manoeuvre; he could side with the manufacturer only to the extent that 'it was a question of the creation of employment in Hamburg, or one of the prevention of job losses'. He could not, however, 'criticise or fight against the measures of the party' as such.[218]

This complex mixture of special initiatives against Jewish businesses from the Propaganda Ministry, and interventions from the Reich Economics Ministry and the Hamburg Legation in Berlin, led to a highly variable, creeping process of displacement of Jews from their 'cultural businesses' in Hamburg. Many, like the art dealer Walter Dosse (mentioned above as the owner of the 'Burstah art gallery'), wound up their businesses in the spring of 1935 because they saw that, at best, further interventions would give them a prolonged, but no more than temporary, reprieve. They never obtained a long-term guarantee that they would be able to continue in the business. Moreover, many had already experienced discrimination before this time. Thus, the Hamburg Gestapo gave the owner of the Henschel & Müller bookstore, Hans Henschel, who among other things ran a specialist orientalist antiquarian store, instructions not to sell any more books from the period before 1800 'since he lacked the prerequisites for dealing with German cultural goods'.[219] In addition, after 1933 he lost several public contracts for book deliveries to libraries and foreign schools. In February 1936, Henschel therefore sold his business at a greatly reduced price to two Hamburg book dealers.[220]

Dr Kurt Enoch, owner of the *Oskar Enoch* and *Gebrüder Enoch Verlag* companies, emigrated to Paris in August 1936 after both firms had been 'Aryanised'. With special permission from the Reich Chamber of Literature and the Reich Office for Exchange Control, Enoch was able to take books with him worth 60,000 RM, having given a commitment to take over the foreign operations of two 'Aryan' publishers Tauchnitz and Albatross in Paris.[221] Enoch, who later rose to be one of the leading publishers in the United States,[222] was able to improve the foreign currency earnings of both publishing houses and as a Jewish emigré was put into the service of the German national economy.

As a so-called 'foreign currency earner', the Hamburg antique dealer Heinrich Bachrach also had some concessions made for him, operating an antique business on *Neue Jungfernstieg* and exporting extensively to Britain. In 1936, Bachrach was even allowed to establish a branch in London with the support of the Hamburg Chamber of Commerce and the Exchange Bureau of the Regional Finance Office of the Lower Elbe region. In addition, the Reich Economy Ministry intervened with the Reich Chamber of Culture on Bachrach's behalf.[223] However, after the Reich Chamber of Culture announced that Bachrach had been banned from the profession in August 1935, the RKK finally indicated in a letter to the Reich Economy Ministry on 14 December 1937 that, because of his 'political unreliability', a removal of the ban was out of the question.[224] In response to the ban, Bachrach did not return to Hamburg from his travels in England. The criminal proceedings opened against him over currency exchange matters finally ended with his citizenship being taken away[225] and the seizure of his entire German assets by the German Reich.

With special permission, five more bookstore owners and publishers who were 'non-Aryan' or who were 'associated' with Jews were able to stay in business until 1937. They were Hans Burghagen, owner of the Johannes Burghagen Publishing House, Adolf Busch Jr., owner of the Rathaus bookstore, Eva Dunk, owner of the Dr Weltsch-Weishut bookstore, Volkmar Scheel, owner of the bookstore that bore his name, and Otto Kurnitzky, owner of the lending library and bookstore named after Dr S. Menzel.[226]

The total number of 'non-Aryans' in Hamburg excluded from the Reich Chamber of Culture was approximately three hundred. By June 1938, seventy members engaged in fine arts were thrown out of the Chamber, including twenty-seven art dealers, seventeen artists, eleven architects and eight more commercial artists.[227] How many of them had previously been self-employed is not known. Forty-seven Hamburg 'non-Aryans' were thrown out of the Reich Chamber of Literature or had their applications for membership rejected.[228] An especially high number of 'non-Aryan' musicians and music teachers from Hamburg were affected. By January 1937, one hundred and thirty-seven of them were excluded from the Reich Chamber of Culture, including ninety-five musicians and singers and forty-two music teachers.[229]

While the exclusion of Jews from the 'cultural economy' proceeded without a recognisable normative legal basis, and dragged on for almost three years, occupational restrictions in other areas were implemented on the basis of statutory measures that made it possible to end all of the economic activities of the Jews affected, stifling opposition at its source: the Reich Interior Ministry sent professional bans to the Jewish owners of all pharmacies in March 1936, forcing them to lease their stores in accordance with the first regulation of the 'Law on the Leasing and Administration of Public Pharmacies'.[230]

It was no coincidence that Jews working in pharmacies faced such exceptionally tough measures. A licencing situation existed whereby the state had taken pharmacies out of the market economy, and the number of approved pharmacies was limited by the state while a large number of approved pharmacists remained without a place to work, often waiting for long periods before they were granted a licence. The displacement of Jewish pharmacists defused this precarious situation and offered an easy way out of the structural dilemma without having to deal with its causes.

In Hamburg, the consequences of this structural problem had emerged in a particularly acute form. Most self-employed pharmacists in Hamburg had a 'real licence', which, unlike a 'personal licence', could be sold or passed on[231] as long as the pharmacist who took on the licence had the necessary professional qualifications. This meant, however, that a considerable part of Hamburg's pharmacies were, in practice, working outside the control of the state. The mismatch between the number of licences available and the number of practitioners was so great that Hamburg pharmacists had to wait an average of twenty-four years after qualifying before gaining a licence.[232]

After 1933, Hamburg's National Socialists had exacerbated this problem still further, granting licences to young National Socialist activists at the expense of older practitioners,[233] thereby unleashing a Reich-wide uproar. The leader of the Professional Society of German Pharmacists condemned the licencing practice in Hamburg for its 'bad decisions' that he would not want 'to approve under any circumstances from the viewpoint of the Movement'.[234] In view of the severe internal party criticism of this situation, the President of the Health and Welfare Department alleged that the profession in Hamburg was 'overly Jewish', making it necessary to give preferential treatment to National Socialists.[235] It is therefore not surprising that the Hamburg authorities did not oppose the measures taken against Jewish pharmacists – though they had taken the part of Jews active in the 'cultural business' – seeing that the ban on Jewish phar-

*von Bolschwing ?*

macists had relieved them from dealing with the precarious situation into which they had manoeuvred themselves.

At the end of 1935, there were still nineteen Jewish pharmacists in Hamburg.[236] They were forced to lease out their practices from March 1936. More detailed information about thirteen of these pharmacists can be found in the restitution documents of the Hamburg regional court.[237] Eleven of the pharmacists possessed a 'real licence', the other two had 'personal licences'. The effective professional ban of March 1936 caught them completely off guard. Up to that point their income had not suffered greatly in spite of the boycott calls.[238] One of the pharmacists, Paul Freundlich, had even modernised his whole pharmacy operation a short time before.[239] Faced with the decision of whether to sell their 'real licence' or to lease the pharmacy out, six of the pharmacists decided to sell immediately, while five others initially leased their practices.

As both the sale and leasing of Jewish pharmacies removed them from control by the state, a 'special trade' took up the opportunities this presented: the difficult situation of Jewish owners was lucrative, as it would become once again with the 'Aryanisations' of later years. This arose most clearly among brokers and lawyers. They were presented with lucrative opportunities to negotiate deals between Jewish business owners who wished to sell up and potential buyers, or to prepare sales and leasing contracts, earning them large sums of money as 'Aryanisation specialists'. All of Hamburg's Jewish pharmacies were 'Aryanised' through the good offices of real estate dealer Ernst Zobel, who earned an average fee from each sales contract of 5000 RM.[240]

Those who had decided to lease their pharmacy – this included both the five pharmacists with 'real licences' and the two with 'personal licences', who of course had no option but to sell – had to accept considerable reductions to their current income. Until 1935, Manfred Pardo, owner of a pharmacy at the *Winterhuder Marktplatz*, had received an average net profit of 23,687 RM annually. After leasing his pharmacy he was left with only 8855 RM as annual rent and 4800 RM for renting out the pharmacy premises.[241]

In deciding to emigrate in 1938, three more Jewish pharmacists chose to sell their businesses, while the remaining four were 'Aryanised' in 1939. These sales were conducted under direct state control after 31 January 1939, when the licences of all Jewish pharmacists were revoked and the Hamburg Reich Governor ordered the sale or relicensing of the remaining pharmacies[242] in pursuit of the regulation on the 'Assignment of Jewish Property' of 3 December 1938.[243] The 'Aryanisation' of the rest of the pharmacies in question once more worked to the advantage of National Socialist functionaries, including one NSDAP local group leader.[244] The example of the pharmacies of Hamburg shows how important the 'Aryanisations' were in the calculations of the National Socialists. Wide-

spread nepotism allowed them to secure the unconditional loyalty of their followers, who in turn were pocketing the 'wages' for their antisemitic activism.

Of the thirteen Jewish pharmacists mentioned, only seven survived the
'Third Reich'. Three died shortly before or after the sale of their pharmacies, and
three were deported and murdered with their families.[245]

## The Initiating Role of the NSDAP and the
## Registration of Jewish Enterprises

On the whole, the Hamburg administration, including its National Socialist leadership, implemented anti-Jewish policy with notable restraint and in special cases
even exercised restraint where this seemed necessary for economic reasons. By
contrast, the NSDAP party apparatus sought to strike a public profile as the leading exponent of radical antisemitism. Detached from any public responsibility,
Hamburg NSDAP officials presented themselves as guardians of the National
Socialist *Weltanschauung* and attempted to place pressure on the Hamburg administration – which from the NSDAP perspective seemed 'feeble' – through antisemitic actions aimed, on the one hand, at radicalising anti-Jewish policy and, on
the other, at underlining their claim to a leading role in the 'Jewish question'.

The underlying approach of party officials was typified in the description in a
letter sent by an 'old fighter' to *Regierender Bürgermeister* Krogmann in October
1935. In the letter, the man deplored the alleged inactivity of Hamburg in the field
of anti-Jewish policy, focusing his criticism on the activity of Jews as collectors for
the Hamburg State Lottery.[246] While the NSDAP had pursued its antisemitic propaganda 'with great success', 'the Jewish question was ignored' by the state of
Hamburg and there was 'no trace' of any attempt to deal with it. The letter culminated in the assertion: 'We old party comrades do not want to have fought and
shed blood so that international capitalist Jewish circles can run their lucrative
businesses and exploit the German people.' The letter from these 'old party comrades' had an effect in that Mayor Krogmann ordered that Jewish collectors be laid
off by the Hamburg State Lottery, not immediately but 'bit by bit'.[247]

The destructive potential which the NSDAP's grassroots supporters were
able to stir up had already been shown by the antisemitic terror unleashed in the
spring of 1933. It is true that in Hamburg there had been no boycott like the
'Christmas boycotts' in Nuremberg and Munich, for example,[248] nor had party
groups stormed Jewish stores, smashing them up and beating owners and customers alike, as had become widespread in small cities and in the provinces.[249]
Nevertheless, the antisemitic street attacks of the NSDAP also revived in Hamburg in 1935. The NSDAP orchestrated an antisemitic demonstration in the

Rothenburgsort quarter on 11 May 1935 in front of Jewish stores on Billhorner Röhrendamm in which NSDAP members shouted, among other things 'Perish Judah' and 'Down with the Jewish traitors'.[250] Apparently the Jewish store attendants felt so little threatened by this transparent propaganda piece that only two of fifteen Jewish store owners closed their shop for the day.[251]

Another NSDAP initiative which attracted just as little popular support was a bill-posting operation in Hamburg launched in May 1935. Posters now appeared on the windows of Jewish stores carrying the message: 'Traitors buy from Jews'.[252] However, only a few customers were frightened off by this. One SA sergeant reported that the Jewish owner of the Walter Bucky department store had told him 'with a wide grin': 'Well, this morning there was a whole load of traitors out there.'[253]

In 1935, larger street operations focused on Altona and Harburg-Wilhelmsburg where, in August 1935, the SA and other organisations embarked upon an anti-Jewish propaganda campaign.[254] As early as July 1935, almost all the shop windows of Jewish businesses had been smeared with colour or antisemitic slogans had been stuck to them.[255] The head of the state police station in Harburg-Wilhelmsburg reported to the headquarters of the secret police in Berlin that such activities attracted hardly 'any sympathy from the bulk of the population', instead they provoked the 'very strongest rejection'.[256] Above all, the direct effect of such actions remained comparatively slight. The NSDAP's 'mob antisemitism' increasingly played an initiating function in terms of anti-Jewish policy, while the public administration, the Chamber of Commerce and other institutions generally held back. Only in this way can we explain why it was that the economic apparatus of the Hamburg NSDAP *Gau* achieved such a dominant position in questions of 'Aryanisation' while it remained almost completely without significance in other policy areas.[257] In addition, the NSDAP's street actions gradually changed the political climate, restricting the space within which others could act and preparing the way for the antisemitic developments to come.

An important role in the poisoning of the public climate was played by the National Socialist press, which provided the journalistic accompaniment for the antisemitic hate campaign. In August 1935, approximately two hundred '*Stürmer* stands' were set up in Hamburg, with 'sponsorship' from local NSDAP groups and centres.[258] In addition the NSDAP party newspaper, the *Hamburger Tageblatt*, published a string of anti-Jewish hate articles in an attempt to stir up a situation that would be ripe for a pogrom. In July 1935, it used some antisemitic attacks on the Kurfürstendamm in Berlin as an opportunity to publish a series of articles under the title 'Jews with a clean slate', promising to expose the 'dangerous force of the Jews in the economy'.[259] In September 1935, the *Hamburger Tageblatt* printed a directory of 'ethnic German' businesses as a supplement, under the title 'Guide to the Aryan Firms in Greater Hamburg', allegedly intended to fulfil the 'urgent desire' of many party members to be able – the supplement noted – to avoid buyers shopping in 'non-Aryan' businesses, for which 'ignorance' on their part was largely to blame.[260]

Thus Hamburg's party newspaper rushed ahead in one of the most disputed aspects of anti-Jewish policy. Any prohibition on party members and state employees buying in Jewish stores, every organised or covert boycott of Jewish firms, could only be effectively put into action, particularly in the large cities, if there was a successful attempt to classify Jewish enterprise systematically, making clear which firms were, according to National Socialist terminology, 'Jewish' or 'Aryan'.

The latter question was only fully dealt with in a secret instruction released by the Reich Economics Ministry on 4 January 1938.[261] Up until this point, the Reich Economics Ministry had repeatedly striven to prevent the development of a systematic definition of Jewish companies – 'on labour market policy grounds and out of consideration for the stabilisation needed by the economy as a whole', as Reich Economics Minister Schacht stated on 19 March 1936 before the Chamber of Trade and Industry of Nuremberg.[262] On this question too, however, the Minister possessed 'only a moderate amount of influence on individual events in the province',[263] particularly since he had himself gone against his own position in a discussion with the Reich Interior Ministry on 23 September 1935, expressly endorsing the duty of Jewish retail businesses to mark themselves as such.[264]

In many cities and regions, however, instructions from Berlin were given little attention and a close cooperation between the party organisation, the administration and the trade and industrial associations had long been successful in bypassing the orders of the Economics Ministry. In 1935, the NSDAP local leadership in Duisburg had drawn up a directory of Jewish businesses, which the city administration soon took over.[265] In Munich and Bielefeld, too, the city authorities had prepared similar directories against the instructions of the Reich Economics Ministry.[266]

In Hamburg, the *Hamburger Tageblatt*'s consumer directory for 'Aryan' stores met with a mixed response. Many 'Aryan' businesses in Hamburg had shown no interest in being included in a consumer guide in a National Socialist newspaper. Thus the editorial team noted, somewhat sheepishly, that the compilation only contained firms that 'set value on being treated as Aryan'.[267]

In the years that followed, a number of party organisations attempted, on several occasions, to win over the Hamburg Chamber of Commerce to the creation of a comprehensive compilation of Jewish businesses. In October 1935, one member of the Racial Policy Office of the Hamburg NSDAP proposed to require a 'race' certificate from all trading companies in order to be able to create an archive of 'Jewish' and 'Aryan' firms. As a model he suggested the registers that the

Racial Policy Office had created for doctors and other professions.[268] In its response, the Chamber of Commerce informed him coolly that it could only accept this proposal if it received a direct instruction from the Reich Economics Ministry[269] – which, given the orientation of that Ministry's policies, could be discounted. The Chamber of Commerce's rejection corresponded to its practice of restricting information in racial questions and underlined once more its restraint in terms of anti-Jewish policy.

The *NS-Hago* and the office of the *Gau* Economics Adviser chose a rather unusual means to compile a company directory. They assigned a private detective agency to do the necessary research, without informing either the Chamber of Commerce, the Retail Association or the Hamburg Economics Department.[270] When the Chamber of Commerce protested against the work being done by the private detective agency, a meeting between the Chamber of Commerce, *NS-Hago*, NSDAP *Gau* Economics Adviser and the Economics Department became necessary, at which the representative of the *NS-Hago* 'immediately became very excited, banged his fist on the table'[271] and acted as if he were 'outraged' at the attitude taken by the Chamber of Commerce. He justified his secrecy with the argument that the data in question was solely to be used for the instruction of party members. Incensed by the unexpected resistance to the project, he decided to provide only the Economics Department and not the Chamber of Commerce with a copy of the completed directory of 'ethnic German' firms.

As these manoeuvres illustrate, there was no prospect in Hamburg of concerted cooperation in the registration of Jewish firms. While the party organisations were creating their respective directories, similar activities on the part of the Chamber of Commerce and the Hamburg city authorities remained out of the question. It was only in December 1937 that the Welfare Department became the first Hamburg administrative department to register its Jewish suppliers systematically, after Reich Governor Kaufmann had made known that they were to give no more contracts to Jewish firms.[272]

On the whole, however, the Hamburg administration began its systematic registration of Jewish commercial concerns only in July 1938, after the Reich Interior Ministry had issued a circular ordering the introduction of directories of this kind.[273] In the region known as 'Old Hamburg' they were prepared by the police headquarters; in the areas incorporated after 1937 (Harburg-Wilhelmsburg, Altona, and Wandsbek) the former city tax offices took charge of them. On 7 December 1938, the Hamburg state administration reported to the Reich Interior Ministry its compliance with the instruction and presented a directory listing eight hundred Jewish enterprises in the area of 'Old Hamburg' alone.[274]

Before the Hamburg administration changed tack, the authorities in Hamburg that were 'directly under Reich control' had already embarked on the systematic registration of Jewish firms. From the beginning of 1938, the Regional Finance Department circulated an internal 'List of Non-Aryans Liable to Evade Taxes', and from the beginning of April 1938 a 'List of Jewish Export Companies'.[275] In December 1938, the Northwestern Section of the SS security service compiled a 'List of Influential and Wealthy Jews'.[276] The Gestapo also developed its own 'Index of Jews' as did the Foreign Exchange Office of the Regional Finance President and the German Labour Front (*Deutsche Arbeitsfront*, DAF). As far as can be reconstructed, the systematic collation of these different sources, and thereby the creation of a system of control in Hamburg without loopholes, did not begin before August 1938.[277] There was no campaign to register Hamburg's Jewish businesses in advance of, or exceeding, the rules developed at Reich level.

## Anti-Jewish Policy in Comparative Perspective: Hamburg and Munich

Seen in the context of anti-Jewish policy at Reich level, Hamburg did not develop an independent approach of its own. On the one hand, the city moved for the most part within the guidelines laid down at Reich level, on the other, the confusion of different measures and different authorities covering the area also prevented the adoption of a clear policy. The centrifugal tendencies in anti-Jewish policy thus did not simply reflect the polycratic tendencies of National Socialist rule and contradictions in anti-Jewish policy on the Reich level. There was also the tactical restraint of the Hamburg party and state leadership, who themselves had not developed clear specifications that could have served as guidelines for a regional anti-Jewish policy. The practice of anti-Jewish policy in Hamburg was thus characterised more by the fact that it had no particular profile than by the possession of any specific feature.

Although there was still a small amount of room for manoeuvre, before 1938, for those in Hamburg who wished to uphold minimal ethical standards and to withstand the thoroughgoing implementation of the National Socialists' racist paradigm, it would be wrong to see the city as an island of humanity in a sea of antisemitic barbarism. It consistently took part in Reich-wide actions like the boycott of 1 April 1933 or in the implementation of national laws like the Civil Service Act. In no way would it be fair to say that the city implemented the laws – as Hamburg's first postwar mayor, Petersen, solemnly declared – 'consistently later and without the ruthlessness ... [shown] elsewhere'.[278] There is no justification for speaking of a 'later' or even of a considerate application of anti-Jewish laws of the Reich in Hamburg. However, it would be correct to say that Hamburg's state leadership did not exacerbate the anti-Jewish policy forged at the

Reich level with measures of its own, and it made hardly any effort to take a prominent position by going beyond the application of the Reich laws. This differentiated Hamburg from many cities and regions in the Reich in which the National Socialists went far beyond the bounds set by Reich policy with their own radical anti-Jewish initiatives. This regional diversity will become clear from a comparison between Hamburg and the Bavarian capital, Munich, which, from 1935, styled itself as the 'Capital of the Movement'.

In Munich at the beginning of 1933, the National Socialist city government under Mayor (*Oberbürgermeister*) Karl Fiehler had introduced exceptionally radical antisemitic measures that went far beyond the policy developed at Reich level.[279] From the beginning of 1933, Jewish firms were prevented from taking public contracts by order of the *Oberbürgermeister* and by decision of the city council, while in Hamburg this policy took definitive shape only in 1937/38. In Munich, the systematic registration of Jewish enterprises began in 1934, in Hamburg, again, only in 1937/38. Whereas in special cases the Hamburg administration intervened in favour of Jewish firms until 1937 – if only on the grounds that this was a matter of retaining employment – there is no evidence that similar activities were undertaken by the Munich city administration. In Munich, the city authorities were refusing to give Jews passports as early as 1933, and at the beginning of 1936 they introduced the criterion of 'racial inadequacy' which meant that Jews could not be given passports. In Hamburg, similar restrictions were introduced for the first time in the wake of Reich-wide instructions in 1937-38. In Munich, Jews were refused entry to city swimming pools in 1933, by public announcement; in Hamburg, the water company issued a limited ban on entry in 1937, covering the so-called 'family bath days'.[280] In Munich, the renaming of streets that had Jewish names was completed by 1938, whereas in Hamburg, this process had barely been prepared, and was characteristically put into effect only after the corresponding decree from the Reich Interior Ministry of 1938.[281]

While the Chamber of Industry and Commerce in Munich was prepared to give information about Jewish firms from 1934, and thereby to facilitate their displacement from the economy, the Chamber of Commerce in Hamburg was rather more restrictive in its approach to releasing such information.

In both cities, Jewish citizens were subject to violent attacks and antisemitic campaigns at the hands of National Socialists from 1933. In Munich, the situation differed from that which obtained in Hamburg in so far as many Jewish business people had been arrested at the beginning of 1933. NSDAP 'Christmas' boycotts against Jewish businesses were then organised, and in 1935 stores were even occupied by force, employees and customers alike being beaten up. There were no comparable attacks in Hamburg at this time.

Whereas Munich almost always embarked upon new measures before the Reich as a whole did, and did not shrink from open confrontation with some of those responsible for anti-Jewish policy at Reich level, even accusing them of having an 'un-National Socialist' attitude, in Hamburg, many anti-Jewish measures were implemented subject to a characteristic 'time-lag'. Here, those responsible for policy subordinated themselves much more strictly to the conditions laid down at Reich level, but at the same time also developed their own special approach to the question in not following the general trend towards the radicalisation of anti-Jewish policy seen elsewhere on the regional level.

The reasons for this notable regional divergence need not lie in any especially antisemitic motivation on the part of Munich's decision-makers. Hamburg's Mayor, Krogmann, and the Hamburg Gauleiter and Reich Governor, Kaufmann, were – as we have already seen from a review of their public speeches – no less antisemitic by inclination than the Mayor of Munich, Fiehler, or the Gauleiter of Upper Bavaria, Wagner. Similarly, it appears difficult to work on the assumption that Munich, being the 'Capital of the Movement', was far more National Socialist and antisemitic than Hamburg. Though Munich was among the earlier centres of the NSDAP, forming the hub of its Bavarian power base, and where more generally radical right-wing antisemitic sentiment was articulated very freely and forcefully after the suppression of the Munich Soviet Republic,[282] nevertheless right-wing extremism never dominated the political culture of the city – shaped as it was by Catholic conservativism and social democracy. At the beginning of the 1920s, Hamburg had been a seat of the right-wing German populist *Deutsch-völkische Schutz- und Trutz-Bund* and the *Deutschnationale Handlungsgehilfen-Verband*, and thus became a centre of antisemitic agitation[283] without being wholly antisemitic or dominated by the extreme right. In the final phase of the Weimar Republic, the vote received by the NSDAP in Munich was not only under the average figure for the Reich as a whole, it was also below the percentage of the vote won by the NSDAP in Hamburg. In July 1932, the NSDAP gained 37.3 per cent of the vote in the Reichstag elections at the national level, 33.7 per cent in Hamburg and 28.9 per cent in Munich.[284] It was not the Catholic South but the Protestant North and East which provided the core of NSDAP support in 1932/33.[285] The title 'Capital of the Movement' may have been a reflection of the strength of the commitment of leading Munich National Socialists to their particular ideological principles, but it in no way reflected the attachment of the population in the city to National Socialism. It is possible, on the other hand, that antisemitic prejudices were more widespread in the Catholic conservative, strongly anti-modern environment surrounding the 'Bavarian People's Party' (*Bayerische Volkspartei*, BVP)[286] than in the Protestant-secular city of Hamburg where antisemitism was frowned upon in the working class and among the economic elite, but this assumption remains speculative given the lack of empirical evidence to support it.[287]

A crucial influence on the divergent attitudes adopted in the two cities was the particular structure of the Hamburg economy and the long crisis into which it had plunged. Its unbalanced economic reliance on foreign trade meant that Hamburg depended far more on its international competitive position – and therefore also on international attitudes to National Socialist Germany – than did the Munich economy, run by the middle class and with a far more diversified commercial structure.[288] The Hamburg National Socialists thus saw themselves, for many reasons, forced to take a cautious approach to the local electorate. In this way, in view of the opposition to National Socialist racial policy among leading traders, shipowners and shipyard owners of the older generation, Hamburg party leaders could not make themselves simple representatives of the interests of middle-class antisemites, whereas the middle-class ideologically based antisemitism of the Munich National Socialists encountered little structural or mental resistance. This did not mean that the widespread resistance of the older generation of businessmen in Hamburg was rooted in fundamental opposition to National Socialist racial doctrine. Their attitude was based much more on the feeling that state-initiated measures against Jewish enterprises ran against a basic political principle of free trade liberalism, that state intervention in the economy should be as limited as possible.

The calculations made in Hamburg's anti-Jewish policy also derived from the continuing structural crisis of the city's economy. A policy which aimed at the speedy displacement and liquidation of Jewish enterprises would, in this situation, have intensified the unemployment problem and endangered the fulfilment of a central National Socialist pledge. This aspect was of special importance in Hamburg in so far as the unemployment figures there were decreasing, but slowly. The number of unemployed people on welfare in Hamburg decreased by 37.1 per cent from March 1933 to September 1934, while in Munich it fell by 60.3 per cent.[289] In February 1936, the unemployed receiving support represented 7.36 per cent of the population as a whole in Hamburg, while in Munich the figure was only 3.7 per cent.[290] In March 1938, the unemployment rate in Hamburg, though it had meanwhile fallen drastically, was still almost two-and-a-half times higher than in Munich.[291]

As an officially recognised 'distressed area', Hamburg also depended more heavily on the support and favour of the Reich than did Munich. Above all, the creation of new, arms-related industries presupposed a programme of systematic assistance from the Reich. Hamburg's leadership could not have afforded a continuing confrontation with the Reich Economics Ministry such as that which continued to bubble in the case of Munich. They were, on the contrary, careful to leave a 'good impression' at Reich level.[292] In addition, the constitutional position of Hamburg as a city-state directly accountable to the Reich linked Hamburg closer to the policy making of the Reich than was the case in Munich, since before 1938 Hamburg had no defined sphere of communal autonomy with respect to the coordination of the regional states of the Reich.

Only in 1938 were the regional peculiarities of anti-Jewish policy largely eliminated, though before this there had been tendencies pointing towards greater homogenisation.[293] Under the growing influence of the SS, the policy was radicalised and centralised to a point at which hardly any room for regional divergence from Reich policy was left. Moreover, the reasons for the tactical caution that had previously been exercised had now disappeared. On the one hand, the marginalisation of the Jewish population remaining after the emigration of many Jews in 1938/39 was so fierce that in a short time they were separated from their non-Jewish environment and thrust like pariahs out of society. From the point of view of the National Socialists this also minimised the risk of an undesirable solidarity with them. On the other hand, increasing economic activity had also provided full employment in the Hamburg economy in 1938/39. Job losses through the liquidation of Jewish concerns could now be absorbed with ease. If one could ever have spoken of a 'protective shield' for Jewish enterprises, in 1938/39 it no longer existed. This accelerated not only the displacement of Jewish firms from the economy, it also determined the character of the 'Aryanisations' now undertaken; they could be organised without constraints from this point of view because of the economic booty the policy would provide. While, until 1938, Hamburg had been somewhat restrained in its regional policy, it now intensified its anti-Jewish measures. The deportation of the Jews from the 'Old Reich' in the autumn of 1941 was due in part to an initiative on the part of the Hamburg Gauleiter, Kaufmann, who had pressed Hitler for an acceleration of the evacuation of Hamburg's Jews.[294]

## Notes

1.  Cf. Adam, *Judenpolitik*, pp. 82–90.
2.  *Archiv des Instituts für die Geschichte der deutschen Juden in Hamburg*, 14-001.2, Max Plaut memoirs, '*Die jüdische Gemeinde in Hamburg 1933–1943*' (copy of a taped interview from 1973), p. 5.

3. *Statistik des Hamburgischen Staates*, Issue XXXIII, *Die Volks-, Berufs- und Betriebszählung of 16. Juni 1925*, Part 2, Hamburg, 1928, p. 82, *Übersicht 67* (*Die Wohnbevölkerung in 20 deutschen Großstädten im Jahre 1925 nach Wirtschaftsabteilungen*).

4. Ibid., p. 80, *Übersicht 66* (*Die Wohnbevölkerung in den Ländern und Landesteilen nach Wirtschaftsabteilungen 1925*).

5. Cf. Birgit Wulff, *Arbeitslosigkeit und Arbeitsbeschaffungsmaßnahmen in Hamburg 1933-1939. Eine Untersuchung zur nationalsozialistischen Wirtschafts- und Sozialpolitik*, Frankfurt am Main, 1987, p. 143.

6. Cited from a letter from Kaufmann to Rudolf Heß of 27 August 1934, BAK, R 43 II/1344, p. 59.

7. Cit. as in StAHH, *Staatsamt*, 91, notes by the Hamburg *Vertretung* in Berlin, 2 November 1934.

8. StAHH, *Senatskanzlei-Präsialabteilung*, 1933 A 99, Senate minutes of 2 August 1933.

9. Letter from Karl Doelmann (Milwaukee, Wisconsin) to the Mayor (undated), ibid.

10. Almo Trading & Importing Company, New York, to the Hamburg *Handelskammer*, 5 November 1935, *Archiv Handelskammer*, 100.B.1.16.

11. Cf. Genschel, *Verdrängung*, p. 77.

12. Cf. *Nazis against the world - the counter boycott is the only defensive weapon against Hitlerism's world threat to civilization, selected speeches from world leaders of public opinion, issued by the Non-Sectarian Anti Nazi League to Champion Human Rights*, New York, 1934.

13. Speech by Hitler to the Conference of Reich Governors, 6 July 1933, citation as in *Akten der Reichskanzlei. Die Regierung Hitler*, Part I 1933/34, ed. Karl-Heinz Minuth, Boppard am Rhein, 1983, pp. 629–636, here p. 631.

14. Citation as per the minutes of a conversation in the *Reichsministerium des Innern* on 25 April 1933, StAHH, *Senatskanzlei-Personalabteilung* (Senate Chancellery-Personnel Division), 1933 Ja 13 (unpag.).

15. *Reichspropagandaminister* Goebbels to the *Deutschen Industrie- und Handelstag*, 9 June 1933, copy in BAP, *Deutsche Reichsbank*, 7309 (unpag.).

16. Circular from the *Reichsminister des Innern*, 17 January 1934, StAHH, *Staatsamt*, 106 (unpag.).

17. Cf. Friedrich Facius, *Wirtschaft und Staat. Die Entwicklung der staatlichen Wirtschaftsverwaltung in Deutschland vom 17. Jahrhundert bis 1945*, Boppard am Rhein, 1959, p. 147.

18. Thus *inter alia* in Willi A. Boelcke, *Die deutsche Wirtschaft 1930–1945. Interna des Reichswirtschaftsministeriums*, Düsseldorf, 1983, p. 210. Similar judgements of the role played by Schacht can be found in Adam, *Judenpolitik*, p. 173. Strikingly divergent arguments made on the basis of new sources are made by Albert Fischer, *Hjalmar Schacht*, particularly in examining Schacht's antisemitism and the relative ineffectiveness of his interventions.

19. Cf. Barkai, *Boykott*, pp. 65–121.

20. On the National Socialist assumption of power in Hamburg and the figures which follow, see Henning Timpke, ed., *Dokumente zur Gleichschaltung des Landes Hamburg 1933*, Frankfurt am Main, 1967, esp. pp. 15–43. On the development of the regime's legislation and administration, see Uwe Lohalm, *Hamburgs nationalsozialistische Diktatur: Verfassung und Verwaltung 1933 bis 1945* (publication of the *Landeszentrale für politische Bildung*), Hamburg, 1997.

21. See StAHH, *Senatskanzlei-Präsialabteilung* 1935 A85/1 (implementation of the *Landesverwaltungsgesetz* of 14 September 1933).

22. Appointment of Kaufmann in BAK, R 43 II/1346, p. 11.

23. Thus Krogmann had to hand over the leadership of the Hamburg *Landesregierung* to him personally and thereby take part in his own fall from power. See the letter from the Mayor to the Hamburg *Reichsstatthalter* of 22 May 1936, StAHH, *Krogmann Familie I* (Carl Vincent Krogmann), C 15 IV/1.

24. Cf. his protest letter to Gauleiter Kaufmann of 25 September 1936 ('Dear Karl!'), which declares *inter alia*: 'I know on the other hand that it is not always easy for you, time and again to be standing up for me, and I am grateful to you that you have done this more than once. I consider it to be almost a miracle that I as a party member from '33 still remain at my post and I am eternally thankful to my Lord God that he has now already allowed me to take part in the construction of our Reich for almost four years ... I will do my duty, wherever Hitler and Providence place me. My admiration for you has always, despite your error, remained the same, and I believe, it may sound supercilious, in Hamburg you have no truer comrade than I.' StAHH, *Krogmann Familie I* (Carl Vincent Krogmann), C 15 IV/1, letter (written by hand) of 25 September 1936.

25. According to information given by Prof. Dr Werner Jochmann and Dr Geert Seelig in conversation with the author, the widespread nickname of '*regierte Bürgermeister*' also related to the relationship between Krogmann and his wife Emerentia, and Krogmann was also mockingly referred to as 'His Emerenz, the *regierte Bürgermeister*'.

26. Decree by Kaufmann on the functions of the *Erster Beigeordnete* (First Councillor) of 20 May 1938, StAHH, *Senatskanzlei-Präsialabteilung*, 1940 A1.

27. These were, *inter alia*, the heads of the *NSDAP-Gauamt für Kommunalpolitik* (NSDAP Gau Office for Municipal Policy), the Hamburg Red Cross *Landesleitung* (state leadership) and the Chair of the *Deutsch-Französischen Gesellschaft in den Hansestädten*.

28. Citation following his unpublished memoirs, StAHH, *Krogmann Familie I* (Carl Vincent Krogmann), C 18, manuscript, p. 229. A part of this memoir appeared in 1976 under the title *Es ging um Deutschlands Zukunft 1932–1939*, Leoni, 1976.

29. 'Fanaticism' was one of those terms by which Krogmann described *himself* in his unpublished memoirs, StAHH, *Krogmann Familie I* (Carl Vincent Krogmann), C 18, manuscript, p. 439.

30. Cf. Krogmann's speech at the '*Liebesmahl*' of the *Ostasiatischen Verein* of 11 March 1933, *Archiv FZH*, diary of C.V. Krogmann, 11 K/4.

31. This was a theme in many interventions written in favour of persons of 'non-Aryan' extraction that were brought to Krogmann. See StAHH, *Krogmann Familie I* (Carl Vincent Krogmann), C 15, I 7, diary entries of 8, 11 and 28 August 1933.

32. Ibid., entry of 12 May 1933, relating a conversation with the President of the *Handelskammer*, Carl Ludwig Nottebohm, whom he informed that the exclusion of Jewish members 'would be absolutely necessary'.

33. Letter from Krogmann to Wilhelm Keppler of 26 April 1933, *Archiv FZH*, diary of C.V. Krogmann, 11 K/4.

34. *Archiv FZH*, diary of C.V. Krogmann, 11 K/5, entry of 5 February 1935.

35. Krogmann said, *inter alia*, 'The Jew wants only to persuade. He is at the same time unconvincing because idealism is completely alien to him. In persuasion however he is master and therefore he primarily selects those occupations in whose exercise the gift of persuasion promises advantages. Thus the Jew becomes a tradesman in order to persuade a customer to buy inferior goods, thus he becomes a newspaper journalist, in order to make the world believe that Jews are the chosen people, thus he becomes a lawyer so as to turn the truth on its head, and thus he becomes a doctor and persuades people that they are ill, so as to be able then to talk them around again to being healthy.' StAHH, *Krogmann Familie I* (Carl Vincent Krogmann), C 15 VI/3, speech manuscript, pp. 6a and 6b.

36. Cf., for instance, the speech by Kaufmann to the *NSDAP-Kreis Innenstadt*, delivered in February 1936, in which he explained: 'The Jew has used everything, has stirred everyone up against each other – he always has his finger in the pie. If Jewry today replies with propaganda campaigns, boycott and murder, then we need not be surprised by this. But we will take care that

it will never again exercise influence in German life.' Cited in *Hamburger Tageblatt*, 22 February 1936.

37. Cf. Kaufmann's speech to the *Hamburg Nationalklub von 1919* of 6 May 1938: 'No one sees this more than I do, because I am beset with these mistakes and must get rid of everything that shows itself to be an abuse.' Cited in BAP, *Reichssicherheitshauptamt* (Reich Security Headquarters), St 3/510, p. 20. See also the statement Kaufmann made to Hamburg industrialists in May 1935, in which he spoke of the 'derailing' of his Hamburg party comrades, *Hamburger Tageblatt*, 18 May 1935.

38. On Kaufmann's 'sentimental socialism' and his regional economic lobbying in favour of Hamburg industry, see Frank Bajohr, 'Gauleiter in Hamburg. Zur Person und Tätigkeit Karl Kaufmanns', in *VfZ* 43 (1995), pp. 267–295, here pp. 285–290.

39. *Hamburger Tageblatt*, 13 August 1935.

40. *Hamburger Tageblatt*, 31 August 1935: 'Gauleiter Streicher's appeal'.

41. See *Archiv FZH*, 12, personal file of Karl Kaufmann, speech to the Hamburg *handelskammer* of January 1939, manuscript excerpt, p. 13. Cf. also below, Ch. VI.

42. StAHH, *Staatsamt*, 106, *Regierungsdirektor* (Permanent Secretary) Eiffe to the *Reichs- und Preußische Wirtschaftsministerium*, 30 October 1936.

43. For analysis of the example given by Hitler, see Hans Mommsen, 'Hitlers Stellung im nationalsozialistischen Herrschaftssystem', in Gerhard Hirschfeld and Lothar Kettenacker, eds, *Der 'Führerstaat': Mythos und Realität*, Stuttgart, 1981, pp. 43–70.

44. Cf. Dieter Rebentisch and Karl Teppe, eds, *Verwaltung contra Menschenführung im Staat Hitlers. Studien zum politisch-administrativen System*, Göttingen, 1986.

45. However, in the field of economic policy Hamburg had *inter alia* a *Sonderbeauftragten für Wirtschaftsförderung und Vierjahresplan* (Special Representative for Economic Research and the Four-Year Plan), a *Wirtschaftsbeauftragte* under the *Reichsstatthalter*, an Aryanisation official, a *Sonderbeauftragten* for Hamburg's relations to the *Reichswerke* Hermann Göring and a *Sonderbeauftragte* for work on the Siegfried Line.

46. Walter Petwaidic, *Die autoritäre Anarchie. Streiflichter des deutschen Zusammenbruchs*, Hamburg, 1946.

47. A collection of the most varied range of research perspectives on the structure of the National Socialist state can be found in Michael Ruck, 'Führerabsolutismus und polykratisches Herrschaftsgefüge - Verfassungsstrukturen des NS-Staates', in Karl Dietrich Bracher, Manfred Funke and Hans-Adolf Jacobsen, eds, *Deutschland 1933–1945. Neue Studien zur nationalsozialistischen Herrschaft*, Düsseldorf, 1992, pp. 32–56.

48. Hans Mommsen, *Nationalsozialismus*, in *Sowjetsystem und demokratische Gesellschaft*, Vol. 4, Freiburg, 1971, pp. 695–713, citation p. 713.

49. Martin Broszat, *Der Staat Hitlers. Grundlegung und Entwicklung seiner inneren Verfassung*, Munich, 1969, citation p. 439.

50. Dieter Rebentisch, *Führerstaat und Verwaltung im Zweiten Weltkrieg. Verfassungsentwicklung und Verwaltungspolitik 1939–1945*, Stuttgart, 1989, p. 533.

51. In an internal discussion in the *Reichsinnenministerium*, the *Ministerpräsident* of Prussia, Hermann Göring, described the commissars as 'plagues on the land' who were the sources of the 'greatest mischief'. Cf. minutes of the conversation in the *Reichsinnenministerium* on 25 April 1933, StAHH, *Senatskanzlei-Personalabteilung* I, 1933 Ja 13 (unpag.).

52. StAHH, *Senatskanzlei-Präsidialabteilung*, 1933 A 61, list of the *Sonderstaatskommissare*, 1 September 1933.

53. StAHH, *Krogmann Familie I* (Carl Vincent Krogmann), C 18, unpublished memoirs, p. 438: 'When the Gauleiter, under the influence of Ahrens, asked me at the beginning of February

1933 whether I would be ready to take over the Office of the First Mayor, I understood nothing about policy nor anything about administration.'

54.  See below, esp. the sub-chapter 'Public contracts and Jewish enterprises'.
55.  StAHH, *Staatsverwaltung-Allgemeine Abteilung*, A I 12, compendium of the *Reichssonderbehörden* in Hamburg.
56.  Cf. Ludwig Eiber, 'Unter Führung des NSDAP-Gauleiters. Die Hamburger Staatspolizei
(1933–1937)', in Gerhard Paul and Klaus Michael Mallmann, eds, *Die Gestapo - Mythos und
Realität*, Darmstadt, 1995, pp. 101–117; Michael Wildt, 'Der Hamburger Gestapochef Bruno
Streckenbach. Eine nationalsozialistische Karriere', in Frank Bajohr and Joachim Szodrzynski,
eds, *Hamburg in der NS-Zeit. Ergebnisse neuerer Forschungen*, Hamburg, 1995, pp. 93–123.
57.  See in this connection the letter from Kaufmann to Hermann Göring of 4 September 1942, in
the National Archives in Washington, Miscellaneous German Records Collection, T 84, Roll 7.
58.  On the respective areas of responsibility of the various offices and agencies, see StAHH, *Senatskanzlei-Personalabteilung* II, 454.
59.  On the activity of the *Gauwirtschaftsberater* in Hamburg, see below, chapters IV, V and VI.
60.  Cf. Peter Diehl-Thiele, *Partei und Staat im Dritten Reich. Untersuchungen zum Verhältnis von
NSDAP und allgemeiner innerer Staatsverwaltung 1933–1945*, Munich, 1969, p. 173ff.
61.  StAHH, *Staatsverwaltung-Allgemeine Abteilung*, A II 8, order from the *Reichsverteidigungskom-
missar* (Reich Defence Commissar) to the Hamburg *Reichsverteidigungsbezirk* (Reich Defence
District) on the decentralisation of the administration, 11 August 1943.
62.  See below in this chapter, 'The Initiating Role of the Hamburg NSDAP and the Registration
of Jewish Enterprises'.
63.  *Hamburger Tageblatt*, 19 October 1936: 'To the stocks with them!'
64.  StAHH, NSDAP, D 4a, letter from *Kreisamtsleiter* Wichmann of 23 October 1941.
65.  Between 1933 and 1945 the Hamburg *Handelskammer* was renamed and transformed numerous times. It was during this time known as the *Industrie- und Handelskammer* – the 'Chamber
of Industry and Trade' – (from 1935) and then the *Gauwirtschaftskammer* – 'Gau Chamber of
Economics' – (after 1942–43), and regained its traditional title of *Handelskammer* in May
1945. So as to preserve a unity of terminology, in the following the traditional appellation of
*Handelskammer* ('Chamber of Commerce') will be used throughout. See also Hans Bielfeldt,
'Citykammer, Gauwirtschaftskammer, Handelskammer', in *Staat und Wirtschaft. Beiträge zur
Geschichte der Handelskammer Hamburg*, Hamburg, 1980, pp. 61–133.
66.  On changes in the personnel at the *Handelskammer*, see Bielfeldt, 'Politik und Personalia im
Dritten Reich', in *Staat und Wirtschaft*, pp. 135–225, here p. 135ff.
67.  Cf. on this point the unpublished memoirs of Carl Vincent Krogmann, *Der Vaterstadt zuliebe
(Erinnerungen 1918–1933)*, p. 190ff., StAHH, *Krogmann Familie I* (Carl Vincent Krogmann),
C 18.
68.  Note by *Reg. Dir.* Köhn of 14 November 1934 on a conversation with *Präses* Hübbe, StAHH,
*Deputation für Handel, Schiffahrt und Gewerbe II*, S XIII, A 1.24.
69.  Communication from the *Handelskammer* of 30 November 1935 to *Fa. Rewe, Archiv Handelskammer*, 100.B.1.22.
70.  Ibid., memorandum of 18 May 1936 (marked Dr Krause).
71.  *Sonderarchiv Moskau*, 500-3-316, p. 461, annual report for 1937 of *SD-Referat II* 112, *Oberabschnitt Nord-West*, 14 January 1938. The annual reports of the SD regional sections for 1937
and 1938 are accessible to academic researchers in the *Archiv FZH*, 93121. Cf. Michael Wildt,
ed., *Die Judenpolitik des SD 1935 bis 1938*, Munich, 1995, p. 49.
72.  *Hamburger Tageblatt*, 26 April 1935, ' "Nazi-Afteker" rechnet ab.'
73.  *Hamburger Tageblatt*, 23 July 1935, 'Lawyer's Wife Defends Jews'.
74.  Ibid.

75. Citation as in StAHH, *Staatliche Pressestelle I-IV*, 7050, Vol. II, manuscript of Krogmann's speech of 9 March 1935, p. 2.

76. StAHH, *Krogmann Familie I* (Carl Vincent Krogmann), C 15, III/3, letter from the General Consul of the Union of South Africa to Krogmann, 11 March 1935.

77. Ibid.

78. Diary of Cornelius Freiherr von Berenberg-Goßler (private collection), entries of 31 March and 1 April 1933: 'I feel ashamed in front of my acquaintances because of the Nazis' measures against the Jews.'

79. Cit. in Bielfeldt, 'Politik', in *Staat und Wirtschaft*, p. 157.

80. On the concept of the *Kriegsjugendgeneration*, the 'young generation' during the war, see Ernst Günther Gründel, *Die Sendung der Jungen Generation. Versuch einer umfassenden revolutionären Sinndeutung der Krise*, Munich, 1932; on the mark left by *völkisch* antisemitism on the middle-class *Kriegsjugendgeneration*, particularly among students, see Ulrich Herbert, '"Generation der Sachlichkeit". Die völkische Studentenbewegung der frühen zwanziger Jahre in Deutschland', in Frank Bajohr, Werner Johe and Uwe Lohalm, eds, *Zivilisation und Barbarei. Die widersprüchlichen Potentiale der Moderne*, Hamburg, 1991, pp. 115–144.

81. Rosenbaum refers explicitly to the wide dissemination of this periodical among the younger middle-class citizens of Hamburg, see Bielfeldt, 'Politik', in *Staat und Wirtschaft*, p. 157.

82. H.V. Hübbe and Dr Haage to the *Reichs- und Preußische Wirtschaftsministerium*, 9 April 1936, *Archiv Handelskammer*, 100.B.1.27.

83. Citation in Bielfeldt, 'Politik', in *Staat und Wirtschaft*, p. 167.

84. 'Hold the door open!' Hamburg 1931, StAHH, *Familie de Chapeaurouge*, U 91; excerpts from the brochure were published by Werner Jochmann in *Nationalsozialismus und Revolution. Ursprung und Geschichte der NSDAP in Hamburg 1922-1933, Dokumente*, Frankfurt am Main, 1963, pp. 341-347.

85. Max Warburg (*Aus meinen Aufzeichnungen*, ed. Eric Warburg, New York, 1952, p. 148) deplored the 'great alarm of the not very courageous Hübbe'.

86. On the political activity of Witthoefft, see StAHH, Arnold Otto Meyer Co., private correspondence, Franz Heinrich Witthoefft, 24. Also cp. Ursula Büttner, *Hamburg in der Staats- und Wirtschaftskrise 1928–1931*, Hamburg, 1982, pp. 365–368.

87. Cf. StAHH, *Fa. Arnold Otto Meyer*, 3, Vol. 2, letter from Witthoefft to Max Warburg, 24 July 1933.

88. StAHH, *Fa. Arnold Otto Meyer*, 3, Vol. 1, condolence letter from Witthoefft to Max Warburg on the death of Carl Melchior and Aby Warburg (undated, beginning of 1934).

89. Peter Ernst Witthoefft to F.H. Witthoefft, 7 November 1933, StAHH, *Fa. Arnold Otto Meyer*, 12.

90. Peter Ernst Witthoefft to F.H. Witthoefft, 3 November 1933, ibid.

91. For an example of the antisemitism of Sloman (born in 1885) see the leaflet he published 'Biological High Treason' (*Biologischer Hochverrat*, distributed by the *Reichsgesundheitsverlag*, Prague, 1943). Here, Sloman describes the reproaches made against racial hygiene, for example that it would lower women to the level of 'child-bearing machines', a 'common cliché of Jewish propaganda, which was disseminated time and again by the Jewish side in the liberal times, precisely to prevent the expansion of the Aryan peoples.' (p. 24).

92. Cf. the diary of Cornelius Freiherr von Berenberg-Goßler (private collection), 1939, entry of 18 April 1939. On Berenberg-Goßler see also Renate Hauschild-Thiessen, 'Cornelius Freiherr von Berenberg-Goßler und das Dritte Reich', *Hamburgische Geschichts- und Heimatblätter*, Vol. 12, Issue 1/1988, pp. 14–32.

93. Cit. in Stefanie von Viereck, *Hinter weißen Fassaden. Alwin Münchmeyer – ein Bankier betrachtet sein Leben*, Hamburg, 1988, p. 136.

94. On the role of the *Handelskammer* in "Aryanisation" from 1938, see Ch. V.

95. Speech by Kaufmann to the Hamburg *Handelskammer*, January 1939, *Archiv FZH*, 12 (personal papers of Kaufmann).

96. *Reichsgesetzblatt* ("Reich Law Gazette", *RGBl*) 1933, Part I, p. 175.

97. Barkai, *Boykott*, p. 35.

98. On the pre-history and passage of the BBG, see Adam, *Judenpolitik*, pp. 51–64 and Hans Mommsen, *Beamtentum im Dritten Reich*, Stuttgart, 1966, pp. 39–61.

99. Wolfgang Wippermann, *Das Leben in Frankfurt zur NS-Zeit, Vol. 1, Die nationalsozialistische Judenverfolgung*, Frankfurt am Main, 1986, p. 55.

100. Cf. Knipping, *Geschichte*, p. 23.

101. StAHH, Senate records for 1933, plenum, p. 314, Senate resolution of 10 April 1933.

102. See the reports of the various authorities in StAHH, *Senatskanzlei-Personalabteilung* I, 1933 Ja 13.

103. See the list in StAHH, *Staatliche Pressestelle I–IV*, 7655.

104. Compare my study *Nationalsozialismus und Korruption*, Frankfurt, 2001.

105. Cf. *1. VO zur Durchführung des BBG*, 11 April 1933, *RGBl* 1933, Part I, p. 195, Abs.2.1.

106. Circular from RMdI re. interpretation of § 3 of the BBG, 1 September 1933, StAHH, *Senatskanzlei-Personalabteilung* I, 1933 Ja 13.

107. See StAHH, *Justizverwaltung I*, XII Aa Vol. 2b 21, note of 27 September 1933.

108. Ibid. The note of 27 September makes mention *inter alia* of members of the Petersen, Mestern and Mumssen families.

109. Cf. *2. VO zur Durchführung des BBG*, 4 May 1933, § 3.1, *RGBl* 1933, Part I, p. 234.

110. StAHH, *Senatskanzlei-Personalabteilung I*, 1933 Ja 29 (Right of the *Reichsstatthalter* to appoint and dismiss officials).

111. See StAHH, Senate records of 1933, plenum, p. 906, sitting of 18 October 1933.

112. StAHH, *Senatskanzlei-Personalabteilung I*, 1933 Ja 13, inventory of 18 July 1938 on the implementation of the BBG in the area covered by the *Reichs- und Preußischen Ministeriums für Wissenschaft, Erziehung und Volksbildung* (the Ministry for Science, Education and Popular Education).

113. See Eckart Krause, Ludwig Huber and Holger Fischer, eds, *Hochschulalltag im 'Dritten Reich'. Die Hamburger Universität 1933–1945*, 3 vols, Berlin, Hamburg, 1991; Angela Bottin, *Enge Zeit. Spuren Vertriebener und Verfolgter der Hamburger Universität*, Berlin, Hamburg, 1992.

114. StAHH, *Senatskanzlei-Personalabteilung I*, 1933 Ja 13, figures from the Hamburg *Staatsamt*, 7 December 1936.

115. Ibid.

116. Among them numbered some teachers Dr Walter Bacher, Edith Knack, Gertrud Pardo and Bella Spanier, a state vetinarian Dr Bruno Feibel and a police chief, Isidor Grabanski. See StAHH, *Senatskanzlei-Personalabteilung I*, 1933 Ja 13c, communication from the personnel department of the Hamburg *Staatsamt* to the Gestapo, 5 June 1934.

117. Cf. Leo Lippmann, *Mein Leben und meine amtliche Tätigkeit. Aus dem Nachlaß herausgegeben von Werner Jochmann*, Hamburg, 1964, p. 624.

118. See StAHH, Hamburg *Oberlandesgericht-Verwaltung*, Abl. 6, 2021, E/1a/5, lists of judges and state attorneys dismissed under the BBG.

119. Cf. the certificate of installation of Albrecht Dreves, private collection of Geerd Dahms.

120. See the ancestry research papers for Albrecht Dreves, private collection of Geerd Dahms.

121. Cit. in StAHH, Senate records for 1933, plenum, p. 983, sitting of 29 November 1933.

122. See the biography of Dreves in the works newspaper of the *Hamburger Freihafen-Lagerhaus-Gesellschaft*, No. 1/1937, p. 5.

123. Cf. letter from the *Gaupersonalamt* of the Hamburg NSDAP to the Hamburg *Staatsamt,* 24 July 1935, StAHH, *Senatskanzlei-Personalabteilung I,* 1935 Ma 9/15.

124. Ibid., memorandum of 9 September 1935.

125. The case is comprehensively documented in StAHH, *Senatskanzlei-Präsidialabteilung,* 1936 S II 447. Cf. also Beate Meyer, '"Besser ist doch, man taucht unter". Zur Verfolgung der "Halbjuden" in Hamburg', in Bajohr and Szodrzynski, eds, *Hamburg,* pp. 125–150, here p. 128 f.

126. Ibid., letter from the *Reichs- und Preußischen Wirtschaftsministerium* to the Hamburg *Staatsamt,* 25 November 1936.

127. See StAHH, *Senatskanzlei-Personalabteilung I,* 1934 Ma 1/200.

128. Ibid., letter from Julius Plaut to the *Reichsstatthalter,* 14 June 1934.

129. Ibid., communication from the *Fürsorgebehörde* to the Hamburg *NSDAP-Gauleitung,* 14 September 1934.

130. According to the *1. VO zum Reichsbürgergesetz* of 14 November 1935, § 4, Section 2, Jewish officials had until 31 December 1935 to retire. See *RGBl* 1935, Part I, p. 1333 f.

131. List of employees and workers who returned to work who had been dismissed through § 4 of the BBG. StAHH, *Senatskanzlei-Personalabteilung II,* 36 UA 1.

132. Circular from the *Reichsstattshalter* re. certificates of Aryan abstraction, 11 March 1937, StAHH, *Senatskanzlei-Personalabteilung I,* 1933 Ja 31 b.

133. StAHH, *Senatskanzlei-Personalabteilung II,* 156, order of the *Senatskommissar für Beamtenangelegenheiten,* 20 November 1933.

134. StAHH, *Senatskanzlei-Personalabteilung I,* 1933 Ja 31 b, note of 20 July 1934.

135. Ibid., note of 26 May 1937.

136. StAHH, *Senatskanzlei-Personalabteilung I,* 1933 Ja 13, order of the Senate, 23 May 1933.

137. *Hamburger Nachrichten,* 14 September 1933.

138. Decree of the *Reichsarbeitsministerium* (Labour Ministry) on the dismissal of doctors from duty in hospitals, 22 April 1933, *RGBl* 1933, Part I, p. 222f.

139. *Hamburger Tageblatt,* 20 November 1934.

140. *Verzeichnis der jüdischen Ärzte, Zahnärzte, Dentisten, Bandagisten, Optiker in Hamburg, Altona, Wandsbek* (1936). If one were to add to this the figures for Jewish doctors in Altona and Wandsbek, the number of Jewish doctors in Hamburg would rise to 293 and that of doctors working in medical insurance to 176.

141. The share of the total figure of 340 doctors in 1934 which the 166 doctors represented was 48.8%. As, however, in 1933 barely 20% of Jewish doctors had already emigrated and doctors who did not work in insurance would have had to make a majority of those doctors who had emigrated, it would not be unreasonable to start from a total figure of approximately 400 Jewish doctors. The 166 authorised health insurance doctors therefore made up 41.5% of the total. The actual proportion of Jewish doctors continuing to practice in medical insurance work might lie between these two figures, 48.8 and 41.5%. On the proportion of Jewish doctors who emigrated, see Stefan Leibfried, 'Stationen der Abwehr. Berufsverbote für Ärzte im Deutschen Reich 1933–1938', *Bulletin of the Leo Baeck Institute,* Year 21, No. 62/1982, pp. 3–39, here p. 11.

142. See Leibfried, 'Stationen', p. 11. In view of this numerical ratio I am not able to follow the thesis of John A. Grenville that the exclusion of Jewish doctors in Hamburg was undertaken in an especially radical fashion. The cases he cited do not support his thesis for the reason that he exclusively refers to established Jewish doctors and university lecturers who were dismissed according to the conditions laid down in the BBG. Cf. John A. Grenville, 'Juden, "Nichtarier" und "Deutsche Ärzte". Die Anpassung der Ärzte im Dritten Reich', in Büttner, ed., *Die Deutschen,* pp. 191–206. On the dismissal of Jewish doctors, see also Werner Friedrich Kümmel, '"Die Ausschaltung". Wie die National Socialisten die jüdischen und politisch mißliebi-

gen Ärzte aus dem Berufe verdrängten', in Johanna Bleker and Norbert Jachertz, eds, *Medizin im Nationalsozialismus*, Köln, 1989, pp. 30–37.

143. *Ärzteblatt für Norddeutschland*, 1938, p. 466f.

144. According to the *4. VO zum Reichsbürgergesetz*, 25 July 1938, *RGBl* 1938, Part I, p. 969f.

145. According to a statement made by Dr Berthold Hannes on 3 June 1954 (*Archiv FZH* 6262), in 1939 there were a total of fourteen Jewish *Krankenbehandler* active in Hamburg.

146. *Hamburger Nachrichten*, 1 September 1933.

147. *RGBl* 1934, Part I, pp. 399–409.

148. Letter from Holzmann of 11 October 1934 to Senator Dr Rothenberger, StAHH, *Medizinalkollegium*, I C 5.

149. Ibid., statement by Matthies of 8 October 1934.

150. Cf. Heiko Morisse, *Rechtsanwälte im Nationalsozialismus. Zur Funktion der Ehrengerichtsbarkeit*, Hamburg, 1995, p. 23, who determined the number of Jewish lawyers in Hamburg on the basis of personnel records.

151. See Siegfried Ostrowski, 'Vom Schicksal jüdischer Ärzte im Dritten Reich. Ein Augenzeugenbericht aus den Jahren 1933–1939', *Bulletin of the Leo Baeck Institute*, Year 6, No. 24/1963, pp. 313–351, here p. 314.

152. *RGBl* 1933, Part I, p. 188.

153. StAHH, *Justizverwaltung I*, II Ba, Vol. 2, No. 6, excerpt from the Senate minutes, 27 March 1933.

154. *Hamburgisches Justizverwaltungsblatt*, 13 April 1933, directive from Rothenberger of 4 April 1933.

155. See on this point Lothar Gruchmann, *Justiz im Dritten Reich 1933–1940. Anpassung und Unterwerfung in der Ära Gürtner*, Munich, 1988, p. 124ff. On developments in Prussia see Tillmann Krach, *Jüdische Rechtsanwälte in Preußen. Über die Bedeutung der freien Advokatur und ihre Zerstörung durch den Nationalsozialismus*, Munich, 1991.

156. Directive from Rothenberger of 31 March 1933, StAHH, *Justizverwaltung I*, II Ba, Vol. 2, 3.

157. Letter by Rothenberger in StAHH, Hamburg *Oberlandesgericht-Verwaltung* (Supreme State Court-Administration), file 6, 2000-2a/3.

158. Official note of 6 April 1933 for Senator Rothenberger, StAHH, *Justizverwaltung I*, XII Aa, Vol. 2b, 15.

159. List of names of lawyers who lost their jobs in StAHH, Hamburg *Oberlandesgericht-Verwaltung*, file 6, 2021 E 1a/5.

160. Calculated according to the figures given in Gruchmann, *Justiz*, p. 151. In Hamburg, as in the Reich as a whole, the number of Jewish lawyers decreased rapidly in the period which followed. The last 68 Jewish lawyers in Hamburg finally lost their positions on 30 November 1938 on the basis of the *5. VO zum Reichsbürgergesetz* of 27 September 1938 (*RGBl* 1938, Part I, p. 1403). Only nine lawyers were allowed then to continue to work as 'legal consultants'. Cf. StAHH, *Amtsgericht Hamburg-Verwaltung* (Hamburg Administrative Court-Administration), 3170

161. Records of meeting, p. 7f., StAHH, *Justizverwaltung I*, II Ba, Vol. 2, 4.

162. Ibid., records of meeting, p. 15.

163. On Rothenberger's life, see also Klaus Bästlein, 'Vom hanseatischen Richtertum zum nationalsozialistischen Justizverbrechen. Zur Person und Tätigkeit Curt Rothenbergers 1896–1959', in Justizbehörde Hamburg, ed., *'Für Führer, Volk und Vaterland …' Hamburger Justiz im Nationalsozialismus*, Hamburg, 1992, pp. 74–145.

164. Already in July 1933 the Reich Finance Ministry had excluded 'non-Aryan' sales offices from making deliveries in exchange for low interest loans. On 7 March 1934, these conditions were renewed in another decree. See Joseph Walk, ed., *Das Sonderrecht für die Juden im NS-Staat*, Heidelberg, Karlsruhe, 1981, pp. 39 and 73.

165. Guidelines for the Assigning of Public Contracts, 14 July 1933, StAHH, *Senatskanzlei-Präsidialabteilung*, 1935 A 35.

166. On the decrees of the *Reichswirtschaftsministerium* of 1 March and 31 May 1938, see Walk, *Sonderrecht*, pp. 217 and 227. The decree of the *Reichswirtschaftsministerium* of 17 March 1938, not mentioned by Walk, can be found in StAHH, *Sozialbehörde I*, WA 10.18, p. 143.

167. Walk, *Sonderrecht*, p. 4.

168. Fliedner, *Judenverfolgung*, p. 115.

169. Walk, *Sonderrecht*, p. 6.

170. Goertz, *Juden*, p. 94.

171. Bruss, *Bremer Juden*, p. 49f. In Bremen the resolution was however withdrawn again in October 1933.

172. Werner, *Hakenkreuz*, p. 73.

173. Knipping, *Geschichte*, p. 35.

174. Hanke, *Geschichte*, p. 100f.; Selig, 'Boykott', in Mensing and Prinz, eds, *Irrlicht*, pp. 178–202, here p. 187ff.

175. As cited in Genschel, *Verdrängung*, p. 82.

176. StAHH, *Sozialbehörde I*, WA 10.18, p. 3.

177. See on this point StAHH, *Senatskanzlei-Präsidialabteilung*, 1935 A 35, official note of October 1934.

178. Confidential circular from Mayor Ahrens, 22 October 1934, StAHH, *Innere Verwaltung (Büro Senator Richter)* [Interior Administration (Office of Senator Richter)], A II 4, p. 7f.

179. StAHH, *Innere Verwaltung (Büro Senator Richter)*, A II 9, letter from *Innensenator* Richter to the Hamburg *Staatsamt*, 10 August 1935.

180. Ibid., letter from the Hamburg *Staatsamt* to the *Senator der inneren Verwaltung* of 4 September 1935.

181. On the attitude of the *Fürsorgebehörde*, see Lohalm, 'Fürsorge', in Herzig, ed., *Juden*, pp. 499–514. Unfortunately, the sources available from other departments do not contain any comparably detailed references to the practice of giving out public contracts. In the following, the primary focus is on the welfare authorities.

182. StAHH, *Sozialbehörde I*, WA 10.18, circular of 14 November 1933.

183. StAHH, NSDAP, B 202, President of the *Gesundheits- und Fürsorgebehörde* (Health and Welfare Department) to *SA-Oberführer* Heuser, 4 January 1935.

184. StAHH, *Sozialbehörde II*, O 21.50-11, p. 38, communication from the *Gewerbekammer* to the *Gesundheits- und Fürsorgebehörde*, 28 May 1934.

185. StAHH, *Sozialbehörde II*, O 21.50-3, pp. 56-58, letter from an optician, Bruno Weser, to the President of the *Fürsorgeamt* (Welfare Office), 31 May 1934.

186. Ibid., communication from the *Orthozentrische Kneifer GmbH*, 22 May 1934, to Abt. 111 of the *Gesundheits- und Fürsorgebehörde*.

187. StAHH, *Sozialbehörde I*, WA 10.18, p. 17, communication from *Wohlfahrtsstelle* (Welfare Office) VI to the *Gesundheits- und Fürsorgebehörde*, 26 August 1935.

188. StAHH, *Sozialbehörde I*, VG 29.10, Vol. 1, communication from the Bucky firm, 31 May 1935, to the *Fürsorgebehörde*.

189. StAHH, *Sozialbehörde I*, WA 10.18, letter from *Verbindungsreferent* Dr Becker to the President of the *Gesundheits- und Fürsorgebehörde*, 25 July 1935.

190. Ibid., note of 19 August 1935.

191. Ibid., letter from Ofterdinger, 29 August 1935.

192. Ibid., circulars from the *Reichs- und Preußische Wirtschaftsminister* of 14 October 1935, and 4 November 1935.

193. StAHH, *Senatskanzlei-Präsidialabteilung*, 1935 A 35, Hamburg *Staatsamt* to the *Senator der Inneren Verwaltung*, 5 October 1935.

194. Draft letter from the *Regierende Bürgermeister* to the *Wirtschaftsbeauftragte des Führers* (1935), StAHH, *Verwaltung für Wirtschaft, Technik und Arbeit*, III 7.

195. On the attitude of Hitler and the discussion over the definitive clarification of the legal position of Jews in economic affairs called for by the *Reichswirtschaftsministerium* in 1935–36, see Fischer, *Hjalmar Schacht*, pp. 184–192.

196. This appeared not only in the assignment of public contracts to Jewish enterprises. For example, the officials of the town council of Wandsbek had to give assurances in writing on behalf of themselves and their members that they would not but in Jewish stores and not to retain any private dealings with Jews. This kind of binding regulation did not exist in Hamburg and was also not introduced in the 'Greater Hamburg Act'. Cf. StAHH, *Senatskanzlei-Personalabteilung I*, 1935 Ja 10, order from *Oberbürgermeister* Ziegler of Wandsbek, 13 August 1937.

197. StAHH, *Sozialbehörde I*, WA 10.18, p. 41, note by the *Wirtschaftsabteilung* of the *Fürsorgebehörde*, 15 May 1937.

198. Ibid., p. 49f., letter from Prellwitz to the President of the Hamburg *Fürsorgebehörde*, 15 May 1937.

199. Ibid., p. 53, memorandum of 7 December 1937.

200. Ibid., note by Büsing of 2 March 1938.

201. The validity of credit vouchers for Jewish businesses has until now been treated only tentatively in regional historical research. No case has been published in which – as was the case in Hamburg – vouchers were likewise valid for Jewish stores up until 1938. In Frankfurt am Main, Munich, Nuremberg, Offenbach, Dortmund and Marburg, for instance, they were already not valid in 1933, and in Bünde by 1935. In Duisburg in 1935, the mayor prevented welfare recipients buying in Jewish stores from having their state support withdrawn, and the campaign was limited to notices which warned against buying in Jewish stores. See, *inter alia*, *Dokumente*, p. 180; Müller, *Geschichte*, p. 213; Werner, *Geschichte*, p. 85; Knipping, *Geschichte*, p. 35; Händler-Lachmann and Werther, *Vergessene Geschäfte*, p. 67; Norbert Sahrhage, *'Juden sind in dieser Stadt unerwünscht!' Die Geschichte der Synagogengemeinde Bünde im 'Dritten Reich'*, Bielefeld, 1988, p. 32; von Roden, *Geschichte*, p. 817.

202. Cf. the *Reichskulturkammergesetz* of 28 September 1933, *RGBl* 1933, Part I, p. 661f. On the launch of the RKK see also Volker Dahm, 'Anfänge und Ideologie der Reichskulturkammer. Die "Berufsgemeinschaft" als Instrument kulturpolitischer Steuerung und sozialer Reglementierung', *VfZ* 34 (1986), pp. 53–84.

203. These were, as laid down in the *Reichskulturkammergesetz*, the *Reichsschrifttumskammer* (Reich Chamber of Literarature), the *Reichspressekammer* (Reich Press Chamber), the *Reichsrundfunkkammer* (Reich Chamber of Broadcasting), the *Reichstheaterkammer* (Reich Theatre Chamber), the *Reichsmusikkammer* (Reich Chamber of Music), the *Reichskammer der bildenden Künste* (Reich Chamber of Fine Arts) and the *Reichsfilmkammer* (Reich Film Chamber).

204. As representative of many such assumptions, see the above-mentioned work by Walk, *Sonderrecht*, p. 52.

205. On the *1. VO zur Durchführung des Reichskulturkammergesetz*, see *RGBl* 1933, Part I, pp. 797–800. See also Karl-Friedrich Schrieber, *Die Reichskulturkammer. Organisation und Ziele der deutschen Kulturpolitik*, Berlin, 1934, p. 28f.

206. On the assumption that the *Propagandaministerium* had first begun its initiatives after the passage of the Nuremberg laws in order to prejudice the expected economic anti-Jewish legislation, see Genschel, *Verdrängung*, p. 116, and Adam, *Judenpolitik*, p. 132. In fact, a majority of the Jewish art, book and antique store owners excluded from the RKK in Hamburg had already received a communication informing them of their exclusion in the spring of 1935. On the

forced exclusion of Jewish publishers and bookstore owners from the beginning of 1935 see also the well-founded and very well-sourced study of Volker Dahm, *Das jüdische Buch im Dritten Reich, Part 1: Die Ausschaltung der jüdischen Autoren, Verleger und Buchhändler*, Frankfurt am Main, 1979, p. 99ff.

207. Cf. StAHH, *Staatsamt*, 106, notes by the *Wirtschaftsbehörde* and the *Staatsamt* of 25 and 28 March 1935.
208. Ibid., communication from the Hamburg *Wirtschaftsbehörde* to the *Staatsamt*, 25 March 1935.
209. Ibid., letter from *Wirtschaftsreferent* Langguth to the *Reichswirtschaftsministerium*, 15 January 1934.
210. Ibid., letter from the Hamburg *Gesandter* in Berlin, Peter Ernst Eiffe, to the President of the *Reichskammer für bildende Künste*, 6 April 1935.
211. Ibid., Hamburg *Vertretung* in Berlin to *Staatsamt*, 4 May 1935.
212. Ibid.
213. This interpretation is shared *inter alia* by Genschel, *Verdrängung*, p. 116; Adam, *Judenpolitik*, p. 132f.; Fischer, *Hjalmar Schacht*, p. 183f.
214. Circular from Hinkel of 22 January 1936, BAK, R 56, V/102. Also cp. Dahm, *Das jüdische Buch*, p. 116ff.
215. This process is described in detail in Dahm, *Das jüdische Buch*, pp. 121–134.
216. StAHH, *Staatsamt*, 106, Hamburg *Vertretung* in Berlin to *Staatsamt* of 31 March 1937.
217. Ibid., note of 31 March 1937.
218. Ibid., communication from the Hamburg *Vertretung* in Berlin to the *Staatsamt* of 11 June 1936.
219. *Archiv des Wiedergutmachungsamtes beim Landgericht Hamburg* (Archiv WgA LGHH), Z 31541, p. 17, cited as per the note by Dr A. Katterfeldt of 24 November 1977.
220. Ibid., p. 1, written statement by Dr H.J. Kölln of 29 December 1958.
221. StAHH, *Oberfinanzpräsident* (Regional Finance President), F 464, p. 27, communication from the *Reichsstelle für Devisenbewirtschaftung* (Reich Office for Foreign Exchange Control) to the Hamburg *Devisenstelle*, 19 June 1936.
222. Enoch functioned *inter alia* as Director of the 'New American Library' and of the 'American Book Publishers Council'. Cf. *Memoirs of Kurt Enoch, written for his family, privately printed by his wife Margaret M. Enoch*, New York, 1984.
223. StAHH, *Oberfinanzpräsident*, R 1937/679, p. 144, letter from the Hamburg *Industrie- und Handelskammer* to the *Devisenstelle des Oberfinanzpräsidenten*, 6 November 1937.
224. Ibid., p. 192, President of the *Reichskulturkammer* (RKK) to the *Reichswirtschaftsministerium*, 14 December 1937. This decision on the part of the RKK was now accepted without protest by the *Reichswirtschaftsministerium*, which had fought on Bachrach's behalf for two years and had always circumvented the decisions of the RKK – an indication of the final antisemitic 'change of course' in the *Reichswirtschaftsministerium* of 1937/38.
225. According to a decree issued by the *Devisenfahndungsamt* (Foreign Exchange Investigation Office) on 21 November 1938, Jews who were involved in foreign exchange investigations could be subjected to an accelerated procedure of denaturalisation which ended in the comprehensive confiscation of all of the assets of the Jews affected. Bachrach was stripped of his citizenship at the end of December 1938, and on 14 March 1939, the Hamburg Gestapo instructed the 'state police to take possession' of his property. Ibid., Vol. II, p. 331, note from the *Devisenstelle* of 27 December 1938; p. 344, communication from the Gestapo to the *Devisenstelle* of 14 March 1939.
226. Berlin Document Centre, RKK 2011, RSK – *Juden, Judenliste der Reichsschrifttumskammer*, 15 March 1937.

227. Ibid., RKK 2011, *Reichskammer für bildende Künste*, letter from the President of the RKdbK to the *Reichsministerium für Volksaufklärung und Propaganda* (Ministry for Public Enlightenment and Propaganda), 8 June 1938.

228. Ibid., RKK 2011, RLA, list of non-Aryan members, excluded or rejected, 27 August 1938, sent to the *Reichsministerium für Volksaufklärung und Propaganda.*

229. Ibid., Jl4 RMK, Parts I-V.

230. On the order of 26 March 1936, see *RGBl* 1936, Part I, p. 317f., Article 3: 'Jews are not permitted to be leaseholders. Public pharmacies with Jewish owners are subject to mandatory leasing.' The law published on 13 December 1935 contained a still more explicitly anti-Jewish clause and essentially restricted obligatory leasing to those who were 'unreliable for national and moral reasons'. Cf. *Gesetz über die Verpachtung und Verwaltung öffentlicher Apotheken* (Law on the Leasing and Administration of Public Pharmacies) of 13 December 1935, *RGBl* 1935, Part I, pp. 1445–1447. On the persecution of Jewish pharmacists under National Socialism see also Frank Leimkugel, *Wege jüdischer Apotheker*, Frankfurt am Main, 1991.

231. This *Realkonzession* was valid for the so-called 'old Hamburg' pharmacies that had already been in existence before the release of the Hamburg *Medizinalordnung* of 20 February 1818. Cf. *Archiv WgA LGHH*, Z 64-1, p. 38.

232. StAHH, *Medizinalkollegium*, I D 6b, Vol. 10, p. 204, President of the *Gesundheits- und Fürsorgebehörde* to the *Senator der Inneren Verwaltung*, 5 April 1935.

233. In April 1934 the Hamburg *Gesundheits- und Fürsorgebehörde* had placed National Socialist functionaries in five out of eight pharmacies that had become available. These were *NSDAP-Kreisleiter* Hans Rehmke, *SA-Obertruppführer* August Heilhecker, *SA-Sanitätsstandartenführer* Karl Weißkopf, *SA-Standartenführer* Hermann Oeser and the regional head of the *Standesgemeinschaft Deutscher Apotheker* (Professional Society of German Pharmacists), Carl Hörmann. See ibid., p. 127, letter from the President of the *Gesundheits- und Fürsorgebehörde* to the *Senator der Inneren Verwaltung* (draft), January 1935.

234. Ibid., p. 57, communication from the *Standesgemeinschaft Deutscher Apotheker* to the Hamburg *Referent für das Gesundheitswesen*, Burger (a pharmacist), 1 June 1934.

235. Ibid., p. 58. President of the *Gesundheits- und Fürsorgebehörde* to the *Standesgemeinschaft Deutscher Apotheker*, 8 June 1934.

236. See StAHH, NSDAP, B 202, list of Jewish pharmacies of 26 October 1935.

237. See *Archiv WgA LGHH*, Z 64-1 (Central-Apotheke, Karl Förder), Z 869-1 (Apotheke am Georgsplatz, Dr Berthold Jutrosinski), Z 2630-1 (Hansa-Apotheke, Paul Freundlich), Z 24542 (Hammerbrook-Apotheke, Wilhelm Fromme), Z 162-2 (Löwen-Apotheke, Dr Werner Bukofzer), Z 455 (Victoria-Apotheke, Felix Wolpe), Z 160-1 (Apotheke zum Freihafen, Max Mandowsky), Z 555-2 (Engel-Apotheke, Arthur Hirsch), Z 4557 (Hirsch-Apotheke, Louis Böhm), Z 657 (Apotheke Zum Ritter St.Georg, Max Wolfsohn), Z 269 (Schwanen-Apotheke, Erwin Memelsdorff), Z 354-1 (Victoria-Apotheke, Georg Schaeffer), Z 65-8 (Apotheke am Winterhuder Marktplatz, Manfred Pardo).

238. On shifts in the income of the Jewish pharmacies in Hamburg see *inter alia Archiv WgA LGHH*, Z 269, p. 51, Z 455, p. 58f. Substantial losses – as far as can be reconstructed – were suffered by just one pharmacy, the 'Apotheke zum Freihafen', owned by Max Mandowsky. In its direct neighbourhood *SA-Standartenführer* Oeser was allowed to establish a new pharmacy in 1934 so as to estrange Mandowsky from customers among the officials at the port. Cf. ibid., Z 160-1, p. 96. In 1950 the President of the *Apothekerkammer* stated that the granting of the concession to Oeser had been 'clearly based on a preference based on political motives'. (p. 72, statement of 15 December 1950).

239. Cf. Galerie Morgenland, ed., *Wurzeln*, p. 42.

240. *Archiv WgA LGHH*, Z 64-1, p. 21, statement by Ernst Zobel, 3 September 1951.

241. *Archiv WgA LGHH*, Z 65-8, second count, p. 12, pharmacy leasing contract of 24 June 1936.
242. *RGBl* 1939, Part I, p. 47f.
243. *RGBl* 1938, Part I, p. 1709.
244. See *inter alia Archiv WgA LGHH*, 65-8, second count, p. 24ff., on the pharmacy on the Winterhuder Marktplatz, whose concession was held by Walter Draheim, an *NSDAP-Ortsgruppenleiter* since 1930.
245. The restitution files of the *Wiedergutmachungamtes beim Landgericht Hamburg* record that the three pharmacists were: Louis Böhm, deported to Minsk with a daughter and two grandchildren and murdered on 18 November 1941; Max Wolfsohn, deported with his wife to Theresienstadt on 15 July 1942, from there to Minsk on 23 September 1942 where he was killed; and Paul Freundlich, deported with his wife on 11 July 1942 and killed in Auschwitz. At the time of the deportation, Böhm was 78 years old, Wolfsohn 70 years old and Freundlich 63 years old. The younger Jewish pharmacists had already emigrated.
246. StAHH, *Verwaltung für Wirtschaft, Technik und Arbeit*, III 7, letter from H. Peters to 'Oberbürgermeister (*sic*) Kroogmann (*sic*)', 27 October 1935.
247. Ibid., note by the *Verwaltung für Wirtschaft, Technik und Arbeit*, 29 November 1935.
248. Cf. Müller, *Geschichte*, p. 220f; Hanke, *Geschichte*, p. 127f.
249. On these violent excesses, see Genschel, *Verdrängung*, p. 109; Händler-Lachmann and Werther, *Vergessene Geschäfte*, p. 77; Schultheis, *Juden*, pp. 88f, 141, 149, 218ff., 322, 383, 440, 490.
250. Special Archives, Moscow, 721-1-2339, p. 35, letter from the *Landesverbands Nordwestdeutschland des Centralvereins deutscher Staatsbürger jüdischen Glaubens* to the *Centralverein Berlin*, 14 May 1935.
251. This did not prevent the National Socialist press from inflating the attacks into the 'spontaneous demonstration' of allegedly 'thousands of inhabitants of Rothenburgsort': 'Men and women of the working classes of our people surrounded the Jewish stores and induced the Jewish aliens to close their shops.' *Hamburger Tageblatt*, 12 May 1935.
252. Special Archives, Moscow, 721-1-2339, p. 31, letter from the *Landesverbands Nordwestdeutschland des Centralvereins deutscher Staatsbürger jüdischen Glaubens* to the *Centralverein Berlin*, 22 May 1935.
253. StAHH, NSDAP, B 202, Report by *SA-Scharführer* Voigt, 1 August 1935.
254. Cf. the reports of the state police stations in Altona and Harburg-Wilhelmsburg, *Geheimes Staatsarchiv Preußischer Kulturbesitz* (Secret State Archive for Prussian Cultural Estate), Berlin-Dahlem, Rep. 90P, reports 12.1, p. 20; reports 3.3, p. 72.
255. Cited in ibid, reports 3.3, p. 71, report of the Gestapo station in Harburg-Wilhelmsburg to the *Geheime Staatspolizeiamt* (Head Office of the Secret State Police) in Berlin, August 1935. One placard read, among other things, 'O Lord give us back to Moses again / give, that he his brothers in faith / will lead into the promised land; give, that the sea will part itself again / and that the high column of water / will stand steady as a wall of rock / and if into its watery insides / the whole mob of Jews is [thrown] within/ O Lord, then shut the flap / and all peoples will have peace.'
256. Ibid., p. 61.
257. See below, Ch. IV.
258. *Deutschland-Berichte der Sopade*, Year 2, 1935 (reproduction, Frankfurt am Main, 1980), p. 933.
259. 'Jews with white waistcoats – a factual report by Edwin Knocker', *Hamburger Tageblatt*, 20–29 July 1935.
260. 'Guide to the Aryan firms of Greater Hamburg', supplement to the *Hamburger Tageblatt*, 27 September 1935.
261. Cf. Walk, *Sonderrecht*, p. 210.

262. Communication from the *Reichs- und Preußischen Wirtschaftsminister* to the *Reichswirtschafts-kammer* of 28 April 1936, *Archiv FZH*, 227–11.
263. Thus Albert Fischer, *Hjalmar Schacht*, p. 183.
264. See Fischer, *Hjalmar Schacht*, p. 184f.
265. From Roden, *Duisburger Juden*, Vol. II, p. 817.
266. Hanke, *Geschichte*, p. 148; Helmut M. Hanko, 'Kommunalpolitik in der "Hauptstadt der Bewegung" 1933–1935. Zwischen "revolutionärer" Umgestaltung und Verwaltungskontinuität', in Martin Broszat, Elke Fröhlich and Anton Grossmann, eds, *Bayern in der NS-Zeit*, Vol. III, Munich, 1981, pp. 329–441, here p. 422; Joachim Meynert and Friedhelm Schäffer, *Die Juden in der Stadt Bielefeld während der Zeit des Nationalsozialismus*, Bielefeld, 1983, p. 52f.
267. *Hamburger Tageblatt*, 27 September 1935. For similar reactions from "Aryan" businessmen in Mannheim, see Fliedner, *Judenverfolgung*, p. 120.
268. *Archiv Handelskammer*, 100.A.1.6, letter from P. Kuntze to the Hamburg *Handelskammer*, 11 October 1935.
269. Ibid., Hamburg *Handelskammer* to P. Kuntze, 17 October 1935.
270. Ibid., note by Dr Leuckfeld (an attorney), 23 May 1936.
271. Citation from ibid.
272. Cf. the survey of Jewish firms in StAHH, *Sozialbehörde I*, WA 10.18.
273. On the circular from the RIM of 14 July 1938 on the implementation of the 3rd decree of the Reich Citizenship Law, see Walk, *Sonderrecht*, p. 233.
274. Communication im StAHH, *Oberfinanzpräsident*, 42 UA 7.
275. *Liste der reichsfluchtsteuerfähigen Nichtarier* and *Liste der jüdischen Ausfuhrfirmen*. Both lists can be found in StAHH, *Oberfinanzpräsident*, 19.
276. *Sonderarchiv Moskau*, 500-1-659, pp. 56–58.
277. For instance, on 26 August 1938, the Altona *Steueramt* (Tax Office) announced that it had gone back to the creation of a trade directory on the basis of the documents of DAF, of the *Handelskammer*, of the police headquarters and its own commercial tax lists. An official order from the *Devisenstelle* of the *Oberfinanzpräsident* on 8 August 1938 referred all employees to the identification of Jews in area "R" listed in the card index in the *Devisenstelle* as well as in the card indexes of the Gestapo and the Statistical Office of the Hamburg *Gemeindeverwaltung* (municipal authorities). See StAHH, *Steuerverwaltung I*, I A 122; ibid, *Oberfinanzpräsident*, 9 UA 8.
278. Citation as in Werner Johe, 'Bürgermeister Rudolf Petersen', in *Jahrbuch des Instituts für Deutsche Geschichte*/Tel-Aviv, 3 (1974), pp. 379–415, here p. 413.
279. For the following information on Munich anti-Jewish policy, see Hanke, *Geschichte*; Hanko, *Kommunalpolitik*; Selig, *Boykott*; Ulrike Haerendel, 'Das Rathaus unterm Hakenkreuz – Aufstieg und Ende der "Hauptstadt der Bewegung" 1933 bis 1945', in Richard Bauer, ed., *Geschichte der Stadt München*, Munich, 1992, pp. 369–393.
280. See StAHH, *Innere Verwaltung (Büro Senator Richter)*, A V 7, p. 15, *Hamburger Wasserwerke* to Senator Richter, 2 April 1937. While the Munich orders were decreed and implemented 'from above', in Hamburg instructions for antisemitic initiatives proceeded 'from below'. Cf. the letter written by Frau H. Markmann, Othmarschen, Moltkestrasse 77, to the Kellinghusenstrasse bath authorities on 24 November 1936: 'For we Aryans, it is a revolting feeling to have to bathe in a pool with Jews.' After further unrepeatable abusive antisemitic letters were received by the Gestapo and the *Verbindungsreferent* (Liaison Officer) of the Hamburg NSDAP, *Innensenator* Richter and *Reichsstatthalter* Kaufmann agreed on a regulation for Hamburg altering the bathing regulations so that Jews were no longer allowed to swim on family bathing days. Cf. ibid, Senator Richter to the Hamburg *Reichsstatthalter*, 30 November 1936, p. 10.

281. On the renaming of Jewish streets in Hamburg, see Galerie Morgenland, ed., *Wurzeln*, pp. 86–88.

282. Cf. Gershom Scholem, *Von Berlin nach Jerusalem. Jugenderinnerungen*, Frankfurt am Main, 1977, p. 172f., who described the atmosphere in Munich as 'unbearable'.

283. Cf. Uwe Lohalm, *Völkischer Radikalismus. Die Geschichte des Deutschvölkischen Schutz- und Trutz-Bundes 1919–1923*, Hamburg, 1970; Iris Hamel, *Völkischer Verband und nationale Gewerkschaft. Der Deutschnationale Handlungsgehilfen-Verband 1893–1933*, Frankfurt am Main, 1967.

284. Figures given in Ursula Büttner, *Politische Gerechtigkeit und sozialer Geist. Hamburg zur Zeit der Weimarer Republik*, Hamburg, 1985, p. 288; Hellmuth Auerbach, 'Vom Trommler zum Führer. Hitler und das nationale Münchner Bürgertum', in Mensing and Prinz, *Irrlicht*, pp. 67–91, here p. 89. In the Reichstag elections of March 1933, the percentage of the total vote cast for the NSDAP was 43.9% on the Reich level, in Hamburg it was 38.8% and in Munich 37.8%.

285. See Jürgen Falter, *Hitlers Wähler*, Munich, 1991, pp. 154–163.

286. On the Munich BVP see Wilfried Rudloff, 'Notjahre - Stadtpolitik in Krieg, Inflation und Weltwirtschaftskrise 1914 bis 1933', in Bauer, *München*, pp. 336–368, esp. pp. 354–357.

287. The relationship between Catholicism and antisemitism has still yet to be sufficiently researched. The view that anti-Jewish prejudices were widespread in Catholicism is put by Olaf Blaschke, 'Wider die "Herrschaft des modern-jüdischen Geistes": Der Katholizismus zwischen traditionellem Antijudaismus und modernem Antisemitismus', in Wilfried Loth, ed., *Deutscher Katholizismus im Umbruch zur Moderne*, Stuttgart, 1991, pp. 236–265; a considerably more cautious picture is given by Wilhelm Damberg, 'Katholizismus und Antisemitismus in West-falen. Ein Desiderat', in Herzig, Teppe and Determann, eds, *Verdrängung*, pp. 44–61.

288. Whereas in Hamburg in June 1933 47.3% of all people in employment worked in trade and transport-related businesses, the percentage in Munich was 34.2%. The proportions employed in industry in the two cities were reversed: 40.2% in Munich, 33.8% in Hamburg. Cf. *Statistisches Jahrbuch deutscher Gemeinden 1935*, p. 2. On the structure of the Munich economy see also Claudia Brunner, *Arbeitslosigkeit in München 1927 bis 1933. Kommunalpolitik in der Krise*, Munich, 1992, pp. 72–78.

289. *Statistisches Jahrbuch deutscher Gemeinden 1935*, p. 155.

290. Calculation according to the figures in the *Statistisches Jahrbuch deutscher Gemeinden 1936*, pp. 416 and 430.

291. As a proportion of the total population, in Hamburg the figure was 2.46% (26,910 unemployed), and in Munich 1.12% (8520 unemployed).

292. Cf. the circular from *Regierenden Bürgermeister* Krogmann of 29 January 1934, which instructed the agencies of the Hamburg Administration to aim to give a 'good impression'. *Archiv FZH*, 323513.

293. For instance through the coordinating function of the *Deutschen Gemeindetag*. Cf. Gruner, *Arbeitseinsatz*, pp. 31ff., 332.

294. See the letter from Kaufmann to Göring of 4 September 1942, National Archives Washington, Miscellaneous German Records Collection, T 84, Roll 7. See also Bajohr, *Gauleiter*, pp. 290–292.

# Chapter III

# JEWISH BUSINESSMEN

## *Economic Situation and Individual and Political Strategies*

### The Demographic and Economic Situation of Hamburg's Jews

In the first half of the nineteenth century, Hamburg's Jewish community was the largest in Germany. At the turn of the century, however, it had fallen to fourth place, behind those of Berlin, Frankfurt am Main and Breslau.[1] Although the number of Jews in Hamburg rose steadily until 1925, the percentage which they represented in the total population in the state of Hamburg fell more dramatically than in almost any other city in the German Reich. Jews made up 4.87 percent of the population in 1811; by June 1933 this had fallen to 1.39 percent, decreasing to a little over a quarter of the original figure.[2] In 1932, therefore, contemporaries were already warning of the 'physical disappearance of the Jewish community'[3] in Hamburg.

Three factors were responsible for the decline of the Jewish percentage of the population.

First, the birth rate of the Jewish population had dropped steadily in the nineteenth century. Around the turn of the century it was exactly half that of the population in Hamburg as a whole.[4] Only in the 1920s did the birth rate for the total population of approximately fifteen births for every one thousand inhabitants per annum fall to the level it had reached among the Jewish population. The Jews of Hamburg had thus accomplished the transition to two-child families a generation earlier than the population as a whole, reflecting both their higher social status and their socialisation into a middle- or upper-class, big city pattern.

Secondly, the Jewish community in Hamburg had only been affected to a limited extent by the immigration of Jews into the large German cities. The number of 'Eastern Jews' in Hamburg was markedly lower than it was in the other large cities.[5]

---

Notes for this chapter begin on page 135.

In other words, the Jewish community of Hamburg was the only one in the whole of the German Reich in which the proportion of locally born Jews (at 50.8%) was higher than that of those born elsewhere (the average for all the major cities combined was 38%). The fact that Hamburg's Jewish community was comparatively settled was related to the lower than average level of immigration it attracted.

Third, the Jewish community in Hamburg lost many members to Jewish-Christian 'mixed marriages', the number of which was well above the average for the Reich as a whole. In the 1920s, almost half of all marriages by Jews were 'mixed marriages'.[6] The weakening of religious ties on both Christian and Jewish sides promoted the development of such marriages, as did the desire of many Jews for integration into their non-Jewish surroundings. The proportion of those people who in National Socialist terminology were described as '*Mischlinge*' was correspondingly high. According to the results of the census of May 1939, in Hamburg the statistics suggested that for every hundred so-called 'full Jews' there were seventy-seven '*Mischlinge*', while the Reich average was only thirty-five, in Berlin the figure was thirty-two, in Breslau twenty-two and in Frankfurt am Main only nineteen.[7] The high number of 'mixed marriages' and '*Mischlinge*' in Hamburg can therefore be seen as indicative of the extent to which the barriers between Jewish and non-Jewish populations had been removed.

An examination of the occupational structure of the Jews of Hamburg in 1925 and 1933[8] shows the overwhelming predominance of the 'commerce and transport' sector in the economic activities of the Jews, while the proportion of Jews engaged in the industrial sector remained far behind and was still further below the average figure for Jews engaged in industry across the Reich as a whole.[9] However, whereas the sectoral employment structures of the Jewish and non-Jewish population across the Reich were distinctly divergent,[10] in Hamburg they had largely converged, as Tables 4 and 5 show.[11] The peculiarities of the Jewish employment structure corresponded to the traditional dominance of commerce and to the below-average development of industry in Hamburg more strongly than was the case in other parts of the Reich.

The occupational position (Table 6) of the Jews of Hamburg deviated sharply from that of the Hamburg population as a whole, however.[12] The proportion of Jews who were self-employed was three times the figure for the whole population, and the proportion of employees in the Jewish population was clearly higher than in Hamburg in general. The percentage of Jews in the working class was, by contrast, far less than the figure for Hamburg as a whole: at between 6.7 percent and 8.0 percent, not even a fifth of the figure for the whole population. This glaring difference in social position was rooted in the centuries' old occupational restrictions on Jews, which they had been able to escape in earlier times by becoming self-employed traders and manufacturers.

As Table 7 shows, Hamburg's self-employed Jews were primarily active in commerce: as wholesalers, in the import/export trade, as real estate agents, and as second-hand goods and raw materials dealers and retailers. Within the retail trade, they were predominantly owners of textile and clothing stores of different types.[13] In 1937 there were still a total of one hundred and seventy-five Jewish textile merchants in Hamburg. Of the one hundred and fifteen specialist stores for ladies' and girls' clothing alone, forty-nine were in Jewish hands.[14] Among the most important textile stores were the clothing stores of Hirschfeld Brothers (*Gebr. Hirschfeld*), Robinsohn Brothers, Feldberg Brothers, and the Heinrich Colm East India House, all of which were based in the centre of Hamburg, and the Gazelle corset store which had branches in most quarters in the city.

Just as Jews were particularly focused on textile retailing, so too those self-employed Jews engaged in manufacturing were primarily involved in the clothing business. Among the biggest enterprises some of the most notable were the textile factory Rappolt & Sons, with over six hundred employees, and raincoat producers such as 'Sturmflut' and Hans Steinberg.

In other branches of Hamburg industry, Jewish firms were rare. The only ones worthy of mention are a few chemical concerns like the Julius Schindler oil works or the Rudolf Reich company, a producer of white lead and wood-turpentine oil. Similarly, Jewish enterprises were clearly underrepresented at the port. In Hamburg there were only two Jewish shipping companies – *Fairplay Schleppdampfschiffs-Reederei Richard Borchardt* and Arnold Bernstein Shipping – and a Jewish shipyard, *Paul Berendsohn Köhlbrand-Werft*.

The concentration of independent Jewish activity in other areas of the economy is easy to reconstruct on the basis of Table 7. In the banking, stock market and insurance sectors, self-employed Jews were primarily engaged as bankers, as stock brokers and as insurance brokers, while among self-employed workers in the public and private service sectors Jews were predominantly doctors and lawyers.

As Table 9 shows, the residential areas in which Hamburg's Jews preferred to live were only to a limited extent determined by their proximity to the places in which they worked.[15] The Jewish population tended to live in the outer districts of Hamburg where there were almost no Jewish enterprises, and most Jewish firms were established in the centre of the city – not in the Harvestehude, Rotherbaum or Eimsbüttel quarters where over fifty percent of the Jews of Hamburg lived but only twenty-three percent of Jewish companies were based.

The total number of Jewish businesses in Hamburg is difficult to determine, and changes in the total figure after 1933 even more so. A list composed by the NSDAP *Gau* Economics Adviser in 1938 suggested that there were a total of 1201 Jewish enterprises[16] and that their original number in Hamburg totalled one thousand five hundred.[17] It follows that by 1938 only twenty percent of Jewish companies had sold their business to an 'Aryan' or had to stop trading altogether. For this very same period, Avraham Barkai estimated the decrease in the number of Jewish businesses in the Reich as a whole at between sixty and seventy percent.[18] Was there really such a major difference between developments in Hamburg and in the rest of the Reich?

There is much to be said for the argument that Jews were able to maintain their businesses in Hamburg substantially longer than elsewhere. The disinclination of the National Socialist state and party leadership in Hamburg to develop a harsher anti-Jewish regional policy than that of the Reich, and their restraint in dealing with the economic activities of Jews due to the peculiar economic position and economic structure of Hamburg, may have contributed to this development. One of the leading members of the Hamburg Advisory Board for Jewish Economic Relief (*Hamburger Beratungsstelle für jüdische Wirtschaftshilfe*), Dr Ernst Loewenberg, recalled in his memoirs that the 'Aryanisation' of Jewish businesses in Hamburg developed 'only slowly' in Hamburg and that emigration occurred later in Hamburg than elsewhere 'because living conditions here were better than in any other place in the Reich'.[19]

That there was a 'delayed Aryanisation' in Hamburg appears even more clearly after taking into account the timing of the transfer of Jewish enterprises into 'Aryan' hands in Hamburg. In so far as it can be reconstructed from the restitution documents of the State Court of Hamburg, the highpoint of the 'Aryanisation' process was reached as late as 1938 and 1939, developing rather slowly before that time.[20] The *Gau* Economics Adviser's figure of one thousand five hundred Jewish enterprises in Hamburg at the beginning of the 'Aryanisation' process appears reasonable in comparison with the number of Jewish businesses in Frankfurt, where at the beginning of 1934 a total of 1,713 were counted.[21] In the census of June 1933, 26,158 'believing Jews' lived in Frankfurt. Thus the figure of one thousand five hundred Jewish enterprises for a total population of 16,973 Jews in Hamburg – 19,410 if the Jewish populations in Altona, Wandsbek and Harburg-Wilhelmsburg are included – does not seem too low.

However, all of these figures must be subjected to fundamental, source-critical considerations. The *Gau* Economics Adviser could hardly have registered Jewish enterprises in Hamburg before 1935/36. The starting-point of one thousand five hundred would therefore not have included those Jewish businesses that had been liquidated or sold before this time. Moreover, the 'Aryanisations' in Hamburg of which we know from the restitution documents – dating overwhelmingly from a later period – include neither liquidated Jewish enterprises nor 'Aryanisations' concluded in the initial phase of the National Socialist regime that were still conducted in half-fair circumstances and for which no requests for restitution were submitted. The number of businesses 'Aryanised' up to 1936/37 was, therefore, certainly higher than the figure given in Table 11.

Finally, in the light of these calculations the statement of Avraham Barkai that the decrease in Jewish enterprises across the Reich was between sixty and seventy percent appears questionable and the rough estimate on which his figure is based should be reviewed. For 1 April 1938, Alf Krüger, the 'Adviser on Jewish affairs' (*Judenreferent*) of the Reich Economics Ministry, gave the number of Jewish enterprises as 39,552.[22] For January 1933, Barkai puts the number of Jewish business concerns at one hundred thousand,[23] based on the total of one hundred and thirty-two thousand self-employed Jewish businessmen given in the occupational census of 1925. However, as all full and limited partnerships as well as doctors and lawyers or even peddlers were counted as 'self-employed businessmen', their number only loosely corresponded to the actual number of enterprises in operation. Extrapolating from the figure of one hundred thousand down to the level of individual cities and regions, at this time Frankfurt would have had over five thousand instead of 1713, and in Hamburg there would have had to be over three thousand instead of one thousand five hundred – both of which seem too high.[24]

The figures for Jewish businesses in different cities and regions diverge considerably and do not provide greater statistical clarity on the Reich level. In the Meschede area twenty percent of all Jewish enterprises had been liquidated or 'Aryanised' by 1938. This corresponded to a figure of forty-one percent for the Jewish textile industry of Baden and Württemberg, fifty percent in Bochum and nearly seventy percent in Marburg – figures which strongly reflect the divergence in regional practices of 'Aryanisation'.[25] Nevertheless, the tendency seems to have developed whereby the speed of the process of displacement of Jewish enterprises was in inverse proportion to the size of the locality concerned: the smaller the town or community the faster and earlier liquidations and 'Aryanisations' of Jewish companies were completed.[26]

In all likelihood the drop in the number of Jewish businesses by 1938 in Hamburg was more than twenty percent, still clearly under the average for the Reich as a whole. The decrease in Jewish businesses in Hamburg was smaller than in Germany as a whole, because, as one of the largest cities, Hamburg provided considerably better conditions for Jewish firms than small cities and rural communities where repressive measures like boycotts were carried out more easily and, most importantly, could be conducted in a controlled manner.

This also corresponds with figures for the turnover and earnings of Jewish businesses in Hamburg up to 1938.[27] Of the twenty firms covered in Table 10 – which of course should not be taken as representative of the whole picture – twelve registered substantial increases in turnover and income, the business activities of five firms stagnated, but only three experienced clear losses. Even if such a small sample should not be overestimated, it is still possible to say that the recovery of the market in the 1930s did not bypass Jewish companies.[28] Although most of these firms no longer received public contracts directly, as suppliers to those companies that did, they often profited indirectly from improvement in the economic situation created by state orders.[29] This tendency emerged rather more clearly in industry, in wholesaling and in imports than in the retail trade, which was hit more heavily by a decline in business and loss of income. As is shown by the turnover figures for Campbell & Co., Europe's largest and most modern optician, or by those of the Heinrich Colm East India House, despite this general tendency, Jewish retail enterprises with secure market positions were able to maintain their position in spite of the conditions they worked in under the National Socialists.

## Spotlight on the Everyday Business of Jewish Enterprises after 1933 – Three Examples

Figures for the turnover and income of Jewish enterprises after 1933 give us information about some aspects of their everyday operations under the National Socialists, but they reflect neither the efforts they had to make in order to reach this size of turnover, nor the repression to which Jewish firms were exposed. These issues will be examined in the following section in the light of three examples of enterprises that continued to operate in Hamburg.

In a vivid report, Hans J. Robinsohn, co-proprietor and 'Works Leader' (*Betriebsführer*) of the Robinsohn Brothers fashion store, described in some depth the prevailing business climate in which Jewish firms worked after 1933.[30] Up until the end of 1937 the business situation of the firm, which had celebrated its fortieth anniversary in March 1932, was 'fairly constant'. Following a relatively brief period of arbitrary and open violence, the company was forcibly 'Aryanised' at the beginning of 1939. Before 1937, the company's turnover remained level, not benefitting from the increases which one might have expected to follow from the improved economic situation. The business was still in the black, but its net earnings after 1933 had nearly halved in comparison with its income figures in the mid-1920s.[31] The wholesale and mail-order trades were particularly affected by a loss of business, since many post office workers in the province denounced their recipients to local party officials and the customers were then abused and subjected to economic reprisals. Similarly, purchases of materials by seamstresses were hit by the 'rabid antisemitic campaign by the heads of the guild'.[32] The number of state officials who conducted credit purchases from the fashion house as private customers fell off because they feared 'written evidence' of the sale would lead to denunciation and dismissal.

Neither state nor administration intervened directly in business life before the end of 1937, which in Robinsohn's judgment was unusual in comparison with other regions: 'What was possible in Hamburg would have led immediately to the concentration camps in Nuremberg.'[33] Only the refreshment room for clients had to be closed after pressure from the government, since the firm would otherwise have had to be declared a 'department store' and would then have been burdened with special taxes.

Conditions within the firm developed along paradoxical lines after 1933. On the one hand, the Law for the Regulation of National Labour (*Gesetz zur Ordnung der nationalen Arbeit*) of January 1934 granted unlimited freedom even to Jewish 'works leaders', but, on the other hand, the company had to act without legal protection in a hostile environment – a situation which the National Socialist-dominated Council of Trust (*Vertrauensrat*) attempted to exploit. Each dismissal of an 'Aryan' employee, and every position given to a Jew, provoked enormous arguments. In such conflicts Robinsohn sought to demonstrate 'calm and firmness', against his inner feelings about the situation, and to take his stand on the basis of a legal status which, in the reality of the 'Third Reich', had long ago been undermined: 'As in the [Roman] arena, the smallest sign of fear, of insecurity or vacillation here was also the most dangerous thing.'[34]

The slightest problems could reveal how fragile the legal position of the company in fact was:

> An awkwardly drafted advertisement led to the threat of a trial on the grounds of unfair competition. A foreign customer who had not paid provided the excuse for an investigation of whether or not behind this there was some syphoning-off of capital. When a very much younger cousin arranged for a model to try on a slightly indecent carnival dress ordered by a customer, the *Vertrauensrat* made it out to be something approaching a sexual scandal; only through my greatest efforts could I prevent it being sent up to 'higher authorities'.[35]

Robinsohn also reported that the company's own chauffeurs sometimes reproached customers when delivering goods because they had ordered goods from a Jewish department store.[36]

If the suppliers and the large majority of private customers had not remained faithful to the company, the fashion store would have run into serious economic difficulties well before 1937/38. That the decline of the company had taken a long time, in spite of all restrictions placed on it, also rested on the fact that the company's owners were particularly committed to their business. In the summer of 1933, they modernised their operations and fitted new shop windows as advertising spaces – a demonstrative measure which attracted attention as well as sympathy. Through focused public relations, 'the most careful service' and special goods promotions, the proportion of 'chance customers' was raised. The ethnic origins of the owners of the company also attracted 'protest customers', who bought in Jewish stores just in order to show their rejection of National Socialism. The company's mail-order business was handled through a specially created 'cover firm' so as to protect the customers from reprisal. The owners confidently defended the firm and only in 1938/39 did they encounter open force when, during the 'Reich Crystal Night', the fashion store was stormed, demolished and plundered.

The Jewish textile manufacturers Rappolt & Sons found themselves in a similar situation. Founded long before, in the middle of the nineteenth century, the company was one of the largest Jewish industrial concerns in Hamburg, employing six hundred and ten staff and two hundred more working from their homes. Under the 'Eres' seal of quality[37] the company manufactured clothing – primarily coats – characterised by a particularly high quality of material and machine processing. After 1933, however, this strategy opened the company to antisemitic propaganda from competing firms who denounced 'Eres' as a 'Jewish label'.[38] At the same time, the exports of the Rappolt firm had fallen by 1935 from fifty percent to ten percent of the company's total turnover because the company was boycotted abroad as a 'German firm'.[39] In the Reich Economics Ministry the management's requests for support met with little willingness to be of assistance.[40] Moreover, after 1933, officials in National Socialist organisations also meddled in Rappolt's internal affairs. When speeches were made in praise of the company boss – a Jew – during an excursion organised for Rappolt's Berlin factory workers, the German Labour Front (*Deutsche Arbeitsfront*, DAF) called a factory meeting in order to condemn what, in their view, was improper behaviour. In the event, the DAF official responsible was unable to speak, being drowned out by employees – including NSDAP members. At that, the DAF demanded that the company managers dismiss those employees who had so vociferously attacked their speaker. When the firm refused to make the dismissals, the DAF asked the persons concerned to give up their jobs of their own volition.[41]

The antisemitic agitation of the 'Adefa' was a far greater threat to the continued existence of the business than such incidents. Adefa – the 'Syndicate of German Manufacturers in the Clothing Industry' (*Arbeitsgemeinschaft deutscher Fabrikanten der Bekleidungsindustrie*)[42] – was founded in June 1933, combining approximately five hundred ladies' and menswear manufacturing firms.[43] They provided a special label for the clothing of their member firms ('Adefa – the sign of goods made by Aryan hands'),[44] arranged numerous fashion shows from which Jewish firms were excluded, and also violently attacked retailers for including clothing from Jewish companies in their collection. Representatives of Adefa member companies threatened retailers with denunciation if they continued to sell clothing with the 'Eres' label from the Rappolt company, or if they displayed the 'Eres' logo in their store window.[45]

In its public self-portrayal Adefa sought to boost the egotism of their members through crude ideological arguments, hoping to expand their share of the market under the National Socialist regime. For instance, the publicity department of Adefa distributed the opening speech of *Gau* Economics Adviser Otto Jung at the Adefa show in the autumn of 1937, which demanded 'that Germans in all income brackets finally be sent a tasteful clothing kit which suits their type and their attitude, and that is not associated with a type of fashionable Bolshevism, invented by the fashion mania of alien races in order to exploit the German people'.[46]

The success of such agitation was limited, however, since many customers still preferred fashionable clothing to a 'tasteful clothing kit'. Even National Socialist store owners complained of the lack of goods of high quality and elegance made by non-Jewish clothing manufacturers, and claimed that they were therefore dependent on Jewish suppliers in order to satisfy the requirements of their clientele.[47] The many years that Jewish textile concerns had in the market, their experience and their skills were not going to be easily eliminated by political pressure, and likewise, despite the antisemitic propaganda, the much-decried 'Eres' label of Rappolt retained its reputation as a sign of high quality.

After the loss in turnover of 1935, Rappolt was almost able to double its textile imports in 1936 with the help of a firm based abroad.[48] By means of ongoing rationalisation, in 1937 it tripled its income over the previous year.[49] When the management sold the company to 'Aryan' businessmen in 1938, they handed over a solvent operation that paid all its bills, as far as was possible, from cash accounts, and having hardly drawn on any bank credit at all. Their 'Aryan' successors subsequently acknowledged the success of the company's labelling policy by renaming the company 'Eres KG', thereby explicitly retaining a product name which, in spite of antisemitic agitation against it, had become generally accepted as a mark of quality.[50]

The official chicanery to which Jewish firms could be subjected after 1933 is clear from a third example of everyday business at the optician Campbell & Co. In 1900, Jewish master optician Julius Flaschner had acquired Campbell & Co., founded in 1816, and by 1933 had built up a business which was considered the 'best equipped sales office for optical products in Germany',[51] and even as 'the largest optical retail store in the continent'.[52] To take only its main outlet at Neuer Wall 30, modernised and renovated in the autumn of 1930 – in the midst of the global economic crisis – Flaschner employed a total of forty-five staff. A further branch had been established in 1924 at Schulterblatt 156a. Flaschner's business profited especially from his close business relations with the

Carl Zeiss company in Jena, which used Flaschner's business as a 'display window'[53] for its exports.

After 1933, the Flaschner family was systematically harassed by the Gestapo. Flaschner's wife was related to the former Vice-President of the Berlin police force, Dr Bernhard Weiß, whose energetic support for the Weimar Republic made him into one of the most hated opponents of the National Socialists. In National Socialist propaganda, he was given the nickname 'Isidor'.[54] In March 1933, Weiß briefly went into hiding at Flaschner's, after his apartment in Berlin was stormed by the SA. Though Weiß and his wife were ultimately able to emigrate to London by way of Czechoslovakia, their twelve-year old daughter remained at first with her relatives in Hamburg and was only able to follow her parents in 1934.

Before 1934, regular house searches by the Gestapo were part of the daily life of the Flaschner family, which soon saw itself subjected to a full-blown witch-hunt. In January 1934, the Hamburg Finance Authorities initiated an enquiry into alleged evasion of foreign exchange controls against Flaschner. The authorities accused him of having taken inflated mortgages in the renovation of his store in 1930 and transferring them abroad.[55] While Flaschner was at the spa in Baden-Baden in the spring of 1934, two detectives arrived with a warrant for his arrest. Unnerved by the permanent harassment he faced, he fled abroad, a move which was held against him by the National Socialists as an acknowledgement of guilt.

At the end of May 1934, the *Amtliche Anzeiger* published a 'wanted' poster for Flaschner after the public prosecutor's office at the Hanseatic Special Court (*Hanseatisches Sondergericht*) had issued an instruction for his remand for 'crimes of high treason'.[56] At this point, the Hamburg Welfare Department deleted Campbell & Co. from its list of suppliers. One of the serious consequences of this measure was that it prompted denunciations from competing firms which saw an opportunity to join the list of suppliers to the welfare authorities. One competitor of Flaschner wrote to the Welfare Department on 6 June 1934, noting 'I know that Flaschner is a cousin of the former chief of police Isidor Weiß [*sic*] in Berlin, who has now gone to live abroad.'[57] Another asserted that he did not want 'to take second place behind those whose inferiority has ultimately and notoriously been proven by their escape and pursuit by warrant from the public prosecutor's office. I refer to the Campbell company at Neuerwall, whose strings are now still being pulled by the hands of a Polish Jew.'[58]

If Campbell's experienced attorney and the Council of Trust had not kept their nerve in this situation, it would probably have been difficult to avoid the collapse of the firm. They turned to the Hamburg Director of the German Labour Front, the Trustee of Labour, the Union of Health Insurers in Greater Hamburg and the Health and Welfare Departments, rejecting the accusations

made against Flaschner as absurd.[59] They also drew attention to the fact that
Flaschner could not have moved his wealth abroad because, in 1930, there was
still free movement of currency and Flaschner would hardly have invested
300,000 RM in his business if at that point in time he were planning to move his
property abroad. Confronted by the initiative taken by the attorney and the
Council of Trust, the institutions involved now consented to a detailed examination of the facts of the matter. This investigation revealed not only that Flaschner
had not smuggled any currency abroad, but that, on the contrary, he had even
brought in currency from Holland and thereby had been 'trading in the interests
of the national economy' – as the Hamburg State Finance Office now expressly
certified.[60] The public prosecutor's office then abandoned its enquiries, Flaschner
returned to Germany and the Welfare Department once more placed him on the
list of suppliers to the authorities. In the period from July 1935 to August 1936
alone, the Campbell firm received a total of seven hundred and fifty-eight orders
from the Department.[61] From 1935 to 1937 the company was able to raise its
annual turnover from 601,200 RM to 790,700 RM.[62] In August 1938 the company had one of the highest turnovers in its history.[63] At this point in time, the
company had already been banned from advertising publicly. A few months later,
Campbell & Co. was 'Aryanised'.[64]

## The 'Jewish Economic Sector': Opportunities and Limits

From 1933 onwards, the pressure exerted by persecution from the National
Socialists drew the heterogeneous Jewish community in Hamburg closer
together. Representatives of various religious groups agreed on a truce and the
newly elected Chair of the Committee of Representatives of the German Israelite
Community (*Deutsch-Israelitische Gemeinde*, DIG), Dr Ernst Loewenberg,
demanded that 'all differences – which noone wants to deny – [be] set aside in
working together'.[65]

One crucial factor in forging this agreement was the worsening economic situation of many Jews, which placed new demands on the Jewish community.
Those Jews who had been dismissed now looked for new jobs which, in almost all
cases, they could only find in Jewish companies; retailers in difficulty sought
financial assistance; young people searched for positions as trainees and apprentices; immigrants sought advice and financial support. With their growing exclusion from German society these needs could soon only be met within a 'Jewish
economic sector'[66] which had to be developed after 1933.

These new demands could at least be addressed on the basis of a tradition of
Jewish self-help that had been taking on increasing importance before 1933 in the

course of the global economic crisis. In Hamburg's Jewish community, the most notable self-help institutions included the 'Israelite Employment Association' (*Israelitische Stellenvermittlungsverein*), which aimed to find 'Sabbath free' positions for Jews, an 'Israelite Institute for Advances' (*Israelitische Vorschuß-Institut*) that granted community members interest-free loans in exchange for a surety,[67] 'Jewish Middle-Class Aid' (*Jüdische Mittelstandshilfe*) and the 'Jewish Vocational Advisory Board' (*Jüdische Berufsberatungsstelle*) which had been founded in Hamburg in October 1926.[68]

After 1933, the 'Advisory Board for Jewish Economic Relief' (*Beratungsstelle für jüdische Wirtschaftshilfe*) systematised these hitherto somewhat disorganised activities and expanded its work into new fields of activity. Under the chairmanship of Dr Rudolf Samson, a lawyer, the Hamburg Advisory Board – also responsible for the Jews of Schleswig-Holstein, Lübeck, Oldenburg and some areas in the province of Hanover – had been founded in the spring of 1933 as a subsidiary of the 'Central Committee of German Jews for Relief and Reconstruction' (*Zentralausschuss der deutschen Juden für Hilfe und Aufbau*).[69] At least half of its income derived from donations and subsidies made by the German Israelite Community and the 'Reich Representation of German Jews' (*Reichsvertretung der deutschen Juden*).[70]

The work of the Advisory Board extended over three areas in particular: occupational retraining and vocational training for youth; welfare provision for emigrés and returnees, and economic assistance in the narrower sense. In the area of occupational retraining and vocational training for youth, the Advisory Board created further educational courses for businessmen in languages, stenography and record keeping; organised retraining courses in carpentry, sewing and tailoring; educated young people in gardening and housekeeping; opened a factory where carpentry and lock-making were taught, and oversaw a number of 'Hachsharah' units providing professional training for Zionist-inclined youth who wanted to emigrate to Palestine.[71] The concentration on agricultural and handicraft training clearly reflected the exclusion of Jewish youth from the academic professions and the poor employment situation in the commercial world.

By 1938, the Migration Welfare Service of the Advisory Board had helped a total of 2,745 people to emigrate,[72] while the Board itself gave economic assistance and economic and occupational advice, and granted loans as well. Dr Ernst Loewenberg recalled in his memoirs that it was of the utmost importance that doctors and lawyers, who had until that point been predominantly entrusted with 'Aryan' patients and clients, had to be helped to build up a 'Jewish practice'.[73]

Beyond that, the Advisory Board helped in readjustment to a reduced standard of living, in the conclusion of settlements with creditors and in the regulation of rent arrears. The Board lent small sums to those establishing new lives elsewhere in Germany or abroad, for the acquisition of goods or the establishment of smaller businesses. Thus, Loewenberg recalled, 'with scant means some kind of existence' could 'be maintained for some years'.[74] Just in the period before May 1934, one thousand eight hundred people received aid from the Hamburg Advisory Board.[75] According to another source in the first half of 1934 it dealt with a total of 4,807 cases.[76]

In addition, the 'Union of Self-Employed Jewish Artisans and Tradesmen of Greater Hamburg' (the *Verein selbständiger jüdischer Handwerker und Gewerbetreibender zu Groß-Hamburg*, VSHG), founded in 1906, arranged credit for its members from the credit bank of the German Israelite Community, posted collective advertisements in the community's publication, the *Hamburger Familienblatt*, and every year published a membership list divided into different professions, which it sent to all Jewish households in the region of Hamburg.[77] This was supposed to make it easier for Hamburg's Jews to buy directly from Jewish stores or to order goods from Jewish firms. In 1934 the Union's membership doubled to four hundred and twenty [78] – a further indication of growing cooperation between Jewish manufacturers.

The *Hamburger Familienblatt* of the Israelite Community was filled with public calls for Jews to consider buying from Jewish firms as an appropriate response to their situation. In June 1934, Chief Rabbi Dr Joseph Carlebach demanded that community members support Jewish restaurant owners by patronising their restaurants.[79] In July 1935 the *Familienblatt* implored its readers in an article on 'The Jews' Common Economic Fate': 'Jewish manufacturers today therefore more than ever before have cause and claim to expect from the Jews who share in their fate that they remember Jewish business people in their orders and in hiring and in the satisfaction of their needs, and to consider them in all areas that they can.'[80]

The demanding tone of the appeal suggests that not all Jews in Hamburg felt obliged to buy in Jewish stores. It is, of course, impossible to determine with any precision the scope of purchases made by Jews out of solidarity with other Jews, which might have compensated to some small extent for drops in their income. An early indication of its real effectiveness is provided by several complaints from 'Aryan' businessmen, particularly in the Grindel quarter, that they were being 'boycotted' by Jews and therefore claimed a right to fiscal relief through a temporary decree controlling sales, residential, trade and housing taxes.[81]

Conversely, circulars from the VSHG, which also called for Jews to purchase from Jewish companies, often met with open resistance in the Committee of Representatives of the German Israelite Community, where arguments were raised against taking a 'one-sided' approach to Jewish firms.[82] Despite complaints from Jewish manufacturers, the administrators of the Community still gave assignments to non-Jewish businesses after 1933.[83] In June 1936, in the Committee of Representatives, the representative of the middle classes bemoaned the fact 'that even people who occupy prominent positions in Jewish life "boycott" Jewish artisans and manufacturers, in other words they do not buy or order from them'.[84] In October 1936, the VSHG failed in an attempt to oblige at least the employees of the German Israelite Community and other Jewish organisations to buy from other Jews and show their solidarity. The community executive chose instead 'to refrain' from 'taking measures affecting these persons'.[85]

The first factor that lurked behind this stubborn refusal to allow purchases to be made in the Jewish economic sector alone, or to instruct that this be mandatory, was the desire not to give more support to the exceptional pressure towards ghettoisation which isolated the community and was destroying their contacts with their non-Jewish environment. Secondly, a moral principle was also being expressed through this attitude: that like would not be repaid with like and the calls for a boycott from the National Socialists ought not to be met with the same from the Jewish community, particularly since their effectiveness was probably very slight.

Unencumbered by such moral scruples, however, the National Socialists intensified their extreme pressure and burdened the Jews collectively with new restrictions. In 1935 they excluded Jews from receiving deliveries from the winter welfare aid organisation. This meant that a Jewish Winter Relief Aid had to be founded, giving support primarily to the unemployed, welfare recipients and poor pensioners.[86]

In January 1936, 2,904 out of 16,300 people – 17.8 percent of the whole community – were given support by Jewish Winter Relief Aid in Hamburg,[87] while in the Reich as a whole, 20.5 percent of all Jews received winter help.[88] In Hamburg, the revenues of Jewish Winter Relief Aid – drawn primarily from deducting a fixed percentage of the incomes of salaried personnel and tradesmen – were maintained at a relatively constant level for a long time. They sank from 242,400 RM in the winter of 1935/36 to 216,700 RM in the winter of 1937/38, but were cut in half in 1938/39 to 102,300 RM, although in 1938/39 most 'donated far more' of their income than had previously been the case.[89] Until that point, the figure for those who had to be supported in Hamburg had been under the average figure for communities across the Reich. However, it shot up in 1938/39 to thirty-nine percent, while on the Reich level at this time the average was still just under twenty-five percent.[90]

These figures reinforce the impression that the economic conditions of Hamburg's Jews in comparison with the average for the Reich were initially somewhat more favourable, but rapidly worsened in 1938. To that extent, 1938 was a veritable *annus horribilis* for the Jews of Hamburg, almost completely smashing their economic means of subsistence, driving many wealthy businessmen into emigration and leaving an increasingly pauperised Jewish community behind, more and more dependent on social welfare. In 1936, the German Israelite Community gave out approximately thirty-nine percent of its budget for expenditure on 'Welfare', while the Hamburg Jewish Religious Federation (*Jüdische Religionsverband*) spent sixty percent of its budget in 1939 on welfare services; in 1940 this figure rose to sixty-eight percent. Real welfare service expenditure had almost trebled from 1936 to 1940 from 522,955 RM to 1,446,716 RM.[91]

To afford their many expenses, the German Israelite Community had to levy higher and higher communal taxes on their members. In 1933/34 these amounted to fifteen percent of the Reich income tax, but gradually rose by 1939 to thirty percent, or one percent of an individual's assets.[92] In 1935 the community's executive even considered going beyond that and levying a 'Communal Capital Export Tax'[93] – a plan which was implemented by the Gestapo at the end of 1938, this time as a mandatory payment.

The growing welfare expenditure increasingly narrowed the room for satisfying the needs of Jewish firms for economic assistance. In 1936, the community's Committee of Representatives refused a subsidy of 300 RM to the VSHG for the printing of a membership list to be made available to Jewish householders. 'We have to take the point of view that we want to do everything for education, welfare and religion', as the Community's financial adviser, Dr Leo Lippmann, said in explaining the rejection of the subsidy request. For this reason, financial expenditure for the support of Jewish tradesmen was 'not justifiable'.[94]

Here, the tight financial constraints on the construction of a Jewish economic sector revealed themselves. The Jewish community was already overloaded with having to finance communal life and welfare. The Advisory Board for Jewish Economic Relief concentrated its energy on occupational training and retraining. At the same time, it had little to offer to Jewish traders, either in terms of advice or the provision of small loans. On the contrary, Jewish company owners gave the community far more, in tax payments, in donations and in providing employment, than they received. Moreover, the proportion of the population of Hamburg that was Jewish was not large enough to provide a self-sufficient stable Jewish economic life in the city. Because widely varying figures for the changing numbers in the Jewish community have been given, their total number for the years 1933–1939 cannot be stated precisely. The local SD regional section, *Oberabschnitt Nord-West*, for instance, estimated the number of 'believing Jews' in Hamburg on 31 December 1937 at 'c. 16,000',[95] while the Gestapo gave a figure of 15,308[96] and Jewish Winter Relief Aid proceeded on the basis that there were only 14,265.[97] According to the figure which is chosen, the number of Jews in Hamburg between June 1933 and December 1937 decreased by between six and sixteen percent, while the average decline in the Reich as a whole in this period was thirty percent. The proportion of Jews in the population of Hamburg remained constant for a long time after 1933 because the total population of Hamburg also decreased over the course of the period.[98] According to the figures given by the Hamburg Advisory Board for Jewish Economic Relief, by the end of 1937, 5,000 Jews in Hamburg – almost thirty percent of the population of 1933 – had emigrated,[99] but these losses may have been partly compensated for by immigration from rural areas and small towns in the surrounding area.

According to the figures given by the SD, in 1937 a total of eight hundred and ninety-six Jews from Hamburg emigrated abroad, and seven hundred and ninety-one departed for other parts of Germany. At the same time, however, 1,106 Jews moved to Hamburg.[100] They included, on the one hand, some particularly poor people, described by the SD as a 'Jewish proletariat'. These preferred to move into the main German cities in the hope of receiving support from the well-endowed urban Jewish communities. On the other hand, the SD reported, they also included many business people who were 'excluded from almost every commercial activity in the country'.[101] In Hamburg and other metropolitan cities they could, by contrast, still hope for a better standard of living and greater working opportunities.

Nevertheless, the total figure of approximately fifteen thousand Jews was not sufficient to keep the more than one thousand Jewish businesses even near to alive. Only in Berlin, where at the end of 1937 nearly one hundred and forty thousand Jews still lived, were the structural preconditions favourable for an autonomous Jewish economic sector. If Jewish enterprises in Hamburg had been able to maintain their operations on a limited level up to 1937, in spite of all the restrictions on them, it was primarily due to two factors. One was that several firm owners were able to overcome the restrictions imposed upon them through their own individual counter-strategies. For example, Hartmann von der Porten, the Jewish owner of the Von der Porten & Frank company, continued to secure public contracts for his business by founding another company under the name of his attorney, creaming off all of the contracts given out by the authorities that had in the meantime been lost by other businesses owned by Jews.[102] Other Jewish enterprises also secured public contracts or import quotas by accepting 'Aryan' partners to represent them to the outside world.[103] One Jewish entrepreneur even bought into an 'Aryan' competitor through his non-Jewish wife.[104]

As is shown by the example of the companies covered here, Robinsohn Brothers, Rappolt & Sons and Campbell & Co., the exceptionally repressive environment had unleashed a strong desire for self-assertion and entrepreneurial energy, to perform better than the competition and to respond to the conditions of the market with especial flexibility and creativity – both through carefully targetted advertisements, by developing their product range and through special offers, and through modernisation, rationalisation and reducing costs. The latter aspect certainly restricted the ability of Jewish firms to increase their staff sizes, with the result that unemployed Jews could only find a limited number of jobs in Jewish enterprises, particularly since, in larger firms, the National Socialist Council of Trust presented an obstacle which had first to be overcome in any attempt to take on another employee.[105]

In some economic areas, Jewish businesses made special adjustments to the needs of particular groups of buyers. While in the textile sector, firms like Rappolt & Sons or the fashion stores of Hirschfeld Brothers and Robinsohn Brothers produced or supplied goods of particularly high quality, oriented towards high-income groups that felt strongly about quality, other Jewish textile retailers – including a large number of door-to-door salesmen – had hitherto specialised in meeting the needs of sections of the population with little money to whom they sold particularly cheap mass-produced goods and even granted opportunities for paying for cheap clothing by instalment, making buying from Jewish traders even more attractive to the poorer sections of the population.[106] In December 1935, the chief of the Gestapo at Harburg-Wilhelmsburg noted that, 'as [was the case] before, members of the public at large still did a brisk trade at Jewish retail businesses'.[107] The welfare offices stressed again and again that welfare recipients in particular showed a 'strong inclination' to buy in Jewish stores, and the SD still complained in January 1938 that customers with a small income 'did not think of avoiding Jewish stores'.[108] Moreover, anti-Jewish agitation seemed 'not to have any impact on a large part of the population'.[109]

This brings us to the second factor that permitted many Jewish firms to survive even under the restrictions now placed on them. The appeals of the National Socialists to boycott Jewish stores and businesses had no impact on the majority of the population. As the National Socialist party press complained, even party members bought in Jewish stores.[110] Most suppliers also seemed little affected, before 1938, by the antisemitic circulars distributed by their professional associations, maintaining financially lucrative business relations with their Jewish clients.[111] Some went so far as to complain in the Chamber of Commerce about the antisemitic measures which had been implemented thus far, since they increased the number of contracts which Jewish firms cancelled and the deliveries they sent back, thereby also endangering the material basis of their 'Aryan' business partners.[112]

Boycott appeals from the National Socialists only found an echo among the minority of convinced antisemites, the core of National Socialist functionaries and parts of the population which, like officials, were particularly susceptible to social pressure. As mentioned, the calls for a boycott also fell on fertile soil among middle-class retailers, traders and craftsmen, a section of the population in which anti-semitism was particularly virulent. However, the extent to which other motives were decisive in making the majority of the population ignore the boycott – resistance to antisemitism, compassion or outright sympathy, economic self-interest, long-standing business relations, customer loyalty, habit, the particularly high quality or cheap range of goods offered – cannot now be reconstructed or evaluated precisely. Even on the basis of a cautious estimate, the relative lack of impact that the boycotts had does not support the argument that the German population as a whole shared in the programme of an 'eliminationist antisemitism'.[113]

## Attempts to Rescue Property

The determination of many Jewish tradesmen in Hamburg to conserve their businesses was strengthened after 1933 by the fact that the National Socialist state made emigration, the only realistic alternative, so unattractive through taxes and compulsory levies that many Jews preferred to remain in Germany rather than to leave, which in many cases could only be done at the cost of confiscation of their property. Only at the beginning of the National Socialist period did the possibility of transferring large parts of one's personal assets abroad still exist. In 1934, the National Socialist state limited these transfers and began a process of ever-greater financial oppression. This was done by the use of two instruments.[114]

First, there was the Reich Flight Tax which the Brüning government introduced in 1931 on the grounds that it was needed to meet Germany's reparation payments – after 1933, this was steadily increased and became in practice a compulsory levy against Jews. Originally applied only to fortunes over 200,000 RM, in May 1934 it had been expanded to cover assets above 50,000 RM. In the last financial year of the Weimar Republic, 1932/33, income from the tax had amounted to approximately 0.9 million RM. Under the National Socialists, this had risen to 342 million RM for the financial year 1938/39. In February 1938, the register of 'non-Aryans subject to the Reich Flight Tax' at the Hamburg Finance Offices listed a total of eight hundred and seventy-seven persons.[115]

Secondly, the rescue of property was made more difficult by the so-called 'Disagio' on the transfer of capital: payment from the accounts of emigrés that had been blocked and moved to the German Gold Discount Bank (*Deutsche Golddiskontbank*, Dego). As late as January 1934, these payments amounted to approximately twenty percent of the total sums transferred. By August 1934 they had risen to sixty-five percent, in June 1935 to sixty-eight percent, in October 1936 to eighty-one percent and in June 1938 to ninety percent. From September 1939 the amount deducted was almost the whole of the account: ninety-six percent.[116] Because the 'Aryanisation' of Jewish property in most cases followed from the emigration of the property's former owner, the National Socialists were able to confiscate a major part of the assets of Jews through the Dego deduction alone.

After the November pogrom of 1938, the list of financial policies aimed at destroying the Jewish community through the 'Jewish capital levy' was completed by a compulsory contribution, at a value of 1 billion RM, levied in five bands up to a level of five percent of total assets owned and through a special emigration levy at a rate of twenty percent of the Reich Flight Tax which the Hamburg Gestapo demanded from every emigré.

Soon after 1933, it became clear that a fiscal policy had been instituted that targeted only Jews who were emigrating. It was a policy which was in contradiction to another fundamental goal of National Socialist anti-Jewish policy – to accelerate the emigration of Jews from Germany. This conflict of objectives within the regime was not completely resolved until 1938/39, when the regime introduced a double strategy of forcing emigration by terrorising Jews and by expropriating them. This meant that earlier on there were still limited opportunities to accommodate the rescue of Jewish property with the intentions of the National Socialist regime.

The 'Haavara agreement' of the summer of 1933 between the Reich Economics Ministry and a number of Jewish organisations was the most significant attempt to tie together the naturally heterogeneous interests of capital transfer and Jewish emigration.[117] This enabled Jewish emigrés going to Palestine to transfer their Reich Marks into Palestine Pounds. Sums were taken from an emigré's blocked RM account and used to finance the export of German goods to Palestine. The emigré was then refunded an equivalent in Palestine Pounds to the sum transferred in RM that Jewish importers had deposited for the purchase of German goods.

In Germany the 'Palestine Trust' (*Palästina-Treuhandstelle*, Paltreu) was established to send funds to Palestine by means of a 'Haavara' (Hebrew for transfer) arranged by the Anglo-Palestine Bank. From 1933–1939, fifty-two thousand German Jews emigrated to Palestine, and thanks to the 'Haavara Agreement' they were able to take 140 million RM with them. While the advantages of the agreement for the emigrés were obvious, the National Socialists signed up to the 'Haavara' procedure for three reasons: it undermined the calls for a general boycott of German exports, promoted the export economy and accelerated the emigration of Jews from Germany.[118]

The effect of the 'Haavara agreement' on the emigration of Jews from Hamburg and on the rescue of their property was only slight. According to the reports of the SD, in 1936 fourteen percent of Jewish emigrés from Hamburg went to Palestine, and in 1937 it was a mere eight and a half percent.[119] The proportion of Jewish business proprietors emigrating from Hamburg who chose to go to Palestine was even smaller, their preferred destinations being primarily the US and Great Britain.[120]

Besides the 'Haavara agreement', there were a few opportunities for organised property transfer. For instance, Jews could establish themselves as coffee growers in Brazil and use their Reich Marks to acquire land from 'Parana Plantations Ltd.', which used the money for buying German railway rolling stock.[121] Similarly emigrés could transfer up to 50,000 RM to Italy at short notice if they paid a Dego levy of forty percent.[122]

For Jewish emigration outside Palestine, another procedure for transferring funds was in operation from May 1937, organised by the 'General Trusteeship for Jewish Emigration Ltd.' (*Allgemeine Treuhandstelle für die jüdische Auswanderung GmbH*, Altreu).[123] From October 1937, the following basic rates applied to an Altreu transfer: a person was allowed to transfer a maximum of 30,000 RM and would lose between fifty percent and seventy-three percent of this in exchanging currency, while the maximum transfer sum for a family of four or more amounted to 50,000 RM with additional foreign exchange losses of fifty to seventy percent.[124] From September 1938, the transfer rates – already low – worsened further.[125] One part of the exchange gains was channelled into an Altreu fund at the Reich Representation of Jews in Germany, and this funded the emigration of Jews with no means of their own. Up until June 1938 three million Reich Marks were received by the Altreu fund, enabling 2,500 poor Jews to emigrate. At least 2,100 Jews were helped to emigrate by the 'small capitalist and middle-class transfer' operation of the Altreu, the maximum amount that could be transferred being 50,000 RM.[126] Using these figures to calculate the number of emigrés for the one-and-a-half year period up to the outbreak of war would suggest a total of under ten thousand emigrated with assistance from the Altreu procedure. The significance of the Altreu for emigration and the transfer of property was therefore smaller than that of Paltreu/Haavara, with which it clashed fiercely over the use of foreign exchange income.[127] Moreover, the Altreu procedure cut out the mass of Jewish company owners in Hamburg because the limits on the sums which could be transferred meant it was attractive only for people with small estates and – through the Altreu fund – for emigrés with no substantial means of their own.

The success which other organisations experienced in rescuing Jewish property cannot be accurately reconstructed because of the paucity of historical sources. For instance, we have little material on the 'Society for the Promotion of Economic Interests of Jews Living or Formerly Resident in Germany Ltd.' (*Gesellschaft zur Förderung wirtschaftlicher Interessen von in Deutschland wohnhaften oder wohnhaft gewesenen Juden m.b.H*, known by the abbreviation FWI), founded in 1934, which focused on trying to organise property exchanges[128] with which German Jews could acquire properties abroad.

In view of the limited opportunities for the organised transfer of property, some Jewish company proprietors attempted to move parts of their property abroad separately so as to save it from the threat of confiscation. The range of businessmen choosing this approach stretched from jewellers, who exchanged their property for high-value jewels and fled with them abroad,[129] through emigrés who smuggled jewellery, cash or valuable pieces of artwork amongst the possessions they were allowed to take,[130] to exporters who let earnings from foreign exchange accounts remain where they were without offering it to the Reichsbank for purchase.[131]

One Jewish export firm from Hamburg invited emigrés to invest their Reich Marks in foreign accounts at a rate of 1:4, thus obtaining a more favourable exchange rate than they would have according to the official restrictions on their accounts. The export firm used the Reich Mark surplus of seventy-five percent to subsidise its own exports. It had a high reputation among the supervisory state offices because its Reich Mark subsidies enabled them to sell even the less valuable German exports abroad without taking advantage of state support via the additional export procedures. The illegal transfer of capital collapsed when a 1938 company audit uncovered foreign accounts worth over a million Reich Marks which had no corresponding accounts in Germany.[132]

Such cases of 'illegal' property transfers were relentlessly pursued by customs and foreign exchange investigators, although the tax and levy policy of the National Socialist state represented injustice dressed up in legal garb, manoeuvring Jewish property owners into a corner which provoked them into looking for 'illegal' solutions. It was not the 'German people's property' that Jews 'sold' abroad, as an inspector from the Hamburg Customs Investigation Unit put it in a report on the enquiry,[133] but family inheritance and the fruits earned by individuals during a long life of work. At least in some cases, they were attempting to save these assets because they would otherwise be expropriated without compensation.

In a landmark judgment in 1953 the Hamburg Supreme Administrative Court ruled that the 'illegal' modes of saving property were justified measures of self-defence, because German Jews, unlike non-Jewish Germans, were in practice forced into exile, not wishing to meet with 'a completely uncertain personal fate'. 'If this group of people on the one hand was forced to emigrate and thereby to take their assets abroad, they were equally forcibly subjected to exchange control regulations, the Reich Flight Tax and the other charges levied on the transfer of capital, and this state attack on the property of those affected by the National Socialist persecution was thus not justified and not in accordance with the bases of law and order. Those victims who protected themselves against this attack on their property were acting in self-defence in the sense of § 53 StGB.'[134]

Even if the form of the 'illegal' rescue of property was probably more wide-spread than appears the case from the documents relating to the enquiry by the customs and foreign exchange investigation unit, it was nevertheless clear that it was only practiced by a small minority of the Jews of Hamburg. The many exchange controls on Jewish companies implemented in 1937 resulted in most Jewish company proprietors adhering with alarming correctness to all of the repressive conditions imposed by the National Socialist exchange control regulations. They did without any secret capital transfers and the majority allowed themselves to be robbed in the course of their emigration.[135] There is no need to explain why Jews took 'illegal' paths to save their property, but rather to explain why it was that the large majority did not, and instead obeyed the laws of a state which branded them as second class, continually instigating new rafts of measures to steal their money. In the diaries of the Dresden novelist Victor Klemperer, an important motive for this behaviour becomes clear, namely to give the lie to anti-semitic propaganda by precise adherence to the laws and thereby to defend their identity as Germans against attributions made from other countries.[136] A representative example of this type of approach is the case of Dr Ernst Loewenberg, Chair of the Committee of Representatives of the German Israelite Community, who reacted with confusion when his sons held up those who smuggled property out of Germany as 'heroes' and themselves smuggled packets of meat into Germany after a trip abroad. Plagued by moral and pedagogical doubts, he wrote in his memoirs: 'There is no injustice in a country in which there is no justice. But what is to become of children who have grown up with such relative concepts of right and wrong?'[137]

## The Political Initiatives of Hamburg Banker Max Warburg 1933-38

The Hamburg bank, M.M. Warburg & Co., played a crucial role in all forms of the organised transfer of property by Jewish emigrés. Almost seventy-five percent of all emigré transfers through the 'Haavara agreement' were handled by the bank. With capital funds of 18 million RM and a balance sheet total of 120 million RM it was one of the ten largest private banks in the German Reich at the time the National Socialists came to power.[138]

A significant factor in the bank's great importance for the foreign trade of Hamburg was its international connections. Many importers in Hamburg used M.M. Warburg & Co. for the commercial credits they needed. In 1933, the bank was represented on 108 supervisory boards of firms in Hamburg and elsewhere; among these were firms as important as HAPAG, Beiersdorf Co., Blohm & Voß, Klöckner-Werke and Rudolph Karstadt Co. Before 1933, Max Warburg, the leading partner in the bank, was as influential in the economic and financial policy making of the Reich as he was in that of Hamburg itself – a member of the Chamber of Commerce of Hamburg, the General Council of the Reichsbank and the Reich Underwriters' Syndicate, and advisor to the Hamburg Finance Deputation.

Warburg lost all of his most important positions and supervisory board memberships after the National Socialists came to power except his seat on the Reich Underwriters' Syndicate. The number of clients banking with M.M. Warburg & Co. went down from 5,241 in 1930 to 1,875 at the end of 1933 – essentially because of changes in the economy and in foreign trade, not because of political factors – and only slowly climbed again in the years that followed. While the significance of the bank for the economy of Hamburg declined after 1933, for the Jewish community as a whole, and the Jewish economic sector in particular, it took on a central role. After 1933 it won over many Jewish customers and was also committed to the sale of their enterprises and to rescuing their property.

As Chair of the 'Aid Association of German Jews' (*Hilfsverein der deutschen Juden*), Max Warburg steadily broadened his (originally mainly charitable) commitments to the Jewish community and increasingly acted as a representative of the political interests of the harried Jewish minority in Germany. In his person various German Jewish traditions combined. A German-Jewish patriot and at the same time a citizen of the world, Warburg defended the legal position of Jews in Germany and underlined their solidarity with their fatherland in spite of the discrimination they faced from the National Socialists. He also promoted Jewish emigration from Germany, including to Palestine, which he – unlike many Zionists – did not see as the territory of a future Jewish nation state but as a model of peaceful coexistence between different religions and cultures. According to his political vision there had to be a '*pénétration pacifique*', 'without taking territorial possession in a political sense. Alongside Arabs, Catholics, Protestants, the Jews would live together on the same soil in the Holy Land, not as rulers but also not as [mere] subjects',[139] as Warburg put it in December 1934.

Just as Warburg's thinking about the future of the Jews moved between the two poles of self-assertion in Germany and emigration abroad, so too did the political initiatives by which he sought to improve the situation of Jews in Germany after 1933 through reaching a settlement with the National Socialist regime. In his memoirs, published privately in 1952, Warburg only hinted at this discreetly.[140] He may well have found the experience of illusions destroyed and continual failure too depressing to expand upon in all their details, either for a wider public or for his own satisfaction. Nevertheless, they are certainly worthy of the attention of historical researchers because of his efforts to reason with, and to moderate, National Socialist anti-Jewish policy in helping Jews in Germany to secure their legal position. The collapse of this attempt casts a revealing light on National Socialist anti-Jewish policy as a whole, which was, at most, prepared and equipped for temporary tactical concessions, but not for the acceptance of binding rules.

Max Warburg's contacts with various representatives of the National Socialist regime began in March 1933 when Dr Otto Wagener, a member of the NSDAP leadership, visited him on Hitler's behalf and in an informal conversation sought to sound out the attitude of German Jews and to gauge the opportunities for and limits to communication with them.[141] The conversation took place at a time when the National Socialists were isolated internationally and faced many boycott movements. The regime hoped that the German Jews would support their efforts to moderate the impact of their antisemitic policies abroad. The discussion focused on the anti-Jewish measures which had been advanced in the NSDAP's manifesto. As expected, Wagener and Warburg reached neither an agreement nor even an understanding. According to Wagener's report, Warburg expressed understanding for occupational restrictions on Jews, but pressed for supporting measures for a professional restructuring and rejected the forced resettlement of the so-called 'Eastern Jews' which the National Socialists had urged. The discussion between Wagener and Warburg – though it was originally the National Socialists' initiative to make contact with a prominent German Jew – was revived only episodically, as the fears of the National Socialists about the extent of the anti-German boycotts, and about what they saw as the power of 'world Jewry' behind the boycotts, soon evaporated. Consequently, the new regime's interest in further conversations or even agreements rapidly declined. The conversation – at least for Warburg – may have kindled the illusion that it might be possible to reach a binding agreement with the National Socialists that would moderate the persecution of the Jews in Germany.

In Spring 1933, Warburg took part in an initiative with other leading Jewish personalities aimed at winning over non-Jewish business leaders to a joint attempt to water down the anti-Jewish policy of the National Socialists. The initiative was launched by Max Warburg, his partner Carl Melchior and former Undersecretary of State, Hans Schäffer, and aimed to use the fears of many non-Jewish entrepreneurs of the National Socialists' attempts to reorganise the German economy so as to retain as many economic opportunities for Jews as possible.[142] This led to the formulation of two memoranda and a meeting on 28 June 1933 which included the Chairman of the Reich Association of German Industry, Gustav Krupp von Bohlen, Carl Friedrich von Siemens and Kurt Schmitt, who was appointed Reich Economics Minister by Hitler a day later.

The memoranda deplored the National Socialists' ongoing interventions in the economy, which endangered the economic livelihood of both Jews and non-

Jews, pressed for opportunities for professional training and retraining (so as to counter the unbalanced concentration of Jews in the independent professions on a structural level) and also did not exclude the possibility of a directed emigration of Jews from the country. Implicit in both memoranda, which were heavily influenced by Max Warburg, was a rejection of racial antisemitism, attributing the existing distribution of Jews in different occupations to historical and cultural causes.

In the event, the joint initiative of Jewish and non-Jewish businessmen did not materialise, the memoranda disappeared into the files and the political authorities were never approached. The reasons for this can only be guessed at. Did the participants fail to agree on how to proceed together? Peter Hayes conjectures that they saw such interventions as obsolete once the National Socialists' anti-Jewish policy appeared to take a more moderate direction in mid-1933.[143] Indeed, Hitler declared on 6 July 1933 that the National Socialist revolution was officially 'concluded', appointed a participant in the scheme, Kurt Schmitt, to head the Reich Economics Ministry, and suggested the possibility of a controlled emigration through the 'Haavara agreement' which did not simply pillage the financial resources of the emigrés.

A problem for this interpretation, however, lies in the fact that in the summer of 1933 Max Warburg still believed the situation of the Jews to be intolerable and continued in his efforts to influence non-Jewish businessmen to oppose the anti-Jewish policy of the National Socialist regime. For him, the initiative was by no means one 'of the last attempts in this direction'.[144] Its three central elements – unhindered economic operations, promotion of Jewish professional training and retraining, and organised emigration under acceptable conditions – continued to form the basis of his political activities until 1938 and he continued to hope for a *modus vivendi* with the political leaders in Germany until the end.

In August 1933, Warburg turned to Emil Helfferich, who, as Chair of the Supervisory Board of HAPAG and Chair of the Hamburg-Bremen East Asia Association, was one of the most influential sympathisers of the NSDAP among the business class of Hamburg. Helfferich then reported the drift of the conversation to the mayor, Carl Vincent Krogmann, who noted in his diary on 25 August:

> He told me, very interesting, that Herr Warburg had gone to him and said to him that he spoke in the name of all Jewish associations and communities. He then asked whether it would be possible to arrive at some agreement with the NSDAP. He completely understood that the Jews could no longer be active in the administration and could no longer lead the large enterprises, but one had still to grant them some rights. The misery in Jewish circles would be quite extraordinarily large. Larger sums would be collected in England, but if things continued like this the Jews here in Germany would all starve. They were again trying in England to settle large numbers

of Jews in Palestine, but that could take place only to a limited extent. Herr Helfferich thought one ought to try at least once to bring about a discussion with leading National Socialists. He thought that the Jews would now be ready for comprehensive concessions.[145]

It is unlikely that Krogmann's diary notes reproduced Warburg's remarks literally. Nevertheless, the way in which Helfferich and Krogmann received them suggests the problematic aspects of Warburg's initiative, which clearly carried the risk of reinforcing antisemitic stereotypes. To men like Helfferich and Krogmann the Jews seemed like a strictly led collectivity, ready at any time to be led, which by their own admission had placed its representatives in an untenable position. Now – under political pressure – they were ready to make the 'comprehensive concessions' necessary. Following this kind of logic the antisemitic policy of the National Socialists had proven justified and the Jews had been made to give way. To follow up on Warburg's initiative appeared in this perspective to be an issue of compassion – so that the Jews would not 'all starve'. There was another lesson to be drawn from this, however: if political pressure had led to a compliant attitude once, did it not follow that continuing pressure would lead to further 'concessions'?

In this antisemitic mode of thought, Mayor Krogmann may have been induced to answer Warburg's initiative with public professions of racial antisemitism. Emil Helfferich described Krogmann's antisemitic fanaticism in his memoirs as 'political rectitude', which had disappointed some observers, 'including Max Warburg, who had expected him to be compromising'.[146] In a letter to Helfferich, Warburg referred to Krogmann's speech of 9 March 1935, delivered to the East Asia Association, writing that he was 'shaken … that that kind of speech is endured even in Hamburg and by prominent figures in Hamburg'.[147] He rejected Krogmann's remarks about the allegedly 'humane' treatment of the Jews in Germany, instead characterising their situation as a 'cold pogrom'. Despite all of his disappointments Warburg still believed in a future for Jews even in National Socialist Germany and closed his letter to Helfferich with the observation that it was 'characterised by love but also by concern for Germany'.[148]

Although Helfferich never replied to him, and despite the fact that he had no success with his initiatives, Warburg continued to seek to engage in a dialogue with Germany's political leaders in subsequent years. According to his own testimony, he found his partners in dialogue primarily among those representatives of the middle class collaborating with the National Socialists who had entered into government in 1933, but had continually lost influence since then. Besides Franz von Papen, Warburg met frequently with Schacht (President of the Reichsbank and Reich Economics Minister), who continued to play a kind of protective role for M.M. Warburg & Co. until 1937/38, but who could not, and would not, contain the antisemitic policy of the regime[149] because his own views were coloured by a bourgeois-conservative salon antisemitism. According to Warburg, Schacht had told him: 'I am not so uncultured as to be an antisemite. But there are many Jews whom I do not like.'[150] Nevertheless, the contact between the two was so close that Schacht entrusted internal information about the regime to him such as the illegal foreign exchange affairs of Propaganda Minister Goebbels.[151]

In about 1935/36, Warburg tried to negotiate the creation of an international liquidation bank with Schacht and the Reich Economics Ministry, the capital for the bank being supplied by American and British Jews.[152] As was the case with the 'Haavara agreement', German export goods would be bought in exchange for the transfer of the property of Jewish emigrés from Germany. Warburg's plan was based on a yearly capital sum of 250 million RM, which would clear the way for a multilateral clearing agreement within a few years, enabling more than one hundred thousand Jews to emigrate. Warburg's project was ill-starred from the outset. At the beginning of January 1936, the American and British press published the plan and thereby mobilised the opponents of the project on both sides. American Jews refused to give the National Socialists material rewards for their antisemitism through the promotion of German exports. Nor was there ever a consensus within the Reich Representation of German Jews over the objectives of the project because the representatives of Zionist organisations were concentrating exclusively on emigration to Palestine.

Despite the evident disunity of the Jewish organisations, and the fact that the antisemitic stereotype of a 'world Jewry' acting in unity had been shown to be a chimera, the Foreign Office and the Reich Propaganda Ministry suspected that the plan hid an international Jewish move to damage the German Reich financially. On 28 January 1936, the German Embassy in London transmitted a report to both ministries from a London 'source' that claimed: 'The Jews hope by this means to impoverish Germany to such extent that she will subsequently be brought to the verge of bankruptcy.'[153]

Grown mistrustful on account of reports like this, the Foreign Office and the Propaganda Ministry began to make enquiries placing the Reich Economics Ministry under pressure. Deputy Undersecretary Pohl in the Reich Economics Ministry, who had often met with Warburg, appeased them by explaining that the conversations were of a 'provisional and in any case a non-committal character'.[154] Schacht indicated to Warburg that he no longer had sufficient political room for manoeuvre to make agreements of this order of magnitude.[155] Warburg's emigration plans had thus been shattered by interdepartmental disputes within the National Socialist polycracy and the rejectionist attitude of potential Jewish financiers in the US. With the founding of the 'Altreu' in 1937, the plans could only be carried out on a smaller scale.

Although Warburg's initiatives had all met with failure, in 1937 he embarked upon a new – and at the same time final – attempt to influence National Socialist policy towards the Jews. Through his former party colleague Walther Dauch, a former Reichstag delegate of the DVP who was responsible for the Kaiser-Wilhelm-Gesellschaft in Berlin, Warburg sought to arrange a meeting with Reich Interior Minister Frick in order to discuss with him a plan for further Jewish emigration.[156] Although Frick's attitude was 'rather negative', a discussion with his Undersecretary of State, Dr Wilhelm Stuckart, materialised on 10 August 1937, which Herbert Göring, a cousin of Hermann Göring, had arranged for Warburg.[157]

Wilhelm Stuckart, who led the 'Constitution and Legislation' department in the Reich Interior Ministry and who held the rank of an *SS-Standartenführer* from 1936,[158] had made a name for himself in the designing of anti-Jewish policy as a commentator on the Nuremberg race laws.[159] What induced a pronounced antisemite like Stuckart, who later took part in the 'Wannsee conference' as a representative of the Interior Ministry and who was thus involved in the so-called 'Final Solution of the Jewish Question', to wish to hold a meeting with a leading representative of Germany's Jews to discuss anti-Jewish policy? The answer was given in a memorandum that Warburg sent to Stuckart two weeks after the meeting. The memorandum suggested that on both sides the focus of the conversation had been 'to use all means to promote the emigration of the Jews from Germany'.[160] For a long time various institutions of the National Socialist regime – including the Reich Interior Ministry – had striven to develop a fundamental approach to the Jews that would have the appearance of 'respectability', in contrast to the 'mob antisemitism' of the National Socialist party grassroots that was deemed to lack vision.[161] This had led the security service of the SS, the SD, to press early on for the forced emigration of the Jews,[162] which Stuckart was evidently also considering.

It appears that any commonalities between Stuckart and Warburg were probably quickly exhausted, since what Warburg said in their two-hour discussion on 10 August 1937 corresponded closely to his previous initiatives and amounted to a fundamental revision of National Socialist anti-Jewish policy. Given that at the end of their conversation Stuckart asked Warburg once more to put his remarks in writing, Warburg's approach was probably similar to the ideas in the abovementioned memorandum of 23 August that Warburg had written with the assistance of his counsel, Dr Kurt Sieveking.[163]

As in all of his political initiatives from Spring 1933 onwards, Warburg pressed once more in this memorandum for appropriate opportunities for professional training for Jewish emigrés – in non-Jewish businesses as well as Jewish ones – so as to improve their career prospects in the countries to which they were going. In order to prevent the emigrés from losing too much of their money or property when emigrating, the upper limit on the movement of property in calculating the Reich Flight Tax, which was fixed at 50,000 RM, ought to be raised and a part of the tax revenues should be used to finance the emigration costs of poor Jews. Because material support for emigration through the Jewish aid organisations was coupled to the emigrés' solvency, Warburg urged a whole catalogue of measures to promote this, ranging from the removal of gift tax to allowing Jews to participate unhindered in commercial affairs. Furthermore, the restrictive conditions for Jews to get passports should also be loosened so that personal 'exploratory journeys' could be made to their intended host countries to sound out the prospects for employment there. Finally, Warburg urged the official recognition of the Reich Representation of Jews in Germany as an interlocutor for the government. In advocating a 'methodically organised, commercially funded and not-too-rushed emigration', Warburg raised the prospect of financial backing through an English loan syndicate at a value of 1.5 million pounds sterling.

Warburg had endeavored to find a solution for the inherent contradictions of National Socialist anti-Jewish policy, simultaneously pursuing the aims of radically destroying the Jewish community, plundering it financially and accelerating emigration to the widest range of destinations possible. Warburg's vision of a 'rational' emigration plan offered material incentives for emigration and did away with the existing restrictions. At the same time, Warburg rejected any form of forced emigration and pressed for the protection of the property and financial affairs of all Jews who wished to remain in Germany, targeting his project at a controlled migration of only part of the community.

Warburg himself judged the chances that his project would succeed rather sceptically. Following the meeting with Stuckart he told Walther Dauch that the meeting was 'satisfying in so far as I could say everything that I had to say and also got the feeling that I have been correctly understood. Whether all that leads to practical results, however, I cannot judge. In any case I feel relieved.'[164] These were not the words of a man who was completely convinced of the prospects that his plan would succeed. On the same day, Warburg telephoned Reich Economics Minister Schacht to tell him of the meeting, receiving the reply: 'Thank you for the information and I would like to congratulate you on this initiative, which is quite right.'[165]

Stuckart reacted to Warburg's initiative in a most dilatory fashion. This was not least due to the fact that by 1937 the authority of the Reich Interior Ministry in the area of anti-Jewish policy had already been so badly eroded that it could 'neither exercise a determining influence formally nor in terms of content', as Dieter Rebentisch described the powers of the Reich Interior Ministry.[166] In a three-page summary of his plan, Warburg himself linked its realisation to nothing less than the agreement of the Deputy of the Führer, the DAF, the Reich

Food Estate, the Reich Interior, Economics, Finance and Labour Ministries as well as the Reich Minister for Science, Education and Popular Education and the Commissioner for the Four Year Plan. Quite apart from this, a number of important decision-makers in policy on Jewish affairs were missing from this list, focused as it was on ministers: Himmler as *Reichsführer* SS and Chief of the German Police and Hitler as the real centre of power. Moreover, among those institutions that were mentioned, probably none of them would have pushed for the end of economic discrimination against the Jews or for security for their material well-being.

Moreover, Warburg's initiative of 1937/38 came at a time when the policy towards Jews was finally developing in the opposite direction, and the economic discrimination against the Jews intensified drastically. On 27 November 1937, Warburg sent two further memorandums to Stuckart on the 'Position and Possibilities for the Emigration of Jews from Germany to Countries Overseas' and on the 'Promotion of the Emigration of Jews Without Much Money'. On this occasion he listed a whole range of recently introduced measures which in practice countered the prerequisites of his basic aim to secure the material welfare of the Jews in Germany: reductions in quotas for raw materials for Jewish companies, the exclusion of Jews from professional associations in the commercial sphere, attacks by party and police authorities, 'unofficial' boycotts, withdrawal of trading licences and authentication cards, dismissals and forced sales of businesses.[167]

Max Warburg's request for a further conversation was ducked by Stuckart. On 4 January 1938, Stuckart wrote to tell him that he was not in a position 'due to extremely heavy work obligations' to name a discussion date in the near future. However, the specific questions which he had promised to deal with in August 1937 were 'all being dealt with'.[168] Though Stuckart raised the vague prospect of a further conversation in February 1938, it seems not to have come to anything. So ended this last attempt by Warburg to counter the increasing radicalisation of anti-Jewish policy through agreements with the National Socialists, and thereby to alleviate the situation of the German Jews.

Max Warburg's initiatives, for which he had more than once gone to the limits of self-respect, collapsed primarily for two reasons. His endeavours to steer the anti-Jewish policy of the National Socialist regime along more moderate lines and to create a secured legal status for the German Jews did not come to terms with the particularly racist quality of National Socialist antisemitism, reflected not only by the worldview of the 'Führer'[169] but also in a wider sense by the National Socialist movement, where antisemitism played an important role in the ideological and emotional integration of the National Socialists. Already in *Mein Kampf*, Hitler had presented this view with unmistakable clarity: 'There can be no pacts with the Jews, but only the harsh either/or.'[170] Those who dehumanised the Jews and saw them as nothing more than an incarnation of evil, as the enemy *par excellence* and as a 'parasite on the people'[171] were hardly going to accept agreements on principle with them, and anyone who urged moderation was denounced by these fanatics as 'traitors' to the principles of the National Socialist *Weltanschauung.* This was of course the experience of bourgeois collaborators like Reich Economics Minister Schacht, who were soon so inescapably caught up in the ideological pitfalls of the National Socialist dictatorship that in practice they had become agents of anti-Jewish policy without being able to exercise real influence over it. In the end Schacht informed Warburg with resignation that Hitler had many times reacted to his reservations against anti-Jewish policy by flying into a 'mad rage'. He could do no more since 'his tongue had now been burnt often enough'.[172]

However, Warburg's initiatives did obstruct the polycratic tendencies of the National Socialist regime, tendencies which led not to stabilisation of policy making but, through internal competition, conflict and an anarchic distribution of powers to the cumulative radicalisation of the system.[173] With respect to anti-Jewish policy there was no prospect of gaining a consensus among the various decision-makers – let alone one arrived at on the basis of moderation and restraint – particularly since Hitler avoided such directives and tended to prefer radical 'solutions'. Since the regime was trying to rid itself of all normative foundations in nearly every policy field, it was virtually inconceivable that it could have been prepared to agree to a normative moderation in the ideologically loaded area of anti-Jewish policy.

The National Socialists were only ready to make temporary concessions, not to establish lasting arrangements. The failure of Warburg's initiatives did not invalidate the moral basis of his approach, but clarified the narrow limits which the National Socialist dictatorship set on all attempts to make agreements that might erect dams of humanity against the barbaric onslaught against the Jews.

# Notes

1. In 1933 the number of Jews in Berlin was 160,564, in Frankfurt am Main 26,158, in Breslau 20,202, in Hamburg 16,885 (in the city) and 16,973 (in the state), in Cologne 14,816 and in Leipzig 11,564. See *Statistik des Deutschen Reiches*, Vol. 451, Issue 5, Berlin, 1936, p. 10. On the development of the Jewish community in Hamburg from the nineteenth century to the collapse of the National Socialist regime, see the instructive overview by Ina Lorenz, 'Die jüdische Gemeinde Hamburg 1860–1943. Kaiserreich-Weimarer Republik-NS-Staat', in Herzig, ed., *Juden*, Hamburg, 1991, pp. 77–100.
2. Cf. Table 1, Appendix.
3. R.E. May, 'Die Entwicklung der jüdischen Mischehen und ihre Wirkung auf die jüdische Gemeinschaft (1932)', published by Lorenz, *Juden in Hamburg*, p. 68.
4. See Lorenz, *Juden in Hamburg*, p. XLVIff.
5. See Table 2, Appendix.
6. See Lorenz, *Juden in Hamburg*, p. LVIII.
7. Cf. 'Die Juden und jüdischen Mischlinge nach der Rassenzugehörigkeit', in *Aus Hamburgs Verwaltung und Wirtschaft*, Special Issue 5, August 1941, p. 20.
8. See Tables 4 and 5, Appendix.
9. According to the census of 16 June 1933, in the Reich as a whole 19.1% of Jews in employment worked in the industrial sector, in Hamburg only 10.26%. The figure for Jews working in trade and transport across the Reich as a whole was 52.5%, in Hamburg 57.65%. See *Statistik des Deutschen Reiches*, Vol. 451, Issue 5, Berlin, 1936, p. 25.
10. The average proportion of those employed in agriculture and forestry across the Reich was 21%, and among the Jewish population only 1%. In the industrial and artisan sectors the figures were 38.8% and 19.1%, while in the trade and transport sector the Jewish population was many times more that of the Reich as a whole at 52.5% to 16.9%. Cf. *Statistik des Deutschen Reiches*, Vol. 451, Issue 5, Berlin, 1936, p. 25.
11. See Tables 4 and 5, Appendix.
12. Cf. Table 6, Appendix.
13. See Table 12, Appendix.
14. Communication from the Hamburg *Handelskammer* to the *Geheime Staatspolizei* (Secret State Police), 8 October 1937, *Archiv Handelskammer*, 100.B.1.7.
15. See Table 9, Appendix.
16. See Table 9, Appendix.
17. *Hamburger Tageblatt*, 2 December 1938.
18. Barkai, *Boykott*, p. 123.
19. Unpublished autobiography of Dr Ernst Loewenberg (private collection), pp. 46, 81.
20. See Table 11, Appendix.
21. *Dokumente zur Geschichte der Frankfurter Juden*, p. 183ff.
22. Krüger, *Lösung*, p. 44.
23. Barkai, *Boykott*, pp. 14, 207.
24. In contrast to the figures given by Barkai, Genschel gave a far lower estimation of the decrease in the number of Jewish businesses. In parallel with the developments of emigration figures, he calculated the proportion of 'Aryanised' businesses at the end of 1937 at 25%. However, he gives no evidence for his evaluation. Cf. Genschel, *Verdrängung*, p. 136.
25. See Kratzsch, *'Entjudung'*; Toury, *Textilunternehmer*, p. 243; Händler-Lachmann and Werther, *Vergessene Geschäfte*, p. 129.
26. This shows the comparison made by Alex Bruns-Wüstefeld between the cities of Heidelberg (1933 c. 80,000 inhabitants), Göttingen (c. 50,000 inhabitants) and Marburg (c. 30,000

inhabitants). Whereas in Heidelberg at the beginning of 1938 53% of all Jewish businesses that had been in existence in 1933 continued to trade, in Göttingen the figure was 44% and in Marburg 31%. Cf. Bruns-Wüstefeld, *Lohnende Geschäfte*, pp. 120–125.

27.  See Table 10, Appendix.

28.  Similar conclusions are also reached by Toury for Jewish textile enterprises in Baden und Württemberg. Cf. Toury, *Textilunternehmer*, p. 140f.

29.  Those bodies which referred to this aspect included the Hamburg Chamber of Commerce in an inventory of October 1937 treating 'Jewish influence in Hamburg industry', *Archiv Handelskammer*, 100.B.1.7.

30.  Hans J. Robinsohn, 'Ein Versuch, sich zu behaupten', in *Tradition*, 3, Issue 4/1958, pp. 197–206.

31.  Statement by Hans Robinsohn in *Archiv WgA LGHH*, Z 3511-1, p. 415.

32.  Robinsohn, *Versuch*, p. 200.

33.  Ibid., p. 198.

34.  Ibid., p. 201.

35.  Ibid., p. 201f.

36.  Statement by Hans Robinsohn in *Archiv WgA LGHH*, Z 3511-1, p. 416.

37.  'Eres' was the colloquial abbreviation of the company name (Eres = R.S. = *Rappolt & Söhne*).

38.  StAHH, *Staatsamt*, 106, communication from *Rappolt & Söhne* to the *Reichs- und Preußische Wirtschaftsministerium*, 22 May 1936.

39.  *Archiv M.M. Warburg & Co.*, file marked '*Nicht durch das Sekretariat*', *Rappolt & Söhne* file, memorandum of 4 October 1935.

40.  See communication from Hamburg *Vertretung* in Berlin to the *Staatsamt*, 11 June 1936, StAHH, *Staatsamt*, 106.

41.  The outcome of this conflict, in which the *Reichswirtschaftsministerium* was also involved, cannot be reconstructed with any precision. On this incident, see the confidential communication from the Hamburg *Vertretung* in Berlin to the *Staatsamt* of 6 September 1935, StAHH, *Staatsamt*, 106.

42.  See BAP, *Reichswirtschaftsministerium*, 8646 (Adefa-Stiftung). In 1934 Adefa replaced the adjective '*deutsch*' with '*deutscharisch*' – 'German Aryan' instead of just 'German' – but in November 1938 it returned to its original title. In August 1939, Adefa was dissolved after the last Jewish textile enterprises had been 'Aryanised' or liquidated.

43.  Toury, *Textilunternehmer*, p. 250.

44.  *Hamburger Tageblatt*, 4 February 1938.

45.  Cf. the letter from one representative, Bernhard Eidmann, to the Ludwig Bertram/Gera Co. of 13 February 1936, StAHH, *Staatsamt*, 106.

46.  Talk by *Gauwirtschaftsberater* Otto Jung, in connection with the opening of the fifteenth Adefa fall show in 1937, *Archiv Handelskammer*, 100.B.1.11.

47.  Cf. Kratzsch, *Gauwirtschaftsapparat*, p. 140f.

48.  StAHH, *Staatsamt*, 106, communication from *Rappolt & Söhne* to the *Reichs- und Preußische Wirtschaftsministerium* of 22 May 1936.

49.  See the detailed records of turnover in the *Archiv M.M. Warburg & Co.*, file marked '*Nicht durch das Sekretariat*', *Rappolt & Co.*

50.  Cf. the communication from Rappolt's successors, *Rappolt & Söhne (Nachf.)*, to the *Amtsgericht Hamburg* of 26 August 1941, by which they requested an exception be granted enabling them to continue to style the company '*Eres KG*'. *Archiv Handelskammer*, 100.B.1.31.

51.  Citation as in *Archiv M.M. Warburg & Co.*, 22056 (*Campbell & Co.*), note on the 'Aryanization of an optical business in Hamburg', October 1938.

52. Citation as in StAHH, *Senatskanzlei-Präsidialabteilung*, 1939 SII 28, communication from H. Droege/A. Kreusler to the *Reichsstatthalter*, 7 January 1939.

53. Citation as in ibid.

54. Dietz Bering, *Kampf um Namen. Bernhard Weiß gegen Joseph Goebbels*, Stuttgart, 1991.

55. StAHH, *Sozialbehörde I*, WA 58.53, p. 7f., statement by Carl Rhein and Walter Müller of 11 June 1934.

56. See *Amtlicher Anzeiger* of 26 May 1934, StAHH, *Sozialbehörde I*, WA 58.53.

57. Citation in StAHH, *Sozialbehörde II*, O 21.50.3, notes of 6 June 1934.

58. Ibid., communication from *Orthozentrische Kneifer GmbH* to the *Gesundheits- und Fürsorgebehörde* of 4 July 1934.

59. StAHH, *Sozialbehörde I*, WA 58.53, p. 7f., statement by Carl Rhein and Walter Müller of 11 June 1934.

60. StAHH, *Sozialbehörde I*, WA 58.53, note of 1 April 1935.

61. Ibid., inventory of 11 September 1936.

62. Cf. Table 10, Appendix.

63. See inventory of income in the *Archiv M.M. Warburg & Co.*, 22056 (*Campbell & Co.*), note on the 'Aryanisation of an optical business in Hamburg', October 1938, p. 4.

64. On the 'Aryanization' of Campbell & Co. see below, Ch. VI.

65. StAHH, *Jüdische Gemeinden*, 360b, p. 52, minutes of the 30th session of the *Repräsantantenkollegium* of 21 June 1933.

66. See in this connnection Barkai, *Boykott*, pp. 57–59, 91–96; S. Adler-Rudel, *Jüdische Selbsthilfe unter dem Naziregime 1933–1939*, Tübingen, 1974; Clemens Vollnhals, 'Jüdische Selbsthilfe bis 1938', in Wolfgang Benz, ed., *Die Juden in Deutschland 1933–1945*, Munich, 1988, pp. 314–411.

67. *Hamburger Familienblatt für die israelitischen Gemeinden Hamburg, Altona, Wandsbek und Harburg* (hereafter: *Hamburger Familienblatt*), 20 September 1933, p. 2. The *Israelitische Vorschuß-Institut* had been operating in Hamburg since 1816.

68. See Lorenz, *Juden in Hamburg*, p. 1074ff.

69. *Hilfe und Aufbau in Hamburg April 1933 bis Dezember 1934*, published by the *Hilfsausschuß der vereinigten jüdischen Organisationen Hamburgs*, Hamburg, 1935.

70. Leo Lippmann, '... daß ich wie ein guter Deutscher empfinde und handele.' *Zur Geschichte der Deutsch-Israelitischen Gemeinde in Hamburg in der Zeit vom Herbst 1935 bis zum Ende 1942*, Hamburg, 1994, p. 51.

71. *Hilfe und Aufbau in Hamburg*, pp. 20–22.

72. Lippmann, *Deutscher*, p. 52.

73. Autobiography of Dr Ernst Loewenberg (private collection), p. 40.

74. Ibid.

75. Figures according to *Hamburger Familienblatt*, 17 May 1934, p. 1.

76. Adler-Rudel, *Selbsthilfe*, p. 123.

77. On the activities of the VSHG see *Hamburger Familienblatt*, 25 January 1934, p. 3; StAHH, *Jüdische Gemeinden* 360b, p. 62, enclosure 1 of 18 June 1933. Unfortunately no copy of the membership register was retained, as it could have provided more precise information on the trading structure of Jewish businesses in Hamburg.

78. StAHH, *Jüdische Gemeinden*, 325, p. 30.

79. *Hamburger Familienblatt*, 21 June 1934, p. 2.

80. '*Jüdische Verbundenheit im Wirtschaftsschicksal*', *Hamburger Familienblatt*, 25 July 1935.

81. StAHH, *Steuerverwaltung I*, Ia 50b, communication from the *Detaillistenkammer* (Retailers' Association) to the *Deputation für Handel, Schiffahrt und Gewerbe* (Trade, Shipping and Industry Deputation) of 14 September 1933.

82. StAHH, *Jüdische Gemeinden*, 297, Vol. 22, p. 93, minutes of the meeting of the board of the DIG of 17 September 1934.
83. Ibid., p. 132, minutes of the meeting of the board of 15 January 1935.
84. StAHH, *Jüdische Gemeinden*, 360b, p. 165, meeting of the *Repräsentantenkollegium* of 8 June 1936.
85. StAHH, *Jüdische Gemeinden*, 297, Vol. 22, p. 371, minutes of the meeting of the board of the DIG of 21 October 1936.
86. See Adler-Rudel, *Selbsthilfe*, pp. 161–165.
87. Information leaflet published by the *Reichsvertretung der Juden in Deutschland*, No. 1/2 (January/February) 1936, p. 4.
88. Adler-Rudel, *Selbsthilfe*, p. 165.
89. Lippmann, *Deutscher*, p. 64.
90. Adler-Rudel, *Selbsthilfe*, p. 165. The figure of 39% refers however to all of the 'Hanseatic cities' together.
91. Figures from Lippmann, *Deutscher*, p. 46.
92. See the inventory in the *Archiv WgA LGHH, Rundordner 'Allgemeines'.*
93. StAHH, *Jüdische Gemeinden*, 297, Vol. 22, p. 251, minutes of the executive board meeting of 3 December 1935.
94. Citation as in StAHH, *Jüdische Gemeinden*, 360b, p. 165, minutes of the sitting of the *Repräsentantenkollegium* of 8 June 1936.
95. Special Archives, Moscow, 500-3-316, p. 454, annual report of *Referat II 112* of *SD-Oberabschnitt Nord-West*, 14 January 1938.
96. StAHH, *Amtsgericht Hamburg - Verwaltung*, Abl. 1987, 3170, note of 12 August 1938.
97. StAHH, *Jüdische Gemeinden*, 329c, p. 362.
98. See Table 1, Appendix.
99. Figures according to Lippmann, *Deutscher*, p. 52.
100. Special Archives, Moscow, 500-3-316, p. 454, annual report of *Referat II 112* of *SD-Oberabschnitt Nord-West*, 14 January 1938.
101. Cited as per ibid., p. 454.
102. *Archiv WgA LGHH*, Z 2912-1, p. 30, communication from Dr Rodekau of 5 April 1951. The balance of profits between the two companies was regulated by a secret 'treaty of friendship' concluded on 3 August 1936 (pp. 32–34).
103. E.g. *Fa. Delmonte & Koopmann*, which operated a canned fish wholesale business and for tactical reasons from 1933 took on an 'Aryan' partner. *Archiv WgA LGHH*, Z 29, pp. 30–33, communication from Martin Friedländer of 18 March 1948.
104. The entrepreneur in question was Hans-Siegfried Steinberg, proprietor of the Hamburg raincoat manufacturer *Hans Steinberg & Co*, who, by using his wife as a partner, bought into Hamburg raincoat manufacturer *H. Becker & Co. GmbH, Archiv WgA LGHH*, Z 2790-5, p. 19.
105. See Robinsohn, *Versuch*, p. 202.
106. The particular attraction of Jewish businesses for poor sections of the population is stressed in reports from various German regions. Cf. Kershaw, *Persecution*, p. 266.
107. *Geheimes Staatsarchiv Preußischer Kulturbesitz*, Berlin-Dahlem, Rep. 90P, Report 3.3, p. 96, report by the head of the state police station at Harburg-Wilhelmsburg to the *Geheime Staatspolizeiamt* in Berlin, December 1935.
108. *Sonderarchiv Moskau*, 500-3-316, p. 453, annual report of *Referat II 112* of *SD-Oberabschnitts Nord-West*, 14 January 1938.
109. Ibid., p. 465.
110. *Hamburger Tageblatt*, 26 April 1935.

111. Cf. Robinsohn, *Versuch*, p. 199, who reported that until 1937 there had been 'no difficulties' with suppliers. In many cases they had retained 'good human relations' with them which would by themselves have been sufficient 'to make the boycott unworkable through [these] suppliers'. 'In one case a company proprietor, the head of his "*Fachschaft*", meaning of his branch of industry for the whole of Germany, had described to me the inconsistency of his situation: on the one hand he was obliged to pass on antisemitic representations in connection with demands for boycotts to the members of his *Fachschaft*; on the other hand, he was not thinking of doing without his [Jewish] customers.'

112. Cf. the communication from *Fa. Bischoff & Rodatz GmbH* to the Hamburg *Handelskammer* of 31 August 1935, *Archiv Handelskammer*, 100.B.1.5.

113. Cf. Goldhagen, *Hitler's Willing Executioners*, pp. 80–163.

114. On discrimination against Jews in taxation and on the following particulars of figures in this respect, see Günther Felix, 'Scheinlegalität und Rechtsbeugung - Finanzverwaltung, Steuergerichtsbarkeit und Judenverfolgung im "Dritten Reich"', in *Steuer & Studium* 5/1995, pp. 197–204; Dorothee Mußgnug, *Die Reichsfluchtsteuer 1931–1953*, Berlin, 1993; Martin Tarrab-Maslaton, *Rechtliche Strukturen der Diskriminierung der Juden im Dritten Reich*, Berlin, 1993.

115. StAHH, *Oberfinanzpräsident*, 19, "List of non-Aryans subject to the Reich capital export tax as the situation stands at 31 January 1938".

116. A table of deductions for the years 1934–1939 can be found in StAHH, *Oberfinanzpräsident*, 47 UA 14.

117. On the 'Haavara agreement', see Werner Feilchenfeld, Dolf Michaelis and Ludwig Pinner, *Haavara-Transfer nach Palästina und Einwanderung deutscher Juden 1933–1939*, Tübingen, 1972; Yehuda Bauer, *Jews for Sale? Nazi-Jewish Negotiations 1933–1945*, New Haven and London 1994, esp. pp. 8–29; Avraham Barkai, 'German Interests in the Haavara-Transfer Agreement 1933–1939', *LBI YB* 35 (1990), pp. 245–266.

118. See on this Barkai, *German Interests*.

119. *Sonderarchiv Moskau*, 500-3-316, p. 452, annual report for 1937 of *Referat II 112* of SD-Oberabschnitt Nord-West, 14 January 1938.

120. See Table 13, Appendix.

121. StAHH, *Oberfinanzpräsident*, 14, note of 27 November 1935.

122. Ibid., circular from the *Reichsstelle für Devisenbewirtschaftung* to the *Leiter* of the *Devisenstelle*, 21 December 1935.

123. On Altreu, see Feilchenfeld, Michaelis and Pinner, *Haavara-Transfer*, pp. 79–81.

124. StAHH, *Oberfinanzpräsident*, 14, transfer table of 26 October 1937.

125. See StAHH, *Familie Plaut*, D 25, excerpt from the minutes of the advisory council of the Altreu of 7 September 1938. From then on the transfer sum was limited to a maximum of 40,000 RM. In extreme cases losses through currency exchanges could be as high as 88%.

126. Figures from ibid., progress report of the Altreu of 9 June 1938.

127. Already in their progress report of June 1938 the Altreu accused Paltreu of having a 'one-sided Zionist' point of view and criticised its high transfer charges, whose maintenance appeared 'most highly problematic'. In a letter from the secretariat of M.M. Warburg & Co. to Dr Ernst Spiegelberg/Amsterdam of 10 September 1938 this was described as a 'family quarrel'. StAHH, *Familie Plaut*, D 25.

128. *Archiv M.M. Warburg & Co.*, FWI files, paper by Dr Alfred Levi of 13 January 1936 ('Some words on the liquidation of Jewish wealth'). Levi pointed out in this connection that most foreign suppliers would have 'proven exceptionally unfavourable' to exchanges of property (p. 4).

129. *Archiv WgA LGHH*, Z 3422-1, p. 14f.

130. StAHH, *Oberfinanzpräsident*, Str 545, p. 1.

131. Ibid., Str 366, p. 78ff.

132. Ibid., Str 678, Vol. 1, pp. 2–75.
133. Ibid., p. 17, Investigation Report of the *Zollinspektor* (Customs Inspector) *Westphal.*
134. *Archiv WgA LGHH*, Z 2831-1, Vol. II, pp. 77–85, judgment of the *Hamburgische Oberver-waltungsgericht* Bf. I 652/52 of 29 May 1953, citation p. 84.
135. For individual cases of this, see below, Ch. VI.
136. Victor Klemperer, *Ich will Zeugnis ablegen bis zum letzten. Tagebücher 1933–1945*, 2 vols, Berlin, 1995.
137. Autobiography of Dr Ernst Loewenberg (private collection), p. 77.
138. On the development of M.M. Warburg & Co. and the following statements, see Christopher Kopper, *Nationalsozialistische Bankenpolitik am Beispiel des Bankhauses M.M. Warburg & Co. in Hamburg*, Bochum (master's thesis), 1988; Eduard Rosenbaum and A.J. Sherman, *Das Bankhaus M.M. Warburg & Co. 1798–1938*, Hamburg, 1978; Ron Chernow, *Die Warburgs: Odyssee einer Familie*, Berlin, 1994.
139. *Archiv M.M. Warburg & Co., Max M. Warburg*, 1934 (Jewish Agency), lecture of December 1934. 'What can America do in the Jewish question?' (manuscript, p. 12).
140. Cf. Warburg, *Aufzeichnungen.*
141. See Avraham Barkai, 'Max Warburg im Jahre 1933. Mißglückte Versuche zur Milderung der Judenverfolgung', in Peter Freimark, Alice Jankowski and Ina S. Lorenz, eds, *Juden in Deutschland. Emanzipation, Integration, Verfolgung und Vernichtung*, Hamburg, 1991, pp. 390–405.
142. On the initiative see besides Barkai, *Max Warburg*, also Peter Hayes, *Big Business*, pp. 254–281, here p. 257f., and Hans Schäffer, 'Meine Zusammenarbeit mit Carl Melchior', in *Carl Melchior: Ein Buch des Gedenkens und der Freundschaft*, Tübingen, 1967, pp. 35–106, here p. 102f.
143. Hayes, *Big Business*, p. 258.
144. As Barkai conjectured in *Max Warburg*, p. 403.
145. StAHH, *Familie Krogmann I* (Carl Vincent Krogmann), C 15, I 7, entry of 25 August 1933.
146. Helfferich, *Tatsachen*, p. 47f.
147. *Archiv M.M. Warburg & Co.*, Carl Melchior/Max Warburg 1935, *Mappe* 180, letter from Max Warburg to Emil Helfferich of 13 March 1935.
148. Ibid..
149. Cf. Albert Fischer, *Schacht.*
150. Citation from the archives of M.M. Warburg & Co., Max Warburg, 1934 (Jewish Agency), draft 'for Dr Schueller (on his questions).'
151. Warburg later shared this information with the American Ambassador, William E. Dodd. See William E. Dodd Jr. and Martha Dodd, eds, *Ambassador Dodd's Diary 1933–1938*, New York, 1941, p. 280, entry of 27 November 1935: 'Max Warburg reported today that he and Dr Schacht had not been able to do anything to relieve the Jewish situation. His information about the financial abuses here, especially the Goebbels group activity, was the same I had heard from other sources.'
152. Cf. Kopper, *Bankenpolitik*, p. 102f.; Chernow, *Warburgs*, p. 528ff.; Abraham Margaliot, 'The Reaction of the Jewish Public in Germany to the Nuremberg Laws', *Yad Vashem Studies* 12 (1977), pp. 75–107.
153. Report from the German Embassy in London to the *Reichsministerium für Volksaufklärung und Propaganda*, 28 January 1936, *Akten der Partei-Kanzlei der NSDAP*, ed. by the *Institut für Zeitgeschichte*, Part I, Munich, 1983, No. 21503.
154. *Reichs- und Preußische Wirtschaftsministerium* to the *Reichsminister des Auswärtigen* (Minister for Foreign Affairs), 18 February 1936, ibid., No. 21574.
155. Chernow, *Warburgs*, p. 529.
156. *Archiv M.M. Warburg & Co.*, Z I 5, Walther Dauch to Max Warburg, 22 May 1937.
157. Ibid., Herbert L.W. Göring to Max Warburg, 6 July 1937.

158. On the career of Stuckart, see Rebentisch, *Führerstaat*, pp. 105–110.

159. Cf. Wilhelm Stuckart and Hans Globke, *Kommentare zur deutschen Rassegesetzgebung*, Vol. I, '*Reichsbürgergesetz von 15. September, 1935. Gesetz zum Schutz des deutschen Blutes und der deutschen Ehre von 15. September, 1935. Gesetz zum Schutz der Erbgesundheit des deutschen Volkes (Erbgesundheitsgesetz) von 18. Oktober, 1935. Nebst allen Ausführungsbestimmungen und einschlägigen Gesetzen und Verordnungen erläutert von Dr Wilhelm Stuckart, Staatssekretär, und Dr Hans Globke, Oberregierungsrat, beide im Reichs- und Preußischen Ministerium des Innern,*' Munich and Berlin, 1936.

160. *Archiv M.M. Warburg & Co.*, Z I 5, Warburg's memorandum of 23 August 1937, p. 1.

161. Cf. Ulrich Herbert, *Best. Biographische Studien über Radikalismus, Weltanschauung und Vernunft 1903-1989*, Bonn, 1996, pp. 203–224.

162. Wildt, ed., *Judenpolitik*.

163. For the following comments, see *Archiv M.M. Warburg & Co.*, Z I 5, Max Warburg's memorandum of 23 August 1937.

164. Ibid., Max Warburg to Walther Dauch, 10 August 1937.

165. Ibid., 'Note for secret records', 10 August 1937.

166. Rebentisch, *Führerstaat*, p. 97. On the position of the *Reichsinnenministerium* in Jewish affairs, see also the testimonial of Bernhard Lösener, 'Als Rassereferent im Reichsministerium des Innern', *VfZ* 9 (1961), pp. 264–313.

167. *Archiv M.M. Warburg & Co.*, Z I 5, Warburg to Stuckart, 27 November 1937.

168. Ibid., Stuckart to Warburg, 4 January 1938.

169. See Jäckel, *Hitlers Weltanschauung*, pp. 55–95.

170. Adolf Hitler, *Mein Kampf*, Vol. I, 17th impression, Munich, 1933, p. 225.

171. Ibid., Vol. I, p. 335.

172. Citation from *Archiv M.M. Warburg & Co.*, Max Warburg, 1934 (Jewish Agency), draft 'for Dr Schueller (on his questions).'

173. On the concept of 'cumulative radicalization' and on the 'functionalist' view of the National Socialist system, see Hans Mommsen, 'Der Nationalsozialismus. Kumulative Radikalisierung und Selbstzerstörung des Regimes', in *Meyers Enzyklopädisches Lexikon*, Vol. 16, Mannheim, *inter alia*, 1976, pp. 785–790; Broszat, *Staat Hitlers*, applied to National Socialist anti-Jewish policy by Adam, *Judenpolitik*; Hans Mommsen, 'Die Realisierung des Utopischen. Die "Endlösung der Judenfrage" im "Dritten Reich"', in *GG* 9 (1983), pp. 381–420.

# Chapter IV

# TRANSITION TO THE SYSTEMATIC 'DE-JUDAISATION' OF THE HAMBURG ECONOMY, 1936–37

Until 1936/37 the economic position of the Jews of Hamburg remained in a state of suspense. On the one hand, many Jewish employees had lost their jobs in the spring of 1933; Jewish state employees had been dismissed; Jewish doctors and lawyers had lost their licences; Jewish pharmacists and self-employed businessmen working in the 'cultural economy' had to give up their livelihoods, and Jewish company owners were confronted with countless infringements on their everyday business affairs, as well as through both open and hidden boycotts. On the other hand the 'Aryanisation' of Jewish businesses had made little progress at this time: at least in Hamburg, many businesses increased their earnings and had in some cases even received state support and patronage; credit vouchers from welfare offices could still be used in Jewish stores; the 'Nuremberg laws' of 1935 had thus far had little impact on the economic situation of the Jews; and the rules with which the economic activities of the Jews were to be regulated, though they had been publicly announced, had yet to see the light of day. At this point there was no sense in which one could speak of a systematic policy of 'de-Judaising' the Hamburg economy.

Two years later the situation had completely changed. At the turn of 1938/39 all of Hamburg's Jewish retail businesses were closed down, the businesses that remained were either being sold or wound up, hundreds of company owners were imprisoned in concentration camps, and Jews were robbed remorselessly. Even if there was much that seems to support Avraham Barkai's interpretation that the years after 1933 saw a continuum of economic displacement and discrimination, the dramatic radicalisation after 1937, and particularly in 1938,

---

cannot be overlooked, depriving the Jews at almost one stroke of all prospects for making a living.

This radicalisation took place at a time when the German Reich had largely overcome the impact of the global economic crisis, rearmament and preparations for war were now in their final stages and the diplomatic situation of National Socialist Germany had been so consolidated that the statesmen of the Western democracies were prepared to stretch out to them the hand of 'appeasement'. This gave the National Socialists important room for manoeuvre in which, in order to prepare for the war against the enemy 'outside', they turned against what in their view was the enemy 'within' – the German Jews.

However, when exactly did the qualitative leap in the 'elimination' of the Jews from economic affairs begin? Historians such as Uwe Dietrich Adam and Helmut Genschel have dated this shift to the end of 1937, connecting it with the departure of Schacht from the Reich Economics Ministry.[1] Though Avraham Barkai and Albert Fischer have rightly relativised Schacht's 'protective hand' policy,[2] there is nevertheless no doubt that his political demise had an important function as a catalyst of the acceleration of 'Aryanisation'.[3] However, the thrust which radicalised anti-Jewish policy took place even before this. This brings institutions into view whose significance for the 'Aryanisation' of Jewish property has often been underestimated: the Office of the *Gau* Economics Adviser of the NSDAP and the Foreign Exchange and Customs Investigators of the Regional Finance Offices. These were the first institutions to push for and systematise the 'de-Judaisation' of the Hamburg economy in 1936/37.

## The NSDAP Gau Economics Adviser as an Authority for 'Aryanisations'

Among the offices of the Hamburg NSDAP which were involved in the propagation of the 'de-Judaisation of the economy', the Office of the *Gau* Economics Adviser (*Amt des Gauwirtschaftsberaters*, GWB) played a dominant role.[4] In Hamburg business circles it was generally known as *der Gau*. The Office was under the authority of the Commission for Economic Policy of NSDAP Reichsamtsleiter Bernhard Köhler in Munich, who promoted, among other things, an 'economic race conflict'. In Hamburg, the Office of the *Gau* Economics Adviser functioned as a springboard for the activities and the careers of a group of young National Socialist economic policy-makers who were particularly focused on translating ideological principles into the management of economic affairs. At the time of the seizure of power by the National Socialists in 1933, the first *Gau* Economics Adviser of Hamburg, Dr Gustav Schlotterer, was 27 years old, his successor Carlo

Otte was 25, and Otte's successor, Dr Otto Wolff, was 26. All three belonged to the 'generation of war youth' (*Kriegsjugendgeneration*), came from petty bourgeois backgrounds, had entered the NSDAP in their youth, carried high honorific ranks in the SS[5] and were highly ideological, ambitious and career-oriented, having begun their careers as commercial employees or in the middle ranks of the civil service and then – at least in the cases of Schlotterer and Wolff – gaining further academic qualifications.[6] The *Gau* Economics Advisers and their staff formed a specifically National Socialist economic élite. In age, origin, political orientation and personal life experience they differed sharply from Hamburg's traditional economic élite of the older generation, who, as a rule, came from 'long-established' upper-middle class families and, as self-employed businessmen, took a pragmatic view of the economy shaped strongly by the experience of managing their own businesses.

The first *Gau* Economics Adviser Dr Gustav Schlotterer[7] held office until 1935, also working in this period as President of the Hamburg Economics Department, before he moved, in 1935, into the Reich Economics Ministry. There he took a leading role in the 'de-Judaisation' of Eastern Europe and of its economy, as '*spiritus rector*'[8] of National Socialist *Großraum* planning, head of both the Eastern Department of the Reich Economics Ministry and the Economics Section of the Ministry for the East. As an old Hamburg National Socialist he took particular account in this connection of the interests of Hamburg's commercial groups, which, faced with the loss of its overseas trade links after the outbreak of war in 1939, were pressing for compensation.[9]

As his successor, Schlotterer's former deputy, Carlo Otte[10] led the Office of the *Gau* Economics Adviser from 1935 to 1940. This gave him considerable responsibility for the 'Aryanisations' carried out in Hamburg. High school graduate and commercial employee, he was clearly the intellectual inferior of his predecessor, and in some respects his behaviour once in office revealed that he was 'not equal to this position', as one former colleague noted in describing him.[11] Otte sought to hide his lack of competence and life experience behind an 'unbelievably arrogant and presumptuous manner'.[12] Nevertheless as a 'fanatic idealist' Otte succeeded in gaining the unrestricted trust of Gauleiter Kaufmann, to whom he was 'faithfully devoted' and to whom he was also subordinated in a disciplinary sense, as was laid down in the Party statutes. This emerged even more clearly over the course of 1940 when Otte was named to head the Principal National Economy Section in the Reich Commissariat for the Occupied Territories in Norway. Although he was thereafter permanently absent from Hamburg, Kaufmann formally continued to give his henchman Otte the title of Hamburg *Gau* Economics Adviser and in his absence in 1942 named him both Senator and Councillor of the Hamburg Municipal Administration. After the war was won, Otte was intended to be head of the Hamburg Economics Department.[13]

Even during his term in office as *Gau* Economics Adviser, Otte was increasingly overshadowed by his principal collaborator Dr Otto Wolff,[14] who had been given overall charge of numerous 'Aryanisations', including that of M.M. Warburg & Co., and who led the Office of the *Gau* Economics Adviser on a temporary basis from 1940. He was considered an intelligent and unscrupulous person who 'wanted to earn power, reputation and wealth at any price'.[15] The future Hamburg Justice Senator Biermann-Ratjen characterised Wolff as one 'of the worst and most brutal supporters of absolute antisemitism in the economy'.[16] Within the briefest time, Wolff had understood how to unite important positions of power in the economy, party and state in his hand, as a board member of HAPAG, acting *Gau* Economics Adviser and Head of the Economics Command in *Wehrkreis X*, and he thereby played a leading role in the organisation of the war economy of Hamburg. As with the behaviour of Otte, Wolff's showy manner was 'not appreciated' by many representatives of the Hamburg economy, since it 'deviated not inconsiderably from the traditions of the Hamburg bourgeoisie'.[17] In the war, Wolff occupied himself, among other things, with the liquidation of Jewish property across the whole of Europe, which he arranged to be transferred by a variety of means to Hamburg.[18]

The institutional weight that the *Gau* Economics Adviser could set against the Chamber of Commerce and the state economics administration was, in general, extremely small. According to statutory provisions, the members of the Office of the *Gau* Economics Adviser were supposed to work primarily in an honorary capacity,[19] though Otte and Wolff were full-time party officials. Of the three Hamburg *Gau* Economics Advisers only Otte, who held no other state office, endeavoured to build up his team institutionally. Since the records of the Office of the *Gau* Economics Adviser were completely destroyed, the development of its personnel and finances can only be reconstructed with difficulty. Apart from allocations from the NSDAP, it received, among its other sources of income, regular allowances from the State of Hamburg and from the Chamber of Commerce.[20] In accordance with the Reich guidelines of the NSDAP, the Office of the *Gau* Economics Adviser ought to have been divided into three sections: economic questions, press and propaganda, and training and presentations, to which further specialists and correspondents were added, but the Hamburg *Gau* Economics Adviser had his own 'Aryanisation Section', which from 1936 was led by Karl Frie (b. 1913, diploma in national economics).[21] A further colleague of the *Gau* Economics Adviser, Dr Eduard Hoffmann (b. 1900), as head of the 'Hamburg Real Estate-Administration Corporation of 1938' worked on the 'de-Judaisation' of land ownership in Hamburg.[22] Beyond that, the *Gau* Economics Adviser had a number of informal working partners, including the lawyer Dr Arthur Kramm (b. 1907), a personal acquaintance of Dr Otto Wolff who had

prepared many 'Aryanisation contracts'. What linked people such as Frie, Hoffmann and Kramm with the young Hamburg *Gau* Economics Advisers was a date
of birth after 1900, the experience of being a child or young person during the
war, academic education, career ambitions and ideological conviction.

In the district leadership circles of the Hamburg NSDAP – there was a total
of ten districts after 1937 – the Office of the *Gau* Economics Adviser was represented by 'District *Gau* Economics Advisers' who again had corresponding
assistants at the local group leadership level. For them, the implementation of
anti-Jewish measures primarily meant controlling and spying on those involved.

In order to preserve the finances of the *Gau* Economics Adviser and at the
same time to increase their institutional influence, Otte established, from
1934/35 onwards, so-called 'Liaison Offices' in the Chamber of Commerce, the
Hamburg State Economics Department and individual industrial associations,
endowing them with supervisory functions. These offices had to be financed by
the institutions in which they were placed. However, more far-reaching control of
the Hamburg economy proved beyond the reach of the *Gau* Economics Adviser,
nor did he have much influence over the city's economic policy. In many cases the
'Liaison Offices' participated *pro forma* in the meetings of the institutions to
which they were attached, but had no real influence. For this reason, the liaison
officer of the *Gau* Economics Adviser was characterised by a counsel of the
Chamber of Commerce as a 'stupid oaf' whose knowledge of the actual work of
the Chamber of Commerce comprised 'only as much as he had to know'.[23] Institutionally, the hastily assembled apparatus of the Office of the *Gau* Economics
Adviser, with its few, even partly honorific, members, was hopelessly inferior to
the established economics institutions like the Chamber of Commerce or the
Hamburg State Economics Department. The political influence of the *Gau* Economics Adviser was almost exclusively tied to whether or not he succeeded in
occupying further formal responsibilities in the state and economics administration beyond the unimportant party office itself, as Schlotterer and Wolff were able
to, but not Otte. The low institutional standing of the *Gau* Economics Adviser
also emerges clearly from the fact that Gauleiter Kaufmann did not avail himself
of the party machine in central economic questions, but established new specialist offices like the 'Special Agents for Economic Development and the Four Year
Plan'. For the established economic institutions this special service was a considerably greater rival than the NSDAP's *Gau* economics apparatus.

Only in one area did the *Gau* Economics Adviser wield any dominant influence: with respect to 'Aryanisation' and to the 'de-Judaisation' of the economy.
This was one of the fundamental ideological objectives of the NSDAP and
seemed an appropriate area to require the participation of party organisations
responsible for economic questions. Accordingly there was a conspicuous contrast

between the influence of the *Gau* Economics Advisers over 'Aryanisation', on the one hand, and their influence over other economic interests, like the establishment of industries and the creation of employment, on the other. The Hamburg Chamber of Commerce, which had seemed extremely reluctant to accept the extension of the influence of the *Gau* Economics Adviser with respect to the registration of Jewish businesses, was astonishingly prepared for this when it came to 'Aryanisations'. Even where the Chamber of Commerce had an indirect influence, as with the appointment of consultants for the assessment of the value of goods in warehouses, it tried to pass the responsibility on to another institution. In November 1938, the Chamber of Commerce still referred applicants who wished to 'Aryanise' a Jewish enterprise to the *Gau* Economics Adviser, claiming that they had 'nothing to do' with such questions and that such Jewish enterprises were 'not known' to them.[24] The Chamber of Commerce, it appeared, had a manifest interest in focusing the energies and activities of the National Socialist *Gau* economics apparatus on the field of 'Aryanisations' so as to be able to limit its impact in other areas more effectively. Moreover, through this division of labour the Chamber of Commerce evaded the delicate problem of having to open proceedings against Jewish firms which had often been members for over a hundred years. For Jewish firms this division of labour was fatal, because they were exposed to the unrestrained attacks of mostly younger, ideologically driven antisemites who conceived of the 'de-Judaisation' of the economy in terms of their *Weltanschauung*, a task which had to be implemented ruthlessly.

In the early years of the National Socialist regime the Office of the Hamburg *Gau* Economics Adviser had still acted with restraint in Jewish affairs.[25] In the above-mentioned conflicts over Beiersdorf AG and Deutscher Tuchversand, Schlotterer and Otte upheld the position of the Reich Economics Ministry and the Hamburg Senate according to which the retention of employment and economic stability were the highest priorities. With the removal from office of the Chairman of the Hamburg Dressmakers in 1934, Otte had even criticised the campaign to exclude the Jews that was being waged by the antisemites of the commercial middle class.

Around 1935/36, by contrast, evidence first appears that anti-Jewish activities were being undertaken by the Office of the *Gau* Economics Adviser. In November 1935, Otte sought, in letters to the HAPAG and Blohm & Voß, to cut off their business relations with 'non-Aryan' suppliers.[26] Neither firm, however, was much impressed by the intervention of the *Gau* Economics Adviser, and both rejected any rupture of business ties and referred to the existing orders from the Reich Economics Ministry that forbade 'individual actions' against Jewish enterprises.[27]

In 1936, the regional economics machinery of the NSDAP across the Reich attempted to establish its responsibility for supervising and authorising 'Aryanisations'. Even so, the timing and extent of its participation differed considerably in each individual region. For example, the *Gau* Economics Adviser of Baden's NSDAP founded a committee in February 1936, with permission from the Chief Minister of Baden, charged with dealing with all questions connected to the activities of Jews in economic affairs from that time onwards.[28] Besides the *Gau* Economics Adviser, the committee included the Labour Trustee and two senior government advisers from the Finance and Economics Ministry in Karlsruhe. He had thereby established his authorisation for participating in the 'Aryanisations' on a formal basis, but still had to tread carefully with the bureaucracy in the Ministry while it continued to try to put the brakes on a radicalisation of 'de-Judaisation policy'.[29]

In *Gau Westfalen-Süd*, on the other hand, the *Gau* Economics Adviser claimed a right to take part in decision making on 'Aryanisations' in open conflict with the local administration in the area.[30] He supported his case formally with a directive from the Deputy Gauleiter of October 1936, which granted him the right to participate in the 'Aryanisation' of clothing and confectionary firms, although he had soon expanded this authorisation to the whole economy. The designation of the *Gau* Economics Adviser as the figure responsible for 'Aryanisations' thus in practice devolved upon him through self-appointment.

The Hamburg *Gau* Economics Adviser may well have taken on responsibility for 'Aryanisation' in 1936 in a similar way. The Hamburg Chamber of Commerce's institutional restraint provided favourable conditions for such acts of self-empowerment. Karl Frie, appointed to work on 'Aryanisation' by the Hamburg *Gau* Economics Adviser in 1936, had already systematised the programme and was about to finish the registration of Jewish companies by this time.[31] There is no evidence in surviving records of the formal appointment of the *Gau* Economics Adviser to this role by the Gauleiter before 14 June 1938, when a directive from Kaufmann laid down comprehensive regulations for the procedure of 'Aryanisation'.[32] Nevertheless it would not have been possible for the *Gau* Economics Adviser to have enforced his claim to authority without the support of the Gauleiter. The owner of the Jewish import company Eichholz & Löser, which in 1935 desired its 'Aryan' attorney to take over a part of the firm in order to recover import quotas that it had already lost, reported that the conclusion of a contract had been delayed until spring 1936 through 'aggravations' from the Gauleiter and the *Gau* Economics Adviser.[33] Why the *Gau* Economics Adviser intervened here with the help of the Gauleiter becomes clear from the circumstances surrounding the negotiations over the contract: the attorney had offered a share in the profits to his Jewish employer,[34] which for the *Gau* Economics Adviser was not compatible with the objective of a rigorous 'de-Judaisation' policy and, in the official terminology of the time, was considered an undesirable disguise for Jewish operations in the economy. This incident not only documents the relatively early time at which the Hamburg *Gau* Economics Adviser was dealing with authorisation for 'Aryanisation' contracts, but also shows his close cooperation with the Gauleiter and the political support given by the Gauleiter for the activities of the *Gau* Economics Adviser. In January 1937, for instance, Kaufmann authorised him to inspect files and request information from the Lower Elbe Regional Finance Office.[35]

News of the powers given to the *Gau* Economics Adviser for supervising 'Aryanisations' spread quickly among Jewish company owners. For example, Max Warburg drew the attention of his Jewish interlocutors from 1937 to the fact that the negotiations over the sale of their firm must have been conducted 'by Otte'.[36]

'Aryanisation contracts' in Hamburg could only be concluded without mandatory authorisations before 1936, though in a few special cases they were also still carried out unsupervised later. Only in this phase was it possible for Jewish proprietors to sell their concerns in conditions of some fairness. One of the last businesses that changed its owner in this way was the Hamburg raincoat factory, Hans Steinberg & Co., sold on 1 July 1936. The company warehouse was sold at eight percent above the price at which it was valued. On top of that, the buyer compensated the Jewish owner both for taking over his established product names and also to keep his goodwill.[37] None of these three arrangements, which all corresponded to the usual customs maintained during the sale of a firm, would have been approved by the *Gau* Economics Adviser in this form.

In an article written for the *Hamburger Tageblatt* of 2 December 1938, the *Gau* Economics Adviser clarified the principles which he had established for granting authorisation for 'Aryanisations'. In the article, he explained to the public of Hamburg that he had been 'giving systematic' and 'focused' attention to the 'de-Judaisation' process 'already long before the publication of the instruction from the Reich Economics Ministry of 26 April 1938' – meaning the ordinance on the registration of Jewish property[38] – in order to implement 'the economic policy demands of the party programme'. He had made his permission dependent on five fundamental demands:

First of all, great value was to be attached to the political reliability of the buyer. Buyers would preferably be members of the younger generation of businessmen or NSDAP members 'who had suffered economic disadvantage in the struggle for the Movement' – a commonly used phrase at that time, which was intended to justify the nepotism of the National Socialists. Secondly, the national economy's need for the Jewish firm would have to be proven, and if it could not be then the firm would not be 'Aryanised' but liquidated on the spot. Thirdly, in accordance with the middle-class oriented political ideas of the NSDAP 'the formation of conglomerates' through the sale of Jewish enterprises was to be avoided. This led automatically to a preference for buyers who were not from the economic establishment, but who wished to establish themselves in business for the first time by means of the 'Aryanisation' in question. Fourthly, after 'Aryanisation', a company was to be completely freed of 'Jewish influence'. This demand was aimed, among other objectives, at the dismissal of all leading Jewish employees as well as at the alteration of 'typical Jewish' company names. Fifth and finally, in authorising the sales contract care should be taken 'that the Jew did not receive an inappropriately high price'. The discussion which follows focuses on a few specific examples in some detail to see how the translation of these demands worked in practice.

An important focus of concern for the *Gau* Economics Adviser in the authorisation of an 'Aryanisation' project was to drive down the sale price of the Jewish company as far as was possible. In principle, therefore, he did not authorise any payments for the 'goodwill' of the enterprise, meaning for the immaterial value of the firm based on its market position, product range, customer groups, business relationships, distribution arrangements or the company's reputation. Only in one of the cases examined did he grant a small amount for 'goodwill', namely in the 'Aryanisation' of the Jewish wholesaler Zinner & Lippstadt in 1937, which traded in cheese and fats. In addition to a payment of 4000 RM for equipment, the total amount for which the company was sold also included 12,000 RM for the 'goodwill' of an enterprise which, in 1936 alone, had earned a profit of over 84,000 RM.[39] The approach of the *Gau* Economics Adviser was thus not an especially obliging one. The purchase price which he fixed arbitrarily – he had told an employee of a Jewish owner that 'there is no question of holding a discussion over calculating the price'[40] – was only sufficient to settle existing commitments so that the proprietor, Olga Lippstadt, came out of the sale of her 'most highly regarded' firm 'poor as a church mouse'.[41]

In all other cases, the *Gau* Economics Adviser refused a 'goodwill' payment even where it was already subject to a contractual agreement between the Jewish proprietor and the 'Aryan' buyer. For example, in screening the 'Aryanisation' of the Simon Arendt fashion store, which also changed owners in 1937, the *Gau* Economics Adviser deleted the agreed 45,000 RM for 'goodwill' and turned against the buyer 'very reproachingly because he was still giving a sum of money to a Jew in compensation for goodwill'.[42]

Payments to Jewish proprietors were only allowed for stocks, business premises and equipment. This rule was particularly disastrous for Jewish owners of trading enterprises who, in selling their business, in essence only received a sum compensating them for the value of their office furniture. Moreover the *Gau* Economics Adviser had issued instructions that stocks and equipment be valued at lower than the going market rate. Their value ought – as one former valuer evasively put it – 'to be made very carefully with regard to its later utility'.[43] In any case, the *Gau* Economics Adviser attached no importance to the exactitude of the valuation. When a valuer from the bicycle industry admitted that he was unable to value the worth of a warehouse of radio sets, *Gau* Economics Adviser Otte instructed him that he should simply 'make a rough estimate'.[44]

In view of the attendant circumstances it is not surprising that the purchase price determined by the *Gau* Economics Adviser was frequently less than the amount that the purchaser was prepared to pay voluntarily, although they themselves would of course have had no interest in paying a high price. At the end of 1937, the *Gau* Economics Adviser pushed down the sale price for the Jewish firm Max Rosenberg & Co., a vegetable and tropical fruit wholesaler, from 36,000 RM to 12,500 RM. The purchaser was the official in the NSDAP *Gau* responsible for the fruit trade, though he did not appear personally as the buyer, but had his attorney act as a front man. The extremely low sale price was so embarrassing, even to the National Socialist, that he paid an additional 3,500 RM to the Jewish owner by way of 'consolation', 'so that the thing would not leave him in too much pain', as he later solemnly testified in court.[45]

In selling the Franz Simon textile business to two party members, the *Gau* Economics Adviser lowered the buying price from 390,000 to 290,000 RM;[46] in the 'Aryanisation' of the second-hand goods company M.H. Lissauer & Co. in January 1938, he halved it from 20,000 to 10,000 RM,[47] and in the sale of the Rudolf Reich company, a manufacturer of white lead and wood turpentine, he cut out 60,000 RM from the contracted price, against the will of the buyer.[48]

All of the interventions of the *Gau* Economics Adviser must be considered to have lacked a legal foundation and took place only by virtue of his self-authorisation. On a strict legal basis, no Jewish company owner could have been forced to give permission that their enterprise be sold before 26 April 1938. In practice, however, the *Gau* Economics Adviser had tied his control network so tightly around Jewish companies by systematic registration – through his informants on the local level in county and town quarters and through control of the trade register – that barely a sale of a Jewish enterprise could take place without his mandatory authorisation.[49]

Similarly, no formal legal basis existed for the classification of an enterprise as 'Jewish', a procedure which formed the basis for all authorised 'Aryanisations' until January 1938. The Office of the *Gau* Economics Adviser decided by the most arbitrary criteria whether or not a company owner was to be considered Jewish. Dr Otto Wolff counted one company owner as a 'Jew' even though he protested that he was a 'Jewish *Mischling*' according to National Socialist race laws. When even an official from the NSDAP raised doubts about this classification, Wolff signalled to him that he only had 'to look at [his] ears to know that he is really a Jew'.[50]

The *Gau* Economics Adviser's oscillation between arbitrary behaviour and arrogation of powers had drastic consequences for Jewish company proprietors. It suddenly lowered the value of their business and at the same time accelerated its sale, although the *Gau* Economics Adviser at first did not possess any authority to force Jewish owners to sell their companies. On the one hand, the number of potential buyers was rising, knowing they would do good business because of the restrictions on authorisation to trade. On the other hand, it became ever clearer to the Jewish owners that there was no future for them to carry on doing business in the Germany of the National Socialists. To save what could be saved now gave them a substantial motive to sell.

## Excursus: The End of the Walter Bamberger Travel Agency

When the Office of NSDAP *Gau* Economics Adviser was given responsibility for authorising 'Aryanisations' in 1936/37, it meant that the party organisation of the Hamburg NSDAP had succeeded for the first time in gaining a dominant position in the 'de-Judaisation' of the economy. At the same time, this guaranteed that all sales of Jewish enterprises would in future be subjected to the discriminatory rules of a National Socialist party organ – and thereby to conditions which systematically disadvantaged Jewish owners.

At this time Hamburg's National Socialists were also intervening indirectly in the business activities of Jewish enterprises that were particularly out of favour with them on political grounds. To this end they used an instrument that they had already begun to test out from 1933 in campaigns and boycotts: a system of controls through indirect means and of political pressure, targetted especially at individual 'Aryan' businesses, so as to obstruct their relationships with Jewish business partners who, it was hoped, would thus be made 'willing to sell'. As we have seen was true in the interventions of the *Gau* Economics Adviser in the cases of Blohm & Voß and HAPAG, such covert intrigues did not always lead to success. In other cases, however, firms gave in to the pressure exerted on them and so contributed to the economic ruin of their Jewish commercial partners.

In 1936/37, the Jewish travel agent Walter Bamberger, situated at Pferdemarkt in Hamburg, fell victim to a conspiracy of this type. In the 1920s, Bamberger had built up his business into the biggest travel agency in Hamburg besides HAPAG, employing around 25 people.[51]

The success of the Bamberger company was based in particular on three main foci of its business activities. Firstly, as an agent for the *Mitteleuropäisches Reisebüro*, which had a monopoly on sales of railway tickets outside German stations, the Bamberger travel agency functioned as an official ticket-issuing department of the German state railways and for all other European railways. The annual turnover of Reich railway tickets alone totalled over one million RM. Secondly, Bamberger in collaboration with the 'Hamburg-South American Steamboat Company' (*Hamburg-Südamerikanische Dampfschiffahrts-Gesellschaft*, HSDG) had developed a programme of sea voyages combined with excursions on land that reached out to a wide section of the public under the slogan 'popular group tours by sea'. The travel agent's commission was two percent of the gross takings from passengers. Thirdly, Bamberger specialised in a concept with a wide clientele – short journeys and single events that ranged from special weekend excursions with the national railways to 'popular' theatre events at a standard price.

Through these activities, which – as the former Hamburg Transport Adviser noted – 'were laid on by no other travel agent in Hamburg',[52] Bamberger became one of the city's pioneers in modern style mass tourism. At the same time, however, he had dared to move into terrain that the National Socialists claimed for themselves through their organisation 'Strength through Joy' (*Kraft durch Freude*). In order to eliminate unwanted competition, which was preventing them from gaining a monopoly of organised mass leisure activities, they put pressure on the *Mitteleuropäisches Reisebüro* and on the *Hamburg-Südamerikanische Dampfschiffahrts-Gesellschaft* with the aim of destroying the economic basis of the Bamberger travel agency.

In December 1936, the HSDG was the first to give way and cut its business ties with Bamberger – against its will, as it underlined after 1945.[53] In February 1937 the *Mitteleuropäisches Reisebüro* followed their example and heeded the 'complaints' of the National Socialists, not without stressing the 'enormous successes' of their cooperation with Bamberger and adding that their business relations were 'always pleasant'.[54]

Robbed of the two most substantial operations on which his enterprise was built, Bamberger had to agree to the sale of his business on 1 April 1937 to German Africa Lines (*Deutsche Afrika-Linien*), which also became the agent for *Mitteleuropäisches Reisebüro* and took full advantage of Bamberger's distressed condition. The sale price of 55,000 RM did not even correspond to the annual profits of the company which, under normal circumstances, would have amounted to five or six times that sum.

Within only a few weeks the combination of pressure from the National Socialists and the servility of Bamberger's commercial partners had brought about the economic downfall of a once thriving business, forcing its 'Aryanisation'. After the sale of the company, Walter Bamberger's 'popular' travel operations that had made his business in Hamburg so well-known – as the Hamburg transport adviser recalled – were 'taken over by "Strength through Joy"'.[55]

## Foreign Exchange Control as Pacemaker for the Process of Expropriation

In 1936/37, the National Socialist state accelerated its repression of Jewish companies through finance policy mechanisms. Two institutions now became central to the expropriation of businesses from Jewish owners that are only seldom mentioned in connection with anti-Jewish policy and whose role has been largely neglected in historical research: Customs Investigation Offices and Regional Finance Offices (*Landesfinanzämter*, renamed *Oberfinanzdirektionen* in 1937) which, as intermediaries for the Foreign Exchange Control Offices established by the Reich Economics Ministry, were placed under the Reich Office for Foreign Exchange Control in 1934.[56]

The fact that researchers have kept conspicuously clear of these institutions in the past is not just a product of the particular problems posed by the nature of the sources. Their preoccupations seem to reflect a feeling that this area, and also, indirectly, the 'illegal' rescue of Jewish property, lay in a morally delicate terrain on which firmly established perpetrator-victim categories tend to become blurred. Firstly, the active role Jews proved to have in saving their property appears not to fit the stereotype of the victim, helpless in the face of their persecution. Secondly, the Foreign Exchange Control Offices and the Customs Investigation Unit did not seem to correspond to the picture of a typical National Socialist institution involved in anti-Jewish persecution. Indeed, foreign exchange controls and thus controls on the traffic of currency between Germany and other countries had been introduced in 1931 under the Brüning government. Because of this, the Regional Finance Offices responsible for this area after 1945 succeeded in persuading the public that their behaviour had always remained within the bounds of normal legal rules.[57] However, examining the behaviour of these institutions in concrete individual cases reveals a complicated and confused situation that cannot be framed within a simple dualistic schema of 'illegal' action and official reaction and that does not fit the model of 'challenge' and 'response'. In 1936/37, supervision of currency exchange in the National Socialist state had been radicalised by separating the responses of the Foreign Exchange Control Offices and Customs Investigation Unit from the behaviour of the Jews and allowing both institutions to become pacemakers in the liquidation of Jewish enterprises. Even a vaguely suspicious factor, indeed even the fact of being Jewish, was now enough to prompt measures confiscating property and enforcing the liquidation of companies. This radicalisation was the result of a long process during which specific exchange control regulations and the work of authorising and supervisory mechanisms were steadily extended.[58]

The legal bases for the escalation of control and licencing activity was formed by the 'Law against Betraying the German National Economy'[59] of 12 June 1933 and the 'Law on Exchange Control'[60] of 4 February 1935. Thenceforth, not only was a licence necessary for acquiring foreign currency with Reich Marks or for transferring Reich Marks abroad, but also for buying gold, precious metals and securities. A licence was likewise required for payments to a foreigner in Reich Marks and had to be made via a blocked account that limited the foreigner's ability to dispose over the payment. Foreign currency automatically had 'to be offered' to the Reichsbank.

In addition to the Reichsbank and the Regional Finance Office Foreign Exchange Control Divisions established in 1931, after 1933 a whole range of new control and supervisory institutions were formed. These included the 'Reich Office for Exchange Control'[61] established in September 1933, which in 1934 took over the supervision of Foreign Exchange Control Offices, and the initial twenty-five and later twenty-eight 'Supervisory Offices' that controlled goods traffic nationwide from 1934. Precise delineations of authority were hardly possible in this administrative jungle. The Law on Exchange Control of 4 February 1935 even legalised this anarchic pattern of authority by laying down in Paragraph 5 that a decision still remained valid if 'a Foreign Exchange Control Office had made it, although a Supervisory Office or the Reichsbank would have been responsible for it; the same applies to decisions of a Supervisory Office or the Reichsbank'.[62]

In Hamburg, its economy being oriented towards foreign trade, the licencing and control authorities quickly expanded into large institutions. There were three hundred and thirty civil servants and employees under Senior Executive Officer (*Oberregierungsrat*) Josef Krebs in the Foreign Exchange Control Office[63] of the Lower Elbe Regional Finance Office (*Landesfinanzamt Unterelbe*) – renamed the Hamburg Regional Finance Office (*Oberfinanzdirektion Hamburg*) in 1937 – nearly as many as the Reich Economics Ministry had in 1933. The Foreign Exchange Control Office was divided into a 'Licencing Department' under Reichsbank Chief Inspector Clausnitzer and a 'Supervision Department', directed by *Regierungsrat* Klesper. It focused on monitoring, checking and prosecution in the strict sense. The office worked closely with the Hamburg Customs Investigation Unit under Senior Customs Officer Hackbarth, which was itself placed under the Customs Division of the Regional Finance Office and Regional Finance President and had four Chief Customs Inspectors, twenty-four Customs Inspectors and an unknown number of Senior Customs Secretaries and Customs Secretaries.[64]

The fact that the anti-Jewish discrimination exercised by these supervisory institutions was radicalised was primarily due to three factors. The first factor related to the establishment of the Foreign Exchange Investigation Unit in Berlin on 1 August 1936. On 7 July 1936, Prussian Minister President Hermann Göring designated *SS-Gruppenführer* Reinhard Heydrich as head of the 'Raw Materials and Foreign Exchange Staff', formed in April 1936, to establish a Foreign Exchange Investigation Unit. He referred to a conversation on 24 June in which they had defined the areas in which the new office would work.[65] This was not to be the last assignment that Heydrich was given by Göring in the wider context of anti-Jewish policy.[66] The appointment of Heydrich secured not only the personal and ideological influence of the SS over foreign exchange investigations but also represented a defeat for Reich Economics Minister Schacht and Reich Finance Minister Schwerin von Krosigk.[67] Among other things, the move subordinated the Customs Investigation Units in a material sense to the Foreign Exchange Investigation Office and placed all foreign exchange investigation authorities at the disposal, indeed under the central leadership, of Heydrich, in particular 'for more serious cases involving foreign exchange investigations that above all else have a political significance'.[68] The Foreign Exchange Investigation Office was even supposed to undertake the 'legal policy evaluation' of such cases.

In a speech given after the war, the head of the Hamburg Foreign Exchange Control Office, *Oberregierungsrat* Krebs, claimed that the Foreign Exchange Investigation Office and the customs investigations that had been done on 'direct instructions of Heydrich' were responsible for the anti-Jewish radicalisation of foreign exchange policy,[69] and similarly an employee in the Office of the Hamburg *Gau* Economics Adviser reported that foreign exchange and customs investigations had been pursued with especial vigour in 'Aryanisation' cases. *Gau* Economics Adviser Otte had 'particular difficulties with the Customs Investigation Office, which in the "Aryanisation" of cases falling under its authority pursued a course which Otte rejected uncompromisingly. The Customs Investigation Office had various contacts in the highest reaches of the SS and it was already a serious matter to go against the designs of the Customs Investigation Office.'[70]

Although both statements can be seen as clearly apologetic, responsibility for anti-Jewish measures being passed on to the Foreign Exchange Control Office or the *Gau* Economics Adviser, to Heydrich, the SS, the Foreign Exchange Investigation Office or the customs investigators, there is – as will be shown below – no doubt about the significance of the Foreign Exchange Investigation Office for the radicalisation of anti-Jewish policy.

This is confirmed by the fact that on 1 December 1936, as a result of their 'legal policy evaluation' of foreign exchange offences, a successful modification in foreign exchange law was declared which constituted the second radicalising factor in the anti-Jewish policy of the institutions supervising foreign exchange controls.[71] A newly inserted Paragraph 37a now permitted the foreign exchange control offices to prohibit anyone suspected of trying to send capital abroad from disposing of their property, to establish trusts to govern the property and to find 'other protective arrangements' that would be 'needed for preventing the intended trafficking in property'. However, from 1936/37, or, at the latest, from 1938, all Jews were seen as potential smugglers of capital, so that the former Hamburg *Gau* Economics Adviser Dr Gustav Schlotterer, now representing the Reich Economics Minister, instructed all foreign exchange control offices to treat each and every Jew interested in emigration as suspect smugglers of capital.[72] Thus, the new Paragraph 37a developed into a clause dealing with dispossession in general and enforcing the liquidation of property held by Jews in particular. From December 1936 to October 1939, in Hamburg Foreign Exchange Control Offices alone 1,314 blocking orders were issued against Jews following the provisions of this paragraph.[73]

The blocking orders that deprived Jewish company proprietors of their right to manage and represent their enterprise set a complex bureaucratic procedure in motion, almost completely incapacitating those Jews affected by it. Blocking orders from the Regional Finance Office went to banks, savings banks and post offices so as to freeze Jewish assets; to domestic and foreign business partners so as to confiscate any accounts receivable; to firms in which the Jews concerned played a role so as to freeze their investments and income; to the Gestapo, in order to confiscate their passports; to the Finance Office, in order to check tax arrears and the flight of capital; to the Customs Investigation Unit and the General Customs Office, so as to check possible failure to pay customs arrears; to the Reichsbank and the German Gold Discount Bank, in order to freeze assets held there; to the Chamber of Commerce and – when a case was related to the operations of an export firm – to the supervisory office responsible.[74]

As the surviving case records of the Hamburg Customs Office show, frequently the presumption of some irregularity was, by itself, sufficient for the Jews concerned to be incarcerated for a long time, delivering them into the hands of the bureaucratic machinery of the National Socialist state. In implementing these blocking orders the Customs Office had gone back to the extensive lists of so-called 'unreliable Jews' which it had systematically drawn up and had also transmitted to police headquarters and to the Gestapo.[75]

The third element in the radicalisation of the expropriation policy must be seen in the context of the extension of the foreign exchange investigation service in 1936/37. A decree from the Reich Economics Minister of 22 October 1936, and a corresponding circular from the Head of the Foreign Exchange Control Office of 19 November 1936, initiated the intensification of the Foreign Exchange Control Office's activities beyond its previous remit.[76] At the beginning of 1935 there were still ten permanent foreign exchange examiners in Hamburg, but their numbers had risen by the beginning of 1936 to twenty and in 1937 to thirty-two.[77] The number of examinations carried out rose from 1,044 in 1936 to 1,543 in 1937, and then to 1,967 in 1938.[78]

According to the decree from the Reich Economics Ministry, all businesses that were involved in any foreign exchange operations worth mentioning were to be examined periodically, every three years. In practice, however, Jewish firms were confronted with up to seven account and foreign exchange checks every year.[79] Thus, any formal offence on the rule book, which in view of the complexity of German foreign exchange law was virtually inevitable, could threaten the very existence of Jewish enterprises.

Altogether, foreign exchange policy had, through legislative authorisation and executive extension, been so radicalised that the supervisory institutions could react to vaguely suspicious developments with far-reaching measures that aimed to liquidate Jewish firms and Jewish property. Often this developed into a spiral of ever-more radical responses, with harsh measures by the state leading to counter-reactions that triggered still harsher measures. For instance, coercive measures aimed by a supervisory body at Jews who dealt in raw materials could start a process that ended with the liquidation of a host of Jewish firms in the fields of raw materials and scrap. The body charged with the supervision of woollen goods, for instance, forced some Jewish traders to sell their stocks at a fixed price on the grounds that they were suspected of overpricing. It then deposited the proceeds in a blocked account from which the traders could not withdraw their money without permission and from which the fines imposed upon them had to be paid. In reaction to these coercive measures some Jewish traders fled abroad in order to take their threatened property to safety. This in turn led the Foreign Exchange Investigation Office in Berlin to instruct all Foreign Exchange Control Offices to step up the seizure of property and place blocking orders against Jewish traders dealing in raw materials under Paragraph 37a.[80]

This type of connection between an increasingly radical foreign exchange policy and the liquidation of Jewish enterprises will be examined in more detail in the following section by focusing on Jewish firms in a variety of economic sectors. This investigation focuses our attention on the question of how, and with what results, Foreign Exchange Control Offices and customs investigators used the instrument of the preventative blocking order in daily practice.

## Foreign Exchange Policy and the Liquidation or 'Aryanisation' of Jewish Enterprises – Five Examples

### The Walter Jacoby firm, sugar exporters

The Walter Jacoby firm was one of the Jewish enterprises in the transit trade exposed to increased pressures from exchange offices and customs investigators from 1937 onwards. Founded in 1889, it exported German sugar until 1931 when the owner, Walter Jacoby, switched his business to transit trade in sugar, particularly between Czechoslovakia, England and the Northern European states.[81]

The transit trade of Jewish firms aroused the suspicion of both exchange offices and customs investigators because it inevitably involved debts being accrued by the companies abroad which – it was often suspected – would be used to evade customs duties. This distrust developed in 1937 into active repression, targeted directly against all Jewish transit trading firms independently of the behaviour of any individual entrepreneur.

At the end of 1937, the Customs Investigation Office deprived the company owner, Walter Jacoby, of his passport, thereby causing his business extensive losses since Jacoby could no longer prepare and conclude transactions abroad.[82] The Foreign Exchange Control Office moved in, and, at the beginning of January 1938, although no concrete grounds for suspicion had been presented, carried out a detailed three-day examination of the Jacoby firm which the owner felt to be humiliating and discriminatory. With the exception of a marginal point that was not even punished with a reprimand, let alone a fine, this examination did not bring to light any hint of an offence against foreign exchange regulations.

Krebs, the head of the Foreign Exchange Control Office, justified the draconian treatment of the Jewish transit trade firms – passport withdrawal, business restrictions, exacting controls – on the grounds of the 'Reich's need for security'. In a letter to the main Hamburg office of the Reichsbank he asserted: 'It must be assumed that at least all Jews with property have tried at one point to move their domicile abroad, thus creating the urgent danger that in this way considerable net assets will be taken abroad.'[83]

In addition to the measures imposed up to that time, he wished to compel Jewish transit trade companies to pass their income through a German bank, despite the fact that the charges imposed by German banks for collecting incoming receipts were 1.5 to two percent higher than those of foreign banks, diminishing the profits that went to transit traders by this percentage.

For the Jacoby firm, as for other Jewish enterprises, this created unbearable trading conditions. Although Jacoby was not guilty of any transgression, he was not allowed the unrestricted use of his passport. On special request he was allowed to make just one business trip to England in January 1938. This still left his business without an adequate basis for long-term activity, particularly since, in the eyes of his foreign business partners, this made Jacoby appear unreliable: the fact that he had to beg for his passport whenever he needed to conclude a transaction, and then could expect to have to make constant interventions to get it, endangered not only his own business but also the funds of his business partners. For this reason, Jacoby did not return to Hamburg from a business trip to England in January 1938 and his company fell prey to the foreign exchange needs of the National Socialist authorities. In letters to a business partner and an employee, he described his difficult position and made clear that he had not left

Germany of his own free will: 'I assume that you know how I was mistreated at the beginning of this month. I have told my English business associates of the conditions compelling my stay here, and believe after everything that I have experienced that I can neither offer my English friends nor my Czech business associates the long-term security for business deals that one expects from a firm of my standing ... Dear Herr H., we have known each other for over 30 years, and you will understand that I am not taking the step that is forced upon me with a light heart, but precisely because we have known each other for so long you will understand me.'[84]

Jacoby informed an employee of his that his English business partner had given him to understand 'that the aggravation of my personal situation still makes it precarious to conduct business with the company in the long term',[85] and added on a personal note: 'You will understand that I am only acting due to urgent pressure and that it causes me unending sorrow to separate myself from you after such a long time of working together, but the circumstances are stronger than I am and you will understand all of this. Do not be angry with me, dear Fräulein S., it strikes me to the soul that in business we must go our separate ways.'

The Foreign Exchange Control Office and the Customs Investigation Unit, which had clearly provoked the step taken by Jacoby and, accordingly, also expected it, immediately took measures in response to his flight. On 21 January 1938, the Foreign Exchange Control Office issued a blocking order under Paragraph 37a of the Foreign Exchange Law which robbed Jacoby of all rights over his company or his private property.[86] The following day, the Foreign Exchange Investigation Office confiscated Jacoby's private property, including his furniture and the contents of his home.[87] The Gestapo issued a wanted notice and instructed that Jacoby be arrested on his return,[88] while the Hamburg-Altstadt Finance Office published a 'tax wanted' notice (*Steuersteckbrief*) for Jacoby in the Hamburg newspapers.[89] The Foreign Exchange Control Office rejected out of hand his request to buy back his confiscated furniture and private memorabilia with foreign currency and to dispose of the company through its 'Aryanisation'.[90] On 25 January 1938, the *Gau* Economics Adviser nominated a 'trustee' to look after the abandoned company[91] who dealt with its ongoing unfinished business and liquidated the company in September 1938.[92] On 5 April 1939, the Foreign Exchange Control Office closed the books on the whole affair by moving that Jacoby's citizenship be taken away from him. Jacoby's denaturalisation was published in the official journal of the Reich (*Reichsanzeiger*) on 30 September 1939.[93]

### *J. Jacobi & Co.*

While dealing with the Walter Jacoby firm, the Hamburg Foreign Exchange Control Office also began proceedings against the Jewish transit trade firm *J. Jacobi &*

*Co.* On 11 March 1933, its owner, Sandor Weißenstein, who had taken the firm over in 1933 from his uncle Paul Haim, returned from a honeymoon in Switzerland and was summoned to the Foreign Exchange Control Office where, behind locked iron doors, he was 'questioned in the well-known and infamous way',[94] as Weißenstein later recalled it. Although the Foreign Exchange Control Office could not confirm its suspicion that he had smuggled foreign currency for his uncle, two days later it issued a blocking order under Paragraph 37a which deprived Weißenstein of the right to manage and represent his firm. The only reason given for this was, 'Herr Weißenstein is a Jew and as a member of the Jewish race there is a risk that he will attempt to evade the currency laws and move his domestic assets abroad.'[95] The explanation made clear that, at this point in time, being of 'Jewish race' was enough to remove Jewish company owners from the positions they had in their enterprises, regardless of their personal conduct or the letter of the law.

When Weißenstein's attempts to have the blocking order removed failed, he went to London where he had the foreign assets of his firm blocked. The Hamburg Foreign Exchange Control Office reacted in the usual way to these moves: it set up an auditor as trustee who liquidated the company and transferred the estate to an 'Aryan' businessman, Walter H., who told his business associates on 3 May 1938 that he 'had taken over the management of J. Jacobi & Co. which was in the process of being liquidated'.[96]

For the company's Jewish owner, this manoeuvre, camouflaged as liquidation, was a perfidious, covert form of 'Aryanisation' because the liquidation procedure gave him no chance of securing even a half-acceptable price for his company. At the end of May 1938, an infuriated Weißenstein sent a letter to his business colleagues from London, writing:

> Herewith I bring to the attention of my business associates that I have forsaken Hamburg after having fought, with practically no effect, against measures that would have practically paralysed my firm. I was subjected to such a comprehensive incapacitation, although detailed official scrutiny had not identified any violation of existing laws, that during the rather hostile hearing I had to explain that I did not intend to continue to direct the company from Hamburg under the restrictions imposed upon me. My firm was, without my agreement, taken over by Herr Walter O. H. and I reserve for myself the right to take whatever steps against the above-named Herr H. appear to me to be necessary to protect my rights in this connection.[97]

Yet Weißenstein could not prevent the liquidation and de facto 'Aryanisation' of his company. The only items he was able to take away from Hamburg to London were a few objects from his private home. Even so, claiming that while marrying in 1937 he had invested his fortune in material assets and household goods, customs investigators imposed an additional payment to the German Gold Discount Bank of over 10,000 RM[98] which had to be settled by his father-in-law.[99]

### Labowsky & Co.

Founded in 1914, Labowsky & Co., which imported and exported bicycle parts, was one of the key Jewish trading firms still conducting large transactions in 1936/37. In 1937 alone, Labowsky & Co. delivered almost £15,000 to the Reichsbank in foreign exchange.[100] This was no protection, however, against the repression meted out by the Foreign Exchange Control Office, which instituted a preliminary investigation at the end of 1937 against the owner, Walter Labowsky, and his partner, Sally de Leeuw, a Dutch Jew. The pretext was 80 RM that had not been settled from a transaction the company had undertaken.[101]

The owners now prepared to emigrate to Amsterdam, giving their most trusted employee power of attorney over their affairs, and on 20 January 1938 the Foreign Exchange Control Office issued a blocking order under Paragraph 37a of the Foreign Exchange Law.[102] Labowsky and de Leeuw thus lost their right to represent the firm. In addition, to use the domestic and foreign assets of their company would require the permission of the Foreign Exchange Control Office.

After this outright expropriation, the two owners emigrated to the Netherlands, recovering the foreign assets of their company and founding a new company in Amsterdam under the name Novex Trading.[103] Their choice to emigrate had been provoked by the Foreign Exchange Control Office and the couple did not make the decision lightly. On 24 March 1938, they wrote to their attorneys: 'You know the circumstances that caused us to leave Hamburg, and you will be able to imagine that only with heavy hearts were we able to transfer a company that represented the sum of our own life's work.'[104]

The couple's understandable demand for appropriate compensation for their business was sharply rejected by the Foreign Exchange Control Office, which was prosecuting both of them for foreign exchange offences.[105] It remains unclear why the two owners proved remarkably accommodating in the period that followed: they paid a fine of 4,100 RM, even paid back £660 from the funds they had received and on 1 May 1938 transferred the firm to their attorneys without themselves keeping any sum in compensation for the company.[106] The opening balance of the company assets now revealed a surplus of 33,000 RM, while the 'goodwill' of the business was worth at least 90,000 RM. The claims of the owners on the German Gold Discount Bank to the value of over 40,000 RM were also transferred to the new owners,[107] who thereby received over 70,000 RM, in addition to an outstanding company, without having to pay Labowsky and de Leeuw a *Pfennig*. This case, too, confirmed that the blocking order issued under Paragraph 37a meant no more in practice than expropriation without remuneration.

This form of 'Aryanisation' was correspondingly lucrative for the buyer. The new owners of Labowsky & Co. were even granted a generous 6,500 RM from the total of 18,000 RM taken in 'De-Judaisation Gains Tax' (*Entjudungsgewinnsteuer*).

Despite their readiness to cooperate, the former owners could not have hoped for a comparably accommodating attitude. If they had hoped to protect their new company's business relationships in Germany by taking an accommodating approach, then this proved to be an expensive miscalculation. Prompted by the Hamburg Foreign Exchange Control Office, the Reich Office for Foreign Trade (*Reichsstelle für den Außenhandel*) in Berlin included their new firm, Novex Trading, in a 'Directory of Insecure Companies Abroad' (*Kartei der unsicheren Firmen des Auslandes*). This meant that German firms were 'warned by German officialdom' against maintaining business relations with the company.[108]

The founder of the company, Walter Labowsky, did not outlive the National Socialist regime. In 1943, three years after the German occupation of the Netherlands, he was deported to the concentration camp at Theresienstadt.[109] From then onwards there is no trace of him. Nothing is known of the fate of his business partner, Sally de Leeuw.

### Gotthold & Co./Metallwerk Peute GmbH

From 1936/37, the radical methods of the Foreign Exchange Control Office and the Customs Investigation Unit began to be turned not only against Jewish trading concerns in the narrower sense but also against firms in the industrial sector. This can be seen from the example of *Gotthold & Co./Metallwerk Peute GmbH*, founded in 1908, which actually consisted of two separate firms – '*Metallwerk Hamburg*' (later renamed *Metallwerk Peute*) which smelted unrefined metals and the trading enterprise *Gotthold & Co.*, which sold the products of the metal works and in addition operated a transit trade in scrap metal.[110]

The Jewish owners of both undertakings were two brothers, Herbert and John Gotthold, and a former attorney, Hermann Bauer, who had risen to the position of joint owner. The senior partner, Herbert Gotthold, was one of the founders of the Hamburg Metals Exchange and officiated as a member of the boards of the German Metal Traders' Union (*Deutscher Metallhändler-Verein*) and the Hamburg Metal Union (*Hamburger Metall-Verein*).[111] From the outset, the development of the firm was subject to enormous changes of fortune. After a great upswing in the First World War, when the metal works developed a special process to smelt used zinc fuses, the enterprise suffered great losses in the period of the great inflation, forcing it into a temporary business relationship with Hugo Stinnes. In the 1930s, however, the business had developed well and somewhat consolidated its position. In 1936/37, *Gotthold & Co./Metallwerk Peute GmbH* was still the largest German supplier of metal to Fascist Italy.[112]

Although the company's development remained unimpaired during the first four years of National Socialist rule, the impact of the antisemitic climate on the private life of the owners was clear enough. In 1936, Herbert Gotthold had been forced to sell his house at Parkallee 47 to escape the antisemitic harassment to which he was subjected by his immediate neighbours. He later recalled that it had become unbearable to live in the house 'where [our] windows were hit, our children were harassed by neighbours, and our fruit was stolen from the garden'.[113] The house was sold for 33,000 RM, only a fraction of the original price of 115,000 RM.

In 1937, the Foreign Exchange Control Office and the Customs Investigation Unit suddenly began to attack the business. In September 1937, it became known that the co-proprietor, Herr Bauer, had saved several thousand Dutch Guilders in a separate account belonging to the Felix Kramarsky company in Amsterdam[114] which did not appear in the company accounts. Bauer and Herbert and John Gotthold were arrested and proceedings were opened against them for foreign exchange violations. In addition, the Foreign Exchange Control Office and Customs Investigation Unit installed a certified public accountant as trustee who prepared the 'Aryanisation' of the business. By May 1938 he had negotiated a sales contract with Franz S., an NSDAP 'veteran' who chaired the NS Metals Group of the Hamburg party organisation. The purchase price of 100,000 RM lay well under half the value of the firm and just covered the existing commitments of the enterprise. The 'Aryanisation' was in fact an expropriation without remuneration. 'I know I bought too cheaply', the National Socialist buyer admitted to the wives of the arrested owners. To settle his bad conscience, he promised them a private payment of 200,000 RM which he then did not deliver. As he later explained, it 'could have cost him his head and his neck'.[115]

On 4 May 1938, the owners were led out of prison to a notary in order to sign a sales contract that had been drawn up without their participation. If they refused to sign, an official from the Customs Investigation Unit threatened that they would be placed in a concentration camp.[116]

The foreign exchange proceedings ended in October 1938 in what was a fiasco for the Foreign Exchange Control Office. The Hamburg District Court (*Landgericht Hamburg*) acquitted the senior partner Herbert Gotthold while his brother John was given a fine which was deemed to have been served already on the grounds of the 13-month period he had been in the remand prison.[117] The co-proprietor, Hermann Bauer, received a two-year jail sentence. After the verdict had been rendered, the Gotthold brothers were arrested again. The Foreign Exchange Control Office issued a blocking order under Paragraph 37a of the Foreign Exchange Law because the Customs Investigation Office insisted on the payment of a 'ransom' of 10,000 Guilders to balance off the foreign exchange assets that had allegedly been concealed abroad.[118] The Gotthold brothers thus had to pay for an offence of which the Hamburg District Court had legally acquitted them only shortly before. Their Dutch relatives had to pay the 'ransom' before they could travel to the Netherlands, emigrating to England from there.

### The Arnold Bernstein Shipping Company

Founded in 1912, the Arnold Bernstein Shipping Company (*Reederei Arnold Bernstein*) was one of the largest Jewish businesses in Germany and even in the mid-1930s still employed more than a thousand sailors.[119] Its founder and owner, Arnold Bernstein, the son of a grain and liquor dealer, laid the foundation for his firm's success after the First World War, first by transporting ore, coal and wood around the Baltic Sea and then specialising in importing American automobiles and tractors to Europe. Using converted cargo ships, Bernstein was able to ship 93,000 automobiles to Europe in the years 1928–1935 alone.[120]

The shipping company was part of a group of firms linked together through their owner. Bernstein owned *Arnold Bernstein Schiffahrt GmbH, Hamburg*, with a total of 15 ships, and *Red Star Linie GmbH, Hamburg*, which he had taken over in February 1935, serving the route between Antwerp and New York. A decisive factor in the acquisition of *Red Star Linie* was the fact that its ships possessed a licence to transport goods without restriction, the 'General Cargo' licence, while the ships of the Bernstein Lines were only permitted to carry unpacked special freight. Another firm in the Bernstein group was the Palestine Shipping Company, Haifa, which provided freight and passenger services to Trieste and Palestine from 1934 onwards.

As was the case with all of the other large German shipping lines, Arnold Bernstein had survived the years of the global economic crisis and consolidated his enterprises only because of the credit assistance he received. For this he had to turn to the American capital market because the National Socialists were not granting Jewish shipping lines sufficient subsidies to compete. Among the principal creditors of the Bernstein Lines were Erie Railroad Company and Chemical Bank & Trust Company, both headquartered in New York.

From 1936, the Hamburg Foreign Exchange Control Office adopted an increasingly hostile attitude to his enterprises. That year saw the Office follow up for the first time on its suspicions that Bernstein's Palestine Shipping Company might have been helping Jews to shift their assets abroad: the absurdity of the claim emerged in November 1936 when the shipping line had to terminate its operations and submit a petition for bankruptcy because it had not been able to find customers for its ships.[121] Reporting on a foreign exchange investigation of September 1936, one auditor speculated that Bernstein had in fact lost his independent decision-making powers and had handed them over to his American creditors, because this was the 'essence of American capitalism'.[122] It was no wonder that the dissemination of just one more rumour in January 1937 was enough to lead to the introduction of a concerted campaign against the Jewish shipowner.

On 18 January 1937, an *Obersturmführer* of the Marine SA working at the shipping company spread the rumour that Bernstein and two of his attorneys wanted to leave for Antwerp.[123] A day later the following institutions were intervening in the case: the Foreign Exchange Control Office, the Customs Investigation Office, the Secret State Police, the public prosecutor at the Hamburg Special Court (*Sondergericht Hamburg*) and the Foreign Exchange Investigation Office (*Devisenfahndungsamt*) in Berlin, which, from this point on, was to coordinate and radicalise the measures taken against the company.[124] A few days later, on 25 January 1937, Bernstein was arrested in the Hotel Esplanade in Berlin. At the same time the Customs Investigation Office seized the company's ledgers in order to search them for any incriminating material.

What it was that the participating institutions – infected by an antisemitic psychosis – were accusing the Jewish shipowner of cannot be reconstructed with any precision from the case records, where suspicions about illicit capital movements between the different enterprises alternated with indications of purely formal offences.[125] Bernstein's attorney, Dr Stumme, put it to him frankly that it was not as if he had violated any foreign exchange regulations; he was rather the victim of a targetted conspiracy: 'You must know that the only purpose of the action against you from the outset was to eliminate Jewish influence over this large, successful enterprise.'[126]

When Bernstein was imprisoned on remand, the former chairman of the board of HAPAG, Marius Böger, was assigned the duty of managing his enterprises in trust.[127] In May 1937, the National Socialists attached one condition to Bernstein's release: that he transfer all of his companies to the trustee, Böger. This arrangement, which dispossessed Bernstein without compensation although it would at the same time have saved him from a long period in detention, collapsed because of the inglorious behaviour of the firm's principal American creditor, Chemical Bank & Trust Company, which dropped its demand for the release of Bernstein in order to gain better terms for itself.[128] This led to a show trial at the Hamburg Special Court (*Sondergericht*) in November 1937 as a result of which, Bernstein was condemned to two-and-a-half years in a penitentiary. While the trial was still underway, he had to sign a transfer agreement that robbed him of all rights to be involved in the management of his businesses. Bernstein recalled later that the only ray of light in this trial had been the speech of the second of his two defence lawyers, Dr Gerd Bucerius. Bernstein characterised Bucerius as one 'of the most capable men I have ever met, very liberal, warm-hearted, and courageous'.[129] Like Bernstein's first defence lawyer, Dr Stumme, Bucerius was also of the opinion that the trial was a stage-managed 'farce'. However, whereas a fearful Stumme avoided any word of recognition for Bernstein in his summing up, Bucerius came down vehemently in favour of his client, as Bernstein recalled in his memoirs:

> He described my life as an uninterrupted proof of my patriotism and of my readiness to serve my country and my compatriots. He mentioned my exceptional decorations from the war and how in 1919, when thousands of people were starving in Hamburg, I had opened a public soup kitchen at which everyone received a warm meal and where more than a thousand people were fed every day, for which I had paid out my own pocket. He reported how I had built up a large passenger and freight line from nothing and expanded German shipping to Belgium and Holland, and that in these years I had brought in more than $20 million for Germany and had created jobs for more than a thousand German sailors. He mentioned that my honourable conduct, my sense of responsibility and my ability had gained respect for me at home and abroad, and made me a model of German prestige and German economic power. The speech of this especially able and courageous man was like a clear, fresh wind that had blown into the stifling, devilish atmosphere.[130]

The courageous summing up of his defence attorney, Bucerius, did nothing to modify the verdict against Bernstein. While still in detention, Bernstein had watched his successor, Böger, quickly bring the shipping company to the brink of ruin as Bernstein's former business associates were boycotting the 'Aryanised' enterprise. He recalled in his memoirs: 'On the one hand, I felt a certain satisfaction that the thief who had robbed me of my property could not reap the fruit of his crime and that the Chemical Bank, which had dropped me and took part in the theft, was now in danger of losing its investment. At the same time, however, it made me sad to see how the work of so many years and so many successful battles was now in danger of being destroyed.'[131]

In March 1939, Bernstein's businesses were sold to the company that had once been his greatest competitor, the Holland America Line (*Holland-Amerika-Linie*). A few weeks before the outbreak of the Second World War, on 25 July 1939, Bernstein was let out of jail after having paid $30,000 that he had had to borrow from a friend abroad.[132] Two days later he left Hamburg and went via Southampton to New York. Hardly anything was left of his former wealth beyond three pairs of trousers, three old coats, three pairs of shoes and eight pairs of woollen socks, listed in his goods removal register.[133]

## The Foreign Exchange Control Office of the Regional Finance President and the Radicalisation of the Normative State

Almost no other model has influenced the interpretation of National Socialist anti-Jewish policy more lastingly than Ernst Fraenkel's study, first published in

1940, of the National Socialist *Doppelstaat* – the 'dual state' – according to which National Socialism juxtaposed a 'prerogative state' (*Maßnahmenstaat*), freed of normative ties and of restrictions on state intervention, with a 'normative state' (*Normenstaat*) whose actions were still subject to a codified legal order.[134] In particular, Fraenkel's study served as a primary inspiration to structuralist interpretations of National Socialist anti-Jewish policy. Thus Uwe Dietrich Adam's study of 'Anti-Jewish Policy in the Third Reich' viewed its eruptions into more radical phases as the 'external reflection of the struggle between the totalitarian pretensions of National Socialism and the rudiments of the normative state'.[135]

It is interesting that when Fraenkel described the crucial difference between normative state and prerogative state, the example he chose to use as an illustration was the Foreign Exchange Control Office: 'However extensive the discretion of an administrative agency – such as the Foreign Exchange Control Offices – this discretion can be exercised only within the limits of its clearly defined jurisdiction. Were the Foreign Exchange Control Office to exceed its jurisdiction, its acts could be declared null and void in a proceeding before the ordinary courts.'[136]

The preventive utilisation of Paragraph 37a of the Foreign Exchange Law in the examples given above has already shown the actual potential for an administrative authority of the normative state to escalate policy. Although it was formally possible to object against the dispossession at the Reich Office for Foreign Exchange Control – without being able to delay the procedure – not a single case is known of this happening in Hamburg, let alone one which was successful. To try to explain the radicalisation of National Socialist anti-Jewish policy solely in terms of the displacement of the normative state by the prerogative state overlooks this radicalisation within the normative state itself, which also contributed to the spiral of repression against the Jews. This radicalisation can be identified without difficulty in the everyday working methods of the Foreign Exchange Control Office.

Until 1935, the Jewish background of a defendant was not even mentioned by the Foreign Exchange Control Office in its investigations of foreign exchange offences. In 1934, when the Hamburg Foreign Exchange Control Office investigated Otto Arenson, referring to a brother-in-law, Julius Barmat, who had smuggled furs to the Netherlands as 'goods on commission', it did not hint at his Jewish background.[137] Two years later he would probably have been described as 'the Jew Arenson', the investigator would probably have referred to the 'Barmat Scandal' during the Weimar Republic,[138] and the supposed or actual misdemeanours of the accused would have been denounced as 'typically Jewish'.

From 1936 onward, nearly all investigation reports against Jews were peppered with antisemitic remarks. 'Jewish unscrupulousness'[139] and 'garbled Jewish ways of speaking' were joined by 'Jewish black marketeers'[140] and the 'dirty machinations' with which 'Jews who just want to emigrate shamelessly exploit the mechanisms of our economic life so as to transfer Jewish capital illegally' and thus 'to sell off the German people's assets at giveaway prices'.[141] Writing of a Jewish suspect, the President of the Regional Finance Office (*Präsident* of the *Landesfinanzamt*, later *Oberfinanzpräsident*), Georg Rauschning, went so far as to note that it was a feature 'of the Jewish nature, which knows no Fatherland and instead graces those countries with their presence in which they believe themselves able to enrich themselves at the expense of the host country'. The Jew was therefore 'an enemy of the people from whom the Reich and its economy should be freed'.[142]

Rauschning had been in office before 1933, and first became a member of the NSDAP in 1937.[143] It is still unclear whether his statements indicate that he was adapting himself to the antisemitic *Zeitgeist* or whether the political conditions of the time were activating antisemitic views which he already held before then. What is evident, both from his behaviour and from that of the officials in the Hamburg Foreign Exchange Control Office, however, is their inability to understand the situation of the Jews in National Socialist Germany. Why did they ignore the constraints under which Jews acted in the proceedings against 'illegal' attempts to salvage their assets, instead of giving an antisemitic interpretation of their behaviour, while members of the judiciary, for instance, occasionally came to a different assessment of the situation?[144]

If these men saw the constraints under which Jews laboured, then some fundamental questions about the self-understanding of finance officials as loyal servants of the state need to be addressed. Did they know they served an unjust regime which was persecuting and creating discriminatory legislation to deal with a minority group? Even more poignantly, did they know that they themselves were helping to effect this state-perpetrated injustice? If they did, this insight was so uncomfortable and fraught with consequences that officials who were not antisemites sought to escape it. In order to suppress their confusion, these men turned aggressively against the causes of their self-doubt rather than give way to it and reconsider their behaviour in a self-critical way.

In pursuing so-called 'foreign exchange offences', the Hamburg Foreign Exchange Control Office worked closely with the Customs Investigation Unit. Although the two institutions both operated under a common roof in the Regional Finance Office, delineating the authority of the two bodies in practice proved unfeasible. In a circular of January 1936, the President of the Regional Finance Office stipulated that the Foreign Exchange Control Office was to deal with general foreign exchange offences while the Customs Investigation Unit was to focus on currency import and export offences in the narrower sense. At the same time he invited the Foreign Exchange Control Office to follow the directive of the Reich Economics Minister 'to avail itself of the services of the Office of the

Customs Investigation Unit in the pursuit of general foreign exchange offences'.[145] Soon it found itself involved in the daily practice of secretly drawing on the Customs Investigation Unit in investigations of the operations of Jewish firms, the customs investigators camouflaging themselves as employees of the Foreign Exchange Control Office and only going into action as officials of the Customs Investigation Unit if it should prove 'to be necessary', as a circular from the Foreign Exchange Control Office ominously put it.[146]

The reports of the Foreign Exchange Control Office and Customs Investigation Unit were steeped in the same antisemitic language. The Customs Investigation Office described the 'foreign exchange offence' of a Jew as 'typically Jewish' behaviour, and even as indicative of an international Jewish conspiracy. In May 1937, the head of the Customs Investigation Unit, *Zollrat* Hackbarth, spoke in relation to an operation undertaken in pursuit of one investigation as a 'penetration into a closed Jewish front'. He claimed that 'Jews of German citizenship in Germany and abroad had united and deliberately and doggedly organised the illegal transfer of domestic Jewish assets'.[147]

Although the Foreign Exchange Control Office saw a formal definition of the powers of the Customs Investigation Unit as an important step to ensure it would not be institutionally superfluous,[148] in their close cooperation there was a blurring not only of areas of responsibility but also of the everyday operational practice of both institutions to a point where they were inseparable. This radicalised the behaviour of the Foreign Exchange Control Office in so far as the Customs Investigation Unit understood itself as an institution of the prerogative state, patterned after the Foreign Exchange Investigation Office (*Devisenfahndungsamt*) and the Gestapo. Like these institutions, the Customs Investigation Unit increasingly overstepped its normative boundaries and expanded its authority to areas that did not fall within its traditional range of tasks. For instance, it enquired into the sexual partners and sexual practices of Jews suspected of sending foreign exchange abroad, in order to initiate proceedings on the grounds of 'racial disgrace' (*Rassenschande*), proceedings which the Customs Investigation Unit was in no way empowered to pursue.[149] Its cooperation with the Secret State Police was so close that it even conducted interrogations on behalf of the Gestapo, 'since very extensive material presented itself and the office space at the Gestapo was very limited', as a report of the Customs Investigation Unit put it.[150]

The Foreign Exchange Control Office and the Customs Investigation Unit both increasingly developed investigative methods free of normative or even basic constitutional limitations. After 1945, an observer who was intimately familiar with their procedural methods, the Jewish lawyer Dr Friedrich Rosenhaft, recalled that from 1933, both institutions became 'fully' involved in the 'lawless exercise of power and acts of terror'. They used the complex tax and foreign exchange laws, 'grossly exaggerating' small items and making the financial penalties that were imposed 'into a significant source of income for the state'. The heads of the offices had compiled 'success statistics', given biased information to the courts and to the district attorney's office and applied ever-more radical methods 'in order to soften up their victims at the time of the first, "sudden" seizures and prepare them to make "declarations of submission"'.[151]

The methods of the Foreign Exchange Control Office and Customs Investigation Unit and the intensification of the antisemitic climate in 1937/38 sometimes led to a situation in which Jews in hearings before the Foreign Exchange Control Office or the Customs Investigation Unit confessed to 'offences' that they had not committed at all. By making such fictitious 'confessions', Jewish defendants were led to believe that the investigation and proceedings would be averted by the payment of a financial penalty. The hope was to evade the scrutiny of the authorities as quickly as possible, avoiding the case being handed to the Public Prosecutor's Office, which held incalculable risks for Jewish defendants: a long period of detention on remand; preventive restrictions on their assets under Paragraph 37a during their detention; legal proceedings under discriminatory conditions and with limited opportunities to prepare a defence, and possibly a prison sentence followed by incarceration in a concentration camp, destroying any opportunity for emigration.

The Foreign Exchange Control Office and Customs Investigation Unit regularly agreed to a 'deal' on the basis of a 'confession' if they had no evidence against the suspect and were themselves convinced of his innocence. In these cases, in addition to the official file containing the concocted confession, they also drew up a 'secret file' in which the actual circumstances of the case were recorded. How the Foreign Exchange Control Office and Customs Investigation Unit handled such a proceeding in practice, in defiance of all legal principles, will be described in more detail below on the basis of a concrete example.

On 12 September 1938, Leopold Garfunkel, as proprietor of Frank & Co., a store selling ladies' and children's fashionwear, was arrested by the Hamburg Customs Investigation Office. The basis on which the arrest was made was a 'confidential communication' from a 'contact', according to which Garfunkel had untruthfully indicated that he had received a loan of 30,000 RM from his relatives in Manchester, England, in order to gain certain pecuniary benefits when emigrating.[152] In reality the sum came from his own funds.

Garfunkel's hearing did not furnish any clues about the truth or otherwise of the confidential communication. Further clues or evidence that would have stood up in court did not exist. In this situation, in order to end the investigative procedure, Garfunkel made a proposal to the officials which was minuted and placed in a secret file. It read as follows: 'He [Garfunkel – F.B.] asked the officials at the hearing whether they would refrain from apprehending him if it were confessed that the 30,000 RM in question did not belong to his dead sister's daughters living in Manchester but were instead his own property. Since this confession does not correspond to the facts, however, it is therefore false.'[153]

The examining officials declared themselves satisfied with this 'agreement' and created a further, falsified minute that went into the official foreign exchange case records. In this note, the passage described the same events in the following words: 'I admit truthfully that it is not true, as I stated in my hearing yesterday, that the 30,000 RM belongs to my mother or more precisely the children of my dead sister. It is rather the case that this 30,000 RM has always been my own property.'[154]

In return for this 'confession' the officials at the hearing promised the end of investigations, which were to be concluded with a financial penalty following from an examination of the facts. In a minute written by the Foreign Exchange Control Office, Garfunkel's motives were described with telling frankness: 'The behaviour of G. is to be explained by the fact that *Volljuden* [i.e., those of full Jewish parentage] in Germany are now subjected to substantial actions and prefer to end an affair of this kind by payment of a sum of money instead of exposing themselves to further measures through a lengthy process of proving their innocence.'[155]

The note reveals how far the methods of the Foreign Exchange Control Office and Customs Investigation Unit had already departed from legal principles. The investigating authorities did not have to deliver proof of an act: it was for the accused to furnish 'proof of innocence'. Meticulous examinations of the evidence, conscientious auditing and detailed searches using the professional tools of foreign exchange examiners, tax inspectors and customs investigation officers were no longer necessary because, under the pressures exerted by the conditions of the time, Jews placed confessions on the record 'voluntarily'. On this basis, sizeable fines could be collected in investigation proceedings, in Garfunkel's case at least 50,000 RM, boosting the 'success statistics' of the investigating authorities.

Within a few years of 1933, extralegal approaches had been established by officials of the normative state which spared them from the nuisance of having to search for evidence. In this they were imitating the methods of the prerogative state, which, although it was seen as an institutional threat, nevertheless provided a model of methods that others could emulate. Where Jews and their legal representatives did not take account of these developments in their calculations when subjected to foreign exchange proceedings, but lodged appeals that were formally still available to them, serious consequences could follow.

This was the experience, for instance, of Dr Conrad Baasch, a lawyer engaged to represent Jews in numerous foreign exchange cases and who, in doing so, had openly denounced the behaviour of the Foreign Exchange Control Office. *Oberregierungsrat* Dr Fischer from the Tax Investigation Service (*Steuerfahndungsdienst*) consequently accused him of having shown himself to be 'most peculiarly engaged in the Jewish problem for a German lawyer'.[156] When, in April 1936, the head of the Hamburg Gestapo, Bruno Streckenbach, made enquiries into the behaviour of Baasch at the Regional Finance Office, the officials of the Foreign Exchange Control Office and those of the Regional Finance Office spotted an opportunity to get rid of the hated attorney. On 1 September the President of the Regional Finance Office, Georg Rauschning, sent the Gestapo an eighteen-page dossier on Baasch. Baasch was described as a personality who was 'no lawyer in the National Socialist sense', but who adhered to 'the purely liberal legal ideas of a bygone past'.[157] He was trying through 'the correct observation of purely formalistic regulations' to evade legal obligations 'that were laid down in the interests of *Volk* and state'. The dossier climaxed in the statement: 'It can easily be seen that such a "lawyer" would be particularly sought out by Jews and, especially in the context of the current struggle of the state and people to defend themselves against this alien race, for whose members the above is the representative, they would be attracted to him automatically.'[158]

On 21 September 1936, Baasch was taken into custody by the Gestapo as an enemy of the state and the people, and on 8 May 1937, in a show trial before the Hamburg Special Court, he was condemned to three years in prison for 'treachery'.[159] In addition, he lost his licence to act as an attorney and was classified as permanently 'unworthy of military service'. The representatives of the normative state – led by the President of the Regional Finance Office – had thereby set an example of a lawyer and in doing so revealed their own relationship to normative thought: they saw guarantees of legal procedure as a 'liberal legal idea' and normative principles as 'purely formalistic regulations'. The Baasch Case showed the extent to which the attitudes and operational practice of the normative state had been radicalised after three-and-a-half years of National Socialist rule.

The administrative approach of the bureaucratic *Normenstaat* has frequently been described by historians as harshly systematic and legalistic, an approach which could execute a political crime *sine ira et studio*, but which at the same time worked with great efficiency because it was cast in a legal form and according to regulations and could therefore be 'worked out' in the context of a 'normal' administrative procedure. This procedure – according to Michael Zimmermann, for example – was the product of an 'administrative routine that, as a strictly formalised, rule-bound procedure, was accustomed to avoiding concrete meaning, the correctness of the formal procedure being the decisive criterion of success'.[160] The modern bureaucracy's complexity and division of labour had, moreover, parcelled up the concrete responsibility of the individuals involved, minimizing, and also completely hiding, the moral consequences of their actions. Bureaucratic actions were thus taken in isolation, with the terrible result that the National

Socialist policies of discrimination, dispossession and annihilation barely seemed to be directly connected to each other any longer. Because of 'the moral indifference of the institution-specific ethos', the bureaucratic normative state was 'a suitable executive aide' for the National Socialists.[161]

The behaviour of the Hamburg Foreign Exchange Control Office can only be partially understood within this interpretative framework, however, heavily influenced as it is by the discussion of the pathologies of modernity.[162] The Office's approach did not distinguish itself primarily by a cold, bureaucratic legalism but is better understood – going beyond a superficial dualism between antisemitic ideologues and bureaucrats dedicated to service – in terms of internal processes of change in the normative state itself, which tended to depart from normative approaches, and by seeing this departure as an extension of its room for manoeuvre and as a liberation from constitutional restrictions. The plethora of antisemitic arguments in the files of the Foreign Exchange Control Office raises questions as to whether antisemitic ideology and conviction did not play a considerable role in this development.

## On the Significance of the 'Change of Course' in the Reich Economics Ministry at the end of 1937

Apart from the self-authorisation of the *Gau* Economic Adviser to licence 'Aryanisations' and the intensification of exchange control policy, the dismissal of Hjalmar Schacht and Hermann Göring's assumption of power as acting head of the Reich Economics Ministry marked a further step in the radicalisation of the 'de-Judaisation' of the economy in Hamburg and in the Reich.[163] There is, however, little cause to classify this as a 'decisive turning-point' in the displacement of the Jews from the economy, or in racist policy more generally.[164] Such an evaluation, firstly, overlooks the fact that the personnel reshuffle in the Reich Economics Ministry made no difference to the fundamentals of anti-Jewish policy – it was rather the result of a struggle for power between the Reich Economics Minister and the Plenipotentiary for the Four-Year Plan over the tempo of the preparation for war and over the underlying orientation of German economic policy in the future. Secondly, the 'Schacht era' had been no 'period of grace' for the economic activities of Jews, and, third, Göring's assumption of office prompted no systematic Reich-wide 'Aryanisation policy' on the part of the government, whose rather unmethodical ordinances continued to lag behind the dynamism displayed at the regional level. A poignant example of this dilatory approach, already seeming almost wholly out of touch with reality, is supplied by a circular on the exclusion of Jews from public orders issued by the Reich Economics Ministry on 1 March 1938,[165] a measure which had been carried out long before that time in most regions.

The changes made at the end of 1937 were, as a whole, rather symbolic and atmospheric in nature. With Hermann Göring, a henchman of Hitler had taken over the Office of the Reich Economics Minister and because of this many NSDAP functionaries in cities and regions around Germany felt encouraged to intensify their anti-Jewish measures.[166] His assumption of office acted as a catalyst, particularly since the Reich Economics Ministry now visibly abandoned its moderate approach to 'de-Judaisation'. The department once charged with the 'Prevention of Illegal Interventions in the Economy' (*Referat Abwehr unzulässiger Eingriffe in die Wirtschaft*), also known internally as the 'Jewish Protection Department', now mutated into the 'Jewish Department' (*Judenreferat*)[167] and then into the 'Jewish Questions' Division (*Abteilung Judenfragen*) under the direction of *SA-Führer* Alf Krüger ('*Judenkrüger*'), who later made a name for himself as the official commentator on anti-Jewish economic legislation.[168]

The material changes in anti-Jewish economic policy were essentially limited to three aspects.

On 27 November 1937, a decree from the Reich Economics Ministry instructed supervisory bodies to grant absolute 'priority' to non-Jewish importers and to limit the quotas of Jewish firms correspondingly.[169] Even before this, however, some supervisory bodies had either reduced or completely eliminated the import quotas of Jewish firms by themselves. Jewish importers of grain, feeds, seeds and herbs had already been excluded from competing for quotas in 1936 on the grounds that they were a threat to the Reich food supply.[170] In addition, before the decree of the Reich Economics Ministry was issued, the quotas held by Jewish importers of skins, bristle and coffee were also eliminated or restricted.[171]

In general, the supervisory bodies went far beyond the terms of the decree, telling Jewish importers that their import quotas were cancelled completely in order to force the 'Aryanisation' of their enterprises. In doing so they were also giving way to the pressure of 'Aryan' firms looking to increase their own import quotas through the elimination of their Jewish competitors.[172] The owner of the Rudolf Reich company recalled that from the autumn of 1937 – before Göring's decree – he had received weekly requests from the Supervisory Office for Oils and Fats (*Überwachungsstelle für Öle und Fette*) to sell his company.[173] In other cases the supervisory bodies threatened to eliminate Jewish partners,[174] thereby arrogating to themselves the position of the 'Aryanisation' authorities and extending their influence over the regulation of questions relating to company property.

Robbed of their business base, most of Hamburg's Jewish import and export firms were compelled to initiate their own 'Aryanisation' at the end of 1937.[175] *Oberregierungsrat* Gotthardt of the Reich Economics Ministry, the department head in the 'Jewish Questions' Division, later judged the restriction and cancellation of import quotas to have been of decisive significance in the displacement of the Jews from economic affairs. In a position paper on 'The Jewish Question in Economic Policy' written in March 1939 he told the Reich Economics Chamber (the *Reichswirtschaftskammer*): 'The economic exclusion of the Jews began in November and December 1937 with the curtailment of the quotas of importers. This set off a great wave of de-Judaisations.'[176]

The next phase in the radicalisation of anti-Jewish economic policy began at the beginning of January 1938, when the Reich Economics Ministry for the first time announced a binding definition of the term 'Jewish commercial concern' (*jüdischer Gewerbebetrieb*).[177] An enterprise was 'Jewish' if it had a Jewish owner; a commercial company or limited partnership was Jewish if it had a Jewish partner; a commercial concern belonging to a legal entity was Jewish if it was in law represented by a Jew, and a supervisory board was Jewish if more than one quarter of its members were Jews or Jews had decisive shares of the capital or voting rights. Where the bureaucratic registration and classification of Jewish enterprises had not already been accomplished, the decree assisted in advancing the process enormously.

Thirdly, a confidential circular from the Reich Interior Ministry, signed by Reinhard Heydrich on 16 November 1937, decreed that only in exceptional cases were Jews to be granted passports for foreign travel.[178] For example, an exception might be made where it served the 'German national economic interest', which a Jewish businessman had to prove by presenting a written reference from the relevant Chamber of Industry and Commerce. Even this procedure, burdensome enough as it was, did not offer any legal guarantees as the opposition of the Gestapo office responsible was enough to block the granting of a passport or for the passport to be withdrawn.

In December 1937, the Hamburg Chief of Police estimated that approximately twelve thousand Jews from Hamburg still had passports.[179] This figure was soon reduced by the withdrawal of passports from those Jews that the Foreign Exchange Control Office or the Gestapo classed as 'not absolutely trustworthy'.[180] In May 1938, the Reich Economics Ministry tightened these regulations further, obliging Chambers of Industry and Commerce to apply a 'stricter standard' in judging cases and to restrict the granting of passports in future to a single trip abroad.[181] The Ministry thereby began to submit all Jewish enterprises that retained international commercial links to a costly bureaucratic procedure, which increasingly restricted their freedom of movement. From August 1938 onwards, they also had to present an *Unbedenklichkeitsbescheinigung* to the Foreign Exchange Control Office certifying that they had no debts or taxes outstanding.[182]

It was this kind of bureaucratic harassment, and not the passage of comprehensive laws, that expedited the exclusion of the Jews from the German economy and the 'Aryanisation' of their enterprises in 1937/38. This development encouraged the regional NSDAP functionaries to intensify their attacks on Jews. At the beginning of March 1938, the *Gau* Inspector, Dr Hellmuth Becker, who was also the 'liaison officer' (*Verbindungsreferent*) between the NSDAP and the administration in Hamburg, announced publicly that, in future, Jewish stores in Hamburg would be marked out 'as [they were] in other cities in the Reich'.[183] Though this announcement was never translated into practical action – in Schleswig-Holstein, Bremen and Hanover the marking of Jewish businesses was introduced in 1938[184] – it nevertheless signalled an intensification of anti-Jewish policy in Hamburg. According to Becker, the time had passed when 'we were still extraordinarily tolerant here' in Hamburg.[185] Harassment and antisemitic repression now increased. In March 1938, for instance, the Hamburg Office for Price Supervision, with help from the Gestapo, struck out against Jewish traders in raw materials. Allegations that prices were excessive led to the imposition of enormous fines and were used 'to carry out a thorough and comprehensive overhaul of the raw materials trade in Hamburg', as the National Socialist *Hamburger Tageblatt* described this form of 'Aryanisation' by attrition.[186] Antisemitic measures like these were a signal to all Jewish company proprietors that it was no longer possible for them to manage their enterprises under tolerable conditions. The 'Aryanisation' of Jewish business thus entered its decisive phase.

## Notes

1. Adam, *Judenpolitik*, p. 172ff.; Genschel, *Verdrängung*, p. 144ff.
2. Barkai, *Boycott*, pp. 59–63; Fischer, *Hjalmar Schacht*.
3. Cf. Kopper, *Bankenpolitik*.
4. On the activities of the *Gauwirtschaftsberater*, see the regional case studies in Kratzsch, *Gauwirtschaftsapparat*.
5. Schlotterer and Otte reached the rank in the SS of *SS-Oberführer*, Wolff that of *SS-Standartenführer*. See Berlin Document Centre, Schlotterer, Gustav; Otte, Carlo; Wolff, Otto, SS-O.
6. Whether this characterization of the Hamburg *Gauwirtschaftsberater* is generalisable or, on the contrary, is specific to Hamburg, must remain open given the lack of empirical comparative studies. Gerhard Kratzsch, in his examination of *Gau Westfalen-Süd*, comes to another conclusion. There the personnel of the *Gau* economics machinery was comprised of 'well-situated entrepreneurs and businessmen, managing directors from the chambers of industry and commerce, factory managers, and the managers of enterprises and savings banks'. See Kratzsch, '"Entjudung"', in Herzig, Teppe and Determann, eds, *Verdrängung*, pp. 91–114, here p. 97.
7. On Schlotterer's biography, see Berlin Document Centre: Schlotterer, Gustav, SS-O; b. 1906 in Biberach a.d. Riß, 1923 entered the NSDAP, 1921–24 commercial employee, 1925 studies

at the Mannheim School of Trade, 1929 at the Political Science Faculty of Tübingen University, 1930 Dr rer.pol., 1931–1933 Chief Economics Correspondent of the *Hamburger Tageblatt*, May 1933 *Regierungsdirektor* and then 1933–1935 President of the *Behörde für Wirtschaft in Hamburg* (Hamburg Economics Authority), until 1935 Regional Economics Adviser in Hamburg, 1935 *Ministerialrat* (Ministerial Counsellor) in the *Reichswirtschaftsministerium*, 1938 *Ministerialdirigent*, 1941 *Ministerialdirektor* (Permanent Secretary), 1941–1944 *Leiter der Fachgruppe Wirtschaft im Ministerium für die besetzten Ostgebiete* (the Specialist Economics Group in the Ministry for the Occupied Eastern Territories).

8. Thus the evaluation of Ludolf Herbst, *Der Totale Krieg und die Ordnung der Wirtschaft. Die Kriegswirtschaft im Spannungsfeld von Politik, Ideologie und Propaganda 1939–1945*, Stuttgart, 1982, p. 133.

9. See below, Chapter VII.

10. On Otte's biography, see Berlin Document Centre, Otte, Carlo, SS-O, b. 1908 in Hamburg, 1914–1923 secondary school, 1923–26 commercial training, 1930 NSDAP, 1935–1945 Regional Economics Adviser in Hamburg, 1940–1945 *Leiter der Hauptabteilung Volkswirtschaft beim Reichskommissar Norwegen* (the Chief Economics Division of the Reich Commissariat of Norway) in Oslo, 1942 Hamburg Senator and Councillor of the Hanseatic City of Hamburg. In 1949 Otte was classified by the Denazification Committee for the Lüneburg region in Category IV (Fellow Traveller) ('Supported National Socialism, without however having promoted it greatly'). Cf. StAHH, *Senatskanzlei-Personalakten* (Senate Chancellery – Personnel Records), A 53, p. 26.

11. Thus the evaluation of Otte's colleague Dr Hans Köhler of 24 July 1948. Cf. also the report of the *Kriminalamt* (Crime Detection Office) of the Hamburg Police. Both can be found in BAK, Z 42 IV/6178, pp. 31-35.

12. Citation as in ibid.

13. StAHH, *Senatskanzlei-Personalakten*, A 53, p. 16, circular from the *Reichsstatthalter*, 12 June 1942.

14. On Wolff's biography, see Berlin Document Centre, Wolff, Otto, SS-O and BAK, Z 42 IV/191: b. 1907 in Kiel, 1928 *Abitur* (final school exams), 1931 Secretary, Reich Railways, 1934 inspector, Reich Railways, extracurricular studies at Hamburg University, national economics, 1934 economics diploma, 1935 Dr rer.pol., 1930 member of the NSDAP, 1936 Chief Assistant to the Regional Economics Adviser, 1940 acting *Gauwirtschaftsberater* and Head of the Economics Command in *Wehrkreis X*, HAPAG board member, Chair of the Armaments Commission in *Wehrkreis X*, *Wehrkreis* representative of the *Reichsminister für Bewaffnung und Munition* (the Reich Minister for Armaments and Munition).

15. See Bielfeldt, 'Politik', in *Staat und Wirtschaft*, p. 171; Statement by Dr Hans Köhler of 24 July 1948, BAK, Z 42 IV/6178, p. 34.

16. *Archiv WgA LGHH*, Z 995-2, p. 34, communication from Biermann-Ratjen, 24 October 1951.

17. BAK, Z 42/IV/191, p. 50, declaration of the *Ministerialdirektor*, Dr Günther Bergemann, 3 December 1947.

18. See below, Chapter VII.

19. *Organisationsbuch der NSDAP*, 4th edition, Munich, 1937, p. 335.

20. Cf. Bielfeldt, 'Politik', in *Staat und Wirtschaft*, p. 171ff.; communication from Otte to Mayor Krogmann of 9 July 1936, StAHH, *Finanzdeputation IV*, VuO IIA, 11n IX B.

21. Statement by Karl Frie before the Hamburg *Wiedergutmachungskammer*, 30 May 1951, *Archiv WgA LGHH*, Z 995-2, p. 167ff.

22. StAHH, *Hamburger Stiftung von 1937*, 24, p. 41., note on a conversation with Dr Eduard Hoffmann of 12 February 1947.

23. Citation found in Bielfeldt, 'Politik', in *Staat und Wirtschaft*, p. 170.

24. *Archiv Handelskammer*, 100.B.1.19, communications from the *Handelskammer* to Karl O. Mohr, 22 November 1938, and to Karl Eggers, 8 December 1938.

25. The restraint on the part of the Hamburg Regional Economics Adviser has a parallel in the attitude of the Regional Economics Adviser in the Westfalen-Süd Region. Cf. Kratzsch, *Gauwirtschaftsapparat*, p. 116ff.

26. *Archiv Handelskammer*, 100.B.1.4., *Gauwirtschaftsberater* to the *Handelskammer*, 26 November 1935.

27. Ibid., HAPAG to *NSDAP-Gauleitung* Hamburg, 25 November 1935; Blohm & Voß to *Handelskammer*, 5 December 1935.

28. Cf. Fliedner, *Judenverfolgung*, p. 114.

29. Ibid., p. 144.

30. Kratzsch, *Gauwirtschaftsapparat*, p. 150ff.

31. Statement by Karl Frie before the *Wiedergutmachungskammer* in Hamburg, 30 May 1951, *Archiv WgA LGHH*, Z 995-2, p. 167ff.

32. See Kaufmann's instruction of 18 June 1938, StAHH, *Staatsverwaltung – Allgemeine Abteilung* (State Administration – General Division), A III 2, p. 17ff.

33. *Archiv WgA LGHH*, Z 286-3, Statement by Edgar Eichholz, 10 February 1950, p. 11.

34. Ibid.

35. StAHH, *Oberfinanzpräsident*, 1, *Reichsstatthalter* Kaufmann to the President of the Hamburg *Landesfinanzamt*, 12 January 1937.

36. See, e.g., the note by Max M. Warburg on a conversation with Julius Flaschner of 29 December 1937, *Archiv M.M. Warburg & Co.*, No. 22056 (*Campbell & Co.*).

37. *Archiv WgA LGHH*, Z 2790-5, resolution of the First *Wiedergutmachungskammer* of *Landgericht Hamburg* (1 Wik 59/53), 16 June 1953, p. 19.

38. *RGBl* 1938, Part I, p. 414ff.

39. *Archiv WgA LGHH*, Z 421-1, sales contract of 24 December 1937, p. 64; company accounts, p. 67.

40. Ibid., p. 11, letter from C.H.A. Meier to Gustav Ely of 9 December 1937.

41. Ibid., p. 12, letter from Drs. Samson/Seidl to the *Landgericht Hamburg*, 29 February 1952.

42. Ibid., Z 184-7, p. 3ff.

43. Ibid., Z 1489, p. 107, statement by Hans Röglin, 15 September 1954.

44. Ibid., p. 108, statement by Werner F. Gebhardt, 25 September 1954.

45. Ibid., Z 986-1, p. 21, examination of 2 July 1951.

46. Ibid., Z 5737-2, p. 19, letter from Dr Stumme, 24 February 1953.

47. Ibid., Z 15202, p. 14, letter from Carlos Malter, 8 February 1954.

48. Ibid., Z 131, p. 5, letter from Dr Neuhäuser, 30 March 1950.

49. One single exception is presented by the Jewish partner of *J. Feigin & Co.*, who in February 1938 was still able to sell his share of the business without the authorization of the *Gauwirtschaftsberater*. Cf. ibid., Z 13144-1, p. 96ff., declaration by J. Trubowitsch, 17 July 1954.

50. Ibid., Z 995-1, p. 47, declaration by Herbert Meyer of 22 September 1950.

51. On the development of the business and the following statements, see ibid., Z 2102-1, pp. 7–9, 30–32, enclosure I, pp. 39–41, enclosure II, p. 22.

52. Ibid., p. 32, statement by former *Senatsrat* Paul Hübner, 18 January 1950.

53. Ibid., enclosure II, p. 22, report by the *Hamburg-Südamerikanische Dampfschiffahrts-Gesellschaft* of 2 December 1949.

54. Ibid., enclosure I, p. 23, communication from the *Deutsche Bundesbahn* of 18 January 1950.

55. Ibid., p. 31, statement by former *Senatsrat* Paul Hübner, 29 November 1950.

56. The growing use of finance policy to attack the German Jews has even today still been largely unexamined. In his memoirs, the Finance Minister of the 'Third Reich', Lutz Graf Schwerin

von Krosigk, diminished the extent of his coresponsibility for the persecution of the Jews beyond recognition (Lutz Graf Schwerin von Krosigk, *Staatsbankrott. Die Geschichte der Finanzpolitik des Deutschen Reiches von 1920 bis 1945, geschrieben vom letzten Reichsfinanzminister*, Göttingen, 1974). The otherwise distinguished analysis of Stefan Mehl, *Das Reichsfinanzministerium und die Verfolgung der deutschen Juden*, Berlin, 1990, also does not delve into the radicalisation process outlined here. The *Reichswirtschaftsministerium* indirectly took part in this radicalisation process through its subordinate authorities, the *Reichsstelle für Devisenbewirtschaftung* and the supervisory bodies. An overview of the activities of the *Devisenstelle* and *Zollfahndung* in Hamburg – the first – can be found in Gaby Zürn, 'Forcierte Auswanderung und Enteignung 1933 bis 1941: Beispiele Hamburger Juden', in Herzig, ed., *Juden*, pp. 487–514.

57. This argument played a central role in the restitution of Jewish property after 1945, in which the Hamburg *Oberfinanzdirektionen* represented the interests of the German Reich. Cf. Spannuth, *Rückerstattung*, esp. p. 137ff.

58. Helmuth Wolthat, 'Devisenbewirtschaftung und zwischenstaatlicher Zahlungsverkehr', in *Grundlagen, Aufbau und Wirtschaftsordnung des nationalsozialistischen Staates*, Vol. 3, Berlin/Vienna, 1939; Rudolf Stucken, *Deutsche Geld- und Kreditpolitik 1914–1963*, Tübingen, 1964; on the connection with and the beginning of foreign exchange control, see Harold James, *Deutschland in der Weltwirtschaftskrise 1924–1936*, Stuttgart, 1988; Reiner Meister, *Die große Depression. Zwangslagen und Handlungsspielräume der Wirtschafts- und Finanzpolitik in Deutschland 1929–1932*, Regensburg 1991.

59. *RGBl* 1933, Part I, pp. 360–363.

60. *RGBl* 1935, Part I, pp. 106–113.

61. *RGBl* 1933, Part I, pp. 1079 ff. and 1088.

62. *RGBl* 1935, Part I, p. 106.

63. Statement given by Krebs, by then a retired senior government offical, on 30 July 1968, *Archiv WgA LGHH*, Z 21091-1, p. 149ff. According to an inventory of 4 March 1939, at this time there were 278 people working in the *Devisenstelle*. See StAHH, *Landesfinanzpräsident*, 9 UA 1, Certification of the personal references of the senior officials and specialists in the *Devisenstelle* of 4 March 1939.

64. *Hamburger Adreßbuch*, 1937 edition, p. 35.

65. BAK, R 58, 23a, p. 144, *Ministerpräsident Generaloberst* Göring to *SS-Gruppenführer* Heydrich, 7 July 1936.

66. On the assignment of Heydrich on 31 July 1941 to prepare a 'Total Solution of the Jewish Question', and on the demographic policy behind it, see Aly, *'Endlösung'*, pp. 270ff., 304–308, 391.

67. It is significant that, in his memoirs, Schwerin von Krosigk outlines in some detail the clash with Himmler and the SS over the protection of customs border (Schwerin von Krosigk, *Staatsbankrott*, pp. 263–269), a conflict won by the *Reichsfinanzministerium*, but says nothing about the increasing competences that the SS won in founding the *Devisenfahndungsamt*.

68. BAK, R 58, 23a, p. 163ff., circular from Heydrich to all state police stations, 22 September 1936; StAHH, *Oberfinanzpräsident*, 4, Circular from the *Reichsstelle für Devisenbewirtschaftung* to the Presidents of the *Landesfinanzämter* and *Devisenstellen* of 16 September 1936.

69. Statement by Krebs of 30 July 1968, *Archiv WgA LGHH*, Z 21091-1, p. 150.

70. BAK, Z 42, IV/6178, p. 33, statement by Dr Hans Köhler of 24 July 1948.

71. *RGBl* 1936, Part I, p. 1000ff. *Gesetz zur Änderung des Gesetzes über die Devisenbewirtschaftung* (Law Modifying the Law on Foreign Exchange Control) of 1 December 1936.

72. StAHH, *Oberfinanzpräsident*, 9 UA 3, *Reichs- und Preußischer Wirtschaftsminister* (then Dr Schlotterer) to the *Oberfinanzpräsidenten - Devisenstellen*, 14 May 1938; *Devisenfahndungsamt* to the *Zollfahndungsstellen*, 14 November 1938.

73. Ibid., 10, report by the *Oberfinanzpräsident* for the *Reichswirtschaftsministerium*, October 1939.
74. Ibid., 9 UA 4, *Devisenstelle* to *Abt. F/Str.* of 27 December 1937.
75. List of 94 'unreliable Jews', 21 January 1938, in ibid., 42 UA 6.
76. Ibid., 1, circular from the *Devisenstelle* 'to all specialist areas', 19 November 1936.
77. Ibid., 4, Report on the 'Development of the Foreign Exchange Examination Service'.
78. Ibid., note on 'investigative tasks completed'.
79. Cf. for instance *Fa. Julius Lachmann*, which in the years 1935–1937 was subjected to fifteen account and currency examinations. Ibid., *Str. 677*, p. 10.
80. On the whole process, see ibid., 4, circular from the *Devisenfahndung*, 8 September 1937 re. *Auswanderung jüdischer Rohproduktenhändler* (emigration of Jewish raw material traders).
81. See on this ibid., *Str 441*, Vol. 1, p. 17ff., report on the sugar exports of Jacoby Co., above-mentioned foreign exchange examination of 7 January 1938.
82. Ibid., p. 15, letter from Jacoby to the *Zollfahndungsstelle*, 7 January 1938.
83. Ibid., enclosure (unpag.), letter from *Oberregierungsrat* Krebs to the head office of the Reichsbank in Hamburg, 19 January 1938.
84. Ibid., p. 68, letter from Jacoby to *B. Reuter & Co.*, 21 January 1938.
85. This and the following citation from ibid., R 1938/5, Vol. 1, letter from Jacoby of 20 January 1938 (unpag.).
86. Ibid., *Str 441*, Vol. 1, p. 27, note from the *Devisenstelle*, 21 January 1938.
87. Ibid., p. 63, memorandum from the *Zollfahndungsstelle*, 22 January 1938.
88. Ibid., p. 80, note from the *Devisenstelle* of 2 February 1938.
89. *Hamburger Tageblatt*, 22 September 1938.
90. StAHH, *Oberfinanzpräsident*, Str 441, Vol. 1, p. 88, communication from the *Devisenstelle* to Jacoby, 4 February 1938.
91. Ibid., p. 60, note by the *Devisenstelle*, 1 February 1938.
92. Ibid., p. 190, letter from Paul Eiler to the *Devisenstelle*, 21 September 1938.
93. Ibid., unpag., communication from the *Devisenstelle* to the Gestapo, 5 April 1939; note by the *Devisenstelle*, 9 December 1940.
94. *Archiv WgA LGHH*, Z 3190-1, p. 41ff., letter from Crasemann of 23 April 1951.
95. Ibid., p. 41.
96. Ibid., p. 50, circular from Walter O. H., 3 May 1938.
97. StAHH, *Oberfinanzpräsident*, F-2385, circular from Weißenstein to his business associates (May 1938), p. 27.
98. Ibid., p. 30, report of the *Zollfahndungsstelle*, 29 July 1938.
99. Ibid., p. 35.
100. Ibid., Str 423, Vol. 1, p. 137.
101. Ibid., p. 16, report of the *Devisenstelle* on a foreign exchange examination at Labowsky & Co., 13 January 1938.
102. Ibid., Vol. 2, p. 120.
103. Ibid., Vol. 1, p. 41, 'Inventory of the sums that Herr Labowsky has taken to Holland'.
104. Ibid., p. 9.
105. Ibid., p. 78, communication from the *Devisenstelle* to Labowsky of 31 March 1938.
106. Ibid., p. 137, communication from the *Devisenstelle* to the *Reichswirtschaftsministerium* of 6 July 1938.
107. Ibid., p. 149, communication from the *Devisenstelle* of 3 August 1938 to the *Deutsche Golddiskontbank*.
108. Ibid., p. 187, communication from the *Außenhandelsstelle für Hamburg und die Nordmark* to the *Devisenstelle*, 28 February 1939.

109. Jürgen Sielemann, ed., *Hamburger jüdische Opfer des Nationalsozialismus. Gedenkbuch*, Hamburg, 1995, p. 225.
110. On the development of the firm, see *Archiv WgA LGHH*, Z 2869-1, Vol. I, pp. 13–27, Klabunde to the *Amt für Wiedergutmachung*, 31 October 1949; pp. 59–64, *curriculum vitae* of Herbert Gotthold of 3 November 1954.
111. Ibid., *curriculum vitae* of Gotthold, p. 59.
112. Ibid., communication from Klabunde, p. 19.
113. Solemn testimony of Herbert Gotthold, 8 November 1954, ibid., p. 55.
114. StAHH, *Oberfinanzpräsident*, Str 401, Vol. 1, p. 1, confidential memorandum of 27 September 1937. The response of the *Devisenstelle* was given by Hermann Bauer during his examination on 7 October 1937. See ibid., p. 23.
115. Citation following *Archiv WgA LGHH*, Z 2869-1, Vol. II, communication from Klabunde to the *Wiedergutmachungsamt beim Landgericht Hamburg*, 5 January 1951, pp. 5–19, here p. 14.
116. Ibid., p. 10.
117. Ibid., pp. 20–30, Judgment of the Hamburg *Landgericht*, 11 KMa 18/38, 24 October 1938.
118. Ibid., communication from Klabunde, 5 January 1951, pp. 5–19; Z 2869-3, p. 8ff., communication from the Hamburg *Landesfinanzamt* to the *Wiedergutmachungsamt beim Landgericht Hamburg*, 24 October 1950.
119. On the history and development of the Bernstein shipping company, see StAHH, *Oberfinanzpräsident*, Str 347, Vol. 1, p. 1ff., report on the foreign exchange control revisions carried out from 9–25 May 1935; *Archiv WgA LGHH*, Z 2660, pp. 13–20, Petition of Arnold Bernstein, New York, 18 December 1948. At the beginning of the 1960s, Bernstein compiled a long autobiographical manuscript in New York. Excerpts have been published in Monika Richarz, ed., *Jüdisches Leben in Deutschland, Vol. 3, Selbstzeugnisse zur Sozialgeschichte 1918–1945*, Stuttgart, 1982, pp. 172–182, and Limberg and Rübsaat, eds, *Deutsche*, pp. 104–113.
120. Figures can be found in StAHH, *Oberfinanzpräsident*, Str 347, Vol. 1, p. 7.
121. Ibid., Vol. 2, note by the *Zollfahndungsstelle Berlin* of 7 January 1936 re. Adolf Bloch; communication from Dr Samson to the *Reichsbankhauptstelle Hamburg* of 18 February 1937 (unpag.).
122. Ibid., Vol. 1, Report on the investigation of the Bernstein firms under § 34 DevGes of 30 September 1935, from 21–29 September (unpag.).
123. Ibid., Report in *Sachen Arnold Bernstein, Reederei* (undat., unpag.).
124. Ibid., *Devisenfahndungsamt* to *Zollfahndungsstelle Hamburg*, 20 January 1937 (unpag.).
125. Ibid., foreign exchange examination reports of 6 July and 30 September 1936 (unpag.).
126. Citation as in Limberg and Rübsaat, *Deutsche*, p. 104.
127. StAHH, *Oberfinanzpräsident*, Str 347, Vol. 2, communication from Böger to the President of the *Landesfinanzamt - Devisenstelle*, 23 April 1937 (unpag.).
128. Limberg and Rübsaat, eds, *Deutsche*, p. 105ff.
129. Ibid., p. 107.
130. Ibid., p. 110ff.
131. Ibid., p. 113.
132. StAHH, *Oberfinanzpräsident*, F 135, p. 5, Property declaration of 27 June 1939.
133. Ibid., p. 24, property removal register of 10 July 1939.
134. Ernst Fraenkel, *The Dual State: A contribution to the theory of dictatorship*, New York, 1941; on the theoretical foundations of the 'dual state' among the National Socialists, see Ulrich Herbert, *Best*, pp. 177–180.
135. Adam, *Judenpolitik*, p. 359.
136. Fraenkel, *Dual State*, p. 70.
137. StAHH, *Oberfinanzpräsident*, Str 4, p. 2ff., Report from the *Devisenstelle*, 12 April 1934.

138. On the Barmat Affair see Stephan Malinowski, 'Politische Skandale als Zerrspiegel der Demokratie. Die Fälle Barmat und Sklarek im Kalkül der Weimarer Rechten', *Jahrbuch für Antisemitismusforschung*, Year 5, Frankfurt am Main, 1996, pp. 46–65.

139. StAHH, *Oberfinanzpräsident*, Str 629, p. 96, Report of the *Devisenstelle*, 21 January 1939.

140. Ibid., R 1936/276, p. 35, Report of the President of the *Landesfinanzamt* to the *Reichsminister der Finanzen*, 2 May 1936.

141. Ibid., Str 678, Vol. 1, pp. 10, 17, Report of the *Devisenstelle*, 27 October 1939.

142. Citation as in ibid., R 1936/276, pp. 1ff., 38, President of the *Landesfinanzamt Unterelbe* to the *Reichsminister der Finanzen*, 2 May 1936.

143. Cf. Berlin Document Centre, personal records of Rauschning, Georg.

144. See, e.g., the judgment of the *Amtsgericht Hamburg* 11 Ms 14/39, 16 August 1939 (Chair: *Amtsgerichtsdirektor* Krause) against five Jews who wanted to smuggle money and family jewellery abroad through an 'Aryan' middleman, who nevertheless robbed them of their property. The *Amtsgericht* treated the accused with remarkable mildness, giving as a reason, 'that all five defendants had as Jews been badly affected by the November legislation of the year 1938'. There was thus a 'pressure' on the Jews, 'who as a result of the November legislation of the year 1938 had to emigrate and, after they had been forced to give up the major part of their money, wanted to secure a few valuables for the remainder of their stay abroad'. It was therefore appropriate 'to hand out to the same milder punishments than it would have been if the case were otherwise'. The judgment can be found in StAHH, *Oberfinanzpräsident*, Str 668, citations from p. 6.

145. StAHH, *Oberfinanzpräsident*, 4, Circular of the *Landesfinanzamtspräsident*, 22 January 1936.

146. Ibid., 9 UA 4, Circular of the *Devisenstelle*, 21 May 1938 re. Cooperation between the *Devisenstelle* and the *Zollfahndungsstelle*.

147. Ibid., Str 294, Vol. 1, Report of the *Zollfahndungsstelle*, May 1937.

148. Ibid., 4, letter from the head of the *Devisenstelle* to the *Oberfinanzpräsident*, 16 June 1937, re. Delimitation of the Areas of Work of the *Devisenstelle* and *Zollfahndungsstelle* in foreign exchange matters.

149. Ibid., Str 687, p. 27ff.

150. Ibid., Str 668, Report of examination by *Zollsekretär* Hellmann and *Zollsekretär* Pils, 27 March 1939.

151. Statement by Dr Friedrich Rosenhaft of 25 August 1950, *Archiv WgA LGHH*, Z 1001-1, p. 16ff.

152. StAHH, *Oberfinanzpräsident*, Str 492, p. 3.

153. Ibid., p. 12, cited from the secret files of the *Zollfahndungsstelle*.

154. Ibid., p. 9, minutes of customs investigation, 13 September 1938.

155. Ibid., p. 11, note by the *Devisenstelle*, 23 September 1938.

156. *Archiv WgA LGHH*, Z 1001-1, p. 68, 'General remarks on the continuing behaviour of the lawyer Dr B.' (for Dr Fischer).

157. StAHH, *Oberfinanzpräsident*, 65, confidential letter from the President of the *Landesfinanzamt* to the *Geheime Staatspolizei*, 1 September 1936.

158. Citation following ibid., p. 3.

159. *Archiv WgA LGHH*, 1001-2, p. 2.

160. Thus Michael Zimmermann on the behaviour of the bureaucracy with regard to the question of deportations: Michael Zimmermann, 'Eine Deportation nach Auschwitz. Zur Rolle des Banalen bei der Durchsetzung des Monströsen', in Heide Gerstenberger and Dorothea Schmidt, eds, *Normalität oder Normalisierung? Geschichtswerkstätten und Faschismusanalyse*, Münster, 1987, pp. 84–96, citation p. 94.

161. Zimmermann, *Deportation*, p. 94.

162. See *inter alia* Zygmunt Bauman, *Modernity and the Holocaust*, Cambridge, 1989.

163. Cf. Genschel, *Verdrängung*, p. 144ff.

164. Thus Adam, *Judenpolitik*, p. 173. For critiques of Adam's position, see Fischer, *Hjalmar Schacht*, and Barkai, *Boycott*, pp. 59–63.

165. Walk, *Sonderrecht*, p. 217.

166. See Kratzsch, *Gauwirtschaftsapparat*, p. 115, who cited the communication of one *GWB-Geschäftsführer* to an *Oberbürgermeister* in which it was stated that after Göring took office 'it was thereby certain that the Jewish influence on the economy would be checked'.

167. See Boelcke, *Wirtschaft*, p. 210ff.

168. Krüger, *Lösung*, p. 44.

169. See Walk, *Sonderrecht*, p. 207.

170. *Archiv WgA LGHH*, Z 286-3, pp. 10–12, communication from Edgar Eichholz, 10 February 1950; ibid., Z 4221-1, p. 27, communication from Dr Heidrich, 19 April 1951.

171. *Archiv M.M. Warburg & Co.*, Z I 5, communication from Leo Lippmann to Max Warburg, 15 September 1937.

172. *Archiv WgA LGHH*, Z 2036-4, p. 21ff., communication from Max Steidtmann, 25 September 1950.

173. Ibid., Z 131, p. 29.

174. Ibid., Z 32-1 (Sparig & Co.), p. 46ff., letter from Dr Kleinwort, 21 June 1951.

175. Examples *inter alia* in ibid., Z 29 (Delmonte & Koopmann Co.), Z 742 (Johannes A. Petersen & Co.), Z 2554-1 (Chemische Industrielle & Co. Ltd., Nachf. Adolf Rimberg), Z 180-7 (Guttmann & Widawer Co.), Z 2036-4 (Steidtmann & Nagel Co.).

176. *Archiv Handelskammer*, 100.B.1.31, lecture by ORR Gotthardt before the *Reichswirtschaftkammer*, 20 March 1939, on 'The Jewish Question in Economic Policy' (MS), p. 2.

177. Ibid., The *Reichs- und Preußische Wirtschaftsminister* to the *Arbeitsgemeinschaft der Industrie- und Handelskammern*, 4 January 1938.

178. StAHH, *Oberfinanzpräsident*, 9 UA 5, confidential decree of the *Reichs- und Preußisches Ministerium des Innern*, 16 November 1937.

179. Ibid., confidential communication from the *Polizeipräsident* to the Hamburg *Devisenstelle*, 23 December 1937.

180. Ibid., confidential circular from the head of the *Devisenstelle*, 29 December 1937.

181. Ibid., confidential circular from the *Reichs- und Preußischen Wirtschaftsminister* to the *Arbeitsgemeinschaft der Industrie- und Handelskammern in der Reichswirtschaftskammer*, 11 May 1938.

182. Ibid., letter from the Head of the *Devisenstelle* to *Sachgebiet R*, 25 August 1938.

183. *Hamburger Tageblatt*, 5 March 1938.

184. *Sonderarchiv Moskau*, 500-3-316, p. 819, annual report for 1938 of *Referat* II 112 in *SD-Oberabschnitt Nord-West*.

185. Cited from *Hamburger Tageblatt*, 5 March 1938.

186. *Hamburger Tageblatt*, 9 April 1938.

# Chapter V

# 'ARYANISATION' UNDER APPARENTLY LEGAL CONDITIONS (APRIL–NOVEMBER 1938)

## Actors and Decision-Makers Responsible for 'Aryanisation' after 26 April 1938

The process of 'Aryanisation' and the liquidation of Jewish enterprises had been accelerated in 1937/38 by a combination of ministerial measures and growing official chicanery. This raised the question of how the National Socialist state would react to one of the greatest changes in property ownership of modern German history which until then had only been regulated by self-appointed authorities like the *Gau* Economics Advisers.

The 'Ordinance on the Registration of the Property of Jews' (*Verordnung über die Anmeldung des Vermögens von Juden*)[1], signed on 26 April 1938 by the Representative for the Four-Year Plan and by the Reich Interior Minister, was the first of a series of laws and ordinances that translated the process of 'Aryanisation' into legal forms with the intention of securing the financial, economic and political interests of the German Reich. The ordinance of 26 April affected all Jews – as defined by the Nuremberg laws – whose property was valued at more than 5000 RM, obliging them to register their property and have its value assessed. In the property register detailed records were compiled of their agricultural and forest property, real estate, industrial property, capital goods, and even of their personal assets like jewellery, private collections and works of art.[2]

Still more drastically, an order issued by Göring on the same day infringed on the right of Jews to dispose of their property.[3] This meant that selling, leasing or re-opening a commercial operation required the granting of permission, 'legal-

---

ising' the informal obligation that already existed to obtain an authorisation for an 'Aryanisation'.

At the same time, however, the central government increasingly removed itself from the practicalities of the 'Aryanisation' process. An executive decree issued by Göring on 5 July 1938 limited the decision-making powers of the Reich Economics Ministry to cover 'Aryanisations' of Jewish enterprises with over one thousand employees – in all other cases the Reich Economics Ministry was to function merely as an appeals authority.[4] Beyond this, Göring reserved for himself all the measures that might be necessary in order – as it was ambiguously phrased – 'to ensure that the utilisation of the registered property be in conformity with the interests of the German economy'.

The bodies that were actually used to authorise 'Aryanisations', however, were the regional administrative authorities above the local level. Depending on the state and region they were in, these institutions diverged enormously: in Berlin, the Chief of Police; in Prussia and Bavaria the district presidents; in Saxony the heads of the district authorities (*Kreishauptleute*); in most other states either the state government or the interior ministry, but in Hamburg, as it was tersely phrased, 'the Reich Governor'. This made Hamburg *Gauleiter* Kaufmann the only Reich Governor in the German Reich assigned to act as the authorizing body for 'Aryanisations' *ad personam*. Moreover, since Hamburg had no Jewish commercial operations with over a thousand employees whose 'Aryanisation' fell under the decision-making powers of the Reich Economics Ministry, Kaufmann's competence in fact extended over all 'Aryanisations' in Hamburg.

The prominence given to Kaufmann in the ministerial decree of 26 April took account of his paramount position of power in Hamburg, which had been strengthened further by the Greater Hamburg Act of 1937 (*Groß-Hamburg-Gesetz*). The reorganisation of the administration had the effect of demoting the '*Regierenden Bürgermeister*', Krogmann, to the rank of an *Erster Beigeordneter* (First Councillor), and made Kaufmann the head of both the newly created Hamburg state administration and the municipal administration, these positions being collectively referred to under the overall title 'Reich Governor in Hamburg' (*Der Reichsstatthalter in Hamburg*).

If the Reich Governor's Office had to process declarations of property as well as authorisations for 'Aryanisation' contracts, it would have been completely overwhelmed. The question therefore arose as to how Kaufmann would, in future, regulate the 'Aryanisation' procedure and thereby balance conflicting interests against each other. For instance, the Hamburg Municipal Administration, which was subject to the German Municipal Regulations, pressed to be able to participate in the 'Aryanisation' of Jewish retail stores and workshops although, according to the wording of the decree, this was actually the responsibility of the

Hamburg state administration as the superior administrative authority.[5] At the
same time, according to Göring's executive decree of 5 July 1938, the local chamber of commerce had to be involved in the procedure. However, what was most
in need of clarification was the position that the *Gau* Economics Adviser would
assume, having previously functioned as the sole authorising body.

After Kaufmann transferred his authority for the registration of Jewish property to the Chief of Police, he gave instructions to the institutions involved on 18
June 1938, covering the implementation of 'Aryanisations' in Hamburg.[6] Kaufmann, though reserving for himself the right of making the final decision, otherwise delegated his decision-making competences to these institutions. Applicants
had to present to the Reich Governor a sales contract that was ready to be concluded, together with the last balance sheet and with an appraisal by an expert
appointed by the Chamber of Commerce or Handicrafts. If it was a retail store or
craft workshop, the responsibility for investigating and making a decision lay
jointly with the Economics Division of the Hamburg State Administration
(*Abteilung 5*), the Department for Trade, Shipping and Industry of the Hamburg
Municipal Administration, the Retail Division of the Chamber of Commerce or
the Chamber of Handicrafts and the *Gau* Economics Adviser. In all other cases –
for Jewish wholesale firms or industrial operations, for example – responsibility
initially lay exclusively with the *Gau* Economics Adviser, who was able to obtain
opinions from other institutions, though he did not have to. Beyond this he
could also alter sales contracts presented to him at his own discretion. If the Economics Division of the Hamburg State Administration was not in agreement
with a decision of the *Gau* Economics Adviser, it could not simply revise it but
had to present the case to the *Gau* Economics Adviser again and place it before
the President of the State Administration, who, as the paladin of the Gauleiter,
had no inclination to go against decisions taken by organs of the party.[7]

What, at first sight, appeared to be a balancing of different interests revealed,
on closer examination, the continuing dominance of the *Gau* Economics Adviser
in all questions relating to 'Aryanisation', though the intention of the legislator
had been that the *Gau* Economics Adviser was only to participate in this process
in a consultative capacity. In practice, no sales contract could be approved in
Hamburg if the *Gau* Economics Adviser opposed it. The statutory regulation of
'Aryanisation' was thus only a legal façade. In reality 'Aryanisation' was still determined by the despotic designs of the National Socialist party organisation while
the officials responsible for 'Aryanisation' in the state administration were rele-
gated to a minor role.

One significant factor behind the influence of the *Gau* Economics Adviser
was the peculiar constitution of Hamburg as a 'City *Gau*'. Whereas in a rural
'Area *Gau*', like Westfalen-Süd, the local police authorities and the mayor took

decisions and the *Gau* Economics Adviser then examined their decision,[8] in Hamburg the *Gau* Economics Adviser formulated the decision himself (as long as the business in question was not a retail enterprise or craft workshop). In this respect, in the conditions which pertained in Hamburg, the *Gau* Economics Adviser could be not unfairly described as an 'ideal executive organ in the continuing process of displacing' Jewish enterprises.[9]

Only in cases dealing with the 'Aryanisation' of retail businesses and craft workshops did he have to come to terms with the Retail Section of the Chamber of Commerce, the Chamber of Handicrafts and the Department for Trade, Shipping and Industry. Here too, however, he had a pivotal position by extending his influence into the negotiation of sales contracts where before he simply gave permission after contracts had been drawn up. In August 1938, he came to an agreement with the Chamber of Commerce, which was actually responsible for the appointment of consultants, that consultants 'who are appointed as specialists without the agreement of the *Gau* Economics Adviser will not be recognised'.[10] Thenceforth, prospective buyers and Jewish proprietors had to turn first to the *Gau* Economics Adviser, who then recommended one or more consultants as specialist auditors. After his formal appointment by the Chamber of Commerce, the consultant had to go back to the *Gau* Economics Adviser from whom he received more detailed instructions on how to value the Jewish enterprise. The *Gau* Economics Adviser was thus assured from the outset that stocks and inventories would be deliberately valued at the lowest level possible. In the 'Aryanisation' of large enterprises the *Gau* Economics Adviser had legal advisers like the National Socialist lawyer Dr Arthur Kramm working for him who fashioned sales contracts in absolute conformity with the principles he laid down; giving preference to party comrades, young businessmen and those starting out in business, preventing the formation of big companies, valuing Jewish enterprises at low levels, and completing the thorough 'de-Judaisation' of companies through the dismissal of Jewish employees.[11] The Chamber of Commerce and the Hamburg Administration only received contracts for scrutiny that had already been 'decided' along the lines laid down by the *Gau* Economics Adviser.

### The Participation of Commercial Institutions in the 'Aryanisation' and Liquidation of Jewish Enterprises

The readiness with which the Chamber of Commerce allowed its competence for the appointment of consultants to be curtailed by the *Gau* Economics Adviser appeared to confirm the attitude that leading figures in the commercial economy had taken towards anti-Jewish policy as somewhat passive observers who were keeping out of developments which they found indecent but who did nothing to protect Jewish businessmen who had been threatened.

At the beginning of 1938, however, signs that there would be a change of position were multiplying. By this point in time, the damage caused by the global economic crisis had finally been overcome, eliminating a factor that had affected Hamburg's export-oriented economy for considerably longer than it had other regions of the German Reich. Restrictions on the 'Aryanisation' of Jewish enterprises no longer appeared to be necessary for the advancement of economic policy. The 'change of course' in the Reich Economics Ministry of 1937/38 disposed of a delaying factor in anti-Jewish economic policy, which now became inexorably more radical. The foreign policy 'successes' of the National Socialist dictatorship in 1938 also consolidated its position, as many expected them to lead to a long period of National Socialist rule. Moreover, from 1938/39 the National Socialist policy of expansion opened a new, lucrative dimension for the Hamburg economy through the 'Aryanisation' of Jewish enterprises in the territories that had been annexed.[12]

Some element of compulsion may also have played a role in this change of position. In 1938 the National Socialists increased their pressure on the commercial economy to break off existing business relations with Jewish enterprises. Such official pressure can be seen in the 'Ordinance Against Support for the Camouflaging of Jewish Commercial Enterprises' (*Verordnung gegen die Unterstützung der Tarnung jüdischer Gewerbebetriebe*) of 22 April 1938,[13] which threatened German citizens with imprisonment if they were involved in 'deliberately masking the Jewish character of a commercial enterprise to deceive the population or the authorities'. This vaguely formulated directive sparked off a mood of insecurity in Hamburg's business circles and numerous enquiries about it were received by the Hamburg Chamber of Commerce. Thus, for example, *Rhenania Ossag AG*, which had business ties with Shell – a company suspected of being 'Jewish' – was considering marking the signs at its gas stations: 'Don't fill up with Jews' in order to fulfil its duty to supply information under the anti-camouflage regulations.[14]

The Hamburg Chamber of Commerce went far beyond the stipulations of the directive, recommending, for instance, that all non-Jewish employees in Jewish enterprises make totally clear in every legal transaction that they worked for a Jewish firm. According to the Chamber of Commerce, this would 'protect decent German businessmen from coming into conflict with criminal law'.[15] In this phrase, the Chamber of Commerce had subtly formulated the unspoken message of the anti-camouflage regulation that to be party to business ties with Jews could, under certain circumstances, become dangerous. Economic contacts with Jews were not criminalised outright, but were nevertheless stigmatised as indecent.

This was sure to move 'decent German' businessmen to keep their distance from Jewish businesses in the future so as to steer clear of possible complications.

The new attitude towards the destruction of the economic affairs of the Jews emerged clearly in the approach taken by the Hamburg Chamber of Commerce at the beginning of 1938. For example, in January 1938 Chairman (*Präses*) Joachim de la Camp, who had presided over the Chamber of Commerce since 1937, informed the *Gau* Economics Adviser that he had agreed a procedure with the President of the Executive Committee of the Stock Exchange (*Gesamtbörsenvorstand*) that action could be taken against undesirable 'non-Aryan' company proprietors – for instance, those who the Chairman felt had camouflaged themselves improperly with an 'Aryan' company name – even without legal regulations to justify it. This meant that the Stock Exchange could recall the proprietor's licence: 'In this way it will be possible, without violating the existing legal framework, to get rid of particular difficulties for which no special legal procedures have been established.'[16] Another development symptomatic of the Chamber of Commerce's change in attitude was the response of the Head of its Department for Commodity Trade, Hans E.B. Kruse, and his lawyer, Dr Leuckfeld, to the request of a Jewish company to rent out a customs warehouse to use for starting up a refining operation. Pressed for guidance from the Hamburg Economics Department, the Chamber of Commerce opposed the request on the grounds that 'the applicant is a non-Aryan and in addition the company to be created here would be under non-Aryan management'.[17] That it turned down the establishment of an enterprise providing new jobs simply by reference to the 'non-Aryan' origins of the applicant suggests that the Chamber of Commerce was no longer indifferent to the anti-Jewish economic policy, and now accepted it.

The Hamburg Chamber of Commerce now openly took the side of the 'Aryan' purchasers in sales negotiations undertaken in pursuit of company 'Aryanisations', also supporting them in their subsequent efforts to evade the contractual obligations they had entered into with Jewish proprietors. Dr Haage, a lawyer, wrote to Dr Eller, the head of the Berlin office of the Hamburg Chamber of Commerce, drawing his attention to 'serious loopholes' in the 'Ordinance on the Registration of the Property of Jews' of 26 April 1938.[18] For example, it provided no long-term indemnification agreements for Jewish employees, who were not to be obliged to obtain a licence with the result that Jews still received pensions that were so high it was 'completely unbelievable'[19] (Dr Eller) and therefore could not 'in the circumstances be described as appropriate'[20] (Dr Haage).

The Hamburg Chamber of Commerce also argued that legal contracts between Jewish and non-Jewish businesses should be open for termination without notice. It referred to the Spaten Brewery of Munich, which had granted a Jewish firm in Hamburg a ten-year contract for exclusive rights to the African market and wished to end the contract without notice.[21]

Finally, the Chamber of Commerce also took up the cases of those purchasers of Jewish property who had signed their contracts before 26 April 1938. Their contracts were to be subjected to the same restrictive requirements as contracts concluded after the April decree, in particular where these contracts still made 'goodwill' payments. In response to a demand made by the Reich Economics Ministry, Haage found a perfidious justification for this in arguing for the equality of opportunity of all Jewish proprietors: 'If a Jew sold his enterprise after 26.4.1938, he receives nothing for goodwill. It is not clear why a Jew who had concluded a contract before this deadline should still make claims today for remuneration for any goodwill that might arise.'[22]

Statements like this no longer held the slightest trace of the restraint in anti-Jewish policy which the Chamber of Commerce had exercised in the first years of National Socialist rule. Chamber of Commerce employees now took strongly antisemitic stances and actively placed Jewish firms under pressure. As an example of this, in 1938, the Hamburg Chamber of Commerce demanded that Jaques Heimann, the owner of *Schlesische Furnierwerke AG*, 'Aryanise' his enterprise, and an employee of the Chamber of Commerce poured scorn on Heimann's attorney by calling him a 'Jewish slave'.[23]

Those industrial associations representing middle-class interests whose initiatives had already gone far beyond National Socialist anti-Jewish policy in 1933 could also now be included institutionally in the process of 'de-Judaisation'. For instance, the Retail Trade Groups (*Fachgruppen des Einzelhandels*) sent a representative to the Hamburg 'Committee for Aryanisation and Liquidation of Jewish Operations' (*Ausschuß für Arisierungen und Liquidierungen jüdischer Betriebe*) which took the decision as to whether a Jewish retail business was to be dissolved or 'Aryanised'.[24] Presided over by both the Department for Trade, Shipping and Industry and the *Gau* Economics Adviser, the Committee enabled representatives of commerce and trade to force the liquidation of Jewish retail enterprises and thereby to eliminate unwanted competition. It is not surprising that, of the three hundred Jewish retail stores still trading in November 1938, only one third were 'Aryanised' and two-thirds were liquidated.[25] The resolutions of the committee were secret, and its decisions taken mostly on the basis of information that was not recorded in writing. This clandestine procedure protected the participants from complaints and hid the corruption and nepotism that increasingly affected the process of 'Aryanisation'. In justifying this procedure the Department for Trade, Shipping and Industry informed the Complaints Office of the Hamburg Municipal Authority that factors had often played a role in decisions 'that lay in the person of the applicant but that in most cases were not recorded in the minutes and which, since it was often a question of strictly confidential information from offices of the party, the administration or industrial associations, also could not be written down in legal documents just like that.'[26]

Similarly, representatives of commerce and industry were involved in the creation of the directory of Jewish industrial concerns prescribed by the third ordinance of the Reich Citizenship Law of 14 June 1938.[27] Professional associations divulged the names and addresses of the Jews in their profession and some businessmen also worked as consultants where there were questions about the extent of 'Jewish influence' within a company. The type of standards that this created can be seen from the advice of one businessman, who described a company as being under Jewish influence because its 'sales metods [sic] had often been reprimanded by the trade association', while he classified another as not Jewish because the owner was 'known as a calm, decent coleague [sic]'.[28]

The primary objective of the heads of professional associations and economic groups was to press for the 'elimination' of Jewish enterprises. In August 1938, the Head of the District Sub-Group for Haulage within the Reich Transport Group for Haulage and Storage, a Dr Gröseling, believed the time had come for 'the German haulage industry to cleanse itself of the Jewish firms that were still in existence'.[29] He therefore asked the Hamburg *Gau* Economics Adviser 'to make this purification of our industry here in Hamburg obligatory', pleading, in addition, for legal measures to shut down Jewish enterprises and proposing that Jewish businesses have their currency exchange licences withdrawn. The heads of other professional bodies forced their members to break off all trading links with Jewish enterprises. That the methods used were harsh is shown by what happened in July 1938 when the cattle agents and butchers of the Hamburg cattle market were obliged to boycott Jewish butchers.[30] Two butchers did not keep to this 'agreement' and in October 1938 found themselves denounced by name on the noticeboard of the Hamburg cattle market. The notice, written on 12 October 1938, described them as 'Jew suppliers' and demanded that they fasten a sign on their stall in future with the inscription 'Meat is delivered to Jews here'.[31] This public stigmatisation had its intended effect. Five days later the overseer of the Hamburg cattle market stated with satisfaction that, 'thanks to the discipline and the National Socialist convictions' of the cattle agents and butchers, all Jewish butchers had stopped making purchases in the Hamburg slaughterhouse.[32] He forbade them from entering the slaughterhouse area. Ruined by the organised compulsory boycott, Jewish butchers had to stop trading.

## Repressive Measures and the Context of 'Aryanisation', 1938

The discriminatory practices of the 'Aryanisation' process, which had crystallised by the time of the authorisation of contracts by the *Gau* Economics Adviser, intensified further in the course of 1938. Outwardly, the National Socialists still clothed their anti-Jewish initiatives in the garb of legality and suggested to the public through legal licencing procedures that they were implemented according to the principles of law, order and fairness – according to the principles of 'merit and decency', as the National Socialist press put it.[33] Moreover, in the officially licenced sales contract, which appeared at first sight to relate to a 'normal' transfer of property, the conditions under which sales were made were virtually undetectable.

In fact, however, the Jewish proprietor was not only confronted with anti-Jewish measures in the narrower area of economic affairs, but, with the passage of the 'Nuremberg Laws' of 1935, he was also subjected to special legislation that marked him out as a citizen with inferior rights and provided repressive regulations governing his everyday life. Compounding their worsening legal position, pressure on Jewish proprietors grew, the business conduct of their competitors became more ruthless, and inside their own enterprises the balance of power between Jewish owners and their mostly non-Jewish employees also shifted.

An example of this conjuncture of external and internal pressure can be seen in the 'Aryanisation' of the Rothschild & Leers chemical factory, which made oils, vaseline and petroleum products, or imported them from England and Scandinavia.[34] In 1936, one of the two owners, Dr Salomon Rothschild, was arrested by the Gestapo after an anonymous denunciation for *Rassenschande*. In respect to the rigidly discriminatory practices of the Hamburg judicial machine in such cases, which between 1936 and 1943 proceeded against a total of 1577 persons and found 429 guilty,[35] such denunciations constituted one of the most important means of placing pressure on Jewish company owners. Hans Robinsohn, who made a detailed analysis of the proceedings of the Hamburg District Court (*Landgericht*), concluded from his investigation that grounds for legal proceedings in cases where *Rassenschande* was alleged, 'were not infrequently reported for business motives, namely in order to exclude a competitor or in order to evade contractual obligations'.[36]

This use of the *Rassenschande* slander for economic purposes can be found in the records of the Hamburg Customs Investigation Office, which was supposed to investigate in criminal matters involving foreign exchange, but which, at the same time, routinely asked Jewish suspects about intimate details of their private lives. If the foreign exchange investigations did not produce sufficient grounds on which to initiate criminal proceedings, the charge of *Rassenschande* could serve the same purpose from the perspective of the Customs Investigation Office: to destroy the business of a Jewish proprietor. Many Jews actually suspected of try-ing to send capital abroad had to undergo a degrading ritual of questioning about their sex life.[37] Many an 'Aryanisation' began with a investigation into alleged *Rassenschande*.[38]

Dr Salomon Rothschild was able to avoid lengthy incarceration only because a company employee – as Rothschild's lawyer recalled after 1945 – 'allowed her virginity to be examined in the port hospital and in this way provided proof that no sexual relationship had ever existed between herself and the applicant'.[39] Roth-schild suspected that the anonymous denunciation originated with an employee who took over the business in July 1938 with the help of a financial backer who, it emerged, was a close acquaintance of Gauleiter Kaufmann. Because of this, all the attempts of the Jewish proprietor to do business with those purchasers who had offered a higher price for the company than his employee had broken down. Since the company's goodwill could not be compensated, the Jewish proprietor only received a modest amount for the company inventory. The valuation of the inventory by a licenced valuer was concluded within just fifteen minutes. Several months after the conclusion of the sale, the new owner of the firm threatened his former employer with a lawsuit if he did not immediately return 10,000 RM of the sale price. He justified this demand with the allegation that the valuation of the manufacturing plant had been too high. When the former owner refused to comply, his successor brought in the Gestapo, stopping his passport four days before his emigration to the USA and threatening to drag out emigration proce-dures or to make his emigration completely impossible. The former proprietor gave in to this extortion and handed over the 10,000 RM demanded.[40]

The 'Aryanisation' outlined here was typical in so far as the most unscrupu-lous adversaries of Jewish businessmen were generally drawn from among the employees of their businesses. Many made use of the weakened legal position of the Jewish owner and the falling market value of their enterprise without giving the owner any consideration, greedily making common cause behind the backs of the Jewish owner with party organisations like the Office of the *Gau* Economics Adviser, thus giving themselves a favourable opportunity to acquire the enterprise at the expense of their former employer.[41] 'Now we also want to be in the top slot', one employee told his Jewish employer after he had cancelled the lease of the business behind his back and procured a new lease for himself.[42] After 1945, many Jewish proprietors complained that under the National Socialists some of their employees had behaved like members of the 'master race' (*Herrenmen-schen*).[43] Frequently they sabotaged sales negotiations by bringing in National Socialist organisations, or they grabbed a personal share in the profits of an 'Aryanised' enterprise through secret arrangements with prospective 'Aryan' buy-ers.[44] The lawyer of the Jewish firm Maaß & Riege, which imported coffee and cocoa from South America, as well as other goods, had party officials accept him as a partner in the enterprise. Since he had no financial means, he also forced the Jewish proprietor to make a 'contribution' with which he gained a partnership in the 'Aryanised' company.[45]

Another of the repressive conditions in which the 'Aryanisations' of 1938 took place was the systematic devaluation of Jewish enterprises during the evaluation of sale prices – a development that had already set in with the authorisation of sales contracts by the *Gau* Economics Adviser, and which was then continued in 1938. Nonetheless, there was a considerable divergence in the price levels imposed, depending both on the branch of industry and region. The officials responsible for 'Aryanisation' in Württemberg conceded only half of the expert's estimate of the value of inventory and machinery.[46] In Hamburg, the only certainty in the conduct of firm valuations after 26 April 1938 was that any 'goodwill' payments were totally out of the question. In contrast to Württemberg, however, the expert evaluation was generally accepted in full. Even so, these could still vary enormously, depending on the instruction given by the *Gau* Economics Adviser. In a few cases, warehouse stocks were valued at retail prices.[47] For the most part, however, assessors based their assessments on the bankruptcy value of a business, which only amounted to half of the retail price.[48] In one extreme case a Chamber of Commerce official even invited the purchaser to buy the business for approximately ten to fifteen percent of the value of the inventory and bluntly suggested that he 'not be stupid and make the most of the existing situation'.[49] Sometimes the detailing of inventories, which, during the annual stock-taking for the enterprise, had lasted a number of days, only lasted a few hours, and often only a few minutes, as was the case for Rothschild & Leers.

A Jewish proprietor faced the prospect of further losses if his enterprise was still owed large sums at the time of 'Aryanisation'. According to a ruling by Hamburg's Gauleiter and Governor, Kaufmann, accounts receivable were not to be added to the sale price so as to eliminate the opportunity for Jewish proprietors to hide sums of money.[50] Only in a few cases were accounts receivable included in the sales contract, and even these were mostly assessed at very low levels.[51] In other cases Jewish proprietors had to recover the sums they were owed themselves after the completion of an 'Aryanisation', while 'Aryan' buyers were only rarely contractually bound to collect debts on behalf of the previous owner. Neither of these two options was to the advantage of the Jewish proprietor. In the first case, his legal position after the conclusion of the 'Aryanisation' had worsened so much that many debtors no longer fulfilled their obligation to pay, guessing that the proprietor did not have enough time to enter into a lengthy legal dispute with them. Under the time pressures introduced by their emigration plans, many Jewish proprietors were able to recover only a fraction of the accounts due to them.

If, in the second case, the 'Aryan' purchaser was obliged to collect the debts, the result for the Jews affected was for the most part no better. The buyer was hardly going to take any interest in an activity that required time and expenditure, but promised no gain in return. In addition, they did not wish to repel the clientèle of their newly acquired company by insisting on the collection of debts.[52]

Particularly high losses were suffered in the 'Aryanisations' of the firms of Jewish importers and exporters. Many Jewish wholesale businesses had, over the years, accumulated 'hidden reserves' through pricing their stocks at low levels so as to be better able to cushion themselves from sudden price slumps.[53] These 'hidden reserves' now proved to be very handy for the buyers because the reserves did not have to be taken into consideration when determining sale prices. Similarly, payments to Jewish businessmen in compensation for losses were dropped in the framing of the Additional Export Procedure (*Zusatzausfuhrverfahren*) without remuneration. The Additional Export Procedure was introduced by Reich Economics Minister Schacht in 1935, in order to stabilise the German export industry.[54] It granted export companies compensation for losses suffered to international competitors as a result of the general currency devaluation that the German Reich had not matched. Due to the relative overvaluation of the Reichsmark, many export businesses were no longer covering their domestic costs. As a result, an export business that could not cover its costs without state compensation was reimbursed by the German Gold Discount Bank, mostly in the form of interest-free securities, so-called 'Scrips'. In this way, many Jewish trading firms had accumulated considerable amounts in compensation that were excluded from 'Aryanisation' contracts and lost without any remuneration. The German Gold Discount Bank did not recognise Scrips demands from 'non-Aryans' planning to emigrate because they suspected that, after emigrating, Jewish businessmen would recover their outstanding foreign claims and would offend against the exchange laws in force.[55] The Jewish trading company *Gebrüder Haas* lost over 30,000 RM, *Ephraim, Gumpel & Co.* over 75,000 RM and the *Albert Geo Simon* company over 164,000 RM in compensation for losses suffered.[56] These Scrips demands on the German Gold Discount Bank could nevertheless, typically with permission from the Reich Economics Ministry, be carried over to the 'Aryan' buyer without the buyer being obliged to pay compensation to the Jewish proprietor.[57]

In the repressive climate of the 'Aryanisations' of 1938, it seemed clear to all of those involved in the process that the final 'de-Judaisation' of the German economy was inevitable and that it was now only a question of when it would take place. This lowered the market value of Jewish enterprises and reduced their owner's room for manoeuvre. The attempt to secure a lucrative share in the 'Aryanisation market' for themselves led to a general race for enrichment and to the use of ever-cruder methods by potential buyers, who often had party officials pass the message to a Jewish proprietor that if he did not sell his business 'something might befall' him and his family.[58] If, however, a prospective buyer had first obtained the necessary political backing from the Office of the *Gau* Economics Adviser or other party agencies, he would generally play for time and delay the conclusion of a contract so as to take advantage of the sinking market value of the Jewish enterprise and drive down the purchase price. The buyer of *Chemische Industrielle Gesellschaft mbH*, a Jewish commercial firm specializing in gloss oil imports, behaved in just this way. On 20 August 1938, the buyer concluded a sales contract with the company's Jewish proprietor, Adolf Rimberg, which the Hamburg Reich Governor licenced on 9 November 1938.[59] He delayed the transfer of the firm with the bogus argument that he wanted to wait first for permission to be given by the Supervisory Office for the Chemical Industry (*Überwachungsstelle Chemie*). In fact, he took advantage of the precarious position of the Jewish proprietor after the November Pogrom of 1938, and on 16 December coerced him into accepting so-called 'implementing conditions' for the original sales contract, which completely transformed its material content and practically constituted a new contract.[60] The alleged 'implementing conditions' freed the buyer from paying the purchase price if sufficient quotas were not granted to him by the Reich offices responsible – a process over which the Jewish proprietor could have no influence and that formally had no connection with the company sale.

Despite the fact that these conditions discriminated heavily against Jewish proprietors, 'Aryanisations' proved even more serious for those Jews employed by them. When the owners changed, they lost their employment and had hardly any prospect of finding a new job. Only in the initial years of the National Socialist regime did they have any real chance of being taken on after the 'Aryanisation' of a business. Ernst Loewenberg, the Chair of the Representative Committee of the German Israelite Community, recalled in his memoirs that, at this time, existing training contracts for Jewish apprentices were still being fulfilled.[61] In later years it was exceptional that Jewish employees were kept on.[62]

From 1937/38 onwards, almost all sales contracts contained a passage that enforced the immediate dismissal of Jewish employees. 'It is a matter for the buyer to deal with the non-Aryan personnel',[63] as most contracts tersely phrased it. By contrast, formulations in which 'in agreement with the competent party offices a transitional arrangement'[64] was to be agreed upon, or the 'Aryan' buyer was to compensate Jewish personnel, were almost generous.[65]

The wholesale dismissal of Jewish personnel was not always the result of the antisemitic convictions of the 'Aryan' buyer. Although there was no formal obligation to make dismissals in 'Aryanisations', an unspoken pressure from the autho-

rizing institutions mostly ensured that the buyers of Jewish enterprises parted
from their 'non-Aryan' employees. On the one hand, the buyer had to certify –
not only in getting authorisation for the sales contract, but also in the allocation
of foreign exchange and import quotas – that there was no longer any 'Jewish
influence' in his business. Having to give this guarantee at least made it impossible to continue to employ Jewish executive secretaries or managerial staff. On the
other hand, the National Socialist judicial administration made those buyers who
took on Jewish personnel liable for the conduct of their Jewish employees. This
was the experience, for instance, of the buyer of the *Altonaer Engros Lager* company, who took over the business in 1938, merged it with his existing enterprises
and continued to employ the Jewish personnel of the 'Aryanised' company. When
a love affair developed between a Jewish and a non-Jewish employee in his company, he was arrested and condemned by the Hamburg District Court to three
years in penitentiary on the grounds of 'complicity in *Rassenschande*'. Though the
judgment was later overturned, the company proprietor had to spend a total of
thirteen months in prison.[66] Such events quickly got around the business world
of Hamburg, and accelerated the dismissal of Jewish employees more efficiently
than any formal duty to dismiss them would have had because company owners
shrank from such unpleasant consequences and sought to avoid political 'trouble'
by making preemptive dismissals.

### 'De-Judaisation' and Middle-class Interests:
### the 'Aryanisation' of Jewish Chain Stores in Hamburg
### (Bottina Shoes Ltd, Speier's Shoe Store, the Gazelle Corset Store,
### Fiedler's Stocking Store)

With respect to the economic and structural consequences of 'Aryanisation' and
'de-Judaisation', historical research has succeeded in coming to a remarkably uni-
fied judgment. From 1936/37, the two processes considerably strengthened the
concentration of German industry, primarily favouring large enterprises, while
the middle-class economic interests that were particularly keen on 'de-Judaisation' had generally suffered rather more setbacks. According to Helmut Genschel,
one could even speak of the paradoxical result 'that an antisemitism originally
deriving from extreme middle-class pressures' had led 'to extremely anti-middle
class consequences'.[67]

Such judgments are based on contemporary analyses of the concentration of
economic power in 1936–1939, which had clearly identified many factors in
addition to 'de-Judaisation' that favoured concentration: the general expansion of
the German economy after surmounting the global economic crisis; the 'repatri-

ation' of German capital from foreign countries; state control of the economy through control over the allocation of raw materials, investment and labour, particularly in the context of the 'Four Year Plan'; cartel legislation and cartel policy, and, finally, fiscal factors and their contribution to the promotion of the liquidity of domestic enterprises.[68]

Crucially, however, it must be born in mind that the 'de-Judaisation' of the economy was not primarily carried out in the form of 'Aryanisations', but through the liquidation of Jewish enterprises, which, from the perspective of many middle-class company owners, eliminated an undesirable source of competition and which therefore represented a wholly desirable measure from a middle-class perspective. If, in January 1939, the highest-ranking middle-class functionary in Hamburg, Christian Bartholatus, Chair of the *NS-Hago*, reported the closing of two thousand Hamburg corner stores as a political success, this was primarily an allusion to the massive liquidation of Jewish commercial concerns in 1938/39.[69] Ludolf Herbst is therefore correct in interpreting the liquidation of Jewish businesses as easing competition for the middle-class economy, though he too proceeds from the hypothesis that 'Aryanisation' accelerated the process of concentration of power in the German economy.[70]

By contrast, Götz Aly and Susanne Heim have presented the liquidation of Jewish enterprises on the model provided by Vienna as the product of a holistic process of government planning combining 'racist ideology and national economic rationalisation', and also turning against inefficient non-Jewish enterprises.[71] They interpret the 'de-Judaisation' of the economy of Vienna as part of a 'drive towards planning and rationalisation',[72] eliminating the so-called 'overcrowding' of numerous branches of the economy and thereby becoming a model for subsequent National Socialist occupation and extermination policies in East Europe. In reality, however, 'de-Judaisation' in Vienna proved to be a combination of outright pogrom and undirected self-enrichment for National Socialist party men[73] – it was the opposite of a controlled process. Moreover, the economistic/functionalist reduction of 'de-Judaisation' by Aly and Heim overlooks the central significance of the racist/antisemitic *Weltanschauung* for the destruction of the economic livelihood of the Jews. Not even in their public statements did the National Socialists attempt to veil their anti-Semitic/racist policy with economic motives, or to justify 'de-Judaisation' to possible sceptics as a modernisation program needed for economic reasons. 'The Jewish question is a *völkisch* and racial and not an economic question', announced the National Socialist economics service *Die Deutsche Volkswirtschaft* in November 1938, emphasising accordingly that the displacement of the Jews from the economy was primarily 'a political measure'.[74]

To be sure, this political measure did have economic consequences. The following section examines these economic effects in the light of 'Aryanisations' effected in Hamburg, focusing particularly on the commercial middle class, whom researchers have generally assumed to be in favour of industrial concentration even if it was disadvantageous to them. In analysing this, the peculiar economic structure of the Hanseatic city has to be taken into consideration, marked as it was by a less than average degree of industrialisation, and a higher than average proportion of commercial enterprises of all kinds.[75]

In the initial years of National Socialist rule in Hamburg, the leadership of the city, as the campaigns against the Beiersdorf and Deutscher Tuchversand companies have shown, still intervened for tactical reasons against radical liquidation initiatives promoted by the commercial middle classes, because they were giving their highest priority to the economic consolidation of the city. At the highpoint of the 'Aryanisations' and 'de-Judaisation measures', which coincided with the final surmounting of the economic crisis even in Hamburg, priorities had shifted. The prominence which was now being given to the promotion of the middle class was made clear by the Hamburg Economics Adviser at the beginning of December 1938, when he revealed the definitive principles that would apply to the 'Aryanisation' of Jewish enterprises in Hamburg. According to his guidelines, among the most important principles behind 'Aryanisation' in Hamburg were, 'that it should not result in the creation of any industrial combines' and that it should 'not enlarge capital-rich firms'; instead, care would be taken to give preference to those prospective buyers 'who appeared technically to be in the new generation'.[76]

These principles related not only to middle-class interests, but were also directed against established industrial enterprises. In the few exceptional cases in which an applicant was able to take over more than one Jewish firm, the applicants were therefore not owners of established enterprises, but new entrepreneurs who, by means of an 'Aryanisation', sought to build an independent existence for themselves.[77] Because of the state's control of trade and foreign exchange, the bilateralisation of trade relations, the allocation of quotas and the introduction of import quotas, the wholesale trade and international commerce that were particularly characteristic of the Hamburg economy had developed into a 'closed shop', making it practically impossible for young businessmen to establish an independent business. Moreover, the total volume of German external trade stagnated at a level so low it was less than half of what it had been before the global economic crisis,[78] making the establishment of new enterprises even more difficult. 'Aryanisation' opened one of the few opportunities for those starting out in industry and for the younger generation of businessmen to overcome the entrance barriers that had been created by the National Socialists' control of the economy.

Since the available sources only give a limited amount of information about the careers and economic background of 'Aryan' buyers, the proportion of those taken by established enterprises on the one hand, and those by first-time owners or making sidewards moves from other companies on the other, cannot be calculated precisely. The proportion of established enterprises might be estimated at roughly one third.[79] The concentration of economic power that these changes in ownership directly effected was thus limited. In this, however, it should be noted that behind some 'Aryanisations' by new entrepreneurs lay a hidden concentration of economic power, as capital-rich financiers stood behind them in the background, and banks in particular acquired formal participation rights in the 'Aryanisations' they financed, and thereby accumulated economic influence in the 'Aryanised' successor companies. Deutsche Bank and Dresdner Bank, among others, became involved in the 'Aryanisation market', targeted the market for observation, financed numerous company purchases and acquired participation rights in the 'Aryanised' firms.[80]

In contrast to the limited concentration of enterprises through changes of ownership – primarily in industry – there was a remarkable number of decartelisations and deconcentrations that were carried out with the advantage of middle-class economic interests in mind. This development was particularly noticeable in the 'Aryanisation' of Jewish chain stores. These were companies in the retail trade with several sales outlets, but under a common management and administration as well as a centralised purchasing system similar to that of a wholesale business. In what follows, their 'Aryanisation' will be examined more closely on the basis of particular examples from Hamburg that describe an important facet in the relation between 'Aryanisation' and middle-class economic interests.

The first of the companies examined in this connection, *Bottina Schuh GmbH*, was closely connected to *Otto Klausner GmbH*, which had operated a shoe wholesale business since 1898, and in 1929 had an annual turnover of over 9 million RM.[81] Its owner, Otto Klausner, entered the shoe retailing business in 1923, and founded *Bottina Schuh GmbH* with a total of eighteen branches in North and Central Germany. The seat of the company headquarters and the mail order department was in Berlin, but five of the eighteen branches were established in Hamburg.[82] After the assumption of power by the National Socialists in 1933, the turnover in some branches stagnated and in some cases even declined,[83] but at the same time the company recorded substantial increases in its mail order business. The total sales of *Bottina Schuh GmbH* were raised by these gains from 6.1 million RM in 1933 to 7.1 million RM in 1937.[84]

In 1937, a district head of the German Labour Front (*Deutsche Arbeitsfront*, DAF) in Berlin pressed, for the first time, for the 'Aryanisation' of the business, and if it refused, threatened that the company would face a press campaign in *Der Stürmer*.[85] At this, the managing director of *Bottina GmbH*, Walter Pauli, embarked on negotiations with a number of prospective buyers. Negotiations developed furthest in 1938 with *Conrad Tack & Co. AG*, which itself operated approximately one hundred and fifty shoe stores, and aimed to reorganise their branch operations through the acquisition of *Bottina*. The purchase collapsed, however, because of the opposition of the DAF, the Berlin *Gau* Economics Adviser, the deputy Gauleiter of Berlin and the Head of the Reich Trade Group (*Reichsgruppe Handel*), *SS-Obergruppenführer* Franz Hayler, who urged the liquidation of the enterprise.[86] The Reich Economics Ministry, which, because of the size of the *Bottina Schuh GmbH*, had to give its authorisation for the sale, gave in to this pressure in August 1938. It decided that the continued trading of the company was 'not in the interest of National Socialist economic policy'.[87] The Reich Economics Ministry placed a liquidator in the company and instructed the Head of the Reich Trade Group to recommend 'splitting up the businesses into independent commercial operations'.[88]

The decision to liquidate the firm is worthy of note in that it led to the loss (at the time already foreseeable) of at least one hundred and fifty jobs in the company headquarters and mail order department. Under the leadership of Hjalmar Schacht, the Reich Economics Ministry had consistently rejected a radical mass liquidation of Jewish enterprises, arguing that they had to avoid economic setbacks and job losses. In the political and economic conditions of 1938, the scales had visibly tipped. Middle-class interests in the Reich Trade Group had the upper hand, with the Group urging that Jewish branch operations 'had to be disposed of'.[89]

The eighteen branches of *Bottina Schuh GmbH*, including the five stores in Hamburg, were therefore sold to individuals at giveaway prices and transformed into independent retail stores. In the process the owner, Ella Klausner – the widow of the founder of the company, Otto Klausner, who had died in 1932 – was stripped of her property with practically no compensation. She later emigrated to the Netherlands and, after the German occupation of 1940, was deported and murdered.

*Schuhwarenhaus Speier*, a company with its headquarters in Frankfurt am Main, also had five of its forty-three branches in Hamburg. The five shoe stores located in central Hamburg,[90] which belonged to the Jewish businessman Max Rosenbaum and his partners Louis Löb and Ernst Braunschweiger, constituted an independent company under the name '*Max Rosenbaum jr., Niederlage von Speiers Schuhwarenhaus*'. They sold the product range of the Frankfurt central office but were otherwise an independent chain of stores.[91]

The five branches were not 'Aryanised' in one go in 1938, but were broken off one after the other in the course of the year through underhanded political machinations. In this case, too, the initiative came from an employee of the DAF, who at the beginning of 1938 wanted to acquire the shoe store at Neuer Wall 13. He therefore pressed the landlord of the premises not to extend Rosenbaum's lease, due to run out in September 1938.[92] The actual beneficiary of this initiative, however, was the manager of the branch, who, working behind the scenes, deceived his Jewish employer and managed to gain possession of a new lease. Possession of the branch made him independent. He took over the personnel at the branch, and paid a mere 900 RM for the value of the inventory, while the stocks of the branch were divided among the four shoe stores still in existence.[93] In the same way – without a formal sales contract – the owners also lost their branch at Schulterblatt 142, which was also taken over by the current store manager after the lease had run out. The manager paid 545 RM for the store inventory and 6500 RM for the stocks, which were transferred to a blocked account on which the owner could not freely draw.[94]

While the third branch at Hamburger Straße 127 had to be liquidated, an SA *Standartenführer* from Bünningstedt near Ahrensburg, who was completely unfamiliar with commercial affairs, acquired the remaining branches at Neuer Wall 61 and Großer Burstah 34. On 15 October 1938, he concluded a sales contract with the owners, but eleven days later, in close coordination with the Hamburg *Gau* Economics Adviser, forced the owners into signing a supplementary contract from which the assumption of company liabilities originally agreed upon was deleted.[95] The final authorisation of the sales was executed on 15 November 1938, when the managing director Louis Löb (also a partner) was incarcerated in Sachsenhausen concentration camp.[96] The sale price of around 80,000 RM, which included no 'goodwill' payment, went into another blocked account and eighty-five percent of this was placed at the disposal of the buyer through the *Hamburger Commerz- und Privatbank AG*. Though Löb and Braunschweiger were still able to emigrate in time, the owner, Max Rosenbaum, was deported in 1941 to the Litzmannstadt (Łódz) Ghetto where he died in 1942.[97]

The largest Jewish chain store in Hamburg was *Korsetthaus Gazelle*, a retail firm for ladies' underwear and corsets that, in Hamburg alone, had over eighteen branches. Its owner, Ferdinand Isenberg, had gradually built up his business since 1907 into one of the largest enterprises in the field in the Reich. In 1938, the company was not 'Aryanised' as a chain store, but was broken up by the methods outlined above. At the beginning of 1939, a trust established after the November Pogrom sold eleven of the stores in Hamburg[98] to former saleswomen and wound up the remaining seven branches without a sale. In four cases, the sale was financed by private backers not involved in the trade who, in this way, obtained a part of the enterprise without even having to obtain formal authorisation for the company transfer. The very low purchase price paid in all of these cases covered the liquidation values of the inventory and of the undervalued stock.

In 1938, Ferdinand Isenberg, whose company had been completely ravaged, was arrested, charged with *Rassenschande*, and put into a cell at Fuhlsbüttel police

station where he committed suicide on 18 February 1939.[99] After the National
Socialists had destroyed Isenberg's life work, taken his property and driven him to
suicide, they went further still and attacked the dignity of the dead company
owner posthumously. Two days after his death, the *Hamburger Tageblatt* considered it appropriate to publish a lead article informing the public of the suicide of
the man they described as the 'race violator' 'Israel Isenberg' [*sic*] under the headline 'The end of a haggling Jew'.[100]

The fourth of the chain operations dealt with here, *Fiedlers' Strumpfläden*
(Fiedlers' hosiery), which had three branches in Hamburg, was also shut down in
1938 by a trustee assigned to the enterprise after the owner, Bernhard Rosen, had
emigrated to the Netherlands in July 1938.[101] While the trustee wound up the
branches at Hamburger Straße 6 and Bahrenfelder Straße 125 without a sale, he
sold the Große Bergstraße 123 branch to the former senior saleswoman of the
business, who was able to acquire the inventory without payment and the stocks
at retail price but with a reduction of a third. The owner did not receive a penny
of the proceeds from the sale or the liquidation, because they were completely
consumed by obligatory payments, taxes and – last but by no means least – by the
trustee's fee.

To summarise the results of the 'Aryanisation' of the four Jewish branch operations outlined above, with a combined total of thirty-one sales outlets in 1938,
the four enterprises were split up within a short period into twenty independent
operations, while ten sales outlets were liquidated and wound up. This not only
relativises generalisations about the tendency of 'Aryanisation' to increase concentration in industry, it also underlines the importance to be placed on middle-
class economic interests in the principal phase of 'Aryanisation'. If there was
concentration in some economic sectors because 'Aryanised' enterprises were
absorbed by existing enterprises, particularly in industry and private banking,[102]
then there were countervailing developments in the retail trade. It was particularly
common for the 'Aryanisation' of Jewish branch operations to be used by
National Socialist officials as an instrument to favour the middle class, giving former employees a chance to build an independent business for themselves. To be
sure, efforts at decartelisation and deconcentration such as these were limited to
the Jewish enterprises bought and sold at giveaway prices under the political conditions of 1938, and when owners no longer had any opportunity to defend
themselves. Asked by the Reparations Chamber (*Wiedergutmachungskammer*)
whether the deconcentration of businesses was a general characteristic of National
Socialist economic policy, the former Chairman of the Federation of the German
Shoe Industry (*Hauptverband der deutschen Schuhindustrie*) replied: 'I know of no
case in which an Aryan branch operation was broken up because middle-class
interests demanded it.'[103]

'Aryanisation' Between the Interests of the Reich and the Regions:
The Hamburg Reich Governor and the Sale of Much Sought-After
'Jewish Property' (Kraftwagen-Handels und Betriebsgesellschaft
mbH, M.M. Warburg & Co., Köhlbrand-Werft Paul Berendsohn,
Fairplay Schleppdampfschiffs-Reederei Richard Borchardt)

Though the Ordinance on the Registration of the Property of Jews of 26 April
1938, and the orders and directives that followed, revealed that the Reich had a
structural design for the 'Aryanisation' of Jewish property, its political implementation was transferred to the regional authorities while the Reich Economics Ministry only took decisions for large Jewish enterprises, and in all other cases was
involved merely as an appeals body. At the same time, the boundaries between
decision-makers at different levels were blurred by the dynamics of the National
Socialist system of governance.[104] Through the *Gleichschaltung* of the German
*Länder* and their transformation into *Reichsgaue* in 1937/38, Hamburg had lost
the sovereign rights it previously enjoyed. In this process, the *Hansestadt* had to
transfer many of its powers to the rapidly expanding 'Special Reich Authorities'
(*Reichssonderbehörden*), which numbered among the most important executors of
the interests of the Reich at the regional level. There was no need for any centralisation of the 'Aryanisation' process in order to involve the Reich or 'to guarantee
the utilisation of property due for registration in the interests of German industry', as it was put by Göring in an order of 24 November 1938.[105]

In the context of 'Aryanisation', the Special Reich Authorities often functioned as a transmission belt for the area-specific interests of the ministries and
institutions of the Reich, which were often oriented towards the arms industry. A
typical instance of the use made of the Special Reich Authorities is to be found in
a circular from the Reich Post Minister to Reich Post Managers on 11 January
1939, in which they were requested to register, before 15 February, all 'assets in
Jewish hands' that 'could be used with advantage by the *Deutsche Reichspost*'.[106]
Such orders guaranteed that the interests of the Reich were articulated in the
implementation of 'Aryanisation'. They did not, however, ensure the primacy of
Reich interests in every case, a result which could only have been secured through
an authorisation procedure centralised at the Reich level. If their interests collided
with the political aims of regional powerbrokers such as the *Gau* Economics
Adviser or the Gauleiter, the Reich Authorities possessed no direct means of influence, because the authorisation of 'Aryanisations' was concentrated at the regional
level by the ordinance of 26 April 1938. However, they could contest decisions
through the Reich Economics Ministry and if necessary have them revised – a
procedure that regional decision-makers realised they had to avoid if their authority was not to be damaged by frequent interventions from the Reich Economics

Ministry. Because of this, all of the participants in the process made an effort, even in the preparation of a decision, to balance the divergent interests of the parties involved. In practice, these divergences of interest shrank to a few, if mostly lucrative, cases, and in Hamburg more than ninety percent of the 'Aryanisations' that can be reconstructed from the surviving sources were carried out without the formal participation of the Reich. Only one person in Hamburg always had to strike a balance between Reich and regional interests, namely Gauleiter and Reich Governor Kaufmann, who stood at the institutional intersection of both decision-making levels as the highest 'sovereign decision-maker' in 'Reichsgau' Hamburg and as a regional representative of the Reich government. He was, moreover, the highest authorising instance for 'Aryanisations' in Hamburg.

That Reich and regional interests did not always harmonise with each other can be seen from the 'Aryanisation' of *Kraftwagen-Handels- und Betriebsgesellschaft mbH*, a Jewish automobile trading company on Hamburg's Repsoldstraße occupying a large plot of land with a big automobile centre of more than two thousand square metres.[107] Because the management of the Hamburg Reich Post Office was urgently seeking places to park its vehicles, at the beginning of 1939 it pressed the Hamburg *Gau* Economics Adviser for a takeover of the business.

The latter, however, showed little inclination to let the Reichspost have the enterprise, reporting that he had succeeded only shortly before then in 'forcing ... the Jew' – meaning the owner, Eduard Hertz – 'into the Aryanisation of his business'.[108] The *Gau* Economics Adviser had decided he would prefer an employee of the firm to be the new proprietor. With respect to the Reichspost, he referred to the earlier application of an employee, against which there could be no objection from both a material and a political point of view. Behind this argument, however, lay concerns pertaining to the principles governing the relationship between the state and the economy. Both the *Gau* Economics Adviser and the Hamburg Chamber of Handicrafts rejected the Reichspost takeover on the grounds that this would have meant 'an expansion of the public services of the Reichspost that the private sector did not want'.[109] The promotion of the private sector in Hamburg in preference to the expansion of the publicly owned economic sector was remarkable in that the National Socialists justified it primarily with reference to regional economic interests. When this led to the former employee being given the business, the managers of the Hamburg Reichspost brought in the Reich Ministries for Post and Economics in an attempt to reverse the decision.

This move created a situation which called for the intervention of the Hamburg Reich Governor. In order to forestall an intervention from the Reich Economics Ministry, if it would prove at all possible, he assigned Senator Wilhelm von Allwörden 'to reach a satisfactory settlement of the affair' with the President of the

Reichspost Office on an informal basis, and reprimanded the Hamburg institutions involved for the approach they had taken, which in his view was 'inappropriate'.[110] At this, the buyer of the business and the Reichspost Office came to an agreement that acknowledged the sale to the former employee, but obliged him to provide the Reichspost with whatever space it might need for its vehicles.

While the Hamburg Reich Governor gave priority to the interests of the Reich in order to settle this affair, which was not that significant in terms of Hamburg's economy, in other cases he gave greater weight to the regional interests of Hamburg. This was clear in the 'Aryanisation' of the banking house M.M. Warburg & Co., one of the largest private banks in the German Reich.[111] Even after 1933, the bank, founded in 1798, was able to preserve its preeminent position in the Hamburg economy. The special significance of M.M. Warburg & Co. was a product of its international reputation, the wide reach of its international connections and the large volume of foreign credit dealt with by the company on which its position as a significant international commercial bank was founded. The bank's reimbursement credits financed the commodity imports of a number of international trading concerns and companies in the raw materials processing industries in Hamburg. When, at the beginning of 1938, Max Warburg initiated the 'Aryanisation' of his business after Reichsbank President Schacht had informed him that his bank could no longer be a member of the Reich Underwriting Consortium (*Reichsanleihekonsortium*),[112] Hamburg's National Socialists made every effort to keep the bank functioning as an important factor in Hamburg's economy.

In view of the size and significance of the banking house, the Reich Economics Ministry had, at first, taken overall control of its 'Aryanisation'. Already in these initial stages, however, the Hamburg Reich Governor was involving himself in the negotiations, and conveyed his political views to the Reich Economic Ministry on 19 March 1938.[113] This was unusual in that Reich Governor Kaufmann did not intervene in most 'Aryanisations', or only became involved in their final phase. According to his letter, M.M. Warburg & Co. was not to be liquidated or sold to a large foreign bank, but, in view of its foreign connections and its significance for the Hamburg economy, was to be allowed to remain an independent enterprise. Consequently, the transformation of the bank into a limited partnership was also designed to prevent a credit institute from outside the area obtaining a minority shareholding, so giving it a veto over the bank's affairs.[114] These demands took account of the significance of the enterprise for the Hamburg economy and were aimed, in particular, at securing the bank's valuable reimbursement credit lines for Hamburg's international commercial firms.

The Reich Economics Ministry acknowledged the special regional interests of Hamburg in the 'Aryanisation' of M.M. Warburg & Co., and made clear from the way it divided responsibilities for the case within the ministry that it accepted the conditions set out by Reich Governor Kaufmann. The fact that *Ministerialdirigent* Dr Gustav Schlotterer, the Deputy Head of the Foreign Economic Department of the Reich Economics Ministry, took overall charge, meant that the proceedings were being directed by a man who had been the Hamburg *Gau* Economics Adviser and President of the Hamburg Economics Department until 1935, and who was a close and trusted friend of Kaufmann.[115]

According to the formal division of responsibilities in the ministry, *Ministerialdirektor* Kurt Lange, Principal Head of the Monetary and Credit Affairs Department (*Hauptabteilungsleiter für Geld- und Kreditwesen*), should actually have been responsible for the 'Aryanisation' of M.M. Warburg & Co. He, too, was no stranger to the state and party leadership of Hamburg, having been President of the Hamburg Audit Department until the beginning of 1936.[116] In this office, however, he had denounced the corruption of Hamburg's senators[117] and, as a member of the security service of the SS (*Sicherheitsdienst*, or SD), made the problem known within the party, with the result that the *Regierende Bürgermeister*, Krogmann, suspended him from his offices,[118] an official investigation was initiated against him, and later, when the corruption scandal could no longer be hushed up, he was 'promoted away' into the newly created Authority for the Four-Year Plan. For a character as difficult as Lange to be entrusted with the 'Aryanisation' of M.M. Warburg & Co. would have been interpreted as a hostile act by the state and party leadership of Hamburg. The unexpected appointment of Schlotterer, known as a representative of the interests of Hamburg in the Reich Economics Ministry, indicated to the Reich Governor, by contrast, that the Ministry was ready to meet his demands.

The Warburg family gained nothing from these backstage manoeuvres. Because their ideas about the sale of the business were not diametrically opposed to those of the Hamburg National Socialists, and the latter were avoiding giving any appearance of repression so as not to attract any international attention, which would have diminished the value of the bank, Max Warburg got the impression that 'even this government felt it was appropriate to treat us with a consideration that they at any rate had not demonstrated with all of the other firms'.[119]

Up until that time, therefore, the owners had a relatively free hand in the choice of partners and of the new company management. The choice of the new managers, comprising the company's long-time general representative Dr Rudolf Brinckmann and international trader Paul Wirtz from Hamburg, met with the regional economic interests of the Hamburg National Socialists and consequently they did not oppose it. The Hamburg Reich Governor only mounted persistent opposition to the desire of the Warburgs to be formally involved as voting partners. Writing to the Reich Economics Ministry, he explained that such involvement was 'not acceptable'[120] and when the responsibility for the authorisation of 'Aryanisations' was transferred to him on 26 April 1938, he only gave his authorisation for the former owners to retain a 'sleeping' stake.

After the 'Aryanisation' of the bank in May 1938, it finally became clear that the allegedly 'friendly Aryanisation'[121] was an illusion that had primarily been designed to deceive international opinion. Both the Reich and Hamburg's National Socialists were now implementing those demands that they had left out of the official proceedings, and if they were still doing so informally then it was with all the more effectiveness. The Hamburg *Gau* Economics Adviser enforced the dissolution of the 'sleeping' partnership, ordered the accelerated dismissal of the Jewish employees, extorted an 'Aryanisation contribution' from the new owners and placed two National Socialist 'supervisors' in the company.[122] The Reich used all the means available to it in terms of tax and duty policy and completely stripped the former Jewish owners during their emigration.[123] Fritz Warburg was arrested in the course of the seizures following 'Reich Crystal Night' in 1938, and was imprisoned for several months, serving as a potential hostage should there be international repercussions. Only in May 1939, after the intervention of the Hamburg banker Cornelius Freiherr von Berenberg-Goßler with Heydrich and Himmler's adjutant Karl Wolff was Warburg released.[124]

The Reich leadership and the National Socialists in Hamburg had successfully pursued their goals in the 'Aryanisation' of M.M. Warburg & Co., displaying both great persistence and remarkable elasticity. In the effective expropriation of the Jewish owners the success of the one in preserving the bank for Hamburg's regional economy was as complete as the success of the other in its concern for the financial interests of the Reich. Most striking, however, was the remarkable lack of friction displayed in the balancing of the interests of Hamburg and the Reich during the first stages of the operation.

A further example of this balance between Reich and regional interests is offered by the 'Aryanisation' of the only Jewish shipyard in the Hanseatic city, *Köhlbrand-Werft Paul Berendsohn*. Its owner, Paul Berendsohn, had erected the shipyard in 1921, on an area near Altenwerder known as '*Korbmachersand*', after working for twenty years as a technician, lawyer and company director.[125] Making use of gaps in the market, Berendsohn had specialised in the construction and repair of river and coastal motorships and in breaking up old ships, and also built steamboats for export to China and suction dredgers for use in the Baltic. Though his shipyard was one of the smaller ones in Hamburg, with about one hundred and twenty employees, its flexibility made it a particularly productive enterprise. Even under the National Socialist regime this remained so, in spite of the 'humiliating degradations' which the ruling National Socialists inflicted on him, as he remarked bitterly afterwards.[126] He and his family were not allowed to take part in a procession through Altenwerder, although the village owed its connection to the electricity grid to him. Painted in big red letters, the motto 'Perish Judah' adorned the floating pontoons of his shipyard. He had to leave the hoisting of the flag at his shipyard to one of his workers because he was officially forbidden to do it, and, in July 1938, *Der Stürmer* launched an offensive propaganda campaign in which Berendsohn was accused of 'selling off' German property.[127]

Negotiations for the sale of his business to an 'Aryan' were already being staged at this time, after all his attempts to transfer the shipyard to his 'half-Jewish' son had collapsed. On 25 March 1938, after a conversation with Dr Arthur Kramm, the confidant of the Hamburg *Gau* Economics Adviser, his lawyer had told him that this kind of arrangement was out of the question because 'political changes in ownership had first to take into consideration those businessmen who were setting themselves up in the industry'.[128]

When the negotiations for the 'Aryanisation' of the shipyard became known in Hamburg business circles, there was no lack of potential buyers for the lucrative enterprise. At the beginning of May 1938, a Hamburg businessman turned to the Assistant to the *Gau* Economics Adviser, Dr Otto Wolff,[129] as well as to Mayor Krogmann, in order to put pressure on Berendsohn, who was unwilling to sell. 'That in the Third Reich one might not be able by an appropriate payment to induce a non-Aryan to sell is difficult for me to understand',[130] he wrote in a thinly veiled request for the application of openly coercive measures. Such measures could only be implemented in an indirect form before November 1938, when the National Socialist regime finally went over to openly coercive 'Aryanisation'.

The affair took an unexpected turn when the 'Industrial Research Company Ltd.' (*Wirtschaftliche Forschungsgesellschaft mbH*, Wifo), a tool of the Reich Economics Ministry, began to take interest in the Berendsohn shipyard. A sales contract was finally concluded between the *Wirtschaftliche Forschungsgesellschaft* and Berendsohn through a real estate agent who had been appointed to the task, and the contract was then submitted to Hamburg Reich Governor Kaufmann for authorisation.

Kaufmann saw the conclusion of the contract as unfortunate, as he would have preferred to sell the shipyard to a private concern from Hamburg, or to acquire the attractive harbor land for the State of Hamburg, rather than to sell it to Wifo. If, however, he refused authorisation for the sales that had been drawn up, he could count on there being a complaint to the Reich Economics Ministry, which would certainly have revised the decision of the Hamburg Reich Governor in favour of Wifo. In this situation, no other option remained open to him than to seek a balance between regional and Reich interests through an informal and formal supplement to the sales contract.

Berendsohn's equipment stocks, the largest in the port of Hamburg, were separated from the business on the initiative of the *Gau* Economics Adviser and transferred to another part of the harbour.[131] On the express wish of the Reich Governor, a purchase option for the State of Hamburg was inserted in the contract that documented the special regional interests of Hamburg in this particular 'Aryanisation'.[132] Kaufmann's long-term goal of securing the shipyard's land for the Hansestadt was realised just five years later when Wifo lost interest in its acquisition, and in the spring of 1943 the business was sold to the State of Hamburg for 1.9 million RM. In 1938, Wifo had paid Berendsohn a mere 400,000 RM for his shipyard. This sum had not even been sufficient to settle the mortgage payments of 215,000 RM and to pay taxes and obligatory duties to the tune of 231,000 RM, with the result that in 1943, at the time of the sale to the city, the once-wealthy shipyard owner was, at the age of sixty-five, having to perform unskilled work in an American plastic factory in order to support his family after their emigration.[133] Once more, Hamburg and the Reich had arranged a balanced reconciliation of their interests at the expense of a Jewish proprietor.

A fourth and final example of this coordination of interests is offered by the 'Aryanisation' of *Fairplay Schleppdampfschiffs-Reederei Richard Borchardt.* The business was founded in 1905, and after the death of the company's founder, Richard Borchardt, was headed by his wife Lucy, generally known in the port in Hamburg as 'Mother Borchardt'. The company possessed a total of more than seventeen tugboats, of which two were stationed in Cuxhaven and used as tugboats on the high seas, and one cargo steamer that was predominantly used in the Mediterranean.[134] It was the only shipping company in Germany that enabled young Jews to train as sailors in the context of a '*Hachscharah*' before emigrating to Palestine.[135]

The discrimination faced by the company in the first years of the National Socialist regime had been kept within defined limits,[136] but anti-Jewish discrimination increased from 1937 onward: a competitor, *Bugsier-, Reederei- und Bergungs-AG*, denounced Fairplay as a 'non-Aryan company' at the Reich Transport Group for Sea Shipping (*Reichsverkehrsgruppe Seeschiffahrt*);[137] the Hamburg Foreign Exchange Control Office questioned whether the shipping company's accounts receivable were too high and withdrew its 'General Currency Exchange Authorisation' (*Allgemeine Devisenverwendungsgenehmigung*);[138] the Hamburg Chamber of Commerce rejected a travel expense claim Lucy Borchardt had made for a journey of several weeks to Palestine,[139] and the Reich Office for Foreign Exchange Control even demanded the introduction of security measures against the shipping company under Paragraph 37a of the Foreign Exchange Law.[140] The Hamburg Foreign Exchange Control Office at first refrained from adopting openly repressive measures. When the 'suspicions' of the foreign exchange auditors that the shipping company was preparing to make an illegal capital transfer could 'not be confirmed', however, the company was presented with a 'cautionary fine' of 15,000 RM for allegedly 'negligent behaviour'.[141]

In view of this acute threat, the owner, Lucy Borchardt, turned to Max Warburg in 1938. Warburg advised her strongly to sell her enterprise as quickly as possible.[142] At the beginning of June 1938, a Dutch shipping line offered 2 million RM for the transfer of the shipping company.[143] Because of the foreign exchange transfer regulations then in force, Borchardt would have been able to take only a fraction of this sum with her when she emigrated. She therefore made an unusual proposition to the licencing authorities in Hamburg, i.e., the *Gau* Economics Adviser and the Reich Governor. The majority of the enterprise was to be transferred to a foundation controlled by the Reich Governor, and the owners in return were to be granted permission to sail four of their ships abroad – three tugboats, *Fairplay X, Fairplay XIV* and *Fairplay IV*, as well as a cargo steamer, the *Lucy Borchardt* – so that they could build a new business for themselves there.[144] Up to that point, there had been no other 'Aryanisation' in Hamburg in which a Jewish enterprise was transformed into a foundation and the owners received 'indemnity in kind' instead of a sum of money. Two factors primarily induced the Hamburg Reich Governor to go along with this unusual suggestion.

The first motive derived from a combination of tactical restraint and the propaganda value of such a move. The 'Fairplay' tugboats were one of the international 'business cards' of the port of Hamburg, and the company had more than four hundred towing contracts with foreign firms. Therefore, for Hamburg's National Socialists a policy of restraint was important in this case, as it had been with respect to M.M. Warburg & Co. It avoided international attention and hid the repressive nature of 'Aryanisation' behind a façade of 'well-meaning generosity'. One auditor noted in a letter to the Foreign Exchange Control Office that this arrangement with the Jewish owners meant that 'foreign agitation' would be 'countered effectively ... because the fact that the former owners were able to build a new business for themselves after their emigration abroad [would] very quickly become known even in foreign shipping circles', particularly since the Jewish proprietors would be obliged 'to promote the business of Hamburg' abroad.[145]

The second motive behind the peculiar modalities of the establishment and organisation of the foundation, which the Reich Governor secretly headed, was that it opened up an opportunity for him to use the proceeds of the business for his own personal priorities. Although the purpose of the foundation was primarily focused on social measures like support for needy company employees or the promotion of the 'general welfare of the people',[146] in practice, the '*Hamburger Stiftung von 1937*' founded by Kaufmann had already shown how the boundaries between welfare and corruption were becoming blurred under the influence of the Gauleiter.[147] The foundation's statute, adopted on 11 August 1938, gave Kaufmann the right to nominate the members of the board of the foundation and to reappoint them at any time. The appointment of the company director, the use of company profits and amendments to the company by-laws, were tied to the agreement of the Reich Governor, who had the right to dissolve the foundation as well.[148] Kaufmann placed two confidants on the board of the foundation: Dr Otto Wolff, Assistant to the *Gau* Economics Adviser and a shipowner, Heinrich Christian ('Heinz') Horn, whom he later also appointed as his personal adviser in 1942 when he was entrusted with the office of Reich Commissar for German Shipping. The managing director he appointed was the veteran National Socialist Wilhelm Theodor Algermissen, who clearly did not see himself as a compliant assistant of the Gauleiter and whose conduct contributed to the fact that the Jewish proprietors were able to return to take back their business completely after 1945.[149] Algermissen opposed repeated attempts by Kaufmann to dissolve the foundation and to transfer the enterprise to his personal favourite, Heinz Horn.[150]

In sum, the advantages of the contract with the Jewish proprietors for the authorities in Hamburg were obvious: Hamburg's port economy would retain the business and its international contacts – something that could be broadcast to the rest of the world for propaganda purposes – and Hamburg's state and party leadership would gain direct control of an important enterprise in the private sector.

The Reich authorities viewed the arrangement with scepticism and expressed their doubts about the effects on foreign exchange policy,[151] yet they found themselves in a situation similar to that of the Hamburg Reich Governor when authorising the sales contract for the *Köhlbrand* shipyard. Formally, they had no means of intervening, because the Reich Governor was responsible for granting authorisations and there was no other body to appeal to that could enable the Reich Economics Ministry to intervene. Consequently, even they had to try to push through the interests of the Reich informally in this case, which, as always, they achieved at the expense of the Jewish proprietors.

The Reich Economics Ministry and the Hamburg Foreign Exchange Control Office insisted that the owners could only take three, instead of the agreed four, ships abroad with them.[152] The remaining fortunes of the Borchardt family, including three other properties in Hamburg, were also subjected to restrictive foreign exchange transfer regulations. The interests of the Reich were also protected when the harbour tugboats were taken: ten of the remaining sixteen *Fairplay* vessels were chartered to the Navy.[153]

After the sale was finalised and the owner, Lucy Borchardt, had emigrated to England, the Reich gradually took possession of the rest of her property. To this end, the Foreign Exchange Control Office carried out a fiscal 'business audit' in 1939, whose results allegedly revealed that the former proprietor had substantial tax arrears. In addition, the foreign exchange auditors reproached her for having concealed from the licencing authorities the actual value of the steamer, the *Lucy Borchardt*, that had been taken abroad.[154]

The allegation of tax arrears appeared implausible from the outset, as regular audits had produced no such evidence before and, in emigrating, the owner had been issued with a certificate by the Tax Office showing that no tax was due. Now the same Tax Office was requesting that the agents for Lucy Borchardt 'sell the properties belonging to Frau Borchardt as soon as possible' and pay the proceeds to the Tax Office in order to settle the alleged tax arrears.[155] In actual fact, it ought to have been the Fairplay Foundation that had to raise the sum, as the former owner had come to an agreement to this effect with the Foundation's executive board. When the alleged tax arrears had to be paid, however, the chair of the executive board, Dr Otto Wolff, could not remember any such agreement having been made.

The owners, therefore, lost all the proceeds from the sale of their properties. The Tax Office seized 71,000 RM in compensation for alleged tax arrears, while 42,000 RM was confiscated for capital gains tax. After the settlement of mortgages and the payment of notarial and broker's fees and so-called 'licencing costs', only 20,000 RM remained, deposited in a blocked emigrant's account.[156] On 25 November, the Hamburg Gestapo completed the plundering of the fortunes of the Borchardts and ordered the state police to secure the family's remaining property on the basis of the ordinance issued by the Reich President for the Protection of People and State (*Reichspräsident zum Schutz von Volk und Staat*) on 28 February 1933, two weeks after Lucy Borchardt had gone into exile.[157]

## Notes

1. *RGBl* 1938, Part I, p. 414ff.
2. StAHH, *Staatsverwaltung*, D I, A 7, Instructions for filling in the property register.
3. Order based on the *Verordnung über die Anmeldung des Vermögens von Juden*, 26 April 1938, *RGBl* 1938, Part I, p. 415ff.
4. See Genschel, *Verdrängung*, p. 157; Krüger, *Lösung*, p. 262ff.
5. StAHH, *Staatsverwaltung - Allgemeine Abteilung*, A III 2, communication from the *Verwaltung für Handel, Schiffahrt und Gewerbe* to the *Hauptverwaltungsamt*, 12 May 1938.
6. Ibid., Kaufmann's order of 18 June 1938.
7. Indeed, there is no case in the surviving files in which the President of the *Staatsverwaltung* went against the decision of the *Gauwirtschaftsberater*.
8. See Kratzsch, *Gauwirtschaftsapparat*, p. 180.
9. Thus Barkai, *Boycott*, p. 64. Cf., by contrast, the formalistic critique of Kratzsch, *Gauwirtschaftsapparat*, p. 116, fn. 21, based on the relationships pertaining in *Westfalen-Süd*.

10. *Archiv Handelskammer,* 49.C.28, Note on the 'Appointment of Specialists in matters concerning the de-Judaization of firms', 17 August 1938. Cf. also ibid., communication from the *Handelskammer* to the specialist auditor re. 'Experts-Activities in the Reorganization of Jewish Firms', 9 September 1938.

11. See the public announcements of the GWB in the *Hamburger Tageblatt,* 2 December 1938.

12. See below, Ch. VII.

13. *RGBl* 1938, Part I, p. 404.

14. *Archiv Handelskammer,* 100.A.2.2, letter from the *Handelskammer* lawyer, Dr Haage, to the Berlin office of the *Hamburger Handelskammer,* 28 April 1938.

15. Ibid., communication from the *Hamburger Handelskammer* to the *Reichswirtschaftsministerium/Sonderreferat Judenfragen* (undated, May 1938).

16. *Archiv Handelskammer,* 100.A.4.1, letter from *Präses* de la Camp and the *Handelskammer* attorney, Dr Haage, to *NSDAP-Gauwirtschaftsberater* Otte, 12 January 1938.

17. StAHH, *Deputation für Handel, Schiffahrt und Gewerbe II,* VI B 3 32 Sch 21, communication from the *Handelskammer* to the *Behörde für Handel, Schiffahrt und Gewerbe,* 21 March 1938.

18. *Archiv Handelskammer,* 100.B.1.19, letter from Dr Haage to Dr Eller, 6 October 1938.

19. Ibid., letter from attorney Dr Eller/Berlin office to the *Hamburger Handelskammer,* 13 May 1939.

20. Ibid., letter from Dr Haage to Dr Eller, 6 October 1938.

21. Ibid., letter from Dr Haage to the Berlin office of the *Hamburger Handelskammer,* 24 October 1938.

22. Ibid., letter from Dr Haage to Dr Eller, 11 May 1939.

23. *Archiv WgA LGHH,* Z 211-2, pp. 14–17, letter from Drs. Behn *inter alia,* 5 June 1950; *II. Zählung,* pp. 23-25, eyewitness statement by Margarethe Gressmann of 19 December 1952.

24. *Archiv Handelskammer,* 100.A.2.6, Vol. 1, Minutes of the sitting of the Committee for the Aryanization and Liquidation of Jewish Operations (*Ausschuss für Arisierungen und Liquidierungen jüdischer Betriebe*) on 22 August 1938. According to the minutes, the representatives of commercial industry present were Bartels of the Working Group for Clothing, Textile and Leather (*Fachgruppe Bekleidung, Textil und Leder*), Wulff of the Working Group for Healthcare, Chemicals and Optics (*Fachgruppe Gesundheitspflege, Chemie und Optik*), Lehmann of the Working Group for Foodstuff and Semi-Luxury Goods (*Fachgruppe Nahrungs- und Genußmittel*), Maasch and Klapproth of the Tobacco Working Group (*Fachgruppe Tabak*), Westerich of the Arts and Crafts, Paper and Toys Working Group (*Fachgruppe Kunstgewerbe, Papier und Spielwaren*), *Assessor* Köhler of the Working Groups for Ironmongery, Electronics and Household Appliances, for Radio and for Jewellery, Gold and Silverware, and Clocks (*Fachgruppen Eisenwaren, Elektro und Hausgerät, Rundfunk, Juwelen, Gold- und Silberwaren, Uhren*), Prediger of the Working Division for Lighting (*Fachabteilung Beleuchtung*) and Nennecke from the Working Division for Office Machinery (*Fachabteilung Büromaschinen*).

25. *Hamburger Fremdenblatt,* 11 January 1939.

26. StAHH, *Senatskanzlei - Präsidialabteilung,* 1938 S II 657, communication from the *Verwaltung für Handel, Schiffahrt und Gewerbe* to *Staatsrat* Dr Becker/*Einspruchsstelle,* 7 January 1939.

27. *RGBl* 1938, Part I, p. 627ff.

28. *Archiv Handelskammer,* 100.A.2.6, letter from Max Rieck to *Geschäftstelle Harburg I* of the *Hamburger Handelskammer,* 12 October 1938.

29. *Archiv Handelskammer,* 100.B.1.21, communication from *Bezirksuntergruppe Spedition* to *Gauleitung Hamburg* of the *NSDAP/Gauwirtschaftsberater,* 11 August 1938.

30. *Justizbehörde Hamburg, Oberstaatsanwalt beim Landgericht Hamburg,* Trial 11 Js 1446/38, p. 38, communication from the *Marktgemeinschaft für Schlachtviehverwertung Hamburg* to the *Oberstaatsanwalt beim Landgericht Hamburg,* 27 March 1939.

31. Ibid., p. 39, Announcement re. supply to Jewish butchers, 12 October 1938.

32. Ibid., p. 40, Announcement re. Jewish butchers, 17 October 1938.

33. Cf. the article 'Arisierung – eine Gesinnungsfrage', *Völkischer Beobachter*, 11 September 1938.

34. On the 'Aryanisation' of this factory, see *Archiv WgA LGHH*, Z 3103-1, 3103-3.

35. Hans Robinsohn, *Justiz als politische Verfolgung. Die Rechtsprechung in 'Rassenschandefällen' beim Landgericht Hamburg 1936–1943*, Stuttgart, 1977, p. 17ff.

36. Robinsohn, *Justiz*, p. 18.

37. For a typical example, see the questioning of a Jewish businessman on 24 April 1939, StAHH, *Oberfinanzpräsident*, Str 687, p. 27ff., which, among other things, had to identify whether he had 'perverse sexual intercourse' and which sexual partners he had had since 1935.

38. *Archiv WgA LGHH*, Z 1367-1 (Hamburger Bleiwerk Ltd), Z 120 (Korsetthaus Gazelle), Z 995-1 (Julius Lachmann Co.), Z 4221-1 (Arnold Vogl Co.).

39. Ibid., Z 3103-1, pp. 30–35, letter from Dr Hagedorn, 16 April 1951, citation p. 33.

40. Ibid., pp. 14–17, letter from Dr Hagedorn, 20 December 1950.

41. Ibid., Z 2522-1 (Maaß & Riege Co.), Z 1159-1 (Schuhwarenhaus Speier), Z 995 (Julius Lachmann Co.).

42. Ibid., Z 1159-1, p. 40a, letter from Dr Samson, 28 February 1951.

43. Ibid., Z 180-7 (Guttmann & Widawer Co.), citation p. 25.

44. Ibid., Z 995-1 (Julius Lachmann Co.), p. 6, letter from Dr Samwer, 8 March 1950.

45. Ibid., Z 2522-1, p. 38, communication from Dr Oppenheim, 14 October 1950.

46. *Archiv Handelskammer*, 100.B.1.19, communication from the *Württembergische Industrie- und Handels-Beratungs- und Vermittlungszentrale Stuttgart* to the *Hamburger Handelskammer*, 22 October 1938.

47. *Archiv WgA LGHH*, Z 184-7, p. 8c.

48. Ibid., Z 28741, p. 30, eyewitness statement by auditor Gustav von Bargen, 18 February 1969.

49. Citation as in ibid., Z 1175-1, p. 9, letter from Irma Beuttenmüller to the *Wiedergutmachungsamt beim Landgericht Hamburg*, 6 July 1950.

50. Ibid., Z 1258-2, p. 35ff. Sales contract for *C. Feldten Nachf. GmbH*, 19 December 1938, with conditions imposed by the *Reichsstatthalter*, 31 December 1938.

51. One example of this was the sales contract for the Maaß & Riege Company, 21 October 1938, ibid., Z 2522-1, pp. 21–24.

52. See in this connection the 'Aryanization' of the Goldschmidt & Mindus Company in which the buyer had been obliged to collect outstanding debts and the debtors only partially fulfilled their payment obligations. In a note of 11 November 1950, (ibid., Z 1489, p. 28ff. re. interim statement on the Goldschmidt & Mindus file) this is related in the following way: 'The new firm did not however bother itself with this since it was primarily concerned to retain the clientèle of the Goldschmidt & Mindus Company.'

53. On the problem of 'hidden reserves' in Jewish trading enterprises, see ibid., Z 995-2 (*Fa. Georg & Co.*), p. 75ff., letter from Dr Robert Lachmann of 11 September 1950.

54. On the ZAV and the points that follow, see *Bestimmungen des Reichswirtschaftsministers über die Förderung zusätzlicher Ausfuhr*, Berlin, 1937; Leonhard Schiffler, *ABC des Außenhandels*, Hamburg, 1937; Theodor Pütz, *Die deutsche Außenwirtschaft im Engpaß der Jahre 1933–1937*, Berlin, 1938.

55. For the Dego's argumentation see the report of auditor Willy Rönnau, 21 October 1958, *Archiv WgA LGHH*, Z 360-1, p. 540ff.

56. See ibid., Z 29562 (*Fa. Gebr. Haas*), p. 17; Z 747-5 (*Fa. Ephraim, Gumpel & Co*), pp. 4-12; Z 360-1 (*Fa. Albert Geo Simon*), p. 542.

57. Cf. ibid., Z 360-1, p. 542 (*Fa. Albert Geo Simon*); StAHH, *Oberfinanzpräsident*, Str 423, Vol. 1, p. 149 (*Fa. Labowsky & Co.*).

58. Ibid., Z 742, main file, p. 3, account of Gerson Nahm, 24 August 1946.
59. Ibid., Z 2554-1, pp. 13–29, legal submission by Dr Greve, 6 September 1951.
60. Ibid., p. 184, Judgment 2 Wik 200/51 of the Second *Wiedergutmachungskammer* of the *Landgericht Hamburg*, 25 August 1953.
61. Autobiography of Dr Ernst Loewenberg (private collection), p. 43.
62. See, e.g., *Archiv WgA LGHH*, Z 265 (*Fa. Alex Loewenberg*).
63. Ibid., Z 1159-4 (*Fa. Schuhwarenhaus Speier*), p. 14ff., sales contract of 15 October 1938.
64. Ibid., Z 421-1 (*Fa. Zinner & Lippstadt*), p. 64ff.
65. Ibid., Z 750, main file, (*Fa. Gebr. Feldberg*), pp. 11-14.
66. Cf. ibid., Z 13399-1, second count, p. 4ff., letter from Dr Harm of 10 November 1952.
67. Genschel, *Verdrängung*, p. 213; on the process of concentration of economic power see also Dieter Swatek, *Unternehmenskonzentration als Ergebnis und Mittel nationalsozialistischer Wirtschaftspolitik*, Berlin, 1972. For the thesis that middle-class interests were of marginal significance in the context of National Socialist policy, see Heinrich August Winkler, 'Der entbehrliche Stand. Zur Mittelstandspolitik im 'Dritten Reich'', *Archiv für Sozialgeschichte*, Vol. XVII, 1977, pp. 1–40.
68. See Günter Keiser, 'Der jüngste Konzentrationsprozeß', *Die Wirtschaftskurve*, Vol. 18 (1939), Issue 2, pp. 136–156; compare also Swatek, *Unternehmenskonzentration*.
69. *Hamburger Fremdenblatt*, 11 January 1939.
70. Herbst, *Krieg*, p. 158ff.
71. Aly and Heim, *Vordenker*, pp. 33–43.
72. Ibid., p. 42
73. Cf. Witek, ''Arisierungen' in Wien', in Talos, Hanisch and Neugebauer, eds, *NS-Herrschaft*, pp. 199–216.
74. *Die Deutsche Volkswirtschaft*, No. 33/1938, p. 1197ff.
75. This is significant in so far as the process of the 'de-Judaisation' of industry – especially of the large industries – was frequently undertaken by affiliating a Jewish enterprise to large industrial concerns, and this unquestionably accelerated the process of industrial concentration. Cf. Keiser, *Konzentrationsprozeß*; on heavy industry see also Gerhard Th. Mollin, *Montankonzerne und 'Drittes Reich'*, Göttingen, 1988, esp. p. 183ff; Hayes, *Big Business*.
76. *Hamburger Tageblatt*, 2 December 1938.
77. In one case a prospective buyer was even able to acquire five Jewish firms. This was an ethnic German returning from South America who had only come to Hamburg in March 1939 in order to establish an independent business there. Cf. *Archiv WgA LGHH*, Z 360-1, p. 761ff.
78. In 1929 the total volume of German foreign trade still amounted to 26.93 billion RM. In the National Socialist period, it reached a high-point in 1937 with 11,379 billion RM, less than half (42.25%) of its initial value in 1929. See Dietmar Petzina, *Die deutsche Wirtschaft in der Zwischenkriegszeit*, Wiesbaden, 1977, p. 123.
79. This assessment rests, however, on a very narrow set of data because the files of the *Wiedergutmachungsamt beim Landgericht Hamburg* only give adequate information about the buyers of Jewish property then required to make restitution in 56 cases. In 20 of the 56 cases (35.7%), the Jewish enterprises had been taken over by established firms from Hamburg or elsewhere. Address books and trade registers prove to be poor tools for research since many buyers came from outside Hamburg or did not live in the city.
80. Cf. OMGUS, *Ermittlungen gegen die Deutsche Bank*, Nördlingen, 1985, pp. 165–175; Harold James, 'Die Deutsche Bank und die Diktatur 1933–1945', in Lothar Gall *et al.*, *Die Deutsche Bank 1870–1995*, Munich, 1995, pp. 315–408, here p. 344ff.; OMGUS, *Dresdner Bank*, pp. 76–84.

81. On the history of the firms, see *Archiv WgA LGHH*, Z 5387-4, pp. 4–8, communication from K. Balaszeskul of 2 April 1951.
82. The five branches stood at Eimsbütteler Str. 60, Neuer Steinweg 70, Hamburger Str. 64, Hammerbrookstr. 103 and Billhorner Röhrendamm 192/6. Of the remaining branches, 2 were in Leipzig, 2 in Plauen and one each in Berlin, Hof, Jena, Hanover, Zwickau, Potsdam, Chemnitz, Bremen and Gera. See ibid., Z 20074, p. 34ff., Z 5387-1, pp. 8–15, Exposé on the *Otto Klausner GmbH* and *Bottina Schuhgesellschaft mbH* companies, 20 November 1937.
83. On the turnover of the five Hamburg branches, see Table 10, Appendix.
84. *Archiv WgA LGHH*, Z 5387-1, p. 9, Exposé of 20 November 1937.
85. Ibid., p. 74ff., Statement by the former Managing Director, Walter Pauli, to the Bremen *Wiedergutmachungskammer*, 9 December 1953.
86. Ibid., Statement by Pauli, p. 76ff., letter from Dr Ernst Asch to Ella Klausner, 17 August 1938, p. 71.
87. Ibid., p. 48 (enclosure), citation as in the minutes of the shareholders' meeting of 14 September 1938.
88. Citation as in ibid.
89. Ibid., p. 76, citation from a conversation between *Geschäftsführer* Walter Pauli and an official from *Reichsgruppe Handel*, statement by Walter Pauli, 9 December 1953.
90. Three of the five branches (Neuer Wall 13 and 61, and Großer Burstah 34) occupied a desirable location in the centre of the city of Hamburg. The business addresses of the other two branches were Schulterblatt 142 and Hamburger Str. 127.
91. *Archiv WgA LGHH*, Z 1159-1, p. 2, Proprietors' property register (undated).
92. Ibid., p. 46ff., eyewitness statement by Hans Gloede of 18 April 1951, p. 50ff., eyewitness statement by Adolf Schierhorn of 15 May 1951.
93. Ibid., pp. 40a–40d, communication from Drs. Samson and Seidl of 1 February 1950.
94. Ibid., Z 1159-3, p. 22ff., communication from H. Günther, 12 June 1953.
95. For the sales contract of 15 October 1938 and the additional contract of 26 October 1938, see ibid., Z 1159-4, p. 14ff. The additional contract opened with the passage: 'The Office of the Gau Economics Adviser desires that in the aforementioned contract the following alterations still be made.'
96. Ibid., pp. 93–95, communication from Drs. Samson and Seidl, 1 June 1953.
97. *Hamburger jüdische Opfer*, p. 345.
98. Those sold were the branches at Mönckebergstr. 29, Steindamm 13, Hamburger Str. 30, Hamburger Str. 96, Schulterblatt 140, Neuer Wall 17, Billhorner Röhrendamm 156, Dammtorstr. 38, Reichenstr. 24, Hoheluftchaussee 30 and Lüneburger Str. 44. For all of the (mostly female) buyers, without exception, the takeover proved not to be very lucrative: all the branches were destroyed by bombing in the war until the last store at Mönckebergstr. 29 was closed in 1943 for infringement of price regulations. On the 'Aryanisation' of *Korsetthaus Gazelle* see *Archiv WgA LGHH*, Z 120-1-11.
99. *Hamburger jüdische Opfer*, p. 186.
100. *Hamburger Tageblatt*, 20 February 1939.
101. On the 'Aryanization' of '*Fiedlers' Strumpfläden*' see *Archiv WgA LGHH*, Z 1175-1, p. 4ff., communication from Dr Herbert Pardo of 25 May 1950.
102. In the private banking sector, the number of enterprises slumped from 1350 in 1932 to 520 in 1939; see Keiser, *Konzentrationsprozeß*, p. 148.
103. *Archiv WgA LGHH*, Z 5387-1, p. 79, eyewitness statement by Otto Weigel of 9 December 1953.
104. Cf. Rebentisch, *Führerstaat*, esp. pp. 231–282.

105. Second Order under the *Verordnung über die Anmeldung des Vermögens von Juden*, 24 November 1938, *RGBl* 1938, Part I, p. 1668.

106. StAHH, *Senatskanzlei - Präsidialabteilung*, 1939 S II 298, Circular from the *Reichspostminister* to *Reichspostdirektionen*, 11 January 1939.

107. On the following particulars see the letter from the President of the Hamburg *Reichspostdirektion* to the *Reichspostminister*, 7 February 1939, StAHH, *Senatskanzlei - Präsidialabteilung*, 1939 S II 298.

108. Citation as in ibid.

109. Ibid., communication from the *Verwaltung für Handel, Schiffahrt und Gewerbe* to the *Einspruchsstelle* of 6 April 1939.

110. Ibid., letter from the *Reichsstatthalter* to Senator von Allwörden, 10 June 1939.

111. On the history and 'Aryanisation' of M.M. Warburg & Co., see Kopper, *Bankenpolitik*, ibid., *Marktwirtschaft*; Chernow, *Warburgs*; Rosenbaum and Sherman, *M.M. Warburg & Co.*

112. Warburg, *Aufzeichnungen*, p. 154.

113. StAHH, *Staatsamt*, 106, letter from the *Reichsstatthalter* in Hamburg (on behalf of von Allwörden) to *Reichswirtschaftsministerium Hauptabteilung V*, 19 March 1938.

114. On Kaufmann's demands, see ibid.

115. On the career and personality of Schlotterer see Ch. IV, fn. 7.

116. On the career of Lange, see Berlin Document Centre, personal file for Lange; *Deutsche Allgemeine Zeitung*, 6 February 1938: Lange Kurt, b. 1895, Diploma – businessman; 1 October 1930 entered NSDAP; 1931–1933 member of NSDAP *Fraktion* in the Hamburg *Bürgerschaft*; *NSFK-Standartenführer*; 1933–1936 President of the Hamburg Audit Division; 1936–1938 Division Head in the *Amt für Deutsche Roh- und Werkstoffe* (the Office for German Raw and Processed Materials); 1938 *Ministerialdirektor* in the *Reichswirtschaftsministerium* and *Hauptabteilungsleiter für Geld- und Kreditwesen*.

117. StAHH, *Senatskommission für den höheren Verwaltungsdienst*, G 2c HV 1936 IV, letter from Lange to *Reichsstatthalter* Kaufmann, 30 August 1935.

118. Ibid., letter from Krogmann to Lange, 10 February 1936.

119. Citation as in Kopper, *Bankenpolitik*, p. 124ff.

120. StAHH, *Staatsamt*, 106, letter from the *Reichsstatthalter* in Hamburg (on behalf of von Allwörden) to *Reichswirtschaftsministerium Hauptabteilung V*, 19 March 1938.

121. Thus the somewhat euphemistic characterization presented by Genschel, *Verdrängung*, pp. 237–240.

122. *Archiv M.M. Warburg & Co.*, 11060, Transformation of M.M. Warburg & Co. into a limited partnership, file 1, letter from the Hamburg *Gauwirtschaftsberater* to M.M. Warburg & Co., 2 December 1938.

123. See below, Ch. VI.

124. See the diary of Cornelius Freiherr von Berenberg-Goßler (private collection), entry of 18 April 1939: 'I have the impression that Warburg is regarded as a prominent Jew so as to be a hostage in case of foreign entanglements.' On 27 April 1939, he noted: 'I am writing to Berlin, to Wolff at the Secret State Police, and offer that in his own emigration Fritz Warburg will give financial means to enable 100 Jewish children and some Jews without means to emigrate.' On 4 May 1939, he negotiated terms with an emissary of Wolff, *SS-Sturmbannführer* Lischka. On 10 May he noted with relief: 'Thank God at midday today Dr Fritz Warburg and his wife finally went off abroad, so they are saved!'

125. *Archiv WgA LGHH*, Z 191-1, pp. 10–12, biography of Berendsohn (undated).

126. Ibid., p. 11.

127. *Der Stürmer*, sixteenth year, No. 29/July 1938, p. 6.

128. *Archiv WgA LGHH*, Z 191-1, p. 14, letter from Dr J. Frahm to Paul Berendsohn, 25 March 1938.

129. StAHH, *Deputation für Handel, Schiffahrt und Gewerbe II*, special papers, XXXIII D 2, letter from Rolff P. Weitzmann to Dr Otto Wolf (*sic*), 9 May 1938.

130. Ibid., cited from a letter from Rolff P. Weitzmann to *Bürgermeister* Krogmann, 9 May 1938.

131. *Archiv WgA LGHH*, Z 191-1, p. 11, biography of Berendsohn.

132. Ibid., p. 25, sales contract of 6 August 1938.

133. Ibid., p. 12, biography of Berendsohn.

134. On the history of the firm see StAHH, *Oberfinanzpräsident*, R 1937/234, pp. 4–18, report of the *Devisenstelle des LFA Hamburg* on the foreign exchange investigation conducted on 5–8 February 1937 at *Fairplay Schleppdampfschiffs-Reederei Richard Borchardt*, 9 February 1937; *Fairplay Schleppdampfschiffs-Reederei Richard Borchard GmbH 1905–1980. Zum 75 jährigen Jubiläum der Fairplay-Reederei*, n.p., n.d.

135. *Fairplay Schleppdampfschiffs-Reederei*, p. 22; also details now in Ina Lorenz, *Seefahrts-Hachschara in Hamburg (1935–1938). Lucy Borchardt: 'Die einzige jüdische Reederin der Welt'*, in Hans-Wilhelm Eckardt and Klaus Richter, eds, *Bewahren und Berichten. Festschrift für Hans-Dieter Loose zum 60. Geburtstag*, Hamburg, 1997, pp. 445–472.

136. Evidently the Hamburg Shipping Authority had even occasionally thought to appoint the Jewish firm as '*Hafen-Musterbetrieb*' (the port's model enterprise), cf. ibid.

137. StAHH, *Deputation für Handel, Schiffahrt und Gewerbe II*, XXI A 15a, communication from *Bugsier-, Reederei- und Bergungs-AG* to the *Reichsverkehrsgruppe Seeschiffahrt*, 20 December 1937.

138. StAHH, R 1937/234, pp. 4–18, report on the investigation of the *Devisenstelle*, 9 February 1937.

139. Ibid., p. 56, communication from the *Handelskammer* to the *Devisenstelle*, 3 June 1937.

140. Ibid., p. 79, *Reichsstelle für Devisenbewirtschaftung* to the *Devisenstelle*, 15 June 1937.

141. Ibid., note by the *Devisenstelle* of 12 January 1938 (unpag.).

142. *Archiv M.M. Warburg & Co.*, 10936, Note re. *Fairplay Schleppdampfschiffs-Reederei*, 1 March 1938.

143. StAHH, *Oberfinanzpräsident*, F 189, Vol. 1, p. 21, confidential communication from the *Kon. Ned. Stoomboot Maatschappij* to Lucy Borchardt, 2 June 1938.

144. Ibid., p. 10, letter from Max Frenzel addressed to the *Oberfinanzpräsident – Devisenstelle*, 2 July 1938.

145. Ibid., pp. 3–5, letter from auditor Max Frenzel addressed to the *Oberfinanzpräsident – Devisenstelle*, 2 July 1938, citations p. 5.

146. Ibid., p. 3.

147. On the Hamburg Foundation of 1937 see Bajohr, *Hamburgs 'Führer'*, p. 69; on the importance of 'Aryanisation contributions' in the finances of the foundation, see below, Ch. VI.

148. Cf. Statute of the *Fairplay-Stiftung*, 11 August 1938, *Archiv M.M. Warburg & Co.*, 18240.

149. *Fairplay Schleppdampfschiffs-Reederei*, p. 25.

150. *Archiv M.M. Warburg & Co.*, 10936, Note by Dr Kurt Sieveking re. *Fairplay*, 7 November 1939.

151. StAHH, *Oberfinanzpräsident*, F 189, Vol. 1, p. 1, letter from Max Frenzel to the *Oberfinanzpräsident*, 13 July 1938.

152. Ibid., p. 27, letter from the *Reichswirtschaftsministerium* to the *Devisenstelle*, 8 August 1938.

153. StAHH, *Deputation für Handel, Schiffahrt und Gewerbe II*, special papers, XXI A 15a 94, letter (sender not recorded) to Senator von Allwörden 're. *Fairplay Dampfschiff-Schlepperei*' (*sic*), 13 January 1940.

154. *Archiv WgA LGHH*, Z 86-2, pp. 31–35, letter from Herbert W. Samuel, 30 March 1950 (with citations from the examination report).
155. StAHH, *Oberfinanzpräsident*, F 189, Vol. 2, p. 33, letter from the *Finanzamt Hamburg-Nord* to Herbert W. Samuel (a lawyer), 24 April 1940.
156. Ibid., p. 167, letter from Herbert W. Samuel addressed to the *Oberfinanzpräsident – Devisenstelle*, 21 December 1940.
157. Ibid., Minute on the file folder of F 189, Vol. 2.

# Chapter VI

# SELLING OFF AND LIQUIDATING ENTERPRISES AND THE RACE FOR PERSONAL ENRICHMENT

### *'De-Judaisation' and 'Aryanisation' from November 1938*

---

## The 'Reich Crystal Night' as a Radicalising Factor

In the course of 1938, the exclusion of the Jews from the economy in Hamburg had accelerated considerably. Important Jewish enterprises had changed owners during the year, and the sale of the large fashion store *Gebrüder Feldberg* on Mönckebergstraße in May 1938[1] had shown that 'Aryanisation' was increasingly being extended to Jewish retail enterprises. Well before the autumn this process of exclusion had become irreversible. The National Socialist regime had consolidated its rule both domestically and in terms of foreign policy after overcoming the economic crisis, stepping up its rearmament and annexing Austria and the Sudetenland. The National Socialists were now unlikely to tolerate the economic operations of Jews on a long-term basis or even for a period of any significant length.

An end to the oft-announced 'de-Judaisation' of the economy was still not in sight, however. In the autumn of 1938, approximately twelve hundred Jewish commercial businesses were still functioning in Hamburg.[2] If the 'Aryanisations' were to continue at their former pace, the destruction of the economic livelihood of the Jews would take several years. The pace of anti-Jewish policy, seen by radical antisemites as too slow, was primarily a product of its inherent contradictions. For instance, the financial plundering of Jews during their emigration had a counterproductive impact on the desired 'de-Judaisation' of the economy, because

---

Notes for this chapter begin on page 262.

many Jews preferred to remain in Germany under repressive conditions rather than embarking upon a poverty-stricken existence abroad.

The rulers of the National Socialist state finally reacted to this dilemma in November 1938, in a way that was typical of their entire policy. Instead of seeking to resolve the conflict between competing goals, setting priorities and weighing divergent interests against each other, they radicalised all of their previous measures simultaneously, with the result that at the end of 1938, a policy crystallised in which open terror was combined with organised compulsory emigration and mandatory 'Aryanisations'. In this way, the lengthy, and at first gradual, process of 'excluding' the Jews from economic life was completed within a few months.

The Reich-wide pogrom that took place during the night of 9–10 November 1938[3] played a central role in radicalising anti-Jewish policy. However, researchers are still divided over whether this marked a decisive 'turning-point'[4] in anti-Jewish policy, or merely represented an intensified 'continuation of the earlier policy', at least as regards the economic displacement of the Jews.[5] At any event, there is no dispute over the fact that anti-Jewish policy had attained a new level of ruthlessness and brutality even before 9 November 1938. This is documented by the apprehension, in June 1938, of Jews with previous convictions who were deported to concentration camps as part of the 'Reich Work-Shy' campaign (*Aktion Arbeitsscheu Reich*).[6] A Jew who had committed no more than a petty offence was automatically included in the list of those to be arrested. The total number of Hamburg Jews detained in June 1938 is unknown. At least forty-one of them died in concentration camps or as a result of later deportation and extermination measures.[7]

In another example, on 27–28 October 1938, more than 17,000 Jews of Polish origin were arrested, taken to the German–Polish border by rail and pushed across the border near Zbaszyn, Chojnice and other towns on the Polish side.[8] In Hamburg, nearly one thousand Jews fell victim to this sudden campaign of arrests. Most did not even have time to take personal necessities like underwear or coats with them, and some store owners also had to leave their businesses in a hurry. Some Jews were able to assign Jewish 'legal counsels' to represent their interests by collective or individual powers of attorney,[9] while in other cases the District Courts appointed 'Trustees for Absentees' (*Abwesenheitspfleger*) in order to secure 'abandoned' properties. Through the mediation of their representatives some of the expellees were able to return to Hamburg at the beginning of 1939 and then had to emigrate within a strictly limited time period. In total, at least three hundred and fifty-five of Hamburg's Jews who had been expelled were later murdered.[10]

Although anti-Jewish policy had thus begun to escalate before 9 November 1938, the significance of the November Pogrom as a radicalising factor cannot be doubted. The pogroms that were stage-managed after the murder of Ernst vom

Rath, Secretary of the German Legation in Paris, marked both the highpoint and the end of a 'mob antisemitism', of which the National Socialist SA and pronounced antisemites like Gauleiter Julius Streicher or Reichspropagandaminister Goebbels were particularly prominent practitioners.[11] In the tradition of East European pogroms, this 'mob antisemitism' exposed Jews to terrible persecution – in the night of 9–10 November alone, over one hundred people were killed, almost two hundred synagogues and seven and a half thousand stores destroyed – though it largely exhausted itself in a hate-filled street violence that was clearly distinguished by its lack of perspective from the harsh, systematic and bureaucratically perfected mass murder of later years. The significance of the November Pogrom as a radicalising factor does not lie in the campaigns of killing and destruction themselves, but rather in the measures taken subsequently and dressed up in a bureaucratic, legal garb. They destroyed the basis of the economic livelihood of the Jews within a few months.

In contrast with a few of the legends that have found their way into serious historical research,[12] the synagogues, businesses and apartments of the Jews in Hamburg were also systematically destroyed, and by units of the Hamburg SA and SS at that. Particularly heavy devastation was caused by the SA and SS units charged with the pogrom in the business quarter at Neuer Wall, near Hamburg's city hall, where shop fronts were demolished, their stocks half-plundered and models in the windows of fashion stores dumped in the Alster canal nearby.[13] Hans Robinsohn of the *Gebr. Robinsohn* fashion store recalled in his memoirs that:

> The ground and first floors looked as if they had been bombed. Every window was smashed. In the airwell, heavy cabinets and desks had been thrown to the ground from the first floor. Typewriters were smashed with crowbars, all the card index files were bent, all the store window manikins thrown through the windows into the Alster canal behind the buildings, [and] large rolls of material had gone the same way. All of the glass tables and closets were destroyed. In one stairway all of the toilet facilities had been systematically smashed to pieces. The splinters of glass and wood lay so deep that we set up two first aid stations where injuries to the feet, legs, hands and arms of the employees who were cleaning up were taken care of.[14]

In Harburg, and in some quarters of Hamburg, the pogrom also continued, despite official bans on violence into the following day, because National Socialist officials there were not satisfied with the extent of the destruction caused during the previous night.[15]

Hamburg's Gauleiter and Reich Governor, Kaufmann, allegedly stayed in Hamburg on the evening of 9 November 1938, and did not travel to Munich where many Gauleiters and senior party leaders were celebrating the fifteenth anniversary of the November Putsch of 1923 at the Bürgerbräukeller. According to the testimony he gave in 1948, during questioning by prosecuting attorneys, he had been informed of the anti-Jewish attacks on the evening of 9 November by the head of the Hamburg Gestapo, Bruno Streckenbach. In response, he had given his local chiefs unambiguous instructions to prevent any vandalism of this kind.[16] This testimony is not really credible: Kaufmann's position in Hamburg was so powerful that it is unthinkable that so many acts of vandalism could have taken place if he had not at least tolerated them. At the same time, however, there are no grounds for believing that it was Kaufmann who gave the orders for the attacks. In Hamburg, the orders were instead given to Hamburg's SA and SS by regional SA and SS leaders and were clearly tolerated by Kaufmann. *SA-Oberabschnitt 'Nordsee'* received an order from *SA-Gruppenführer* Böhmker, who instructed his *Unterführer* from Munich, first by telephone and then even in writing, 'to destroy all Jewish businesses immediately', 'to set fire' to the synagogues and 'to shoot' any Jews who resisted 'immediately'.[17] The annual report for 1938 of the SD *Oberabschnitt* responsible for Hamburg correspondingly stated, under the heading of work done on 'Jewry', that the pogrom had been 'executed by the SA and SS'.[18]

In the first days after the pogrom, the Gestapo arrested at least 879 Jews of Hamburg who were either kept for a lengthy period in the police prison in Fuhlsbüttel or were transported from there to concentration camps, generally to the camp at Oranienburg.[19] If, up until the November Pogrom, some wealthy Jewish businessmen still hoped for tolerable conditions in which to be able to continue not only their professional work, but also their private lives in Germany, this hope finally proved illusory in November 1938. The experience of utter humiliation during their imprisonment marked the end of all security for them and prompted the numbers of emigrants in the first months of 1939 to rise quickly. By the end of 1938 almost 4,100 Jews had emigrated from Hamburg.[20]

One of those arrested was the Hamburg businessman Edgar Eichholz, who owned the import firm Eichholz & Loeser. As early as 1936, he had been forced to sell part of his firm to his lawyer when his import quotas for grain were taken away, but he continued to live in considerable prosperity and possessed all of the trappings of a well-situated, Hanseatic businessman, with his own respected company, residence, servants and automobile. On 11 November 1938, he was arrested in the office of his company and kept for several weeks in the police prison at Fuhlsbüttel. After his release he reported his prison experiences to his son:

When I was in the process of leaving the office at 1 o'clock, two civilians entered with a question about whether the company was pure Aryan. No, proprietor, come along. Empty all your pockets, take at most 10.- M with you, a clock, pencils, leave everything there. Off to city hall. Wait there, questioning, you are still under arrest, down into a dark hole with a plank bed and pissoir. Half an hour, then what seemed to be a lousy petty cash boy came in. A further half hour, Herr Clavier, who in his time had been our supplier and is my age. Then taken away by green prisoner transport van. In the courtyard of city hall two lanky SS. And now the abuse was let loose. Quick, quick, you Jewish pig, can't you stretch your legs, little so-and-so, we'll teach you now. And jabbed and kicked into the green van. And still more Jews came into the vehicle. A total of 31. Some of them had been given a bloody beating. And then into the prison at Fuhlsbüttel. There with the same people, at a speed that could never be fast enough, out of the cars with kicks, pokes and scolding, and then standing to attention with faces against the wall of the passage, one beside the other. I can tell you, it was agony, especially since everything was new and still unexpected, especially the scolding, the unrepeatable expressions, the poking.

At four o'clock we were like this in one room, finding ourselves, after 5 people had come into the room before us, a colorfully mixed group of 36 people there, of whom I knew Clavier, a certain Levy from the corn exchange, Heymann from Christensen, Heymann & Lüthge, and Friedmann from Eppendorfer Landstraße, better people there, such as, e.g., Dr Fritz Warburg and Dr Carl August Cohn, who, as I later became aware, both found themselves in a room above us, and also simple people like servants, newspaper salesmen, artisans, men from 17 years up to 68.

The cursing of the 22-23 year-old SS 'sergeants', as they were called, and dry black bread too ... What more should I tell you of the atrocious insults and the mean treatment of a sadistic kind from this small sergeant; it was, as it later turned out, easy compared with everything that had to be gone through by those who had been arrested in the first two days and taken to Oranienburg.

After 14 days there was a piece of paper so that we could let our relatives know of our whereabouts. Everything had to be written with a 1 centimeter-long stump, [and] the sergeant tore up the letters that had been arduously cobbled together with so much love: Are you Jewish pigs saying we should censor this scrawl? In four weeks you will be able to write again ... We were supposed to have been allowed to move about outside every day except Sunday for 20 minutes, weather permitting. Three times a week at most we were thus taken to the prison yard for exercise. One thinks of old people, harassed because they could no longer straighten their knees correctly.[21]

During his time in prison, Eichholz must have recognised that neither his social status as such nor the conviction which he emphasised at other points of being a 'good German' protected him from harassment. 'Better people' saw themselves subjected to the same discriminating prison conditions as 'lousy petty cash boys'. At the same time, Eichholz registered speechlessly that National Socialism had practically turned upside down the value system of the bourgeois society that he trusted and in which he, like most Jewish businessmen, had grown up: venerable dignitaries, successful Hanseatic businessmen who had once belonged to the leading stratum of society in Hamburg now had to stand to attention before adolescent 'sergeants' to be harassed and abused by them. One Hamburger, deported to Sachsenhausen concentration camp, recalled that elderly and wealthy Jews were treated with especial sadism by the young SS guards,[22] and if their physiognomy resembled the propaganda cliché of the 'Jewish bigwig', they were seen as a suitable target for the SS guards to take out not only their antisemitic hatred, but also their social frustrations. Whether they were baptised Christians or believing Jews, whether they approved or disapproved of the murder of Legation Counsellor vom Rath which the National Socialists had used as a welcome pretext for the pogrom, whether they were 'national' thinking, highly decorated front officers or pacifist-inclined internationalists, successful entrepreneurs or bankrupts, punctual taxpayers or defaulters, whether they had kept or had violated the law – all this did not have the slightest significance in overfilled prison cells or in the barracks of concentration camps, where they were helpless in the face of the oppression meted out by their guards. Neither their social status, their behaviour or their convictions could protect them from a worse fate, only a speedy emigration – this was the lesson learned from the bitter experience of the National Socialist terror unleashed after November 1938.

The non-Jewish bourgeoisie of Hamburg also anxiously watched as the bases of bourgeois security were undermined by street violence, pillage and arbitrary arrests, particularly because no-one doubted the organised character of the pogrom, soon widely dubbed *Reichskristallnacht* ('Reich Crystal Night') in response to the National Socialists' deceitful propaganda about 'spontaneous popular anger'. 'Old terms are being overturned, and everything is darker than ever',[23] Nikolaus Sieveking, a nephew of a previous mayor, Mönckeberg, noted in his diary on 16 November 1938. Although Sieveking was one of the most vehement opponents of National Socialism among Hamburg's bourgeoisie from 1933 onward, in November 1938, in a spirit of self-criticism, he asked himself whether he was not guilty, too. To Sieveking, the November Pogrom was:

> something that concerns us all and from which we cannot be released: not only because according to our upbringing and character we must be and remain unable to understand any of these things, but also because we have to become clear about how far we are all together *guilty* [emphasis in original] of them. Today is a real day for repentance. Real resistance to this whole development has been lacking from its beginning, and it has buried us with the force of an avalanche. If there is still hope that a decent society will one day become a reality, then we generate it from the experience of these developments, [knowing] how they once were and how they have often been.[24]

Like Sieveking, the Hamburg banker Cornelius Freiherr von Berenberg-Goßler was also one of the convinced opponents of National Socialism. He had numerous Jewish friends, businessmen and bankers, for whom he fought with remarkable courage. From those like the banker Kurt Rosenmayer, who went to see him after his release from prison 'with head shorn',[25] and who, like the banker George Behrens, '[could] hardly reach out a hand due to frostbite',[26] he learned many

details of the abuse they had suffered. His friend and partner, Percy Hamberg, did
not survive the tortures and died on Christmas Day 1938. Although he lay in a
sanatorium in a deep depression, the National Socialists had also arrested him after
the pogrom and taken him to the penitentiary at Strelitz.[27] 'Every decent-thinking
man must dissociate himself with abhorrence from this Nazi Party',[28] Berenberg-
Goßler noted with outrage in his diary on 13 November 1938. A few days later he
formulated his critique of the National Socialist regime still more absolutely:

> Almost everyone is talking about the unbelievably mean treatment of the Jews, who
> are being locked up and robbed. 'For what will it profit a man, if he gains the whole
> world and forfeits his life?' Again and again I find myself thinking about this biblical
> saying. What are all the successes and conquests of Hitler beside this bestial abuse
> that fills all decent men across the whole world with abhorrence. Rather a small,
> decently led state than a large Reich like Germany is today, without law and decency,
> with a government of robbers and murderers.[29]

Sieveking and Berenberg-Goßler felt confirmed in their fundamental rejection of National Socialism by the regime's abuse of the Jews. The category of
'decency' played a central role in their critique, Sieveking, for instance, evoking
the 'community of the decent' and Berenberg-Goßler deploring the lack of 'law
and decency'. A leadership of a state which trampled on human dignity through
arbitrary arrests and the theft of property was indecent in their view, placing itself
on a level with thieves and murderers and deserving no support even if it was able
to show economic and foreign policy 'successes'. In their understanding, the concept of 'decency' included achievements of modern civilisation such as the rule of
law and respect for individual human dignity. Accordingly Berenberg-Goßler
described the treatment of the Jews in his journal as a 'disgrace in front of the
civilised world'.[30]

This general critique of National Socialism, which they could only entrust to
their diaries, and (even more so) their understanding of decency, were minority
views among the Hamburg bourgeoisie and the population as a whole. Nevertheless numerous hints appear in the diary of Berenberg-Goßler that the pogrom
was viewed as 'indecent', 'unworthy' or 'despicable', both in his own bourgeois
environment and also in wider circles of the population.[31] SD reports also
recorded rejection and scepticism towards the pogrom from supporters of the
National Socialists and noted 'that even party members rejected the manner in
which the operation was carried out'.[32] At the same time, the criticism of the
majority of the population was not aimed at anti-Jewish policy as such, but was
limited to the methods used in implementing it, in particular to the destruction
of material assets that disavowed the constant appeals of the National Socialists to
save and sacrifice for the common good.[33] It was not anti-Jewish policy that was

'indecent' in the eyes of the majority of the population, but rather uncontrolled excesses, pillage and the destruction of 'national wealth'. If one can believe the reports of the SD, parts of the population were therefore completely 'in agreement' with the demolition of synagogues, whereas the destruction of businesses and private residences encountered 'strong opposition'.[34] In this perspective 'decency' degenerated into a category stripped of all normative implications that should have followed from it, and could, in extreme cases, be perverted into a purely formal attitude that was quite compatible with mass murder.[35]

Gauleiter Kaufmann meticulously registered the opinions and attitudes of the population towards the November Pogrom. In January 1939, he used a speech he delivered to the Hamburg Chamber of Commerce as an opportunity to distance himself carefully from the excesses of 'Reich Crystal Night', thus giving expression to the general critique of these excesses while at the same time pressing a far wider perspective on his audience, namely the prospect of a speedy 'final regulation of the Jewish problem'. Kaufmann went on at some length:

> I am one of those convinced National Socialists who are of the opinion that the quickest lawful final regulation of the Jewish problem is the best solution (lively applause). I am one of the extreme opponents of anyone who believes that a problem of this kind, which positively must be solved, can only be solved with methods that normally would be despicable. Out of this conviction I have also attempted in Hamburg – and I believe that the method used in Hamburg has been limited to the extent that was really necessary – to avoid any act whose method did not correspond to the solution of the problem and whose mentality would sometimes lead to the precise opposite of what was intended, which ultimately represents an unworthy solution in terms of being conscious of our power and of our whole situation (lively applause). I believe that this opinion has found express acknowledgement at high quarters from General Field Marshall Göring[36] (lively applause). It is in fact quite incomprehensible that this should happen at a time when we should be so careful in handling the assets of our nation, when, to give one example, the pursuit of progress makes destroying assets problematical. This means that it is not [really] the property of the Jews that has been destroyed, but something that our nation is in dire need of (shouts: very true!). But I believe that we have learned from this, and I can guarantee that such things will never be repeated. That of course does not rule out the possibility that we will now also bring these problems, which had to be raised, to their final regulation. This is of course also a question that now really had to be dealt with and resolved, that will be resolved and that is best solved when it is done by legal means and as quickly as possible. The rest of the world will resign itself to this situation, with more or less of a fuss.[37]

To his bourgeois audience, Kaufmann presented himself as a National Socialist capable of making criticisms and who knew how to interpret the voice of the people correctly, even if he cynically played down the excesses of the pogrom in Hamburg as being limited to the 'extent really necessary' and concealed his personal responsibility for them. In the future, no 'mob antisemitism', no useless destruction of material goods and no street terror was to unsettle the security of non-Jewish '*Volksgenossen*' (national comrades). Further negative effects on popular opinion should instead be avoided by a speedy 'final regulation' of the problem. This meant using the state apparatus instead of the street fighters of the SA. In other words, the 'exclusion' of the Jews would only escape criticism from the non-Jewish population if it was perpetrated by the state and dressed in legal garb, and not as a pogrom that was seen by the population as a potential threat to its own position. This was the conclusion that Kaufmann and the National Socialist state leadership had drawn from the 'Reich Crystal Night'. No unbroken line of continuity ran between the November Pogrom and the subsequent mass murder of the Jews.[38] The 'Reich Crystal Night' marked the highpoint of 'mob antisemitism', but also lastingly discredited it.[39] In its place a policy was now introduced that aimed at much more radical and fundamental 'solutions'. What was camouflaged from the outside with the blanket of reform and moderation in reality signified a drastic radicalisation of anti-Jewish policy. It was not the pogrom, but Kaufmann's call for a 'final regulation' that bore more than a semantic commonality with the subsequent 'final solution'.

## The Liquidation and Forced 'Aryanisation' of Jewish Businesses

On the very day after the pogrom, 10 November 1938, Hitler, in conversation with Goebbels and Göring, had given instructions for the final 'exclusion' of the Jews from the economy.[40] Two days later the leadership of the National Socialist state, at a meeting in the Reich Ministry for Aviation in Berlin, agreed to intensify all existing anti-Jewish measures at one and the same time. On 12 November 1938, the compulsory 'Aryanisation' and liquidation of Jewish enterprises was instituted through the first Ordinance on the Exclusion of the Jews from German Economic Life (*Verordnung zur Ausschaltung der Juden aus dem deutschen Wirtschaftsleben*), Jews being forbidden from operating retail and mail order businesses as well as workshops after 1 January 1939.[41] According to an implementation directive of 23 November, these enterprises were to be totally liquidated if the continued operation of the enterprise through its 'Aryanisation' was not essential for the supply of the population.[42] Where businesses were liquidated, their Jewish proprietors were forbidden from selling their stocks to the population. Instead they had to offer their goods to the professional association responsible, and thereby, indirectly, to their competitors. The 'Ordinance on the Utilisation of Jewish Property' (*Verordnung über den Einsatz des jüdischen Vermögens*) of 3 December 1938, finally allowed the higher administrative authorities

– the Reich Governor in Hamburg – to liquidate or 'Aryanise' all Jewish commercial concerns and real estate.[43] Securities had to be deposited in a foreign exchange bank, and jewels, jewellery and works of art had to be offered to a public purchasing office.

Alongside the elimination of the economic livelihoods of the Jews, the National Socialists also intensified their repression through financial policy. The 'Ordinance on the Restoration of Street Scenery at Jewish Commercial Concerns' (*Verordnung zur Wiederherstellung des Straßenbildes bei jüdischen Gewerbebetrieben*) issued by Göring on 12 November, placed the burden of clearing the damage caused by the pogrom on the victims and seized their insurance claims for the coffers of the Reich.[44] The 'Ordinance on an Expiation Payment by Jews of German Citizenship' (*Verordnung über eine Sühneleistung der Juden deutscher Staatsangehörigkeit*) published on the same day, required of them an additional mandatory contribution of one billion RM, levied in five instalments to total five percent of the assets they held personally at the time.[45] In December 1938, the Gestapo in Hamburg introduced an additional 'emigration levy' (*Auswandererabgabe*) valued at twenty percent of 'Reich Flight Tax' payments. It had already wound up the existing institutions of the Jewish community, and on 2 December 1938, appointed the former community attorney Dr Max Plaut as the sole director of the Jewish Religious Federation of Hamburg (*Jüdische Religionsverband*) and of all other Jewish organisations.[46] The proceeds of the 'emigration levy', amounting to 1.3 million RM in Hamburg by March 1939, were originally intended to facilitate the emigration of Jews without means of their own, but ultimately had to be used to pay the budget deficit of the Jewish Religious Federation.[47]

The introduction of the Emigré Tax signalled that after the November Pogrom the emigration of the Jews was also going to be enforced by the state. On 12 November 1938, the participants at the meeting in the Reich Aviation Ministry agreed to establish a Central Reich Office for Jewish Emigration (*Reichszentrale für jüdische Auswanderung*) under the direction of the Head of the Security Police and the SD, Reinhard Heydrich. The model used for this was the 'Central Office for Jewish Emigration' (*Zentralstelle für jüdische Auswanderung*) established in Vienna in the spring of 1938 under the direction of Adolf Eichmann, which, through the use of force, had secured the emigration of over fifty thousand Austrian Jews within a few months.[48]

The decisions and directives issued after the November Pogrom introduced not only a new phase in the radicalisation of anti-Jewish policy, but also one of centralisation in which regional discrepancies in anti-Jewish policy were largely levelled out. With respect to the economic 'exclusion' of the Jews, however, the 'division of labour' employed thus far remained in force. While, in the regions, the *Gau* Economics Advisers and regional authorities authorised 'Aryanisations' and liquidations of Jewish enterprises, and now also of Jewish real estate, the Reich limited itself to confiscating the proceeds of sales and other Jewish assets through taxes, compulsory contributions and foreign exchange transfer ordinances. In January 1939, the Reich authorities withdrew more or less completely from the 'Aryanisation' process in Hamburg when the Reich Economics Ministry delegated its only means for exercising influence, namely its function as an appeals instance, to the 'Complaints Office' of the Hamburg Reich Governor,[49] headed by an intimate of Gauleiter Kaufmann, *Gau* Inspector Dr Hellmuth Becker. The move meant that the Reich had limited its activities definitively to the confiscation of the fortunes of Jews.

Attempts to skim off the proceeds of 'Aryanisations' through a Reich-wide 'De-Judaisation Gains Tax' (*Entjudungsgewinnsteuer*), however, had little success. The Ordinance on the Utilisation of Jewish Property, promulgated on 3 December 1938, allowed the authorising bodies to levy a payment on 'Aryanisations' on behalf of the German Reich.[50] According to a directive from the Reich Economics Ministry of 8 February 1939, the payment was to amount to seventy percent of the difference between the official valuation and the sale price actually paid. On 10 June 1940, Hermann Göring, as Head of the Four-Year Plan, also issued an 'Ordinance on the Scrutiny of De-Judaisation Transactions' (*Verordnung über die Nachprüfung von Entjudungsgeschäften*).[51] This provided for a compensation payment for all 'Aryanisation' sales conducted since 30 January 1933 in which the buyer had received 'inadequate pecuniary benefit'. This could have been taken to mean that the directive was to be applied retroactively to almost all 'Aryanisations' as enriching the buyer at the expense of the Jewish proprietor was virtually characteristic of such sales. In Hamburg this directive was hardly applied at all. It only raised about 50 million RM, and a mere fraction of this total was set aside for the use of the Reich. The futility of the Reich's attempts to cream off the proceeds of 'Aryanisations' underlines once again that the Reich institutions exercised hardly any influence over the actual practice of these 'Aryanisations', and that regional state and party decision-makers preferred to allow the proceeds to go to their personal favourites or to be deposited in dubious special accounts rather than to transfer them to the Reich.[52]

After November 1938, there was little change to the formal division of responsibilities for 'Aryanisation' and liquidation of Jewish enterprises in Hamburg. The Ordinance on the Utilisation of Jewish Property of 3 December 1938 had once more acknowledged the position of the Reich Governor as the highest authorising body. On 14 November 1938, Kaufmann had transferred his competence for 'Aryanisations' to Senator Wilhelm von Allwörden,[53] who functioned as both his Economics Representative and as Head of the Hamburg Department for Trade, Shipping and Industry. Allwörden hardly ever went into action as

'Aryanisation' Commissioner because heart-muscle damage confined him to six months in hospital from November 1938.[54]

The *Gau* Economics Adviser continued to hold a dominant position in the 'Aryanisation' of Jewish enterprises. This emerged in the days following the November Pogrom when he appointed 'trustees' for those Jewish enterprises whose owners had been arrested.[55] Formally, he had absolutely no authority to do this because the installation of trustees was connected to the issuance of a blocking order under Paragraph 37a of the Foreign Exchange Law that could only be granted by the Foreign Exchange Control Office of the Regional Finance President. The Foreign Exchange Control Office, caught unawares by the *Gau* Economics Adviser, made no protest once the facts had been established on the ground and 'legalised' his arbitrary procedure by formally assigning the 'trustees' with their charge.[56]

This self-authorisation, typical of the behaviour of the *Gau* Economics Adviser and unquestionably given political cover by Gauleiter Kaufmann, had consequences for the 'Aryanisation' of Jewish businesses from November 1938 because, without exception, the trustees were members of the NSDAP[57] who saw themselves not as representatives of the state but as the *Gau* Economics Adviser's political appointees and thus as party functionaries. One trustee formally installed by the Foreign Exchange Control Office, for example, wrote straight back to the Office that he had 'been asked by the NSDAP to resign from his trusteeship' and, just weeks after the end of his period in office, demonstratively presented himself for a final meeting at the Foreign Exchange Control Office.[58] It was, therefore, no accident that in the final phase of 'Aryanisation' those who acquired Jewish businesses were overwhelmingly NSDAP members. The stronger the direct influence of the party and the weaker the position of Jewish firm proprietors, the more favourable conditions became for National Socialists and convinced antisemites. In the early years of the National Socialist regime, they hardly figured among those involved in 'Aryanisations' because these presupposed an arrangement with the Jewish proprietor which could not easily have been forced on him. After many Jewish company owners had been transported to concentration camps and had lost their influence over their businesses, party members became all the more insistent in demanding a share in the booty.

The final phase of 'Aryanisation' had no impact on the informal dominance of the party organisation – represented by the *Gau* Economics Adviser – even if the Department for Trade, Shipping and Industry was formally responsible for the authorisation of sales contracts for Jewish businesses and real estate. By contrast, the Hamburg Economics Department, the specialised groups for the commercial economy and the Chamber of Commerce had great influence over the decision as to whether Jewish businesses were to be liquidated or 'Aryanised'. Within a short period, an agreement was reached among all participants in November 1938 to liquidate two hundred of the three hundred remaining Jewish retail businesses and a majority of the approximately three hundred Jewish craft workshops.[59]

Helmut Genschel has argued that, after the November Pogrom, the state successfully undermined the NSDAP's claim to the leading role in the 'Aryanisation' process and 'Aryanisations' were now 'modified in favour of the state and gradually, with a bureaucratic thoroughness, transformed into a system'.[60] In this he drew on a number of sources, including an order from Göring of 10 December 1938 which, in agreement with the Deputy to the Führer, laid down that 'Aryanisation' was a 'function of the state' which was to take place 'only on a strictly legal basis' and that the proceeds from 'Aryanisations' were therefore to be delivered 'only to the Reich'.[61]

From the perspective of Hamburg, however, orders of this kind, far from being regarded as energetic attempts to implement a sovereign right of the state, were rather seen as helpless attempts to ensure that developments that had run out of control did not go completely off-track. The installation of 'trustees' had already revealed the actual balance of power in Hamburg and thus the de facto downgrading of the state vis-à-vis the party. In addition, the particular circumstances surrounding the 'Aryanisations' effected after November 1938 were far removed from evidencing a formalisation and bureaucratisation of the authorisation procedure. After the arrest of many Jewish firm owners a feverish race for enrichment set in. In no other phase of the 'Aryanisation' process did enrichment from Jewish enterprises become more extensive than in the period of 'legal' regulations enacted from 1938 onward. This development was made still more significant in Hamburg by the relative delay in the 'Aryanisations' there, a number of lucrative businesses still lying in Jewish hands in November 1938. Of the approximately twelve hundred Jewish enterprises existing in the autumn of 1938, practically none were still operating a year later.[62] The 'Aryanisation' and liquidation of the remaining Jewish enterprises was therefore completed within an extremely short period and assumed almost volcanic proportions around 1938/39. More than eighteen hundred prospective buyers applied during the 'Aryanisation' of the one hundred Jewish retail businesses alone.[63] In the atmosphere that developed, everything had to be sold, and even larger enterprises changed hands within ten minutes.[64] Some trustees sold off the stocks of Jewish enterprises at rock-bottom prices,[65] sales of stocks for which it had taken ten days to do the annual inventory were completed within two hours[66] and some buyers cut short the sales negotiations and the authorisation procedure by donning their party uniforms and summarily chasing the Jewish proprietor from their business.[67] The formal façade of the authorisation procedure for 'Aryanisations' was, therefore, in many cases merely a sham.

The authorisation of the sales contract was increasingly reduced to a pure act of acknowledgment, and authorisations were no longer preceded by any detailed checks. The beneficiaries of these conditions were often National Socialists who sought to use political patronage to secure lucrative enterprises for themselves. In one case, a former salesman took over a Jewish firm who, shortly before, had been dismissed from his position on the grounds that he was a 'non-Aryan'.[68] In the final phase of the 'Aryanisation' process, the authorising bodies no longer even required an 'Aryan certificate' from the buyers.

As the transfer of businesses after November 1938 shows, Jewish company owners had now become mere objects, lacking all influence, no longer possessing any genuine options from which to negotiate. Anyone who was arrested after the pogrom looked on helplessly while his enterprise was sold or liquidated. 'The Nazi authorities and *Gau* Economics Offices decreed the sale and the Jewish business owner could only watch as he was ruined',[69] as Paul Schiff described the position faced by the prisoners. Schiff, a volunteer in the First World War who had been a front-line officer, was the owner of the wholesale enterprise *Gebr. Frank*. On 15 November 1938, he was placed in custody at the Fuhlsbüttel police jail. The 'trustee' who was installed sold the business for around 29,000 RM to an applicant who was a member of both the NSDAP and the SS. In October 1938, the value of the stocks alone was still calculated for tax purposes at around 80,000 RM, but it was lowered in order to 'facilitate endorsement [of the sale] by the Assistant to the *Gau* Economics Adviser'.[70] In custody, Schiff had no influence and was finally let out of the police prison to sign the contract.

Fritz Lobbenberg, who was deported to the Sachsenhausen concentration camp and owned a retail store selling jewellery, umbrellas and leatherware at Jungfernstieg 33 under the company name *J. Lobbenberg*, had a similar experience.[71] When he was released in December 1938, he found that during his absence the 'trustee' had sold his entire stock to his competitors. The jewellery had been taken by a member of the SS who ran the *Wiener Schmuckkästchen* firm at *Neuer Wall*, while the rest of the stock had been transferred to a specialist umbrella store. The store furnishings and the cash register had been given to a long-serving saleswoman who used them to build up an independent business for herself. The former owner received a trifling amount for the sale with which he ultimately paid the travel expenses for his emigration to Jamaica.

These opportunities for enrichment were largely taken up by NSDAP members after November 1938. Many a National Socialist was now able to come into possession of a business even if it was not intended for 'Aryanisation', but was due to be liquidated. One interested buyer introduced himself to the textile business owner Martin Josephs and to the liquidator appointed by the authorities in December 1938, indicating that he had been 'assigned by the NSDAP' to take

over the business.[72] Neither the liquidator nor the authorising bodies contradicted this groundless claim, and the buyer was ultimately able to acquire the
business at a giveaway price even where an order to liquidate the company had
been given. Sale or liquidation made no difference to the owner during this phase,
since even a formal business sale would not have provided greater remuneration.
'For me it was completely indifferent which "party comrade" took advantage of
my lack of rights at the time',[73] one company owner wrote of this situation.

If several National Socialists applied to take over a Jewish business, intense
struggles could develop behind the scenes involving many institutions and organisations. The 'Aryanisation' of *Ostindienhaus Heinrich Colm* at *Neuer Wall* 13/15
was typical of these conflicts. A ladies' clothing store enjoying the best possible
economic fortunes, it employed around seventy workers and consistently increased
its turnover even after 1933. The enterprise was run as a limited partnership
whose shares were distributed between the Jewish founder of the firm, Heinrich
Colm, his non-Jewish wife and his two 'half-Jewish' children.

The owners' attempts to transfer the business to the non-Jewish wife were
rejected on the grounds that after over twenty-five years of marriage with the
company founder she was 'too Judaised'.[74] For similar reasons, the takeover of the
business by a long-standing employee collapsed when the employee was classified
as 'politically unreliable' by the Department for Trade, Shipping and Industry.[75]
Just one day after the pogrom, the Hamburg *Gau* Economics Adviser installed his
party colleague Hans Sixt Freiherr von Jena as 'trustee' for the lucrative enterprise,
for which there were thirty-seven applications from potential buyers. The contract
was given to a textile businessman and party member from Perleberg with whom
the trustee and the Jewish proprietor concluded a sales contract on 15 December
1938. The buyer had already sounded out the political terrain through a confidant, who received a commission of 4,500 RM.[76] The buyer then paid the Jewish proprietors 23,000 RM for an enterprise that, in the year 1937 alone, had
turned over 776,000 RM. In addition, the contract designated a monthly payment of 550 RM and partnership for the 'half-Jewish' son of the owner.

This contract was contested by two National Socialists, one of whom was a
'*Gau* Professional Official' for the DAF. They had also applied to take over the
business before the sale. Now they threatened the Jewish owners with the
Gestapo, brought in the Office for Trade and Handicraft of the NSDAP,[77] and
pointed out the fact that the authorising body actually responsible, the Department for Trade, Shipping and Industry, had already expressed its support for their
becoming the new owners on 10 December 1938. Consequently, on 13 January
1939 when the Department for Trade, Shipping and Industry declared the sales
contract concluded on 15 December 1938 to be invalid, the original buyer complained to the Reich Economics Ministry. The Ministry then refused to intervene.

In the end, the affair deteriorated into a conflict between the *Gau* Economics Adviser, on the one hand, and the Department for Trade, Shipping and Industry, on the other. The *Gau* Economics Adviser took the side of the original buyers,[78] in large part because he did not want to contradict a decision of his trustee, while the Department supported the two plaintiffs with the argument that taking over the enterprise would give them a start in business while the other party was already running an enterprise in Perleberg.[79] The Reich Governor finally settled the argument in favour of the *Gau* Economics Adviser and repudiated the position of the Department for Trade, Shipping and Industry, overturning its rejection and acknowledging the original contract of 15 December 1938[80] – a process that affirmed the informal primacy of the NSDAP over the municipal authorities in the 'Aryanisation' of Jewish property.

The victims of these conflicts were the Jewish owners. The monthly payment of 550 RM to the 'half-Jewish' son of the owner originally agreed was reduced in the context of the appeal process to 250 RM. The reason given for this by the official in the Office of the *Gau* Economics Adviser was that the son had a 'very Jewish' appearance and so there could be no place for him in the business.[81]

At the outbreak of war in 1939, the liquidation and 'Aryanisation' of Jewish enterprises in Hamburg was practically complete. Only a few enterprises owned by foreign Jews were able to continue beyond this time as they were not at first subject to 'compulsory Aryanisation' under the Ordinance on the Utilisation of Jewish Property of 3 December 1938. On special orders from the Reich Economics Ministry, however, the enterprises of Polish, Czech, Norwegian, Danish, Dutch, Belgian and Luxemburgian Jews were gradually drawn into the 'Aryanisation' process.[82] All other enterprises owned by foreign Jews were ultimately placed under the Reich Commissioner for Dealing with Enemy Property – for example, the *Kühlhaus Rosshafen AG* enterprise in Hamburg, owned by British Jews, was placed under mandatory administration by court order in July 1940.[83]

## The Seizure of Real Estate Owned Privately by Jews

In contrast to the destruction of the economic livelihood of the Jews in Hamburg, it would be inaccurate to speak of the systematic 'Aryanisation' and expropriation of their real estate, even at the end of 1938. According to an inventory of 15 October 1938, a total of 2,043 properties in the Hanseatic City of Hamburg were held by Jewish proprietors at this point in time, representing 2.25 percent of the total figure of all properties.[84] This percentage was higher in the state territory of 'old Hamburg', at 3.7 percent (1,665 properties), than in the city quarters added to Hamburg in 1937/38, Altona (1.1 percent, 310 properties), Harburg-Wilhelmsburg (0.5 percent, 43 properties) or Wandsbek (0.3 percent, 25 properties). Of the properties in the former state territory of Hamburg 13.2 percent were business premises, 19.2 percent were properties with a mixed use, 48 percent rented residences and 14.7 percent properties containing owner-occupied one-family houses, mostly villas in the Rotherbaum and Harvestehude quarters. The high proportion of rented properties, and properties used for more than one purpose, partly in quarters with small numbers of Jewish residents like Hamburg-Neustadt, nevertheless spoke of a high number of wealthy Jewish property owners who earned their income through letting out residential and business properties.

On 1 April 1938, the number of properties in the old Hamburg state territory owned by Jews was still 1,877. At this point, a programme of systematic fiscal discrimination was launched against Jewish proprietors, their exemption from real estate taxes, for instance, being withdrawn from them on 19 April 1938.[85] One week later the Ordinance on the Registration of the Property of Jews of 26 April 1938 (*Verordnung über die Anmeldung des Vermögens von Juden*) introduced registration of all of their real estate, which could still be sold, however, with no prior authorisation. At the same time, the 'Aryanisation' of Jewish enterprises, the repression of Jews through financial policy measures and the general pressure for Jews to emigrate, also triggered a growing number of real estate sales without a formal regulatory mechanism. In addition, just prior to 1938, the National Socialists had found ways to force Jewish proprietors to sell their property regardless of legal principles.

A characteristic case occurred in Hamburg in 1937, when a lucrative department store property in the centre of Hamburg – on the corner of Jungfernstieg 4/5 and Reesendamm 1/3 – changed hands.[86] Up until 1931, the building, which belonged to Dr Gerhard Sostberg and Max Isaac, housed the fashion store *Hirsch & Cie.*, in which Max Isaac had a financial stake. When *Hirsch & Cie.* ran into difficulties during the global economic crisis and had to stop trading, the property and building were used to take out, *inter alia*, an interest-free mortgage of 300,000 RM to satisfy the demands of creditors. A further mortgage of 200,000 RM was also taken out in the favour of a Jewish creditor.

Around 1932/33, the owners succeeded once more in letting their buildings at a profit. It is not without a certain irony that the Jewish proprietors from now on accommodated in their building the American department store chain *Woolworth GmbH* as well as the National Socialist party newspaper, the *Hamburger Tageblatt.*

At the beginning of 1937, the publishing director of the *Hamburger Tageblatt*, Edgar Brinkmann, pressed the Jewish proprietors to sell the building, which, following consultations with the Munich headquarters of the publishing house Eher & Co., he wanted to turn into a National Socialist 'Press Building'. Because he felt the sale price of 2.5 million RM demanded was too high, he put pressure on the Jewish owners of the building by means of an ingenious plan. Through two lawyers who were given full powers of attorney, the Jewish creditors were forced to sell their credit for 200,000 RM to the partners in the *Hamburger Tageblatt* at a price of 80,000 RM. The money was loaned to them by the businessman Philipp F. Reemtsma, who had befriended Brinkmann. In possession of the mortgage, the *Hamburger Tageblatt* now initiated compulsory foreclosure proceedings against the Jewish owners with respect to alleged arrears in interest payments, with the aim of earning themselves a favourable position to take over their building. In the meantime, however, it was decided that the location for the publishing house of the *Hamburger Nachrichten* was to be at the Speersort, so the interest of the *Hamburger Tageblatt* in acquiring the property on Jungfernstieg and Reesendamm suddenly subsided. Woolworth GmbH, until then an uninvolved third party, now profited from the new situation. It bought the property for 1.5 million RM from the Jewish proprietors, who had lost all leverage to negotiate on the price because of the threat of the compulsory foreclosure proceedings. The directors of the *Hamburger Tageblatt* received a considerable windfall from the mortgage, for which they had paid only 80,000 RM, but was refunded by Woolworth at the full value of 200,000 RM. After Philipp F. Reemtsma's loan of 80,000 RM had been repaid with interest, the victims of this cooperation between the National Socialists and an American department store chain were the Jewish proprietors, who had been forced to sell their property at well under half of its market value.

Although this example suggests the informal opportunities the National Socialists had to force Jews to sell their property if necessary, by mid-1938 the Hamburg Gauleiter was also formally enforcing seizures of private property owned by Jews, primarily in order to regulate the sale of real estate. The occasion for his intervention was offered by the Law on Changes in the Commercial Law of the German Reich (*Gesetz zur Änderung der Gewerbeordnung für das Deutsche Reich*) of 6 July 1938, which forbade Jews from trading in real estate as well as from acting as brokers or house and real estate agents.[87] After all properties in Hamburg owned by Jews – previously entrusted to the care of Jewish real estate agencies – were placed on a register with the help of the housing and real estate associations,[88] the Gauleiter transferred them to compulsory administration by a newly created real estate corporation, the 'Hamburg Real Estate Administration Corporation of 1938 Ltd.' (*Hamburger Grundstücks-Verwaltungsgesellschaft von 1938 mbH*, GVG).[89] The corporation was established and managed without legal legitimation after the law of 6 July 1938 had provided no regulations for the compulsory administration of real estate owned by Jews. In the current state of research, we cannot say whether the GVG was founded by Kaufmann copying models from other regions of the Reich or whether it was a development specific to Hamburg.[90]

Properties owned by Jews could be transferred to the control of the GVG in two different ways. On the one hand, the GVG 'Aryanised' the existing Jewish real estate agencies and took over the properties they had previously managed.[91] On the other, those properties for which a blocking order had been issued under Paragraph 37a of the Foreign Exchange Law could be handed over by the GVG to a trustee administration.

If compulsory administration by the GVG itself lacked any legal basis, the circumstances of its establishment reinforced the climate of injustice and corruption. The initial capital with which the GVG was established came from 'Aryanisation contributions' that Gauleiter and Reich Governor Kaufmann had made available to the GVG.[92] In order to hide this connection, a number of moves were made, including the establishment of 'Hanseatic Property Management and Trust Company Limited' (*Hanseatische Vermögensverwaltungs- und Treuhand-Gesellschaft mbH, Treuhansa*), directed by one of the partners, the National Socialist Hans Sixt Freiherr von Jena.[93] That the GVG was nevertheless established, de facto, by the Gauleiter and Reich Governor is clear from Paragraph 16 of the articles of association which stipulated that the net profits of the GVG were to be 'placed in principle at the disposal of the Reich Governor in Hamburg for social uses'.[94] These 'social uses' – as Kaufmann's payment orders verify – included financing the NSDAP and the 'liquidation of the debts of deserving party comrades'.[95] The managing director of the GVG, who worked together with Dr Eduard Hoffmann, was a colleague from the Office of the NSDAP *Gau* Economics Adviser.[96] By establishing the GVG, the Gauleiter was pursuing three political goals in particular:[97]

1. The GVG was primarily intended to administer the properties of Jewish owners and only to sell off a limited number of them so as to prevent a surplus being sold that would lead to a fall in prices across the whole real estate market.
2. The GVG gave the Gauleiter a direct avenue to enrich himself, to gain further influence and to seize properties owned by Jews.
3. The GVG was useful as a collection point for 'Aryanisation contributions' and served the Gauleiter, and indirectly the Hamburg NSDAP, as a hidden source of income.

These activities so clearly contravened the fundamentals of justice and morality that even the *Gau* Economics Adviser in Hamburg, Otte, confided to one of his colleagues that the GVG gave him an 'uneasy feeling'.[98] Among Jewish real estate owners, the GVG was soon so notorious that at the end of 1938 some preferred to sell their property at giveaway prices than to leave it to fall into the hands of GVG executors.[99]

The Ordinance on the Utilisation of Jewish Property of 3 December 1938 introduced a state licencing requirement for the sale of properties as well as the possibility of an enforced sale.[100] In Hamburg, it meant that the Department for Trade, Shipping and Industry was made responsible for the authorisation of sales contracts, while in Berlin this activity was taken over from the Real Estate Price-Setting Offices by the Berlin District Offices.[101] It would, nevertheless, be inaccurate to speak of the municipal authorities taking a leading role in the 'Aryanisation' of Jewish real estate sales. The Hamburg Economics Department was reduced, in practice, to serving as an executive organ of the Gauleiter and the NSDAP. On the one hand, the Gauleiter and Reich Governor also worked as the highest instance in the authorisation of real estate sales so that the Economics Department was dependent on Kaufmann's deciding vote. On the other, the NSDAP also participated in the 'Aryanisation' of Jewish real estate in two ways, first through the *Gau* Economics Adviser and secondly through the GVG. Each sales contract submitted in Hamburg was presented to the *Gau* Economics Adviser for examination and comment first. Only after he had given his agreement was the sales contract passed on to the Department for Trade, Shipping and Industry, which fixed the sale price in accordance with the specifications laid down by the *Gau* Economics Adviser. In Hamburg, the price varied from one property to the next between the 'moderate market value' and the standard value of the property, which, for many real estate sales, was still knocked down considerably.[102] In no case did the Jewish proprietor receive the actual market value of his property. After establishing the price, the Economics Department brought the GVG into the procedure, which negotiated with the buyer over the size of his 'Aryanisation contribution'.[103] These contributions were transferred to a special 'trust account' that did not appear in the books of the GVG even though it was established under the name of the GVG's managing director. The exclusive right to use the account lay with the Gauleiter and Reich Governor, who also gave final approval to sales contracts that had been submitted.

This procedure guaranteed unlimited opportunities of influence to the Gauleiter and to party organisations. Through the GVG, they could directly control part of the properties of Jewish owners, reject applicants for the properties who in their view were unsuitable, to a large degree determine prices and secure properties for the State of Hamburg, for the NSDAP, for party functionaries or for other acceptable prospective buyers. The Jewish proprietors were correspondingly helpless when faced with the machinations of the authorising institutions, which, on the basis of the following three examples, can only be hinted at.

In December 1938, the Jewish interior decorator, Kurt Clavier, had sought to sell his property at Harvestehuder Weg 11 before emigrating to South Africa.[104] However, an offer from the Egyptian Consulate to buy it for 165,000

RM was not authorised by the Reich Governor, who wanted the building to be the headquarters of the State of Hamburg. On 31 January 1939, Kaufmann therefore made the GVG the trustee for the property, on which a blocking order had been placed under Paragraph 37a of the Foreign Exchange Law. On 15 March 1939, the property was finally 'offered' to the City of Hamburg, which acquired it fourteen days later at a price of 125,000 RM and then installed some of the departments of the Hamburg state administration and the NSDAP. The sale price had been reduced by about 40,000 RM, and, on top of that, it was transferred to a blocked account which the Jewish owner could only access with permission from the Foreign Exchange Control Office.

Similarly the purchase of a large property of three thousand square metres on Scheffelstraße belonging to Elli Lippmann was clearly a crass form of self-enrichment.[105] Her husband, Carl Lippmann, had bought the property in 1925 for 117,000 RM and laid down a large fruit garden and a tennis court. For this, Lippmann had invested a further 14,000 RM. In March 1940, his wife had to sell the property to Rudolf August Oetker of the *Dr August Oetker/Bielefeld* company, who bought it in order to complement his private property on Bellevue. A price of 58,000 RM had been envisaged, which did not amount to even half the price it had been bought for. This was reduced once again to 45,500 RM in a notice from the Reich Governor authorising the sale on 13 June 1940. A complaint from the Jewish proprietor was rebuffed on the grounds that the reduction of the sale price had been made in light of 'national economic interests', although it concerned a garden property for which absolutely no business use had been proposed.

The third example, the sale of a property at Hamburger Straße 88, is raised here because it relates to the complete financial plundering of a Jewish proprietor in the course of the sale of his property.[106] On 7 December 1938, a Jewish proprietor, Bernhard Stern, sold his property for 54,000 RM to an acquaintance. After the deduction of all 'charges' levied, he was left with just 90 RM. The proceeds of the sale were reduced not only by having to pay for mortgages, real estate tax, broker's fees and handling charges to the GVG, but also by a sale price reduction ordered on the grounds of an alleged 'defect' and by an 'Aryanisation contribution' to the GVG of 5000 RM. In this case the 'Aryanisation contribution' was not imposed upon the buyer but on the Jewish proprietor, effectively confiscating the whole of the sale proceeds with the exception of the symbolic sum of 90 RM.

For many Jews, the sale of their properties was so financially unattractive that they only sold their real estate if they needed the proceeds to pay off taxes and compulsory levies, and not all owners parted with their properties when they emigrated. Some even preferred an official trustee administration that left them with a formal right to the property rather than agree to a sale which, because of foreign exchange transfer regulations, generally robbed them of their property completely.

Whereas continuing to manage a business usually presupposed the personal presence of the firm owner, a property could be administered without problems even after the owner had emigrated.

Moreover, the National Socialists only exercised selective – not general – pressure on Jewish real estate owners to sell up. On 28 December 1938, Hermann Göring, after a meeting with Hitler, ordered that the 'Aryanisation of house ownership be placed at the end of the whole Aryanisation process' and the 'Aryanisation' of Jewish businesses be given the highest priority.[107] The National Socialists' caution was linked directly to the plans for ghettoising the Jews in specified residential areas and concentrating them in 'Jewish houses' (*Judenhäuser*). The implementation of these plans presupposed that Jews could own real estate – the alternative would have been to place an obligation on 'Aryan' homeowners to establish 'Jewish houses'.

The combination of all of these factors meant that only a third of the properties of Jews in Hamburg were 'Aryanised' before October 1939, by which time the 'Aryanisation' and liquidation of Jewish enterprises had been completed.[108] According to an assessment by the GVG's Managing Director, Dr Hoffmann, who based his calculations on a total figure of 2,400 properties in 1938, at this point in time there were still 1,600 owned by Jews, and among these approximately a thousand were rented residential properties. The GVG, which was assigned three to four properties by the Hamburg Economics Department per week, in due course administered four hundred properties, but sold only one hundred and twenty of them.

The majority of properties owned by Jews were seized on behalf of the German Reich in 1941/42. The two documents that served as the legal bases for this were the 'Decree of the Führer and Reich Chancellor on the Utilisation of the Requisitioned Property of Enemies of the Reich' (*Erlaß des Führers und Reichskanzlers über die Verwertung des eingezogenen Vermögens von Reichsfeinden*)[109] of 29 May 1941, which, along with other measures, was applied at the time of the deportation of Jews living in Germany,[110] and the Eleventh Ordinance of the Reich Citizen's Law of 25 November 1941, which deprived all Jews who had emigrated abroad of their German citizenship and seized their property, placing it under the official administration of the Reich.[111]

The administration of the property seized in this way was the responsibility of the Reich Finance Minister and the Regional Finance President in Berlin, who, nevertheless, delegated their powers to the regional finance offices responsible,[112] where, from the end of 1941, agencies were established for the 'utilisation of requisitioned property'.[113] Those properties owned by a Jew that were not assigned to the Reich by the Eleventh Ordinance of the Reich Citizenship Law were frequently placed at the disposal of the 'Reich Commissioner for Dealing with

Enemy Property' (*Reichskommissar für die Behandlung feindlichen Vermögens*).[114]
He assigned private individuals or companies to manage the official administration – in the case of Hamburg this was primarily the GVG, which thereby developed into the largest administration body for dealing with the real estate property
of Jews.[115] Thus, in contrast to the 'Aryanisation' and liquidation of Jewish enterprises, for which the state had hardly taken any action and which had focused on
funnelling off property assets through taxes, it profited directly from the seizure
of land, which was only partly 'Aryanised' in private hands and was mostly put
under state control.

## The Financial Despoliation of Individual Jews

While the Reich authorities had largely been kept out of the implementation of
the 'Aryanisation' and liquidation of Jewish enterprises, they were all the more
vigorously involved in the attempts to cream off as many of the assets of the Jews
in favour of the Reich as they could. Anyone who emigrated in 1938/39 succeeded in keeping no more than a fraction of his or her property from falling into
the hands of the authorities.[116] In the following section, a few examples of expro-
priations that took place in Hamburg are described to show how tax and compulsory levies led to the complete financial ruin of Jewish proprietors:

In July 1938, Albert Aronson was still one of the most prosperous businessmen in Hamburg.[117] He was the sole proprietor of the chocolate factory *Reese &
Wichmann GmbH*, of the cigarette import firm *Havana-Import-Compagnie* and of
thirty-six properties, some of which were in an excellent location. The total value
of his property was over 4 million RM. When Aronson emigrated to London six
weeks later, he could only take 1.7 percent of his property to safety abroad. In
order to obtain cash for his emigration, he had taken out a credit for 800,000 RM
at his bank, M.M. Warburg & Co., of which only 66,000 RM (£5,413) was
transferred while 734,000 RM went as a part payment to the German Gold Discount Bank. To repay the credit, Aronson had to sell most of his properties at a
pittance and both of his firms were 'Aryanised'. The proceeds of the firm sales,
which amounted to 800,000 RM (no match for the firms' actual values), were
transferred to a blocked account that Aronson was not allowed free access to. The
Hamburg Regional Finance Office had issued a blocking order against him on 12
July 1938. In order to obtain his passport, Aronson had to pay 613,713 RM in
Reich Flight Tax, 245,410 RM for the 'Jewish Property Levy' (*Judenvermögens-
abgabe*) and 100,000 RM to a secret fund owned by the Hamburg Gauleiter.
Under the Eleventh Implementation Regulation of the Reich Citizens' Law of 25
November 1941, the remaining cash assets and the remainder of the properties

were confiscated for the use of the German Reich, which thereby acquired 98.3 percent of his property.

As a second example, we turn to the Hamburg private bank M.M. Warburg & Co., which, as we have seen, was transformed in 1938 from a family enterprise into a limited partnership.[118] In the course of this 'Aryanisation', the Warburg family was only fully compensated for the balance-sheet value of the net assets, 11.6 million RM. However, the actual sale proceeds were reduced to 6.4 million RM because, among other reasons, the value of its daughter enterprise in Amsterdam, Warburg & Co., was taken into account in the sale price. Of this 6.4 million RM, 3 million RM remained initially as a 'sleeping contribution' to the enterprise, though this soon had to be liquidated. Thereafter, the sale proceeds were completely drained away by taxes and levies; the Warburgs paid 850,000 RM in Reich Flight Tax, 1,000,000 RM as a fee for the process of authorising the 'Aryanisation', 1,221,000 RM for the Jewish property levy and a 450,000 RM emigration levy. In order to continue to be able to direct Warburg & Co. in Amsterdam as a family enterprise, they had to transfer an additional 1,200,000 RM in Dutch guilders into a blocked Reichsmark account, for which a fee of ninety percent was payable to the German Gold Discount Bank. The Bank thus robbed them of a further 1,080,000 RM. What appeared at first sight to be a fair and even a 'friendly "Aryanisation"',[119] on closer examination becomes a total financial pillaging. Even the outwardly moderate forms of this property transfer did nothing to alleviate this situation as seemingly appropriate financial compensation to the Jewish proprietor was largely siphoned off by the tight net of National Socialist tax and levy policies.[120]

Rudolph Levinson also had to go through this bitter experience, resigning at the end of 1938 as a partner in *Sparig & Co.*, a company which imported spices and other goods. The expected financial payment of 126,000 RM, which did not fully recompense the hidden reserves or the 'goodwill' of the business and which was, in addition, based on an undervaluation of the stocks, was reduced to around 100,000 RM on the intervention of the *Gau* Economics Adviser. In trying to justify its actions the *Gau* leadership noted that it could not permit such a 'great weakening of the firm'.[121] This sum was subsequently almost completely wiped out. Levinson had to pay 32,000 RM in Reich Flight Tax and 22,000 RM as a 'Jewish property levy'. In order to obtain $160 in cash for his emigration to the USA, Levinson had to make a payment of 15,500 RM on account to the German Gold Discount Bank. After he had paid a further 6,500 RM for his passage abroad, the inspection of his removal goods by the Hamburg Customs Investigation Unit robbed Levinson of the rest of his possessions. The Customs Secretary responsible maintained in his report of the examination that the property being taken abroad had been purchased after 1933, for which a levy had to be paid to the German Gold Discount Bank, amounting not to the listed value of 3,352.15 RM, but to 3,802.29 RM.[122] From the difference between the two he judged that there had been an illegal capital movement of 450.14 RM for which he fined Levinson 19,000 RM. Of his one-time fortune, Levinson was left with only the goods he was taking with him, $160 and a credit of 934.55 RM, from which a further 720 RM had to be paid to a removal firm.[123]

A fourth example of the financial despoliation of Jewish property is presented by the case of Robert Schwarz, the main partner of the S.R. Levy & Co. import firm, which imported bristle, horsehair and fibrous material, and was one of the biggest importers in Hamburg. After Schwarz had been imprisoned on a charge of *Rassenschande* in 1937, the Foreign Exchange Control Office issued a blocking order in August 1938 under Paragraph 37a of the Foreign Exchange Law[124] and placed a 'trustee' in the company. Schwarz had to sell his firm to a party favourite in the autumn of 1938, against his will. The proceeds of the sale totalled 700,000 RM, although the value of his enterprise was over two million RM and a stream of prospective buyers had offered considerably higher amounts for the company.[125] Because the buyer promised a 'contribution' to the heads of the Hamburg *Gau*, the amount received by the Jewish proprietor was reduced by a further 100,000 RM, which was paid into an account of the Gauleiter for the 'Hamburg Foundation of 1937'.[126] After Schwarz emigrated to England in January 1939, leaving most of his assets in Germany, his property was confiscated by a particularly sinister underhand manoeuvre. On 2 March 1939, the Office for Price-Setting and Supervision of Prices of the Department for Trade, Shipping and Industry (*Preisbildungs- und Preisüberwachungsstelle der Verwaltung für Handel, Schiffahrt und Gewerbe*) imposed a penalty tax of 500,000 RM on Schwarz, alleging 'offences against the Overseas Price Regulation [*Auslandspreisverordnung*]'.[127] That this was a fabricated charge issued purely in order to confiscate his property is clear from a report by the 'trustee', who, as a chartered accountant sworn to audit the business documents of *S.R. Levy & Co.*, had checked them in detail, and determined in his conclusion: 'In the course of my audit, I have not established that there were any symptoms that might have suggested offences against the foreign exchange regulations or other laws or regulations issued to protect German industry.'[128]

Schwarz immediately lodged a complaint against the fine at the beginning of March 1939, but it was only processed in mid-August 1939 and met with a terse rejection from the Reich Governor.[129] This meant that the Office for Price-Setting won enough time to seize all of the assets Robert Schwarz had left in Germany, including the sale proceeds of the 'Aryanisation', savings accounts, securities and life insurance. Nor did they shrink from illegally confiscating the private property of his wife and publicly auctioning her gold and silverware as well as two cases of wine.[130]

As the Aronson, Warburg, Levinson and Schwarz cases show, in 1938/39 there were no longer any opportunities for Jewish proprietors to avoid giving plunder by the state authorities a legalistic gloss. Even if previous 'Aryanisations' had preserved a modicum of fairness, providing a level of return from a sale that, under the circumstances, may have been acceptable, this made no difference to the end result, which was complete expropriation. 'Aryanisations' appeared to be governed by a somewhat macabre principle: the more generous and 'friendly' they were initially and the higher the sale proceeds received by the Jewish proprietor, the larger the sums pocketed by the German Reich, which in most cases proved to be the main financial profiteer of the 'Aryanisations'.

As the examples of Rudolph Levinson and Robert Schwarz also showed, the state did not refrain from participating in the plundering of the private property of Jews. Under the Ordinance on the Utilisation of Jewish Property of 3 December 1938, they had to offer to sell their jewellery, jewels and works of art to the German Reich. In Hamburg, the city pawnbroker functioned as a collection point for jewellery and precious metals. A Jewish proprietor only received a maximum of one sixth of the actual value of the gold, diamonds and gems in his private collection. The average price of a gram of refined gold in 1939 was 6 RM, whereas a Jewish owner only received 1 RM. The average price for silver at the same time was twenty *Reichspfennige*. Up until 23 March 1939, Jewish proprietors only received four *Pfennige*, from 23 March 1939 until 10 June 1939, only two and a half, and thereafter less than 2 *Pfennige* – less than an eleventh of its actual value.[131]

In Hamburg alone, the total weight of silver collected amounted to over 20,000 kilograms, of which most was melted down for use in manufacturing armaments. Nevertheless, the State of Hamburg kept 2,000 kg of particularly valuable and artistic silverware, buying it at the smelting furnace. After 1945, a majority of the pieces it had bought were still intact, ready to be returned to their Jewish owners.[132]

The German Reich also took advantage, for its own financial enrichment, of the examinations of goods that Jewish refugees sought to remove abroad. In their pursuit of this, the officials of the Hamburg Customs Investigation Unit stood out for their antisemitic malice and bureaucratic chicanery. Before emigrating, each refugee had to submit in triplicate a detailed register of the goods they were taking to the Foreign Exchange Control Office, which forwarded the register to the Customs Investigation Unit for examination and then gave final approval for the removal of property. Articles purchased after January 1933 had to be listed separately on the register. In the view of the authorities, these had been acquired exclusively for the purpose of emigration and were therefore assessed as a form of capital flight.[133] They could prohibit the items from being taken abroad or saddle them with a high levy that had to be paid to the German Gold Discount

Bank. The very smallest errors could provoke drastic fines and even legal proceedings which could last a long time and stop the projected emigration.

The Jewish businessman, Arthur Menke, was fined 20,000 RM. His list of the goods he was taking abroad described some items – of insignificant value – that had been acquired after 1933. An assessor from the Foreign Exchange Control Office remarked upon this draconian fine: 'Remember, you are a Jew, otherwise nothing would have been said about this small error.'[134]

The most correct behaviour gave refugees no protection from the frequently excessive demands made on them. For instance, in 1939, Fritz Lobbenberg, the owner of the J. Lobbenberg Company mentioned above, had to pay 12,996 RM as a levy to the German Gold Discount Bank for the goods he was taking to Jamaica. Just one fan and a radio, valued at 74 and 480 RM respectively, led the Customs Secretary responsible to impose a five hundred percent surcharge of 2,770 RM.[135]

Most officials in the Customs Investigation Unit had a firm view about the range of private clothes needed for emigration. One Customs Secretary itemised a range of articles in an examination report which he thought were 'not justifiable', because the couple emigrating were, in his opinion, 'in possession of a good and sufficient wardrobe'.[136] After he had checked closely that the underpants of the husband were really – as indicated – used and not new, and thus did not confirm his suspicion of attempted capital flight that would hurt the German Reich, he complained that, among other things, they were taking eight pairs of shoes and two dresses for which he imposed a special levy of five hundred percent of their value. This was even too much for the Foreign Exchange Control Office, which ultimately reduced the surcharge to two hundred percent.[137]

Jews remaining in Germany after 1938/39 were similarly subjected to strict limitations on their property. In taking this up, the Foreign Exchange Control Offices responsible fell back on a 'proven' instrument that had instigated several 'Aryanisations' in Hamburg since the end of 1936, and was now turned against all Jews who owed duties or who were 'liable to the Reich Flight Tax': Paragraph 37a of the Foreign Exchange Law, which reemerged nearly word-for-word as Paragraph 59 of the newly formulated 'Law on Foreign Exchange Control' (*Gesetz über die Devisenbewirtschaftung*) of 12 December 1938.[138] Up until 27 November 1939, in Hamburg alone, 1,372 blocking orders were issued under Paragraph 59.[139] For Jewish property owners this meant transfer of property to a 'limited access blocked account' in a certified foreign exchange bank, and scarce and constantly reduced 'free allowances' for personal living costs and a simultaneous duty to obtain a permit for almost all unscheduled expenses.[140] This gave the Foreign Exchange Control Offices an efficient instrument to keep the living standards of even prosperous Jews at a low level, and later to confiscate their recently acquired property on behalf of the German Reich. The occasion for the confiscation of the property of those Jews who were not protected by being in a 'privileged mixed marriage' was a deportation order. In October 1941, the deportation of Jews from Hamburg had begun. A 'Property Utilisation Office', created especially for this purpose by the Regional Finance President, now took over the confiscation and valuing of their property.[141] In so far as the fate of Jewish businessmen from Hamburg can be reconstructed from the sources, almost every fourth one was deported and then murdered or committed suicide before deportation.[142]

Even after emigration, which approximately two-thirds of company owners completed successfully, the financial oppression of Jewish property owners was by no means over. After Jewish émigrés were deprived of their citizenship, any unsold assets went to the Reich. From 1938 onward, the deprivation of the citizenship of Jewish émigrés was constantly being made easier. According to a confidential order issued by Reichsführer SS Himmler, from 1939 onward, Jews could be deprived of citizenship if they displayed 'typically Jewish behaviour damaging to the people'.[143] With the Eleventh Ordinance of the Reich Citizenship Law of 25 November 1941, it finally became obligatory for Jewish émigrés to be stripped of their citizenship and for their property to be seized.[144] Jews who had emigrated or had been deported could also be declared 'enemies of the Reich', their possessions in Germany being placed under the control of the 'Reich Commissioner for Dealing with Enemy Property'.[145]

In addition to this, the Foreign Exchange Control Office and (even more commonly) the Customs Investigation Unit spied on Jewish émigrés through contact people and 'agents' in order to seek out hidden assets and undetected routes along which capital was being taken abroad. In most cases, however, these investigations only documented the continuing process of the pauperisation of once-prosperous business people and entrepreneurs. One report described the living conditions of Julius Flaschner, who now lived in London, but who had previously been one of the most-respected Jewish businessmen in Hamburg – the owner of the opticians' business Campbell & Co. possessing, until 1938, a private fortune of over one million RM:

> He had rented a small room near his two sons-in-law. The room is packed full just with two simple beds. Two wardrobe trunks standing in the corridor of the apartment serve as a closet. Flaschner appears not to have any income. He replied negatively to my question in this connection noting that he would in any case not be given a work permit. For the purpose of sharing out expenses, the two Flaschners take lunch separately. While Frau Flaschner appears at noon at one son-in-law's, Herr Flaschner takes his lunch with the other son-in-law.[146]

A few weeks before, on 22 May 1939, the main Gestapo office in Hamburg had ordered the confiscation of the assets left by Flaschner in Germany, and these were then taken over by the German Reich. While Flaschner had to live in London with temporary furniture under the poorest conditions, the Hamburg auctioneer Heinrich Schopmann was publishing a large newspaper advertisement in which he offered for auction 'the used, valuable and highly modern entirely furnished villa at Abteistraße No. 25 belonging to the married couple Julius Israel Flaschner (Jewish possession) that has passed into the hands of the Reich'.[147] This was not a euphemism for wardrobe trunks transformed for use as closets: among other things there were a 'French music salon in the style of Louis XVI', 'golden lounge furniture with silk damask cover', a 'fireplace in white marble', a 'gentleman's room in oak', a 'living room in the original Biedermeier', a Steinway grand piano as well as numerous oil paintings by French masters. The contrast to the living conditions of the Flaschners in exile could hardly have been more striking. This example, and that of many others, makes clear how successfully the German Reich had plundered the possessions of Jews after the 'Aryanisation' and liquidation of their enterprises.

## Corruption and Nepotism

After the November Pogrom, when Hermann Göring announced at the meeting of 12 November 1938 that Jewish businesses were to be quickly liquidated or 'Aryanised' he took the opportunity to refer to the 'difficulties' that had resulted from the 'Aryanisation' of Jewish enterprises in the past. Speaking just to this inside circle of leading National Socialists, Göring was astonishingly frank:

> It is humanly understandable that there are strenuous attempts to place party comrades in these businesses and thus to give them a certain remuneration. In this respect, I have seen appalling things in the past that so enriched the small chauffeurs of Gauleiters that they thereby ultimately accumulated a fortune of half a million for themselves. The gentlemen know about it? Is it correct, however? (Agreement) These things are of course impossible. I will not shy away from intervening ruthlessly where there are shady dealings. If it should be a question of a prominent person making the offence possible, then within two hours I will be with the Führer and quite plainly report on this mess.[148]

What the Head of the Four-Year Plan describes here as a 'mess' was not a matter of occasional misdemeanours by individual functionaries, but of the characteristic structural features of the 'Führerstaat': corruption and nepotism,[149] which were also a defining feature of the 'Aryanisation' process. After the National Socialist regime had done away with, or brought into line, all potential institutions of control – such as the independent press, parliaments or law courts – the quest for enrichment assumed such proportions among NSDAP functionaries that corruption became a serious domestic political problem. Not the least serious of its consequences were the numerous complaints made by the people about 'bigshot' National Socialist 'golden pheasants'.[150]

Göring's threat to take such incidents to Hitler personally was more a gesture of helplessness than a signal of an earnest campaign against corruption. It was, moreover, an empty threat, since Hitler would normally have covered up the misdeeds of his subordinates,[151] particularly if they were passed to him by a man whose corruptibility and baroque drive for splendour was well-known across the Reich. From the Hamburg firms *Reemtsma* and *Rhenania-Ossag AG* alone Göring received regular payments and gifts of artwork worth several million RM in all.[152]

On the regional level, after 1933 a policy favouring cliques and clientship developed that honoured the 'idealistic' commitment of National Socialist functionaries with material rewards. Corruption and nepotism were the instruments that served the Gauleiters in particular to secure the political loyalty of their party comrades through a system of privileges.[153] As the public coffers could not be plundered by the NSDAP without limit, and because NSDAP Reich Treasurer Schwarz was subjecting the regional organisations of the party to an austerity regime, many Gauleiters used 'Aryanisations' as welcome sources of income. They regarded Jewish property as their own personal estate with which they could satisfy the desire of the party and of its functionaries for enrichment. Helmut Genschel has suggested this connection between 'Aryanisation' and corruption by reference to the *Gau* in Franconia, where, among other things, the *Gau* leadership took in twenty-five percent of the sale prices obtained in 'Aryanisations'.[154] At the same time, however, he characterised these developments as 'atypical', attributing them primarily to the rabid antisemitism of the Gauleiter, Julius Streicher.

In reality, the developments in Franconia represented only the tip of an iceberg – almost every *Gau* practiced similar methods. The heads of the *Gau* in Thuringia took ten percent of the sale price of all 'Aryanisations' in order to finance old-age pensions for 'veterans' of the NSDAP.[155] In *Gau Saarpfalz* Jewish proprietors even had to pay forty percent of the proceeds of a sale into a special account of the *Gau* leadership.[156] Enrichment deriving from Jewish property assumed still more glaring dimensions in the occupied territories after 1939. One study focusing on the 'final solution' in East Poland has concluded that there was a 'structural connection between killing the Jews and corruption.'[157]

In Hamburg, Gauleiter and Reich Governor Kaufmann had created a personal finance fund outside the city budget through the establishment of the 'Hamburg Foundation of 1937' (*Hamburger Stiftung von 1937*) with which he financed the party organisations of the NSDAP, personal favourites and the 'liquidation of the debts of deserving old party comrades.'[158] Even the statute of the foundation barely covered up these spending priorities, expressly foreseeing that it would 'promote patriotic institutions (in particular organisations of the NSDAP)' and would 'support comrades of the party and people in need of help.'[159] The chairman of the foundation was the Hamburg Finance Senator, *SS-Oberführer* Dr Hans Nieland, though the power to authorise arrangements for payments was reserved for the Reich Governor alone.[160] At least 854,000 RM of the foundation's capital derived from the 'Aryanisation contributions' that had to be paid by buyers and occasionally by Jewish proprietors.[161]

The mechanics of the collection of 'Aryanisation contributions' can be seen more clearly in the 'Aryanisation' of the M.M. Warburg & Co. bank. On 24 August 1938, Dr Otto Wolff of the Office of the *Gau* Economics Adviser wrote to the new partner of the bank, Dr Rudolf Brinckmann, because, he said, after examining the documents 'some questions' remained that would have to be clarified in conversation with the coffee-broker, C.C. Fritz Meyer.[162] Meyer had served in 1933 as the National Socialist President of the Hamburg lower house, the *Bürgerschaft*, and, as Hamburg 'State Councillor' (*Staatsrat*) and 'Senior Councillor' (*Ratsherrenältester*) of the Hamburg Council (*Ratsherrenversammlung*). He was one of the closest political confidants of the Gauleiter, as well as being one of the few 'veteran' National Socialists in Hamburg's commercial circles. On 2 September, he suggested that Brinckmann had 'obtained an unusually large profit' through the takeover of the bank and that the '*Karl-Kaufmann-Stiftung*' – as the 'Hamburg Foundation of 1937' was known at the time – should therefore be given an appropriate contribution.[163] Brinckmann countered that Meyer's demand was unjustified, arguing he had made no financial gain from the 'Aryanisation' and he could therefore only foresee a contribution possibly being made in the following year at the earliest.

This rejection, which Meyer responded to 'visibly disappointed', could, however, only be sustained by Brinckmann and his business partner Wirtz for a few weeks. After the November Pogrom, they feared drastic consequences for their business. As Cornelius von Berenberg-Goßler noted in his diary, Wirtz was 'beside himself over the antisemitic wave' and was seriously thinking about liquidating the bank.[164] In a conversation with *Gau* Economics Adviser Otte on 18 November 1938, Brinckmann and Wirtz therefore promised not only the 'contributions' demanded but also the employment of National Socialists after the *Gau* Economics Adviser 'recommended' they should 'employ such people as are recognised in political affairs in order to make outwardly clear the separation from the past'.[165] On 19 December 1938, Brinckmann and Wirtz transferred 25,000 RM to an account belonging to the Reich Governor and announced the payment of an equal sum for the next year. In January 1939, they also placed two National Socialists in the company who the *Gau* Economics Adviser had recommended to them.[166]

The 'Aryanisation contributions' gathered in these ways were not only deployed in the covert financing of the NSDAP, their organisations and the political favourites of the Gauleiter,[167] but also for acquiring Jewish property. Using a special fund of the Foundation, Gauleiter Kaufmann bought all of the shares of the chemical manufacturer *Siegfried Kroch AG* in Hamburg-Wandsbek. The enterprise, founded in 1901 by Siegfried Kroch, chiefly produced leather and textile oils and auxiliary products for metalwork.[168] The Kroch family emigrated to England in 1936, and in 1938 they attempted to sell their shares at the best possible price.[169] The negotiations over the sale collapsed, however, in part as a result of the strict conditions imposed by the *Gau* Economics Adviser, who would only authorise a payment of 95,000 RM instead of the sale price demanded of 180,000 RM. After the November Pogrom, a 'trustee' put in charge of the enterprise sold all of the shares in the company for 62,000 RM to Dr Gerhard Goß-mann and Walter Günther in June 1939. Goßmann, who had been unemployed before this time, testified that the two businessmen paid 'not a *Pfennig*' for the shares. They were merely 'used as a front'[170] to mask the actual buyer, the Hamburg Foundation of 1937, and thereby Reich Governor Kaufmann, who clearly wished to use the profits from the factory as a source of income for his foundation. As a reward for acting as front men, Goßmann moved onto the Executive Committee and Günther onto the Supervisory Board of the 'Aryanised' company, *Kroch AG*. The transaction was contrived by Dr Eduard Hoffmann of the Office of the *Gau* Economics Adviser,[171] who also functioned as Managing Director of the Hamburg Real Estate Administration Corporation of 1938 (*Hamburgische Grundstücks-Verwaltungsgesellschaft von 1938*), and who, in this position, requisitioned 'Aryanisation contributions'. A network of corruption and obscure financial transfers had been put together which was essentially based on the exploitation of Jewish property.

At the centre of this network stood the Hamburg Foundation of 1937, which still continued to operate after 1945.[172] The Foundation also profited from the 'Aryanisation' of Jewish-owned real estate, receiving at least 425,000 RM in 'Aryanisation contributions' from the Hamburg Real Estate Administration Corporation of 1938.[173] This latter body also demanded money from the buyers of real estate properties, though the 'contribution' was frequently subtracted from the sale price and thus shifted onto the Jewish seller.[174]

Jewish-owned properties in prestigious locations exercised a special fascination on the Hamburg NSDAP and its leading functionaries. Gauleiter and Reich Governor Kaufmann established his headquarters in a Jewish upper-middle class villa, the so-called 'Budge-Palais'.[175] His deputy – Under-Secretary of State Ahrens – and many other functionaries of the Hamburg NSDAP had bought Jewish residences on advantageous conditions in the course of the 'real estate Aryanisation'.[176]

Uninhibited, the departments of the Hamburg NSDAP also acquired for themselves the properties of Jewish owners. The '*Gau* Leader School' of the Hamburg NSDAP was established in a property in Barsbüttel that had belonged to a Jewish financier who had owned the 'German-American Petroleum Company' (*Deutsch-Amerikanische Petroleum-Gesellschaft*). Although the value of the property amounted to over 450,000 RM, the NSDAP *Gau* Treasurer paid a mere 60,000 RM (into a blocked account) for it. This sale price he described with cynical frankness as 'so laughably low … that it could at most be reckoned as a kind of token payment'.[177] In 1942, the SS was able to buy the villa on the Außenalster lake as a 'guest house' for a still cheaper price. After the Jewish proprietor died of a heart attack during an interrogation, the Gestapo forced his executor to sell the property. Though the buyer was not the SS, but the 'Hamburg Electricity Works' (*Hamburger Elektrizitätswerke AG*, HEW), its General Manager, Helmut Otte, was a brother of the *Gau* Economics Adviser and a prominent member of the SS, and he ultimately transferred the property to the SS free of charge.[178]

Although the Gauleiter generally kept out of the 'Aryanisation' procedure, in several cases he did use his position as the highest authorising body to the benefit of NSDAP functionaries. He refused permission for some sales contracts that had been submitted and ensured that the Jewish enterprises concerned went instead to local and district leaders of the NSDAP, even if these men had never been involved in commercial affairs, let alone managed an enterprise.[179]

An example of the nepotism with which the Gauleiter bound his subordinates to unconditional loyalty is offered by the 'Aryanisation' of *Herz & Co.*, which, among other things, used cocoa wastes to make cocoa butter and cocoa fat. The Special Representative for Economic Development and the Four-Year Plan, *Senatsdirektor* Essen, had thoroughly checked the applications for the firm that had been made and, on this basis, granted the Department for Trade, Shipping and Industry authorisation to proceed.[180] A few days later Kaufmann rescinded the decision[181] and, on 12 May 1939, transferred the business to NSDAP *Kreisleiter* Carl Döscher, to his brother, and to NSDAP *Ortsgruppenleiter* Pahl, none of whom had any commercial experience and who, therefore, had not been taken into consideration by Essen.

The problems caused by their lack of commercial knowledge soon showed themselves. A few months after the 'Aryanisation' of *Herz & Co.*, its new proprietors turned to the Hamburg Economics Department for aid, requesting additional supplies of raw materials for processing.[182] Only thanks to continuous political protection were the owners able to make considerable personal incomes in 1940 and 1941. A tax inspection in 1942 made clear, however, that the firm did not keep accounts and had to be assessed for all kinds of taxes afresh.[183] As a result of their 'unorthodox' management of the enterprise, the owners also came into conflict with the stipulations of the War Economy Directive (*Kriegswirtschaftsverordnung*). In 1942 *Kreisleiter* Döscher was convicted and sentenced to one and a half years in prison – extended to two years the following year – because he had made deliveries of large quantities of cocoa fat and mustard oil without taking ration coupons in return.[184]

During the 'Aryanisation' of the well-known opticians' business Campbell & Co., Kaufmann supported the application of a 'party comrade' as a potential buyer.[185] In December 1938, the owner of the enterprise, Julius Flaschner, had concluded a sales contract with Carl Rhein, his attorney of many years, and *Optikermeister* Schönberg, the trustee put in charge of the company. Kaufmann then dismissed Schönberg, who had been given his post by the *Gau* Economics Adviser, and appointed a new trustee in his place, a fellow optician, Bruno Weser, on 21 December 1938. One week later, Weser, as a compliant protegé of the Gauleiter, sold the business to NSDAP *Ortsgruppenleiter* Arthur Riebniger. In addition, the head of *NS-Hago*, Christian Bartholatus, joined the lucrative enterprise as a 'sleeping partner'.

The many other buyers of Jewish property who profited directly from the political protection of the *Gau* leadership included Benno Richter, the brother of the Hamburg Senator for the Interior, SA *Gruppenführer* Alfred Richter, who was granted a branch of the Salberg fashion accessory enterprise on Jungfernstieg,[186] and SA *Standartenführer* Walther Finger, who took over two branches of the Speier shoe store.[187]

A number of other decision-makers involved in National Socialist anti-Jewish policy in Hamburg also used their influence for personal gain. The 'Jewish Affairs Adviser' (*Judenreferent*) of the Hamburg Gestapo, Claus Göttsche, set aside over 237,000 RM for his personal use from a Gestapo account holding the proceeds of Jewish properties which had been auctioned.[188] The Head of the Labour Detachment for 'Jews and Gypsies' with the Hamburg Labour Office (*Arbeitseinsatz für 'Juden und Zigeuner' beim Hamburger Arbeitsamt*), Willibald Schallert, systematically enriched himself at the expense of the Jews placed under him, squeezing their property out of them, abusing women sexually and denouncing those who fell out of favour with him to the Gestapo, which arranged for deportations to Auschwitz straightaway.[189] That National Socialist anti-Jewish policy was practiced under conditions like these unmasks their official, pseudomoralistic rationales for 'Aryanisation', which, National Socialist propaganda told the public, would be implemented on the basis of 'merit and decency'.[190]

The German Reich took hardly any steps to reverse the damage to its own financial interests that this corruption caused. It would be idle to speculate about whether the Reich turned a blind eye to the corruption of National Socialist functionaries as a tribute to the 'Movement'. The National Socialist '*Führerstaat*'

possessed no efficient mechanisms of control to tackle corruption on the structural level. An effective system of control was blocked primarily by three circumstances: the dictatorial elimination of any critical public opinion; the 'Führer
Principle', which was aimed at attaining unconditional loyalty, not at checking
power, and which favoured the formation of Mafia-like cliques; and most importantly, the abolition of the rights of the victims, who were left defenceless against
arbitrary Nazi rule.

## The Behaviour of Those who Acquired Jewish Property – a Typology

While the fate of persecuted Jewish proprietors can at least be reconstructed from
the available archives in general terms, the surviving sources are largely silent about
the biographies of the 'Aryans' who bought their property. This contrast becomes
especially clear in the files of the Restitution Chambers (*Wiedergutmachungskam-
mern*) of the Hamburg District Court (*Landgericht Hamburg*), in which there are
frequently extensive 'Life Records' (*Lebensberichte*) on Jewish proprietors that
vividly reflect their experiences of persecution. The buyers, in contrast, were not
interested in a detailed reconstruction of the sales procedures and therefore sought
to exclude precise information about their background and their participation in
the 'Aryanisation' from the proceedings. As all the files of the authorising bodies
were systematically destroyed at the end of the war – including, for example, the
holdings of the *Gau* Economics Adviser, which contained political and economic
assessments of buyers – a collective biographical analysis of these buyers, i.e., a
social/structural analysis of their age, their social position and their party and
organisational affiliations, is not possible without lengthy research into hundreds
of individual cases. They would probably have confirmed the impression given by
the process of authorising 'Aryanisations' as it developed, as is suggested by the
information provided in individual proceedings: the involvement of established
economic enterprises in the 'Aryanisation' of Jewish firms in Hamburg affected at
most a third of all cases.[191] The process was dominated instead by former employees, business people of the new generation who wished to make themselves independent and who, until now, had found no openings in the state-regulated
commercial system, those switching from established companies, newcomers to
the industry who were driven by the prospect of lucrative businesses, NSDAP
members and functionaries who hoped to use their political connections for their
personal gain as well as profiteers of all sorts involved in work connected with
'Aryanisations' and described by Max Warburg as 'evil subalterns'.[192]

The fact that 'Aryanisations' in Hamburg developed into a programme for the
promotion of newly established businessmen, members of the middle class and

party comrades[193] was, in large degree, due to the structure of Jewish enterprises in the city. Being a trade and services centre, there were only a few large-scale Jewish enterprises in Hamburg that could have excited the interest of significant businesses. Some enterprises, like *Fairplay Schleppdampfschiffs-Reederei Richard Borchardt* or *Köhlbrand-Werft Paul Berendsohn*, had been taken out of the private sector and transferred to public ownership. The great majority of Jewish enterprises were medium-sized and could be acquired with relatively small amounts of capital. These circumstances influenced 'Aryanisations' in Hamburg at least as strongly as the criteria for authorisations laid down by the authorities responsible.

While the sources available do not provide enough information for a precise social/structural analysis, they are quite rich for analysing the behaviour of buyers during the process of 'Aryanisation'. The files of the Restitution Chamber of the Hamburg District Court (*Landgericht*) reveal a range of methods and behavioural strategies and offer a basis for some kind of classification. The diversity of behavioural approaches and choices make clear that, although the buyers were working within a framework that had been preset by the National Socialist ruling powers, they nevertheless actively contributed to the creation of the atmosphere and conditions in which the transfer of property took place. Moreover, a behavioural analysis can correct the cliché according to which 'Aryanisations' always enriched the buyer. First, the buyers in no way represented a homogeneous collective of mercenary profiteers, as is attested by a number of sworn testimonies given by Jewish proprietors after 1945 in favour of 'Aryan' buyers.[194] Second, in spite of the discriminatory context in which Jewish proprietors had to work, not all 'Aryanisations' proved to be good business for the buyers. This applied particularly to foreign trade companies, which made up almost one third of all Jewish enterprises in Hamburg. When these were taken over by an 'Aryan', they were generally boycotted by their Jewish business partners abroad. At the outbreak of war in 1939, almost all business ties were broken off and many enterprises stopped trading or had to keep their heads above water through bartering their wares. During the allied bombings on Hamburg in 1943, more than half of all the commercial concerns of Hamburg were completely destroyed. After 1945, some buyers of Jewish property found themselves confronted with demands for the restitution of an enterprise that had brought absolutely no profit to them at all.[195]

The spectrum of buyers ranged from inconsiderate exploiters, who hoped to plunder Jewish proprietors completely, to sympathetic businessmen who sought to pay appropriate sums for their acquisitions. If, in the following presentation, a behavioural typology is advanced, it should be born in mind that this is based on a sample of some three hundred 'Aryanisations', which is a somewhat narrow base.[196] Around ninety percent of these 'Aryanisations' took place in 1938 and

1939[197] when conditions were particularly oppressive for Jewish proprietors, and this of course also influenced the behaviour of the 'Aryan' buyer. Bearing these qualifications in mind, the buyers of Jewish enterprises can be arranged into three behavioural categories:

The first group – active and unscrupulous profiteers – comprised approximately forty percent of all buyers. Their behaviour was characterised by the fact that, beyond the discriminatory conditions set for the 'Aryanisation', they also took personal initiatives against Jews in order to push down the sale price still further and to exploit the disadvantage in which the owners found themselves without mercy. They were not satisfied with the undervaluation of inventory and stocks or with cuts in the 'goodwill', and often presented themselves to the proprietors as representing the NSDAP[198] to intimidate them and show them they would not be accepted as equal partners in a negotiation. Beyond this, some blackmailed Jewish proprietors with threats of denunciation or threats to bring in the Gestapo, and had their passports stopped.[199] Many refused to abide by contractual obligations or appeared in party uniform and were presumptuous enough to forbid the Jewish proprietors from continuing to manage their businesses.[200] NSDAP members and employees of Jewish firms both appeared in this group with particular frequency. Many 'Aryanisations' that were effected in such circumstances took place in 1939, when the progress made in stripping the rights of Jewish proprietors facilitated the task of the buyer seeking enrichment.

A second group of buyers of Jewish property, also comprising about forty percent of the total, are best characterised as 'sleeping partners'. They sought their own personal profit in the context of the 'Aryanisations' – for example, through the undervaluing of inventory and stocks – but did not expose themselves beyond that, and were anxious to handle the 'Aryanisation' in a form that outwardly appeared to be correct. On the whole they behaved rather inconspicuously, on the one hand foregoing an alliance with the authorising bodies that would have worked to their ruthless advantage but, on the other, not taking any steps to provide Jewish proprietors with fair compensation for their property. Some buyers in this group nurtured the illusion of a 'normal' property transfer and were therefore unsympathetic to the claims of Jewish owners when it came to restitution proceedings after 1945.[201]

The remaining twenty percent – in other words the smallest group of buyers – fit into the category of well-meaning, sympathetic business people who sought to give appropriate compensation to Jewish proprietors. Many buyers in this group had personal friends who were Jews. Often they were only prepared to make a purchase at the request of these friends. In these sales, a closer examination shows that the buyer and Jewish proprietor had forged a secret alliance against the authorising bodies. Frequently they sought to hide the 'goodwill' payment, which could not be made officially, in other, artificially inflated items in the accounts,[202] or to make secret payments to the Jewish proprietor.[203] Though well-intentioned, due to the rigid imposition of taxes and levies and difficulties with their implementation, such transactions rarely fulfilled their aims, namely to make appropriate amends to the Jewish proprietor. Some Jewish proprietors therefore went completely without payment and instead made a secret arrangement with the buyer defining the acquisition as a trust that would be dissolved again when the National Socialist regime fell.[204]

A few buyers went beyond this to take measures that were illegal under the prevailing laws. For example, they transferred the firm's accounts receivable to the Jewish proprietor abroad, hiding them in the sales contract,[205] or paid a secret monthly pension that went unspecified in the purchase agreement.[206] One buyer even personally smuggled Swiss watches and gold chains to Amsterdam and sent the 'goodwill' abroad in a money bag in order to give the Jewish proprietor complete compensation.[207] Even under the repressive conditions of National Socialist rule it was quite possible for a buyer who had the corresponding will to arrange a fair solution for the Jewish proprietor. Still, such acts carried a considerable personal risk for the buyer, and they also cast a revealing light on the reversal of fundamental moral principles created by 'Aryanisations'. Anyone who felt duty-bound by the traditional principles of the honour of a businessman and sought not to take advantage of the undeserved plight of others – in other words anyone who in this respect wished to remain decent – had to become a 'criminal' and to offend against the existing laws. In the moral dilemma of the well-meaning buyer, the amorality of 'Aryanisations' revealed itself in all clarity.

### Other Beneficiaries

From the mid-1930s an informal 'Aryanisation market' had developed, both in Germany in general and Hamburg in particular, based on a number of 'trade' practices surrounding the sale and utilisation of the property of Jews. Thus, a large number of brokers and lawyers watched the market looking for suitable acquisitions, forged contacts between proprietors and buyers and executed the contracts that followed. High commissions turned the 'Aryanisations' of Jewish property into a lucrative business.

In Hamburg, the National Socialist attorney Dr Arthur Kramm – who has already been referred to a number of times, and who enjoyed a relationship of particular trust with the *Gau* leadership – secured a quasi-monopoly over the sale of the larger Jewish enterprises.[208] As a legal adviser and middleman for the *Gau* Economics Adviser, he was able to raise his annual income from 6,000 RM in

1936 to over 73,000 RM in 1939.[209] Other brokers and attorneys specialised in particular branches of the economy. In Hamburg, all Jewish drugstores were 'Aryanised' through the services of the real estate agent Ernst Zobel. An example of the large sums of money to be made from this is provided by the G.W. Unger fashion business on the Jungfernstieg, which changed hands for 200,000 RM. The attorney who prepared the contract, Dr Droege, Chair of the Hanseatic Association of Lawyers (*Anwaltskammer*), received a fee of 30,000 RM. He justified this high demand with the characteristic argument 'that the contract ultimately only came off thanks to his good connections'.[210] That Dr Droege also functioned at the same time as President of the 'Pro Honore' Association formed to combat the 'problem of bribery' serves to indicate another dimension of the moral decline of business habits during the National Socialist rule.

Other attorneys used their special position in the context of sales negotiations to their own advantage by making themselves owners of the businesses awaiting 'Aryanisation' or by acquiring partnerships in them. Kurt Bauer, owner of the Felsenthal automobile sales company, recalled that his attorney of many years, to whom he had entrusted the protection of his interests in the 'Aryanisation' of his firm, had unscrupulously abused his trust and had taken over the firm himself with support from the *Gau* leadership.[211]

The German banking industry worked alongside brokers and attorneys in this 'Aryanisation market'. Deutsche Bank and Dresdner Bank, to give two examples, both kept a watchful eye on the market, financed numerous firm sales and acquired shares in the 'Aryanised' firms.[212]

Such lucrative business dealings resulted not only from sales, but also through administering trusteeships over Jewish property, mostly set up in pursuance to orders from Regional Finance Offices under Paragraph 37a of the Foreign Exchange Law. In Hamburg, the trustees and liquidators appointed were, exclusively, members of the NSDAP.[213] Particularly prominent in this respect was the 'Hanseatic Property Management and Trustee Company Ltd' (*Hanseatische Vermögensverwaltungs- und Treuhand-Gesellschaft mbH*, Treuhansa), managed by the National Socialist Hans Sixt Freiherr von Jena.[214] From the proceeds of the sale or liquidation of Jewish enterprises, the 'trustees' not only allocated princely salaries to themselves, they also acquired the companies under administration or secured a share in the company during the negotiations over a sale.[215]

Wherever there were 'Aryanisations', criminal elements were also at work who used the distress of the Jews in Germany to their own advantage without the slightest consideration. This environment ranged from criminals who, in a mafia-like manner, extorted 'protection money' from Jewish firms[216] to unscrupulous lawyers who posed as the saviors of Jews in distress and then ran off with substantial fee advances.[217] Others claimed to have close relationships with Hamburg's leading National Socialists, enticed distressed Jews with far-reaching promises and took large sums from them without giving in return what they had led their clients to expect.[218]

When the number of Jews pressurised into emigration rose sharply in 1938, an illegal trade in entry visas developed and a considerable number of people enriched themselves from this commerce. As the Hamburg Emigration Department (*Auswanderungsamt Hamburg*) reported to the Reich Office for Emigration (*Reichsstelle für Auswanderung*), so-called 'emigration agents' were receiving substantial bribes for procuring visas.[219] In the Hamburg consulates of a number of countries in South and Central America, many consuls and their employees were involved in the corrupt business of providing the life-saving visas. For one entry visa to Argentina a bribe of 5,000 RM per person had to be paid, while a visa to Haiti could be obtained for just 1,000 RM. The Jewish Religious Federation of Hamburg (*Jüdische Religionsverband Hamburg*) put on a brave face when it encountered this nasty practice, taking part in the payment of bribes in order to enable at least some Jews who had no means of their own to escape.[220]

The Uruguayan Consul General, Rivas, deputy doyen of the consular corps in Hamburg, proved to be particularly unscrupulous in using Jews desperate to leave the country. In the knowledge that the market value of his visas was high, he was wont to go 'shopping' in exclusive Jewish stores without paying.[221] In close cooperation with his – predominantly Jewish – employees at the consulate, he not only took substantial bribes, but also demanded various 'fees' and hard currency as security which he illegally transferred abroad. In 1939, the Hamburg Lower Court (*Amtsgericht*) finally prosecuted five Jewish employees of the Uruguayan Consulate General for embezzlement and foreign exchange violations.[222] It described the behaviour of the Consul General as 'unbelievable' and accused the defendants of having 'enriched themselves in the most frivolous of ways' and of having 'sucked' Jewish emigrants 'dry'. It was 'outrageous', the Court felt it had to tell the Jewish defendants, 'to pounce on people who find themselves in a state of distress in order to rob them blind'.[223] For a Court in the National Socialist period to issue such moralistic reproaches was not entirely devoid of cynical hypocrisy. The robbery of defenceless people by techniques thinly veiled in legal language was, after all, part of the everyday working methods of the National Socialist state.

# Notes

1. *Archiv WgA LGHH*, Z 750, pp. 11–14, sales contract of 17 May 1938.
2. See Table 9, Appendix.
3. On the November Pogrom, see *inter alia* Hermann Graml, *Reichskristallnacht. Antisemitismus und Judenverfolgung im Dritten Reich*, Munich, 1988; Hans-Jürgen Döscher, *'Reichskristallnacht'. Die Novemberpogrome 1938*, Frankfurt am Main/Berlin, 1988; Wolfgang Benz, 'Der November-Pogrom 1938', in Benz, ed., *Juden*, pp. 499-544; Pehle, ed., *Judenpogrom*.
4. On this position see Adam, *Judenpolitik*, p. 204ff.; Benz, *November-Pogrom*, p. 499; Ulrich Herbert, 'Von der 'Reichskristallnacht' zum 'Holocaust'. Der 9. November und das Ende des 'Radauantisemitismus'', in ibid., *Arbeit, Volkstum, Weltanschauung. Über Fremde und Deutsche im 20. Jahrhundert*, Frankfurt am Main, 1995, pp. 59–77.
5. Thus Avraham Barkai, 'Schicksalsjahr 1938', in Pehle, ed., *Judenpogrom*, pp. 94–117.
6. Cf. Wolfgang Ayaß, '"Ein Gebot der nationalen Arbeitsdisziplin". Die Aktion "Arbeitsscheu Reich" 1938', in *Feinderklärung und Prävention. Kriminalbiologie, Zigeunerforschung und Asozialpolitik (Beiträge zur nationalsozialistischen Gesundheits- und Sozialpolitik, No. 6)*, Berlin, 1988, pp. 43–74; Patrick Wagner, *Volksgemeinschaft ohne Verbrecher. Konzeptionen und Praxis der Kriminalpolizei in der Zeit der Weimarer Republik und des Nationalsozialismus*, Hamburg, 1996, pp. 279–292.
7. On the basis of the deportation list (*Archiv der Mahn- und Gedenkstätte Sachsenhausen*, R 201, M3, pp. 55–82) and the memorial book for Jewish victims of National Socialism in Hamburg, the following 41 persons were included in the numbers: Heinz Abraham, Max Blumenthal, Albert Bohn, Leo Ehrlich, Siegfried Feldheim, Walter Freund, Berthold Freundlich, Walther Goldberg, Julius Goldschmidt, Alfons von Halle, Felix von Halle, Jacob Hecht, Martin Heynemann, Gustav Holstein, Hugo Horwitz, Joseph Ludwig, Max Karfunkel, Arthur Krebs, Leo Lazarus, Dr Leonhard Lazarus, David Levy, Alfons Liebenthal, Siegfried Liebreich, Sally Loeb, Fritz Mainzer, Max Mendel, Hugo Moses, Nathan Neumann, Siegfried Neumann, Alfred Oppenheim, Alfred Pein, Theodor Reiss, Bruno Rosenbaum, Siegfried Rosenblum, John Salomon, Isidor Selig, Leo Silberstein, Hermann Sonn, Lippmann Weinberg, Max Wolf, Adolf Wolff.
8. Cf., *inter alia*, Trude Maurer, 'Abschiebung und Attentat. Die Ausweisung der polnischen Juden und der Vorwand für die 'Kristallnacht'', in Pehle, ed., *Judenpogrom*, pp. 52–73.
9. StAHH, *Oberfinanzpräsident*, 9 UA 9, letter from Dr Urias to the *Devisenstelle*, 3 December 1938.
10. See *Hamburger Jüdische Opfer*, p. XVIIff.
11. On this argument see, *inter alia*, Herbert, *'Reichskristallnacht'*.
12. Cf., for example, the comment of Hermann Graml, *Reichskristallnacht*, p. 25: Gauleiter Kaufmann in Hamburg had 'strictly forbidden' the November Pogrom of 1938, so it had 'to be plotted by [National Socialist] commandos from the neighbouring regions'. At the 'Nuremberg trials' Kaufmann maintained this although it was not the truth. On the actual events, see below. In a comprehensive treatment Jürgen Sielemann has shown almost all of the details given by Kaufmann and other decision-makers of the time to have been lies based on expedience or aiming at self-protection. Cf. Jürgen Sielemann, 'Fragen und Antworten zur 'Reichskristallnacht' in Hamburg', in Eckardt and Richter, eds, *Bewahren*, pp. 473–501.
13. See the diary entries of 10 November 1938 written by Luise Solmitz (*Archiv FZH*, 11/S 11), Cornelius von Berenberg-Goßler (private collection) and Nikolaus Sieveking (private collection).
14. Robinsohn, *Versuch*, p. 204ff.
15. On the pogrom in Harburg see BAK, Z 42 IV/1668, p. 78a.

16. Statement by Kaufmann of 13 September 1948 to the *Oberstaatsanwaltschaft des Landgerichtes Hamburg, Archiv FZH*, 12 (Drescher, personal file).

17. Thus the wording of Böhmker's order in the *Archiv FZH*, 6263.

18. *Sonderarchiv Moskau*, 500-3-316, p. 822, annual report for 1938 of *Referat II 112* in SD-Oberabschnitt Nord-West.

19. *Archiv FZH*, 35363, list of expenses incurred in the introduction of protective custody by the Secret State Police in November 1938 (with prisoner lists): on 10 November a total of 217 Hamburg Jews were arrested, 473 on 11 November, 77 on 12 November, 51 on 14 November, 55 on 15 November and 6 on 17 November.

20. Statement released by the Hamburg Chief of Police and published in the *Hamburger Tageblatt*, 9 March 1939.

21. Letter from Edgar Eichholz, 14 February 1939, private collection.

22. See Benz, *Novemberpogrom*, p. 530: 'The SS men, hardly any of whom were over 21 years old, particularly had it in for old, fat, Jewish-looking and socially superior Jews, e.g., rabbis, teachers and lawyers, while they treated sporty-looking Jews more mildly. Thus one former senior civil servant in the legal service who announced himself with his title was treated particularly sharply, and along with him so too was the owner of a large catering business.'

23. Diary of Nikolaus Sieveking, private collection, entry of 16 November 1938.

24. Ibid.

25. Diary of Cornelius Freiherr von Berenberg-Goßler (private collection), entry of 25 November 1938.

26. Ibid., entry of 22 December 1938.

27. Ibid., entry of 16 November 1938.

28. Ibid., entry of 13 November 1938.

29. Ibid., entry of 26 November 1938.

30. Ibid., entry of 24 November 1938.

31. Ibid., entries of 12 and 26 November 1938. For criticisms of the pogrom made by many Hamburgers, see Sielemann, *Fragen und Antworten*, p. 500.

32. *Sonderarchiv Moskau*, 500-3-316, p. 823, annual report for 1938 of *Referat II 112* of SD-Oberabschnitt Nord-West. The criticisms of the pogroms of many convinced National Socialists were also reported by Hamburg agents of the *Sopade*. Cf. *Deutschland-Berichte der Sopade*, fifth year (1938), pp. 1355–1357.

33. Cf. Bankier, *Germans*, p. 87ff.

34. *Sonderarchiv Moskau*, 500-3-316, p. 822, annual report for 1938 of *Referat II 112* in SD-Oberabschnitt Nord-West.

35. The best-known example of this kind of perversion of the concept of 'decency' is offered by the speech of Heinrich Himmler at the *SS Gruppenführer* conference in Posen on 4 October 1943, where he claimed that the SS had 'remained decent' in conducting the mass murder of the Jews. *Der Prozeß gegen die Hauptkriegsverbrecher vor dem Internationalen Militärgerichtshof* (hereafter: *IMG*), Vol. XXIX, Nuremberg, 1949, Document 1919-PS, p. 145. With respect to the Russians, Himmler explained: 'We Germans, the only people in the world to take a decent approach to animals, will also take a decent attitude to these human animals.' Cf. ibid., p. 123.

36. Göring had criticised the destruction of property during the pogrom, among other things. In his speech at the *Reichsluftfahrtministerium* of 12 November 1938, he declared: 'For my part, I would have preferred that you had killed 200 Jews and had not demolished such valuable goods.' Citation as in Döscher, *'Reichskristallnacht'*, p. 131.

37. *Archiv FZH*, 12 (personal file, Kaufmann), speech by Kaufmann to the *Hamburger Handelskammer* on 6 January 1939.

38. Cf. by contrast Wolfgang Benz, *Novemberpogrom*, p. 499, who sees the 'Reich Crystal Night' as the most 'decisive step in the path to the "Final Solution"'.
39. See also Herbert, *'Reichskristallnacht'*, p. 76.
40. Cf. the statement by Göring of 14 March 1946 at the Nuremberg trial, *IMG*, Vol. IX, Nuremberg 1947, p. 312ff.
41. *RGBl* 1938, Part I, p. 1580. The directive was issued by Göring in his position as Representative for the Four-Year Plan.
42. *RGBl* 1938, Part I, p. 1642.
43. *RGBl* 1938, Part I, pp. 1709–1712.
44. *RGBl* 1938, Part I, p. 1581.
45. *RGBl* 1938, Part I, p. 1579.
46. StAHH, Plaut family, D 21, Instruction from the Hamburg *Staatspolizeileitstelle* (on behalf of Göttsche) to Max Plaut, 2 December 1938.
47. On the emigration levy, see Lippmann, *Guter Deutscher*, p. 71ff.
48. Cf. Hans Safrian, *Die Eichmann-Männer*, Vienna, 1993, pp. 23–67.
49. StAHH, *Senatskanzlei - Präsidialabteilung*, 1939 S II 28, Note of 18 January 1939.
50. *RGBl* 1938, Part I, pp. 1709–1712, here p. 1709, Article V, § 15, Deposit 1.
51. *RGBl* 1940, Part I, p. 891ff.
52. More details on the subject of corruption and nepotism are contained later in the chapter.
53. Wilhelm von Allwörden, b. 1892 in Altona, son of a dentist; 1899-1905 elementary school in Altona and Wrist/Holstein; 1906–1909 Further Education College and Trade School; 1919–1930 employee in a retail business; 1925 entry into the NSDAP; 1931–32 full-time Senior Director of *Gau* affairs (*hauptamtlicher Gaugeschäftsführer*) and *SA-Gruppenführer*, from 1933 Hamburg Senator (responsible *inter alia* for Welfare, Social Services, Schools and Culture); 1938 full-time Councillor, Head of the Department for Trade, Shipping and Industry, Economics Representative and 'Aryanization Representative' for the Hamburg Reich Governor; 1942–1945 head of *Hauptabteilung II* in the Reich Ministry for the Occupied Territories; d. 1955 in Hamburg. On Allwörden's career, see StAHH, *Senatskanzlei - Personalakten*, A 50; Berlin Document Centre, SA file for Wilhelm von Allwörden.
54. StAHH, *Senatskanzlei - Personalabteilung II*, 766 UA/2, order from Kaufmann of 14 November 1938. Though Kaufmann held Allwörden fit to perform his duties and thereby gave him the opportunity 'to be able to make decisions in every case even today from the hospital bed', Allwörden was, de facto, no longer involved in any of the larger 'Aryanizations' after November 1938. Cf. ibid., communication from the *Verwaltung für Handel, Schiffahrt und Gewerbe* to the *Stadtrechtsamt*, 17 December 1938.
55. StAHH, *Oberfinanzpräsident*, 9 UA 6, communication from the *Devisenstelle* to *Zollinspektor* Bösche and *Assessor* Dr Kroog of 15 November 1938; letter from the *Gauwirtschaftsberater* to the *Devisenstelle*, 17 November 1938.
56. Ibid., list of the trusteeships as of 2 December 1938.
57. See StAHH, *Bürgerschaft II*, C II d 1, Vol. 2, list of the trustees put in place by the GWB. These included 'party comrades' Hans Sixt Freiherr von Jena, Edgar Koritz, Hermann Schönberg, Kurt Post, Karl Knapp, Dr Johann Krumm, Dr Erich Grundmann, Karl Freitag, Adolf Berkelmann, Friedrich Lindener, Dr Karl Kroll, Chr. Franz Schulze, Arnold Wolter, Hans Minnarck, Dr Wolfgang Merck, Dr Hans Juul, Hans Völtzer, Ernst Tospann, Paul Eggerstedt, Friedrich Janssen, Hans F. Dabelstein, Bruno Schwarz, Friedrich Platz, Willy Rönnau, Otto Jandt, Dr Alois Sommer, Hans Tietgen and Dr Werner Hotzel.
58. StAHH, *Oberfinanzpräsident*, Str 441, Vol. 1, p. 193, note from the *Devisenstelle*, 21 February 1939.

59. *Hamburger Fremdenblatt*, 11 January 1939; StAHH, *Oberfinanzpräsident*, 9 UA 6, communication from the *Verwaltung für Handel, Schiffahrt und Gewerbe* to the *Oberfinanzpräsident* of 3 December 1938.

60. Genschel, *Verdrängung*, p. 195.

61. The instruction from Göring of 10 December 1938 was published in *IMG*, Vol. XXVII, Nuremberg 1948, Document 1208-PS, pp. 69–71.

62. See the regular reports of the *Hamburger Gemeindeverwaltung* to the *Reichsstatthalter* re. Register of Jewish Commercial Concerns, StAHH, *Steuerverwaltung I*, I A 122.

63. StAHH, *Senatskanzlei - Präsidialabteilung*, 1938 SII 657, communication from the *Verwaltung für Handel, Schiffahrt und Gewerbe* to the *Einspruchsstelle*, 7 January 1939.

64. For instance *Ostindienhaus Heinrich Colm*. See *Archiv WgA LGHH*, Z 28-1.

65. Ibid., Z 1112-2 (*Fa. J. Lobbenberg*), p. 1, letter from Fritz Lobbenberg to the *Wiedergutmachungsamt beim Landgericht Hamburg*, 29 July 1950.

66. Compare, e.g., the treatment of the business owned by Adolf Lipper, who dealt in watches and gold articles, where thousands of watches and pieces of jewellery were valued in two hours; ibid., Z 963-4, p. 4, communication from Dr Herbert Pardo to the *Wiedergutmachungsamt beim Landgericht Hamburg*, 26 January 1960.

67. Ibid., Z 2588 (*Fa. H.J. Luft*), p. 5, communication from Dr Lappenberg to the *Wiedergutmachungskammer des Landgerichts Hamburg*, 18 July 1951.

68. This was the sales representative Willi Leube, who acquired the A. Buck company, a skin cream manufacturer, in the spring. Cf. ibid., Z 13959, communication from Leube of 15 October 1948, with enclosures (unpag.).

69. *Archiv WgA LGHH*, Z 1382-1, p. 133, solemn testimony of Paul Schiff, 28 June 1954.

70. Ibid., p. 5, communication from Paul Schiff of 16 July 1949.

71. On the liquidation of the business, see ibid., Z 1112-2, p. 42ff., communication from Dr Conrad Baasch, 22 January 1953.

72. Ibid., Z 9879, p. 4, communication from Dagny Ohlekopf of 16 October 1948.

73. Ibid., Z 2889, p. 12, statement by Gustav Hirsch on 7 February 1953.

74. Ibid., Z 28 - main file, p. 14, communication from Werner Colm, 28 July 1948.

75. StAHH, *Senatskanzlei - Präsidialabteilung*, 1939 S II/16, communication from Dr Werdermann to the *Reichswirtschaftsministerium*, 20 January 1939.

76. *Archiv WgA LGHH*, Z 28-1, p. 100, communication from Dr A. Harm, 5 February 1951.

77. StAHH, *Senatskanzlei - Präsidialabteilung*, 1939 S II/16, letter from Fritz Meimerstorf to the NSDAP *Amt für Handel und Handwerk*, 14 January 1939.

78. Ibid., letter from the *Gauwirtschaftsberater* to the *Einspruchsstelle* of the *Reichsstatthalter*, 28 February 1939.

79. Ibid., letter from Dr Werdermann to the *Reichswirtschaftsministerium*, 20 January 1939.

80. Ibid., letter from the *Reichsstatthalter* to Hans Baumann, 3 March 1939.

81. Ibid., letter from the *Gauwirtschaftsberater* to the *Einspruchsstelle* of the *Reichsstatthalter*, 28 February 1939.

82. BAK, R 87/114, p. 9, directive of the *Reichswirtschaftsministerium* of 14 August 1940 re. Treatment of foreign citizens in the exclusion of Jews from German economic affairs.

83. Ibid., R 87/932, p. 31, Resolution of the *Hanseatische Oberlandesgericht* of 2 July 1940, on the basis of §§ 12ff. of the *Verordnung über die Behandlung feindlichen Vermögens* of 12 January 1940.

84. On this and the following events, see Joseph Hunck, 'Juden und jüdischer Grundbesitz in der Hansestadt Hamburg', in *Deutsche Wohnungswirtschaft*, 45th year (1938), p. 653 ff. Hunck's article was published in numerous newspapers, see *inter alia* BAP, *Deutsche Reichsbank*, 3085, p. 43, excerpt from the *Deutschen Bergwerks-Zeitung* of 22 November 1938.

85. Walk, *Sonderrecht*, p. 221, guidelines of the *Reichsinnen- und Reichsfinanzminister* of 19 April 1938 with regard to real estate tax.

86. On the following particulars see *Archiv WgA LGHH*, Z 3511-1, esp. pp. 133–160, Resolution of the First *Wiedergutmachungskammer* of the Hamburg *Landgericht* No. 253/50, 25 April 1952.

87. *RGBl* 1938, Part I, p. 823ff.

88. *Hamburger Tageblatt*, 13 August 1938, 'Jewish real estate agencies have to be announced!'

89. On the creation of the GVG, see the judgments of the *Wiedergutmachungskammer* of the *Hamburger Landgericht*, *Archiv WgA LGHH*, Z 2-8a, p. 49. In a copy of a letter from the GVG to the *Oberfinanzdirektion Westfalen* of 7 December 1938, (p. 39) it is noted: 'Our company has been founded with the express permission of the Reich Governor for the transfer of the management of Jewish real estate which was previously administered by Jewish real estate agencies. Thus all such properties will be managed by our company.'

90. In Berlin, where the 'Aryanisation' of real estate has been more closely examined by researchers, there appears to have been no comparable institution. See Schmidt, '"Arisierungspolitik" des Bezirksamtes', in Metzger *et al.*, eds, *Kommunalverwaltung*, pp. 169-228.

91. Cf., e.g., *Archiv WgA LGHH*, Z 1120-1 ('Aryanisation' of the Moritz Mündheim Jewish real estate agency).

92. StAHH, *Hamburger Stiftung von 1937*, 24, p. 41ff., note on consultation today with Herr Dr Eduard Hoffmann, former Managing Director of the GVG, 12 February 1947.

93. Ibid., p. 5, statement of company auditor *Obersteuerinspektor* Rathjen of 26 November 1945.

94. Citation as found in ibid., p. 6.

95. On the utilization of 'Aryanisation contributions' see StAHH, *Hamburger Stiftung von 1937*, 12, Vol. 1ff.

96. Dr Eduard Hoffmann, b. 1900 in Bremen; from 1 May 1933 member of the NSDAP; 1933–1936 District Economics Adviser (*Kreiswirtschaftsberater*) of the NSDAP in Hamburg, from 1938 employee of the *Hanseatische Verlagsanstalt*, then Managing Director of the GVG. Cf. StAHH, De-Nazification File for Hoffmann.

97. StAHH, *Hamburger Stiftung von 1937*, 24, p. 41ff., note on consultation today with Herr Dr Eduard Hoffmann, former Managing Director of the GVG, 12 February 1947.

98. BAK, Z 42, IV 6178, p. 35, statement by Dr Hans Köhler of 24 July 1948.

99. Cf., *inter alia*, *Archiv WgA LGHH*, Z 286-3, p. 8, communication from Edgar Eichholz of 26 April 1948: 'While I was in concentration camp, my father, out of fear that the whole house would be taken by the *Hamburger Grundstücksverwaltung*, as had already been the case for other Jews, sold at the price still obtainable at the time.'

100. *RGBl* 1938, Part I, pp. 1709–1712.

101. See Schmidt, *'Arisierungspolitik'*.

102. For a comparison of property values and sale proceeds see *inter alia Archiv WgA LGHH*, Z 2-22, *Grundstücksaufstellung Albert Aronson*, pp. 98–108.

103. StAHH, *Hamburger Stiftung von 1937*, 24, p. 41ff., note on consultation today with Herr Dr Eduard Hoffmann, former Managing Director of the GVG, 12 February 1947.

104. On what follows, see *Archiv WgA LGHH*, Z 448-1, p. 18, communication from the *Hansestadt Hamburg -Finanzbehörde/Liegenschaftsverwaltung* of 30 March 1950; ibid., second count, pp. 5–7, Resolution of WiK 263/50 of the Hamburg *Landgericht*, 5 June 1950.

105. On the following, see StAHH, *Firma Ernst Kaufmann*, 68, Letter of complaint from Elli Lippmann to the *Verwaltung für Handel, Schiffahrt und Gewerbe*, undated (June 1940).

106. On the following, see *Archiv WgA LGHH*, Z 606-6, pp. 21–28, communication from Drs. Barber and Labin to the *Wiedergutmachungsamt beim Landgericht Hamburg* of 18 July 1950.

107. StAHH, *Staatsverwaltung*, D IV A 4, confidential express letter from the *Beauftragter für den Vierjahresplan* of 28 December 1938.
108. On the following figures, see StAHH, *Oberfinanzpräsident*, 9 UA 3, note by the *Devisenstelle* of 24 October 1939, on a conversation with 'Dr Hoffmann from the Office of the Hamburg Gau Economics Adviser'.
109. *RGBl* 1941, Part I, p. 303.
110. Cf. also the form for the authorization of seizures, StAHH, *Oberfinanzpräsident*, 48 UA 3.
111. *RGBl* 1941, Part I, p. 722ff.
112. Cf. Mehl, *Reichsfinanzministerium*, pp. 92–104.
113. On the activities of the Hamburg *Vermögensverwertungsstelle*, see StAHH, *Oberfinanzpräsident*, 23.
114. Cf. Stephan H. Lindner, *Das Reichskommissariat für die Behandlung feindlichen Vermögens im Zweiten Weltkrieg*, Stuttgart, 1991, p. 135ff. A list of the real estate properties administered by the *Reichskommissar* in Hamburg can be found in BAK, R 87/9382, pp. 57a–65a.
115. On the management of properties by the GVG see BAK, NS 1/2319, p. 4ff.
116. Also see Zürn, 'Enteignung', in Herzig, ed., *Juden*, pp. 487–514.
117. On the Aronson case and the details that follow, see *Archiv WgA LGHH*, Z 2 - main file, pp. 1–5, communication from Arthur Reimann of 12 December 1945.
118. On the 'Aryanisation' of M.M. Warburg & Co. see above, Ch. V; for the following figures see BAK, Z 45 F, OMGUS-FINAD, 2/181/2, communication from Eric Warburg to the OMGUS Finance Division, 23 January 1946; Kopper, *Bankenpolitik*, p. 125ff.
119. Thus the characterisation in Genschel, *Verdrängung*, pp. 237–240.
120. This applies above all to the period after 1938, when alternatives for the transfer of assets, like the 'Altreu' procedure or the transfers in the context of the Haavara agreement, were no longer available.
121. *Archiv WgA LGHH*, Z 32-1, pp. 46–49, communication from Dr Kleinwort of 21 June 1951.
122. StAHH, *Oberfinanzpräsident*, F 1448, p. 45, report of investigation by *Zollsekretär* Siedler, 23 November 1938.
123. Ibid., p. 54, communication from the *Devisenstelle* to the *Oberfinanzpräsident* of 15 September 1947: 'The assets of 77,000 RM declared by Levinson in August 1938 were almost totally consumed before his emigration by tax payments, payment of the Jewish property levy (*Judenvermögensabgabe*), by the costs of emigration, etc.'
124. Ibid., F 2216, blocking order issued by the *Devisenstelle* on 17 August 1938.
125. After 1945, Schwarz's lawyer, Dr Harm (by then *Regierungspräsident*), noted of this 'Aryanization' praxis: 'The practice of "Aryanization" in Hamburg developed then on the whole in such a way that the Gau Economics Adviser mostly determined the buyer of a company in cooperation with Dr Kramm, who worked solely in this area, so that other offers simply did not come to fruition. This was also the case with respect to Herr Schwarz.' *Archiv WgA LGHH*, Z 3313-1, p. 23, declaration of *Regierungspräsident* Dr Harm of 26 February 1947.
126. On the '*Hamburger Stiftung von 1937*', an illegal fund of the Gauleiter, see the sub-chapter below on 'Corruption and nepotism'.
127. StAHH, *Oberfinanzpräsident*, F 2216, p. 107, communication from the *Verwaltung für Handel, Schiffahrt und Gewerbe* to the *Devisenstelle*, 10 March 1939.
128. Ibid., R 1804/38, p. 27ff., Report of *Wirtschaftsprüfer* Dr Tospann, 12 September 1938.
129. *Archiv WgA LGHH*, Z 23551-UA 5, p. 105, Judgment of the 1. WiK 18/63 of the Hamburg *Landgericht*, 23 December 1964. The *Wiedergutmachungskammer*'s verdict on this procedure read (p. 106): 'Thus one could only deal with the complaint of a person who had been put into a position in which in any case they had no rights.'
130. Ibid., p. 106.

131. StAHH, *Oberfinanzpräsident*, 48 UA 8, memorandum by the Hamburg Regional Finance Office, 10 November 1951; ibid., eyewitness statement by Otto Blumberg, 17 October 1951.

132. Cf. Carl Schellenberg, 'Silver from the Jewish property', in *Neues Hamburg*, Vol. VII, Hamburg, 1952, pp. 89–93.

133. Cf. StAHH, *Oberfinanzpräsident*, 14, circular of the *Reich- und Preußischer Wirtschaftsminister* to the *Oberfinanzpräsident* of 13 May 1938; communication from the *Devisenstelle* to the *Oberfinanzpräsident* re. Removal of Property by Emigrants, 30 August 1938.

134. *Archiv WgA LGHH*, Z 1547-4, p. 13, citation as in a letter from Dr Krauel, 11 September 1951.

135. StAHH, *Oberfinanzpräsident*, F 1536, note by the *Devisenstelle*, 30 January 1939.

136. StAHH, *Oberfinanzpräsident*, F 1539, p. 28, report of investigation by *Zollsekretär* Marquardt of 21 March 1939.

137. Ibid., p. 32, estimate of Dego Levy by the *Devisenstelle*, 28 March 1939.

138. *RGBl* 1938, Part I, pp. 1734–1748, here p. 1742.

139. StAHH, *Oberfinanzpräsident*, 10, p. 63, memorandum by the *Devisenstelle*, 30 November 1939.

140. Ibid., p. 3ff., sample blocking order under § 59 of the Foreign Exchange Control Law.

141. On the activities of the '*Vermögensverwertungsstelle*' see below, Chapter VII.

142. Cf. Table 13, Appendix.

143. StAHH, *Oberfinanzpräsident*, 8, confidential circular from the *Devisenstelle* to the *Sachbearbeiter* of *Gruppe I* and *Sachgebiet F*, 17 June 1939.

144. *RGBl* 1941, Part I, pp. 722–724.

145. StAHH, *Staatsverwaltung*, D I A 7, p. 73, Decree of the Führer on the Utilisation of Property seized from Enemies of the Reich, 29 May 1941; pp. 89, 92, letters from the *Reichskommissar für die Behandlung feindlichen Vermögens* to the *Reichsstatthalter - Staatsverwaltung* of 14 January and 27 April 1943 re. confiscation of the properties of Hermann Levy and Hans Enoch. See also Lindner, *Reichskommissariat*, p. 135ff.

146. StAHH, *Oberfinanzpräsident*, F 527, p. 26ff., Report on Meeting with the Jewish *emigré* Flaschner in London, 28–30 July 1939 (Author: *Steuerrevisor* Albert Fluthwedel).

147. *Archiv WgA LGHH*, Z 60, enclosure 5, p. 29, newspaper advertisement of *W.C.H. Schopmann & Sohn* (undated, the auction took place on 24–25 November 1939).

148. *IMG*, Vol. XXVIII, Nuremberg 1948, Document 1816-PS, p. 499ff.

149. See Frank Bajohr, 'Nationalsozialismus und Korruption', *Mittelweg 36*, Issue 1(1998), pp. 57–77, and Ralph Angermund, 'Korruption im Nationalsozialismus. Eine Skizze', in Christian Jansen, Lutz Niethammer and Bernd Weisbrod, eds, *Von der Aufgabe der Freiheit. Politische Verantwortung und bürgerliche Gesellschaft im 19. und 20. Jahrhundert. Festschrift für Hans Mommsen zum 5. November 1995*, Berlin, 1995, pp. 371–383. See also Rainer Weinert, '*Die Sauberkeit der Verwaltung im Kriege'. Der Rechnungshof des Deutschen Reiches 1938–1946*, Opladen, 1993, p. 133ff.

150. The golden uniforms of senior National Socialists lent them the nickname *Goldfasane*. Cf. *inter alia* Heinz Boberach, ed., *Meldungen aus dem Reich. Die geheimen Lageberichte des Sicherheitsdienstes der SS 1938–1945*, Herrsching 1984, Vol. 16, p. 6260ff.

151. One wartime example has been analysed by Lothar Gruchmann, 'Korruption im Dritten Reich. Zur "Lebensmittelversorgung" der NS-Führerschaft', *VfZ* 42 (1994), pp. 571–593.

152. '*Die Nazikorruption in Hamburg. 1. Bericht der von der Bürgerschaft on 8.März 1946 niedergesetzten Ausschusses betreffend Untersuchung nationalsozialistischer Korruptionsfälle*', Informationsblätter der SPD-Bürgerschaftsfraktion, No. 2/September 1946, p. 12ff.

153. On the case of Hamburg, see Bajohr, *Gauleiter*, pp. 267–295, here pp. 277–280.

154. Genschel, *Verdrängung*, pp. 240–248.

155. BAK, NS 1/554, *Gauschatzmeister Thüringen* to *Reichsschatzmeister Schwarz*, 22 July 1938.
156. Ibid., letter from the *Beauftragter des Reichsschatzmeisters für den Gau Saarpfalz* to the *Reichsrevisionsamt*, 18 November 1938.
157. Thomas Sandkühler, *'Endlösung' in Galizien. Der Judenmord in Ostpolen und die Rettungsinitiativen von Berthold Beitz 1941–1944*, Bonn 1996, p. 201. See also Dieter Pohl, *Nationalsozialistische Judenverfolgung in Ostgalizien 1941–1944. Organization und Durchführung eines staatlichen Massenverbrechens*, Munich, 1996, pp. 116ff., 297ff.
158. Even before the creation of the *Hamburger Stiftung von 1937* Kaufmann had allowed 'old party comrades' to receive regular financial donations from the state budget. See StAHH, *Finanzdeputation IV*, VuO II A 1a XVI B 8b III B, State Budget Plan 1936, Section III 1936-25-41.
159. *Archiv WgA LGHH*, Z 993, p. 124ff., Statutes of the *'Hamburger Stiftung von 1937'*.
160. StAHH, *Hamburger Stiftung von 1937*, 1, § 3 of the Statutes in the version of 18 May 1942: 'The Reich Governor is personally responsible for orders relating to payments'.
161. Ibid., 24, p. 27, letter from the *Oberfinanzpräsident* to the *Bürgermeister* of the Hanseatic city of Hamburg, 8 February 1946; ibid., p. 172, sketch of the origin of foundation property, 21 May 1948.
162. *Archiv M.M. Warburg & Co.*, 11060, file 1 (Transformation of M.M. Warburg & Co. into a limited partnership), letter from the *Gauwirtschaftsberater* (p.p. Dr Wolff) to Dr Brinckmann, 24 August 1938.
163. Ibid., note by Dr Brinckmann of 2 September 1938.
164. Diary of Cornelius Freiherr von Berenberg-Goßler (private collection), entry of 17 November 1938
165. *Archiv M.M. Warburg & Co.*, 11060, file 1 (Transformation of M.M. Warburg & Co. into a limited partnership), letter from the *Gauwirtschaftsberater* to the management of M.M. Warburg & Co., 2 December 1938.
166. Ibid., letter from the *Gauwirtschaftsberater* to the management of M.M. Warburg & Co., 12 December 1938. The National Socialists in question were Toni Kesseler and Ernst Tiede. A further attempt by the *Arbeitsamt* to install 'high quality employees' in the bank was nevertheless dismissed by Wirtz: 'I answered that in the last four weeks we had installed two employees, one at the instigation of the Gau Economics Adviser and one at the instigation of the Gauleiter. Thus our requirements in this respect have been covered.' Ibid., note by Paul Wirtz of 31 January 1939.
167. On individual payments made by the foundation see StAHH, *Hamburger Stiftung von 1937*, 12, Vol. 1ff. On 12 February 1938, for instance, the foundation paid 1000 RM 'to pay off the debts of an old, well-deserving party comrade'; on 8 March 1938, 3000 RM for the music course of the Hitler Youth, to pay for musical instruments; on 8 April 1938, 1000 RM to *Stadtinspektor* Trzaska for staff excursions; on 9 May 1938 214 RM as a 'contribution for a well-deserving party comrade', etc.
168. Cf. the corresponding figures in *Die Chemische Industrie im Deutschen Reich 1939/40. Aufbau, Entwicklung, Werke, Arbeits- and Interessengebiete, Tochtergesellschaften and Beteiligungen, Verträge and Vereinbarungen, Statistik and Finanzen der Unternehmungen der deutschen chemischen Industrie einschließlich Ostmark and Sudetengau*, tenth impression, Berlin, 1939, p. 34ff.
169. For the following details, see *Archiv WgA LGHH*, Z 993, pp. 14–16, 263–283, letters by F.H. Kroch of 25 September 1950, and 21 June 1956 (with enclosures).
170. Ibid., Vol. II, pp. 313–316, Statement by Dr Goßmann of 10 August 1956.
171. Ibid., p. 333, letter from the trustee, Carl Sandvoss, 10 September 1956.
172. The property of the *Hamburger Stiftung von 1937* was seized by the British Occupation Authorities after 1945 and a trusteeship established to deal with its affairs. After the release of its assets in November 1951 it was placed under the management of the Hamburg Social

Department, first as the 'Hamburger Stiftung' and later as the 'Hamburger Sammelstiftung für Bedürftige'. Although the Foundation had not only been the recipient of 'Aryanisation contributions', but also received money from an SS fund, after 1945 the Social Department opposed the claims of Jewish owners for restitution. On its conduct in the Kroch case, see ibid., p. 44ff., communication from the Social Department/Legal Dept., 5 March 1953.

173. StAHH, *Hamburger Stiftung von 1937*, No. 24, p. 10ff., abridged report of the auditor, *Obersteuerinspektor* Rathjen, on the results of previous audits of the *Hamburger Stiftung von 1937*, p. 41, Note on consultation today with Dr Eduard Hoffmann, 12 February 1947.

174. StAHH, *Oberfinanzpräsident*, 9 UA 3, Note of 21 April 1939. According to the note, it was a repeated occurrence 'that the buyer shifted the Aryanization tax imposed upon him onto the Jews by subtracting the Aryanization profit from the amount that was to be transferred to the Jew's blocked account.'

175. Cf. Günter Könke, 'Das Budge-Palais. Entziehung jüdischer Vermögen und Rückerstattung in Hamburg', in Herzig, ed., *Juden*, pp. 657–668.

176. StAHH, Ahrens Family, 5, p. 108.

177. BAK, NS 1/2375-2, note of 16 February 1937.

178. *Archiv WgA LGHH*, Z 1719-2, pp. 20–22, communication from Dr Carl Stumme, 18 July 1951.

179. Cf., e.g., StAHH, *Deputation für Handel, Schiffahrt und Gewerbe II*, XXXIII D 5 ('Aryanisation' of Herz & Co.); ibid., *Senatskanzlei-Präsidialabteilung*, 1939 S II/28 ('Aryanisation' of Campbell & Co.).

180. StAHH, *Deputation für Handel, Schiffahrt and Gewerbe II*, Special papers, XXXIII D 5, Decree of the *Verwaltung für Handel Schiffahrt and Gewerbe*, 4 May 1939.

181. Ibid., communication from the *Verwaltung für Handel, Schiffahrt und Gewerbe* to *Senatsdirektor* Essen of 24 May 1933, re. Decision of the *Reichsstatthalter*, 12 May 1939.

182. Ibid., memorandum, 21 August 1939.

183. *Die Nazikorruption*, p. 13.

184. *Justizbehörde Hamburg*, Judgment of the Hamburg *Landgericht* 11 K Ls W. 502/43 of 4 June 1943, against Carl Döscher.

185. Cf. the corresponding proceedings in StAHH, *Senatskanzlei - Präsidialabteilung*, 1939 S II 28, particularly the notes of 16 and 18 January 1939.

186. *Archiv WgA LGHH*, Z 194 – main file, p. 7, declaration of Gustav Wüstenhöfer, 19 August 1947.

187. Ibid., Z 1159-4, p. 15ff., communication from Dr Samson of 20 November 1950.

188. StAHH, *Oberfinanzpräsident*, 47 UA 13, communication from the *Norddeutschen Bank* to the *Oberfinanzpräsident*, 26 June 1950.

189. Cf. *Justizbehörde Hamburg*, state attorney's preliminary investigation against Willibald Schallert at the Hamburg *Landgericht* on the grounds of offences against humanity, 14 Js 278/48.

190. Cf. the article 'Arisierung – eine Gesinnungsfrage', *Völkischer Beobachter*, 11 September 1938.

191. By contrast, Barkai also stresses the unscrupulous utilisation of 'Aryanisation' by the economic establishment, whereas Hayes – particularly on temporal grounds – argues in a more differentiated way. Cf. Barkai, *Unternehmer*, esp. p. 237; Hayes, *Big Business*.

192. *Archiv M.M. Warburg & Co.*, Hamburg, *Autobiographische Aufzeichnungen Max Warburgs*, New York, 1944, Chapter 'Die Arisierungen 1936–1938', p. 2.

193. This is also confirmed by the analyses by Kratzsch of *Gau Westfalen-Süd.* Cf. Kratzsch, *Gauwirtschaftsapparat*, pp. 216–238.

194. A representative example here is the 'Aryanisation' of the import-export firm H. van Pels & Wolff, whose Jewish partner Max van Pels sold his shares in the business to his 'Aryan' business partner at the beginning of 1938. In a sworn statement after 1945, the Jewish partner stated

that he had 'separated because of an argument that was settled and conducted quite honourably' and his partner not only 'fully bought him out' but also took a 'considerable personal risk' on his behalf in order to retain assets for him with which he could reconstruct his business affairs abroad. See *Archiv WgA LGHH*, Z 13984, p. 18, declaration by Max van Pels/New York of 16 October 1952.

195. On such not untypical cases see ibid., Z 5500-2 (*Fa. Schönthal & Co.*), Z 5432-7 (*Fa. Bernhard Stern*), Z 9343 (*Fa. Dr Emil Marx Nachf.*).

196. This sample of 'Aryanisations' was collated from the available sales contracts and 'Aryanisation lists' in the Hamburg State Archive (*inter alia*, the papers of the *Oberfinanzpräsident*, 9 UA 6, 42 UA 7, 28/1, 28/2) and through research in the restitution papers of the *Wiedergutmachungsamt beim Landgericht Hamburg*.

197. See Table 11, Appendix.

198. *Archiv WgA LGHH*, Z 9879/2894 (*Textilgeschäft Martin Josephs*), Z 2889 (*Fa. H.W. Almind Nachflg.*).

199. Ibid., Z 3103 (*Chemische Fabrik Rothschild & Leers*).

200. Ibid., Z 2588 (*Fa. H.J. Luft*).

201. The *Wiedergutmachung* legislation was thus frequently described as 'immoral and unlawful', and many buyers now styled themselves as the real victims of the political conditions. See, e.g., ibid., Z 3350-1 (*Fa. Inselmann & Co.*), letter from Julius Mehldau to the Hamburg *Landgericht*, 17 February 1953.

202. Ibid., Z 1124 (*Spedition S. Dreyer Sen. Nachf. GmbH*), Z 13410 (*Fa. Julius Engländer & Hinsel*).

203. Ibid., Z 13984 (*Fa. H. van Pels & Wolff*).

204. Ibid., Z 2185-1 (*Fa. Walter Benjamin*).

205. Ibid., Z 14281/14292 (*Fa. Wilhelm Haller*).

206. Ibid., Z 6051 (*Fa. Blankenstein & Bosselmann*).

207. Ibid., Z 15172-1 (*Fa. Julius Hamberg*).

208. On Kramm's involvement in lucrative 'Aryanisations', see ibid., Z 131 (*Fa. Rudolf Reich*), Z 28-1 (*Ostindienhaus Heinrich Colm*), Z 995-1 (*Fa. Julius Lachmann*), Z 995-2 (*Fa. Georg & Co.*).

209. Cf. StAHH, De-Nazification Papers for Kramm. Kramm, b. 1907, an acquaintance of Dr Otto Wolff, entered the NSDAP on 1 May 1933. On 18 October 1935, he received his licence as an attorney.

210. Berlin Document Centre, personal file, Karl Kaufmann - PK, letter (undated) re. G.W. Unger Aryanization.

211. *Archiv FZH*, 6262, Report by Kurt Bauer, 3 October 1951.

212. Cf. OMGUS, *Deutsche Bank*, pp. 165–175; James, *Deutsche Bank*, pp. 315–408, here p. 344ff.; OMGUS, *Dresdner Bank*, pp. 76–84.

213. See the lists of trustees in StAHH, *Bürgerschaft II*, C II d 1, Vol. 2.

214. '*Treuhansa*' was given trusteeships for *inter alia Gebrüder Hirschfeld, Heinrich Abeles & Co., Adolf Salberg, Ostindienhaus Heinrich Colm* and *J. Lobbenberg*.

215. Cf. the case of the wholesale firm Goldschmidt & Mindus, where the trustee von Jena invested 50,000 RM in a personal partnership, *Archiv WgA LGHH*, Z 1489-1, p. 2ff.

216. *Justizbehörde Hamburg*, Judgment of the Hamburg *Amtsgericht*, Dept. 121, against Max Arthur Schlappkohl, 7 March 1939, 7 Js 181/39.

217. Ibid., Judgment of the Hamburg *Landgericht* against Dr Alois Schlosser of 18 July 1941, 6 Js 1336/38; for comparable events in Vienna see Safrian, *Eichmann-Männer*, p. 35ff.

218. Ibid., Judgment of the Hamburg *Landgericht* against Anna Korowitschka of 21 August 1940, 11 Js 121/40.

219. See StAHH, *Auswanderungsamt I*, Section II, A II 13, Vol. III 1938, communication of 21 October 1938.

220. Ibid., interrogation of Dr Max Plaut of 3 October 1938.

221. Interview with Hans Hirschfeld of 9 August 1990, p. 8 (Interviewer Beate Meyer), *Forschungsstelle für Zeitgeschichte in Hamburg/Werkstatt der Erinnerung.*

222. *Justizbehörde Hamburg,* Judgment of the Hamburg *Amtsgericht,* Dept. 131, 3 August 1939, 11 Js 209/39.

223. Ibid., *Urteilstext,* p. 25ff.

# Chapter VII

# LOOKING FOR PROFIT

*Beyond the City Limits*

---

### Hamburg's Industry and
### National Socialist Expansion Policy after 1938–39

Most regional studies that describe the 'Aryanisation' of Jewish enterprises and the liquidation of Jewish property end at the beginning of the war in 1939, when 'Aryanisations' in the 'Old Reich' had largely been completed.[1] Thereafter, the only regional/historical facts that earlier scholarship has focused on are the deportation of the Jewish population and the confiscation of their property. Such a perspective, though, reduces the National Socialist regime to a 'German dictatorship' and negates the tendency of the Reich to expand from 1938–39 onwards, following which the policy of 'de-Judaisation' spread to the annexed territories. Moreover, this process cannot be excluded from a regional/historical analysis, but must be understood as an integral component of regional anti-Jewish policy and the persecution of the Jews in two respects. First, businessmen did not simply come into possession of Jewish enterprises in their own region, they also took them from across occupied Europe, and, second, increasing sections of the population were drawn in as direct beneficiaries of the confiscation of Jewish property.

Accordingly, 'Aryanisations' took on a new lucrative aspect for parts of Hamburg's economy through the National Socialist expansionist policy launched in 1938/39.[2] The extension of 'Aryanisation' beyond Hamburg's city boundaries began with the '*Anschluß*' of Austria in March–April 1938. From the perspective of Gauleiter and Reich Governor Kaufmann, this provided Hamburg's international commercial sector with an opportunity to open up new markets in South-Eastern Europe through the 'Aryanisation' of Jewish intermediaries trading in

---

Notes for this chapter begin on page 282.

Vienna. In order to achieve this, in the spring of 1938 Kaufmann proceeded with almost as much precision as an ordnance survey. 'If one wishes to conquer new countries', Kaufmann explained, what matters is that 'one sets about the conquest of such countries with all tactical intelligence and care in attitude and calculation'.[3]

It began in March 1938, when he called on Hamburg's industry and the Hamburg population to support the 'Hamburg Donation for Austria'.[4] This brought in over one million RM in cash donations and an abundance of gifts in kind that filled twenty-eight railway trucks altogether.[5] The donation campaign went beyond the ostensible purpose of relieving the poverty of Austrian 'compatriots', and had the secret goal of marking out the sphere of interest of the Hamburg economy in Austria. This strategy received further support as a result of the appointment of Gauleiter Josef Bürckel as 'Reich Commissioner for the Reunification of Austria with the German Reich' (*Reichskommissar für die Wiedervereinigung Österreichs mit dem Deutschen Reich*), as Kaufmann and Bürckel enjoyed a long-standing personal friendship. It is, therefore, no surprise that Hamburg's representatives were to be found in the administrative retinue of Bürckel, including Economics Authority Department Head, Dr Walter Emmerich,[6] who worked in the 'State and Economy' department of the Reich Commissioner's Office. There was also the Industrial Association lawyer, Dr Werner Bosch, establishing district offices for arranging public contracts in Austria. Colleagues of the *Gau* Economics Adviser were similarly active in all territories annexed after 1938.[7]

In May 1938, Gauleiter Kaufmann made his first public statement on the results of his efforts. The forum he chose was the 'Hamburg National Club of 1919', bringing together the pro-National Socialist circles within Hamburg's bourgeoisie in general, and the city's businessmen in particular. Among the points which Kaufmann made to the group, he underlined that:

I was in Austria and also in Vienna, and I have a great number of really expert colleagues down there. They are still there and will remain there. And I would also like to invite as many initiatives to develop there as possible. If in Germany the Jews have played a quite enormous role, in Austria it has been far greater still. When I see, for example, that in the haulage business in Vienna, which has a very great importance, almost 95% of the capital and management lies with Jews and its management is in Jewish hands, and if I consider that the foreign trade of Austria is at least 99% managed or influenced by Jews, directly or indirectly, then implementing that wonderful word 'Aryanisation' in Vienna is naturally quite simple. And this is important because a city like Hamburg must have great interest here in coming into the best, closest and most practical contact with the industry of Vienna, and it is also important 1. that the opportunity will be made use of, 2. proceeding correctly and 3. showing daring and even knowing how to use the opportunities of the moment fruitfully as well. What we can do here on the part of the administration has been done. I have not published this in the press. There you have only read of 28 rail cars. That was a sausage thrown on a heap of bacon. Through this I secured a good foothold for Hamburg. It is now for the relevant circles of Hamburg's economy to build this advance party action into a victory in the field. The preparations have been made and you will soon hear specific proposals. I ask you to help me from your side so that we take for Hamburg what is there to be taken.[8]

The total extent of what the Hamburg economy 'took' through 'Aryanisations' in Vienna cannot be determined. It is clear, however, that Hamburg's enterprises in Vienna acquired several Jewish haulage contractors and international commercial businesses.[9]

Through the participation of Hamburg's business community in the 'Aryanisations' in Vienna, the basic pattern for a regional-economic lobbyism had been established that repeated itself in the territorial annexations that followed and that, among other things, were built on the exploitation of Jewish property. The most important elements of this lobbyism, which were to serve the interests of Hamburg's foreign trade particularly well, were the personal initiative of Gauleiter Kaufmann and the positioning of representatives from Hamburg in the administration of the territories that had been annexed.

After the '*Anschluß*' of Austria in 1938, Hamburg's Gauleiter turned his attention to South-East Europe. As the loss of all overseas trade relations had to be counted on if the war that was expected broke out, Kaufmann sought compensating opportunities in the lands to the South-East of Europe. After the establishment of the Protectorate of Bohemia and Moravia he announced 'certain measures that would serve to deepen the relations between Hamburg and South-East Europe'.[10] After the onset of war, the official who mostly represented Hamburg's interests in the Reich Economics Ministry, the Director-General (*Ministerialdirigent*) and former Hamburg *Gau* Economics Adviser Dr Gustav Schlotterer, joined the search for compensation for Hamburg's trading companies whose international business relations had been completely disrupted by the war. He put the view at a meeting of various Reich departments at the beginning of January 1940 'that firms from Hamburg and Bremen could be substitutes for the Jewish representatives that needed replacing in the Balkans'.[11]

A new opportunity to improve the situation of Hamburg's trade by giving it compensation emerged in April 1940, when, with support from Schlotterer, a representative from Hamburg was appointed Economics Minister of the General Government.[12] This was Dr Walter Emmerich, who had already proven himself in 'field work' and who, after his 'period on probation' in Vienna, had been promoted to Hamburg Senate Director and then Senate Counsel. Emmerich not only created new export opportunities in the General Government for companies engaged in foreign commerce, he also appointed forty trade enterprises as 'district wholesalers'. In this function they took over Jewish businesses and their warehouse stocks and were responsible for the sale of the inventory of liquidated Jewish enterprises.[13] That Hamburg's trading ventures alone provided twenty of the forty district wholesalers is not surprising, given Emmerich's appointment as Economics Minister. On the occasion of his birthday, the district wholesalers sang a song for him that they had themselves composed. It was entitled 'Ali Baba and the forty thieves', suggesting how deeply sections of the Hamburg economy had become involved in the National Socialist pillaging programme.

Outside the General Government, many Hamburg firms were active in the newly established '*Warthegau*'. Their activity was supported by the City of Hamburg through an official twinning with Lódz, known as Litzmannstadt from 1939.[14] In May 1943, Arthur Greiser, the Gauleiter of *Wartheland*, publicly praised the multifarious activities of Hamburg in his *Gau* and stressed in particular that 'numerous Hamburg business people had become valuable colleagues in building up German trade' there.[15] Lucrative opportunities were offered to Hamburg businessmen, particularly as representatives and supervisors of large enterprises that had been seized[16] and placed under the control of 'Main Trustee Bureau East' (*Haupttreuhandstelle Ost*, HTO). Its approach to business was soon widely referred to by the common phrase 'You scratch my back and I'll scratch yours'.[17] The activities of Hamburg businessmen also encompassed the 'de-Judaisation' of the economy of the *Warthegau*[18] and marketing the products of the Jewish ghetto in Lódz/Litzmannstadt, which supplied Hamburg department stores such as *Alsterhaus* with clothing.

Similarly, Hamburg businessmen also took part in the 'de-Judaisation' of the economy in Western Europe. In the Netherlands, where there had once been twenty-one thousand Jewish enterprises, many businesses in the clothing industry and other sectors were 'Aryanised' by Hamburg firms.[19] Here too, however, it was the Hamburg companies engaged in international trade which dominated among the buyers, seeking opportunities to compensate for the trade relations they had enjoyed until recently elsewhere. Their activities followed no long-term plan, being oriented to the short-term maintenance of the business concern. This emerges clearly from a letter of 21 December 1940, sent by the Amsterdam branch of the Arnold Otto Meyer Company, a Hamburg firm, to the Audit Office (*Wirtschaftsprüfungsstelle*), which was responsible for the authorisation and supervision of 'Aryanisations' in the Netherlands.[20] In the letter, the company requested the transfer of the Jewish enterprise '*N.V. H. Jacob's Industrie & Maatschappij*', which had commercial establishments in Amsterdam and Antwerp. At its head office in Schiedam, the enterprise operated a modern factory for processing pulses, primarily for the Dutch market. The Hamburg company referred to the 'crisis of our local company regarding the breaking off of all of our [international] business relations' and justified the request on the basis of the 'possibility of shifting our economic activity from overseas to the domestic market, which offers us the conditions needed to help our company to pass through the war years unweakened'. From a financial perspective the takeover of the Jewish enterprise proved extremely lucrative, since – as the Arnold Otto Meyer Company itself noted – the sale price of 165,000 Dutch guilders corresponded to 'only about one quarter of the effective value of this object'.

Hamburg's enterprises worked in the occupied territories in the West with such an intensity that some industrial and trade associations from the Rhine and Ruhr districts felt compelled to protest to the Reich Economics Ministry against the alleged 'exclusionary efforts of Hamburg'.[21] Whereas firms from western Germany had still not received any entry permits for the occupied territories – as the tenor of the letter suggested – Hamburg's businessmen had long been active there. The complainants attributed this preferential treatment to the crisis support that had for some years been given the Hanseatic city, deriving from the time when it was an economically 'distressed area', but guaranteeing it continued preference from the Reich ministries during the war. Responding to these complaints, Gauleiter Kaufmann pleaded for a disciplined approach: 'We do not want to appear like carrion vultures,' he noted to the Hamburg Chamber of Commerce in October 1940, 'but I would prefer to meet a thousand Hamburgers in Rotterdam and Antwerp than to meet none at all.'[22]

In sum, the 'commitment' of Hamburg businesses in National Socialist-controlled areas in Europe provides evidence that some of the moral inhibitions which had still been apparent in anti-Jewish policy in the early years of the National Socialist regime had disappeared to a large extent in the war years. This 'commitment' also made clear the international dimensions of 'Aryanisation', which was in no way limited to Hamburg and the German Reich, but, in the course of the National Socialist war of conquest, stretched across the whole of Europe.

## The Population of Hamburg as Material Beneficiaries of the Murder of the Jews

The conquests of the first years of the war did not only give Hamburg firms access to Jewish businesses. 'Aryanisations' took on a new dimension when potentially the whole population of Hamburg was drawn into the circle of beneficiaries.

Hamburgers in the police and administrative apparatus of the occupied territories were offered direct access to Jewish property. The pillage of the 'Villa Bondy' in Prague in 1939 by Hamburgers who belonged to the Order Police (*Ordnungspolizei*), taking money, jewellery, shares, works of art and so on without any inhibitions, is representative of a multitude of mostly 'unruly' activities aimed at self-enrichment.[23]

At the same time, during the war an unending succession of transports took property confiscated from Jews off to the Hanseatic City. This meant that furnishings of all sorts could be sold and auctioned off to prospective buyers from Hamburg and its North German surroundings. Public auctions began on a large scale in February 1941 when the Gestapo, on the instruction of the Reich Governor, seized the property that Jewish emigrants were waiting to move abroad, but which could no longer be shipped because of the outbreak of war in 1939.[24] This included approximately three to four thousand container-like 'lift vans' which had, until then, been stored in the free port of Hamburg. They contained the property of Jewish emigrants from all parts of Germany as most Jewish refugees left Germany via Hamburg, the traditional port from which emigrants left the country. The proceeds of the auctions found their way to an account of the Gestapo at Deutsche Bank and by the beginning of 1943 totalled 7,200,000 RM.[25] Both auctioneers[26] and removal companies[27] organised much of this form of 'Aryanisation'. In the war years the auctions became a source of much of their profit-making.

The objective of the auctions was 'to take the goods at appropriate prices to the widest possible sections of the population', as the agencies involved publicly reassured the daily press.[28] Preferential treatment was given to those who had been bombed out of their homes, young married couples and expatriates returning to Germany who were cared for by the NSDAP's Organisation for Germans Abroad (*Auslandsorganisation*).[29] Numerous agencies of the state and NSDAP also availed themselves of so-called 'Jewish goods'.[30] The Social Department created a fund for furniture and household goods, the Regional Finance President and the SD area leadership for Hamburg completed their own furnishings with office furniture from this source, the Hamburg Museum of Art (*Kunsthalle*) had a committee that took paintings from the refugees' goods, and Hamburg's Public Libraries were enlarged with books from the private collections that Jews had once owned.[31]

From February 1941 to April 1945, there was hardly a day on which Jewish property was not publicly offered and auctioned off in Hamburg. First, an adequate supply of Jewish property was provided for by the 'Property Utilisation Office' (*Vermögensverwertungsstelle*) of the Hamburg Regional Finance President, which conducted auctions of the furnishings of deported Hamburg Jews from the autumn of 1941.[32] Second, a large amount of Jewish property was taken to Hamburg having been seized in Western Europe in the context of '*Aktion M*' (*Möbel-Aktion*, or 'Furniture Campaign').[33] '*Aktion M*' was preceded in 1940/41 by the organised theft of art and cultural goods by the '*Einsatzstab Reichsleiter* Rosenberg'. On 31 December 1941, Hitler gave his personal consent to extending the registration and seizure of all Jewish property to France, Belgium, Holland and Luxemburg. The organisational implementation was taken over by the Western

Office (*Dienststelle West*) in the Reich Ministry for the Occupied Eastern Territories which cooperated closely in its task with the SS Security Service (*Sicherheitsdienst*). By 1944, the Western Office had sold off the contents of approximately 72,000 apartments owned by Jews, most of whom had been deported to Auschwitz. Their property was at first concentrated at collection points, sorted there with assistance from Jewish slave labourers made available by the SD, and finally sent in a series of shipments to the Reich. Originally, Jewish property was to have been used in the occupied territories for furnishing German agencies and their officials. Due to the destruction caused by bombing, however, most shipments went to the heavily damaged cities of North and Western Germany.[34] The population of Hamburg, which was particularly badly affected by the bombing raids, profited more than most places from the *Möbel-Aktion* deliveries, and the furniture from several thousand apartments belonging to deported Dutch Jews was shipped to the Hanseatic city.[35] The total volume of the 'Jewish goods' that were transported from Holland to Hamburg alone amounted to forty-five shiploads between March 1942 and July 1943, comprising 27,227 tonnes of furniture, furnishing, clothing and other goods.[36] In addition, by 1944 the German Reich Railways (*Deutsche Reichsbahn*) had transported a total of 2,699 railroad cars of Jewish property to Hamburg. Altogether, between 1941 and 1945, the possessions of at least thirty thousand Jewish households from Hamburg, Germany and Western Europe were publicly auctioned in Hamburg. As the surviving lists of the auctioneer suggest that there were approximately ten buyers for the property of one single Jew there must have been – taking into account the many repeat sales – at least one hundred thousand inhabitants in Hamburg and the North German regions directly surrounding it who bought items of Jewish property in the years 1941–1945.[37] These customers ranged from the simple housewife in Hamburg to department stores from the Ems region, which regularly enquired with the auctioneers about new deliveries.[38] One former auctioneer explained, after 1945, that articles owned by Jews were 'mostly given away at knock-down prices' and there had been a considerable discrepancy between their actual value and the auction proceeds, particularly with respect to 'valuable items' like furniture, carpets and furs.[39]

Former Hamburg librarian, Gertrud Seydelmann, reported in her autobiographical recollections how extensively the population on the 'home front' profited from the robberies, in particular through the auctioning of Jewish property:

> We still had no supply problems. Stolen goods or goods paid for with worthless paper money still poured in to us from the whole of the Europe we had occupied and plundered. Our food cards, clothing cards, and shoe-purchase credits were still properly redeemed. Men on leave still brought meat, wine, clothes and tobacco home from the occupied territories. Ships still lay docked in the port with Jewish property

that had been seized in Holland. Simple housewives from the *Veddel* quarter [a work-ing-class district] were suddenly wearing fur coats, trading in coffee and jewellery, had old furniture and carpets from the port, from Holland or from France... Some of my readers also asked me to stock up at the harbour with carpets, furniture, jewellery and furs. It was the stolen property of Dutch Jews who – as I was to learn after the war – had already been carried off to the gas chambers. I wanted to have nothing to do with it. Even in rejecting this I had to beware of the primitive, greedy, money-grubbing people, particularly women. I could not express my true thoughts. Only some, less euphoric women whose husbands I knew to be confessed Social Democrats could I carefully influence, in that I made clear to them where these shiploads full of the best household effects came from and told them the old proverb: 'Ill-gotten goods never prosper.' And they took note of this.[40]

Seydelmann's recollections refer to a gender-specific aspect of the auctions, in which – particularly because of the absence of many men – women were most active, while up until then 'Aryanisation', especially 'Aryanisations' of Jewish busi-nesses, had essentially been a male domain. Furthermore, it was clearly only a minority of the population that was aware of the moral connotations of this prop-erty transfer, although according to the reports in the press and the official auction advertisements there could be no doubt that the goods offered came from Jews. Even someone who knew nothing of the mass murder of the Jews and who believed in the official statements about the 'evacuation' or 'deployment of labour in the East' had to assume that the deported Jews were going to meet with an uncertain fate if they were not even allowed to take personal belongings with them.

On what was this moral indifference based, typical as it was of the general attitude of the German population to the fate of the Jews? There is much to sug-gest that the explanation for this behaviour should be sought in a mixture of desensitisation, indifference, self-preoccupation and a growing decay of ethical standards. This development was promoted, on the one hand, by the brutalising effects of National Socialist policy, which by negative selection systematically honoured inhumane attitudes and patterns of behaviour, and on the other, by the ubiquity of death and dying in the war, which increasingly relativised the value of the life of a human being.

While the German population behaved with moral indifference towards the fate of the Jews, at the same time it met the antisemitic propaganda offensive with which the National Socialist regime promoted the Holocaust from 1941 with indifference, scepticism and open rejection. According to the historian David Bankier, this apparent paradox, and the aversion to the antisemitic propaganda that was expressed in growing apathy, was a manifestation of guilt and fears of retaliation.[41] These feelings were completely suppressed as, with the growing suf-fering caused by the war, many styled themselves as the victims of the war. In par-ticular, those who had been bombed out could, on the basis of this self-definition, repress moral scruples about the acquisition of Jewish property. Their own experience of suffering and the 'omnipresence of death'[42] in the rubble of German cities blunted the suffering of others.

The so-called 'Jewish question' and the genocide of the European Jews that today rightfully stands at the centre of many analyses of the National Socialist regime no longer featured in the consciousness of most Germans, particularly during the second half of the war, as they apathetically focused on the everyday struggle for survival in their bombed-out cities.[43] In addition to this suppression of conscience lay the fact that, in the auctions, the German Reich formally appeared as owner and the buyers could nurture the fiction that this was not the property of deported and murdered Jews, but state property that they were buying, particularly since a majority of the goods offered had belonged to foreign Jews, facilitating the anonymisation and depersonalisation of their property further.

It would, however, be misplaced to characterise the unscrupulous appropriation of the property of deported and murdered Jews as a product of a moral desensitisation that was limited to the broken-down societies of the large cities. One investigation based on life-history interviews about the Swabian community of Baisingen, which had been unaffected by bombing, showed that the residents there overwhelmingly showed no moral scruples about taking part in the auctioning of the property of their Jewish neighbours, and some even went to the authorities and to Jewish villagers before the deportations in order to secure particularly lucrative goods for themselves.[44] Although the residents in the community also took part in auctions if the connection between the goods and their deported owners was not broken apart by a deceitful anonymity, they justified their behaviour with the superficial, self-suggested argument that the possessions were state property because they were auctioned by Finance Officials in the service of the German Reich. Whereas party functionaries of the NSDAP had already availed themselves of the property of deportees, taking particularly valuable goods before the auctions, they had acquired the items 'correctly' and 'from the state' – thus ran the central argument of their justifications, which reduced the moral problematic involved to the form of appropriation. Franziska Becker believed this moral indifference was promoted by poverty and by a materialistic mentality 'which traditionally allowed little sensitivity for interhuman or moral reservations.'[45]

Independent of the specific reasons for the moral indifference of the German population, it must be concluded that through the systematic auctioning of Jewish property the National Socialist state made numerous 'ordinary' Germans into accomplices of its policy of robbery and expansion, and into material beneficiaries of the murder of the Jews – an aspect to which previous research on 'Aryanisation' has given scarcely any attention. What had begun gradually in 1933 with individual property sales, developed into one of the largest transfers of property in modern history. It was finally transformed, in 1938/39, into a policy of pillage by taxation, and ended in the massive theft in which, ultimately, ever greater sections of the German population participated.

# Notes

1. Symptomatic of this is the formulation of Kratzsch, *Gauwirtschaftsapparat*, on the 'de-Judaisation' of the economy in *Gau Westfalen-Süd*: 'It rose very moderately until 1936, strengthened increasingly until spring 1938, rose steeply in 1938, reached a peak in winter 1938/39, then fell swiftly and soon came to an end.' (p. 116).

2. Only the broad outline of this process can be sketched out here because of the destruction of all the thematically relevant papers of the Hamburg *Wirtschaftsverwaltung*.

3. Citation from a speech by Kaufmann to the *Hamburger Nationalklub von 1919* on 6 May 1938, BAP, *Reichssicherheitshauptamt*, St 3/510, p. 10.

4. *Hamburger Tageblatt*, 24 March 1938.

5. *Hamburger Tageblatt*, 2 April 1938.

6. Dr Walter Emmerich, b. 1895; 1914 *Abitur* (high school diploma); 1919–1929 commercial employee and attorney; 1930 doctorate (*Dr rer.pol.*); 1931–1933 teaching assistant (*Assistent*) to Prof. Dr Sieveking; member of the SA in 1933 and the NSDAP in 1937; 1934 head of department in the Hamburg Economics Authority; 1940 Senate attorney (*Senatssyndikus*); 1940–1945 head of the Economics Department (*Hauptabteilung Wirtschaft*) in the General Government, cf. BAK, Z 42, IV/3801, p. 11.

7. *Hamburger Tageblatt*, 13 January 1940: 'Colleagues of the Gau Economics Adviser were sent into the Sudetenland, the *Ostmark* [Austria], the Protectorate and into the General Government and the German territories formerly in Poland.'

8. Speech by Kaufmann to the *Hamburger Nationalklub von 1919* on 6 May 1938, BAP, Reichssicherheitshauptamt, St 3/510, p. 11.

9. See, *inter alia*, StAHH, *Staatsamt*, 106, letter from the *Reichsstatthalter - Gemeindeverwaltung* to the *Reichs- und Preußische Wirtschaftsministerium*, 4 April 1938, re. 'Aryanisation' of the haulage contractor *Eger & Co.* of Vienna by the Hamburg firm *Julius Rudert*. The author of the letter, *Senatsdirektor* Köhn, likewise asked the Ministry for a 'benevolent judgment' in 'similar cases'. On the development of 'Aryanisations' in Vienna, see Witek, 'Arisierungen', in Talos, Hanisch and Neugebauer, eds, *NS-Herrschaft*, pp. 199–214.

10. BAP, *Reichswirtschaftsministerium*, 9572, communication from the *Hamburger Handelskammer* to the *Reichswirtschaftsministerium*, 23 June 1939.

11. Cited from BAP, *Deutsche Reichsbank*, 6612, p. 396, Report on meeting of the economic and statististical department of the Reichsbank of 10 January 1940.

12. BAK, Z 42, IV/3801, p. 17, Statement by *Ministerialdirektor* Dr Bergemann, 3 December 1947.

13. On the work of the *Kreisgroßhändler* see Aly and Heim, *Vordenker*, pp. 232–237; Pohl, *Judenverfolgung*, p. 130.

14. Cf., *inter alia*, the *Hamburger Anzeiger* of 25 February 1943 on the visit of Ventzki, the *Oberbürgermeister* of Litzmannstadt to Hamburg.

15. Cited from *Hamburger Fremdenblatt*, 29 May 1943.

16. Cf., e.g., the work of Hamburg international businessman Kurt Lindener, member of the executive of the Hamburg stock exchange, who managed businesses in Litzmannstadt and Dombrowa from September 1941 to October 1942 and earned a total salary of 23,950 RM for it. This payment provoked 'irritation in the widest circles', *SS-Gruppenführer* Greifelt, head of the *Stabshauptamt* of the *Reichskommissar für die Festigung deutschen Volkstums*, informed the HTO in October 1942. All figures are from BAP, *Rechnungshof des Deutschen Reiches*, 5991, pp. 12–14, conclusions re. the installation of supervisors over the administration and utilisation of the HTO in large enterprises under trustee administrations in Berlin according to the subject files of the HTO, enclosure 2.

17. Citation from BAK, R 58/1002, Report of the commander of the security police and the SD for the district of Galicia, 26 June 1943, re. Attitude of Reich Germans in the Occupied Territories, pp. 107–206, citation from p. 200.

18. See on this Arthur Greiser, *Der Aufbau im Osten*, Jena, 1942.

19. StAHH, *Blohm & Voß*, 341, Vol. 1, p. 1, note by Rudolf Blohm, 5 January 1943: 'In addition in Arnhem and Amsterdam three formerly Jewish concerns were inspected which had been taken over by Hamburg firms by means of Aryanisation with support from German officials in Holland'. On the 'Aryanisation' of Jewish property in the Netherlands, see A.J. van der Leuw, 'Reichskommissariat und Judenvermögen in den Niederlanden', in Rijksinstituut voor Oorlogsdocumentatie, ed., *Studies over Nederland in Oorlogstijd*, Part 1, 's-Gravenhage, 1972, pp. 237–249.

20. On the following citations see: *Archiv des Rijksinstituuts voor Oorlogsdocumentatie/Amsterdam*, Collection 47, File 23b, communication from the N.V. Arnold Otto Meyer company, Amsterdam, to the *Wirtschaftsprüfungsstelle*, 21 December 1940.

21. BAP, *Reichswirtschaftsministerium*, 9573, pp. 224–229.

22. *Archiv FZH*, 32325, p. 29, speech by Kaufmann of 29 October 1940.

23. BAP, *Rechnungshof des Deutschen Reiches*, 5758, letter from the *Rechnungshof des Deutschen Reiches* to the *Reichsprotektor in Böhmen und Mähren*, 21 June 1941. Proceedings against the principal offenders were instigated on the decision of the *SS- und Polizeigericht* in Hamburg on 8 August 1940.

24. *Archiv des Wiedergutmachungsamtes beim Landgericht Hamburg*, file on 'Confiscation of assets by global measures', Guidelines of the Hamburg Gestapo for the Auctioning of Jewish Personal Affects, 20 January 1941.

25. StAHH, *Oberfinanzpräsident*, 47 UA 17 (Alphabetical Register of the Auction Proceeds Received in 1941–1943).

26. Ibid., UA 30 (Register of 22 auctioneers involved in the auctioning of Jewish personal affects).

27. Ibid., 47 UA 2 (Register of 21 removal firms involved in the transporting of Jewish household goods).

28. 'Jüdisches Umzugsgut unter den Hammer', *Hamburger Fremdenblatt*, 29 March 1941.

29. See *Archiv WgA LGHH*, correspondence of the auctioneer, Carl F. Schlüter, 1941–1943 (uncatalogued).

30. On the following events see StAHH, *Oberfinanzpräsident*, 23 (*Handakte* of the head of the *Dienststelle für die Verwertung eingezogenen Vermögens*).

31. StAHH, *Hamburger Öffentliche Bücherhallen*, 14, memoranda of 11 June 1942, 3 August 1942, and 4 and 7 September 1942.

32. On the material aspects of the deportations, see H.G. Adler, *Der verwaltete Mensch. Studien zur Deportation der Juden aus Deutschland*, Tübingen, 1974, p. 491ff.

33.  Cf. the overall performance report of *Dienststelle West* of the *Reichsministerium für die besetzten Ostgebiete*, 8 August 1944, *Archiv WgA LGHH*, Document collection on the '*M-Aktion*', pp. 170–175. On the confiscation of property, especially in Belgium, see Israël Shirman, 'De ekonomische plundering van de Joden in België', in *Bijdragen tot de Geschiedenis van de Tweede Wereldoorlog*, Vol. 3, Brussels, 1974, pp. 163–182. On confiscations in the Netherlands, see Jaques Presser, *Ondergang. De Vervolging en Verdelging van het Nederlandse Jodendom 1940–1945*, 's-Gravenhage 1965, Part 2, pp. 186–223.

34.  Cf. the statistical overview of the transport objectives in the performance report, p. 174. Here it is noted that out of 735 transports with a total of 29,436 railroad wagons, 18,665 wagons went to cities particularly affected by the bombing, 8,191 wagons to central 'Reich Warehouses' and 2,580 wagons to SS divisions and to the *Reichsbahn, Reichspost* and the police. Most transports went to the following *Gaue*: Weser-Ems (5,988 wagons), Hamburg (2,699 wagons), Essen (1,928 wagons), Cologne-Aachen (1,457 wagons) and Mecklenburg, esp. Rostock (1,023 wagons).

35.  StAHH, *Senatskanzlei-Präsidialabteilung*, 1942 S II 538, letter from *Beigeordneter* Martini to *Reichsstatthalter* Kaufmann, 16 October 1942.

36.  *Archiv Rijksinstituut voor Oorlogsdocumentatie/Amsterdam*, file on *M-Aktion*, letter from the head of the *Einsatz* command of *Reichsleiter* Rosenberg in the Netherlands/Amsterdam to *SA-Standartenführer* Dr Koeppen/Berlin, 2 August , 1943, with a comprehensive report on the seizure of apartments in the Netherlands, 26 March 1942 – 31 July 1943.

37.  Cf. die Listen im *Archiv WgA LGHH*, correspondence of the auctioneer, Carl F. Schlüter, 1941–1943 (uncatalogued).

38.  See the letter from the Carl Möddel store of Lingen/Emsland, which dealt in manufactured goods and fashionwear, to the auctioneer Carl F. Schlüter, ibid.

39.  StAHH, *Oberfinanzpräsident*, 15/2/2, report of auctioneer Carl Bleck, 12 January 1951.

40.  Gertrud Seydelmann, *Gefährdete Balance. Ein Leben in Hamburg 1936–1945*, Hamburg, 1996, p. 105ff.

41.  Cf. Bankier, *Germans*, p. 142ff.

42.  Bernd-A. Rusinek, *Gesellschaft in der Katastrophe. Terror, Illegalität, Widerstand - Köln 1944/45*, Essen, 1989, p. 115.

43.  Cf. Kershaw, *Persecution*, pp. 261–289; Mommsen and Obst, *Reaktion*, pp. 374–421.

44.  Franziska Becker, *Gewalt und Gedächtnis. Erinnerungen an die nationalsozialistische Verfolgung einer jüdischen Landgemeinde*, Göttingen, 1994, pp. 77–140.

45.  Ibid., p. 80.

# CONCLUSION

The displacement of Jewish entrepreneurs began in Hamburg, as in the rest of the Reich, directly after the National Socialist seizure of power. Violent attacks on Jews and Jewish businesses, organised boycotts, exclusions from professional associations, the withdrawal of licences for Jewish doctors and lawyers, 'voluntary Aryanisations' of numerous enterprises and mass dismissals of Jewish employees – and not only from public service – marked the beginning of a process that cannot be separated from the subsequent mass 'Aryanisation' of Jewish enterprises and the plundering of their owners. To be sure, this process did not run in unbroken continuity – it was marked by phases of tactical caution on the part of the National Socialists and by other delaying factors, followed by phases of explosive acceleration and radicalisation.

In the early years of the National Socialist regime, antisemitism pressed upwards 'from below', being particularly widespread in the commercial middle class and focused on destroying the economic livelihood of the Jews. As was demonstrated by the campaigns against *Beiersdorf AG* and *Deutscher Tuchversand*, however, this middle-class radical antisemitism was not given unconditional support by the new National Socialist rulers in Hamburg, although '*Regierender Bürgermeister*' Krogmann and Gauleiter and Reich Governor Kaufmann were clearly antisemites. The Hamburg state and party leadership consistently placed importance on implementing anti-Jewish Reich laws like the Law for the Restoration of a Professional Civil Service, but to a large extent avoided radicalising anti-Jewish policy through independent initiatives.

Looked at in the light of comparison with other regions, this was rather unusual, as can be seen for instance from a comparison of anti-Jewish policy in Hamburg with that in Munich and other German cities, where the new rulers proceeded against Jews earlier and with more radical consequences, and where they often far exceeded orders from the Reich. Although there were no public islands of humanity under the conditions imposed by National Socialist rule at that point in time, nevertheless the economic situation and the situation of the Jews concerned became more regionally diverse than the scholarly literature has assumed in the past. Even regional/historical investigations mostly presuppose that there was a homogeneous implementation of all anti-Jewish measures from above downward.

In Hamburg, the policy of destroying the economic life of the Jews by no means remained in a state of suspension free of contradictions up until 1936/37. Despite harassment and boycotts, Jewish enterprises also participated in the slow recovery of the market and occasionally obtained rising profits; despite special measures against independent Jewish entrepreneurs there was still no question of a systematic policy of 'de-Judaisation'. Since Hamburg's state leadership at first avoided unambiguous interventions in anti-Jewish policy, disparate approaches developed within the administration which ranged from combating to support-ing Jewish enterprises and which reflected the particularism of competing author-ities under the National Socialists.

The initial tactical restraint in anti-Jewish policy was justified above all by the economic structure and situation of Hamburg as a port and trading city – and by the need arising from this for a cautious approach to international opinion. Until 1938, Hamburg was officially recognised as an economically 'distressed area' because the unemployment figures there sank only slowly after 1933, and the National Socialist policies of armament and autarchy, though favouring industry and agriculture, inhibited the international commerce which dominated Ham-burg. The results were feelings of discontent and ill-will on the part of the popu-lation. In this situation an offensive against the more than fifteen hundred Jewish enterprises in Hamburg would have exacerbated the economic crisis and would have presented a threat to the stability of the National Socialist regime which the National Socialists in power in Hamburg did not wish to face.

In addition, the economic displacement of the Jews did not meet with undi-vided support in all sections of the population. Thus, the attempt of the National Socialists to provide a valve for antisemitism 'from below' while at the same time to compel the population to boycott Jewish businesses through the boycott of 1 April 1933, proved a failure. Even the Hamburg Chamber of Commerce and lead-ing business circles kept aloof from the economic displacement of the Jews at first. Whereas the younger businessmen from the 'generation of war youth' frequently proved to have an antisemitic orientation, the older generation of businessmen viewed the racial antisemitism of the National Socialists with scepticism and also as a potential threat to their own position, as measures against Jewish enterprises were the outcome of a policy of state intervention in the private sector that was itself undesirable. Even this partial scepticism was generally only expressed pas-sively and at a distance, and not in signs of active solidarity with Jews.

For the Jews, the National Socialist seizure of power led to their progressive isolation. This ended a process of assimilation which had gone considerably farther in Hamburg than in other regions, from whence, for instance, the high number of so-called 'mixed marriages' derived. The policy of 'dissimilation' after 1933 facilitated a return to Judaism, particularly among younger Jews, and promoted the construction of a Jewish community of solidarity which sought to compensate for the hardships caused by economic discrimination. Nevertheless, the opportunities to stabilise the economic situation of those affected within the framework of a 'Jewish economic sector' remained limited. In their struggle to maintain their enterprises, Jewish businessmen were largely thrown onto their own resources. Some harassment or repression could initially be balanced out through increased commitment, flexibility and creativity in Jewish firms. If many Jewish businesses in Hamburg maintained their market position until 1937, this was due above all to the remarkable will of their owners to keep them going.

In 1936/37, however, the phase of temporary restraint came to an end and the National Socialists began to aim at the complete destruction of the economic livelihood of the Jews in the medium term. This was shown by the collapse of all of the attempts of the Hamburg banker Max Warburg to come to a political arrangement with leading National Socialists in order to help the Jews in Germany secure a legal status. The special quality of National Socialist racist anti-semitism, and the political structures which threatened a cumulative radicalisation of anti-Jewish policy, permitted temporary tactical concessions, but allowed for no agreements on principles to be struck on the basis of normative legal guarantees.

In Hamburg, the Bureau of the *Gau* Economics Adviser succeeded in establishing its responsibility for the authorisation of 'Aryanisations' in 1936/37. Until then it had still been possible for Jewish businessmen to sell their business by free agreement at an appropriate price. The conditions on which the *Gau* Economics Adviser granted authorisations ended this freedom to make contracts and ensured that Jewish proprietors from then on would make enormous losses from sales, since payment could only be made for the inventory and stocks and not the actual firm value – the 'goodwill'.

The Hamburg *Gau* Economics Adviser, and those of his employees involved in the 'Aryanisation' process, belonged to a generation of academically educated and ideologically rigid men of ambition who, by their relatively young age alone were distinguished from the traditional notables – the typical industrial leaders of Hamburg – and personified a new, National Socialist economic elite. While the *Gau* offices of the Hamburg NSDAP in general, and the *Gau* Economics Adviser in particular, possessed only a few institutional powers and, in comparison with the state administration, were, at least in Hamburg itself, of subordinate importance, the 'Aryanisation' and 'de-Judaisation' of the economy represented one of the few fields of action in which a *Gau* Office of the NSDAP could exert a dominant influence. This was also linked to the readiness of both the Chamber of Commerce and the Hamburg Economics Department to leave the *Gau* Economics Adviser a free hand in 'Aryanisations' in order to restrict more effectively the 'revolutionary' energies of the men responsible for economic policy in the *Gau* in other respects.

Alongside the Office of the *Gau* Economics Adviser, the Foreign Exchange Control Office of the Regional Finance Office of the Lower Elbe – the *Landesfinanzamt Unterrelbe*, from 1937 renamed the *Oberfinanzdirektion Hamburg* – and the Customs Investigation Unit also worked to intensify the repression of Jewish enterprises from 1936/37 onward. Supported by Paragraph 37a of the Foreign Exchange Law, later Paragraph 59, which allowed all of the proprietorial rights of the Jewish businessman over his property to be withdrawn if there was just a vague suspicion that capital was being smuggled abroad, the Foreign Exchange Control Office set in motion a spiral of repression that ended in the liquidation or 'Aryanisation' of any significant Jewish enterprises. The approach taken by the Foreign Exchange Control Office made clear that the radicalisation of anti-Jewish policy cannot be explained exclusively by the outstripping of the bureaucratic, constitutional order – the 'normative state' (*Normenstaat*) – by the National Socialist 'prerogative state' (*Maßnahmenstaat*), based entirely on measures espoused by different actors within the National Socialist hierarchy. It must rather be seen in terms of radicalisation processes within the 'normative state' itself, where the tendency was to depart from approaches based on a normative legal understanding, freed of the restrictions imposed by a legal state. To this extent, the ideal/typical divisions set out by Fraenkel also became confused so that one should actually speak of the creeping undermining and partial self-destruction of the 'normative state'.

Special ministerial measures and official harassment in 1937/38 accelerated the 'Aryanisation' and liquidation of Jewish businesses. With the Ordinance on the Registration of the Property of Jews (*Verordnung über die Anmeldung des Vermögens von Juden*) of 26 April 1938 and the ordinances that followed, the Reich entered into the process of 'Aryanisation' and 'legalised' the hitherto informal obligation to seek authorisation. Even so, 'de-Judaisation measures' were not centralised at the Reich level and continued to be implemented by regional institutions.

In Hamburg, Reich Governor and Gauleiter Kaufmann functioned as the highest authorising instance, on the one hand regulating the discreet balance between Reich and regional interests in the sale of particularly lucrative businesses and, on the other, recognising the division of powers and practical procedures that had previously been in operation. The Bureau of the *Gau* Economics Adviser also continued to occupy a dominant position in the 'Aryanisation' process, although, according to the ordinances issued by the government of the Reich, he was only entitled to a right to participate in the process.

Over and above this, the Hamburg Economics Department and the bodies representing commerce and industry were now institutionally involved in the exclusionary measures and took part in decisions such as the liquidation or sale of Jewish enterprises. While the Hamburg Chamber of Commerce had behaved rather passively until 1937/38, it now openly intervened on the side of 'Aryan' buyers and supported them in their efforts to slip out of obligations to Jewish property owners. Several factors were significant in this change of approach: the consolidation of the National Socialist regime through domestic as well as foreign policy 'successes', which many expected would lead to a long period of National Socialist rule; the overcoming of the economic crisis even in Hamburg; the fact that the restraint towards Jewish businessmen which had been justified on the basis of economic policy no longer appeared to be necessary; the dynamic of the exclusion process which, in 1938, became irreversible and the institutional involvement of the Chamber of Commerce in 'Aryanisation' in the annexed territories, which, from 1938/39, opened up new, lucrative dimensions of the drive for enrichment, particularly for the economy of Hamburg.

'Aryanisations' had particularly favourable economic consequences for middle-class business, because the liquidation of the mostly middle-class Jewish enterprises relieved the pressure of competition. The systematic break-up of Jewish branch enterprises in Hamburg, which were destroyed and sold off as individual stores, also primarily served to promote the interests of the middle class. Similarly, in authorising 'Aryanisations', the *Gau* Economics Adviser fixed his main guidelines to serve the interests of the middle class, explicitly foreseeing the 'prevention of the formation of large companies' and the 'promotion of a new generation'. It would therefore be wrong to suggest that 'Aryanisations' fostered economic concentration beyond isolated instances, particularly since it was not the established economic enterprises of Hamburg that were predominant among the buyers, but those who were just trying to establish a business for themselves with the help of 'Aryanisations': former employees, businessmen of the new generation who until then had found no openings in the state-regulated foreign commerce system, newcomers to business, others changing occupation and profiteers moving in the political wake of the National Socialists.

For Jewish businessmen the formal 'legalisation' of 'Aryanisation' procedures from 1938 did not mean any increase in predictability and legal security. On the contrary, they increased the arbitrary treatment and repression they faced. For them, the underlying conditions for the sale of businesses worsened more and more in the course of 1938, with the result that the value of their firms sank drastically. The systematic and now institutionalised devaluation of inventory and warehouse stocks, the loss of accounts receivable, hidden reserves, the requirements of the Additional Export Procedure, pressures of the most diverse kind stretching to denunciations and the summary dismissal of all Jewish employees in firm sales, only represent some of the facets of the repressive means by which 'Aryanisations' were carried out in 1938.

Despite all of the repressions there were still more than twelve hundred Jewish enterprises in existence in Hamburg in the autumn of 1938. Their accelerated liquidation or 'Aryanisation' within the months that followed would not have been possible without the events that took place on 'Reich Crystal Night'. Though the violent excesses of the pogrom were rejected by economic circles in Hamburg and even by a section of the supporters of the National Socialists, with the result that Hamburg Gauleiter Kaufmann publicly distanced himself from the acts of violence committed, they nevertheless accelerated the 'final regulation of the Jewish problem', as Kaufmann put it, in so far as the events following '*Kristallnacht*' radicalised and systematised the annihilation of the economic livelihood of the Jews in pseudo-legal forms.

Even now, the legally established compulsory 'Aryanisation' did not lead to a centralisation of the measures taken to exclude the Jews from the economy. Instead, the authorities maintained the 'division of labour' that had previously been operational, according to which the Reich confiscated the property of Jews through a network of taxes and compulsory levies, and almost totally plundered them on emigration, while regional institutions also continued to be given responsibility for liquidation and 'Aryanisation'. These institutions brought the 'de-Judaisation' of those Jewish enterprises still in existence to a conclusion within a few months. Only the expropriation of the private real estate of the Jews extended over a longer period. At the beginning of December 1938, over two hundred Jewish retail businesses were closed down in Hamburg within a few days. The Jewish proprietors were hardly able to exercise any influence over the winding up or sale of their business at this point in time. When numerous company proprietors were arrested after the November Pogrom and thrown into concentration camps, the authorising bodies installed 'trustees' in their abandoned enterprises. These trustees could wind up or sell the enterprises without the agreement of the owner.

In its final phase, 'Aryanisation' in Hamburg resembled a 'race for riches', in which National Socialists in particular came into possession of lucrative enterprises. Corruption and nepotism determined the character of the 'Aryanisations' in this phase. Numerous decision-makers in the Hamburg NSDAP enriched themselves on Jewish property and the Gauleiter used the 'Aryanisations' as a welcome source of income, requiring 'Aryanisation contributions' of owners and buyers which he used to finance the NSDAP and his personal favourites.

Over and above this, attorneys, brokers, banks, trusteeships, 'emigration agents' and many other people and institutions, engaged in an 'exploitative trade' that developed in the economic areas connected with 'Aryanisations', an indication of the fluid transition to a criminal milieu which profited from the vulnerable situation and needs of persecuted Jews.

With the National Socialist policies of expansion and annexation from 1938/39 the circle of beneficiaries broadened to ever-greater sections of the population. From 1941–1945, in Hamburg alone the property of thirty thousand Jews from Hamburg, Germany and Western Europe was publicly auctioned. At least one hundred thousand inhabitants of Hamburg and of its North German neighbouring regions may have acquired items of Jewish property in this period. In addition, numerous Jewish enterprises in Eastern and Western Europe were 'Aryanised' by Hamburg firms. The involvement of Hamburgers in 'Aryanisation' therefore went far beyond the city limits and stretched to the whole of the European territories controlled by the National Socialists.

That many 'ordinary Germans' profited materially from the killing of the Jews, and were thereby morally implicated in the policy of destruction, represented a form of involvement in the genocide that has been barely noted in the literature. Previous debates among researchers have turned either on the question of what the German population knew of the murder of the Jews or on the participation in the killings themselves of 'ordinary men' as they are described in the work of Browning, or 'ordinary Germans' in that of Goldhagen. In sum, the behaviour of the material beneficiaries of the process is indicative of the erosion of moral standards in the German population, and of the extent of the moral indifference with which the Germans reacted to the extermination of the Jews.

# APPENDIX I

*Register of Jewish firms that were 'Aryanised' or liquidated in 1938/39*[1]

| Name of Enterprise | Commercial Field | Seat, Address |
|---|---|---|
| 1. Abeles & Co., Heinrich | Beer importer, general partnership | Kleiner Kielort 3-5 |
| 2. Abraham, Richard | Tobacco and cigarette importer | Brook 2/Freihafen |
| 3. Abrahamssohn, Joel | Discount jobber | Elbstr. 64 |
| 4. Abt, Leopold | Export of iron, glass, porcelain and musical instruments | Sierichstr. 88 |
| 5. Adler, Herbert | Import agents | Schopenstehl 15 |
| 6. Adler, M. | Egg store | Gählerstr. 3 |
| 7. Albrecht, Jacob | Tailor's workshop | Gerhofstr. 3 |
| 8. Allgemeine Bekleidungs-Centrale (ABC) Inh. Kurt Moses | Specialist in menswear and ladieswear | Alter Steinweg 1 |
| 9. Almind, H.W. Nachflg. | Timber trade | Jenischstr. 27 |
| 10. Altonaer Engros Lager | Textile and haberdashery wholesaler | Hamburger Str. 29 |
| 11. Ambor K.G., J. | Hardware manufacture | Spaldingstr. 62 |
| 12. Amles | Textile department store | Wandsbecker Chaussee 154/156 |
| 13. Andermann, Jacob | Egg store | Balduinstr. 22 |
| 14. Andrade, Ivan | Smoking accessories/cigar store | Bellealliancestr. 66 |
| 15. Anker, Carl Leopold | Manufacturer of equipment for brewers and vintners | Humboldtstr. 55 |
| 16. Arendt, Leo | Ladies' hat store | Hamburger Str. 78-80 |
| 17. Arendt, S. | Ladies' clothing | Eimsbütteler Chaussee 15 |
| 18. Arendt, Simon | Ladies' fashion store | Neuer Wall 35 |
| 19. Arndt & Cohn | Import/export | Alter Wall 32 |
| 20. Arnstein, Max | Equipment store | Pinnasberg 30 |
| 21. Ascher, August Sohn | Import and export of porcelain, enamelled goods, wooden and leather goods | Neuer Wall 70/74 |
| 22. Ascher, Arthur Nachflg. | Shipbroker | Große Elbstr. 58 |
| 23. Auerbach, A. | Trader in metals | Brahmsallee 16 |
| 24. Automat-Papier Fabrik | Toilet paper manufacturer | Marienthaler Str. 43 |
| 25. Avanzini, Adolf | Textile retail trade | Zeppelinstr. 15 |
| 26. Bachmann & Co, Moritz | Tanned materials | Neuer Wall 69 |
| 27. Bachrach, Friedrich | Private bank | Adolphsbrücke 11 |
| 28. Bachrach & Loeb | Export of skins | Cremon 11/12 |
| 29. Bäko-Werk | Bakery equipment manufacturer | Hoheluftchaussee 139/141 |
| 30. Baján, Eva | Embroidery store | Grindelallee 147 |
| 31. Bari, S. | Grocery retail trader | Bornstr. 25 |
| 32. Baruch, Louis | Raw wool imports | Paulstr. 11 |

| | | | |
|---|---|---|---|
| 33. | Baumgarten, Betty | Ladies' hats | Flemingstr. 16 |
| 34. | Bebe Schuhe Alfred Behr | Shoe store | Mönckebergstr. 8 |
| 35. | Becker K.G., Sally | Grocery wholesaler | Catharinenstr. 5 |
| 36. | Beckmann, John | Import and export of glass, porcelain, manufactured goods and electrical products | Ferdinandstr. 26/27 |
| 37. | Behr, Bernhard Nachf. | Menswear store | Dietmar-Koel-Str. 2 |
| 38. | Behr & Co., Richard | Import and transit trade | Gertrudenkirchhof 10 |
| 39. | Behr, Gebr. | Manufactured goods | Lübecker Str. 54 |
| 40. | Behrend, Bruno | Sweet manufacturer and wholesaler | Zollstr. 16 |
| 41. | Behrendt & Bodenheimer | Grain importer | Heimhuderstr. 76 |
| 42. | Behrendt & Feilmann | Fabric wholesaler | Alter Wall 61 |
| 43. | Behrens | Ladies' hats | Hoheluftchaussee 26 |
| 44. | Behrens, S. | Radio repair store | Beim Jacobistift 5 |
| 45. | Behrens & Söhne, L. | Private bank | Hermannstr. 31 |
| 46. | Belmonte, Michael | Private bank | Neuer Wall 54/60 |
| 47. | Belmonte, P.& A. | Export agents | Neuer Wall 54/60 |
| 48. | Benenson, Gebr. J. & S. | Import and export of grain and feed | Adolphsbrücke 9/11 |
| 49. | Benjamin, Walther | Citrus fruit import | Oberhafenstr. 5 |
| 50. | Benjamin, Wilhelm | Fabric | Neuer Wall 42 |
| 51. | Benscher, Gotthardt | Leather import and wholesale | Cremon 11-12 |
| 52. | Benzian & Co. | Trade in ores | Hohe Bleichen 8/10 |
| 53. | Berlin, Eduard | Gravestone workshop | Fuhlsbütteler Str. 66 |
| 54. | Berliner Waarenhaus Moritz Cohn | Ladieswear | Bahrenfelder Str. 87 |
| 55. | Bernhard, Hugo | Fabric wholesaler | Große Bäckerstr. 2 |
| 56. | Bernhardt & Stavenhagen | Insurance broker | Mönkedamm 7 |
| 57. | Bernstein, Adolf | Metalware wholesaler | Süderstr. 45 |
| 58. | Bernstein, Nathan | Egg store | Sachsenstr. 18 |
| 59. | Bertel & Krebs | Citrus fruit wholesale | Ifflandstr. 8 |
| 60. | Bertenthal, Oscar | Shoe store | Große Johannisstr. 61 |
| 61. | Betten-Beer | Bed retailer | Wexstr. 38 |
| 62. | Bilak, Julius | Export of groceries, manufactured goods, haberdashery and paperware | Große Bleichen 31 |
| 63. | Bing, Jonas OHG | Insurance broker | Mönckebergstr. 22 |
| 64. | Blanke & Co. | Import of vehicle parts | Klosterallee 5 |
| 65. | Blankenstein & Bosselmann | Specialist in grocery and beverages | Neuer Wall 59 |
| 66. | Blättner, S. | Diamond tool manufacturer | Hohenfelder Str. 1 |
| 67. | Blau & Schindler | Tanned materials | Catharinenstr. 25 |
| 68. | Bleifarbwerk Wilhelmsburg GmbH | Lead manufacturer | Holzbrücke 5 |
| 69. | Blöde, Else | Menswear | Eppendorfer Weg 22 |
| 70. | Blöde, Max | Gentlemen's clothing | Eppendorfer Weg 54 |
| 71. | Blum, Adolf & Popper | Transit vehicle transport | Mönckebergstr. 17 |
| 72. | Blum, Henry | Export agents | Hahntrapp 5 |
| 73. | Blumenthal, August | Export and transit trade | Glockengießerwall 1 |
| 74. | Blumenthal, Louis | Ladies' overcoats | Osterstr. 153a |
| 75. | Bock, Louis | Stamping and engraving | Hinrich-Lohse-Str. 284 |
| 76. | Bock, Max M. | Engineering office | Alfredstr. 61 |
| 77. | Bogopolsky, Simon | Leatherware | Neuer Wall 10 |
| 78. | Bollweg, Ludwig | Export agents | Pferdemarkt 45/51 |
| 79. | Bonneval, Hermann | Cigar retailer | Kaiser-Wilhelm-Str. 59 |
| 80. | Borchardt, James | Stamp trader | Rostocker Str. 3 |
| 81. | Borchardt & Co., Hans | Import and export of raw materials and semi-manufactured goods | Holzbrücke 2 |
| 82. | Bottina Schuh GmbH | Shoe store | Eimsbütteler Str. 60 Neuer Steinweg 70 Hamburger Str. 64 Hammerbrookstr. 103 Billhorner Röhrendamm 192/6 |

| 83. Boysen, Isaak | Menswear | Neuestr. 56 |
|---|---|---|
| 84. Brandt & Wolk OHG | Dyeing works | Alsterdorfer Str. 19 |
| 85. Braun, Bruno | Dried fruit | Schopenstehl 20/21 |
| 86. Braun & Sohn | Grocery import | Schopenstehl 20/21 |
| 87. von Braunschweig & Co. | Raffia import | Repsoldstr. 87/91 |
| 88. Braunschweiger, L. | Household goods retailer | Paulsplatz 12 |
| 89. Breilmann & Co. | Textile retailer | Hohenesch 48/52 |
| 90. Brieger, Heinrich | Trade in technical oils | Königstr. 25 |
| 91. Broches, Salomon | Optician | Grindelallee 115 |
| 92. Brock, Wilhelm | Egg importer | Berliner Tor 8 |
| 93. Bromberg, C. | Export of hardware, machines and tools | Bleichenbrücke 10 |
| 94. Brück, Adolf | Furniture store | Hamburger Str. 152 |
| 95. Buck, A. | Skin cream manufacturer | Woldsenweg 18 |
| 96. Bucky, Carl | Department store | Eimsbütteler Chaussee 4-6 |
| 97. Bucky, Walter | Department store | Hamburger Str. 133 |
| 98. Bud, Adolf | Ladies' and childrenswear store | Eimsbütteler Chaussee 14 |
| 99. Bukschnewski, David | Commercial lab | Gröningerstr. 6 |
| 100. Bume & Co. | Export of machines and ironware | Mönckebergstr. 8 |
| 101. Bundheim, Ernst | Import and export from Crin d'Afrique | Hohe Bleichen 20 |
| 102. Burchard & Co., Valentin | Pharmaceutical factory | Vogelreth 3 |
| 103. Burchardt, Max Berthold | Brokerage | Isestr. 36 I |
| 104. Calmann, E. | Private bank | Neuer Wall 101 |
| 105. Calmon, Edgar | Shoe store | Alsterdorfer Str. 14/16 |
| 106. Camienke, Erich | Photographical equipment | Elbstr. 117 |
| 107. Campell & Co., W. | Specialist store for optical goods, photography, cinema | Neuer Wall 30 Schulterblatt 156a |
| 108. Caspari, Louis | Shoe store | Grindelallee 92 |
| 109. Catz & Co. Trading mbH | Trade representatives | Trostbrücke 4 |
| 110. Chassel, Betty | Textile business | Eppendorfer Weg 192 |
| 111. Chemische Fabrik Michel & Co. KG | Chemical manufacturer | Curschmannstr. 26 |
| 112. Chemische Fabrik Dr. Rothschild & Leers GmbH | Chemical manufacturer | Berzeliusstr. 41 |
| 113. Chemische Fabrik Siegfried Kroch AG | Chemical manufacturer | Bismarckstr. (no number) |
| 114. Chemische Fabrik Dr. Weigert GmbH | Chemical manufacturer | Süderstr. 294 |
| 115. Chemische Industrielle Gesellschaft mbH Nachf. Adolf Rimberg | Trade in chemicals | Colonnaden 49 |
| 116. Christensen, Heymann & Lütge | Grain agent | Hopfensack 20 |
| 117. Cibulski, Gustav | Accessories for shoe manufacturers | Lindenallee 26 |
| 118. Clavier, Kurt | Interior decoration, furniture, decorators | Harvestehuder Weg 11 |
| 119. van Cleef, Benjamin E. | Import of nutwood and varnished wood | Süderstr. 173-175 |
| 120. Cohaco Continentale Handelskompanie Koch & Co. | Import of pulses and seeds | Mattentwiete 1 |
| 121. Cohen, Emil | Milk store | Dillstr. 8 |
| 122. Cohn, Alfred L. | Stationer | Fuhsbütteler Str. 130 |
| 123. Cohn, Judith | Stamp dealer | Bismarckstr. 93 |
| 124. Cohn K.G., Gustav | Import of raw materials from overseas | Reimersbrücke 5 |

| 125. Cohn, Robert | Retailer | Kirchenstr. 6 |
|---|---|---|
| 126. Cohn, Siegmund | Skin import | Albertstr. 32-34 |
| 127. Collette, Glaessner & Co. GmbH | Trade in goods of all sorts | Neuer Wall 73-75 |
| 128. Colonial-Export-Compagnie mbH | Grocery export | Mönckebergstr. 10 |
| 129. Cossen, S. | Jewellery wholesaler | Große Johannisstr. 13 |
| 130. Coutinho, Curt | Wholesale business in fats and bakery commodities | Hohe Bleichen 43/44 |
| 131. 'Die Dame' Inh. Georg Bloch | Ladies' fashion | Große Bleichen 5 |
| 132. Damenhüte Alex Cohen | Ladies' hats | Am Markt 22a |
| 133. Daniel, Max | Private bank | Hansastr. 65 |
| 134. Danziger, Dora | Corset store | Hoheluftchaussee 127 |
| 135. Darm-Import-Kompagnie W. Müller & Co. | Skin imports | Schanzenstr. 60/62 |
| 136. Davidson, Gebr. | Import/export of coffee, hides and balsam | Mönckebergstr. 7 |
| 137. Dawidowitz, Fritz | Shoe store | Mundsburger Damm 54 |
| 138. Delmonte & Koopmann | Import/export of canned fish | Dovenfleth 40 |
| 139. Dessauer, Geschwister | Manufactured goods wholesaler | Hamburger Str. 206a |
| 140. Deutsche Roulo Gesellschaft Thörl & Co. K.G. | Wholesale belts for beating clothes | Spaldingstr. 42 |
| 141. Deutschmann & Augustin | Transport | Kleine Reichenstr. 21/23 |
| 142. Dinkelspiel & Co. | Food processors | Holländ. Brook 3 |
| 143. Dobrowolski, A. | Textile retailer | Lehmweg 51 |
| 144. Doernberg, Robert | Fruit importer | Oberhafenstr. 5 |
| 145. Donner, Adolf | Glass/porcelain/household goods | Steindamm 49 |
| 146. Donner, Gebr. | Household goods | Eppendorfer Weg 6 |
| 147. Dr. Spiegel & Co. Nachf. | Fatty acids | Brandsende 24 |
| 148. Dreyer, S. sen. Nachf. GmbH | Shipping | Oberwärderdamm 16/18 |
| 149. Dreyfuß, Heinrich | Jeweller | Colonnaden 60 |
| 150. Duschenes, Franz | Broker for drugs and chemicals | Steinstr. 12 |
| 151. Dyhrenfurth | Men's fashion | Hammerbrookstr. 2 |
| 152. Eber & Sohn | Raw rubber | Alstertor 1 |
| 153. Ehrenberg, Walter | Drugstore/consumer goods | Rathausstr. 29 |
| 154. Ehrlich, Ernst | Dealer in skins/hides | Neue Burg 29 |
| 155. Ehrlich, M. | Manufactured goods retailer | Pilatuspool 13 |
| 156. Ehrlich, M. | Poultry and sausage retailer | Grindelhof 55 |
| 157. Ehrmann, Alfred | Manufactured goods | Fruchtallee 64 |
| 158. Eichberg, Irma | Children's clothing (production and wholesale) | Große Bergstr. 125 |
| 159. Eichholz & Loeser | Wholesale cereal, oilseeds, feed, groceries | Schulstr. 2 |
| 160. Eisenmann & Co., Max | Motor vehicles | Wandsbeckerstieg 3/11 |
| 161. Ekert & Co. | Sports equipment | Fuhlentwiete 51/53 |
| 162. Elkan & Co., S. | Import/export of steel and pig iron | Magdalenenstr. 33 |
| 163. Engers, Emil | Metal and mineral import | Loogestieg 21 |
| 164. Engländer & Hinsel | Toy and fashion wholesaler | Michaelisstr. 19 |
| 165. Ephraim, Gumpel & Co. | Import/export of textiles, haberdashery and hardware | Mönckebergstr. 5 |
| 166. Epstein, Albert | Import/export of toys, machines, textiles and hardware | Mönckebergstr. 5 |
| 167. Ero Schuh Inh. Rudolf Oberschützky | Shoe store | Große Bleichen 22 |
| 168. Etam Strumpfhaus | Hosiery | Neuer Wall 16/18 Großer Burstah 29 Eppendorfer Baum 25 Mönckebergstr. 17 |
| 169. Ettisch, Daniel | Gentlemen's clothing | Süderstr. 70 |
| 170. Eulenburg, Max Nachf. | Gas wholesaler | Deichstr. 22 |
| 171. Ewo, Inh. Max Salomon | Department store | Große Bergstr. 125 |

| | | |
|---|---|---|
| 172. Fabian, Martin | Textiles | Steindamm 102 |
| 173. Fairplay Schleppdampfschiffs-Reederei Richard Borchardt | Shipping company | Steinhöft 11 |
| 174. Feigin & Co., I. | Grocery and dried fruit importer | Bei den Mühren 70 |
| 175. Feis, Albert | Private bank | Neuer Wall 42 |
| 176. Feldberg, Gebr. | Fashion store | Mönckebergstr. 17 |
| 177. Feldten, C. Nachf. GmbH | Chemicals manufacturer | Erdmannstr. 8 |
| 178. Fiedler, Mandl | Tobacco store | Alter Steinweg 49 |
| 179. Fiedler's Strumpfläden Inh. Bernhard Rosen | Hosiery | Große Bergstr. 123 Hamburger Str. 6 Bahrenfelder Str. 125 |
| 180. Finkels, Abisch | Department store | Bahrenfelder Str. 110/116 |
| 181. Fischer, Hugo | Import/export of haberdashery, foodstuffs and canned goods | Eppendorfer Landstr. 18 |
| 182. Fleischmann, Golda | Specialist work clothing store | Vorsetzen 42 |
| 183. Fränkel, Helmuth | Gold and silverware store | Großer Burstah 5 |
| 184. Frajnd, Max | Shoe store | Billhorner Röhrendamm 112 |
| 185. Franck & Co., M.B. | Private bank | Meßberg 1 |
| 186. Frank, Gebr. | Warehouse for woods and veneers | Jenischstr. 14 |
| 187. Frank & Co | Ladies and childrens' wear | Hamburger Str. 85 |
| 188. Frank & Nielsen | Manufactured goods | Bahnstr. 1/3 |
| 189. Frank, Victor | Private bank | Große Bleichen 31 |
| 190. Frank, Wilhelm | Private bank | Loogestieg 11 |
| 191. Franke, August Nachfl. | Men's laundry | Schaarmarkt 4 |
| 192. Franke, W. Otto | Trade in chemical products | Durchschnitt 19 |
| 193. Frankenberg, Hans | Textile goods | Mönckebergstr. 5 |
| 194. Frankenthal, Gucisa | Leather store | Alter Steinweg 66 |
| 195. Frankfurter & Co., James | Import/export of groceries, hardware and manufactured goods | Große Bäckerstr. 2 |
| 196. Frankfurter & Liebermann | Import/export | Große Bleichen 31 |
| 197. Freudenthal, Georg | Cigar retailer | Reeperbahn 22 |
| 198. Freund & Co., Albert OHG | Import of raw materials from overseas | Neuer Wall 71 |
| 199. Freund, S. & Pels | Building machinery and locomotive factory | Spitalerstr. 7 |
| 200. Friedheim jun., M. | Menswear | Alsterarkaden 11a |
| 201. Friedländer, Max | Cigar retailer | Spaldingstr. 47 |
| 202. Friedländer & Co., J.H. | Cereal and feed wholesaler | Schauenburgerstr. 32 |
| 203. Friedländer & Co., Martin | Export of hardware, textiles, stoneware and haberdashery | Hohe Bleichen 8/10 |
| 204. Friedmann, Geschw. | Toy/baby carriage retailer | Eppendorfer Weg 6 |
| 205. Frisch, Julius Nachfl. H. Löwenstein | Men's hats | Eimsbütteler Chaussee 61 |
| 206. Frischmann, M.A. | Drugstore goods wholesaler | Neuer Wall 54 |
| 207. Frühling, Gustav | Credit house | Müggenkampstr. 70 |
| 208. Fuchs Papierwarenfabriken AG | Paper factory | Kieler Str. 302/306 |
| 209. Fürst & Co., C. | Metal wholesaler | Bugenhagenstr. 6 III |
| 210. Galewski, Marcus | Women's and childrenswear | Steindamm 108/114 |
| 211. Gans, Gebr. | Silk fabric | Neuer Wall 10 |
| 212. Ganz, Robert | Import/export of tools | Schopenstehl 15 |
| 213. Gazelle | Corsets/linen | Graskeller 3 Hamburger Str. 30 Hamburger Str. 96 Hammerbrookstr. 93 Schulterblatt 140 Neuer Wall 17 Billhorner Röhrendamm 156 Dammtorstr. 38 Reichenstr. 24 |

| | | |
|---|---|---|
| | | Wandsbecker Chaussee 167 |
| | | Hoheluftchaussee 30/34 |
| | | Mönckebergstr. 29 |
| | | Steindamm 13 |
| 214. Geller, James | Cigar retailer | Papenstr. 38/40 |
| 215. Gelles, Theodor | Export of haberdashery and manufactured goods | Hopfenmarkt 2 |
| 216. Gerechter, Leopold, Lesser Levy Nachfl. | Underwear manufacture | Rutschbahn 8 |
| 217. Gerson, Adolf | Household appliance and kitchen utensil wholesaler | Eimsbütteler Chaussee 87 |
| 218. Glücksmann, Samuel | Delicatessen/egg store | Hammerbrookstr. 80b |
| 219. Glückstadt, Hanns | Grocery retailer | Heinrich-Barth-Str. 6 |
| 220. Glückstadt & Münden | Postcard manufacturer and wholesale business | Beim Andreasbrunnen 3 |
| 221. Götz, Reinhold | Stamp dealer | Schulstr. 2 |
| 222. Goldberg, Salomon | Egg store | Talstr. 7 |
| 223. Goldmann, M. | Furrier | Steindamm 134/136 |
| 224. Goldner, Julius | Stamp wholesaler | Hohe Bleichen 31/35 |
| 225. Goldrei, Foucard & Son, Charles | Trade in eggs and egg products | Hoheluftchaussee 139/141 |
| 226. Goldschmidt, Albert | Metal foundry | Venusberg 4/5 |
| 227. Goldschmidt, J. Sohn | Private bank | Börsenbrücke 8 |
| 228. Goldschmidt, Nathan | Second-hand goods dealer | Klosterallee 2 |
| 229. Goldschmidt, Rahel | Manufactured goods | Klosterallee 22 |
| 230. Goldschmidt & Co., Harry | Export agents | Neuer Wall 10 |
| 231. Goldschmidt & Mindus | Hardware, bicycle and radio wholesaler | Rödingsmarkt 66/69 |
| 232. Goldstein Wwe. & Sohn, E. | Office equipment retailer | Holzbrücke 11 |
| 233. Goldtree & Liebes | Bulk exports | Neue Burg 29 |
| 234. Graetz, Waldemar | Menswear | Colonnaden 66/68 |
| 235. Greif, Adolf | Specialist work clothing store | Mühlenstr. 8 |
| 236. Greif, Leo | Manufactured goods store | Schlageteistr. 8 |
| 237. Greiner, Rubin | Textile retailer | Eppendorfer Weg 9 |
| 238. Gruber, Sara | Draper | Wexstr. 17 |
| 239. Gross & Co., David | Textiles | Alter Steinweg 63/64 |
| 240. Grossmann, Jacob | Linen | Rutschbahn 3 |
| 241. Grünbaum, Kurt K. | Sugar agent | Bergstr. 7 |
| 242. Grüners Modellhaus | Ladies' clothing | Beim grünen Jäger 25 |
| 243. Gumpert, Conrad | Trade in equipment for bakers | Lange Reihe 29 |
| 244. Gumpert, S. Co. m.b.H. | Manufacture of foodstuffs | Danielstr. 103 |
| 245. Gurwitsch & Co., M. | Tar products | Große Reichenstr. 1 |
| 246. Guttmann & Widawer | Import of coffee, honey and skins | Gerhofstr. 3/5 |
| 247. Haar, D. | Import of egg products | Neue Gröningerstr. 17 |
| 248. Haas & Cie., Gebr. | Veneer trade | Billstr. 158 |
| 249. Haas & Co., Ernst | Import/export of textiles | Steckelhörn 12 |
| 250. Hagedorn & Co., J.P.H. | Cigar retailer | Colonnaden 41 |
| 251. Hahlo, Max B. | Import/export | Steinstr. 23 |
| 252. Halberstadt & Co., Siegfried | Export of manufactured goods, textiles and haberdashery | Neuer Wall 54 |
| 253. von Halle, Hugo | Stationers | Billhorner Röhrendamm 168 |
| 254. von Halle, Philipp | Ladies' drapery store | Graskeller 4 |
| 255. Hamberg, Hermann | Private bank | Neuer Wall 10 |
| 256. Hamberg, Julius | Import of equipment for the paint and dying industry | Königstr. 21 |
| 257. Hamburg-Altonaer Wach- und Schließgesellschaft m.b.H. | Security firm | Fehlandstr. 3-5 |
| 258. Hamburger Bleiwerk, Adolf Bernstein AG | Leadpipe, sheet lead, lead traps and tinpipe factory | Süderstr. 45 |

| | | |
|---|---|---|
| 259. Hamburger Damen-Konfektionshaus GmbH | Ladieswear | Reeperbahn 81/89 |
| 260. Hamburger Krawatten-Centrale Arthur Meyer | Mens' fashion | Große Bleichen 20 |
| 261. Hamburger Spezial-Schokoladenfiguren-Fabrik J. Gold | Chocolate figure manufacturer | Papenstr. 33 |
| 262. Hamburger Textil-Engros-Vertrieb | Textile sales/woollen goods wholesaler | Isestr. 115 |
| 263. Hammerschlag | Hat store | Neuer Wall 52 |
| 264. Hammerschlag, Otto | Export of heavy goods, iron and machines | Königstr. 14/16 |
| 265. 'Hangro' Hanseatischer Großhandel in Konsumwaren Guggenheim & Co. | Drugstore goods wholesaler | Neuer Wall 26/28 |
| 266. Hansa-Trocken-Feuerlöscher GmbH | Fire extinguishers | Amelungstr. 15 |
| 267. Hart, Hermann | Raw materials | Bei den Mühren 91 |
| 268. Hartig, Hugo | Import/export of cellulose, mechanical woodpulp and paper | Burchardstr. 1 |
| 269. Hauer & Labes | Pastry wholesaler | Lohhof 1 |
| 270. Hausner, N. | Bed retailer | Kaiser-Wilhelm-Str. 45 |
| 271. Havana-Import-Compagnie Albert Aronson & Co. | Cigar importer | Wendenstr. 130 |
| 272. Hecht, Edgar | Auctioneer | Esplanade 15 |
| 273. Heilbut, Julius | Private bank | Alstertor 1 |
| 274. Heinemann, Bernhard | Furniture store | Weidenallee 38/40 |
| 275. Heinemann, Julius | Jeweller | Gerhofstr. 2/8 |
| 276. Henschel, Alfred | Opticians | Bergstr. 3 |
| 277. Hepner & Juliusberg | Import/export of tanned goods | Admiralitätsstr. 60/61 |
| 278. Herr & Co. KG, Otto | Roofing, insulation and flooring manufacturer | Husumer Str. 12 |
| 279. Herren-Kleider-Fabrik 'Fortschritt' GmbH | Textile factory/menswear | Hamburger Str. 60-62 Billhorner Röhrendamm 104-104b Wilstorferstr. 25 |
| 280. Hersslik & Co., Julian | Wholesale business/rubberware | Königstr. 14 |
| 281. Hertz, Valeska | Hosiery | Schanzenstr. 121 |
| 282. Herzberg, Gebr. | Export of hardware and electrical appliances | Haynstr. 5 |
| 283. Herz & Co. Ltd | Grinding mill for foodstuffs and feed | Bugenhagenstr. 6 |
| 284. Herzog, Alexander | Stationer | Lübecker Str. 59 |
| 285. Hessberg, Max | Import/export | Fischertwiete 2/Chilehaus |
| 286. Hesse, Otto | Coffee Agent | Sandtorquai 20 |
| 287. van Hessen & Co. mbH | Skin wholesaler | Süderstr. 315 |
| 288. Heymann, J. D. | Furniture/interior furnishing | Neuer Wall 42 |
| 289. Hinrichsen & Co., Adolph | Corset factory | Glashüttenstr. 40 |
| 290. Hirsch, Adolph | Skin wholesaler | Grimm 12 |
| 291. Hirsch, Ephraim | Pawnbroker | Wexstr. 9 |
| 292. Hirsch, Hermann | Soap store | Hudtwalckerstr. 28 |
| 293. Hirsch A.G., Jacob | Metal wholesaler | Alstertor 2 |
| 294. Hirsch & Cie. | Fashion store | Mittelweg 107 |
| 295. Hirschfeld, Gebr. | Clothing store | Neuer Wall 17-23 |
| 296. Hirschfeld, Julius/Meyer, J.W. Nachf. | Shoe store | Steindamm 92 |
| 297. Hirt, Hermann | Fur store | Eppendorfer Landstr. 14 |
| 298. Hockenheimer, Fred S. | Junk wholesaler | Hammer Deich 28/34 |
| 299. Hönigsberg, O. | Egg store | Eppendorfer Weg 134 |
| 300. Holstein, Fritz | Ladies' underwear manufacturer | Süderstr. 176 |
| 301. Horwitz, M. | Stationer | Neumünsterstr. 59 |

| 302. Horwitz & Co., Waldemar | Import/export of textiles, machines, porcelain and painting materials | Neuer Wall 72 |
|---|---|---|
| 303. Hovedissen, Ernst | Export agents | Neuer Wall 10 |
| 304. Hubermann, Hermann | Textile retailer | Große Roosenstr. 23 |
| 305. Hundt & Hebeler | Agents | Catharinenstr. 47/48 |
| 306. Importers Company mbH | Raw material exports | Königstr. 14 |
| 307. Inselmann, L.J. | Radio retailer | Lappenbergsallee 25 |
| 308. 'Iris' Haus für Schmuck und Geschenke, Inh. George Abraham | Jewellery, leather and fashion accessory retailer | Neuer Wall 32 |
| 309. Isaacsohn & Bühring | Import/export of haberdashery, hardware, toys and glassware | Kaiser-Wilhelm-Str. 20-26 |
| 310. Jacob, Philipp, Sana Reformschuhwaren | Shoe store | Brennerstr. 8 |
| 311. Jacobsohn, Elsa | Stationer | Lange Reihe 91 |
| 312. Jacobsohn, Gebr. | Textile retailer | Mühlenstr. 11 |
| 313. Jacobsohn, Siegmund | Stationer | Lange Reihe 93 |
| 314. Jacobson & Co., N. | Import/export of metals and chemicals | Königstr. 15/17 |
| 315. Jacoby, Berthold OHG | Furniture mover and storer | Hoheluftchaussee 150/155 |
| 316. Jägermann, Wolf | Furrier | Gänsemarkt 13 |
| 317. Jeczes, Rosa | Leather store | Herderstr. 28 |
| 318. Jonas Söhne & Co., H.A. | Private bank | Neuer Wall 26/28 |
| 319. Josephs, Martin | Textile business | Alsterdorfer Str. 18 |
| 320. Juda, Joseph | Menswear | Süderstr. 164 |
| 321. Kahn, Albert | Wine store | Breite Str. 147 |
| 322. Kahn, Siegmund | Import of untreated hides | Catharinenstr. 25 |
| 323. Kant & Co., Paul | Exporters | Mönckebergstr. 10 |
| 324. Karo, Moritz | Textile retailer | Wexstr. 33 |
| 325. Katz, L. | Textile retailer | Adolfstr. 159 |
| 326. Katzenstein, Ernst | Stationer | Valentinskamp 29 |
| 327. Katzenstein, Julius | Workshop for furniture, interior decoration and design | Mittelweg 118 |
| 328. Keiler, Ernst jun. | Import/export of untreated asbestos | Neuer Wall 54 |
| 329. Keller & Hess | Coffee importers | Sandtorquai 14/17 |
| 330. Kendziorek, Leo | Drugstore | Wandsbeker Chaussee 159 |
| 331. Keramikhaus Grundstücks-Gesellschaft mbH | Real estate agent | Hamburger Str. 27/28 |
| 332. Kimmelstiel, Ad. | Hat maker | Neuer Wall 39 |
| 333. Kimmelstiel & Co., M. | Stationery | Neuer Wall 39 |
| 334. Knobloch & Co., Hugo | Import/export of groceries, textiles, haberdashery and paper | Esplanade 6 |
| 335. Köhlbrand-Werft Paul Berendsohn | Shipyard | Korbmachersand/ Altenwerder |
| 336. Köpcke, J.J. | Chemical-pharmaceutical factory | Preystr. 4 |
| 337. Kohn, Gebr. | Coal sales, sawmill and cutting works | Eiffestr. 410 |
| 338. Kohn, Gustav KG | Shoe store | Mönckebergstr. 17 |
| 339. Kohn, Martin | Import/export | Königstr. 15 |
| 340. Konfektionsgeschäft 'Billig und Fesch' Käthe Lissauer | Ladies' fashion | Steinweg-Passage 3 |
| 341. Koppel, Rosa | Agents | Rothenbaumchaussee 233 |
| 342. Korn, Geschwister, OHG | Ladies' clothing | Lübecker Str. 1 |
| 343. Korngold, Hermann | Ship plumbing and outfitting | Stubbenhuk 8 |
| 344. Korte, Arthur | Linoleum trader | Burchardstr. 24 |
| 345. Kowarsky, Michael | Import/export of hides and furs | Neuer Wall 54 |
| 346. Kraftwagen-Handels- und Betriebsgesellschaft mbH | Motor vehicle sales business | Repsoldstr. 75/79 |
| 347. Kreph, Elias | Furniture store | Schulterblatt 32 |
| 348. Kreph, Israel | Tobacco wholesaler | Schanzenstr. 71 |
| 349. Krohn, Rudolf | Fruit and vegetable retailer | Schulweg 18 |

| 350. Krombach Söhne, M. | Steam-run brickworks | Haynstr. 8 |
|---|---|---|
| 351. Kronheimer & Co., J. | Import/export | Admiralitätsstr. 71/72 |
| 352. Kugelmann, John | Scrap metal | Bieberstr. 7 |
| 353. Kühl & Co., Carl | Coal store | Isestr. 17 |
| 354. Külper, Leopold | Secondhand goods store | Stellinger Weg 14 |
| 355. Kupke, Gertrud | Embroiderer | Kaiser-Wilhelm-Str. 112 |
| 356. Lachmann, Julius | Import/export | Alsterdamm 15 |
| 357. Laco Export Comp. Kelter & Asch | Export | Bleichenbrücke 25/29 |
| 358. Landauer & Co., F. | Drugstore goods wholesaler | Grimm 22 |
| 359. Landsberger & Sachs | Grocery wholesaler | Catharinenbrücke 1 |
| 360. Lange, Delfs & Co. | Haberdashery wholesaler | Rosenstr. 11 |
| 361. Lanzkron & Mathiason | Chemical exporters | Steckelhörn 11 |
| 362. Laser, Sally | Textile retailer | Sand 1 |
| 363. Laser, Simon | Menswear | Hamburger Str. 8 |
| 364. Lavy & Co., Chs. | Clothing, tie manufacturer | Bleichenbrücke 25/29 |
| 365. Lazarus, Wilhelm | Insurance agency | Bergstr. 11 |
| 366. Lefeld & Co. | Import/export of cocoa beans, feed and wax goods | Woldsenweg 16 |
| 367. de Lemos, J. & Heß | Export of manufactured goods, stationery and hardware | Neuer Wall 54 |
| 368. Leser, Siegmund | Fashionwear store | Steindamm 53 |
| 369. Levy, Alexander | Private bank | Alstertor 1 |
| 370. Levi, Selma | Second hand goods store | Frankenstr. 3 |
| 371. Levy, Leon | Hair wholesaler | Neue Burg 13 |
| 372. Levy, Martin | Auctioneer | Fuhlsbütteler Str. 142 |
| 373. Levy Söhne Inh. Gustav Levy | Tobacconists | Wilmannspark 4 |
| 374. Levy & Co., S.R. | Import/export of bristle, horsehair and fibrous material | Deichstr. 42 |
| 375. Lewandowski, Arthur Ernst | Medical dressings and stamp wholesaler | Grindelberg 9a |
| 376. Lewandowski, Gebr. | Corsets | Jungfernstieg 38 |
| 377. Lewie, Elsa | Coffee/tea/cocoa/sweets | Rothenbaumchaussee 49 |
| 378. Lewin, Max | Cigarette factory | Alter Wall 60 |
| 379. Leyser Alfred | Mens' fashion | Zeughausmarkt 22 |
| 380. Libis, Siegmund | Fabric cleaning | Kanalstr. 160 |
| 381. Lieber, Gustav | Stamp wholesaler | Schanzenstr. 7 |
| 382. Liebes, Max | Export of hides and skins | Graskeller 3 |
| 383. Liefmann Söhne Nachf., R. | Export of textiles, haberdashery, hardware and jewellery | Brandstwiete 24 |
| 384. Lindemann, Siegfried Wwe. & Sohn | Typewriter retailer | Neuer Wall 10 |
| 385. Lindenblüt, Ber | Fur store | Breitenfelder Str. 1a |
| 386. Lindloff | Specialist in ladieswear | Hamburger Str. 41 Große Bergstr. 71/75 |
| 387. Lindor Strumpfläden GmbH | Hosiery | Rödingsmarkt 66/69 |
| 388. Lion, Frederick E. | Private bank | Hermannstr. 34 |
| 389. Lipmann & Co., Carl | Import/export of skins | Wendenstr. 45 |
| 390. Lipper, Adolf | Clock and gold sales business | Hamburger Str. 88 |
| 391. Lippmann, H. | Metal wholesaler | Rödingsmarkt 21 |
| 392. Lippstadt, Martin jr. | Import/export of African plant fibers | Mönckebergstr. 7 |
| 393. Lissauer & Co., M.H. | Second hand | Mönckebergstr. 17 |
| 394. Lisser, Juan | Import/export | Kattrepel 2 |
| 395. Litmann, Max | Cobblers' equipment wholesaler | Lübecker Str. 50 |
| 396. Littmann, Moritz | Footwear retailer | Hamburger Str. 27 |
| 397. Liwerant, Gebr. | Hosiery factory | Fuhlentwiete 51/53 |
| 398. Lobbenberg, J. | Retail business selling jewellery, umbrellas and leather goods | Jungfernstieg 33 |
| 399. Löwe, Elisabeth | Cigar retailer | Im Tale 10 |

| 400. Loewenberg, Alex | Specialist office equipment business | Bleichenbrücke 10 |
|---|---|---|
| 401. Löwenheim, Julius | Radio retailer | Bornstr. 1 |
| 402. Loewenthal, L.J. | Butter | Neue Gröningerstr. 15 |
| 403. Löwenthal, Becker & Co. | Shoe wholesale and exports | Alter Steinweg 42 |
| 404. Londner, Nathan Bernd | Book printers | Große Bergstr. 130a |
| 405. Luft, Hersch Joseph | Draper | Gählersplatz 9-10 |
| 406. Luria & Co. Succs., B. | Import/export | Jungfernstieg 6-7 |
| 407. Maaß & Riege | Import/export | Bugenhagenstr. 5 |
| 408. Magnus, Moritz jr. | Weapon retailer | Düsternstr. 46/50 |
| 409. Magnus, Sigmund | Coal store | Klosterallee 7 |
| 410. Magnus & Co., James | Export of technical articles and metals | Mönckebergstr. 31 |
| 411. Mahler, Louis | Store selling clocks | Krayenkamp 16 |
| 412. Maidanek, Karl | Cobbler and leather store | Bergstr. 73 |
| 413. Marcus, Julius | Manufactured goods retailer | Mühlenstr. 9 |
| 414. Markus, Alfred | Draper | Hamburger Str. 26 |
| 415. Marx, Dr. Emil, Nachf. | Technical oils and fats | Spitalerstr. 12/Semperhaus B |
| 416. Marx, Max | Export agents | Mönckebergstr. 5 |
| 417. Marx & Co., Gebr. | Import/export | Reimersbrücke 5 |
| 418. Mathiason, Alfred | Animal hair trader | Bartelsstr. 65 |
| 419. Mathiason, E. jr. | Private bank | Neuer Wall 70/74 |
| 420. May, Anna | Cigar retailer | Wexstr. 1 |
| 421. May & Co. | Export | Mönckebergstr. 18 |
| 422. Mayer's Kurzwarenhaus | Haberdashery store | Großneumarkt 40 |
| 423. Mees & Co., Willy | Silkware store | Hamburger Str. 21/23 Schulterblatt 144/146 |
| 424. Meier, Joseph, Inh. Max Pommerantz | Mens' and boyswear | Wilstorfer Str. 14 |
| 425. Meier, S. | Mens' and boyswear | Mönckebergstr. 7 |
| 426. Melind & Co., E. | India rubber stamp factory | Rosenstr. 19a |
| 427. Mendel, Nachf., J. | Leather wholesaler | Catharinenstr. 25 |
| 428. Menke & Busse | Citrus fruit importers | Oberhafenstr. 5/Fruchthof (Chilehaus) |
| 429. Meyer, Adolf | Corset and bandage accessories | Königstr. 11-13 |
| 430. Meyer, Albert | Private bank | Oberstr. 61 |
| 431. Meyer, Martin | Feed import/fishfood | Burchardstr. 24 |
| 432. Meyer, Richard | Jeweller | Dammtorstr.1 |
| 433. Meyer & Co. AG, Carl | Export of lamps and glass | Oberwärder Damm 12 |
| 434. Meyer & Co., Oscar | Import/export | Jungfernstieg 2 |
| 435. Meyer & Sohn, Otto | Trade in animal materials | Schauenburger Str. 15/19 |
| 436. Minden, Johanna | Fabric warehouse | Stadthausbrücke 39 |
| 437. Mindus & Co., Felix | Export of jute and cloth products | Hohe Bleichen 31/32 |
| 438. Mingelgrün, Klara | Gentlemen's clothing | Große Johannisstr. 6 |
| 439. Modehaus Sam. Meyer | Finery and fashion accessories | Steindamm 35 |
| 440. Möller, A.J. | Raw tobacco store | Benedictstr. 17 |
| 441. Möller, W. | Jewellery, gold and silverware store | Isestr. 49 |
| 442. Moos, Elias | Import of hides | Bei den Mühren 46/48 |
| 443. Moritz & Pincoffs | Export | Königstr. 14/16 |
| 444. Müller & Co. GmbH | Stamp wholesaler | Schanzenstr. 7 |
| 445. Nachum & Bandmann | Upholstery wholesaler | Kammermannstwiete 3 |
| 446. Nagel, Max | Ladies drapery store | Königstr. 51 |
| 447. Nathan, Gebr. | Stationery and fashion | Gänsemarkt 41 |
| 448. Nathan, Neben & Co. | Menswear | Kaiser-Wilhelm-Str. 115 |
| 449. Neufeld, Hermann | Cigar retailer | Billhorner Röhrendamm 78 |
| 450. Neumann, Arthur | Draper's | Alter Steinweg 47 |
| 451. Neuwirth, Schaja | Mens' and boyswear | Bremer Str. 3 |
| 452. Niederländische Export-Company mbH | Export of chemicals, seeds drugstore goods | Billstr. 173 |

| 453. | Norddeutsche Metallbettstellen-Fabrik GmbH | Metal bed factory | Manteuffelstr. 44/48 |
|------|---------------------------------------------|-------------------|----------------------|
| 454. | Norddeutsche Überseegesellschaft mbH | Import/export of chemicals, paint, paper | Kleine Reichenstr. 1 |
| 455. | Dr. Oberländer, Eugen | Mineral oil importer | Hochallee 46 |
| 456. | Obersky, A. | Corset factory | Steindamm 156 |
| 457. | Oelwerke Julius Schindler GmbH | Fabrication of mineral-based oil lubricants | Hohe Bleichen 28 |
| 458. | Oettinger & Co., Hans N. | Raw tobacco wholesaler | St. Annenufer 6 |
| 459. | Oppenheim, Rudolf | Stamp dealer | Ness 3 |
| 460. | Ostindienhaus Heinrich Colm KG | Clothing store | Neuer Wall 13/15 |
| 461. | Panofsky, Siegmund | Specialist electronics store | Kaiser-Wilhelm-Str. 53 |
| 462. | Papierhaus Erka | Stationer | Kaiser-Wilhelm-Str. 55 |
| 463. | Papierhaus Krohn | Stationer | Steindamm 109 |
| 464. | Pasler, Henry | Cutlery | Holstenstr. 188 |
| 465. | Paul, Alfred | Fruit and vegetable retailer | Eppendorfer Landstr. 29 |
| 466. | van Pels, H. & Wolff | Import/export of chemicals | Billstr. 173 |
| 467. | Pels, James | Export of chemical products | Neuer Wall 54 |
| 468. | Perlstein, Salomon | Produce retailer | Lohmühlenstr. 82 |
| 469. | Petersen & Co., Johannes A. | Import/export of wines and spirits | Borgfelderstr. 66 |
| 470. | Pfifferling, Jacob | Menswear | Schulterblatt 125 |
| 471. | Pfifferling, L. | Stationery and office equipment | Hoheluftchaussee 88 |
| 472. | Philip, Iwan | Machine-tool store | Großer Burstah 5 |
| 473. | Philip Spiro's Sohn | Paper and office equipment | Hermannstr. 21/23 |
| 474. | Philip & Co., Arthur | Hair and wool wholesaler | Kleine Johannisstr. 10 |
| 475. | Pick, Ignaz | Wholesaler, haberdashery and groceries | Deichstr. 9 |
| 476. | Pincus, Leopold | Textile retailer | Silbersackstr. 26 |
| 477. | Pokorny, Egon | Wholesaler, animal materials | Beneckestr. 50 |
| 478. | Polack, James | Jewellery store and clock salesman | Altenwallbrücke 2/4 |
| 479. | von der Porten & Frank | Bristle importers | Alter Steinweg 73/77 |
| 480. | Prag & Co., Carl | Flannels | Loewenstr. 1 |
| 481. | Prager, Arthur | Drugstore | Belleallianceestr. 68 |
| 482. | Prenzlau, Behrens & Lundin GmbH | Import/export of Chinese egg products | St. Annenufer 6-7 |
| 483. | Rappolt & Söhne | Textile factory | Mönckebergstr. 11 |
| 484. | Reese & Wichmann | Chocolate and sweet factory | Wendenstr. 130 |
| 485. | Regenmäntelfabrik Sturmflut GmbH | Raincoat factory | Rödingsmarkt 66/69 |
| 486. | Reich, Rudolf | Metal paint wholesaler | Neuer Wall 41 |
| 487. | Reichwagen & Nölting | Export agents | Mönckebergstr. 3 |
| 488. | Reider, Sonja | Shoe store | Winterhuder Weg 2 |
| 489. | Reimler, Christian Nachf. | Import/export/wholesaler | Pumpen 6/Chilehaus C III |
| 490. | Reiss, Rosenstern & Co. | Light railway factory | Husumer Str. 7 |
| 491. | Reiss & Co., Walter | Import of untreated wool | Mönckebergstr. 5 |
| 492. | Reiter, Inselmann & Co. | Import/export of tar, wood pitch and turpentine | Spitalerstr. 11/ Barkhof, Haus 1 |
| 493. | Rendsburg, Willy | Stationery manufacture and wrapping paper wholesaler | Krayenkamp 9 |
| 494. | Rieder, M., Inh. Joseph Levy | Footwear warehouse | Neuer Steinweg 1/3 |
| 495. | Rieder & Co. | Shoe store | Lappenbergsallee 35 |
| 496. | Rieder & Sohn, M. | Shoe store | Hamburger Str. 164 |
| 497. | Rimberg, M.C. | Fabric warehouse | Elbstr. 96 |
| 498. | Robertson, S.J. | Auctioneer | Stellinger Weg 19 |
| 499. | Robertson & Co., Adolf | Private bank, export agents | Hohe Bleichen 16 |
| 500. | Robinsohn, Gebr. | Clothing store | Neuer Wall 25-33 |
| 501. | Rosenbaum & Wolf | Private bank | Mönckebergstr. 22 |
| 502. | Rosenberg, Fritz | Transport | Hüxter 13 |

| 503. Rosenberg, Gustav | Office equipment retailer | Lilienstr. 15 |
|---|---|---|
| 504. Rosenberg, H. | Export | Spitalerstr. 9 |
| 505. Rosenberg, Julius | Junk dealer | Idastr. 19-21 |
| 506. Rosenberg & Co., Max | Import/export of groceries and citrus fruit | Pumpen 6 |
| 507. Rosendorff, Hugo | Drugstore | Neue Str. 18 |
| 508. Rosenstern & Co. | Borate, tartaric acid, coconut fibre and hide importer | Mönckebergstr. 5 |
| 509. Rosenthal, E. | Department store | Hinrichsenstr. 27 |
| 510. Rosentreter, Samuel | Textile retailer | Große Bergstr. 128 |
| 511. Rosner, Israel | Specialist store for work clothing | Wexstr. 24 |
| 512. Rosner, Hermann | Specialist store for work clothing | Mühlenstr. 9 |
| 513. Rothschild, Behrens & Co. | Office equipment retailer | Mönckebergstr. 18 |
| 514. Rothschild & Baruch | Private bank | Alter Wall 76/78 |
| 515. Rusek, Kalman | Leather store | Kurze Str. 12 |
| 516. Sachs, Samson Inh. Julius Nathan | Hire-purchase business | Hammerbrookstr. 22 |
| 517. Sahm, Heinrich | Cigar retailer | Dragonerstall 9 |
| 518. Salberg, Adolf GmbH | Chainstore dealing in leather and fashion accessories | Jungfernstieg 38 |
| 519. Salinger, Walter | Work clothing | Große Roosenstr. 24 |
| 520. Salm, Alexander S. | Importer of skins | Schäferkampsallee 28 |
| 521. Salomon, Elise | Bread retailer | Valentinskamp 37 |
| 522. Salomon, Friederike | Fashion accessory retailer | Alter Steinweg 48 |
| 523. Salomon, Gebr. | Export agents | Steinhöft 9 |
| 524. Salomon, H.J. | Box manufacturer, woodcutter | Friedrichstr. 59 |
| 525. Samson, D. | Private bank | Neuer Wall 5 |
| 526. Samson, Gebr. | Export of foundry equipment | Schauenburger Str. 2 |
| 527. Samuel & Rosenfeld | Trade in hides and skins | Admiralitätsstr. 71/72 |
| 528. Satz, Adolf L. | Cosmetics store | Hoheluftchaussee 69 Eppendorfer Baum 43 |
| 529. Schapiro, Moisey | Import/export of hides and skins | Hohe Bleichen 8/10 |
| 530. Scheibel, J.F.U. | Hops, malt and brewing equipment | Spitalerstr. 11/Barkhof I |
| 531. Schenkolewski, Max | Woollenwear store | Brahmsallee 4 |
| 532. Schenkolewski, Zacharias | Draper | Peterstr. 3 |
| 533. Schleicht | Ladies' hats | Hamburger Str. 131 |
| 534. Schlesische Furnierwerke AG | Veneer factory and sawmill | Billstr. 23/25 |
| 535. Schlewinsky, Siegfried | Manufactured goods store | Mittelstr. 84 |
| 536. Schlüter & Co., Carl | Wine importer | Borgfelder Str. 66 |
| 537. Schmerler, Moses | Draper | Bremer Str. 5 |
| 538. Schmidt & Co., Gustav | Chemicals manufacturer | Schnackenburgsallee 189 |
| 539. Schnabel, Richard | Drugstore | Grindelhof 64 |
| 540. Schönberg & Schaufeld | Citrus fruit wholesaler | Klosterstr. 36 |
| 541. Schönfeld & Co., Benedict | Export of textiles, toys, bicycles and automobile parts | Burchardstr. 24 |
| 542. Schönfeld & Wolfers | Import/export of textile products | Hohe Bleichen 31/32 |
| 543. Schönthal & Co. | Chemical wholesaler | Neuer Wall 10 |
| 544. Schröter & Co., Louis | Import agents and broker for groceries, dried fruits, spices and canned food | Pumpen 6/ Chilehaus C |
| 545. Schüler & Co., Max | Import/export of paper and cellulose | Kirchenallee 25 |
| 546. Schulz, Josef | Fabric business | Steindamm 107 |
| 547. Schuster, Arthur | Household appliance and kitchen utensil store | Neuer Steinweg 64 |
| 548. Schwarz, Gustav | Private bank | Bergstr. 14 |
| 549. Segall, Louis | Photography store and studio | Süderstr. 73 |
| 550. Seligmann, Gustav | Manufactured goods | Marschländerstr. 8 |
| 551. Seligmann, Moses | Private bank | Bleichenbrücke 3 |

| 552. Simon, Albert Geo | Import/export of manufactured goods, haberdashery and hardware | Kattrepel 2 |
|---|---|---|
| 553. Simon, Franz | Textile department store | Herderstr. 29-31 |
| 554. Simon, Iwan OHG | Cereal importers | Hohe Bleichen 20 |
| 555. Simon, Max jr. | Chemicals manufacturer | Mühlenkamp 65 |
| 556. Simon, S. | Butcher, ship provision and outfitting | Baumwall 4/5 |
| 557. Sipser, Simon | Export of textiles and fashion accessories | Gröningerstr. 23/25 |
| 558. Solmitz & Co. | Private bank | Raboisen 103 |
| 559. Sparig & Co., W. | Import of spices and oilseed | Brauerstr. 27/28 |
| 560. Speier Schuhwarenhaus | Footwear store | Großer Burstah 34<br>Neuer Wall 61<br>Schulterblatt 140/142<br>Hamburger Str. 127<br>Neuer Wall 13 |
| 561. Spiegel & Co., W. | Import/export | Hopfensack 20 |
| 562. Spielwaren-Vertriebs-Gmbh | Toystore | Alter Wall 46 |
| 563. Sporthaus Derby Inh. Elsa Lewin/ Max Blöde | Menswear | Eimsbütteler Chaussee 84 |
| 564. Stapel & Israel | Export | Hochallee 104 |
| 565. Stapelfeld, Geschw. | Furniture and trousseau store | Karlstr. 10 |
| 566. Stavenhagen, J.M. | Wool importer | Alstertor 1 |
| 567. Stechmann & Co., R. | Export of cotton goods and hardware | Kattrepel 2 |
| 568. Steinberg, Ernst August | Specialist store for menswear and work clothing | Große Bergstr. 115/117 |
| 569. Steiner, Jacob | Cosmetic products | Schaarsteinweg 3 |
| 570. Steinhardt, O. & W. | Import/export | Kaiser-Wilhelm-Str. 20/26 |
| 571. Stempel, Adolf | Linen, stockings | Große Johannisstr. 83 |
| 572. Stern, Bernhard | Specialist drapery and trousseau store | Hamburger Str. 88a |
| 573. Stern, Ferdinand GmbH | Ladies' hat store | Schulterblatt 128 |
| 574. Stern, Willi | Export of textile goods, iron, chemicals | Mönkedamm 7 |
| 575. Sternheim, Arthur | Citrus fruit importer | Oberhafenstr. 5/Fruchthof |
| 576. Stoppelmann, Alfred | Wild game and poultry retailer | Billhorner Röhrendamm 163 |
| 577. Strauss, Benno | Leather wholesaler | Mittelweg 44 |
| 578. Streim, Iwan | Soap store | Talstr. 7 |
| 579. Streit, Lina | Furniture store | Zollenbrücke 3 |
| 580. Stryer, Simon | Bed store | Rathausmarkt (Alt.) 2 |
| 581. Teppich-Juster, Juster & Co. | Carpet, furniture, curtains, decorations | Ellerntorbrücke 5 |
| 582. Texta -Textil-Etage | Textiles | Mönckebergstr. 11 |
| 583. Theilheimer, Willy | Seeds | Große Reichenstr. 3 |
| 584. Theiner & Janowitzer | Import/export | Bleichenbrücke 10 |
| 585. Tikotzinsky, O. | Leather store | Herderstr. 12 |
| 586. Tomkins, Hildesheim & Co. | Coffee importers | Sandtorquai 20 |
| 587. Trechmann, Edmund | Cigar wholesaler | Steckelhörn 12 |
| 588. Trier Nachf., Otto | Corset accessories | Kaiser-Wilhelm-Str. 89 |
| 589. Tropisco-Farbengesellschaft mbH | Anti-rust paint | Lilienstr. 36 |
| 590. Tugendhaft, Isaak | Wild game and poultry retailer | Rappstr. 4 |
| 591. Unger, Gustav Wilhelm | Ladies' and mens' fashionwear | Jungfernstieg 7/8<br>Alsterarkaden 3/5 |
| 592. Ventura, Salo | Import of raw tobacco | Breite Str. 34/36 |
| 593. Vogel, Betty | Corset store | Jungfernstieg 42 |
| 594. Vogl, Arnold | Import/export of spices, dried fruit and sardines | Hopfensack 8 |
| 595. Wachs, Paul | Fur store | Wohlers Allee 78 |
| 596. Wagenberg, Max | Furniture factory | Neumann-Reichardt-Str. 29/33 |
| 597. Wagner, L. | Department store | Neuer Steinweg 91-94<br>Elbstr. 70-84 |
| 598. Wagschal, Rahel | Draper | Großneumarkt 15 |

| 599. van der Walde, David | Export of technical appliances | Brandsende 15/17 |
|---|---|---|
| 600. van der Walde, Rudolf | Export of shoe manufacturing equipment, glass, enamel and household goods | Brandsende 15/17 |
| 601. Walden, S. | Menswear | Alter Steinweg 15 |
| 602. Walter, Georg | Ladieswear | Fuhlsbütteler Str. 192 |
| 603. Walzer, Moritz | Furniture and menswear business | Moorstr. 4 |
| 604. Wandsbecker Dampf-Haarwäscherei Frankenthal KG | Animal hide cleaner | Helbingstr. 64-66 |
| 605. Warburg & Co., M.M. | Private bank | Ferdinandstr. 75 |
| 606. Wassermann, Alfred | Radio store | Kleine Johannisstr. 15 |
| 607. Weber, Wilhelm jr. | Export of hardware, car and motorbike accessories | Bleichenbrücke 10 |
| 608. Wegner, F. | Seed wholesaler | Brandstwiete 40/42 |
| 609. Wegner & Co. | Men's underwear factory | Spaldingstr. 160 |
| 610. Weigert, Gebr. | Import/export of groceries | Sandtorquai 27 |
| 611. Weil, Isidoro | Import/export | Schauenburger Str. 1 |
| 612. Wichmann's Flaggengeschäft Inh. Selma Meyer | Flag manufacturers | Rothenbaumchaussee 3 |
| 613. Wiener, M. | Paint and lacquer (factory, storehouse and sales) | Kleine Reichenstr. 5 |
| 614. de Winter & Co., Leo | Dairy produce | Gröningerstr. 14 |
| 615. Wohl & Co. | Import/export of groceries | Heußweg 14 |
| 616. Wolf, Hyman | Import/export of skins | Fischertwiete 1/Chilehaus B |
| 617. Wolf & Heilbrunn | Wholesaler, hides and skins | Große Freiheit 9 |
| 618. Wolff & Co., Franz | Coffee import | Sandtorquai 20 |
| 619. Wolosker & Co., S. | Smoking accessory wholesaler | Bergstr. 27 |
| 620. Wright, J.G. | Mineral water producer | Bartelsstr. 65 |
| 621. Würzberg, Gustav | Clothes store | Holstenstr. 37 |
| 622. Wulfsohn, Walter | Rubber boot wholesaler | Hohe Bleichen 40/42 |
| 623. Zenetti & Holzer | Export of machines and technical appliances | Mattentwiete 38 |
| 624. Zinner, Josef | Leatherware store | Alter Wall 64 |
| 625. Zinner & Lippstadt | Cheese wholesaler | Neue Gröningerstr. 18 |

1. The register is incomplete. According to the figures drawn up by the NSDAP Gau Economics Adviser, in the autumn of 1938 there were still approximately 1,200 Jewish enterprises in Hamburg. The following figures were collated from the files of the Wiedergutmachungsamtes beim Landgericht Hamburg, from Hamburg address books, file 100. B1. 21 in the Archiv der Handelskammer, and a handful of files from the Bestand Oberfinanzpräsident at the Staatsarchiv Hamburg (9 UA 6, 42 UA 7, 19, 28/1, 28/2).

# APPENDIX II
## Tables

---

*Table 1* Number of Jews in Hamburg and percentage of Jews in the total population 1811-1939[1]

| Year | Absolute numbers | % of the total population |
|------|------------------|---------------------------|
| 1811 | 6,429 | 4.87 |
| 1866 | 12,550 | 4.46 |
| 1871 | 13,796 | 4.07 |
| 1890 | 17,877 | 2.87 |
| 1900 | 17,949 | 2.34 |
| 1910 | 19,472 | 1.92 |
| 1925 | 19,904 | 1.73 |
| 1933 | 16,973 | 1.39 |
| Altona 1933 | 2,006 | 0.83 |
| Wandsbek 1933 | 116 | 0.25 |
| Harburg-Wilhelmsburg 1933 | 315 | 0.28 |
| The town of Hamburg 1937 | 15,308 | 1.40 |
| Greater Hamburg 1939 | 10,131[2] | 0.6 |
| *'Mischlinge'* of the 1st & 2nd degree | 7,787 | 0.5 |

1. For the figures for 1811: Ina Lorenz, *Die Juden in Hamburg zur Zeit der Weimarer Republik,* Hamburg 1987, p. XLII; for statistics for 1866–1925 see *Statistisches Jahrbuch für die Freie und Hansestadt Hamburg 1929/30,* Hamburg 1930, p. 27; for figures for 1933 see *Statistik des Deutschen Reiches,* Vol. 451, Issue 5, Berlin 1936, pp. 34, 41; figures for 1937 can be found in StAHH, *Amtsgericht Hamburg - Verwaltung,* ABl. 1987, 3170, Note of Aug. 12, 1938; for the figures for 1939 see: *Aus Hamburgs Verwaltung und Wirtschaft,* Special issue No. 5, 1 August 1941, p. 17. Up until 1937 the figures given relate to the State of Hamburg.
2. This number includes so-called 'Jews by race' *(Rassejuden),* according to the National Socialist definition of the term.

**Table 2** Birthplaces of Jews in the main German cities and in Hamburg, 1933[3]

| Birthplaces | Total figure for the main cities | | Hamburg City | |
|---|---|---|---|---|
| | Numbers | % | Numbers | % |
| German Reich | 250,678 | 70.79 | 14,040 | 83.15 |
| *Those in the communities counted* | 134,715 | 53.74 | 8,571 | 61.05 |
| *Those in the rest of the Reich* | 115,963 | 46.26 | 5,469 | 38.95 |
| Former German territories occupied by other states after 1918 | 38,374 | 10.84 | 552 | 3.27 |
| Other Foreign Countries | 64,721 | 18.28 | 2,228 | 13.20 |
| *Those from Poland* | 41,865 | 11.82 | 869 | 5.15 |
| *Those from Russia* | 4,345 | 1.13 | 174 | 1.03 |
| Unknown | 347 | 0.09 | 65 | 0.38 |
| **Total** | 354,120 | 100 | 16,885 | 100 |
| Those born locally | 134,715 | 38.0 | 8,571 | 50.8 |
| Native Germans[4] | 252,746 | 71.4 | 13,772 | 81.6 |

3. Calculated according to figures in *Statistik des Deutschen Reiches,* Vol. 451, Issue 5, Berlin 1936, pp. 15, 50ff.
4. 'Native' *(einheimisch)* Jews were defined as citizens of the Reich, born either in the German Reich or in former German areas occupied by other states after 1918.

***Table 3***   The Jewish population of Hamburg's quarters, 1933[5]

| City area | Numbers | % of the total population | % of Hamburg Jews |
|---|---|---|---|
| Altona-Nord | 57 | 0.76 | 0.34 |
| Altona-Süd | 30 | 0.30 | 0.18 |
| Neustadt-Nord | 527 | 1.71 | 3.10 |
| Neustadt-Süd | 408 | 1.49 | 2.40 |
| St.Georg-Nord | 264 | 0.77 | 1.56 |
| St.Georg-Süd | 143 | 0.27 | 0.84 |
| St.Pauli-Nord | 406 | 1.18 | 2.39 |
| St.Pauli-Süd | 191 | 0.66 | 1.12 |
| Eimsbüttel | 1,221 | 0.99 | 7.19 |
| Rotherbaum | 3,586 | 12.07 | 21.13 |
| Harvestehude | 3,722 | 12.92 | 21.93 |
| Eppendorf | 2,695 | 3.23 | 15.88 |
| Geestvororte | 198 | 0.55 | 1.17 |
| Winterhude | 1,318 | 2.07 | 7.77 |
| Barmbek-Nordost | 310 | 0.32 | 1.83 |
| Barmbek-Nordwest | 414 | 0.43 | 2.44 |
| Uhlenhorst | 242 | 0.60 | 1.43 |
| Hohenfelde | 345 | 1.06 | 2.03 |
| Eilbek | 166 | 0.30 | 0.98 |
| Borgfelde | 106 | 0.33 | 0.62 |
| Hamm | 400 | 0.41 | 2.36 |
| Horn | 59 | 0.33 | 0.35 |
| Billwärder Ausschlag | 64 | 0.13 | 0.38 |
| remaining quarters | 13 | 0.06 | 0.08 |
| Rural area | 88 | 0.10 | 0.52 |
| **Hamburg State** | **16,973** | **1.39** | **100** |

5.   Calculated from the figures given in *Aus Hamburgs Verwaltung und Wirtschaft*, Year 11, 1934, No. 8, p. 178.

*Table 4*  Occupational structure of the Jews of Hamburg, 1925[6]

| Economic sector | Total working population of Hamburg | | Jewish working population | |
|---|---|---|---|---|
| | Number | % | Number | % |
| A. Agriculture, gardening | 14,385 | 2.2 | 8 | 0.1 |
| B. Industry, mining | 202,259 | 30.5 | 1,285 | 11.7 |
| C. Trade and Transport | 266,540 | 40.2 | 6,588 | 60.1 |
| D. Administration, independent professions | 37,373 | 5.6 | 599 | 5.5 |
| E. Health professions | 22,599 | 3.4 | 509 | 4.7 |
| F. Domestic work | 43,251 | 6.5 | 201 | 1.8 |
| G. Unemployed or without fixed occupation | 76,816 | 11.6 | 1,768 | 16.1 |
| **Total** | 663,223 | 100 | 10,958 | 100 |

*Table 5*  Occupational structure of the Jews of Hamburg, 1933[7]

| Economic sector | Total population of Hamburg | | Hamburg Jews | |
|---|---|---|---|---|
| | Number | % | Number | % |
| A. Agriculture, gardening | 25,553 | 2.10 | 35 | 0.20 |
| B. Industry and Handicraft | 361,640 | 29.68 | 1,742 | 10.26 |
| C. Trade and Transport | 487,545 | 40.01 | 9,784 | 57.65 |
| D. Public service, private services | 141,167 | 11.59 | 2,332 | 13.74 |
| E. Domestic work | 34,068 | 2.8 | 174 | 1.03 |
| F. Unemployed, Self-employed | 168,474 | 13.83 | 2,906 | 17.12 |
| **Total** | 1,218,447 | 100 | 16,973 | 100 |

6.  Table from Lorenz, *Juden,* p. 61. The figures cover the State of Hamburg.
7.  The figures cover not only those in work but also their dependents and thus the whole population of the State of Hamburg. Calculated from: Die Volks-, Berufs- und Betriebszählung in Hamburg am 16.Juni 1933. Nachtrag zum Statistischen Jahrbuch für die Freie und Hansestadt Hamburg, Year 1933/34, Hamburg 1935, p. 17; Statistik des Deutschen Reiches, Vol. 451, Issue 5, Berlin 1936, p. 72.

***Table 6*** Working status of the Jews of Hamburg in 1925 and 1933[8]

| Working status | Working population of Hamburg 1925 (total) | | Jewish working population of Hamburg 1925 | | Jewish working population of Hamburg 1933 | |
|---|---|---|---|---|---|---|
| | Total figure | % | Total figure | % | Total figure | % |
| Self-employed | 93,498 | 15.9 | 4,584 | 49.9 | 3,665 | 45.8 |
| Employees and officials | 186,360 | 31.8 | 3,631 | 39.5 | 3,303 | 41.3 |
| Workers | 250,861 | 42.8 | 611 | 6.7 | 636 | 8.0 |
| Members of family assisting in business | 16,422 | 2.8 | 195 | 2.1 | 251 | 3.1 |
| Domestics | 39,266 | 6.7 | 169 | 1.8 | 146 | 1.8 |
| **Total workers** | 586,407 | 100 | 9,190 | 100 | 8,001 | 100 |

***Table 7*** Distribution of self-employed Jews in selected economic sectors in the State of Hamburg, 1933[9]

| | **Economic sector** | **Numbers** | **%** |
|---|---|---|---|
| Industry and handicraft | Iron, steel, metals, machinery | 18 | 0.50 |
| | Electronics | 9 | 0.25 |
| | Chemicals | 37 | 1.02 |
| | Textiles | 13 | 0.36 |
| | Printing | 24 | 0.66 |
| | Leather/wood/carved materials | 17 | 0.47 |
| | Food and groceries | 35 | 0.96 |
| | Clothing | 164 | 4.52 |
| | Construction | 39 | 1.08 |
| Trade and transport | Trade | 2,431 | 67.03 |
| | *Of which trade in goods* | 1,419 | 39.12 |
| | *Of which trade in real estate* | 915 | 25.22 |
| | Banks/stock exchange/insurance | 217 | 5.98 |
| | Hotel trade | 37 | 1.02 |
| Public service and private services | Administration, education | 228 | 6.29 |
| | *Of which legal and economic services* | 135 | 3.72 |
| | Health service, welfare | 319 | 8.80 |
| | Theater, cinema | 39 | 1.08 |
| **Total** | | 3,627 | 100 |

8. Figures from *Statistisches Jahrbuch für die Freie und Hansestadt Hamburg 1929/30,* Hamburg 1930, p. 29; *Statistik des Deutschen Reiches,* Vol. 451, Issue 5, Berlin 1936, p. 72. The figures cover the State of Hamburg.

9. Calculated from: *Statistik des Deutschen Reiches,* Vol. 451, Issue 5, Berlin 1936, pp. 88–90. The figures cover the State of Hamburg.

**Table 8**  Age structure of Hamburg's Jewish population, 1933[10]

| Age groups | Total for Hamburg | | The Jews of Hamburg | |
|---|---|---|---|---|
| | Numbers | % | Numbers | % |
| under 6 | 72,316 | 6.40 | 751 | 4.45 |
| 6 - 14 | 114,676 | 10.16 | 1,822 | 10.79 |
| 14 - 20 | 68,755 | 6.09 | 911 | 5.39 |
| 20 - 30 | 212,533 | 18.82 | 2,328 | 13.79 |
| 30 - 40 | 209,919 | 18.59 | 2,784 | 16.49 |
| 40 - 50 | 178,131 | 15.77 | 2,629 | 15.57 |
| 50 - 60 | 141,895 | 12.57 | 2,593 | 15.36 |
| 60 - 65 | 49,162 | 4.35 | 1,059 | 6.27 |
| over 65 | 81,920 | 7.25 | 2,008 | 11.89 |
| Total | 1,129,307 | 100 | 16,885 | 100 |

**Table 9**  Jewish Companies in Greater Hamburg, 1938[11]

| | Retail | Handicraft | Other | Total | % of companies |
|---|---|---|---|---|---|
| Kreis 1 | 12 | 30 | 51 | 93 | 7.7 |
| Kreis 2 | 64 | 88 | 122 | 274 | 22.8 |
| Kreis 3 | 119 | 58 | 410 | 587 | 48.9 |
| Kreis 4 | 29 | 12 | 43 | 84 | 7.0 |
| Kreis 5 | 8 | 5 | 15 | 28 | 2.3 |
| Kreis 6 | 20 | 11 | 11 | 42 | 3.5 |
| Kreis 7 | 30 | 19 | 18 | 67 | 5.6 |
| Kreis 8 | 13 | - | 3 | 16 | 1.3 |
| Kreis 9 | 2 | - | - | 2 | 0.17 |
| Kreis 10 | 4 | - | 8 | 12 | 0.7 |
| Total | 301 | 223 | 677 | 1201 | 100 |

10.  Figures from: *Statistisches Jahrbuch für die Freie und Hansestadt Hamburg 1934/35,* Hamburg 1935, p. 9. The figures cover the city of Hamburg.

11.  Calculated from the figures given in the *Hamburger Tageblatt,* 2 Dec. 1938. A precise date for this overview, which was provided by the Office of the NSDAP Gau Economics Adviser, is difficult to arrive at. The register of Jewish enterprises prepared on 7 Dec. 1938, included 800 firms in Old Hamburg (letter from the Reichsstatthalter to the *Reichsinnenministerium,* 7 Dec. 1938, StAHH, *Oberfinanzpräsident,* 8), the tables published detail 1110 enterprises in the area of Old Hamburg (*Kreis* 1–6, 9). They must therefore have been drawn up before December 1938, and were probably drawn up in mid-1938. The districts covered included the following town quarters in Hamburg: *Kreis* 1: Eppendorf, Winterhude, Hoheluft, Lokstedt, Schnelsen, Niendorf, Langenhorn, Fuhlsbüttel, Ohlsdorf, Alsterdorf, Groß-Borstel; *Kreis* 2: Eimsbüttel, Harvestehude, Rotherbaum; *Kreis* 3: St.Pauli, Altstadt, Neustadt, Steinwärder, Waltershof, Finkenwärder; *Kreis* 4: St.Georg, Borgfelde, Hammerbrook, Klostertor, Kleiner Grasbrook, Veddel, Rothenburgsort, Billwärder Ausschlag, Billbrook; *Kreis* 5: Hohenfelde, Eilbek, Hamm, Horn, Billstedt; *Kreis* 6: Barmbek, Uhlenhorst; *Kreis* 7: Altona, Ottensen, Bahrenfeld, Elbvororte; *Kreis* 8: Harburg, Wilhelmsburg, Vororte Süderelbe; *Kreis* 9: Bergedorf, Lohbrügge, Vier- and Marschlande; *Kreis* 10: Wandsbek, Bramfeld, Steilshoop, Farmsen, Walddörfer, Alstertal, Rahlstedt.

***Table 10***   Turnover (T) and Profits (P) of selected Jewish enterprises in the years 1930–1938 in thousands of RM

| | 1930 | 1931 | 1932 | 1933 | 1934 | 1935 | 1936 | 1937 | 1938 | T/P |
|---|---|---|---|---|---|---|---|---|---|---|
| *Wholesale and international trade* | | | | | | | | | | |
| 1. A. Krause & Co.[12] | | 522,190 | 389,826 | 322,134 | 324,435 | 442,275 | 924,513 | | | T |
| 2. Gold-schmidt & Mindus[13] | 1,820,000 | 1,563,000 | 1,621,000 | 1,981,000 | 2,238,000 | 1,900,000 | | | | T |
| 3. Maaß & Riege[14] | | | | 384,000 | 320,000 | 480,000 | 869,000 | 1,054,000 | | T |
| 4. Zinner & Lippstadt[15] | 117,161 | 102,967 | 93,199 | 71,087 | 70,375 | 79,980 | 84,593 | 46,980 | | P |
| 5. Delmonte & Koopmann[16] | | | | | | 52,095 | 77,784 | 163,384 | | P |
| 6. Sparig & Co.[17] | | | | | | 1,543,000 | 2,153,000 | 1,689,000 | | T |
| | | | | | | 39,498 | 83,500 | 92,200 | | P |
| 7. Juan Lisser[18] | | | | | | 346,000 | 540,000 | 568,000 | | T |
| | | | | | | 9800 | 28,400 | 35,800 | | P |
| 8. Albert Geo Simon[19] | | | | | | 441,492 | 837,220 | 982,178 | | T |
| 9. Ephraim, Gumpel & Co.[20] | | | | | 192,000 | 553,000 | 1,200,000 | | | T |
| 10. Chem.-Industr. GmbH[21] | | | | | | | 38,000 | 79,000 | 40,000 | P |
| 11. Labowsky & Co.[22] | | | | | | | 639,579 | 634,255 | | T |

12.   The firm had an export business directed overseas. Figures in StAHH, *Oberfinanzpräsident*, R 1937/16, p. 49.

13.   The firm dealt wholesale in radio equipment, bicycles, and musical instruments. Figures in *Archiv WgA LGHH*, Z 1489-1, 2nd count, p. 74.

14.   The firm had import and export business with South America (incl. in coffee, cocoa and rubber). Figures in *Archiv WgA LGHH*, Z 2522-1, p. 30.

15.   The firm dealt wholesale in cheese and fat products. Figures in *Archiv WgA LGHH*, Z 421-1, p. 66ff.

16.   The firm operated a wholesale and import business in fish conserves. Figures in StAHH, *Oberfinanzpräsident*, R 1937/1484, p. 4.

17.   The firm imported and exported spices. Figures in StAHH, *Oberfinanzpräsident*, F 1448, p. 8.

18.   The firm had import and export business with Guatemala. Figures in *Archiv WgA LGHH*, Z 599-1, p. 39.

19.   The firm was engaged in transit trade with South America. Figures in StAHH, *Oberfinanzpräsident*, F 2112, Vol. 1, p. 11.

20.   The firm had import and export business with South America. Figures in StAHH, *Oberfinanzpräsident*, R 1937/814, p. 5.

21.   The firm imported and traded in gloss oil. Figures in *Archiv WgA LGHH*, Z 2554-1, p. 14.

22.   The firm imported and exported bicycle parts. Figures in StAHH, *Oberfinanzpräsident*, Str 423, Vol. 2, p. 150.

*Table 10 continued*

| | 1930 | 1931 | 1932 | 1933 | 1934 | 1935 | 1936 | 1937 | 1938 | T/P |
|---|---|---|---|---|---|---|---|---|---|---|
| *Retail trade* | | | | | | | | | | |
| 12. Ost-indienhaus H. Colm[23] | 378,000 | 346,000 | 354,000 | 472,000 | 560,000 | 635,000 | 735,000 | 776,000 | 704,000 | T |
| 13. Textilhaus Simon[24] | | | | | | 569,020 | 611,060 | 671,390 | | T |
| 14. Marcus Galewski[25] | | | | | | 47,946 | 52,679 | 46,535 | 54,643 | P |
| 15. Max Pommerantz[26] | | | | 56,858 | 55,278 | 50,970 | 55,124 | 58,863 | | T |
| | | | | 2,645 | 4,013 | 5,084 | 5,165 | 5,264 | | P |
| 16. Adolf Meyer[27] | | | | | | | 6,580 | 8,291 | 4,786 | P |
| 17. Alex Löwenberg[28] | 387,000 | 313,000 | 257,000 | 217,000 | 208,000 | 191,000 | 186,000 | 181,000 | | T |
| 18. Bottina Schuh Gmbh[29] | | | 1,330,283 | 1,149,317 | 1,128,061 | 1,060,940 | 1,031,194 | 1,094,945 | | T |
| 19. Schuhhaus Speier[30] | | | | 73,374 | 84,055 | 77,346 | 74,695 | | | T |
| 20. Campbell & Co.[31] | | | | | | 601,200 | 737,200 | 790,700 | | T |
| *Industrial operations* | | | | | | | | | | |
| 21. Rappolt & Söhne[32] | | | | 3,380,000 | 4,200,000 | 3,950,000 | 4,130,000 | 4,930,000 | | T |

23. The firm was one of the largest clothing stores in Hamburg. Figures in *Archiv WgA LGHH,* Z 28, p. 11.
24. Figures in *Archiv WgA LGHH,* Z 5737-2, p. 35.
25. The firm dealt in ladies' and children's clothing. Figures in *Archiv WgA LGHH,* Z 2217-12, p. 21.
26. The firm operated a retail trade for men's- and boy's-wear. Figures in *Archiv Fst.,* 227-11 (inventory of the *Finanzamt Hamburg-Harburg* of April 24, 1938).
27. The firm dealt in corsets and bandage accessories. Figures in *Archiv WgA LGHH,* Z 3095-2, enclosure, p. 1.
28. The firm sold office supplies. Figures in *Archiv WgA LGHH,* Z 265-1, p. 23.
29. The firm, operating across the Reich, had a total of five shoe stores in Hamburg (Eimsbütteler Chaussee 60, Hamburger Str. 64, Neuer Steinweg 70, Hammerbrookstr.103, Billhorner Röhrendamm 192/6). Figures in *Archiv WgA LGHH,* Z 5387-1, p. 15.
30. The firm had several shoe stores in Hamburg. The turnover figures given are for the branch at Schulterblatt 142. Figures in *Archiv WgA LGHH,* Z 1159-3, p. 24.
31. The firm had Hamburg's largest optician's business. Figures in *Archiv M.M. Warburg & Co.,* 22056 (unpag.).
32. The firm operated a clothing factory. Figures in *Archiv M.M. Warburg & Co.,* file marked 'Nicht durch das Sekretariat', Rappolt & Söhne (unpag.).

*Table 11*   Timing of 'Aryanisations'[33]

| Year | Number of Firms | % |
|------|-----------------|-----|
| 1934 | 1 | 0.3 |
| 1935 | 4 | 1.3 |
| 1936 | 10 | 3.2 |
| 1937 | 12 | 3.9 |
| 1938 | 168 | 54.2 |
| 1939 | 114 | 36.8 |
| 1940 | 1 | 0.3 |
| Total | 310 | 100 |

*Table 12*   Economic sectors of 'Aryanised' businesses in Hamburg[34]

| Sector | Figure | % |
|--------|--------|-----|
| Wholesale, import-export | 132 | 42.60 |
| Handicraft | 11 | 3.55 |
| Industrial operations | 47 | 15.16 |
| Retail businesses | 84 | 27.10 |
| Of which textiles and shoes | 56 | 66.66 |
| Of which groceries | 7 | 8.33 |
| Removal firms | 5 | 1.61 |
| Banks | 5 | 1.61 |
| Agents, representatives | 26 | 8.38 |
| Total | 310 | 100 |

33.  Established by reference to the files of the *Wiedergutmachungsamt beim Landgericht Hamburg*. The figure is incomplete.
34.  Collated from the files of the *Wiedergutmachungsamt beim Landgericht Hamburg* (incomplete).

*Table 13*  Fate of Jewish Proprietors after 'Aryanisation'[35]

|  | Numbers | % |
|---|---|---|
| Deported and murdered | 55 | 18.71 |
| Suicide | 10 | 3.40 |
| Murdered in a camp in Germany | 4 | 1.36 |
| Died in Germany | 18 | 6.12 |
| Deported and survived | 4 | 1.36 |
| Survived in Germany | 4 | 1.36 |
| Emigrated | 199 | 67.69 |
| **Total** | 294 | 100 |
|  |  |  |
| Emigrated to |  |  |
| USA | 59 | 29.65 |
| Great Britain | 41 | 20.60 |
| Netherlands | 21 | 10.55 |
| South and Central America | 21 | 10.55 |
| Palestine | 7 | 3.52 |
| France | 5 | 2.51 |
| Australia/New Zealand | 5 | 2.51 |
| Belgium | 4 | 2.01 |
| Denmark | 3 | 1.51 |
| South Africa | 3 | 1.51 |
| Shanghai | 3 | 1.51 |
| Other | 9 | 4.52 |
| Unknown | 18 | 9.05 |
| **Total** | 199 | 100 |

35.  The table includes only those Hamburg businessmen and women whose fate can be established on the basis of available sources (incl. deportation lists, emigration files, etc.). It cannot be ruled out that a part of the numbers of emigrants recorded here fell victim to the National Socialist persecution in the occupied countries. I would like to thank Jürgen Sielemann and Dagmar Wienrich for reconstructing the subsequent fate of these proprietors.

# APPENDIX III
*Abbreviations*

| | |
|---|---|
| Adefa | *Arbeitsgemeinschaft deutscher (deutsch-arischer) Fabrikanten der Bekleidungsindustrie* – Syndicate of German (German-Aryan) Manufacturers in the Clothing Industry |
| AG | *Aktiengesellschaft* – Joint stock company (Co.) |
| Altreu | *Allgemeine Treuhandstelle für Jüdische Auswanderung GmbH* – General Trusteeship for Jewish Emigration Ltd |
| BAK | *Bundesarchiv Koblenz* – Federal Archive, Koblenz |
| BAP | *Bundesarchiv Potsdam* – Federal Archive, Potsdam |
| BBG | *Gesetz zur Wiederherstellung des Berufsbeamtentums* – Law for the Restoration of the Professional Civil Service |
| BDM | *Bund deutscher Mädel* – League of German Girls |
| BNSDJ | *Bund Nationalsozialistischer Deutscher Juristen* – League of National Socialist German Lawyers |
| DAF | *Deutsche Arbeitsfront* – German Workers' Front |
| DDP | *Deutsche Demokratische Partei* – German Democratic Party |
| Dego | *Deutsche Golddiskontbank* – German Gold Discount Bank |
| DIG | *Deutsch-Israelitische Gemeinde* – German Israelite Community |
| DNVP | *Deutschnationale Volkspartei* – German National Peoples' Party |
| DVP | *Deutsche Volkspartei* – German Peoples' Party |
| FZH | *Forschungsstelle für Zeitgeschichte in Hamburg* – Research Institute for Contemporary History in Hamburg |
| Gestapo | *Geheime Staatspolizei* – Secret State Police |
| GmbH | *Gesellschaft mit beschränkter Haftung* – Limited company (Co. Ltd) |
| GG | *Geschichte und Gesellschaft* |
| GVG | *Hamburger Grundstücksverwaltungs-Gesellschaft von 1938 mbH* – Hamburg Real Estate Administration Corporation of 1938 Ltd |
| GWB | *Gauwirtschaftsberater der NSDAP* – Gau Economics Adviser of the NSDAP |

| | |
|---|---|
| HAPAG | *Hamburg-Amerikanische Paketfahrt-Aktiengesellschaft* – Hamburg-American Parcel Delivery Co. |
| HEW | *Hamburger Elektrizitätswerke AG* – Hamburg Electric Works Co. |
| HJ | *Hitlerjugend* – Hitler Youth |
| HSDG | *Hamburg-Südamerikanische Dampfschiffahrts-Gesellschaft* – Hamburg-South American Steamboat Company |
| HTO | *Haupttreuhandstelle Ost* – Main Trustee Bureau East |
| IMG | *Internationaler Militärgerichtshof (Nürnberg)* – International Military Court (Nuremberg) |
| JTC | Jewish Trust Corporation |
| KG | *Kommanditgesellschaft* – Limited partnership |
| LBI YB | Leo Baeck Institute Yearbook |
| LFA | *Landesfinanzamt* – Regional Finance Office |
| NSBO | *Nationalsozialistische Betriebszellen-Organisation* – National Socialist Factory Cells Organisation |
| NSDAP | *Nationalsozialistische Deutsche Arbeiterpartei* – National Socialist German Workers' Party |
| NS-Hago | *Nationalsozialistische Handwerks-, Handels- und Gewerbeorganisation* – National Socialist Craft, Trade and Commerce Organisation |
| NSV | *Nationalsozialistische Volkswohlfahrt* – National Socialist People's Welfare |
| OMGUS | Office of Military Government for Germany (US) |
| OHG | *Offene Handelsgesellschaft* – General partnership |
| ORR | *Oberregierungsrat* – Senior Executive Officer |
| Paltreu | *Palästina-Treuhandstelle* – Palestine Trusteeship Office |
| RDM | *Reichsverband Deutscher Makler* – Reich Federation of German Real Estate Brokers |
| RGBl | *Reichsgesetzblatt* – Law Gazette of the Reich |
| RIM | *Reichsinnenminister/-ministerium* – Reich Interior Minister/Ministry |
| RKdbK | *Reichskammer der bildenden Künste* – Reich Chamber of Fine Arts |
| RKK | *Reichskulturkammer* – Reich Chamber of Culture |
| RM | *Reichsmark* – Reich Mark |
| RMK | *Reichsmusikkammer* – Reich Chamber of Music |
| RSK | *Reichsschrifttumskammer* – Reich Chamber of Literature |
| RWM | *Reichswirtschaftsminister/-ministerium* – Reich Economics Minister/Ministry |
| SA | *Sturmabteilungen* – NSDAP storm troopers |
| SD | *SS Sicherheitsdienst* – SS Security Service |
| Sopade | Social Democratic Party in exile |
| SPD | *Sozialdemokratische Partei Deutschlands* – Social Democratic Party of Germany |
| SS | *Schutzstaffeln* – NSDAP Protection Squads |
| StAHH | *Staatsarchiv Hamburg* – State Archive of Hamburg |
| URO | United Restitution Organisation |

| | |
|---|---|
| VfZ | *Vierteljahrshefte für Zeitgeschichte* |
| VO | *Verordnung* – decree |
| VSHG | *Verein selbständiger jüdischer Handwerker und Gewerbetreibender zu Groß-Hamburg* – Union of Self-Employed Jewish Artisans and Tradesmen of Greater Hamburg |
| WgA LGHH | *Wiedergutmachungsamt beim Landgericht Hamburg* – Reparations Office of the State Court of Hamburg |
| ZAV | *Zusatzausfuhrverfahren* – Supplementary Export Procedure |
| ZfG | *Zeitschrift für Geschichtswissenschaft* |

# SOURCES

## Archival Sources

1. Staatsarchiv Hamburg (StAHH)
Oberfinanzpräsident
Finanzdeputation IV
Steuerverwaltung I
Jüdische Gemeinden
NSDAP
Verwaltung für Wirtschaft, Technik und Arbeit
Deputation für Handel, Schiffahrt und Gewerbe II
Blohm & Voß
Senatskanzlei - Präsidialabteilung
Senatskanzlei - Personalabteilung I und II
Senatskanzlei - Personalakten
Senatsprotokolle
Staatsverwaltung
Staatsverwaltung - Allgemeine Abteilung
Staatsamt
Staatliche Pressestelle I-IV
Innere Verwaltung (Büro Senator Richter)
Sozialbehörde I und II
Auswanderungsamt I
Justizverwaltung I
Oberlandesgericht - Verwaltung
Amtsgericht Hamburg - Verwaltung
Medizinalkollegium
Aufklärungsausschuß Hamburg-Bremen
Hamburger Stiftung von 1937
Hamburger Öffentliche Bücherhallen
Fa. Arnold Otto Meyer
Familie Ahrens
Familie Burchard

Familie de Chapeaurouge
Familie Krogmann I
Familie Plaut

2. Archiv des Wiedergutmachungsamtes beim Landgericht Hamburg (Archiv WgA
   LGHH)
Restitutionsakten Z 1-31599
Korrespondenz Carl F. Schlüter 1941–1943
Rundordner 'Allgemeines'

3. Bundesarchiv Koblenz (BAK)
Reichsfinanzministerium
Reichswirtschaftsministerium
Reichskanzlei
Reichskulturkammer
Reichssicherheitshauptamt
Reichsorganisationsleiter der NSDAP
Reichsschatzmeister der NSDAP
Partei-Kanzlei
Spruchgerichte in der Britischen Zone

4. Bundesarchiv Potsdam (BAP)
Reichswirtschaftsministerium
Deutsche Reichsbank
Reichssicherheitshauptamt

5. Berlin Document Center
Personalakten NSDAP, SA, SS
Bestand Reichskulturkammer

6. Justizbehörde Hamburg
Ermittlungsverfahren und Urteile des Hanseatischen Sondergerichtes, Oberlandes-
   gerichts Hamburg, Landgerichts Hamburg, Amtsgerichts Hamburg

7. National Archives Washington
Miscellaneous German Records Collection

8. Special Archives, Moscow
Reichssicherheitshauptamt
Centralverein deutscher Staatsbürger jüdischen Glaubens

9. Archives of the Netherlands State Institute for War Documentation (NIOD)
Möbel-Aktion
Collectie 47
HSSPF

10. Archiv der Forschungsstelle für Zeitgeschichte in Hamburg (Archiv FZH)
Personalakten
Judenverfolgung/Berichte
Handelskammer
Hamburg/Senat
Alte Garde/Gau Hamburg
Tagebuch Carl Vincent Krogmann
Tagebuch Luise Solmitz

11. Archiv der Handelskammer Hamburg
Akten 49.C.28, 100A.1.6, 100.A.2.2, 100A.2.6, 100A.4.1, 100B.1.4-100.B.1.31

12. Institut für die Geschichte der deutschen Juden
Lebenserinnerungen Max Plaut

13. Archiv M.M. Warburg & Co.
Einzelkorrespondenz (Nicht durch das Sekretariat)
Autobiographische Aufzeichnungen Max Warburg
Schriftwechsel Max Warburg
Firmenakten

14. Werksarchiv der Beiersdorf AG
Fach 130/132

15. Archiv des Norddeutschen Rundfunks
Rundfunkansprachen Karl Kaufmann

16. Nordelbisches Kirchenarchiv Kiel
Akte B IV

17. Geheimes Staatsarchiv Preußischer Kulturbesitz, Berlin-Dahlem
Lageberichte der Staatspolizeistellen Altona und Harburg-Wilhelmsburg

18. Private collections
Diary of Cornelius Freiherr von Berenberg-Goßler
Diary of Nikolaus Sieveking
Notes of Edgar Eichholz
Autobiography of Dr. Ernst Loewenberg
Personal records of Albrecht Dreves

## Periodicals

**Der Stürmer**
*Völkischer Beobachter*
*Hamburger Tageblatt*
*Hamburger Familienblatt für die israelitischen Gemeinden Hamburg, Altona, Wandsbek und Harburg*
*Hamburger Nachrichten*
*Hamburger Anzeiger*
*Hamburger Fremdenblatt*
*Hamburger Echo*
**Hamburgischer Correspondent**

# Bibliography

Adam, Uwe Dietrich, *Judenpolitik im Dritten Reich*, Düsseldorf 1972.

Adler, H.G., *Der verwaltete Mensch, Studien zur Deportation der Juden aus Deutschland*, Tübingen 1974.

Adler-Rudel, S., *Jüdische Selbsthilfe unter dem Naziregime 1933-1939*, Tübingen 1974.

Institut für Zeitgeschichte, ed., *Akten der Partei-Kanzlei der NSDAP*, Parts I and II, Munich 1983-1992.

Aly, Götz, *'Endlösung'. Völkerverschiebung und der Mord an den europäischen Juden*, Frankfurt am Main 1991.

Aly, Götz, and Heim, Susanne, *Vordenker der Vernichtung. Auschwitz und die deutschen Pläne für eine neue europäische Ordnung*, Hamburg 1991.

Angermund, Ralph, 'Korruption im Nationalsozialismus. Eine Skizze', in Christian Jansen, Lutz Niethammer anΩd Bernd Weisbrod, eds, *Von der Aufgabe der Freiheit. Politische Verantwortung und bürgerliche Gesellschaft im 19. und 20. Jahrhundert. Festschrift für Hans Mommsen zum 5. November 1995*, Berlin 1995, pp. 371–383.

Auerbach, Hellmuth, 'Vom Trommler zum Führer. Hitler und das nationale Münchner Bürgertum', in Björn Mensing and Friedrich Prinz, eds, *Irrlicht im leuchtenden München? Der nationalsozialismus in der 'Hauptstadt der Bewegung'*, Regensburg 1991, pp. 67–91.

Ayaß, Wolfgang, '"Ein Gebot der nationalen Arbeitsdisziplin". Die Aktion "Arbeitsscheu Reich" 1938', in *Feinderklärung und Prävention. Kriminalbiologie, Zigeunerforschung und Asozialenpolitik (Beiträge zur nationalsozialistischen Gesundheits- und Sozialpolitik, Nr. 6)*, Berlin 1988, pp. 43–74.

Bästlein, Klaus, 'Vom hanseatischen Richtertum zum nationalsozialistischen Justizverbrechen. Zur Person und Tätigkeit Curt Rothenbergers 1896-1959', in *Justizbehörde Hamburg*, ed., *"Für Führer, Volk und Vaterland..." Hamburger Justiz im Nationalsozialismus*, Hamburg 1992, pp. 74–145.

Bajohr, Frank, 'Gauleiter in Hamburg. Zur Person und Tätigkeit Karl Kaufmanns', *VfZ* 2/1995, pp. 267–295.

Ibid., 'The Beneficiaries of "Aryanization": Hamburg as a Case Study', *Yad Vashem Studies*, vol. XXVI, Jerusalem 1998, pp. 173–201.

Bajohr, Frank, and Szodrzynski, Joachim, '"Keine jüdische Hautcreme mehr benutzen". Die antisemitische Kampagne gegen die Hamburger Firma Beiersdorf', in Arno Herzig, ed., *Die Juden in Hamburg 1590–1990*, Hamburg 1991, pp. 515–526.

Ibid., ed., *Hamburg in der NS-Zeit. Ergebnisse neuerer Forschungen*, Hamburg 1995.

Bankier, David, *Die öffentliche Meinung im Hitler-Staat. Die "Endlösung" und die Deutschen. Eine Berichtigung*, Berlin 1995.

Barkai, Avraham, *From Boycott to Annihilation: The Economic Struggle of German Jews, 1933–1945*, Hanover and London 1989.

Ibid., '"Schicksalsjahr 1938". Kontinuität und Verschärfung der wirtschaftlichen Ausplünderung der deutschen Juden', in Walter H. Pehle, ed., *Der Judenpogrom 1938. Von der "Reichskristallnacht" zum Völkermord*, Frankfurt am Main 1988, pp. 94–117.

Ibid., 'Deutsche Unternehmer und Judenpolitik im "Dritten Reich"', *GG* 15 (1989), pp. 227–247.

Ibid., 'Volksgemeinschaft, "Arisierung" und der Holocaust', in Arno Herzig and Ina Lorenz, eds, *Verdrängung und Vernichtung der Juden unter dem Nationalsozialismus*, Hamburg 1992, pp. 133–152.

Ibid., 'German Interests in the Haavara-Transfer Agreement 1933–1939', *LBI YB* 35 (1990), pp. 245–266.

Ibid., 'Max Warburg im Jahre 1933. Mißglückte Versuche zur Milderung der Judenverfolgung', in Peter Freimark, Alice Jankowski and Ina S. Lorenz, eds, *Juden in Deutschland. Emigration, Integration, Verfolgung und Vernichtung*, Hamburg 1991, pp. 390–405.

Barnouw, David, 'Die Schneiderei und Bekleidungsfirma Grijpman GmbH. Der Krieg und seine Profiteure', in *1999*, Issue 1/1995, pp. 15–37.

Bauer, Yehuda, *Jews for Sale? Nazi-Jewish Negotiations 1933–1945*, New Haven and London 1994.

Bauman, Zygmunt, *Dialektik der Ordnung. Die Moderne und der Holocaust*, Hamburg 1992.

Becker, Franziska, *Gewalt und Gedächtnis. Erinnerungen an die nationalsozialistische Verfolgung einer jüdischen Landgemeinde*, Göttingen 1994.

Benz, Wolfgang, ed., *Die Juden in Deutschland 1933–1945*, Munich 1988.

Ibid., 'Der November-Pogrom 1938', in ibid., ed., *Die Juden in Deutschland 1933–1945*, Munich 1988, pp. 499–544.

Berding, Helmut, *Moderner Antisemitismus in Deutschland*, Frankfurt am Main 1988.

Bering, Dietz, *Kampf um Namen. Bernhard Weiß gegen Joseph Goebbels*, Stuttgart 1991.

Bielfeldt, Hans, 'Citykammer, Gauwirtschaftskammer, Handelskammer', in *Staat und Wirtschaft. Beiträge zur Geschichte der Handelskammer Hamburg*, Hamburg 1980, pp. 61–133.

Ibid., 'Politik und Personalia im Dritten Reich', in *Staat und Wirtschaft. Beiträge zur Geschichte der Handelskammer Hamburg*, Hamburg 1980, pp. 135–225.

Blaschke, Olaf, 'Wider die "Herrschaft des modern-jüdischen Geistes": Der Katholizismus zwischen traditionellem Antijudaismus und modernem Antisemitismus', in Wilfried Loth, ed., *Deutscher Katholizismus im Umbruch zur Moderne*, Stuttgart 1991, pp. 236–265.

Boberach, Heinz, ed., *Meldungen aus dem Reich. Die geheimen Lageberichte des Sicherheitsdienstes der SS 1938–1945*, Herrsching 1984.

Boelcke, Willi A., *Die deutsche Wirtschaft 1930–1945, Interna des Reichswirtschaftsministeriums*, Düsseldorf 1983.

Bopf, Britta, 'Zur "Arisierung" und den Versuchen der "Wiedergutmachung" in Köln', in Horst Matzerath, Harald Buhlan and Barbara Becker-Jákli, *Versteckte Vergangenheit. Über den Umgang mit der NS-Zeit in Köln*, Cologne 1994, pp. 163–193.

Bottin, Angela, *Enge Zeit. Spuren Vertriebener und Verfolgter der Hamburger Universität*, Berlin, Hamburg 1992.

Broszat, Martin, *Der Staat Hitlers. Grundlegung und Entwicklung seiner inneren Verfassung*, Munich 1969. (English edition: *The Hitler State*, New York, 1981.)

Brunner, Claudia, *Arbeitslosigkeit in München 1927 bis 1933. Kommunalpolitik in der Krise*, Munich 1992.

Bruns-Wüstefeld, Alex, *Lohnende Geschäfte. Die "Entjudung" der Wirtschaft am Beispiel Göttingens*, Hannover 1997

Bruss, Regina, *Die Bremer Juden unter dem Nationalsozialismus*, Bremen 1983.

Büttner, Ursula, ed., *Die Deutschen und die Judenverfolgung im Dritten Reich*, Hamburg 1992.

Ibid., *Hamburg in der Staats- und Wirtschaftskrise 1928–1931*, Hamburg 1982.

Ibid., *Politische Gerechtigkeit und sozialer Geist. Hamburg zur Zeit der Weimarer Republik*, Hamburg 1985.

Ibid., *Not nach der Befreiung. Die Situation der deutschen Juden in der britischen Besatzungszone 1945–1948* (ed. by the Landeszentrale für politische Bildung, Hamburg), Hamburg 1986.

*Die Chemische Industrie im Deutschen Reich 1939/40. Aufbau, Entwicklung, Werke, Arbeits- und Interessengebiete, Tochtergesellschaften und Beteiligungen, Verträge und Vereinbarungen, Statistik und Finanzen der Unternehmungen der deutschen chemischen Industrie einschließlich Ostmark und Sudetengau*, 10th edition, Berlin 1939.

Chernow, Ron, *Die Warburgs. Odyssee einer Familie*, Berlin 1994.

Comité des Delegations Juives, ed., *Das Schwarzbuch. Tatsachen und Dokumente. Die Lage der Juden in Deutschland 1933*, Paris 1934.

Dahm, Volker, *Das jüdische Buch im Dritten Reich. Teil 1: Die Ausschaltung der jüdischen Autoren, Verleger und Buchhändler*, Frankfurt am Main 1979.

Ibid., 'Anfänge und Ideologie der Reichskulturkammer. Die "Berufsgemeinschaft" als Instrument kulturpolitischer Steuerung und sozialer Reglementierung', *VfZ*, 1/1986, pp. 53–86.

Damberg, Wilhelm, 'Katholizismus und Antisemitismus in Westfalen. Ein Desiderat', in Arno Herzig, Karl Teppe and Andreas Determann, eds, *Verdrängung und Vernichtung der Juden in Westfalen*, Münster 1994, pp. 44–61.

*Deutschland-Berichte der Sozialdemokratischen Partei Deutschlands (Sopade) 1934–1940*, 7 vols, Frankfurt am Main 1980.

Diehl-Thiele, Peter, *Partei und Staat im Dritten Reich. Untersuchungen zum Verhältnis von NSDAP und allgemeiner innerer Staatsverwaltung 1933–1945*, Munich 1969.

Diekmann, Irene, 'Boykott - Entrechtung - Pogrom - Deportation. Die "Arisierung" jüdischen Eigentums während der NS-Dikatur. Untersucht und dargestellt an Beispielen aus der Provinz Mark Brandenburg', in Dietrich Eichholtz, ed., *Verfolgung - Alltag - Widerstand. Brandenburg in der NS-Zeit*, Berlin 1993, pp. 207–229.

Diner, Dan, 'Rationalisierung und Methode. Zu einem neuen Erklärungsversuch der "Endlösung"', *VfZ* 40 (1992), pp. 359–382.

Dodd, William E. Jr. and Dodd, Martha, eds, *Ambassador Dodd's Diary 1933–1938*, New York 1941.

Döscher, Hans-Jürgen, *"Reichskristallnacht". Die Novemberpogrome 1938*, Frankfurt am Main, Berlin 1988.

*Dokumente zur Geschichte der Frankfurter Juden 1933–1945*, ed. by the Kommission zur Erforschung der Geschichte der Frankfurter Juden, Frankfurt 1963.

Drobisch, Klaus, Goguel, Rudi and Müller, Werner, *Juden unterm Hakenkreuz*, Berlin 1973.

Eiber, Ludwig, 'Unter Führung des NSDAP-Gauleiters. Die Hamburger Staatspolizei (1933–1937)', in Gerhard Paul and Klaus Michael Mallmann, eds, *Die Gestapo - Mythos und Realität*, Darmstadt 1995, pp. 101–117.

Facius, Friedrich, *Wirtschaft und Staat. Die Entwicklung der staatlichen Wirtschaftsverwaltung in Deutschland vom 17. Jahrhundert bis 1945*, Boppard am Rhein 1959.

*Fairplay Schleppdampfschiffs-Reederei Richard Borchard GmbH 1905–1980. Zum 75jährigen Jubiläum der Fairplay-Reederei*, n.p. 1980.

Falter, Jürgen, *Hitlers Wähler*, Munich 1991.

Feilchenfeld, Werner, Michaelis, Dolf and Pinner, Ludwig, *Haavara-Transfer nach Palästina und Einwanderung deutscher Juden 1933–1939*, Tübingen 1972.

Felix, Günter, 'Scheinlegalität und Rechtsbeugung - Finanzverwaltung, Steuergerichtsbarkeit und Judenverfolgung im "Dritten Reich"', *Steuer & Studium* 5/1995, pp. 197–204.

Ferk, Gabriele, 'Judenverfolgung in Norddeutschland', in Frank Bajohr, ed., *Norddeutschland im Nationalsozialismus*, Hamburg 1993, pp. 280–309.

Fischer, Albert, *Hjalmar Schacht und Deutschlands "Judenfrage". Der "Wirtschaftsdiktator" und die Vertreibung der Juden aus der deutschen Wirtschaft*, Cologne 1995.

Ibid., 'Jüdische Privatbanken im "Dritten Reich"', *Scripta Mercaturae*, Vol. 28, Issue 1/2, 1994, pp. 1–54.

Fliedner, Hans-Joachim, *Die Judenverfolgung in Mannheim 1933–1945*, 2 vols, Stuttgart 1971.

Fraenkel, Ernst, *The Dual State: A contribution to the theory of dictatorship*, New York, 1941.

Frei, Norbert, *National Socialist Rule in Germany: The Führer State 1933–1945*, 2nd edition, Oxford 1993.

Ibid., 'Wie modern war der Nationalsozialismus?', *GG* 19 (1993), pp. 367–387.

Fröhlich, Elke, ed., *Die Tagebücher von Joseph Goebbels. Sämtliche Fragmente*, Parts I and II, Munich 1987–1996.

Galerie Morgenland, ed., *"Wo Wurzeln waren..." Juden in Hamburg-Eimsbüttel 1933–1945*, Hamburg 1993.

Genschel, Helmut, *Die Verdrängung der Juden aus der Wirtschaft im Dritten Reich*, Göttingen 1966.

Goertz, Dieter, *Juden in Oldenburg 1930–1938*, Oldenburg 1938.

Goldhagen, Daniel Jonah, *Hitler's Willing Executioners: Ordinary Germans and the Holocaust*, New York 1996.

Goral-Sternheim, Arie, *Im Schatten der Synagoge*, Hamburg 1989.

Goschler, Constantin, *Wiedergutmachung. Westdeutschland und die Verfolgten des Nationalsozialismus (1945–1954)*, Munich 1992.

Goschler, Constantin, and Herbst, Ludolf, eds, *Wiedergutmachung in der Bundesrepublik Deutschland*, Munich 1989.

Graml, Hermann, *Reichskristallnacht. Antisemitismus und Judenverfolgung im Dritten Reich*, Munich 1988.

Ibid., 'Irregeleitet und in die Irre führend. Widerspruch gegen eine "rationale" Erklärung von Auschwitz', *Jahrbuch für Antisemitismusforschung* 1/1992, pp. 286–295.

Greiser, Arthur, *Der Aufbau im Osten*, Jena 1942.

Grenville, John A., '"Nichtarier" und "Deutsche Ärzte". Die Anpassung der Ärzte im Dritten Reich', in Ursula Büttner, ed., *Die Deutschen und die Judenverfolgung im Dritten Reich*, Hamburg 1992, pp. 191–206.

Gruchmann, Lothar, *Justiz im Dritten Reich 1933–1940. Anpassung und Unterwerfung in der Ära Gürtner*, Munich 1988.

Ibid., 'Korruption im Dritten Reich. Zur "Lebensmittelversorgung" der NS-Führerschaft', *VfZ* 4/1994, pp. 571–593.

Gründel, Ernst Günther, *Die Sendung der Jungen Generation. Versuch einer umfassenden revolutionären Sinndeutung der Krise*, Munich 1932.

Gruner, Wolf, *Der Geschlossene Arbeitseinsatz deutscher Juden. Zur Zwangsarbeit als Element der Verfolgung 1938–1943*, Berlin 1997.

Ibid., 'Die öffentliche Fürsorge und die deutschen Juden 1933–1942. Zur antijüdischen Politik der Städte, des Deutschen Gemeindetages und des Reichsinnenministeriums', *ZfG*, Vol. 45, Issue 7/1997, pp. 597–616.

Ibid., *Judenverfolgung in Berlin 1933–1945. Eine Chronologie der Behördenmaßnahmen in der Reichshauptstadt*, Berlin 1996.

Händler-Lachmann, Barbara and Werther, Thomas, *"Vergessene Geschäfte - verlorene Geschichte". Jüdisches Wirtschaftsleben in Marburg und seine Vernichtung im Nationalsozialismus*, Marburg 1992.

Haerendel, Ulrike, 'Das Rathaus unterm Hakenkreuz - Aufstieg und Ende der "Hauptstadt der Bewegung" 1933 bis 1945', in Richard Bauer, ed., *Geschichte der Stadt München*, Munich 1992, pp. 369–393.

Hamel, Iris, *Völkischer Verband und nationale Gewerkschaft. Der Deutschnationale Handlungsgehilfen-Verband 1893–1933*, Frankfurt am Main 1967.

Hanke, Peter, *Zur Geschichte der Juden in München zwischen 1933 und 1945*, Munich 1967.

Hanko, Helmut M., 'Kommunalpolitik in der "Hauptstadt der Bewegung" 1933–1935. Zwischen "revolutionärer" Umgestaltung und Verwaltungskontinuität', in Martin Broszat, Elke Fröhlich and Anton Grossmann, eds, *Bayern in der NS-Zeit*, Vol. III, Munich 1981, pp. 329–441.

Hauschild-Thiessen, Renate, 'Cornelius Freiherr von Berenberg-Goßler und das Dritte Reich', *Hamburgische Geschichts- und Heimatblätter*, Vol. 12, Issue 1/1988, pp. 14–32.

Hayes, Peter, 'Big Business and "Aryanization" in Germany', *Jahrbuch für Antisemitismusforschung* 3/1994, pp. 254–281.

von Hehl, Ulrich, *Nationalsozialistische Herrschaft*, Munich 1996.

Helfferich, Emil, *1932–1946. Tatsachen*, Jever 1969.

Herbert, Ulrich, *Best. Biographische Studien über Weltanschauung, Radikalismus und Vernunft 1903–1989*, Bonn 1996.

Ibid., 'Arbeit und Vernichtung. Ökonomisches Interesse und Primat der "Weltanschauung" im Nationalsozialismus', in Dan Diner, ed., *Ist der Nationalsozialismus Geschichte? Zu Historisierung und Historikerstreit*, Frankfurt am Main 1987, pp. 198–236.

Ibid., 'Rassismus und rationales Kalkül. Zum Stellenwert utilitaristisch verbrämter Legitimationsstrategien in der nationalsozialistischen "Weltanschauung"', in Wolfgang Schneider, ed., *"Vernichtungspolitik". Eine Debatte über den Zusammenhang von Sozialpolitik und Genozid im nationalsozialistischen Deutschland*, Hamburg 1991, pp. 25–35.

Ibid., '"Generation der Sachlichkeit". Die völkische Studentenbewegung der frühen zwanziger Jahre in Deutschland,' in Frank Bajohr, Werner Johe and Uwe Lohalm, eds, *Zivilisation und Barbarei. Die widersprüchlichen Potentiale der Moderne*, Hamburg 1991, pp. 115–144.

Ibid., 'Von der "Reichskristallnacht" zum "Holocaust". Der 9. November und das Ende des "Radauantisemitismus"', in ibid., *Arbeit, Volkstum, Weltanschauung. Über Fremde und Deutsche im 20. Jahrhundert*, Frankfurt am Main 1995, pp. 59–77.

Herbst, Ludolf, *Der Totale Krieg und die Ordnung der Wirtschaft. Die Kriegswirtschaft im Spannungsfeld von Politik, Ideologie und Propaganda 1939–1945*, Stuttgart 1982.

Ibid., *Das nationalsozialistische Deutschland 1933–1945. Die Entfesselung der Gewalt: Rassismus und Krieg*, Frankfurt am Main 1996.

Herzig, Arno, and Lorenz, Ina, eds, *Verdrängung und Vernichtung der Juden im Nationalsozialismus*, Hamburg 1992.

Herzig, Arno, Teppe, Karl and Determann, Andreas, eds, *Verdrängung und Vernichtung der Juden in Westfalen*, Münster 1994.

Ibid., eds, *Die Juden in Hamburg 1590–1990*, Hamburg 1991.

Hilberg, Raul, *The Destruction of the European Jews*, 3 vols, New York 1985.

Hilfsausschuß der vereinigten jüdischen Organisationen Hamburgs, ed., *Hilfe und Aufbau in Hamburg April 1933 bis Dezember 1934*, Hamburg 1935.

Hirschfeld, Gerhard, and Kettenacker, Lothar, eds, *Der "Führerstaat": Mythos und Realität*, Stuttgart 1981. (English edition: *The Führer State: Myth and Reality*, London 1981.)

Hitler, Adolf, *Mein Kampf*, 17th edition, Munich 1933.

Ibid., *Sämtliche Aufzeichnungen 1905–1924*, eds, Eberhard Jäckel and Axel Kuhn, Stuttgart 1980.

*100 Jahre Beiersdorf 1882–1982*, Hamburg 1982.

Jäckel, Eberhard, *Hitlers Weltanschauung. Entwurf einer Herrschaft*, Stuttgart 1981.

James, Harold, *Deutschland in der Weltwirtschaftskrise 1924–1936*, Stuttgart 1988.

Ibid., 'Die Deutsche Bank und die Diktatur 1933–1945', in Lothar Gall et al, *Die Deutsche Bank 1870–1995*, Munich 1995, pp. 315–408.

Jochmann, Werner, *Nationalsozialismus und Revolution. Ursprung und Geschichte der NSDAP in Hamburg 1922–1933, Dokumente*, Frankfurt am Main 1963.

Johe, Werner, 'Im Dritten Reich 1933–1945', in Werner Jochmann and Hans-Dieter Loose, eds, *Hamburg. Geschichte der Stadt und ihrer Bewohner*, Vol. II, Hamburg 1986, pp. 265–376

Ibid., 'Bürgermeister Rudolf Petersen', *Jahrbuch des Instituts für Deutsche Geschichte*, Tel-Aviv, Vol. 3/1974, pp. 379–415.

Ibid., *Die gleichgeschaltete Justiz. Organisation des Rechtswesens und Politisierung der Rechtsprechung 1933–1945, dargestellt am Beispiel des Oberlandesgerichtsbezirks Hamburg*, Frankfurt am Main 1967.

Kaum, Ekkehard, *Oscar Troplowitz. Forscher - Unternehmer - Bürger*, Hamburg 1982.

Keiser, Günter, 'Der jüngste Konzentrationsprozeß', in *Die Wirtschaftskurve*, Issue 2/1939, pp. 136–156.

Kershaw, Ian, *The Nazi Dictatorship: Problems and Perspectives of Interpretation*, London 1985.

Ibid., 'The Persecution of the Jews and German Popular Opinion in the Third Reich', *LBI YB* 26 (1981), pp. 261–289.

Klemperer, Victor, *Ich will Zeugnis ablegen bis zum letzten. Tagebücher 1933–1945*, 2 vols, Berlin 1995.

Knipping, Ulrich, *Die Geschichte der Juden in Dortmund während der Zeit des Dritten Reiches*, Dortmund 1977.

Kopper, Christopher, *Zwischen Marktwirtschaft und Dirigismus. Bankenpolitik im "Dritten Reich" 1933 bis 1939*, Bonn 1995.

Ibid., *Nationalsozialistische Bankenpolitik am Beispiel des Bankhauses M.M. Warburg & Co. in Hamburg*, Bochum (Master's thesis) 1988.

Krach, Tillmann, *Jüdische Rechtsanwälte in Preußen. Über die Bedeutung der freien Advokatur und ihre Zerstörung durch den Nationalsozialismus*, Munich 1991.

Kratzsch, Gerhard, *Der Gauwirtschaftsapparat der NSDAP. Menschenführung - "Arisierung" - Wehrwirtschaft im Gau Westfalen-Süd*, Münster 1989.

Ibid., 'Die "Entjudung" der mittelständischen Wirtschaft im Regierungsbezirk Arnsberg', in Arno Herzig, Karl Teppe and Andreas Determann, eds, *Verdrängung und Vernichtung der Juden in Westfalen*, Münster 1994, pp. 91–114.

Krause, Eckart, Huber, Ludwig, and Fischer, Holger, eds, *Hochschulalltag im "Dritten Reich". Die Hamburger Universität 1933–1945*, 3 vols, Berlin, Hamburg 1991.

Krüger, Alf, *Die Lösung der Judenfrage in der deutschen Wirtschaft. Kommentar zur Judengesetzgebung*, Berlin 1940.

Kulka, Otto Dov, '"Public Opinion" in Nazi Germany and the "Jewish Question"', in Michael R. Marrus, ed., *The Nazi Holocaust*, Vol. 5, Westport/London 1989, pp. 115–150.

Kümmel, Friedrich, '"Die Ausschaltung". Wie die Nationalsozialisten die jüdischen und politisch mißliebigen Ärzte aus dem Berufe verdrängten', in Johanna Bleker and Norbert Jachertz, eds, *Medizin im Nationalsozialismus*, Cologne 1989, pp. 30–37.

van Laak, Dirk, 'Die Mitwirkenden bei der "Arisierung". Dargestellt am Beispiel der rheinisch-westfälischen Industrieregion 1933–1940', in Ursula Büttner, *Die Deutschen und die Judenverfolgung im Dritten Reich*, Hamburg 1992, pp. 231–257.

Leibfried, Stefan, 'Stationen der Abwehr. Berufsverbote für Ärzte im Deutschen Reich 1933–1938', *Bulletin des Leo Baeck Instituts* 62/1982, pp. 3–39.

Leimkugel, Frank, *Wege jüdischer Apotheker*, Frankfurt am Main 1991.

Lenz, Rudolf, *Karstadt. Ein deutscher Warenhauskonzern 1920–1950*, Stuttgart 1995.

van der Leeuw, A.J., 'Reichskommissariat und Judenvermögen in den Niederlanden', in
Rijksinstituut voor Oorlogsdocumentatie, ed., *Studies over Nederland in Oorlogstijd,*
Part 1, 'S-Gravenhage 1972, pp. 237–249.

Limberg, Margarete, Rübsaat, Hubert, eds, *Sie durften nicht mehr Deutsche sein.
Jüdischer Alltag in Selbstzeugnissen 1933–1938,* Frankfurt am Main 1990.

Lindner, Stephan H., *Das Reichskommissariat für die Behandlung feindlichen Vermögens
im Zweiten Weltkrieg,* Stuttgart 1991.

Lippmann, Leo, *Mein Leben und meine amtliche Tätigkeit. Aus dem Nachlaß
herausgegeben von Werner Jochmann,* Hamburg 1964.

Ibid., *"...daß ich wie ein guter Deutscher empfinde und handele." Zur Geschichte der
Deutsch-Israelitischen Gemeinde in Hamburg in der Zeit vom Herbst 1935 bis zum
Ende 1942,* Hamburg 1994.

Lösener, Bernhard, 'Als Rassereferent im Reichsministerium des Innern', *VfZ,* 9, 1961,
pp. 264–313.

Lohalm, Uwe, *Völkischer Radikalismus. Die Geschichte des Deutschvölkischen Schutz- und
Trutz-Bundes 1919–1923,* Hamburg 1970.

Ibid., 'Hamburgs öffentliche Fürsorge und die Juden 1933 bis 1939', in Arno Herzig,
ed., *Die Juden in Hamburg 1590–1990,* Hamburg 1991, pp. 499–514.

Ibid., *Hamburgs nationalsozialistische Diktatur: Verfassung und Verwaltung 1933 bis 1945*
(published by the Landeszentrale für politische Bildung), Hamburg 1997.

Lorenz, Ina, *Die Juden in Hamburg zur Zeit der Weimarer Republik. Eine Dokumentation,*
2 vols, Hamburg 1987.

Ibid., 'Die jüdische Gemeinde Hamburg 1860–1943. Kaiserreich-Weimarer Republik-
NS-Staat', in Arno Herzig, ed., *Die Juden in Hamburg 1590 bis 1990,* Hamburg
1991, pp. 77–100.

Ibid., 'Seefahrts-Hachschara in Hamburg (1935–1938). Lucy Borchardt: "Die einzige
jüdische Reederin der Welt"', in Hans-Wilhelm Eckardt and Klaus Richter, eds,
*Bewahren und Berichten. Festschrift für Hans-Dieter Loose zum 60. Geburtstag,*
Hamburg 1997, pp. 445–472.

Louven, Astrid, *Die Juden in Wandsbek 1604–1940. Spuren der Erinnerung,* Hamburg 1989.

Ludwig, Johannes, *Boykott - Enteignung - Mord. Die "Entjudung" der deutschen
Wirtschaft,* Hamburg 1989.

Malinowski, Stephan, 'Politische Skandale als Zerrspiegel der Demokratie. Die Fälle
Barmat und Sklarek im Kalkül der Weimarer Rechten', *Jahrbuch für
Antisemitismusforschung,* Vol. 5/1996, pp. 46–65.

Margaliot, Abraham, 'The Reaction of the Jewish Public in Germany to the Nuremberg
Laws', *Yad Vashem Studies* 12 (1977), pp. 75–107.

Matzerath, Horst, *Nationalsozialismus und kommunale Selbstverwaltung,* Stuttgart and
elswhere 1970.

Maurer, Trude, 'Abschiebung und Attentat. Die Ausweisung der polnischen Juden und
der Vorwand für die "Kristallnacht"', in Walter H. Pehle, ed., *Der Judenpogrom 1938.
Von der "Reichskristallnacht" zum Völkermord,* Frankfurt am Main 1988, pp. 52–73.

Mehl, Stefan, *Das Reichsfinanzministerium und die Verfolgung der deutschen Juden,* Berlin
1990.

Meister, Reiner, *Die große Depression. Zwangslagen und Handlungsspielräume der Wirtschafts- und Finanzpolitik in Deutschland 1929–1932*, Regensburg 1991.

Memoirs of Kurt Enoch, written for his family, privately printed by his wife Margaret M. Enoch, New York 1984.

Mensing, Björn, and Prinz, Friedrich, eds, *Irrlicht im leuchtenden München? Der Nationalsozialismus in der "Hauptstadt der Bewegung"*, Regensburg 1991.

Menzel, Curt, 'Minderheitenrecht und Judenfrage. Zwei Vorträge, gehalten am 17.Februar und 28.April 1933 im Bund Nationalsozialistischer Deutscher Juristen in Hamburg', Beuern o.J.

Meynert, Joachim, and Schäffer, Friedhelm, *Die Juden in der Stadt Bielefeld während der Zeit des Nationalsozialismus*, Bielefeld 1983.

Minuth, Karl-Heinz, ed., *Akten der Reichskanzlei. Die Regierung Hitler, Teil I 1933/34*, Boppard am Rhein 1983.

Mollin, Gerhard Th., *Montankonzerne und "Drittes Reich"*, Göttingen 1988.

Mommsen, Hans, *Beamtentum im Dritten Reich*, Stuttgart 1966.

Ibid., 'Hitlers Stellung im nationalsozialistischen Herrschaftssystem', in Gerhard Hirschfeld and Lothar Kettenacker, eds, *Der "Führerstaat": Mythos und Realität*, Stuttgart 1981, pp. 43–70.

Ibid., 'Nationalsozialismus', in: *Sowjetsystem und demokratische Gesellschaft*, Vol. 4, Freiburg 1971, pp. 695–713.

Ibid., 'Kumulative Radikalisierung und Selbstzerstörung des Regimes', in *Meyers Enzyklopädisches Lexikon*, Vol. 16, Mannheim and elsewhere 1976, pp. 785–790.

Ibid., 'Die Realisierung des Utopischen. Die "Endlösung der Judenfrage" im "Dritten Reich"', *GG* 9 (1983), pp. 381–420.

Mommsen, Hans, and Obst, Dieter, 'Die Reaktion der deutschen Bevölkerung auf die Verfolgung der Juden 1933–1945', in Hans Mommsen and Susanne Willems, eds, *Herrschaftsalltag im Dritten Reich*, Düsseldorf 1988, pp. 374–421.

Morisse, Heiko, *Rechtsanwälte im Nationalsozialismus. Zur Funktion der Ehrengerichtsbarkeit*, Hamburg 1995.

Müller, Arnd, *Geschichte der Juden in Nürnberg 1146–1945*, Nuremberg 1968.

Mußgnug, Dorothee, *Die Reichsfluchtsteuer 1931–1953*, Berlin 1993.

Neumann, Franz, *Behemoth. Struktur und Praxis des Nationalsozialismus 1933–1944*, German ed., Frankfurt am Main 1977.

Non-Sectarian Anti-Nazi League to Champion Human Rights, ed., *Nazis against the world - the counter boycott is the only defensive weapon against Hitlerism's world threat to civilisation, selected speeches from world leaders of public opinion*, New York 1934.

OMGUS, *Ermittlungen gegen die Deutsche Bank*, Nördlingen 1985.

Ibid., *Ermittlungen gegen die Dresdner Bank*, Nördlingen 1986.

Ostrowski, Siegfried, 'Vom Schicksal jüdischer Ärzte im Dritten Reich. Ein Augenzeugenbericht aus den Jahren 1933–1939', *Bulletin des Leo Baeck Instituts* 6/1963, pp. 313–351.

Pätzold, Kurt, *Faschismus, Rassenwahn, Judenverfolgung. Eine Studie zur politischen Strategie und Taktik des faschistischen deutschen Imperialismus (1933–1935)*, East Berlin 1975.

Ibid., 'Von der Vertreibung zum Genozid. Zu den Ursachen, Triebkräften und
    Bedingungen der antijüdischen Politik des faschistischen deutschen Imperialismus',
    in Dietrich Eichholtz and Kurt Gossweiler, eds, *Faschismusforschung. Positionen,
    Probleme, Polemik*, Cologne 1980, pp. 181–208.

Paul, Gerhard, *Aufstand der Bilder. Die NS-Propaganda vor 1933*, Bonn 1990.

Pehle, Walter H., ed., *Der Judenpogrom 1938. Von der "Reichskristallnacht" zum
    Völkermord*, Frankfurt am Main 1988.

Petwaidic, Walter, *Die autoritäre Anarchie. Streiflichter des deutschen Zusammenbruchs*,
    Hamburg 1946.

Petzina, Dietmar, *Die deutsche Wirtschaft in der Zwischenkriegszeit*, Wiesbaden 1977.

Plum, Günter, 'Wirtschaft und Erwerbsleben', in Wolfgang Benz, ed., *Die Juden in
    Deutschland 1933–1945*, Munich 1988, pp. 268–313.

Pohl, Dieter, *Nationalsozialistische Judenverfolgung in Ostgalizien 1941–1944.
    Organisation und Durchführung eines Massenverbrechens*, Munich 1996.

Presser, Jaques, *Ondergang. De Vervolging en Verdelging van het Nederlandse Jodendom
    1940–1945*, 'S-Gravenhage 1965.

*Der Prozeß gegen die Hauptkriegsverbrecher vor dem Internationalen Militärgerichtshof*,
    Vol. I-XLII, Nuremberg 1946–1949.

Pütz, Theodor, *Die deutsche Außenwirtschaft im Engpaß der Jahre 1933–1937*, Berlin 1938.

Rebentisch, Dieter, *Führerstaat und Verwaltung im Zweiten Weltkrieg.
    Verfassungsentwicklung und Verwaltungspolitik 1939–1945*, Stuttgart 1989.

Rebentisch, Dieter, and Teppe, Karl, eds, *Verwaltung contra Menschenführung im Staat
    Hitlers. Studien zum politisch-administrativen System*, Göttingen 1986.

Rheingans, Stefan, 'Ab heute in arischem Besitz. Die Ausschaltung der Juden aus der
    Wirtschaft', in Anton M. Keim/Verein für Sozialgeschichte Mainz, eds, *Als die letzten
    Hoffnungen verbrannten, 9./10. November 1938. Mainzer Juden zwischen Integration
    und Vernichtung*, Mainz 1988, pp. 53–66.

Richarz, Monika, ed., *Jüdisches Leben in Deutschland. Selbstzeugnisse zur Sozialgeschichte*,
    Vol. 3, Stuttgart 1982.

Ibid., 'Luftaufnahme - oder die Schwierigkeiten der Heimatforscher mit der jüdischen
    Geschichte', *Babylon*, Issue 8/1991, pp. 27–33.

Robinsohn, Hans, *Justiz als politische Verfolgung. Die Rechtsprechung in
    "Rassenschandefällen" beim Landgericht Hamburg 1936–1943*, Stuttgart 1977.

Ibid., 'Ein Versuch, sich zu behaupten', *Tradition*, Vol. 3, Issue 4/1958, pp. 197–206.

von Roden, Günter, *Geschichte der Duisburger Juden*, Duisburg 1986.

Rosenbaum, Eduard, and Sherman A.J., *Das Bankhaus M.M. Warburg & Co.
    1798–1938*, Hamburg 1978.

Ruck, Michael, 'Führerabsolutismus und polykratisches Herrschaftsgefüge -
    Verfassungsstrukturen des NS-Staates', in Karl Dietrich Bracher, Manfred Funke and
    Hans-Adolf Jacobsen, eds, *Deutschland 1933–1945. Neue Studien zur
    nationalsozialistischen Herrschaft*, Düsseldorf 1992, pp. 32–56.

Ibid., *Bibliographie zum Nationalsozialismus*, Cologne 1995.

Rudloff, Wilfried, 'Notjahre - Stadtpolitik in Krieg, Inflation und Weltwirtschaftskrise
    1914–1933', in Richard Bauer, ed., *Geschichte der Stadt München*, Munich 1992, pp.
    336–368.

Rusinek, Bernd-A., *Gesellschaft in der Katastrophe. Terror, Illegalität, Widerstand - Köln 1944/45*, Essen 1989.

Safrian, Hans, *Die Eichmann-Männer*, Vienna 1993.

Sahrhage, Norbert, *"Juden sind in dieser Stadt unerwünscht!" Die Geschichte der Synagogengemeinde Bünde im "Dritten Reich"*, Bielefeld 1988.

Sandkühler, Thomas, *"Endlösung" in Galizien. Der Judenmord in Ostpolen und die Rettungsinitiativen von Berthold Beitz 1941–1944*, Bonn 1996.

Sauer, Paul, ed., *Dokumente über die Verfolgung der jüdischen Bürger in Baden-Württemberg durch das nationalsozialistische Regime*, 2 vols, Stuttgart 1966.

Schäffer, Hans, 'Meine Zusammenarbeit mit Carl Melchior', in *Carl Melchior. Ein Buch des Gedenkens und der Freundschaft*, Tübingen 1967, pp. 35–106.

Schellenberg, Carl, 'Silber aus jüdischem Besitz', *Neues Hamburg*, Vol. VII, Hamburg 1952, pp. 89–93.

Schiffler, Leonhard, *ABC des Außenhandels*, Hamburg 1937.

Schleunes, Karl A., *The Twisted Road to Auschwitz. Nazi Policy Toward German Jews 1933–1939*, new edition, Urbana and Chicago 1990.

Schmidt, Monika, 'Arisierungspolitik des Bezirksamtes', in Karl-Heinz Metzger et al, eds, *Kommunalverwaltung unterm Hakenkreuz. Berlin Wilmersdorf 1933–1945*, Berlin 1992, pp. 169–228.

Scholem, Gershom, *Von Berlin nach Jerusalem. Jugenderinnerungen*, Frankfurt am Main 1977.

Schreiber, Karl-Friedrich, *Die Reichskulturkammer. Organisation und Ziele der deutschen Kulturpolitik*, Berlin 1934.

Schultheis, Herbert, *Juden in Mainfranken 1933–1945, unter besonderer Berücksichtigung der Deportationen Würzburger Juden*, Bad Neustadt a.d. Saale 1980.

Schwerin von Krosigk, Lutz, *Staatsbankrott. Die Geschichte der Finanzpolitik des Deutschen Reiches von 1920 bis 1945*, Göttingen 1974.

Selig, Wolfram, 'Vom Boykott zur Arisierung. Die "Entjudung" der Wirtschaft in München', in Björn Mensing and Friedrich Prinz, eds, *Irrlicht im leuchtenden München? Der Nationalsozialismus in der "Hauptstadt der Bewegung"*, Regensburg 1991, pp. 178–202.

Seydelmann, Gertrud, *Gefährdete Balance. Ein Leben in Hamburg 1936–1945*, Hamburg 1996.

Sielemann, Jürgen, ed., *Hamburger jüdische Opfer des Nationalsozialismus, Gedenkbuch*, Hamburg 1995.

Ibid., 'Fragen und Antworten zur "Reichskristallnacht" in Hamburg', in Hans-Wilhelm Eckardt and Klaus Richter, eds, *Bewahren und Berichten. Festschrift für Hans-Dieter Loose zum 60. Geburtstag*, Hamburg 1997, pp. 473–501.

Shirman, Israël, 'De ekonomische plundering van de Joden in België', *Bijdragen tot de Geschiedenis van de Tweede Wereldoorlog*, Vol. 3, Brussels 1974, pp. 163–182.

Sloman, Ricardo, ed., *Biologischer Hochverrat*, Prague 1943.

Spannuth, Jan Philipp, *Die Rückerstattung jüdischen Eigentums nach dem Zweiten Weltkrieg. Das Beispiel Hamburg*, Hamburg (master's thesis) 1994.

*Statistisches Jahrbuch für die Freie und Hansestadt Hamburg 1929/30*, Hamburg 1930.

*Statistik des Deutschen Reiches*, Vol. 451, Issue 5, Berlin 1936.

*Statistik des Hamburgischen Staates*, Issue XXXIII, *Die Volks-, Berufs- und Betriebszählung vom 16.Juni 1925*, Hamburg 1928.

Stuckart-Globke, *Kommentare zur deutschen Rassegesetzgebung*, Vol. I, 'Reichsbürgergesetz vom 15.September 1935. Gesetz zum Schutz des deutschen Blutes und der deutschen Ehre vom 15.September 1935. Gesetz zum Schutz der Erbgesundheit des deutschen Volkes (Erbgesundheitsgesetz) vom 18.Oktober 1935. Nebst allen Ausführungsbestimmungen und einschlägigen Gesetzen und Verordnungen erläutert von Dr. Wilhelm Stuckart, Staatssekretär, und Dr. Hans Globke, Oberregierungsrat, beide im Reichs- und Preußischen Ministerium des Innern', Munich and Berlin 1936.

Stucken, Rudolf, *Deutsche Geld- und Kreditpolitik 1914–1963*, Tübingen 1964.

Swatek, Dieter, *Unternehmenskonzentration als Ergebnis und Mittel nationalsozialistischer Wirtschaftspolitik*, Berlin 1972.

Tarrab-Maslaton, Martin, *Rechtliche Strukturen der Diskriminierung der Juden im Dritten Reich*, Berlin 1993.

Thamer, Hans-Ulrich, *Verführung und Gewalt. Deutschland 1933–1945*, Berlin 1986.

Timpke, Henning, ed., *Dokumente zur Gleichschaltung des Landes Hamburg 1933*, Frankfurt am Main 1967.

Toury, Jacob, *Jüdische Textilunternehmer in Baden-Württemberg 1683–1938*, Tübingen 1984.

Uhlig, Heinrich, *Die Warenhäuser im Dritten Reich*, Cologne 1956.

Ulshöfer, Otfried, *Einflußnahme auf Wirtschaftsunternehmungen in den besetzten nord-, west- und südeuropäischen Ländern während des Zweiten Weltkrieges, insbesondere der Erwerb von Beteiligungen (Verflechtungen)*, Tübingen 1958.

von Viereck, Stefanie, *Hinter weißen Fassaden. Alwin Münchmeyer - ein Bankier betrachtet sein Leben*, Hamburg 1988.

*Die Volks-, Berufs- und Betriebszählung in Hamburg am 16.Juni 1933. Nachtrag zum Statistischen Jahrbuch für die Freie und Hansestadt Hamburg*, Year 1933/34, Hamburg 1935.

Vollnhals, Clemens, 'Jüdische Selbsthilfe bis 1938', in Wolfgang Benz, ed., *Die Juden in Deutschland 1933–1945*, Munich 1988, pp. 314–411.

Wagner, Patrick, *Volksgemeinschaft ohne Verbrecher. Konzeptionen und Praxis der Kriminalpolizei in der Zeit der Weimarer Republik und des Nationalsozialismus*, Hamburg 1996.

Walk, Joseph, ed., *Das Sonderrecht für die Juden im NS-Staat*, Heidelberg, Karlsruhe 1981.

Warburg, Max, *Aus meinen Aufzeichnungen*, ed. Eric Warburg, New York 1952.

Weckbecker, Arno, *Die Judenverfolgung in Heidelberg 1933–1945*, Heidelberg 1985.

Ibid., 'Phasen und Fälle der wirtschaftlichen "Arisierung" in Heidelberg 1933–1942', in Norbert Giovannini et al., eds, *Jüdisches Leben in Heidelberg. Studien zu einer unterbrochenen Geschichte*, Heidelberg 1992, pp. 143–152.

Weinert, Rainer, *"Die Sauberkeit der Verwaltung im Kriege". Der Rechnungshof des Deutschen Reiches 1938–1946*, Opladen 1993.

Wendt, Bernd Jürgen, 'Der "Holocaust" im Widerstreit der Deutungen', in Arno Herzig and Ina Lorenz, eds, *Verdrängung und Vernichtung der Juden unter dem Nationalsozialismus*, Hamburg 1992, pp. 29–74.

Werner, Josef, *Hakenkreuz und Judenstern. Das Schicksal der Karlsruher Juden im Dritten Reich*, Karlsruhe 1988.

Werner, Klaus, *Unter der Herrschaft des Nationalsozialismus 1933–1945 (Zur Geschichte der Juden in Offenbach am Main, Vol. 1)*, Offenbach 1988.

Wiesemann, Falk, 'Juden auf dem Lande. Die wirtschaftliche Ausgrenzung der jüdischen Viehhändler in Bayern', in Detlev Peukert and Jürgen Reulecke, eds, *Die Reihen fast geschlossen. Beiträge zur Geschichte des Alltags unterm Nationalsozialismus*, Wuppertal 1981, pp. 381–396.

Wildt, Michael, ed., *Die Judenpolitik des SD 1935 bis 1938. Eine Dokumentation*, Munich 1995.

Ibid., 'Der Hamburger Gestapochef Bruno Streckenbach. Eine nationalsozialistische Karriere', in Frank Bajohr and Joachim Szodrzynski, eds, *Hamburg in der NS-Zeit. Ergebnisse neuerer Forschungen*, Hamburg 1995, pp. 93–123.

Winkler, Heinrich August, 'Der entbehrliche Stand. Zur Mittelstandspolitik im "Dritten Reich"', *Archiv für Sozialgeschichte*, Vol. XVII, 1977, pp. 1–40.

Witek, Hans, '"Arisierungen" in Wien. Aspekte nationalsozialistischer Enteignungspolitik 1938–1940', in. Emmerich Talos et al, eds, *NS-Herrschaft in Österreich 1938–1945*, Vienna 1988.

Wippermann, Wolfgang, *Die nationalsozialistische Judenverfolgung (Das Leben in Frankfurt zur NS-Zeit, Vol. 1)*, Frankfurt am Main 1986.

Wollenberg, Jörg, 'Enteignung des "raffenden" Kapitals durch das "schaffende" Kapital. Zur Arisierung am Beispiel von Nurnberg', in ibid., ed., *"Niemand war dabei und keiner hat's gewußt." Die deutsche Öffentlichkeit und die Judenverfolgung*, Munich/Zürich 1989, pp. 158–187, 263–267.

Wulff, Birgit, *Arbeitslosigkeit und Arbeitsbeschaffungsmaßnahmen in Hamburg 1933–1939. Eine Untersuchung zur nationalsozialistischen Wirtschafts- und Sozialpolitik*, Frankfurt am Main 1987.

Zimmermann, Michael, 'Eine Deportation nach Auschwitz. Zur Rolle des Banalen bei der Durchsetzung des Monströsen', in Heide Gerstenberger and Dorothea Schmidt, eds, *Normalität oder Normalisierung? Geschichtswerkstätten und Faschismusanalyse*, Münster 1987, pp. 84–96.

Zürn, Gaby, 'Forcierte Auswanderung und Enteignung 1933 bis 1941: Beispiele Hamburger Juden', in Arno Herzig, ed., *Die Juden in Hamburg 1590 bis 1990*, Hamburg 1991, pp. 487–514.

# INDEX

Printed in the United States
204848BV00003B/364-390/P